DATE DUE

MAY 17 '91	ILL: Metro-Tech,		
JAN 30 '91	Sent 6-18-92,		
	4 wks use		
FEB 10 '91	ILL: KRS, BU		
MAR 29 '92	1-10-05,		
APR 13 '92			
RT'D JUL 27 '93			
	ILL LDL, 2-2-07		
4 wks use			

FAMILY TRANSITIONS

THE GUILFORD FAMILY THERAPY SERIES
Alan S. Gurman, *Editor*

FAMILY TRANSITIONS: CONTINUITY AND CHANGE OVER THE LIFE CYCLE
Celia Jaes Falicov, *Editor*

FAMILIES AND LARGER SYSTEMS: A FAMILY THERAPIST'S GUIDE THROUGH
THE LABYRINTH
Evan Imber-Black

AFFECTIVE DISORDERS AND THE FAMILY: ASSESSMENT AND TREATMENT
John F. Clarkin, Gretchen L. Haas, and Ira D. Glick, *Editors*

HANDBOOK OF FAMILY THERAPY TRAINING AND SUPERVISION
Howard A. Liddle, Douglas C. Breunlin, and Richard C. Schwartz, *Editors*

MARITAL THERAPY: AN INTEGRATIVE APPROACH
William C. Nichols

FAMILY THERAPY SOURCEBOOK
Fred P. Piercy, Douglas H. Sprenkle, and Associates

SYSTEMIC FAMILY THERAPY: AN INTEGRATIVE APPROACH
William C. Nichols and Craig A. Everett

FAMILY RESOURCES: THE HIDDEN PARTNER IN FAMILY THERAPY
Mark A. Karpel, *Editor*

FAMILY PARADIGMS: THE PRACTICE OF THEORY IN FAMILY THERAPY
Larry L. Constantine

SYSTEMS CONSULTATION: A NEW PERSPECTIVE FOR FAMILY THERAPY
Lyman C. Wynne, Susan H. McDaniel, and Timothy T. Weber, *Editors*

CLINICAL HANDBOOK OF MARITAL THERAPY
Neil S. Jacobson and Alan S. Gurman, *Editors*

MARRIAGE AND MENTAL ILLNESS: A SEX-ROLES PERSPECTIVE
R. Julian Hafner

LIVING THROUGH DIVORCE: A DEVELOPMENTAL APPROACH TO
DIVORCE THERAPY
Joy K. Rice and David G. Rice

GENERATION TO GENERATION: FAMILY PROCESS IN CHURCH AND SYNAGOGUE
Edwin H. Friedman

FAILURES IN FAMILY THERAPY
Sandra B. Coleman, *Editor*

CASEBOOK OF MARITAL THERAPY
Alan S. Gurman, *Editor*

FAMILY TRANSITIONS
Continuity and Change over the Life Cycle

Edited by

CELIA JAES FALICOV
La Jolla Marital and Family Institute
University of California, San Diego

Foreword by Salvador Minuchin

THE GUILFORD PRESS
New York   London

16801425
DLC

11-5-90

For Raul:
Love always
Celia

© 1988 The Guilford Press
A Division of Guilford Publications, Inc.
72 Spring Street, New York, NY 10012

Printed in the United States of America

Last digit is print number: 9 8 7 6 5 4 3 2 1

Library of Congress Cataloging-in-Publication Data
Family transitions.

(The Guilford family therapy series)
Bibliography: p.
Includes index.
1. Family psychotherapy. 2. Family. I. Falicov,
Celia Jaes. II. Series.
RC488.5.F356 1988   616.89'156   87-28119
ISBN 0-89862-074-0

Contributors

LINDA A. BENNETT, PhD, Department of Anthropology, Memphis State University, Memphis, Tennessee

PAULINE BOSS, PhD, Department of Family Social Science, University of Minnesota, St. Paul, Minnesota

JAMES H. BRAY, PhD, Department of Psychology, Texas Woman's University, Houston, Texas

DOUGLAS C. BREUNLIN, MSSA, Family Systems Program, Institute for Juvenile Research, Chicago, Illinois

LEE COMBRINCK-GRAHAM, MD, Institute for Juvenile Research, Chicago, Illinois

CELIA JAES FALICOV, PhD, La Jolla Marital and Family Institute, La Jolla, California, and Department of Psychiatry, University of California, San Diego, California

H. CHARLES FISHMAN, MD, DHS Mental Healthcare, Inc., Plymouth Meeting, Pennsylvania

MANUEL GUTIERREZ, PhD, Aspira Inc. of Pennsylvania, Philadelphia, Pennsylvania

ESTRELLA JOSELEVICH, PhD, Buenos Aires, Argentina

DAVID V. KEITH, MD, Family Therapy Institute, St. Paul, Minnesota

HOWARD A. LIDDLE, EdD, School of Medicine, University of California, San Francisco, California

KATHARINE J. MCAVITY, MSW, Washington Psychological Center, Washington, District of Columbia

MONICA MCGOLDRICK, MSW, Community Mental Health Center, University of Medicine and Dentistry of New Jersey, Piscataway, New Jersey

BRAULIO MONTALVO, MA, The Family Institute, Albuquerque, New Mexico

DAVID H. OLSON, PhD, University of Minnesota, St. Paul, Minnesota

FRANK S. PITTMAN, III, MD, Department of Psychiatry, Emory University, and Department of Psychology, Georgia State University, Atlanta, Georgia

BERNICE L. ROSMAN, PhD, Philadelphia Child Guidance Clinic, Philadelphia, Pennsylvania

ESTER R. SHAPIRO, PhD, Cambridge Hospital, Harvard Medical School, Boston, Massachusetts

THOMAS C. TODD, PhD, Illinois School of Professional Psychology, Evanston, Illinois, and the Center for Family Studies/Family Institute of Chicago, Chicago, Illinois

FROMA WALSH, PhD, University of Chicago, Chicago, Illinois

WENDY L. WATSON, RN, PhD, Faculty of Nursing, University of Calgary, Calgary, Alberta, Canada

J. PAMELA WEINER, MA, PhD cand., Department of Family Social Science University of Minnesota, St. Paul, Minnesota

CARL A. WHITAKER, MD, Department of Psychiatry, University of Wisconsin, Madison, Wisconsin

DONALD S. WILLIAMSON, PhD, Department of Family Medicine, Baylor College of Medicine, Houston, Texas

STEVEN J. WOLIN, MD, Department of Psychiatry and Behavioral Sciences, George Washington University Medical Center, Washington, District of Columbia

LORRAINE M. WRIGHT, RN, PhD, Faculty of Nursing, The University of Calgary, Calgary, Alberta, Canada

LYMAN C. WYNNE, MD, PhD, Department of Psychiatry, University of Rochester Medical Center, Rochester, New York

Family Therapy Development: A Parable

Family therapy was born in the late fifties. She did not, of course, spring full-grown from the brain of Zeus. No, like any other human birth, hers was the product of two families joining together. Very different families they were, indeed—different geographically, with different traditions, rituals, languages, myths, and cognitive styles.

One of the families—the mother's side?—had long-established roots in the Northeast. This was a large family, with many aunts, uncles and cousins, almost all of them with university connections—certainly establishment. Their names were legion: Ackerman, Bowen, Whitaker, Wynne, Fleck, Bell, Auerswald, Minuchin. This family's beliefs were a continuation of psychodynamic belief systems, of course modified, conflicting, and challenging. But there was no doubt of the dialogue or of its lineage: the influence of the past on the present, the importance of mastering experiences in certain stages for the successful and harmonious mastering of the next stages. . . . One could say they were all influenced in their thinking and beliefs by developmental concepts, be it via Freud, Sullivan, Erickson, or even Piaget. These were older uncles whose portraits one could still see in their offices.

This side of the family also believed in the importance of emotions, of unconscious or unwitting processes, and of cataclysmic events like birth, death, murderous rage, sex and incest, reason and unreason, and at times all of these beliefs mixed in strange and confusing ways.

They also had a fastidious way of thinking: They focused on details, forever explaining the root and cause of events, usually searching for causes in the past.

Of course all of these beliefs and meticulous searches burdened them, and they were ready for new ideas, new language and new myths. In effect, they began their own search, but the old belief systems remained there, submerged, but influential, sometimes appearing in broad daylight, other times part of the closet baggage.

The West Coast family was different. They were rebels and revolutionaries. For a start, they rejected their lineage, and proclaimed themselves born full grown from the brow of Bertalanffy, Weiner, Bertrand Russell. . . . Linguists, communication theorists, mystics, and philosophers were selected for parenting, while social theorists and the old-timers in psychology and psychiatry were stoned for their past sins and their temples burned.

The first fully chosen, the grandfather and leader of the bunch of young turks, was Bateson, and with him the other members of the immediate family: Jay Haley, Weakland, Jackson, Virginia Satir. Others joined: Watzlawick, Fish. . . . They had the advantage of living all together in a large castle in Palo Alto. There they began their successful attack on the established truth, proclaimed truth relative, and began to construct a new system of belief that would have the advantage of not being rooted in social issues.

A new language developed: homeostasis, entropy, first and second order change, recursive feedback loop, double-bind. New concepts were written in this language. The family was excited by the sound of the language and hoped that the human family would organize itself to its harmonies.

So Family Therapy was born. At her birth, the members of both families smiled, as all families do at such events, and hoped that the newborn would do *them* proud. Of course there is always rivalry and competition between families at the birth of a first grandchild. And Jay Haley invited Milton[1] to the christening. Milton was a rather strange guest, who belonged to both families, yet belonged to neither. Milton smiled mysteriously.

Family therapy sucked from both breasts and grew up divided. As she developed, as youngsters usually do, she entered into alternative coalitions with the Northeast and the West Coast families. In each coalition she became more competent in some areas, and in equal proportions was made more incompetent in others. Besides, she began to know and differentiate her aunts and uncles, and realized that what had seemed in the beginning a homogeneous family was really a conglomerate—a rambunctious, sometimes opinionated, closely interwoven bunch of relatives. For instance, Aunt Peggy (who is close to Uncle Don) shares with Cousin Lynn an appreciation of the aesthetics of disengaged circular questioning. But on feminist issues she is closer to Cousins Betty, Monica, Virginia, and a number of others in articulating the nature of family power and patriarchal hierarchies. The West Coast side of the family, as it grew, sent offspring to Italy, where Aunt Mara, who is now on distant terms with Uncle Gianfranco and Uncle Luigi, is close to Cousin Tomm in Canada, who still goes to parties with Gianfranco and Luigi. Both sides are full of alliances, coalitions, and paradoxes, like any family.

When Family Therapy began school she sometimes spoke the differentiated language of the West Coast, so rich in universals, and at times the language of the Northeast, still rooted in particulars. Of course signifiers are sometimes confusing. Once when she said "neutrality" she seemed to mean just that. But lately neutrality seems to be shifting to mean an overall goal in the midst of challenge. Sometimes it means something altogether different, as when Aunt Mara tells parents to go to the movies together but not tell the children the plot. And when Family Therapy enjoyed repeating the word *provocazione,* a word frequently used by Cousin Maurizio (who lives in Italy but not in Milan), at times it meant just provocation, and the meaning was clear. But sometimes *provocazione* meant provocation embedded in a field of acceptance, which seems to mean the same thing as neutrality, but maybe that's different in Milan. And Family Therapy learned more and more words, and she was excited by their sound.

As she approached adolescence she began to see that the two families had learned from each other, but they didn't want to admit it. So they gave different names to the concepts that they had learned from the other side of the family. The new labels were usually more complex than the old concepts because the new owners were not yet as familiar with them as the old owners were. And Family Therapy, as older adolescents and young adults do, grew weary of the family squabble because she knew that families will do what they have to do. But the process of integration is going to be in the hands of her children, who will know that their grandparents are nice, but do not understand the world.

As an adult, Family Therapy looked at her assets and found herself rich in systems theory and all the words that kept growing; she also had quite a rich repertory of technique for changing families that were now available to all the family members in the West and the Northeast, Canada, Europe, Rome, Milan, South America, and even Japan. She found that what excited her now was to look at the contexts of families—the social system, the hospital, the court, the welfare system—and she realized she'd always wanted to be a politician.

One thing bothered Family Therapy. While she had all this knowledge and all these dreams, she didn't really know families. Her own development had been in a family skewed toward the excitement of the new, and in the process the painstaking, detailed exploration of the particulars of families had eluded her. And so in the calm way that belongs to mature people, she bestowed her blessing on Celia, who wanted to edit a book on the Family Life Cycle.

In the way characteristic of family reunions, important relatives from both coasts were gathered for this event: the writing of a unique book titled *Family Transitions*. In this book, differences in world views are welcomed in pursuit of a common concern that transcends particular schools: the development and refinement of models and perspectives about the temporal evolution— spontaneous or planned—of family relationships. Like most well-orchestrated family therapy rituals, those participating in the experience of writing or reading this book come away with a greater appreciation of the idiosyncratic confusion, dreams, pains, and hope that belong to family members as they face old and new tasks in the process of living, growing, and dying. There are no simplifications or stereotypes here about stages and tasks but deeper insights into the complexity of how families change and stay the same with the unfolding of life events.

Family theorists will find in this remarkable volume ways to include

Family Therapy Development: A Parable

hitherto neglected dimensions of family change and ways to connect with distant relatives, family sociologists and developmental psychologists. Family therapists who read it will be better equipped to weave their techniques, their exciting words, and their theories in patterns that can heal.

Salvador Minuchin, MD

NOTE

1. For those readers not on a first-name basis with the therapists mentioned in the foreword, they are as follows: Milton H. Erickson, Peggy Papp, Don Bloch, Lynn Hoffman, Betty Carter, Monica McGoldrick, Virginia Goldner, Mara Selvini Palazzoli, Gianfranco Cecchin, Luigi Boscolo, Karl Tomm, Maurizio Andolfi, and Celia Falicov.

Preface

The family has its own growth.—D. W. Winnicott (1965)

In simple words, the quotation above captures the message of this book. In more technical terms, the idea that the family as a unit has its own evolutionary processes is new and relatively unexplored. In spite of increasing interest in the family life cycle as a framework for family therapy, relatively little has been done to elucidate the specific dimensions and processes of spontaneous and therapeutically induced change over the family life cycle.

Until now, the most common approach to family development in both sociology and family therapy has been to provide a modal description of the family life cycle as following a more or less orderly sequence of stages, such as marriage, parenthood, and old age, characterized by developmental tasks and punctuated by transitions. Although that approach has been productive and is further expanded in this volume, other conceptualizations that do not necessarily follow the normative description of the stage-oriented approach offer new perspectives on family development.

Following an introductory chapter that stresses the contributions of life cycle concepts developed in family sociology, crisis theory, and family therapy, and that outlines future directions for the family development framework in family therapy, the volume is divided into four parts. Part One deals with the much needed creation of new conceptual models that integrate the temporality of the life cycle approach with systems theory. Such models have important clinical and research applications and, by their very nature, cut across therapeutic orientations. Olson's (Chapter 2) approach is rooted in family sociology; he integrates family life cycle concepts with his well-known Circumplex Model and presents research results that argue for the utility of that integration. Wynne (Chapter 3) presents a sophisticated model for the development of family relatedness based on the epigenetic principle. In an extension of her relational picture of the family life spiral, Combrinck-Graham (Chapter 4) applies that model to families with sexually developing adolescents. Breunlin (Chapter 5) offers a clinically applicable theory of development based on changes in individual competence that occur through oscillations between higher and lower levels of family functioning.

Part Two presents microscopic and macroscopic perspectives that place family therapy views of development in the context of other disciplines and lift them from the circumscribed arena of the therapist's office. Some chapters also discuss how changing (or static) sociocultural values affect conceptions about individual and family development. Shapiro (Chapter 6) proposes a creative integration of family life cycle stage theory with individual developmental psychology that focuses on a process model of individuation. Using an ecosystemic "lens," Montalvo and Gutierrez (Chapter 7) comment on factors that constrain human development; they discuss the misuse of the "cultural identity" concept in the fields of health, mental health, and education as an explanation of "developmental" failures of Puerto Rican youth and of the behavior of Puerto Rican women interacting with institutions. Bennett, Wolin, and McAvity (Chapter 8) introduce cultural perspectives on life cycle transitions through a carefully constructed paradigm based on the concept of "family identity," a vehicle for cultural transmission over the generations. The timely issue of gender development is introduced in Chapter 9 by Boss and Weiner, who present a critique of family therapists' assumptions about women's development and offer alternative assumptions within a new, more flexible systemic paradigm.

The five chapters in Part Three explore the role of expected and unexpected events in producing family crises and disruptions in the family life cycle. Pittman (Chapter 10) distinguishes different patterns of crises and discusses the appropriate treatment approach for each. In her examination of developmental crises that result from a combination of family evolution and cumulative stress, Joselevich (Chapter 11) offers a conceptual and clinical paradigm that incorporates important ideas about patterns of change in living systems. The impact of chronic illness in a child on the family's organization and development is covered by Rosman (Chapter 12), who also considers the effect of different interventions on the future evolution of families with chronically ill children. Walsh and McGoldrick (Chapter 13) have studied the impact of death and unresolved mourning on the family life cycle and, reciprocally, the influence of family life cycle tasks on the family's response to death. They suggest interventions that facilitate adaptation to loss and that strengthen the family for future passages. Another clinical area in which the life cycle framework has been specifically applied is in the assessment and treatment of substance abuse. Todd (Chapter 14) gives specific guidelines for the application of the life cycle model to substance abuse, connecting the stages of treatment to the stages of addiction at different points in the life cycle.

Although the family development paradigm potentially applies to all family therapy orientations, its importance, meaning, and use depend crucially upon the structure of a given conceptual or therapeutic approach. In Part Four, proponents of the major family therapy approaches—*intergenerational, structural, systemic,* and *symbolic-experiential*—describe how the family life cycle framework is articulated within their orientations. Williamson and Bray (Chapter 15) give an overview of the use of family development concepts in the intergenerational orientations, which is followed by their own "systemic and cybernetic" intergenerational model of individual and family growth. A structural approach is presented by Fishman (Chapter 16), who formulates a structural–developmental assessment schema to help organize therapeutic goals and predict the durability of change. Wright and Watson (Chapter 17), basing their work on the Milan approach, discuss the use of a systemic, nonnormative developmental approach that nonetheless takes into account life cycle stages and transitions. In an intriguing iconoclastic chapter, Keith and Whitaker (Chapter 18) warn about the danger that the life cycle paradigm may simplify the family's complexity. Focusing on the bare bones of development (birth and death), they talk about families evolving through the multigenerational symbolic experience. A final chapter by Liddle (Chapter 19) is included in this section. It deals with the yet unexplored topic of how to use the family development framework in the training context.

All of the chapters are original contributions by leading experts, theoreticians, clinicians, researchers, and trainers. The book has been written for family therapists, but it should also be of interest to individual therapists, developmental psychologists, human development specialists, and family sociologists. Since the volume presents a comprehensive range of approaches that both expands on previous work and presents new models relevant to family development, it could be valuable for teaching family therapy in academic and professional settings. The format of the book was designed to present a variety of orientations and approaches to family development and to emphasize a balanced blend of theory building and clinical application throughout.

My interest in the topic of family development is long standing. As a graduate student on the Committee on Human Development at the University of Chicago, I set out to learn more about the evolution of family systems by conducting longitudinal research on the transition to parenthood. The paucity of conceptual and research tools available then for use in studying the dimensions and processes of change involved in going from a dyadic to a triadic system continues to a large extent today. The memory of the transformations I observed as a student, paired with an enduring interest in understanding developmental processes in the families I see in therapy, provided strong motivation for putting this book together.

Of all the concepts used by family therapists, the family development framework is among the least studied, in spite of its relevance to understanding spontaneous family change and to facilitating therapeutic intervention. As a topic, family development also has the potential of creating bridges with other social sciences, as I have endeavored to explain in the opening chapter. For the families themselves, the life cycle framework represents a meaningful description of universal processes in their lives. As a way of thinking, it encourages a temporal orientation that encompasses past, present, and future, but most of all, it fosters in both clients and therapists a vision of a future, a vision that almost always includes hope and progress. It is my hope, too, that this book finds ways to transform some of the bewildering complexity of its topic into an enriched understanding within those who read it.

REFERENCE

Winnicott, D. W. (1965). *The family and individual development.* London: Tavistock Publications.

Contents

OVERVIEW

1

Family Sociology and Family Therapy Contributions to the Family Development Framework: A Comparative Analysis and Thoughts on Future Trends

CELIA JAES FALICOV
La Jolla Marital and Family Institute
University of California, San Diego

We have a less satisfying explanation of human psychological development than of the life cycle of the fruit fly, which has been an object of study for less than a hundred years.—Jerome Kagan (1984)

Models of individual development over the life cycle have been fairly well established through clinical practice and basic research. By contrast, models of family development are in a nascent, rudimentary stage, in terms of both their internal complexity and their articulation with systems-oriented therapies. There are as yet no clear answers to questions about what parameters change over time in the family as unit, what impedes family development, and what produces the change observable in family transitions.

Current knowledge about family development permits only global description. There are many reasons why we know more about the development of the fruit fly than about the development of the individual or the family. The most prominent one is the complexity of human social, mental, and emotional development, which presents itself at its maximum proportions in any discussion of the family as a growing system.

A well-established French intellectual tradition advises us to straddle at least two disciplines when attempting to understand a complex subject matter. This, of course, makes the subject matter even more complex, but in the long run it also clarifies many issues that would otherwise remain untouched through excessive respect for the boundaries among disciplines. The topic of family development provides an ideal arena for this type of practice insofar as human development really should be an interdisciplinary area of study, inte-

3

grating individual, interpersonal, and family systems approaches. Some attempts to reduce the distance among disciplines concerned with human development are beginning to be made (see Hill & Mattessich, 1979; Lerner & Spanier, 1978).

Family therapy originally borrowed some aspects of the family development framework described by family sociologists in the late 1940s and early 1950s, but a rich body of information, models, and insights about development seldom tapped by family therapists continues to be generated by family sociology and other social sciences. On the other hand, a family systems theory perspective undoubtedly can expand traditional developmental theories, particularly those that focus on the interior of the individual (see Minuchin, 1985).

The contributions of family sociologists to a family development framework are discussed in the first major section of this chapter. It focuses on the importance of family stress theory and on the strengths and limitations of integrating the family development framework with systems-oriented therapies. The second section presents a descriptive critical analysis of the use of family life cycle concepts by the major family therapy orientations. Each theory is examined with regard to its position on the importance of considering life cycle issues in theory and practice, its views about family dysfunction and family development, and its theory about the relationship between developmental and therapeutic change. The third section offers concluding thoughts on the future evolution of an integrative and multidirectional systemic family development framework.

FAMILY SOCIOLOGY VIEWS ON FAMILY DEVELOPMENT

The Family Development Framework

The developmental approach in family sociology stems from the conceptual work done by Evelyn Duvall and Reuben Hill in the late 1940s (Aldous, 1978; Duvall, 1957; Hill & Rodgers, 1964). Designed to meet the challenges of the growing field of family studies, this approach was, from its inception, an eclectic, integrative framework that brought together concepts from rural sociology, child development, and the sociology of work. It also merged concepts from structure–functionalism and symbolic interactionism, the two main philosophical positions in sociology. Even though the concepts were taken from several disparate viewpoints, the end result was a cogent approach that accounted for regularities in family life over time. Over a decade ago, family therapists adopted the bare outlines of the family development framework, but they have seldom seemed to turn to the sociological sources or to collaborate with family sociologists on this subject matter.

Basic Developmental Concepts

The core concept of the developmental framework is the notion that families change in form and function over the life cycle and that they do so in an ordered sequence of *developmental stages.* Three criteria are used for dividing the life cycle into stages: (1) *changes in family size,* usually due to additions or losses of family members, which divides family life into five expanding, stable, and contracting stages (stable stage—childless, expanding stage—childbearing, stable stage—child rearing, contracting stage—launching, and stable stage—empty nest); (2) *changes in age composition,* based on the chronological age of the oldest child from infancy through young adulthood; and (3) *changes in work status* of the breadwinner(s). A synthesis of these categories results in eight stages of development in Duvall's (1957) scheme. (Seven of these stages appear in Table 2-1 in Chapter 2 of this volume.)

Those developmental dimensions were added to a structural-functional conception of the family as a system in which the units, or members, occupy two types of *role positions: age positions* (e.g., child, adolescent) and *relatedness positions* (e.g., husband–wife, father–daughter). New stages of development occur when there are marked changes in *role content* resulting from age changes or from additions or losses of members that require rearrangement of roles. The appropriate role changes become the family's *developmental tasks.*

Among the difficulties presented by this predictable picture of a family gliding smoothly from stage to stage are that it leaves out the stresses that often accompany family change and that it disregards psychological aspects such as the construction that the individual or the family makes of the social role demands. In addition, and perhaps most important, the focus is on the processes *within* stages, with insufficient attention paid to the processes of change *between* stages (Mederer & Hill, 1983). These deficits appear to have been overcome by the introduction of the family stress theory.

Family Stress Theory

The family development framework represented efforts to understand change in families under normal circumstances. Family sociologists also engaged in a parallel effort to understand families under unusual stresses, such as the economic hardships experienced during the Depression of the 1930s (Angell, 1936; Cavan & Ranck, 1938) or the separations endured during World War II (Hill, 1949). The notions of coping, adjustment, and adaptation were used to link the developmental framework and family stress theory by arguing that expectable life cycle changes can be stressful and may require as much ongoing adjustment as sudden, unexpected events (McCubbin & Figley, 1983; McCubbin & Patterson, 1983). The best known scheme for the study of family stress and coping is the ABC—X model (Hill, 1949, 1958; McCubbin *et al.*, 1980; McCubbin & Figley, 1983). The "A" stands for the stressor event, "B" represents the family's coping resources, "C" is the interpretation the family gives to the event, and "X" is the outcome or crisis state. Since 1958, this model has generated a substantial body of research dealing with each of its four aspects. Most recently, the notion of regularities in stresses and strains at different stages in the family life cycle has been developed by Olson (see Chapter 2, this volume).

The equation of normative and nonnormative events proposed by the marriage between the family development framework and family stress theory can be problematic or inaccurate at times, but the integration of concepts related to stress theory, although seldom recognized, proved to be important in a number of ways. First, it introduced an important refinement of the original family life cycle framework. In its early formulation, the family development framework considered stages to be discrete or discontinuous because they required major qualitative reorganization of roles (Hill & Mattessich, 1979). Later on, periods of *transition* between stages were added, taken primarily from Rapaport's (1963) conception of developmental crises. These became the periods of discontinuity between stages, while the processes of change within stages were thought to be continuous, since the family had reached relative structural stability. Second, the introduction of a more in-depth picture of the distributions of stresses and strains over the family life cycle increased the clinical relevance of this model. Third, the notion of a "pile-up of stressors" (Hill, 1949) mirrored more accurately the complex reality most families face—that is, having to cope with several expected and unexpected stresses simultaneously. Fourth, by introducing processes of coping and adaptation, some dynamic elements were added to a model that could appear to be static because of its emphasis on the structural organization of stages. Finally, this addition opened the possibility of seeing family problems or symptoms as unsuccessful efforts at adaptation, a perspective espoused by many family therapists.

Family Development and Family Dysfunction

The family development framework and family stress theory were not intended to address clinical issues. Yet, it is possible to make several inferences from these theories about areas of potential difficulty for evolving families that may be helpful to clinicians. One possible source of stress for families is the incompatibility of developmental tasks among family members. Hill (1986) has observed that some families have more compatibility than others in developmental tasks between parents and children, or among siblings, or even between husband and wife. For example, families with children spaced at regular intervals will experience a smoother "meshing" of tasks than those whose members arrive in distinct "waves." Among the latter are families for whom stage-specific tasks lapse for some time and then need to recur again or be "recycled," such as when a parent who has already raised children in a first marriage has another child after remarrying.

The issue of why some families experience smooth transitions while others go through rough times has been broached by family sociologists (Burr, 1972; Hill, 1986). Hansen and Johnson (1979) believe that smooth transitions result when the family starts to experiment with new patterns gradually, while still retaining the comfort and familiarity of the old patterns. Rough transitions may occur when the gradual phasing in is not possible, either because the family has a limited repertoire of experimental behaviors and becomes "stuck" in old patterns or because an unexpected and severe stress may be superimposed on a normative transition. A number of refinements can come about from Hansen and Johnson's ideas, such as the possibility of breaking down the transitional period into phases of old versus experimental behavior patterns, and even operationalizing phases of transitions as different ratios of established to new patterns (Mederer & Hill, 1983).

The issue of when and how a normal life cycle transition develops into a disorganizing state of crisis that may be accompanied by symptoms is of fundamental importance to family therapists. One basic hypothesis is that difficulties in adapting to the normative transition stem from the overwhelming accumulation of other stresses (Hill, 1949). Boss (1983; Boss & Greenberg, 1984) offers another hypothesis, based on her idea that a period of boundary ambiguity is common during transitions, given the complex role and rule changes and task realignments required. The degree and the duration of the period of boundary ambiguity influence whether life cycle changes produce successful or unsuccessful coping. Joselevich (Chapter 11, this volume) translates models of stress and crisis for the clinical treatment of families facing several simultaneous expected and unexpected changes.

The Family Development Framework and General Systems Theory

Family therapists have assimilated the basic concepts of the family development framework but appear to be less acquainted with efforts by family sociologists to explore the relationship between family development and general systems theory.

In 1971, Hill proposed to examine the family life cycle framework in the light of general systems theory. He started by summarizing four clusters of conceptualizations relevant to the family life cycle framework: (1) the family as a social system that is relatively closed, boundary maintaining, equilibrium seeking, purposive, and adaptive; (2) concepts of structure, such as position, role norms, role clusters, and complexes; (3) concepts of goal orientation and direction; and (4) concepts dealing with orderly sequences or sequential regularities such as stages of development.

Although it would be interesting to compare the two perspectives on all of the four clusters, it is in the first of the conceptualizations that Hill believes the greatest overlap can be found between systems theory and the family developmental framework. There are two areas of similarity and difference in the conceptualization of the family as a social system.

The first area of comparison concerns the phenomenon of *interdependence of parts.* Both perspectives subscribe to the premise of "nonsummativity," which states that the effects of system membership are greater—or sometimes less—than the sum of the behaviors of the individuals composing the system and that change in one part of the system brings about changes in other parts. This assumption is still generally taught as a truism in family therapy training. But systems theorists (Hill cites Buckley [1968] on this issue) have a more complex, less mechanistic view of the interdependence of parts than do family developmentalists, since they *do not* believe that every part of the system is related to all of its companion parts, so that a change in one will inevitably affect all the others. (This hypothesis may help explain why a recent review of research studies on marital satisfaction over the life cycle failed to lend definite support to the theoretical truism that the marital experience is dependent upon the vicissitudes of the family life cycle [Menaghan, 1983], raising the issue about the partial insulation of other subsystems—parental, sibling, individual—from the life cycle events that the family as a whole is undergoing.)

Based on this important difference between systems theory and the family development framework regarding the interdependence of parts, Hill proposed a rewriting of the family life cycle framework to present the interdependence of parts as a variable, changing in degree over the life cycle, low in the beginning of marriage and varying over time afterward. If we were to heed Hill's proposal, the presentation of the family life cycle could take a process-oriented form based on one parameter of systems change: the interconnectedness of family members alternating between degrees of closeness and distance (separateness). In addition, future theories would have to consider relatively independent developments in different family subsystems.

The second area of comparison concerns the *degree of openness and permeability of boundaries* of the family as a social system. In its initial formulation, family development theory regarded the family as a "relatively closed system," changing mostly through the maturation of family members and maintaining equilibrium by warding off incompatible external pressures. This definition of the family as a homeostatic system becomes problematic when one considers that within a developmental perspective, the family is necessarily viewed as a changing structure responsive not only to variance in age, size, and composition but also to societal expectations. Furthermore, the family is anything but static, ideally providing a variety of growth-promoting experiences. How can these two opposite views of the family be reconciled? Hill believes that systems theory can help resolve this dilemma. Systems theory looks at social systems as relatively open internally and externally. It includes notions of positive feedback (Hoffman, 1971; Maruyama, 1963), "mapping for variety" (Cadwallader, 1959), and morphogenesis (Speer, 1970). These notions can help explain change processes in the family that the developmental framework cannot account for with its emphasis on homeostasis, and they can help identify processes at work in relation to family growth and adaptation. In short, "a modern systems perspective would emancipate and liberate the family development framework from the shortcomings of the organismic and the mechanical models from which the framework has drawn so many of its analogies" (Hill, 1971, p. 311). As will be discussed later, these ideas within family sociology parallel family therapy theory as it developed over time, moving from an earlier focus on equilibrium-seeking or homeostatic properties of systems to an emphasis on growth and change-promoting processes.

Family Sociology and Family Therapy

The family life cycle framework has been widely accepted in the social sciences in spite of acknowledged shortcomings. These include its essentially descriptive nature, its emphasis on child over adult development, its focus on nuclear family units, and its tendency, in practice, to appear somewhat oblivious to historical and cultural contexts. Family therapists have incorporated many concepts derived from the traditional family development framework, such as normative age and sex roles, family stages, and phase-specific developmental tasks, and also concur with family sociologists on the assumption that change within stages is continuous but that change during transitions is discontinuous (Hill & Mattessich, 1979). Family therapists have also enriched the original family development scheme by including a three-generational perspective and by adding stages and transitions of divorce and remarriage (Carter & McGoldrick, 1980).

Other potential contributions of family sociology to family therapy come from the research area. The family development framework has been utilized to study normative patterns of marital satisfaction over the family life cycle (Blood & Wolfe, 1960; Klein, Jorgensen, & Miller [cited in Hill & Mattessich; 1979]; Menaghan, 1983; Rollins & Cannon, 1974; Rollins & Feldman, 1970; Spanier, Lewis, & Cole, 1975). An example of this type of research is provided by Olson in Chapter 2 of this volume.

Family sociologists have had the opportunity to apply the family development framework in conceptually organizing the everyday details of family life in the American nuclear family through the perspective of work, marital, and parenting roles in ways that are applicable to research in normal family development. Furthermore, family sociologists have the tools with which to study the constant modifications that the family life cycle undergoes through exposure to sociocultural, economic, and other historical factors and thus to question biased assumptions embedded in the dominant developmental theories, such as Boss and Weiner do in Chapter 9 of this volume.

Hill's proposal to integrate the family development framework with systems theory has rendered only a few, but nevertheless very significant, models for family therapists. Olson has taken precisely the two aspects of systems theory noted by Hill (1971)—the interdependence of parts (cohesion) and the openness and flexibility of the family system to change (adaptability)—and has combined them in the circumplex model (Olson, Russell, & Sprenkle, 1983; Olson, Sprenkle, & Russell, 1979). One of the applications of this model is to chart family life cycle changes along these two system dimensions, as Olson does in Chapter 2 of this volume. By adding the study of clusters of stressors and strains and of the family's coping resources and satisfaction in the various life cycle stages, Olson captures all of the basic elements of a state-of-the-art sociological model of family development. Combrinck-Graham (1983, 1985, and Chapter 4, this volume) presents another example of a sophisticated process model of family development focused on the changes in the interconnectedness of family members, which alternates between centrifugal and centripetal states over a three-generational family life cycle.

The family development framework continues to grow conceptually as theorists compare and integrate theoretical insights from related disciplines, such as life-span developmental psychology, and attempt to ascertain isomorphisms in the development of individuals, families, and even larger systems, such as communities (Hill & Mattessich, 1979). In the applied arena, Hill (1986) has recently extended and modified the original framework for use with single-parent families.

FAMILY LIFE CYCLE CONCEPTS IN FAMILY THERAPY

The family life cycle framework has been productive for family clinicians during the past decade. Some 30 years ago, Pollack (1956), a psychoanalyst, proposed the use of sociological small-group and role theory to provide a safeguard against placing the source of pathology in the individual only and thereby ignoring the family. One of the sociological concepts he selected for integration with psychoanalytic views was the idea of the family as a small social organization that undergoes various phases of development. He then examined various phases of marital and family development in terms of a set of dimensions of need complementarity that take on different primacy and content at various stages. Although Pollack's theory about therapeutic intervention had the sophistication to integrate psychoanalytic concepts (such as regressive or arrested needs) and social role adaptations to cultural demands, his work did not become known by family therapists at that time.

In 1971, a posthumous publication by Scherz, a social worker, presented what appears to be the first description in family therapy terms of how family and individual developmental tasks interrelate and influence each other. Scherz was influenced by the psychodynamic thinking of Erikson and Lidz and by the family sociology concepts of Hill and Parsons, and she made a sensitive translation of these ideas to the therapy situation. She postulated recurrent, universal family tasks that parallel and interdigitate with individual psychological tasks, and the idea that at each stage there has to be a shift in object relations, identifications, and marital equilibrium. She believed that conflict is inherent in family development for several reasons. The needs of the family may be different from the needs of the individual. Conflict also ensues when the children move into developmental stages that are inevitably incompletely resolved by the parents. A high point of stress also occurs when movement toward the next stage is imminent, because there is always conflict between the wish to retain the status quo and the wish for change. This peak of stress was labeled by Scherz as a transitional, developmental, or maturational crisis. Scherz described both the content and the process of the various stages and tasks. O'Connell (1972), who attended Scherz's lectures at the Smith College School for Social Work in 1970, summarized the relational processes involved in family development as intimacy versus distance, acceptance versus competition, enabling versus undermining, exposure versus encapsulation, consolidation versus confusion, and release versus adhesion. O'Connell regarded these processes as ongoing and repetitive, but as assuming different primacy at different moments in the life cycle.

The interest in the family life cycle within social work has continued (Rhodes, 1980; Shilling & Gross, 1979). But it was not until 1973, with the publication of Solomon's general developmental schema that appealed to both psychoanalytic and systems therapists, that the family development framework first became widely known to family therapists. Solomon (1973) conceptualized a schema of family development influenced by Erikson (1963) and by Scherz (1971). The stages Solomon proposed were marriage, the birth of the first child and subsequent childbearing, the individuation of family members, the actual departure of the children, and the integration of loss. Central to each stage are specific developmental tasks that need to be mastered adequately before the family can go on to the next stage. Each task is described first in psychodynamic terms and then in social role terms. For example, in the first stage, marriage, the first task involves each partner's relinquishing the primary gratification experienced in his or her family of origin and investing the marriage as the primary need-meeting relationship. The second task involves the implementation of male and female roles in a variety of marital functions. It is hypothesized that avoidance of developmental tasks leads to chronic difficulties in family interaction, whereas doing the taskwork adequately brings on acute, temporary, stage-specific stress.

Also in 1973, in *Uncommon Therapy,* Jay Haley used the family life cycle framework to conceptualize the clinical work of Milton Erickson. Haley proposed that individual symptoms were an indication that the family was "stuck" around transition points that required changes the family was unable to make. Support for the idea that symptom onset is related to family developmental crises, particularly those that alter family composition through the addition and loss of members, was given in a research study by Hadley *et al.* (1974).

Carter and McGoldrick (1980) charted the life cycle progress of the three-generational American middle-class family and described not only the developmental tasks inherent in each stage but also the transitional difficulties. By describing expectable impasses and by offering possible therapeutic interventions, Carter and McGoldrick's approach significantly increased the clinical relevance of thinking about the family as an evolving unit.

A Descriptive Critical Analysis of the Use of Family Life Cycle Concepts by the Major Family Therapy Orientations

The family life cycle framework has become a substantive concept and a useful therapeutic tool for family therapists. One of its salient characteristics is its applicability across theoretical positions. This distinct advantage ironically could have stunted its own development. Since the framework does not belong to any of the well-articulated family approaches, its conceptualization has remained at a rather global, simple level, and the task of integrating it with other family therapy concepts has not yet even begun.

One way to begin this task is to ask how each of the major family therapy orientations actually uses life cycle concepts in theory and in practice. Although these uses are not always readily discernible, it is possible to deduce them from careful reading, inference, and analysis. An examination of the family life cycle framework from the perspective of the structural, strategic, brief, systemic, psychodynamic/intergenerational, and symbolic–experiential viewpoints in family therapy can help add richness to this framework and increase its articulation with other family therapy concepts, without robbing it of its original advantage of transcending theoretical allegiances.

In this section, I will present my views, for each orientation, on (1) how it utilizes concepts related to the family development framework, (2) what dimensions change over the life cycle and how these changes come about, (3) how family dysfunction is connected with family development, (4) the relationship between a theory of change and a theory of family development, and (5) specific applications and techniques. The evolution of ideas in family therapy has been rapid, which means that sometimes an orientation changes its views on family development over a relatively short period. Whenever possible, I have tried to base my analysis on the most recent published position.

Before embarking on this analysis, I believe it is important to distinguish between the concepts of "family development" and the "family life cycle," to help the reader in understanding similarities and differences among the various family therapy orientations. Although the two terms are not synonymous, family therapists often use them interchangeably. This confusing practice was probably inherited from family sociologists, who used the label "family developmental framework" for their studies of the family life cycle.

The "family life cycle" refers to those nodal events that are tied to the comings and goings of family members, such as the birth and raising of children, the departure of children from the household, retirement, and death (Duvall, 1957). These events produce changes requiring adaptation in the formal (or the symbolic) organization of a family. These changes in family composition require reorganization of roles and rules. The life course of families evolves through a fairly predictable sequence of stages, which appears to be fairly universal in spite of cultural and subcultural variations. The family life cycle is also subject to myriad individual variations in timing and coping strategies, but these changes have been dubbed "normative" for a reason. Much of the human race shares similar biologic time clocks or societal expectations (i.e., entrance into puberty and menopause, entrance into elementary school, and retirement from work), and therefore there is little choice about these changes. Another reason for life cycle commonalities is that the normative patterns act as a guide or a cultural ideal, which, whether valued or denigrated, has some influence on people's perceptions of their lives, if not on their actual life conduct.

"Family development" is an overarching concept, referring to *all* transactional coevolutionary processes connected with the growth of a family. These include processes of continuity and change connected with work or occupational development, relocation, migration and acculturation, acute or chronic illness, or any set of events that significantly alters the texture of family life. Psychological processes such as the development of intimacy in a couple, unmourned grief reactions, invisible loyalties, or the transmission of intergenerational triangles in a family are an integral part of family development. Although there is a regularity and internal logic to many of the processes subsumed under family development (the stages of migration, the stages of alcoholism, the stages of adaptation to illness), each family is different precisely because each can be said to have its own *developmental path,* which evolves from all the different settings in which development takes place, including each family's construction of its past and present.

Life cycle and developmental processes overlap and interact, sometimes synchronically, other times asynchronically (see Wynne, Chapter 3, and Williamson and Bray, Chapter 15, this volume). Because family development is a more inclusive concept, it can subsume processes connected with life cycle changes. Therefore "family development" is used in the following discussion whenever a generic term is needed, whereas "family life cycle" is reserved for the organizational and adaptational changes connected with changes in family composition.

Structural Family Therapy

A developmental way of thinking underlies structural family therapy. Although this orientation gives primacy to issues of family structure, statements about family development can be culled from various publications (Minuchin, 1974; Minuchin & Fishman, 1981).

Structural concepts relevant to family development. Many key constructs used in structural family therapy have explicit or implicit relevance to the family life cycle. The family is viewed as an open sociocultural system in transformation and as a social unit that confronts a series of *developmental tasks* (Minuchin, 1974). As such, the family undergoes natural change over time, progressing through fairly *predictable developmental stages:* couple formation, families with young children, families with school-age or adolescent children, and families with grown children (Minuchin & Fishman, 1981). These stages are punctuated by changes in family composition, by the reorganization of old subsystems and the appearance of new ones, and by changes in boundaries outside and inside the family. The physical and social maturation of children writes much of the timetable for family development because much of the work of structural family therapists is with families that have school-age or adolescent children. The basic life cycle flow is similar for all families, in spite of cultural and other contextual differences.

Demonstrating an early interest in normal development, Minuchin (1974) reported an interview with a nonclinical couple during the stage of family formation. He concluded that the developmental tasks they were facing involved two major processes. One was the spouses' mutual *accommodation* to each other's style in a large number of daily routines. The other process entailed *boundary making,* which involved negotiating the nature of the boundary between the two newlyweds and of the boundary between them and their families of origin and groups of friends. Further, both sets of family-of-origin parents and siblings also faced adjustments and boundary reorganizations in order to accept and support the new family unit.

Central to the structural model is the idea that families go through *periods of transition* when a new member enters the system or when an established member departs. The family life cycle thus evolves through stages of entrance and departure, or joining and separating of family members. These periods of transition (birth of a child, death of a spouse, adolescent launching) often involve changes in the distribution of roles and in the rules that define family boundaries.

The refinement of the concept of boundary into the two parameters— *patterns of proximity* among family members and *hierarchical structure* of the family—proposed by Wood and Talmon (1983) and Wood (1985) provides a means of clarifying the dimensions that change during family transitions. When a structural therapist forms a diagnostic impression of a family, temporal parameters (chronological and maturational) are regularly included along with the structural dimensions of proximity and hierarchy, since functional family structures change naturally to fit with developmental requirements, while dysfunctional ones lag behind. For example, in well-functioning families, a parent–child dyad tends toward greater proximity, or enmeshment, in the early stages of the child's maturation and becomes more disengaged over time. The impact of family proximity on individual development is also taken into consideration. Enmeshed members are said to become limited in the development of autonomy, whereas disengaged members are handicapped in their feeling of belonging to a family or group.

The dimensions pertaining to hierarchies also have a developmental component—that is, parents have executive power over, influence on, and responsibility for their children by virtue of their older age and greater experience. Changes in the hierarchy occur as children mature through adolescence. Perhaps because of its focus on children in two-generational families, structural theory does not fully address the boundary changes that occur during adult development or in the three-generational family.

The relationship between family development and family organization is one of reciprocal influence. Developmental requirements change the organization of the family, but just as often, development adjusts to fit the most functional organization for a particular family.

Family dysfunction and family development. For structural therapists, family dysfunction is linked to developmental processes in several ways:

1. The family restructuring involved during *periods of transition* is stressful. New processes always generate anxiety. Structural problems may be revealed or may develop anew in the form of blurred or rigid boundaries manifested as too much proximity or as a confusion of hierarchies. Although most families change their patterns adaptively, some families will respond to stress in a dysfunctional manner by clinging to the old patterns. These stresses may be connected with the appearance of symptoms and may be misjudged as rigidly pathological rather than as transitional. Thus structural therapists espouse an orientation whereby many families would be treated as needing to accommodate to average stressful transitions (Minuchin, 1974), and they distinguish these families from those that have a more permanent and rigid dysfunction.

2. Functional and dysfunctional patterns are assessed by the *fit* of a system's structural organization to its functional requirements in developmental and social contexts (Aponte & VanDeusen, 1981). It would seem that one of the ways in which the fit is determined is through observations about "age-appropriate behavior," or behaviors, tasks, and privileges that are consonant with the chronological ages of family members. Age expectations then become one of the criteria for evaluating the functional insertion of a member in subsystems, inside and outside the family.

3. The *pace of change* during transitions is also essential to assessing dysfunction. If the transition to the new stage occurs too slowly or too quickly, the results are problematic. For example, the reorganizations that occur after

a divorce cannot be rushed, nor can the transitional structures go on indefinitely (Wood & Talmon, 1983).

4. Other dysfunctions are connected with *developmental lags.* By virtue of his or her position in the family's organization, an overinvolved or underinvolved individual often cannot act in ways appropriate to his or her chronological age within the family. This inability could result in an enduring emotional handicap in other social situations. There are similarities between this notion of developmental deficit and the concept, in the developmental psychology literature, of incompletion or failure in accomplishing a developmental task. There are also similarities with the notion, in the psychoanalytic literature, of fixation at a certain level of development, but in structural family therapy there is no fixed determinism or pessimism about the possibility of recovery and later growth in different contexts. Hence the notion of a "lag" or retardation rather than inalterable loss.

Theory of change and family development. Conceptions about change within the structural orientation emphasize how family therapists have tended to disregard the fact that families are constantly changing, prompted by inside and outside forces. Furthermore, processes of continuity and of change coexist and alternate in a family's adaptation. Utilizing Ilya Prigogine's (Glansdorff & Prigogine, 1971) concept of dissipative structures, Minuchin and Fishman (1981) describe how, in a living system, fluctuations in the customary transactions among family members, occurring either internally or externally, create instabilities that can move the system toward a new structure. Since a fluctuation is not followed by a response that returns the system to a steady state but rather by further amplification, the family may enter a crisis from which the transformation results in a different level of functioning, one that makes coping possible. Both continuous and discontinuous processes can lead to transformations of patterns. (For further discussion of this important topic see the section Key Issues in Family Development in this chapter, and Fishman, Chapter 16, this volume.)

This conceptualization of change also provides a perspective for drawing parallels between family developmental crisis and therapeutic goals, since the therapeutic crisis is said to follow a developmental blueprint. Structural therapy unlocks family members from ineffective interactions and thus helps them restructure the family to adapt to the new developmental or contextual requirements.

> One of the goals of therapy is to move the family to a stage of creative turmoil where what was given must be replaced by a search for new ways. Flexibility must be induced by increasing the system's fluctuations, ultimately moving toward a level of higher complexity. In this sense, therapy is an art that imitates life. Normal family development includes fluctuations, periods of crisis and resolution at a higher level of complexity. Therapy is the process of taking a family that is stuck along the developmental spiral and creating a crisis that will push a family in the direction of their own evolution. (Minuchin & Fishman, 1981, p. 27)

Although the respectful therapeutic push is in the direction of the family's own evolution, structural therapists have a sense of the appropriate direction for change, one that will enable normal development to take place.

Relevant applications and techniques. Developmental concepts have applications at various stages of the therapeutic process. For inclusion in their repertoire of *assessment tools,* structural trainees are encouraged to internalize a model of normative developmental expectations for families with children of different ages. Typical structural assessments include a bridge to explore the age appropriateness of family members' behaviors. For instance, asking about disagreements among family members is a way to explore patterns of conflict resolution (or the lack thereof), but it also serves to make fine discriminations about age-appropriate autonomy or other developmental achievements.

The structural model of assessment is taken a step further by Fishman (Chapter 16, this volume), who integrates a second-order cybernetic approach. He formulates a four-dimensional model of "structural–developmental" assessment to be used at the beginning and at the end of therapy to predict whether developmental processes have been set in motion and therefore whether the change will be *durable.* The four dimensions covered are (1) detecting developmental instabilities, (2) evaluating family organization, (3) collecting individual and family histories, and (4) assessing the family system, a process that involves the therapist both objectively (as observer) and subjectively (as participant).

Developmental frames are also utilized during the *problem definition stage,* since families seem to understand a theme or a reframing that presents either the individual or the family as having missed some crucial aspect of maturation. Developmental analogies can be powerful tools for mobilizing a family, by means of a language that points out complementarities (e.g., "You are acting like a four-year-old" and then, to the parents, "How do you manage to keep him that young?"; Minuchin & Fishman, 1981, p. 197).

Several structural *techniques* seem to have an implicit maturational theme or content that uses *age* as a plastic construction. These could be labeled as *age metaphors* ("Mother and daughter act like twins"); *age predictions* (to an 11-year-old anorectic: "At the point you are 12 you will start eating . . . "); *age differentiations* ("You are sometimes 12 and sometimes 4 years old"); *age enactments* (asking a parent and a child to stand up to see who is taller and who weighs more, and comparing the combined weights of parents with the weight of the child to dramatize hierarchical imbalances); and *objective versus subjective age,* or *chronological versus emotional age* ("You may be 8 but you are acting 14"). (Quotes in parentheses are culled from Minuchin & Fishman, 1981.) Other age-related developmental messages can be found in the way structural therapists manipulate the structure of a session by changing subsystems composition and meeting with various combinations of age groups (older children and parents; peer group; younger and older children).

Treatment goals are also guided by concepts about appropriate family organization in relation to the identified patient's developmental stage and the family's developmental tasks during that stage. Treatment plans and therapeutic techniques are finely tuned in order to accommodate the differences in the parent–child relationship at different stages: childhood, preadolescence, adolescence, or older adolescence (Rosman, 1986).

Sensitivity to developmental issues in the family is extended to the therapist–family match. For example, joining or alliance building and use-of-self interventions are said to work better when the therapist has personally experienced the stage of family development that the family is undergoing.

In this book, two applications of structural family treatment to specific problems emphasize and further expand developmentally oriented thinking. Rosman (Chapter 12) discusses the developmental disruptions and prospective coping in families with a chronically ill member, and Todd (Chapter 14) accords centrality to developmental issues in a structural–strategic approach to the treatment of substance abuse.

Strategic, Brief, and Systemic Family Therapies

In this section, the work done by Haley at the Family Therapy Institute of Washington, DC, by the Brief Therapy Center of the Mental Research Institute (MRI) in Palo Alto, and by the Milan team in Italy will be discussed separately because, in spite of similarities in their theoretical roots, the views of these groups regarding the family life cycle framework differ substantially.

Strategic, brief, and systemic therapy concepts relevant to family development. As noted earlier, Haley was one of the first to introduce the concept of the family life cycle to family therapists when he focused on developmental processes as a background for Milton Erickson's strategic work (Haley, 1973). In so doing, Haley offered several concepts that served to link the family sociologists' model of the family as a group undergoing fairly smooth developmental transitions with the crisis theorists' observations about family problems emerging around transition points. Haley's main thesis was that symptoms appear when there is an interruption or a dislocation in this natural unfolding in the life cycle of a family.

The model of the family life cycle that Haley utilized is based on six stages: the courtship period; marriage and its consequences; childbirth and dealing with the young; middle-marriage difficulties; weaning parents from children; and retirement and old age. The model is straightforward and serves an orienting function with regard to possible crisis points for families. By inference from Haley's general propositions, one can say that hierarchical change is the most important dimension of family development. Haley felt that talking to and about a family in developmental terms was better than trying to construct a family typology or a family symptomatology (Haley, 1971; Stanton, 1981). But he really did not elaborate a model of family functioning over the life cycle. Rather, like most strategic therapists, he remained more interested in developing a model of therapeutic change geared toward solving problems.

The Brief Therapy Center of the MRI (Watzlawick, Weakland, & Fisch, 1974; Weakland, Fisch, Watzlawick, & Bodin, 1974) bases its approach on the fact that all families have problems in living, many of which derive from the difficulties imposed by life cycle transitions. The transitions that the MRI group includes are the change from the voluntary relationship of courtship to the commitment of marriage, and from this to the irreversible commitment to the new family when the first child is born; the sharing of influence with other authorities that is required when children enter school, and such sharing with the children themselves and their peers in the adolescent period; the shift from a child-oriented marital relationship back to a two-party system when the children leave home, and the intensification of the two-party relationship at retirement; and the return to a single life upon the death of one spouse.

In its original work, the Brief Therapy Center of the MRI considered life cycle issues to be very important elements in problem formation. But in more recent writings, life cycle issues seem to have lost their previous significance. For example, in 1974, Weakland *et al.* stated, "We see normal transitional steps in family living as the most common and important 'everyday difficulties' that may lead to problems" (p. 147). Problems would be likely to develop if people treated an ordinary difficulty as a problem or if they treated an ordinary (or worse) difficulty as no problem at all. Despite this strong initial interest, the latest volume of the Brief Therapy Center (Fisch, Weakland, & Segal, 1982) contains no explicit references to life cycle issues, not even in a lengthy case report of a family with an adolescent in difficulty. This absence was later clarified by Fisch (1983) as a change of perspective, whereby the MRI group no longer sees life cycle transitions as having any greater importance than other changes.

The initial writings of the Milan group show sensitivity to family development (Selvini Palazzoli, Cecchin, Prata, & Boscolo, 1978). Although the group's earlier views regarded family systems as primarily stable or homeostatic, its more recent views stress that systems are always changing and evolving and only appear to be stable (Tomm, 1984a). The Milan group is more interested than Haley or the MRI group in how the behavior evolved into its present form (MacKinnon, 1983). A part of systemic therapy's epistemology is always concerned with the evolution of a problem and with how the system's members view themselves now and how they view their own shared history. In this way, the Milan group ends up with a detailed understanding of how family members perceive their past and with more clues as to how the family came to be as it is now. The intention is not to help clients understand or "work through" past emotions but rather to use the information to disrupt, often through "positive connotation," the symptomatic configurations in the present (Hoffman, 1981).

Family dysfunction and family development. Perhaps the best known life cycle aspect of Haley's model is the proposal to define pathology as the interruption of a normal developmental process. The assumption here is that the symptom is an indication that the family is having difficulties getting past a stage in the life cycle. Conceptually, these difficulties are linked to a structural fault: confused or incongruous hierarchies in the family. The goal of therapy is to get the family unstuck and get the life cycle moving again. In spite of its logical weaknesses (Gurman, 1983), the importance of this stance is that it redefines or reframes symptoms for families and for therapists. The family no longer has to search for a cure for the pathological individual but rather has to work at resolving the impasse they are all experiencing.

In its view of dysfunction, the MRI group is not concerned with understanding the origin of family problems but rather with understanding how families maintain the problems through their well-intentioned but unfortunate attempts to resolve them. Contrary to the family's expectations, these attempted solutions lead them to more of the same patterns and prevent the organizational or rule shifts that are necessary for resolving the problem. Wrong solutions come about when family members overemphasize or underemphasize difficulties in living by taking action when it is unnecessary and by not taking action when necessary. Other wrong solutions come about when action is taken at the wrong level: The family attempts first-order change when the life transition requires second-order change, or vice versa. Any of these wrong solutions can calcify into a chronic problem that slows down developmental progress.

For the Milan group, dysfunction "occurs at points of natural transformation when the system is unable to make the leap to a new way of functioning" (MacKinnon, 1983, p. 430). There is a temporal emphasis here, with an evolutionary focus where past and present are connected to the future. Given the family's current "epistemology" (their way of viewing their dilemma), there are no alternatives that would help change their present predicament. Derailments from the family life cycle, such as those precipitated by illness, premature death, or ambiguities in relationships at developmental junctures, are associated with the appearance of symptoms. Flexibility is a determinant feature. Flexible families face and adapt to developmental changes, whereas families that are not flexible enough experience conflict and the subsequent emergence of symptoms around transitional periods. If the family rules do not allow for natural progression through the life cycle, a family member may develop a symptom as a solution to helping the family progress along its evolutionary path (Hoffman, 1981; Tomm, 1984b).

Theory of change and family development. In his original statements about the family life cycle in 1973, Haley did not elaborate on the nature of the transition process beyond the notion that symptoms appear when there is disruption in the unfolding of the cycle. There are several ways to interpret this idea. The best known interpretation is that the life cycle change required at the time of the appearance of the symptom is discontinuous in nature and difficult to achieve, given the family's present organization. Another possibility is that the family is unable to complete an already ongoing and continuous process rather than failing to initiate a new process (Breunlin, 1983). Both possibilities seem plausible. Perhaps under normal circumstances, changes come about in a continuous way, and therapy could somehow imitate this process.

In *Problem-Solving Therapy* (1976), Haley's model of therapy suggests that change is gradual and that it occurs in stages, which may involve alternate and even abnormal family structures as intermediate stages toward the goal. With the publication of *Leaving Home* (1980), Haley made clear links between the life cycle model and a therapy in progressive stages (Breunlin, 1983) to help the family complete the young adult's leaving-home process. The outcome is evaluated in normative developmental terms, such as engaging the young adult in age-appropriate activities like working or living independently. The therapist works systematically in a clear direction toward a predictable goal. Although there is a fundamental shift in family functioning over time, this is accomplished through a gradual, almost plodding digital process that lacks the flair of the analogical communication often associated with discontinuous change. Furthermore, one of the processes involved for the parents appears to be a *gradual learning* to relate to their children as adults (Perrota, 1986). One may argue that this tendency to favor continuous change is apparent primarily in *Leaving Home,* but this is actually where Haley demonstrates a great deal more interest in applying a life cycle model than in his more recent writings.

Consistent with their focus on interactional sequences in the here and now, Watzlawick *et al.* (1974) of the MRI group do not make generalizations about family development over time, but they offer a description of first-order and second-order mechanisms of change that is later expanded and directly applied to the life cycle by Hughes, Berger, and Wright (1978). First-order changes are those that take place within a given set of rules and are aimed at preserving the continuity or stability of the system. Second-order changes involve the creation of new rules and thus facilitate total system reorganization. According to Hughes *et al.* (1978), the family life cycle requires the two types of change. First-order change is relevant to within-stage changes, and second-order change is needed when shifting from stage to stage during family transitions. This theory helps to describe how some families grow chronologically without really changing their interpersonal rules. True developmental change can only be of the second-order type, and it involves a leap to a new family organization, a restructuring that is discontinuous and irreversible (Hoffman, 1980; Weeks & Wright, 1979).

Hoffman (1981) uses Ashby's concept of "step-function" to explain how living systems undergo intervals of constancy separated by discontinuous jumps. In addition to her attending to macroprocesses, Hoffman (1981), using

communications concepts, makes unique contributions toward an understanding of the microprocesses involved in developmental change. She believes
that certain types of communications, labeled as "simple binds," or paradoxical injunctions, give confusing directives that over time create sufficient
pressure for movement into a new stage of development. The receiver, for
instance, an adolescent, may be asked to be simultaneously in a symmetrical
and a complementary relationship with a parent. Since this is an impossible
situation, a leap or a transformation to a new integration must occur. Hoffman
reserves the term "double bind" for those communication sequences that
block this developmental leap.

The Milan group's position relative to the nature of change is that
families constantly evolve, though they are generally unaware that they are
doing so. This type of continuous change occurs in everyday life and helps the
progression through individual and family life cycles. Discontinuous changes
occur with major life events and can also result from therapeutic interventions.
Systems change can occur within the affective, cognitive, or behavioral domains,
but the most profound changes occur in the family's perceptions and beliefs
(MacKinnon, 1983; Wright & Watson, Chapter 17, this volume). A major
difference between the Milan approach and many other approaches is the
avoidance of imparting a developmental direction to the interventions, with a
strict adherence to notions of emergent and multidirectional change. The
Milan group has even developed techniques to avoid focusing on family
transitions lest the therapist be tempted to become too purposive and invested
in producing a particular developmental outcome, and direct the family to
function or to be organized in a particular way. (For a discussion and illustrations of this important topic, see Wright & Watson, Chapter 17, this volume.)

Relevant applications and techniques. Systemic and strategic therapists
rely on the family life cycle as one of their *assessment tools.* For Haley, the
therapist's knowledge of developmental expectations serves as a guideline for
recognizing family crisis points. The MRI Brief Therapy Center takes into
account life cycle values and expectations when learning the language and
values of the family, since this learning facilitates tailoring the interventions to
each family. For the Milan group, the content of a particular hypothesis is
derived from several sources, including information about the particular
family, experience with similar problems, and theory. During the *hypothesis-
generating phase,* the Milan group uses a variety of ideas from various
psychological theories, which include views about human development. The
systemic therapist explores the differences in relationships over time, before
and after significant nodal events in the family's history and in relation to
hypothetical future events (Penn, 1985). The purpose is twofold: "first, to
release new information into the system so that the family members themselves will make the connections between events, relationships or behaviors,
and second, to gather information to validate or invalidate hypotheses"
(MacKinnon, 1983, p. 429).

When moving on to a *definition of the presenting problem,* all of these theories make considerable use of the family life cycle framework. In 1980, Haley integrated his interest in life cycle redefinitions with his problem-solving approach in a therapy for "mad young people" (schizophrenics, substance abusers, or those with other severe symptoms) that regards their problems as family failures to negotiate the leaving-home stage. This type of therapy may well be considered a problem-focused, strategic–developmental approach, although many structural concepts (hierarchies, coalitions) are also essential components.

Stanton and Todd (1982) applied Haley's ideas about the association between severe symptoms in young people and the family's separation difficulties to understanding and treating substance abuse in adolescence and the launching stage. Todd (Chapter 14, this volume) expands the model to include adult substance abuse and offers guidelines for conducting a life cycle diagnosis. He suggests strategies for incorporating (explicitly or implicitly, directly or indirectly) life cycle interventions and also applies a developmental metaphor to the description of the stages of addiction and recovery.

For the MRI group, life cycle interventions are indistinguishable from others, since all interventions are geared toward dealing with unfortunate attempted solutions to human problems. Strategic therapists believe that paradoxical techniques are ideally suited to producing discontinuous leaps and are therefore the treatment of choice for developmental impasses (Hoffman, 1980; Weeks & Wright, 1979). Adding a developmental emphasis to strategic thinking, Coppersmith (1981) describes a useful technique called "developmental reframing," whereby the identified patient is labeled not as "bad" or "mad" but as "young." This intervention interdicts dysfunctional sequences, creates a sense of hope, and, by putting the parents in charge, restructures family boundaries. Thus a strategic reframing creates a different level of family organization in a way that is similar to spontaneous processes of developmental change.

For the Milan group, the redefinitions connected with developmental issues take place in an indirect fashion, perhaps in the form of a reflexive question that stimulates a family to think and act in a new way (Tomm, 1987). An example of this type of question is, "If you decided to convince your son that he was ready to leave home, how would you go about it?" Another approach may be to explore through circular questioning the meaning and belief about a developmental problem, such as finding a connection between an older adolescent's failure to leave home and a belief that this person has an illness, and to intervene when beliefs interfere with problem-solving efforts (Wright & Watson, Chapter 17, this volume).

Haley (1973) applied the metaphor of therapeutic interventions as initiation ceremonies that ease the family's journey to the next developmental stage. Many interventions that fall in the category of *rituals* are used by therapists of the three approaches described in this section, but the Milan group has most explicitly focused on rituals as "spontaneously" facilitating developmental passages. (For illustrations of therapeutic "rites of passage" in families with adolescents, see Quinn, Newfield, & Protinsky, 1985.)

Regarding *therapeutic goals,* Haley appears to have normative outcomes in mind—even if he does so only strategically—and thus directs the therapy to accomplish them, most notably in the leaving-home approach. The MRI Brief Therapy group is not concerned with life cycle goals beyond symptom relief or problem resolution. The Milan group believes that the therapist cannot be directive, because he or she does not know what the future course or evolution of a particular family will or should be. The goal is not to put the family "back on track" but to facilitate a context whereby the family will decide the position that leads to less stress or increased growth, primarily through the introduction of new meanings or actions that will alter the family's patterns.

There are many interventions and techniques that could be labeled structural-developmental, strategic-developmental, or systemic-developmental. Many of these are described in detail in this volume in Chapter 12 by Rosman, Chapter 14 by Todd, Chapter 16 by Fishman, and Chapter 17 by Wright and Watson.

Psychodynamic/Intergenerational Family Therapy

Developmental approaches have characterized psychoanalysis from its inception. The original tenets of psychoanalysis and their later derivatives in object relations theory, ego psychology, interpersonal psychiatry, and self psychology contain a substantial theory of human development. Family therapy derivatives from these individual approaches can be found in the psychodynamic, intergenerational, or multigenerational family therapy orientations.

Ackerman (1959) was perhaps the first proponent of a psychodynamic approach to the family. He pointed out contradictions and ambiguities in Freud's ideas about individual development. For instance, Freud emphasized the role of the family in molding the child's personality but gave priority to inborn instincts and unconscious mental processes over the interpersonal reality of the family environment. Ackerman (1966) struggled to define terms such as "family identity" and bemoaned the lack of appropriate language to describe the joint identity of a family pair or the shared experiences of family members over their life course.

In Theodore Lidz's *The Person: His Development Throughout the Life Cycle* (1968), each chapter addresses a different phase of individual development, following Freud's phases of psychosexual development but integrating the interpersonal and psychosocial theories of Sullivan and Erikson, and Piaget's model of cognitive development. Two features of Lidz's approach to individual development set the stage for the possibility of family development. One is the recognition that development continues beyond adolescence and that the adults in the family are therefore also in the process of change. The other is the emphasis on the interactional nature of development, whereby each family member directly—rather than at a fantasy level—affects the course of the others' development.

Many pioneer family therapists brought their psychoanalytic legacies into the construction of their new, interpersonally oriented theories and practices. Among these are Murray Bowen, Ivan Boszormenyi-Nagy, James Framo, Norman Paul, and Robin Skynner.

Psychodynamic/intergenerational concepts relevant to family development. The concept of stages of development, with predictable sequences, processes, and developmental tasks, appears in a variety of forms in the psychodynamic family orientations. Psychodynamic stages, unlike the sociological family stages, refer to real or fantasized *unconscious* early processes in the family of origin that later determine, or at least color, present and future relationships in the family of procreation. The main concept here is the *transmission of emotional patterns* through the generations in each particular family. In this context, family life cycle stages and transitions appear to be thought of as more superficial and thus are not explicitly focused on. Extensive information-gathering of past events through inquiry and genograms gives important clues about three-generational family stresses and family functioning during life cycle transitions. But this family functioning is largely "inherited" from the functioning of previous generations around similar life cycle events. One possible area of future conceptualization for psychodynamic family therapists is the interaction (with points of synchrony and asynchrony) between multigenerational pattern transmission and family life cycle stages and transitions. McGoldrick and Gerson (1985) have offered useful guidelines for interpreting genograms that help assess the fit among family pattern repetition across generations, life events, and family functioning.

Contemporary psychodynamic theory subscribes to the *epigenetic principle.* This principle states that developmental progress requires the meeting and surmounting of the critical tasks of each developmental phase at the proper time and in the proper sequence. Closely related to this principle is the notion of developmental arrest. Just as some individuals are believed to have reached a certain level of development beyond which little growth is possible, so some families are regarded as having reached a certain *level of development* over the generations, in a fashion similar to the idea of fixation at, or regression to, developmental levels in the Freudian scheme. The notion that not only individuals but also couples and families have fairly fixed levels of development implies ideals or models of optimal development for families against which their present functioning can be judged. These models of family functioning are not generally made explicit, but there are some exceptions, such as that of Skynner (1981), who utilized differences between healthy and dysfunctional families in the Timberlawn study as the basis for determining the ideal norm (Lewis, Beavers, Gossett & Phillips, 1976).

For some psychodynamic theorists, the concepts of anal, oral, and genital stages of individual development continue to be useful tools for evaluating the personality characteristics and the level of development of family members (Skynner, 1981). But the most important developmental concept transferred to family development from the literature on individual development is that of *individuation* or *differentiation of self.* For some writers (Meissner, 1978), the developmental course involves repeated separation–individuation experiences, the most critical being those that take place in the resolution of oedipal attachments and at adolescence. These processes enter cycles of repetition in adulthood because most people are thought to chose spouses who have similar levels of development.

For Bowen (1978), the individual's failure to differentiate from the family of origin is at the core of the multigenerational transmission of family problems. The level of fusion–differentiation is fairly well set and hard to change, but the process of defining oneself within the family's relationships inevitably yields a truer, more authentic intimacy with others, demonstrating that differentiation of self is actually a family process. (For further discussion in this volume, see Chapter 6 by Shapiro and Chapter 15 by Williamson and Bray.) Other intergenerational theories also maintain that present family development is stimulated by an individual's differentiation of self and that repressions, developmental failures, and invisible loyalties are passed on from one generation to the next and become roadblocks to individual and family growth (Boszormenyi-Nagy & Spark, 1973; Paul, 1969; Skynner, 1981; Stierlin, 1974).

Family dysfunction and family development. In psychodynamic theory, *internalized history* is the cause of family stress and symptoms (Wachtel & Wachtel, 1986). Stress and anxiety activate past emotional issues that have been repressed and denied, sometimes for generations. This reactivation and the efforts to avoid it often lead to family dysfunction and can lead to symptoms. For Bowen (Kerr, 1981), relationships are more stressful when the individuals have a low level of differentiation and are fused. This intense *fusion* is usually deflected or "resolved" through distancing, triangling a child, or focusing on the dysfunction of one of the spouses. For Skynner (1981), there is a wish for the spouse "to function in a perpetually gratifying parental role" (p. 43), but the partners avoid direct expression of this need for fear of encountering, once more, the pain felt at the time of the "developmental failure." Intense stress is externalized to another family member, often a child. For Paul (1969), failure to mourn a death in the family leads to fusion, whereby some family members are inducted to take on roles that compensate for the "unmourned loss." For Stierlin (1974), the loss may be not only of persons but of ambitions, skills, or ideals that the parents had to give up for themselves when they separated from their parents and that are manifested in their expectations for their adolescent children. For Boszormenyi-Nagy and Spark (1973), when trustworthiness and accountability are damaged in a family, and "invisible loyalties" prevent expression of injustices felt, family development cannot proceed as expected. Symptoms of blaming others, parentifying a child, or failing as a parent may develop. Well-functioning families can openly change their loyalties as required by life cycle changes, whereas dysfunctional families cannot adapt to these new requirements. For Williamson and Bray (Chapter 15, this volume), symptoms are repeated and well-intentioned, but unfortunately misguided, attempts at resolving intergenerational problems, a hypothesis that marries the intergenerational and strategic approaches.

The question of what triggers an emotion that has been repressed, often for generations, or of what stimuli precipitate such intense anxiety is addressed by these theories only in a very tangential way. Careful reading of case studies reveals that often the trigger may be a life cycle event; for instance, the birth of a baby, who requires nurturance, may stir unresolved yearnings for nurturance in the new parents, or a son's graduation from high school may reawaken unresolved competition between the father and his own father. The life cycle event then becomes a marker for associated emotions.

There have been a few attempts to integrate the psychoanalytic ideas about family development with the family life cycle framework that can be useful in the clinical situation. Skynner (1981) postulates a recurrent dialectical sequence of oral, anal, and genital processes (or dependency, control, and sharing) at each individual and family developmental stage (childhood, adolescence, marriage) and integrates these stages with Duvall's family sociology schema of family development. Pincus and Dare (1978) and Dare (1979) integrate object relations theory with the family life cycle framework.

Another important articulation between psychodynamic concepts and the family life cycle is offered by Barnhill and Longo (1978). They propose that since families pass through and resolve the conflicts of each life cycle stage with varying degrees of success, it can be assumed that there would be some partial fixation or unresolved issues at one or several stages of the life cycle. The family goes on growing while conflictual unresolved points are left behind, often to be reawakened when the family faces new transitions that can prompt it to "regress" to previous levels of functioning. Since the stresses occur around family transitions rather than during the stages, Barnhill and Longo (1978) urge therapists to focus on the transition periods. To help therapists with detection, they offer a classification of nine transitions between stages, ranging from commitment (and marriage) to retirement and old age.

In sum, repressions, fusions, invisible loyalties, introjects, or developmental failures passed on from one generation to the next affect the level of development achieved and represent family vulnerabilities that can generate symptoms or other forms of regression when the life cycle stage requires assumption of new roles for which there are no previous workable models.

Psychoanalytic theory of change and family development. Since psychoanalysis always emphasizes the mastery, or rather the lack of mastery, of previous stages of development, it is, perhaps, as Wachtel and Wachtel (1986) suggest, more a theory about how development is prevented through fixation or developmental arrest than a theory about how development comes about. It is in this sense that psychodynamic theory can be said to be a deficit-oriented model, one that points to crucial unevolved aspects of emotional systems. Nevertheless, a counterpart growth orientation is also present. It is manifested in the striving for optimal family growth that is anticipated as an outcome of therapy. Also, the re-creation of past situations in present relationships is believed to have the potential for resolving some of those past issues.

Individual development appears to be foremost, and this, in turn, stimulates family growth. The articulation of individual and family change hinges largely on the individuation of the self. Shapiro (Chapter 6, this volume) shows how the concept of individuation can provide a bridge between individual and family development by integrating child and adult developmental theories with intergenerational family systems perspectives. Another form of integration of individual and family development is achieved by Williamson and Bray (Chapter 15), with their concept of personal authority in the family system as a critical adult developmental task involving fundamental changes in the power relations with one's parents.

For the intergenerational theories, developmental change is continuous, in a rather deterministic and linear manner. Spontaneous change simply does not occur in intergenerational patterns. Levels of differentiation of self are relatively fixed throughout the family life cycle or change very sluggishly. The tendency toward repetition of old patterns is another indication of the emphasis on resistance to change. Life cycle events may create alterations in the emotional system but not enough to create discontinuities or even large-increment changes. In general, there seems to be considerable pessimism in these theories regarding how much change is possible. An exception is the theory of Williamson and Bray (Chapter 15), who regard life cycle events as "windows," or opportunities, for change. Framo (1981) and Paul (1969) also are more optimistic than others.

Relevant applications and therapeutic interventions. In contrast to their pronounced interest in early childhood experiences in the family, intergenerational approaches have surprisingly little interest in child development. Interventions are focused on the adults of the first and second generations. Current family problems are shadows of the past, which can be truly resolved only by actively changing the interaction of each individual with his or her family of origin.

Barnhill and Longo (1978) recommend attending to the issues related to the fixation point as well as to the current transition difficulty. In this way, new opportunities become available for strengthening the family's ability to cope with stress during future transitions. But most psychodynamic interventions do not really focus on the details of family life cycle reorganizations, presumably because transitional adjustments are considered to be relatively easy to make, except in families in which there is a carry-over of past developmental failures. An exception that attends to both present and past issues is offered by Stierlin (1974). In a fascinating study of the life cycle stage he calls "separating parents from adolescent children," Stierlin found that the achievement of a healthy separation and identity formation in the adolescent son depended on the father's successful working out of his own middle-age crisis, which in turn had connections with his own unresolved past and present issues. The interventions, however, were focused on the here and now of the father–son interaction in order to transform "annihilating fights" into "loving fights" and thus strive for mutual liberation. Williamson (1981, 1982) and Williamson and Bray (Chapter 15, this volume) also are oriented toward dealing with the present developmental task and helping the client achieve a new developmental stage.

Intergenerational theories use psychodynamic concepts for understanding family stresses, but they utilize a variety of techniques that may come from other approaches. As in individual psychoanalytic theory, insight and understanding, not behavioral change, constitute the critical therapeutic agent, but such understanding can occur only when anxiety is low (Nichols, 1984). This prerequisite raises questions about the utility of these approaches for stressful transitions. The techniques are developmental or growth promoting insofar as they are geared toward releasing developmental blocks but not because they necessarily address life cycle issues that the family faces as a group.

An important application of developmental thinking is to explore the therapist's family of origin, both as a didactic experience and as an avenue to attaining more differentiated positions, which will increase a therapist's objectivity. The therapist's family's current position in the life cycle is also important, because it could increase empathy and understanding for the family or produce blocks in the therapist's performance.

Symbolic–Experiential Family Therapy

Experiential family therapy is a professedly atheoretical, highly intuitive, and feeling-oriented approach. Carl Whitaker's symbolic–experiential approach has been influenced by psychodynamic and existential thinking.

In their description of symbolic–experiential family therapy, Whitaker and Keith (1981) consider the family life cycle to be "a great model of evolution in a system, changing while simultaneously maintaining its integrity" (p. 191). The clearest markers of the family life cycle are birth and death, and possibly marriage. The developmental stages of the children largely define family processes. Other markers include relocation, changes in income, and "the time when the father quit drinking, or the mother turned religious" (p. 191). Thus, in addition to well-known family stresses, Whitaker and Keith add crucial idiosyncratic moments for the particular family. All of these life cycle events tend to be underestimated by therapists and families, but they probably have a *cumulative* effect on family functioning as a whole. An example they give of cumulative stress is the family with adolescent children. The children are separating and undergoing an identity crisis, the parents are in a midlife crisis, and the grandparents are facing the old-age crises of retirement and physical change.

Whitaker and Keith (1981) offer another conceptualization of the life cycle by thinking of it as *serial impasses* that occur as "the stress between unification and separation of the individuals is repeatedly erupting and resolving" (p. 192). For example, as the "we" unit of courtship dissolves, another "we" emerges with marriage. The stress is dealt with openly or through other means, such as accidents or distractions, until the sense of "we-ness" is reestablished.

Dysfunction comes about through an impasse in a family life cycle transition or by a family's not adapting to changed circumstances brought about by the developmental dynamics of children's growth, the arrival of a baby, or the death of a parent. Conflicts related to time and living space (i.e., the relocation of one member or of the whole family) can also result in dysfunctional stress. If three or four serious stresses develop in one year, the possibilities for dysfunction are increased (Whitaker & Keith, 1981).

Normal families have an evolutionary sense of time that pushes members along the course of the life cycle. A connection with past generations is experienced, but introjects are brought up to date and modified, which is consonant with this theory's emphasis on becoming (Walsh, 1983). The mechanisms of developmental change are *identity crises* that the family undergoes when faced with illnesses, career changes, or other forms of self-doubt. *Frustration* is another mechanism for accelerating change. The processes involved in these changes are assimilation and accommodation, regression and integration, falling apart and putting things back together in a different way (Whitaker & Keith, 1981).

The usefulness attributed to life cycle thinking by Keith and Whitaker in 1981 is followed up in this book by a provocative, iconoclastic chapter (Chapter 18) in which they debunk the normative use of the family life cycle framework. Like the caption accompanying Rene Magritte's painting of a pipe that warns the viewer that a painting of a pipe is not a pipe, Keith and Whitaker's chapter warns the reader that a life cycle concept is not a life cycle of any real family but rather a representation or a metaphor. In spite of their deconstructive stance, Keith and Whitaker do not merely pop the balloon for those who forget that concepts are very imperfect constructs. Apprehensive about the possibility that desymbolization and simplification could occur through misuse of the family life cycle framework, they offer a view of the life cycle that is complex, symbolic, and unpredictable. This view is, of course, consistent with their theory of families and their theory of therapy. It incorporates intuitions, feelings, and hunches about conscious and unconscious aspects of individuals, families, and therapists in a less ordered and perhaps more true-to-life fashion than the typical normative accounts of the family life cycle. In their hands, the scheme of the life cycle remains a useful metaphor in understanding and talking with families as long as it does not get elevated ("overextended and overcalcified") to concrete descriptions or explanations of family patterns over the life course. The main events of the life cycle that they focus on are births and deaths, real or symbolic. The strongest determinants for family continuity and change are the patterns emanating from the families of origin. Therefore the therapeutic method includes the three-generational group in family consultations where the family history is told. The present crises are discussed in the context of the families of origin, all the time focusing on the symbolic meaning of experiences.

KEY ISSUES IN FAMILY DEVELOPMENT: THOUGHTS ON THE FUTURE EVOLUTION OF THE FAMILY LIFE CYCLE FRAMEWORK IN FAMILY THERAPY

In this section, I summarize and discuss key issues in family development and compare the views on these issues that are held by the family therapy orientations presented in the previous section. (Table 1-1 summarizes the positions of each of these orientations.) Family sociologists' views (see the first major section of this chapter) and some insights from life-span developmental psychology on these key issues are also included. Difficulties that have hampered the conceptual progress of the family life cycle framework are highlighted, and future areas of study are suggested.

The discussion is presented in terms of a number of shifts in emphasis, which I believe will help us focus on areas not yet developed and will balance a tendency toward creating unproductive dichotomies. The discussion covers the following shifts: (1) from the family life cycle concept to a more encompassing concept of family development, (2) from universality to cultural and gender relativity, (3) from stages to transitions, (4) from markers to dimensions and processes, (5) from normality to dysfunction, (6) from dualism to dialectic, and (7) from a deficit to a resource orientation.

Finally, some comments on the directionality and durability of change are included, and a schema is presented that divides life cycle interventions into markers and processes, helping to unify various attempts to utilize life cycle concepts in clinical practice.

From Family Life Cycle to Family Development

The differentiations made earlier between family development and the family life cycle can help us understand what types of temporal lenses are utilized by the various family therapy orientations. During assessment and in planning interventions, the structural, the strategic, and even the systemic schools pay considerable attention to life cycle events as markers of impending or current

Table 1-1. Developmental Concepts in the Major Family Therapy Orientations

Family therapy approach	Dimensions (What changes?)	Processes (How does it change?)	Dysfunction	Theory of change	
				Continuous or discontinuous	Directionality
Structural (Minuchin, Montalvo, Rosman, Fishman)	Family organization; Boundaries: proximity and hierarchies; Age-appropriate attributes	Accommodation; Boundary making	Transitional stress—symptom; Lack of "fit" between structure and developmental requirement; Pace of reorganization too slow or too fast	Families constantly changing while maintaining continuity; Fluctuation from usual pattern → amplification → crisis → new level of coping	Normative blueprint; Therapeutic crisis parallels developmental crisis and adaptation
Strategic (Haley)	Family organization; Hierarchies	Undefined	Developmental lag — Symptom appears when life cycle is interrupted, signaling developmental difficulty; Time deviations (too slow or too fast)	Change can be gradual and in stages, including abnormal intermediate stages; Change can also be discontinuous	Normative blueprint helpful as marker of turning points; Help in passage to next stage and in social adjustment necessary for individual growth
Brief (MRI group)	Family rules	Undefined; Balance of symmetry and complementarity (Hoffman)	Wrong attempted solutions prevent necessary rule shifts; Overemphasis or underemphasis on normal life difficulties	Discontinuous	Normative guidelines but not imposed; Tasks designed to unlock impasse

Systemic (Milan group)	Family beliefs and world views	Three-generational adjustments and readjustments. Focused on each family's perception of its own evolution	System unable to make the leap at points of natural transformation	Continuous and discontinuous	Therapist doesn't know about and can't impose future evolution; can only facilitate it
Psychodynamic/ intergenerational	Individuation or differentiation of self Family develops dialectical pattern of dependency, control, and sharing (Skynner)	Biologic maturation Level of development fairly well fixed	Reactivation of fixated developmental level by life cycle stress Symptom represents a symbolic or denied emotion over the generations	Continuous	Model of optimal functioning in facing and surmounting unfinished developmental tasks
Symbolic–experiential	Undefined Births and deaths— real or symbolic (Whitaker)	Assimilation and accommodation Regression and integration Family identity crisis Falling apart and putting things back together	Situational life cycle stress leads to growth impasses Spouses struggle over modeling families of origin Intergenerational self-esteem legacies	Continuous and discontinuous	Avoid normative model; stress on individuality and creativity

change. The structural school takes normative expectations into account when delineating goals for the family, whereas the Milan systemic approach purposively avoids imparting a normative direction to the therapeutic goals. In comparison, the psychodynamic/intergenerational and symbolic–experiential approaches use the life cycle framework as well as other current aspects of family development (career lines, phases of illness) as background or contextual information only and place more emphasis on a multigenerational historical understanding of family development using other explanatory concepts, such as triangulation, projection, or unresolved grief. This difference in emphasis is dictated in part by the characteristic features of these schools. The structural and strategic models emphasize present family stresses and attempt to label problems as transitional whenever possible. The psychodynamic/intergenerational theories postulate that unresolved past issues are involved in the present problems and thus interpret the problems as being "deeper" than transitional stresses. Although some psychoanalytic family therapists (Barnhill & Longo, 1978; Skynner, 1981) integrate a life cycle framework, they, too, ultimately consider life cycle stresses *per se* as insufficient to bringing about symptomatology unless they uncover a larger problem of past family development.

Several chapters in this book distinguish between family development and the family life cycle and provide tools for using both concepts in family therapy theory and practice. In a systemic relational version of the epigenetic principle of development, Wynne (Chapter 3, this volume) introduces four processes that unfold progressively and cumulatively in relational systems: attachment/caregiving, communicating, joint problem solving, and mutuality. The quality of relating afforded by these evolving processes may be propitious to the inevitable changes brought about by life cycle events, or conversely, the family may not be ready for these changes. Williamson and Bray (Chapter 15) distinguish between life cycle processes and multigenerational family patterning (i.e., differentiation of self, or personal authority in the family system), pointing out that they may not operate synchronically but that both are necessary to understanding a family's functioning at any given time.

The complexity involved in modern families' undergoing multiple transitions requires moving from a description of their current life cycle stresses toward an integration of these stresses with other ongoing and past developmental concerns. The concepts of family development and the family life cycle can be integrated in the study of the family either by using existing developmental models or by creating new ones. The model presented by Carter and McGoldrick (1980) postulates a central concept of the flow of anxiety in families as being both "vertical" and "horizontal." The horizontal flow includes all the anxieties inherent in coping with the stresses of life cycle transitions. The vertical flow of anxiety includes patterns of relating that have been passed down through the generations in a family primarily through the mechanism of triangling. Although normative change is usually stressful, anxiety takes a quantum leap when the horizontal (normative) stress intersects with a vertical (transgenerational) stress. Karpel and Strauss (1983) also integrate the developmental tasks occurring at the current structural level (e.g., change in marital roles following the birth of a baby) with tasks occurring at the "relational ethics" level (e.g., balancing loyalty issues in the families of origin), which always implicate previous developmental issues.

Walsh and McGoldrick (Chapter 13, this volume) develop a multilevel model that integrates past and present dimensions to enable therapists to understand the experience of loss over the family life cycle. The model encompasses four parameters: (1) the family's mourning process, which has its own tasks and evolving sequence; (2) other adaptational factors, such as the timing of the loss and the family's past experiences with unresolved mourning; (3) concurrent tasks of the life cycle stage that the family is undergoing; and (4) the social context of loss, such as gender and cultural influences.

Another example of these new comprehensive models of the family life cycle and family development is provided by Rolland (1987) in a conceptual scheme for thinking about the interface between chronic illness and the life cycle. He combines the time lines and phases in the evolution of a chronic illness with the individual's and the family's current life cycle issues and their transgenerational experiences of illness and loss.

From Universality to Cultural and Gender Relativity

The timing, the tasks, the rituals for transition, the coping mechanisms, and even the meaning attached to the different family life cycle stages vary from culture to culture and from subculture to subculture. Yet the family life cycle framework utilized by family therapists seldom considers the family in its sociocultural contexts. Although many universal similarities do exist among families, use of the normative prototype of the American white Protestant nuclear family life cycle may lead to significant errors in assessment. Cultural differences may lead in some families to a longer stage of interdependence between mother and young children or to the absence of a clear launching stage for young adults or of a marked "empty nest" stage for middle-aged or even older parents, as in the case of the Mexican-American family (Falicov & Karrer, 1980).

Future models of the family life cycle and family development need to consider which dimensions and processes have universal application and which are culture specific. Meanwhile, sensitivity to the fact that there are many normative family life cycles may help us avoid errors that occur by focusing only on cultural similarities or on cultural differences among families (Falicov, 1983). One way to clarify life cycle values is to introduce cultural relativity with regard to issues of family organization and family development in the training of family therapists (Falicov, 1988; Falicov & Brudner-White, 1983).

Cultural values inevitably influence theories about what is expected developmentally and ideals about what is desirable. Developmental theories have normative concepts not only about poor and optimal functioning, and about stagnation and growth, but also about men and women (Hare-Mustin & Maracek, 1986). The tendency either to create cultural stereotypes or to ignore differences by applying the norms of the dominant culture—a tendency that is so prevalent in the area of ethnicity or social class—is also manifested in the area of gender differences. Hare-Mustin (1987; Hare-Mustin & Marecek, 1986) provides both (1) a critique of gender dichotomies in psychoanalytic theory (Freud, Erikson) and moral development theory (Kohlberg, Gilligan) that simplify or exaggerate differences between men and women while obscuring power differentials and (2) a challenge to create gender-sensitive theories of family development that are free from gender stereotypes. Boss and Weiner (Chapter 9, this volume) explore biased assumptions embedded in the developmental models utilized by family therapists and offer new directions for rethinking assumptions about men and women.

Developmental psychology has recently offered models of development that facilitate the study of ecosystemic interactions between the individual and the environment in several sociocultural levels, including social support systems, institutional settings, and cultural values (Bronfenbrenner, 1977; Egan & Cowan, 1979). (For an application of Bronfenbrenner's model to family therapy, see Falicov, 1988, and Melson, 1983.)

Studies in developmental psychology that have implications for gender differences and life cycle issues within a family context can also offer valuable information for family therapists. An interesting illustration is provided by Steinberg (1981), who focused on the triad of a mother and a father and their son undergoing the transition from prepuberty to puberty. Steinberg's data indicate that before the son's puberty, the parents shared equally in the hierarchy of the family. By the time the son was in late puberty, he had risen within the hierarchy at the expense of his mother, who then ranked third. The son gained his new position through repeated interruptions of, and confrontations with, his mother. Initially, the mother's resistance to the son's assertions erupted into considerable conflict, until the father intervened and placed limits on the son's behavior. As the adolescent entered late puberty, the conflict subsided, with the mother having more deference for the son. According to Steinberg, the stimulus for these changes appears to have been the son's physical maturation. It is possible that assertive behaviors learned in the peer group are experimented with at home and that mothers, most likely because of gender-related issues in the society at large, are a more frequent target of experimentation than are fathers. There are multiple implications in these findings for gender differences and for the family life cycle and family organization, not the least of which is that it may be the mother, and not the father and or the adolescent, who undergoes the greatest change in position as a result of the child's maturation.

From Stages to Transitions

Family therapists usually make a distinction between stages and transitions, assuming that change during stages is of a first-order nature, while change during transitions is of a second-order nature (see the subsection Theory of Change and Family Development for Strategic, Brief, and Systemic Family Therapies, p. 20). In spite of this important assumption, distinctions are seldom made among developmental activity within a stage, transitional phenomena between stages, and transitional dysfunctions that can lead to more permanent disturbances. It is often unclear whether changes take place during stages, during transitions, or in both. Given family therapists' assumption that success in negotiating family transitions is crucial for family well-being, it is noteworthy that the language used to describe the life cycle is almost always in terms of age-linked stages, with relatively little attention paid to transitional periods. Exceptions are the MRI Brief Therapy Center group and Barnhill and Longo (1978), who use the language of transitions. Carter and McGoldrick (1980) do refer to transitional changes within a stage framework. Breunlin (Chapter 5, this volume) drops the stage–transition framework altogether in favor of a concept of microtransitions. The work of Pittman (Chapter 10, this volume) and of Joselevich (Chapter 11, this volume) constitutes examples of focusing on turning points.

Two conceptions of stage have been distinguished by developmental psychology (Kohlberg, 1973): the age-linked maturational *social role* conception and the *developmental task* conception, which is not age linked. Both are combined in family therapy theory. In practice, however, therapists tend to label the age-linked stage that the family is going through, such as the family with adolescents, and to assume that the developmental tasks follow from the naming of the stage. The problem with explanations based only on social role criteria is that they tend to become circular. For example, parents and children argue because they are a family with adolescents; we know they are in this stage because parents and children argue. It is a short step from here to the reification of a construct (Keith & Whitaker, Chapter 18, this volume).

A developmental task conception is less age bound and more substantial in its postulation of what constitutes development, and it allows for more variability than the naming of stages alone. It is also possible to postulate developmental tasks independently from stages, as Kantor (1983) does. He elaborates a set of eight developmental tasks (e.g., centralization, decentralization) that stem from the larger culture's value prescriptions and pose dilemmas for the family that can erupt into developmental crises.

The emphasis on stages may be an inheritance of the family sociology model that describes family relationships as qualitatively different from stage to stage, dealing more with what happens *within* than *between* stages. The implication of a focus on stages is that they are long, enduring, and structurally stable, whereas transitions are short and fleeting periods of structural instability (Mederer & Hill, 1983). Thus, paradoxically to its intent in describing temporal change, the traditional family life cycle framework appears to be better equipped for dealing with periods of structural stability rather than periods of change, perhaps because, as was mentioned earlier, the implied systems model used by family sociologists could account better for morphostasis than morphogenesis. Family sociologists made some strides in the direction of correcting this problem with the introduction of family stress theory and with their proposal to integrate general systems theory in order to shed light on the family's developmental change. In family therapy, proposals to incorporate concepts of evolutionary feedback and change in living systems can be viewed as efforts in a similar direction (Hoffman, 1981; Minuchin & Fishman, 1981).

Life-span developmental psychologists have devoted much work to the concept of transition as a passage, or a period of instability where new patterns of behavior are experimented with (Danish, Smyer, & Nowak, 1980; Golan, 1981; Levinson et al., 1978; Schlossberg, 1981). Levinson's (1986) model offers a way of integrating stages and transitions through an alternating series of structure-building (stages) and structure-changing (transitions) periods. In contrast to the notion that developmental change occurs only during transitions, Levinson believes that both periods have crucial developmental tasks. In addition, the period of building and maintaining a structure is no less stressful than the period of dismantling it.

There are also some new proposals from family sociology. One example is Klein, Jorgensen, and Miller's "stage-transitional branching process," which embraces how families get from one stage to the next and adds the idea that changes culminate in "branches," or several levels of new equilibrium (cited in Hill & Mattessich, 1979).

From Markers to Dimensions and Processes

Little attention has been given to delineating the dimensions that change over the family cycle (i.e., *what* changes during particular stages and transitions) or the processes by which those changes take place (i.e., *how* the changes come about). Some schools, such as structural family therapy, have defined the dimensions and processes of life cycle change. For other schools, however, these parameters can be deduced only from other aspects of their theories (see Table 1-1). The reason for this lack of interest in dimensions and processes may be that for family therapists, life cycle events are used mainly as *markers* of impending or present change in family organization and functioning.

A shift may be needed whereby life cycle events are studied in terms of a set of dimensions and processes changing over time rather than as mere markers. Olson's model (see Chapter 2, this volume, and the Family Sociology section in this chapter) and Combrinck-Graham's model (1983, 1985, and Chapter 4, this volume) are examples of models that focus on *dimensions,* such as the interdependence among family members, and then trace or follow changes along these dimensions over the life cycle.

Another approach is to turn toward *process* models of development. These models are interested in tapping broader processes of transformation, those that cut across stages and transcend them and that may take different forms at different stages. Within life-span developmental psychology, there are several examples of this type of broad, macroprocess approach. In Riegel's dialectical theory (1975, 1976), development is not conceived of as lying in either the individual or the social group, but as evolving from the dialectical interaction between the two. He defines "developmental change" as the emergence and eventual resolution of contradictions, conflicts, and asynchronies occurring along four planes of developmental progression: inner/biological, individual/psychological, cultural/sociological, and outer/physical. One of the difficulties with process theories is that they can be more vague and abstract than stage theories, but they are a good, and probably a necessary, complement to stage theories. Weeks and Wright (1979), for example, suggest utilizing Riegel's scheme to construct a dialectic of the family life cycle by combining the four planes of development with Duvall's (1957) life cycle stage progression and viewing each stage simultaneously from the perspective of each of the four planes.

In family therapy, a good example of a process model is Shapiro's work (Chapter 6, this volume), with her application of the process of individuation over the life cycle. Terkelson (1980) and Hoffman (1981) are also interested in the processes of change during transitions. Reiss's (1981) work on paradigm shifts at major life transitions includes the steps involved in the "construction" of a shared concept of crisis and the eventual family reorganization.

From Normality to Dysfunction

Virtually all of the family therapy orientations reviewed assume that family dysfunction can be connected with a developmental impasse and that the aim of therapy is to reestablish the normal life cycle flow. Thus the issue of when and how a normal life cycle transition develops into a disorganizing state of crisis that may be accompanied by symptoms is of fundamental importance to family therapists. Table 1-1 shows that each school's assumption about the relationship between family dysfunction and family development is consistent with the epistemological position that each theory embraces across many topics. In the area of family dysfunction, the family life cycle does not really approximate the status of a unifying framework, because each family therapy approach "reduces" the problem of developmental impasse to its basic premise about dysfunction, leaving us with a plurality of perspectives on the relationship between family dysfunction and family development.

The widespread idea that the symptom signals the family's difficulty in making a life cycle passage deserves further consideration. As an interpretation, it certainly has the power to depathologize the family's present behavior and point toward a clear direction for the family's future. But it has logical problems. Gurman (1983) warned about two fallacies that may accompany a life cycle perspective. One is the fallacy of the "symptomatic signal," that is, the symptom as a signal that the family is having developmental difficulties. This implies that the symptom is a *reflection* of a difficulty, but Gurman's point is that it is also possible that the symptom is not a metaphor but an actual *interference* with developmental progress, as happens when an individual's physical handicap interferes with family progress. The second fallacy is the "nominalist fallacy," which states that a description of an event cannot be an explanation for the event; that is, the explanation cannot be circular.

These fallacies point to a need for further elaboration of the connection between the symptom and the developmental passage. One way to think about this connection is to view the symptom as a manifestation of the stress that the family is experiencing around the transition events. Another way is to observe that the family is rigidly organized and cannot change its organization to fit the new developmental requirements. A third possibility is that a symptom has a meaning or a function or acts as a "solution" that serves to maintain stability in the face of impending change. These various meanings are rooted in different processes of development and have vastly different implications for intervention, but they remain largely unexplored. This is another instance where the family life cycle construct is utilized as a marker, in this case accompanied by another marker, the symptom, with little specification of the macroprocesses or microprocesses involved.

It may be profitable to consider concepts from other fields regarding the connection between family dysfunction and developmental processes. As was discussed earlier, studies conducted by family sociologists raise a number of interesting hypotheses about why families may experience transitions as rough or smooth, and about the degree, duration, and accumulation of adaptational tasks required on the part of the family. Recent studies conducted by developmental psychologists on family transformation at nodal points can provide much needed information about healthy development and a greater understanding of what may go awry with family growth. One such study demonstrates that if there are difficulties with the formation of an autonomous sibling subsystem when a family of two parents and a child expands by adding a second child, the parents become exhausted from intervening between the two children, and a mounting crisis envelops the marital, parental, and parent–child subsystems, making adaptation to this stage problematic (Krepner, Paulsen, & Schuetze, 1982).

There is also some indication that identifying, before and during the transition period, such family variables as the disruption of time schedules, the number of new decisions involving disagreement among family members, and the degree of pretransition family conflict can help therapists assess the degree of distress that a family experiences during transitions and can facilitate the selection of an effective treatment approach (Worthington, 1987).

From Dualism to Dialectic in the Nature of Change

Issues concerning the nature of change are, by definition, the most central matters of developmental theory. The fundamental human struggle to preserve the old while striving to produce or adapt to the new is nowhere more vividly experienced than during life cycle transitions. An interactional or systems approach to human development calls for a dialectical integration of the tendency toward continuity and the tendency toward change (Gollin, 1981; Hultsch & Plemons, 1979; Urban, 1978).

In family therapy (and in family sociology), there has been a significant movement from a focus on homeostatic processes toward an emphasis on change-promoting and evolutionary processes. Tendencies toward continuity and toward change in systems are included, but in a dualistic rather than a dialectical fashion, for instance, by assuming that the changes within stages are continuous and of the first order and that the changes between stages are discontinuous and of the second order, since these processes are believed to operate separately or at best sequentially. For a family to be both *flexible and stable,* however, the tendencies toward change and discontinuity need to occur *simultaneously* with the tendencies toward continuity and stability (Melitto, 1985). What is needed for healthy adaptation and for coping with life cycle or other developmental challenges is an integration or synthesis of the two types of processes, so that a sense of continuity, identity, and stability can be maintained while new behavioral patterns are evolving. Hansen and Johnson (1979) discuss life cycle difficulties that result from one process occurring in the absence of the other. Keeney (1983) also criticized the dualism implied in morphostasis and morphogenesis, stating that "one cannot, in cybernetics, separate stability from change—both are sides of a systemic coin" (p. 70). A theory of family development compatible with this view would address change and stability simultaneously and probably offer alternative explanations for family dysfunction other than the idea that families are "stuck" and unable to bring about discontinuous change. Walsh (1983), Liddle and Saba (1983), Fishman (Chapter 16, this volume), and Breunlin (Chapter 5, this volume) question a "discontinuous only" view of family development.

One way to resolve the tendency to dichotomize and polarize processes that actually flow together is to think of a dynamic balance or ratio between continuous and discontinuous changes at all points in the family life cycle. At times and in some areas, the ratios will change toward more continuity than discontinuity, or vice versa, but one process could never replace the other (Falicov, 1984). It also seems possible that the resolution of a conflict between forces for continuity and forces for change posed as thesis and antithesis can blossom into a developmental synthesis.

The concept of "family identity" introduced by Bennett, Wolin, and McAvity (Chapter 8, this volume) provides an interesting avenue to studying simultaneous and related processes of continuity and change in a family over the generations through the transmission of family rituals. Some continuities may be adaptive, whereas others may have deleterious effects, such as Montalvo and Gutierrez (Chapter 7, this volume) propose with their concept of "cultural identity" as a societal and individual developmental constraint.

Another promising integration of the concepts of continuity and change is offered by Melitto (1985). Based on the work of Heinz Werner and Jean Piaget, he argues that the relationship between morphostasis and morphogenesis depends on the level of organization of the system. For relatively underdeveloped and underorganized systems, negative and positive feedback occurs singly or in sequence. More advanced forms of adaptation that integrate continuity and change are typical of well-developed and well-organized systems. This interpretation of developmental change as a higher level of organization and integration suggests that diverse family therapy approaches can directly or indirectly stimulate developmental growth by increasing the level of organization and differentiation within the family.

From a Deficit to a Resource Orientation

The notion that developmental impasses at one stage can be understood in terms of developmental deficits in completing the tasks of previous stages appears in its strongest form in the psychoanalytic orientations, but to some extent it is a generalized belief for most of the therapeutic approaches. Family sociology and developmental psychology also largely shares this view.

Theories that profess a model of the family and of optimal family functioning, particularly in relation to a concept of levels of development (see Table 1-1), are more likely to adhere to a deficit view of family development and to have a pessimistic outlook regarding the extent to which true change is possible. Other theories are more optimistic about the possibilities for change based on current experiences, even if they adhere to a notion of a hierarchy of stages built one upon another. To obtain a more systemic view of the family life cycle, an epistemological shift may be needed here that conceptualizes more clearly the variations in patterns and the resources for change inherent in each stage. One way to do this may be by focusing on the interplay between the different family subsystems (including individual members) in terms of simultaneous or sequential stages and developmental tasks in ways that generate systems variety and new opportunities for change (Falicov, 1984). Although not originally intended to show a resource orientation, Erikson's (1959) cogwheeling effects between the generations, Stierlin's (1974) coincidence of adult and adolescent tasks, and Combrinck-Graham's (1985) life spiral model offer potential in that direction.

The Directionality and Durability of Change

By definition, the concept of development implies a goal and a direction toward that goal. This uniformity of goals and direction for accomplishing them is being questioned within both developmental psychology (Bronfenbrenner, Kessel, Kessen, & White, 1986) and family therapy.

Most family therapists appear to think that the evolution of family forms during the family life cycle and family development has a specifiable, probably normative end point, but the Milan school sets out to avoid imparting a life cycle developmental direction to the family interventions. Although this may be a difficult and perhaps unrealistic stance for the child-oriented therapies, such as structural family therapy, since children have many well-established maturational regularities, the Milan position highlights an area of theoretical importance. Most conceptualizations of the family life cycle are, of necessity, value laden, incorporating not only contents borrowed from the dominant culture but also the therapist's own developmental preferences. Seldom considered are families' constructions and values about their own life cycles. Much as they do with regard to other cultural issues, therapists should *not* assume similar directions and end points among families faced with similar life cycle transitions (Falicov, 1986, 1988). Rather, a family life cycle assessment should consider the family's own preferences along with the life cycle templates embedded in the therapist's personal and conceptual views (Liddle & Saba, 1983).

Finally, there is the matter of *durability of change.* Developmental change, by definition, is durable if not permanent, in spite of regressions or impasses. Obtaining a new developmental achievement during the course of therapy is one way of ensuring that therapeutic changes are durable rather than fleeting or temporary; durability can be obtained through continuous or discontinuous change (see Fishman, Chapter 16, this volume).

Life Cycle Interventions

Theories of the family life cycle and family development translate into a variegated array of rich applications and interventions. In the second major section of this chapter, these applications were divided into different stages of the therapeutic process: assessment, hypothesis generation, problem definition, intervention techniques, and therapeutic goals. A survey across these aspects of treatment for each theory indicates that regardless of therapeutic orientation, most approaches rely to some extent on the family life cycle as a guide to understanding the family's predicament, to evaluating healthy behavior, and to generating hypotheses about the presenting problem. The stance taken on continuous and discontinuous change determines the choice of therapeutic technique. Therapists who believe that developmental change can come about only through discontinuous change consider paradoxical techniques as ideally suited for developmental impasses.

On the issue of therapeutic goals, the theories vary regarding the extent to which they adhere to the importance of having a model of the family life cycle and to an understanding of spontaneous processes of developmental change as guides for selecting therapeutic goals and appropriate interventions. Structural family therapy shows the greatest interest in such blueprints, whereas the approach of the Milan group and some of the intergenerational approaches, such as that of Bowen, demonstrate the least interest.

The therapeutic interventions reviewed previously (see the section Family Life Cycle Concepts in Family Therapy) are used as avenues to normalizing present, past, and even future behavior; to introducing a philosophical or educational outlook; to imparting a specific developmental direction or presenting an ambiguous picture about possibilities for development; to stimulating life cycle change and transformation of rules through enactment, direct or indirect directives and tasks, circular and reflexive questioning; or promoting insight, role playing the role of the other, and attending to developmental double binds. As diverse in theoretical underpinnings as these interventions are, they could be dubbed "developmental–systemic," since they all have the common thread of a life cycle construction or theme that provides a context, shaping the nature of the therapy experience for the family and the therapist alike.

Life cycle events as markers and processes. In spite of many conceptual differences in theories of dysfunction and theories of change, it appears that in the realm of therapeutic interventions, the various therapeutic orientations utilize the family life cycle approach in surprisingly similar ways. Most family therapists use the family life cycle paradigm as a *context* for assessment and for creating change by regarding family life cycle events either as markers or processes. "Markers" are signals or indicators of impending, recent, or even past change that alert therapists to the presence of expectable behaviors and possibly the experience of stress. Milestones and turning points are common ways of referring to life cycle markers. "Processes" refer to the same life cycle events through dynamic temporal lenses, that is, as having a time for preparation, some course of duration, and an eventual outcome affecting a number of areas or dimensions of family life. Both markers and processes are conceptual constructs (see Reese and Smyer, 1983) that guide assessments, therapeutic interventions, and treatment plans. They can also be manifested at the level of language contents or constructions of reality shared and coevolved with the family.

Examples of markers that are applicable across therapeutic orientations are (1) *stages and transitions,* which include real or symbolic additions and losses of family members and involve physical or psychological (observable and reported) change in individuals' and subsystems' attributes over time; (2) *age-appropriate behaviors,* which focus on the chronological ages of family members (or even the "age" of subsystems, such as years since marriage or remarriage); and (3) *age as a metaphor* for youth, competence, immaturity, and so forth, or for stimulating recollection of parental and grandparental life cycle experiences. Markers are used most frequently in the initial stages of treatment and enjoy widespread use among family therapists.

Useful constructs for addressing life cycle events as developmental *processes* are (1) the language of *proximity* or interdependence (the conflict or dialectic between dependence and autonomy, togetherness and separateness, fusion and differentiation–individuation, centrifugal and centripetal processes); (2) the language of *hierarchies* in interpersonal interactions (the conflict or dialectic between symmetrical and complementary balances, between leader and follower or "master" and "slave" roles) or in social organizations (authoritarian, democratic, or permissive systems); and (3) the language of *adaptation* (the conflict or dialectic between resistance to or acceptance of change, between flexibility and rigidity, between continuous and discontinuous change). These constructs are likely to be used in the middle and late phases of treatment and are compatible with many orientations.

Most family therapists, armed with the concepts of their own therapeutic approaches, detect life cycle instabilities or *markers* and focus on them explicitly or implicitly in order to facilitate a situation that sets in motion developmental *processes* toward new balances in the dimensions of family life.

CONCLUSION

Family therapists appear to have prematurely closed off the complex issues of stability and change and of continuous and discontinuous, qualitative and quantitative, first-order and second-order changes during the family life cycle. The connection between family dysfunction and the family life cycle also needs much more elaboration than has been given to it so far. Most family therapy approaches have rather mechanically endorsed the traditional stage model of the family without examining issues connected with stages and transitions or attempting to delineate the dimensions and processes involved in life cycle change. Future models need to reopen and explore these issues. This can be done within the confines of the various family therapy orientations, creating perhaps a necessary diversity, but also running the risk of a reductionistic approach whereby basic issues of the family life cycle framework become isomorphic to other predictable aspects of those theories. A fresher, more unifying outlook may result from attempts to develop models of the family life cycle that address evolutionary aspects of systems and that focus on the dimensions and processes of change. Several of these new models are developing in family therapy, as well as more complex models that encompass the interface between the family life cycle and other aspects of family development. It is also suggested that when it comes to therapeutic interventions, divergent schools converge in their utilization of family life cycle events as markers and processes of change.

Family therapy has lacked not only a more microscopic look at the issues involved in family development but also the metaperspective for its life cycle models that is enjoyed by other disciplines. Family sociology and developmental psychology are beginning to share common assumptions about life cycle processes and are moving toward interactional and systemic models. Relaxing the boundaries between these disciplines can provide many valuable new paths and supplement incomplete aspects of the family life cycle framework used in family therapy.

REFERENCES

Ackerman, N. W. (1959). The psychoanalytic approach to the family. In J. H. Masserman (Ed.), *Individual and familial dynamics.* New York: Grune & Stratton.

Ackerman, N. W. (1966). *Treating the troubled family.* New York: Basic Books.

Aldous, J. (1978). *Family careers: Developmental change in the family.* New York: Wiley.

Ambron, S. R. & Brodzinsky, D. (1982). *Lifespan human development.* New York: Holt, Rinehart & Winston.

Angell, R. C. (1936). *The family encounters the Depression.* New York: Charles Scribner.

Aponte, H. & VanDeusen, J. (1981). Structural family therapy. In A. S. Gurman, & D. P. Kniskern, (Eds.), *Handbook of family therapy.* New York: Brunner/Mazel.

Barnhill, L. & Longo, D. (1978). Fixation and regression in the family life cycle. *Family Process, 17,* 469–478.

Blood, R. & Wolfe, D. (1960). *Husbands and wives.* Glencoe, IL: Free Press.

Boss, P. G. (1983). The marital relationship: Boundaries and ambiguities. In C. Figley & H. I. McCubbin (Eds.), *Stress and the family* (Vol. 2). New York: Brunner/Mazel.

Boss, P. G. & Greenberg, J. (1984). Family boundary ambiguity: A new variable in family stress theory. *Family Process, 23,* 535–546.

Boszormenyi-Nagy, I. & Spark, G. (1973). *Invisible loyalties: Reciprocity in intergenerational family therapy.* New York: Harper & Row.

Bowen, M. (1978). *Family therapy in clinical practice.* New York: Jason Aronson.

Breulin, D. C. (1983). Therapy in stages: A life cycle view. In M. Liddle (Ed.), *Clinical implications of the family life cycle.* Rockville, MD: Aspen Systems Corporation.

Bronfenbrenner, U. (1977). Toward an experimental ecology of human development. *American Psychologist, 24,* 513–530.

Bronfenbrenner, U., Kessel, F., Kessen, W. & White, S. (1986). Toward a critical social history of developmental psychology: A propaedeutic discussion. *American Psychologist, 41,* 1218–1230.

Buckley, W. (Ed.). (1968). Society as a complex adaptive system. In *Modern systems research for the behavioral scientist.* Chicago: Aldine.

Burr, W. (1972). Role transitions: A reformulation of theory. *Journal of Marriage and the Family, 34,* 407–416.

Cadwallader, M. (1959). The cybernetic analysis of change in complex social organizations. *American Journal of Sociology, 65,* 154–157.

Carter, E. & McGoldrick, M. (Eds.). (1980). *The family life cycle: A framework for family therapy.* New York: Gardner Press.

Cavan, R. & Ranck, K. (1938). *The family and the Depression.* Chicago: University of Chicago Press.

Combrinck-Graham, L. (1983). The family life cycle and families with young children. In H. Liddle (Ed.), *Clinical implications of the family life cycle*. Rockville: Aspen Systems.
Combrinck-Graham, L. (1985). A model for family development. *Family Process, 24:* 139–150.
Coppersmith, E. (1981). Developmental reframing: He's not bad, he's not mad, he's just young. *Journal of Strategic and Systemic Therapies, 1* (1), 1–8.
Danish, S., Smyer, M., & Nowak, C. (1980). Developmental intervention: Enhancing life-event processes. In P. Baltes & O. Brim, Jr. (Eds.), *Life-span development and behavior* (Vol. 3). New York: Academic Press.
Dare, C. (1979). Psychoanalysis and systems in family therapy. *Journal of Family Therapy, 1,* 137–152.
Duvall, E. (1957). *Family development*. Philadelphia: Lippincott.
Egan, G. & Cowan, M. (1979). *People in systems: A model for development in the human systems professions and education*. Monterey, CA: Brooks/Cole.
Erikson, E. (1959). Identity and the life cycle. *Psychological Issues, 1,* 1–171.
Erikson, E. (1963). *Childhood and society* (rev. ed.). New York: W. W. Norton.
Falicov, C. J. (Ed.). (1983). Introduction. *Cultural perspectives in family therapy*. Rockville: Aspen Systems.
Falicov, C. J. (1984). Focus on stages: Commentary to C. Proudfit's developmental analysis of V. Wolf's novel *To the Lighthouse*. *Family Process, 23* (3), 329–334.
Falicov, C. J. (1986). Cross-cultural marriages. In N. Jacobson & A. Gurman (Eds.), *Clinical handbook of marital therapy*. New York: Guilford Press.
Falicov, C. J. (1988). Learning to think culturally in family therapy training. In H. Liddle, D. Breunlin, & R. Schwartz (Eds.), *Family therapy training: Recent trends, perspectives and developments*. New York: Guilford Press.
Falicov, C. J. & Brudner-White, L. (1983). The shifting family triangle: The issue of cultural and contextual relativity. In C. J. Falicov (Ed.), *Cultural perspectives in family therapy*. Rockville: Aspen Systems.
Falicov, C. J. & Karrer, B. (1980). Cultural variations in the family life cycle: the Mexican-American family. In E. Carter & M. McGoldrick (Eds.), *The family life cycle: A framework for family therapy*. New York: Gardner Press.
Fisch, R. (1983). Commentary to L. MacKinnon: Contrasting strategic and Milan therapies. *Family Process, 22* (4), 438–440.
Fisch, R., Weakland, J. & Segal, L. (1982). *The tactics of change*. San Francisco: Jossey-Bass.
Framo, J. (1981). The integration of marital therapy with sessions with family of origin. In A. Gurman & D. Kniskern (Eds.), *Handbook of family therapy*. New York: Brunner/Mazel.
Glansdorff, P. & Prigogine, I. (1971). *Thermodynamic theory of structure, stability and fluctuations*. New York: Wiley.
Golan, N. (1981). *Passing through transitions*. New York: The Free Press.
Gollin, E. (1981). Development and Plasticity. In E. Gollin (Ed.), *Developmental plasticity: Behavioral and biological aspects of variations in development*. New York: Academic Press.
Gurman, A. (1983). The virtues and dangers of a life-cycle perspective in family therapy. *American Journal of Family Therapy, 11* (1), 67–72.
Hadley, T., Jacob, T., Milliones, J., Caplan, J., & Spitz, D. (1974). The relationship between family developmental crisis and the appearance of symptoms in a family member. *Family Process, 13* (2), 207–214.
Haley, J. (1971). A review of the family therapy field. In J. Haley (Ed.), *Changing families*. New York: Grune & Stratton.
Haley, J. (1973). *Uncommon therapy: The psychiatric techniques of Milton H. Erickson*. New York: W. W. Norton.
Haley, J. (1976). *Problem-solving therapy*. San Francisco: Jossey-Bass.
Haley, J. (1980). *Leaving home*. New York: McGraw-Hill.

Hansen, D., & Johnson, V. (1979). Rethinking family stress theory: Definitional aspects. In W. Burr, R. Hill, F. Nye & I. Reiss (Eds.), *Contemporary theories about the family. Vol. I: Research based theories.* New York: The Free Press.

Hare-Mustin, R. (1987). The gender dichotomy in developmental theory. *New Ideas in Psychology, 5* (2), 261-267.

Hare-Mustin, R., & Marecek, J. (1986). Autonomy and gender: some questions for therapists. *Psychotherapy 23* (2), 205-212.

Hill, R. (1949). *Families under stress: Adjustments to the crisis of war, separation and reunion.* New York: Harper & Row.

Hill, R. (1958). Generic features of families under stress. *Social Casework, 49,* 139-150.

Hill, R. (1971). Modern systems theory and the family: A confrontation. *Social Science Information, 10,* 7-26.

Hill, R. (1986). Life cycle stages for types of single parent families: Of family development theory. *Family Relations, 35* (1), 19-30.

Hill, R. & Mattessich, P. (1979). Family development theory and life-span development. In P. Baltes & O. Brim, Jr. (Eds.), *Life-span development and behavior.* New York: Academic Press.

Hill, R. & Rodgers, R. (1964). The developmental approach. In H. Christensen (Ed.), *Handbook of marriage and the family.* Chicago: Rand McNally.

Hoffman, L. (1971). Deviation-amplifying processes in natural groups. In J. Haley (Ed.), *Changing Families.* New York: Grune & Stratton.

Hoffman, L. (1980). The family life cycle and discontinuous change. In E. Carter & M. McGoldrick (Eds.), *The family life cycle: a framework for family therapy.* New York: Gardner Press.

Hoffman, L. (1981). *Foundations of family therapy.* New York: Basic Books.

Hughes, S., Berger, M., & Wright, L. (1978). The family life cycle and clinical intervention. *Journal of Marriage and Family Counseling, 4* (4), 33-40.

Hultsch, D. & Plemons, J. (1979). Life events and life-span development. In P. Baltes & O. Brim, Jr. (Eds.), *Life-span development and behavior.* New York: Academic Press.

Kagan, J. (1984). *The nature of the child.* New York: Basic Books.

Kantor, D. (1983). The structural-analytic approach to the treatment of family developmental crisis. In H. Liddle (Ed.), *Clinical implications of the family life cycle.* Rockville: Aspen Systems.

Karpel, M., & Straus, E. (1983). *Family evaluation.* New York: Gardner Press.

Keeney, B. P. (1983). *Aesthetics of change.* New York: Guilford Press.

Kerr, M. (1981). Family systems theory and therapy. In A. Gurman & D. Kniskern (Eds.), *Handbook of family therapy.* New York: Brunner/Mazel.

Kohlberg, L. (1973). Stages and aging in moral development—some speculations. *Gerontologist, 13,* 497-502.

Krepner, K., Paulsen, S. & Schuetze, Y. (1982). Infant and family development: From triads to tetrads. *Human Development 25,* 373-391.

Lerner, R. & Spanier, G. (Eds.). (1978). *Child influences on marital and family interaction.* New York: Academic Press.

Levinson, D. with Darrow, C., Klein, E., Levinson, M. & McKee, B. (1978). *The seasons of a man's life.* New York: Knopf.

Levinson, D. (1986). A conception of adult development. *American Psychologist 41* (1), 3-13.

Lewis, J. M., Beavers, W. R., Gossett, J. T. & Phillips, V. A. (1976). *No single thread: Psychological health in family systems.* New York: Brunner/Mazel.

Liddle, H. & Saba, G. (1983). Clinical use of the family life cycle. In H. Liddle (Ed.), *Clinical implications of the family life cycle.* Rockville: Aspen Systems.

Lidz, T. (1968). *The person: His development throughout the life cycle.* New York: Basic Books.

MacKinnon, L. (1983). Contrasting strategic and Milan therapies. *Family Process 22*(4), 425-440.

Maruyama, M. (1963). The second cybernetics: Deviation-amplifying mutual causal processes. *American Scientist, 51,* 164-169.

McCubbin, H., & Figley, C. (1983). Bridging normative and catastrophic family stress. In H. McCubbin & C. Figley (Eds.), *Stress and the family: Coping with normative transitions* (Vol. 1). New York: Brunner/Mazel.

McCubbin, H., Joy, C., Cauble, B., Comeau, J., Patterson, J. & Needle, R. (1980). Family Stress and coping: A decade review. *Journal of Marriage and the Family 42*(4), 855-871.

McCubbin, H., & Patterson, J. (1983). The family stress process: The double ABCX model of family adjustment and adaptation. In H. McCubbin, M. Sussman, & J. Patterson (Eds.), *Advances and developments in family stress theory and research.* New York: Haworth.

McGoldrick, M., & Gerson, R. (1985). *Genograms in family assessment.* New York: W. W. Norton.

Mederer, H. & Hill, R. (1983). Critical transitions over the family life span: Theory and research. In H. McCubbin, M. Sussman & J. Patterson (Eds.), *Social stress and the family: Advances and developments in family stress theory and research.* New York: Haworth.

Meissner, W. W. (1978). The conceptualization of marital and family dynamics from a psychoanalytic perspective. In T. Paolino & B. McCrady (Eds.), *Marriage and family therapy.* New York: Brunner/Mazel.

Melitto, R. (1985). Adaptation in family systems: a developmental perspective. *Family Process 24*(1), 89-100.

Melson, G. (1983). Family adaptation to environmental demands. In H. McCubbin & C. Figley (Eds.), *Stress and the family: Coping with normative transitions* (Vol. 1). New York: Brunner/Mazel.

Menaghan, E. (1983). Marital stress and family transitions: A panel analysis. *Journal of marriage and the family 45*(2), 371-386.

Minuchin, P. (1985). Families and individual development: Provocations from the field of family therapy. *Child Development, 56,* 289-302.

Minuchin, S. (1974). *Families and family therapy.* Cambridge: Harvard University Press.

Minuchin, S., & Fishman, H. C. (1981). *Family therapy techniques.* Cambridge: Harvard University Press.

Nichols, M. (1984). *Family therapy: Concepts and methods.* New York: Gardner Press.

O'Connell, P. (1972). Developmental tasks of the family. *Smith College Studies in Social Work, 42*(3), 203-210.

Olson, D. H., Sprenkle, D. H., & Russell, C. S. (1979). Circumplex model of marital and family systems: I. Cohesion and adaptability dimensions, family type and clinical applications. *Family Process, 18,* 3-28.

Olson, D. H., Russell, C. S. & Sprenkle, D. H. (1983). Circumplex model VI: Theoretical update. *Family Process, 22,* 69-83.

Paul, N. (1969). The role of mourning and empathy in conjoint marital therapy. In G. Zuk & I. Boszormenyi-Nagy (Eds.), *Family therapy and disturbed families.* Palo Alto: Science and Behavior Books.

Penn, P. (1985). Feed forward: Future questions, future maps. *Family Process, 24*(3), 299-322.

Perrota, P. (1986). Leaving home: Later stages of treatment. *Family Process, 25*(3), 461-474.

Pincus, L. & Dare, C. (1978). *Secrets in the family.* London: Faber and Faber.

Pollack, O. (1956). Sociological and psychoanalytic concepts in family diagnosis. In B. L. Greene (Ed.), *The psychotherapies of marital disharmony.* New York: Free Press.

Quinn, W., Newfield, N., & Protinsky, H. (1985). Rites of passage in families with adolescents. *Family Process, 24*(1), 101-112.

Rapaport, R. (1963). Normal crises, family structure and mental health. *Family Process, 2,* 68-80.

Reese, H. W. & Smyer, M. A. (1983). The dimensionalization of life events. In E. J. Callahan & K. A. McCluskey (Eds.), *Life-span developmental psychology: Nonnormative life events.* New York: Academic Press.

Reiss, D. (1981). *The family's construction of reality.* Cambridge: Harvard University Press.

Rhodes, S. (1980). A developmental approach to the life cycle of the family. In M. Bloom (Ed.), *Life span development.* New York: Macmillan.

Riegel, K. F. (1975). Adult life crisis: A dialectic interpretation of development. In N. Datan, & L. Ginsberg (Eds.), *Life-span developmental psychology: Normative life crisis.* New York: Academic Press.

Riegel, K. F. (1976). The dialectics of human development. *American Psychologist, 31*(10), 689-700.

Rolland, J. (1987). Chronic illness and the life cycle. *Family Process, 26*(2), 203-222.

Rollins, B. & Cannon, K. (1974). Marital satisfaction over the life cycle: A reevaluation. *Journal of Marriage and the Family, 36,* 271-283.

Rollins, B. & Feldman, H. (1970). Marital satisfaction over the family life cycle. *Journal of Marriage and the Family, 32,* 20-28.

Rosman, B. (1986). Developmental perspectives in family therapy with children. In H. C. Fishman & B. L. Rosman (Eds.), *Evolving models for family change.* New York: Guilford Press.

Scherz, F. H. (1971). Maturational crisis and parent-child interaction. *Social Casework, 52,* 362-369.

Schlossberg, N. K. (1981). A model for analyzing human adaptation to transition. *Counseling Psychologist, 9*(2), 2-18.

Selvini Palazzoli, M., Cecchin, G., Prata, G., & Boscolo, L. (1978). *Paradox and counterparadox.* New York: Jason Aronson.

Shilling, S. M. & Gross, E. J. (1979). Stages of family therapy: A developmental model. *Clinical Social Work Journal, 7*(2), 105-114.

Skynner, R. (1981). An open systems, group analytic approach to family therapy. In A. Gurman & D. Kniskern (Eds.), *Handbook of family therapy.* New York: Brunner/Mazel.

Solomon, M. (1973). A developmental, conceptual premise for family therapy. *Family Process, 12,* 179-188.

Spanier, G., Lewis, R. & Cole, C. (1975). Marital adjustment over the family life cycle: The issue of curvilinearity. *Journal of marriage and the family, 37,* 263-275.

Speer, D. C. (1970). Family systems: Morphostasis or morphogenesis, or is homeostasis enough? *Family Process, 9,* 259-278.

Stanton, M. D. (1981). Strategic approaches to family therapy. In A. Gurman & D. Kniskern, (Eds.), *Handbook of family therapy.* New York: Brunner/Mazel.

Stanton, M. D. & Todd, T. C. and Associates. (1982). *The family therapy of drug abuse and addiction.* New York: Guilford Press.

Steinberg, L. D. (1981). Changes in family relations at puberty. In L. D. Steinberg (Ed.), *The life cycle: Readings in human development.* New York: Columbia University Press.

Stierlin, H. (1974). *Separating parents and adolescents.* New York: Quadrangle.

Terkelson, K. G. (1980). Toward a theory of the family life cycle. In E. Carter & M. McGoldrick (Eds.), *The family life cycle: A framework for family therapy.* New York: Gardner Press.

Tomm, K. (1984a). One perspective on the Milan systemic approach: I. Overview of development, theory and practice. *Journal of Marital and Family Therapy, 10*(2), 113-126.

Tomm, K. (1984b). One perspective on the Milan systemic approach: II. Description of session format, interviewing style and interventions. *Journal of Marital and Family Therapy, 10*(3), 253-271.

Tomm, K. (1987). Interventive interviewing: Part II. Reflexive questioning as a means to enable self-healing. *Family Process, 26*(2), 167-184.

Urban, H. B. (1978). The concept of development from a systems perspective. In P. B. Baltes (Ed.), *Life-span development and behavior* (Vol. 1). New York: Academic Press.

Wachtel, E. F. & Wachtel, P. L. (1986). *Family dynamics in individual psychotherapy.* New York: Guilford Press.

Walsh, F. (1983). The timing of symptoms and critical events in the family life cycle. In H. Liddle (Ed.), *Clinical implications of the family life cycle.* Rockville: Aspen Systems.

Watzlawick, P., Weakland, J. & Fisch, R. (1974). *Change: Principles of problem formation and problem resolution.* New York: Norton.

Weakland, J., Fisch, R., Watzlawick, P. & Bodin, A. (1974). Brief therapy: Focused problem resolution. *Family Process, 13,* 141-168.

Weeks, G. R. & Wright, L. (1979). Dialectics of the family life cycle. *The American Journal of Family Therapy, 7,* 85–91.

Whitaker, C. & Keith, D. (1981). Symbolic-experiential family therapy. In A. Gurman & D. Kniskern (Eds.), *Handbook of family therapy,* New York: Brunner/Mazel.

Williamson, D. S. (1981). Personal authority via termination of the intergenerational hierarchical boundary: A "new" stage in the family life cycle. *Journal of Marital and Family Therapy, 7,* 441–452.

Williamson, D. S. (1982). Personal authority in family experience via termination of the intergenerational hierarhical boundary. Part III: Personal authority defined and the power of play in change-process. *Journal of Marital and Family Therapy, 8,* 309–323.

Winnicott, D. W. (1965). *The family and individual development.* London: Tavistock Publications.

Wood, B. (1985). Proximity and hierarchy: Orthogonal dimensions of family interconnectedness. *Family Process, 24*(4), 487–508.

Wood, B. & Talmon, M. (1983). Family boundaries in transition: A search for alternatives. *Family Process, 22,* 347–357.

Worthington, E. L. (1987). Treatment of families during life transitions: Matching treatment to family response. *Family Process, 26*(2), 295–308.

PART ONE

CONCEPTUALIZATIONS OF FAMILY DEVELOPMENT

2

Family Types, Family Stress, and Family Satisfaction: A Family Development Perspective

DAVID H. OLSON
University of Minnesota, St. Paul

NORMATIVE STUDY OF FAMILY DEVELOPMENT

Although considerable work has been done describing individual development, few studies have focused on the family as it develops over time. Theorists like Erik Erikson (1959) have described the stages of development for individuals across the life cycle. Daniel Levinson and colleagues (1978) focused on the adult stages of development in his book *The Seasons of a Man's Life.* Levinson's book provided the framework for Gail Sheehy's (1976) book *Passages,* which made the life cycle a more popular topic.

Family development, however, has seldom been studied in a systematic and large-scale manner. The pioneering work of Reuben Hill (1964, 1970, 1971) on family development has been used for descriptive purposes, but little is known about family processes and satisfaction within each of the major stages. Consequently, there is a lack of descriptive information about *normative processes* in families at different stages of the family life cycle.

Most of the problems individuals have either begin or end up in the family. As a result, families today are encountering endless challenges and frustrations that both threaten their current structures and strain their available resources. To complicate their problems, society gives only lip service to the importance of families and comes to their rescue only when they are under intense stress and are unable to cope effectively. Only recently have there been conferences and books focusing specifically on family strengths (Stinnett, Chesser, DeFrain, & Knaub, 1980). In addition, Walsh (1982) has edited an excellent book that

This chapter highlights some of the findings regarding family development from the national survey of "normal" families published by Olson and Associates (1983) entitled *Families: What Makes Them Work.* All the research methods are described in *Family Inventories* by Olson & Associates (1982).

describes normal family processes from a variety of theoretical and therapeutic perspectives.

Most studies of families have focused on those that have difficulty coping with a variety of issues, such as drug abuse, spouse abuse, and sexual abuse, and with a range of emotional and physical problems. "Normal" families have primarily been used as control groups and have not been the focus of research in their own right. As a result, we know a great deal about the characteristics of problem families and can only assume that normal families simply lack those characteristics. What we do *not* know about are the positive aspects of families that help them cope and deal effectively with stress over the life cycle.

In contrast to other studies, the study presented in this chapter focuses on the strengths and attributes that help families deal more effectively with stresses and strains (Olson and Associates, 1983). This chapter will focus on a description of what is *normative* for families at various stages of the family life cycle. This includes how family types differ, what families have as strengths, the kinds of stresses they encounter, how they cope with stress, and how satisfied they are with their marriage and family.

Stages of the Family Life Cycle

One of the primary goals of this study was to describe normal family processes at various stages of the family life cycle. Therefore descriptions of the specific stages of the cycle were needed before families were recruited and also when data were analyzed.

Acting upon the belief that the developmental needs of families change as children are born, mature, and leave their homes, my colleagues and I used the classic work of Hill and Rodgers (1964). Their work was particularly valuable in exploring the nature of family development at different stages of the life cycle. Using this developmental framework, we initially located stage divisions by focusing on the ages of children in the family and on corresponding changes that the family encounters as children mature. Based on these criteria, the seven stages that appear in Table 2-1 were used throughout the study.

Description of the Sample

A questionnaire was developed to assess the following dimensions from the perspective of several family members: family stress, family types, family resources, and family satisfaction. A total of 2,692 individuals from 31 states responded to this questionnaire (Olson and Associates, 1983). The sample consisted of 1,140 couples (2,280 adults) and 412 adolescents, 206 males and 206 females. The final numbers of couples and families at the various stages of the family life cycle are summarized in Table 2-1. Our goal was to obtain at least 100 couples and families at each stage of the life cycle, with about 200 families at the adolescent stage. Not only was that goal achieved, but

Table 2-1. Families across the Life Cycle

Stages of the family life cycle	Couples	Adolescents	Total individuals
Stage 1 Young couples without children	121	NA	242
Stage 2 Families with preschoolers (ages 0–5)	148	NA	296
Stage 3 Family with school-age children (ages 6–12)	129	NA	258
Stage 4 Families with adolescents (ages 13–18)	261	350	872
Stage 5 Launching families (first adolescent; age 19)	191	62	444
Stage 6 Empty-nest families (all children gone)	144	NA	288
Stage 7 Retired couples (male over age 65)	146	NA	292
Total	1,140	412	2,692

Note. NA = not applicable.

data were obtained from husbands and wives at all stages and from one adolescent member of each family at the adolescent stage. More details on the data collection methods are available elsewhere (Olson and Associates, 1982).

Characteristics of the Families

Two important characteristics of this study merit special attention. First, this is a study of intact families who, in conventional terms, might be described as "normal," "typical," "nonclinical," or "ordinary." Second, this is a cross-sectional rather than a longitudinal study—groups of families were studied at several points in the family life cycle. Because of these characteristics, one should not make generalizations to all families or to how families change over time. The findings of this cross-sectional study represent snapshots of intact families as they were at one point in time; they do not describe change in the same families across the family life cycle.

One purpose of the study was to examine the nature of families in which married partners with or without children were living together as a single unit in a common household. Therefore conclusions drawn from the study can be applied only to similar kinds of families.

A major criterion for inclusion was membership in an intact family. Although this study includes some reconstituted families and some previously divorced adults, members of other family forms, such as single-parent families, divorced couples, or unmarried cohabiting couples, did not participate. The temptation to apply these findings to such alternative family forms should be avoided.

Although the cross-sectional approach does not allow for an assessment of *changes* from stage to stage, it does provide the opportunity to examine *differences* between families at various stages of the family life cycle. What remains open to question with this approach is which differences are due to differences in family life cycle stages and which are due to the social-historical context within which each group of subjects or age cohort has lived. Thus it is impossible to assess with certainty which dissimilarities are developmental differences and which are due to the varying ages, maturity levels, or historical contexts of the people studied.

Conceptual Model

Family systems at seven stages of the family life cycle were systematically studied on several major theoretical dimensions: family types, family stress, family resources, and marital and family satisfaction (see Figure 2-1). *Family types* were derived from the Circumplex Model, according to which families are classified as balanced, midrange, or extreme types and as falling into one of four quadrants of the model. *Family stress* provides a more in-depth picture of the specific stresses and strains that each family member experiences at each stage of the family life cycle. *Family resources* include such factors as family pride and accord as well as marital resources, which include 11 areas such as communication, conflict resolution, and sexual relationship. *Marital and family satisfaction* focuses on how well these other processes work for family members. Satisfaction with the marriage and satisfaction with family life are seen independently as important outcomes to consider for each family member.

To gain a more panoramic perspective on family life across the life cycle, each of these dimensions is explored in considerable detail. Data will be provided on how couples and families differ on these dimensions across the life cycle. The descriptions provided by the husbands, wives, and adolescent family members will also be compared and contrasted. Because of the differences in reports among family members, this information clearly demonstrates some of the complexity of family life. It also made the data analysis

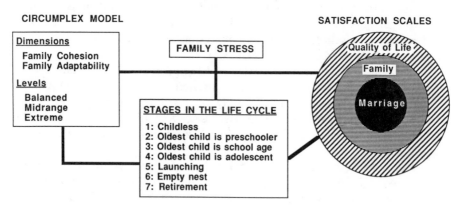

Figure 2-1. Conceptual overview of Circumplex Model, family stress, and family satisfaction.

more challenging and complicated. Following are the questions we asked pertaining to each dimension:

1. How do the *family types* (based on cohesion and adaptability) vary across the family life cycle?
2. What types of *stress* do husbands, wives, and adolescents encounter at various stages of the family life cycle?
3. What are the *family resources* that discriminate between high- and low-stress families?
4. How does *marital and family satisfaction* vary across the family life cycle?

FAMILY COHESION, ADAPTABILITY, AND COMMUNICATION

Family cohesion, adaptability, and communication are three dimensions of family behavior that emerged from a conceptual clustering of more than 50 concepts developed to describe marital and family dynamics. Though some of these concepts have been used for decades (e.g., power and roles), many of them have been developed by individuals observing problem families from a general systems perspective (e.g., pseudomutuality, double binds) (Olson, 1986).

After we reviewed the definitions of many of these concepts, it became apparent that despite the creative terminology, the terms were conceptually similar and dealt with closely related family processes. The first family process, or dimension, *family cohesion*, had to do with the degree to which an individual was separated from or connected to his or her family system. The second dimension was *family adaptability*, which focused on the extent to which the family system was flexible and able to change. The third dimension was *family communication* between various members.

The salience of these three dimensions is that several theoretical models independently have focused on variables related to the cohesion, adaptability, and communication dimensions. Most of these models have been developed in the last 5 years by individuals with a systems perspective on the family. The value and importance of these three dimensions is evidenced by the fact that these theorists and therapists concluded independently that the variables they selected were critical for understanding and treating marital and family systems.

Most of the recent theorizing about family dynamics and intervention has been strongly influenced by general systems theory. The current work has focused on describing both clinical and nonclinical families (Beavers, 1977; French & Guidera, 1974; Kantor & Lehr, 1975; Lewis, Beavers, Gossert, & Philips, 1976) or has been concerned with clinical intervention (Benjamin, 1974, 1977; Constantine, 1983; Epstein, Bishop, & Levin, 1978).

Family Cohesion

"Family cohesion" is defined as the "emotional bonding that family members have toward one another" (Olson and Associates, 1983). Within the Circumplex Model, some of the specific concepts or variables that can be used to diagnose and measure the family cohesion dimensions are emotional bonding, boundaries, coalitions, time, space, friends, decision making, and interests and recreation. There are four levels of cohesion (see Figure 2-2), ranging from disengaged (very low) to separated (low to moderate) to connected (moderate to high) to enmeshed (very high).

It is hypothesized that the central levels of cohesion (separated and connected) are most viable for family functioning. The extremes (disengaged or enmeshed) are generally seen as problematic. Many couples and families who come for treatment often fall into one of these extremes. When cohesion levels are high (enmeshed systems), there is overidentification, so that loyalty to and consensus within the family prevent individuation of family members. At the other extreme (disengaged systems), high levels of autonomy are encouraged, with family members "doing their own thing" and having limited attachment or commitment to the family. It is the central area of the model (separated and connected) where individuals are able to experience and balance being independent from and connected to their families.

Family Adaptability

"Family adaptability" is defined as the "ability of a marital or family system to change its power structure, role relationships, and relationship rules in response to situational and developmental stress" (Olson, 1986). To describe, measure, and diagnose couples on this dimension, a variety of concepts were taken from several social science disciplines, with heavy reliance on family sociology. These concepts include family power (assertiveness, control, discipline), negotiation styles, role relationships, and relationship rules. The four levels of adaptability (see Figure 2-2) range from rigid (very low) to structured (low to moderate) to flexible (moderate to high) to chaotic (very high).

As with cohesion, it is hypothesized that central levels of adaptability (structured and flexible) are more conducive to marital and family functioning, whereas the extremes (rigid and chaotic) are the most problematic for families as they move through the family life cycle.

Basically, adaptability focuses on the ability of the marital and family system to change. Much of the early application of systems theory to families emphasized the rigidity of the family and its tendency to maintain the status quo (Haley, 1959, 1962, 1963). "Morphostasis" was the term used to describe the pattern of rigidity to change, and "morphogenesis" was the potential to develop and grow as a system. Until the work of such theorists as Speer (1970) and Wertheim (1973, 1975), the importance of the potential for change received minimal attention. These authors helped to clarify the fact that systems need both stability and change and that it is the ability to change when appropriate that distinguishes functional couples and families from dysfunctional ones.

Family Communication

The third dimension in the Circumplex Model, family communication, is considered to be a facilitating dimension; that is, it is considered to be critical to movement on the other two dimensions. Because it is a facilitating dimension, communication is not included graphically in the model.

Positive communication skills (i.e., empathy, reflective listening, support-ive comments) enable couples and families to share with each other their changing needs and preferences as they relate to cohesion and adaptability. Negative communication skills (i.e., double messages, double binds, criticism) minimize the ability of a couple or family members to share their feelings, thereby restricting their movement on the other two dimensions.

THE CIRCUMPLEX MODEL

Figure 2-2 illustrates the dimensions of family cohesion (togetherness) and family adaptability (change) and the four levels of each dimension. Combining the dimensions enables us to identify and describe 16 distinct types of marital and family systems. Although it is assumed that it is possible to identify conceptually, measure empirically, and observe clinically all 16 types, it is also assumed that some of the types occur more frequently than others. As with any circumplex model, the more central types are the most common, but it is hypothesized that couples and families having problems fall more frequently into the extreme types.

Once the types were identified and located within the model, it became clear that there were three basic groups of types: balanced, midrange, and extreme. One group had scores at the two central levels on both dimensions (four balanced types); another group was extreme on both dimensions (four extreme types); and the third group was extreme on only one dimension (eight midrange types).

Developmental Hypotheses Derived from the Circumplex Model

One of the assets of a theoretical model is that hypotheses can be deduced and tested in order to evaluate and further develop the model. The following are hypotheses derived from the model:

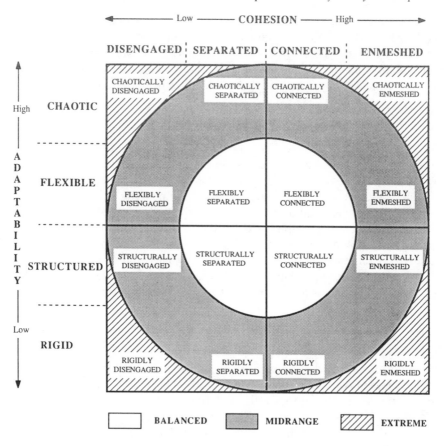

Figure 2-2. Circumplex Model: 16 types of marital and family systems for two dimensions (family cohesion and family adaptability).

Hypothesis 1. Couples/families with balanced (two central levels) cohesion and adaptability will generally function more adequately across the family life cycle than will those at the extremes of these dimensions.

An important issue in the Circumplex Model relates to the definition of "balance." Even though a balanced family system is located on the two central levels of the model, it should *not* be assumed that these families always operate in a "moderate" manner. Being balanced means that a family can experience the extremes on the dimension when appropriate but that they do not typically function at these extremes for long periods.

Hypothesis 2. If the normative expectations of a couple or family support behaviors on one of either of the extremes of the circumplex dimensions, the couple or family will function well as long as all family members are satisfied with these expectations.

Although a curvilinear relationship is generally predicted, some important qualifications must be made in terms of the normative expectations and cultural bias of Hypothesis 1.

The normative expectations in our culture provide two conflicting themes that can create problems for couples and families. One theme is that family members are expected to do things together as a family; the second theme encourages individuals to "do their own thing." The theme of independence becomes more prominent as children approach adolescence, and it has taken on greater importance for increasing numbers of women in our culture. As a result, it has become difficult for many American families to balance these two themes.

Families in our culture still vary greatly in the extent to which they encourage and support individual development in ways that may differ from the family's values. Although parents probably prefer that their children develop values and ideas similar to theirs, most parents allow their children to become somewhat autonomous and differentiated from the family system.

However, a sizable minority of families have normative expectations that strongly emphasize family togetherness, often at the expense of individuation from the family system. Their family norms stress emotion and physical togetherness, and they strive for high levels of consensus and loyalty. Such American ethnic groups as Slovak-Americans (Stein, 1978), Puerto Ricans (Minuchin, Montalvo, Guerney, Rosman, & Schumer, 1967) and Italians (Goetzel, 1973) as well as religious groups such as the Amish (Wittmer, 1973) and the Mormons (Schvaneveldt, 1973) have high expectations regarding family togetherness. These expectations are also common, but less predominant, in many other American families, regardless of their ethnic or religious orientation. Many of these families could be described as extreme on the cohesion dimension (i.e., enmeshed), and they function well as long as all family members are willing to go along with those expectations.

Hypothesis 3. To deal with situational stress and developmental change across the life cycle, balanced families will change their cohesion and adaptability, whereas extreme families will resist change over time.

This hypothesis addresses the issue of change in the family system in response to stress or to accommodate changes in family members, particularly as members change their expectations. The Circumplex Model is dynamic in that it assumes that individuals and families will change, and it hypothesizes that change can be beneficial to the maintenance and improvement of family functioning.

FAMILY DEVELOPMENT AND THE CIRCUMPLEX MODEL

The Circumplex Model allows us to integrate systems theory with family development, a proposal made more than a decade ago by Reuben Hill (1971). Building on the family development approach described by Hill and Rodgers (1964), we hypothesized that families must change as they deal with normal transitions in family life. It was expected, therefore, that the stage of the family life cycle and the composition of the family would have considerable impact on the type of family system that exists.

We hypothesized that at any stage of the family life cycle, there would be a diversity in types of family systems as described in the Circumplex Model. In spite of this diversity, we predicted that families would cluster together in some types more frequently than in others at different stages of the family life cycle.

The Circumplex Model is dynamic in that it assumes that changes can occur in family types over time. Families are free to move in any direction that the situation, stage of the life cycle, or socialization of family members may require. A retrospective look at a family illustrates the dynamic nature of the model.

Steve and Sally were both raised in rather traditional homes. Three years after they were married, they became parents for the first time, and Sally resigned from her teaching job. Because of the dependency needs of their son and their own desire for mutual support during this transition period, they developed a moderately high, but not extreme, level of family cohesion (connected). Also, their upbringing led them to be moderately low, but not rigid, on the adaptability dimension (structured). They were comfortable with a rather traditional, husband-dominant power structure and segregated role relationship, preferring the relative security of these established patterns to the difficulties of continually negotiating them. According to the model, their family type would be described as structurally connected, an option that seemed to be satisfying to them at the time.

Years later, when Sally and Steve's son became a teenager, Sally began to pursue a career. Both parents experienced a good deal of "consciousness raising" about sex roles through the media and through involvement in several growth groups. Because of their son's needs for more autonomy at this age as well as the parents' separate career interests, they began operating at a lower level of cohesiveness, moving from being connected to being more separated.

Furthermore, the family power structure shifted from being husband dominant to a more shared pattern. Sally now exercises much more control in the relationship than she had previously, and the couple struggles almost on a weekly basis to redefine the rules and role relationship that govern their relationship. Although they occasionally yearn for the security of their earlier, more structured relationship, both find excitement and challenge in this more flexible relationship style. In short, flexibly separated best describes their current family organizational pattern.

This brief case history illustrates the dynamic nature of the model, which allows for movement within reasonable limits. The model also seeks to recognize diverse values and legitimizes the various organizational ideals of families.

When one family member desires change, the family system must deal with this request. For example, increasing numbers of married women want to develop more autonomy from their husbands (cohesion dimension) and also want more power and equality in their relationships (adaptability dimension). If their husbands are unwilling to understand and change in accordance with these expectations, the marriages will probably experience increased amounts of stress. Another common example of changing expectations occurs when a child reaches adolescence. Like the wife in the previous example, adolescents often want more freedom, independence, and power in the family system.

Family Cohesion

Family cohesion is a measure of how close to each other family members feel emotionally, or their sense of connectedness to or separateness from other family members. Our study found significant differences between husbands and wives in their perceptions of family cohesion. People at various stages of the family life cycle also reported different levels of cohesion in their families. Thus there were both family-member and stage differences on the measure of family cohesion (see Figure 2-3).

Across the seven stages of the life cycle, wives generally rated their families as more closely knit, or higher on cohesion, than did the husbands. Only at the launching stage (Stage 5) did the wives' average score on cohesion drop slightly below the mean score for husbands. The differences between husbands and wives were greatest in the earlier stages, converged at the launching stage (Stage 5), and then separated again at the empty-nest and retirement stages (Stages 6 and 7). In these latter two stages, wives' scores again significantly exceeded those of the husbands.

Family cohesion appeared to be at its highest among families in the early stages of the family life cycle. Levels of family cohesion were lower among families with adolescent children (Stage 4) and reached the lowest level with families at the launching stage (Stage 5). Levels of cohesion were higher again at the empty-nest and retirement stages, but still lower than the levels reported by couples at the earliest stages of the family life cycle.

From the perspective of family development theory, it seems appropriate that family cohesion differs by stage. It reaches its lowest level during the launching stage, when adolescents are leaving home and attempting to carve out a life-style and identity of their own. These lower levels at the launching stage reflect the efforts of the adolescent to differentiate himself or herself from the family. The result is a diminished sense of togetherness and closeness among all family members at this time. It also seems appropriate that reported levels of cohesion are at their highest in the earliest stage(s), when romantic

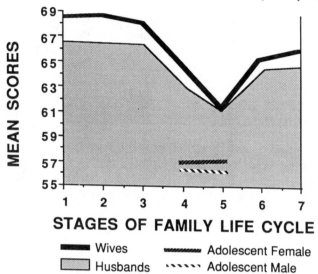

Figure 2-3. Mean scores on family cohesion at different stages of the family life cycle.

and idealistic views of the marital relationship are apt to be at their highest, reflecting a desire for a greater degree of togetherness.

Both male and female adolescents reported significantly lower levels of family cohesion than did either of their parents (see Figure 2-3). Teenagers in both the adolescent and launching stages (Stages 4 and 5) reported lower levels of family cohesion. This finding is consistent with the interpretation that adolescents are seeking to differentiate themselves from their families. To accomplish this task, it is often necessary for them to view their families as less cohesive.

Family Adaptability

Family adaptability is a measure of the extent to which a family can adapt its structure, rules, and roles to meet the challenges presented by the changing needs of the family and its individual members. This is a measure of the ability of the family to change when it is appropriate or necessary.

As with cohesion, perceptions of family adaptability varied significantly at different stages of the family life cycle and among different family members. Wives reported significantly higher levels of family adaptability than did husbands at all of the stages, except at the launching stage (Stage 5). The differences on family adaptability were not as pronounced as were those on cohesion, but the fluctuations between groups were similar to those on cohesion. Scores on family adaptability progressively decreased from the newly married group (Stage 1) through families with adolescents (Stage 4) and then increased again during the two postlaunching stages (Stages 6 and 7).

Unlike the scores on family cohesion (where group means for husbands and wives both reached their low point at the launching stage), husbands' assessments of family adaptability reached a low point in the adolescent stage (Stage 4) and became somewhat higher in each of the succeeding stages. In contrast, the mean for wives' scores on adaptability reached its lowest point during the launching stage and increased in the later two stages.

Adolescents viewed their families as significantly less flexible on adaptability than did their parents. At both the adolescent stage (Stage 4) and the launching stage (Stage 5), teenagers' scores on family adaptability were substantially lower than those of their mothers or fathers. This parent–adolescent contrast was greatest at the adolescent stage. The discrepancy between the generations decreased somewhat with the older adolescents in the launching stage (Stage 5), but they were still significant.

These parent–adolescent differences are also consistent with the generational differences found on cohesion. It is at this time in their lives that adolescents usually seek greater freedom and autonomy from their families, frequently working toward loosening previous family restrictions. Thus, while they are seeking greater flexibility from their families, it is reasonable to expect them to view their families as less flexible. The results reported here on both adaptability and cohesion suggest support for some of the most important developmental tasks that the family development theorists view as germane to the adolescent and launching stages.

FAMILY TYPES ACROSS THE LIFE CYCLE

The proportion of families that fell into each of the three family types—balanced, midrange, and extreme—varied across the seven stages of the family life cycle. The percentage of families representing each type across stages ranged from 55% to 65% for balanced types, from 25% to 40% for midrange types, and from 10% to 20% for extreme types. Although the frequency of each family type did vary among stages, an analysis of variance indicated that these distributions were not significantly different. In other words, there appears to be some consistency regarding the numbers of balanced, midrange, and extreme family types across the life cycle stages.

Adolescents as a group tended to view their families as more extreme and less balanced in comparison with the views of the total group of parents. Although these differences were not found to be statistically significant, they do reflect the fact that adolescents viewed their families as significantly lower on both cohesion and adaptability than did their parents.

Another analysis of the differences in family types across the life cycle was undertaken in order to determine how frequently families fell into each quadrant (I through IV) of the Circumplex Model (see Figure 2-4). The Circumplex Model was divided into four general quadrants rather than the sixteen types. Therefore, each quadrant contained four types of family systems. For this analysis, the stages of the life cycle were reduced from seven to four. The four new stages were called young couples without children (Stage 1), families with young children (Stage 2), families with adolescents (Stage 3), and older couples (Stage 4). Stage 1 remained unchanged. The original Stages 2 and 3 were combined to form the new Stage 2, families with young children up to 12 years of age. The original Stages 4 and 5 were combined to form the new Stage 3, families with adolescents, and Stages 6 and 7 were combined to form the older couples group (Stage 4).

Although more families at all four stages fell into Quadrants II and III, there was considerable variation in the percentage of families in each quadrant across the four stages. A majority (57%) of the young couples without children (Stage 1) fell into Quadrant II, and about one quarter (25%) fell into Quadrant III; very few of them fell into Quadrants I and IV. In contrast, almost half (45%) of families with adolescents (Stage 3) fell into Quadrant III, and about one quarter (28%), into Quadrant II.

Even though fewer families fell into Quadrants I and IV, there were considerably more families in some stages in these quadrants than in other stages. More specifically, about one quarter (26%) of families with young children (Stage 2) fell into Quadrant IV, and there were more families from Stages 3 and 4 than from Stages 1 and 2 in Quadrant I.

NORMATIVE STRESSORS AND STRAINS ACROSS THE LIFE CYCLE

Families face many demands throughout the family life cycle. These demands are often described in terms of family transitions, family passages, family developmental tasks, and family life events. But past research has not documented in any systematic way the specific demands and the most frequent family life stressors at each stage of the life cycle. In this section, I focus on what various family members identify as their major family life stressors.

Husbands and wives were asked to identify the stressors and strains that their families had experienced during the past year. These stressors and strains were recorded on FILE Inventory and were summarized by adding the number of times each was recorded with a "yes" (McCubbin, Patterson, & Wilson, 1980). The ten most frequently cited stressors or strains were identified within each of the seven stages of the family life cycle. The results of this analysis are presented here.

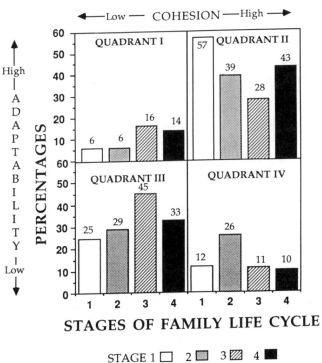

Figure 2-4. Percentages of families falling into each of the four quadrants of the Circumplex Model across four stages of the family life cycle.

The actual numbers of stressors that husbands and wives recorded at different stages of the life cycle are indicated in Figure 2-5. Specifically, wives reported more "demands" than did husbands during the preschool (Stage 2), school-age (Stage 3), launching (Stage 5), and empty-nest (Stage 6) stages of the family life cycle. This brief, initial overview encouraged us to probe more deeply into the distribution of specific stressors and strains that affect families at each stage of the life cycle.

Our analysis focused on the cluster of stressors and strains most characteristic of *each stage* of the family life cycle and on clusters that were consistently mentioned *across all stages* of the cycle. By identifying the ten most frequently cited stressors and strains (recorded by either parent at each stage), and by grouping them into their major categories (e.g., losses, illness, intrafamilial strains), we began to understand more clearly the "pileup" distribution of stressors and strains across the cycle.

The most frequently cited stressors and strains are presented in Table 2-2.

To begin, there was a rather persistent struggle with financial stressors and strains across all stages of the life cycle. Financial strains are clearly problematic for families at the preschool (Stage 2), adolescent (Stage 4), launching (Stage 5), and retirement (Stage 7) stages.

Intrafamilial strains were also problematic across the life cycle, but such strains (e.g., father's time away, husband–wife conflict, chores not getting done) were most apparent during the school-age (Stage 3) and adolescent (Stage 4) stages. It comes as no surprise that work–family strains were also persistent across the cycle. These strains (e.g., increased work responsibilities) were most apparent for the childless (Stage 1) and school-age (Stage 3) stages.

Illnesses and losses of relatives, family members, and close friends appear to be associated with the empty-nest (Stage 6) and retirement (Stage 7) stages. However, it is important to note that illnesses also were cited as major stressors during the childless (Stage 1), preschool (Stage 2), and launching (Stage 5) stages.

As expected, pregnancy stressors and strains were associated with the preschool (Stage 2) stage, and family transitions (e.g., children moving in and out of the family), with the launching (Stage 5) stage. It is surprising to note that marital strains emerged as a major stressor at the empty-nest (Stage 6) stage.

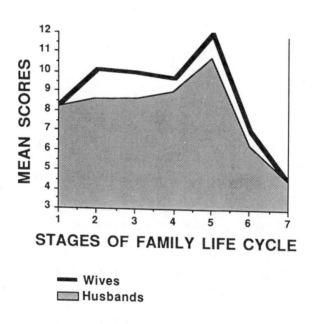

Figure 2-5. Mean number of stressors for husbands and wives across stages of the family life cycle.

Table 2-2. Top Stressors and Strains over the Family Life Cycle

Stressors	Stage 1 Childless	Stage 2 Preschool	Stage 3 School age	Stage 4 Adolescent	Stage 5 Launching	Stage 6 Empty nest	Stage 7 Retirement
Intrafamilial strains	20%	20%	50%	30%	20%	10%	10%
Financial strains	30%	50%	20%	60%	40%	30%	40%
Work–family strains	40%	10%	30%	10%	10%	10%	10%
Illnesses	10%	10%			10%	20%	20%
Marital strains						10%	
Pregnancy		10%					
Family transitions					20%		
Total	100%	100%	100%	100%	100%	100%	100%

CRITICAL FAMILY RESOURCES ACROSS THE LIFE CYCLE

Families face a host of stressors and strains throughout the life cycle. These demands change in terms of their frequency, type, and intensity, making family adjustment and coping difficult tasks. Although some families are unable to manage these demands and may experience such severe consequences as violence, extreme interpersonal conflict, or ill health, many families are able to cope and to endure, and have demonstrated the capacity to make adjustments to challenges throughout the family life cycle. We have deliberately chosen to focus our attention on, and to learn from, those "enduring" or "coping" families.

In attempting to understand how and why these families appear relatively successful in their adjustments to demands, we can gain a deeper appreciation of what it takes to cope with the challenges of becoming a couple, raising children, and entering retirement. We can also gain a fuller understanding of what resources are necessary to increase the family's resistance to stressors.

Given our natural tendency to view high-stress and low-stress families as "problem" and "nonproblem" families, respectively, it is important to emphasize two points. First, families under stress should be viewed along a continuum ranging from "extremely high stress" to "high stress" to "low stress" and, finally, to "extremely low stress." Second, families in this study clustered in the central area of this "stress continuum." In other words, 85% of these "normal" families were classified in the *midrange* of family stress. Because this study focused on normative and developmental processes in families, it is important to emphasize that our analysis does *not* focus on comparing problem and nonproblem families.

Because of our interest in identifying the most "critical" family strengths, coping mechanisms, and resources, we used a stepwise statistical procedure. This procedure selects the variables best able to improve the discrimination between high- and low-stress families.

A brief review of the critical family resources identified for each stage of the life cycle is presented in Table 2-3. (Note that for this analysis, we again used the four stages that we reconstructed for an analysis of family types.) Specifically, the results of this analysis lead us to the following conclusions and propositions about the relationship between family demands and family resources: Family resistance to stress and recovery from distress may well be facilitated, in part, by family and marital strengths. The critical nature of specific family and social resources varies according to the stage of the family life cycle and the demands unique to each stage of family development. The most important resources characteristic of *low-stress families* at each stage are as follows:

1. Young couples without children (Stage 1): family accord, good financial management, satisfactory communication, compatible personality, and shared leisure activities.

Table 2-3. Critical Family Resources in High- and Low-Stress Families

Stage 1 Young couples without children	Stage 2 Families with young children	Stage 3 Families with adolescents	Stage 4 Older couples
Family Strengths			
Family accord	Family accord		
Marital Strengths			
Financial management	Financial management	Financial management	
Communication	Communication		
Personality issues			Communication
		Personality issues	Personality issues
	Family and friends	Family and friends	
Leisure activities			
	Children and marriage		
		Sexual relationship	
Satisfaction Variables			
		Marital satisfaction	
	Family satisfaction		
	Quality of life	Quality of life	

2. Families with young children (Stage 2): family accord, good financial management, good communication, satisfaction with family and friends, a supportive social network, satisfaction with child rearing, a positive appraisal of family life, and satisfaction with life.
3. Families with adolescents (Stage 3): good financial management, compatible personality, a supportive network of family and friends, a positive appraisal of the marital relationship, sexual relationship, and satisfaction with life.
4. Older couples (Stage 4): good marital communication and compatible personality.

Marital and Family Satisfaction

Marital and family satisfaction are primary outcome variables because they reflect the mood and happiness with regard to the overall functioning of the family. This section explores how family satisfaction varies across life cycle stages for husbands, wives, and adolescents. Another question to be explored is, do couples become less satisfied with their marriages when they become parents, and even *less* satisfied when their children enter adolescence?

Marital Satisfaction

There are many ways to define "marital satisfaction"; a useful one was provided by Hawkins (1968), who described it as

> the subjective feelings of happiness, satisfaction and pleasure experienced by a spouse when considering all current aspects of his marriage. This variable is conceived of as a continuum running from much satisfaction to much dissatisfaction. Marital satisfaction is clearly an attitudinal variable and thus, is a property of individual spouses. (p. 648)

In our study, marital satisfaction was measured separately by two different scales. (The use of two independent measures reflects the central place of research on marital satisfaction in the study of families during the last 30 years; Burr, Leigh, Day, & Constantine, 1979; Lewis & Spanier, 1979.) One measure was the short form of the Locke–Wallace Marital Adjustment Scale (Locke & Wallace, 1959). Since the Locke–Wallace scale was employed extensively during the 1960s and 1970s, its use allows us to compare our results to those of many other studies. The second measure of marital satisfaction was from the ENRICH Inventory (Olson, Fournier, & Druckman, 1982). It was developed as a short scale that would be relevant and sensitive to changes in families across the life cycle. Each of the ten items in the scale relates to one of the important content areas in the ENRICH Inventory.

Although the couples in our study were generally satisfied with their marriages, approximately 13% of the males and 16% of the females indicated that they had considered separation or divorce. At all stages of the family life cycle, fewer husbands than wives had considered separation or divorce. The tendency to contemplate separation or divorce was higher for couples in Stage 2 (families with preschoolers) through Stage 5 (launching families). Older couples (at the later two stages) are probably more conservative; these are also the couples who have managed to remain married for 25 or more years.

Our study confirms the findings of a great deal of other recent work indicating that marital satisfaction tends to have the shape of a shallow U-curve (Glenn & McLanahan, 1982; Rollins & Galligan, 1978; Schram, 1979; Spanier & Lewis, 1980; Spanier, Lewis, & Cole, 1975; Waldron & Routh, 1981). Previous research has focused on the decline in satisfaction following the birth of the first child and the subsequent rise in satisfaction as the children are launched from the nest.

However, these data also make clear that these differences in *marital* satisfaction across the family life cycle represent only slight changes in levels of satisfaction. The most dramatic difference in marital and family satisfaction occurs between the launching (Stage 6) and empty-nest (Stage 7) stages. A detailed analysis (*t* tests) of changes across all stages showed significantly higher scores at Stages 6 and 7 than at Stages 2, 3, and 4 for both husbands and wives. Lower levels of satisfaction at these stages of the life cycle have been found in other studies as well.

Husband and wife differences were even less pronounced than were differences across the family life cycle. The magnitude of sex differences that did exist was not related to stage of the life cycle, with the exception of overall satisfaction with the quality of life. Husbands tended to rate their satisfaction with their overall quality of life higher than did their wives, but, again, the difference was small.

Family Satisfaction

Although a wealth of theorizing and research has been done on marital satisfaction, family researchers have rarely concerned themselves with *family satisfaction*. Campbell, Converse, and Rodgers (1976) explicitly differentiated satisfaction with one's family from other forms of satisfaction. For this reason, we developed the Family Satisfaction Scale for our family survey (Olson & Wilson, 1982). A pool of items was compiled to (1) assess family satisfaction on each of the specific subscales of family cohesion and family adaptability and (2) measure satisfaction on these dimensions in a valid and reliable manner.

Fourteen subscales, drawn from the Circumplex Model, were used to assess family satisfaction. Each subject's satisfaction was measured on the eight cohesion subscales: Emotional Bonding, Family Boundaries, Coalitions, Time, Space, Friends, Decision Making, and Interests and Recreation. Satisfaction was also assessed on the six adaptability subscales: Assertiveness, Control, Discipline, Negotiation, Roles, and Rules.

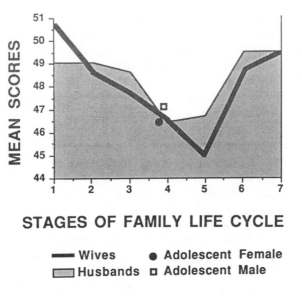

STAGES OF FAMILY LIFE CYCLE

━━ Wives   ● Adolescent Female

▦ Husbands □ Adolescent Male

Figure 2-6. Mean scores of family members on family satisfaction across stages of the family life cycle.

Family satisfaction at different stages of the family life cycle is illustrated in Figure 2-6. As with marital satisfaction, wives' family satisfaction starts out higher than that of husbands in the early years of marriage. Both husbands' and wives' scores drop, with husbands reaching their lowest point at Stage 4, when adolescents are at home. Wives reach their lowest levels of satisfaction (both marital and family) when the adolescents are leaving home (Stage 5). Family satisfaction increases for both husbands and wives during the empty-nest and retirement stages. A more detailed analysis (*t* tests) indicated that satisfaction at the earlier stages (Stages 1 and 2) was significantly higher than at the school-age (Stage 3) and adolescent (Stages 4 and 5) stages for both husbands and wives.

It is interesting to note that reports of adolescents' family satisfaction differ greatly from those of adults. This is partly because group mean scores are used, and because the level of agreement among a father, mother, and adolescent within the same family is very low ($r = .32$).

SUMMARY

This chapter has attempted to provide a panoramic perspective of normative family processes across the family life cycle. We have captured some of the complexity of marriage and of family life but continue to be amazed at the diversity in families. Certain commonalities have emerged in these families however, in terms of their family dynamics, the stressors and strains they face, their methods of coping, and the levels of their marital and family satisfaction.

The couples and families studied were obtained from a stratified, randomly selected sample from seven stages of the family life cycle. To obtain this developmental perspective, data were obtained from couples who were newly married through those in their retirement years.

Because of the cross-sectional design and focus of the study, the sample consisted entirely of intact marriages and families. The families were pre-dominately white, middle-income couples in their first marriage. Almost half (45%) of the sample lived in a community of 25,000 or more, and about one quarter (26%) lived on farms or in rural areas. Each family had an average of three children.

Major differences were found across the stages of the family life cycle and among the various members of the family. Stage differences were consistently found for many of the family characteristics and can be accounted for in at least two ways. First, these differences reflect the unique developmental tasks and different family structures at each stage of the family life cycle. Second, the co-hort differences between, for example, younger and older couples may be a result of the historical contexts in which they live, of the cultural environment and life events they have experienced, and of the norms and values of their culture.

Our data clearly demonstrate the importance of taking stage differences and individual differences into account when planning any type of research study, program, or service involving families. Thus family researchers and program planners should integrate individual and stage differences into their projects. Because of the potency of the stage breakdown used in this study, program planners might want to use the four reconstructed stages for their work rather than the original seven.

In regard to family types based on the Circumplex Model, few differences were observed across stages or between family members in the percentages of balanced, midrange, and extreme types. However, when the dimensions of cohesion and adaptability were considered, significant differences across the stages and among family members on these two dimensions appeared. Generally, wives viewed their families as more cohesive and adaptable than did their husbands. Adolescents reported substantially lower levels of both family cohe-sion and adaptability than their parents. The general trend between stages indicated that levels of adaptability and cohesion dropped through the first four or five stages to a low point at the adolescent and launching stages and then recovered somewhat in the later two stages. These findings clearly indicated differing perceptions among family members and differences between stages.

Family stressors and strains varied considerably at different stages of the life cycle. Although major social and family stressors were important, it was often the day-to-day hassles that appeared to be of importance, since these events have a cumulative impact. This supports the value of assessing the pileup of stressors.

To cope with family stress, individuals in these families tended to rely primarily on internal resources rather than on external supports offered by professionals and community agencies. One important discovery from this study is that marital and family strengths are very significant, positive characteristics of families. Marital strengths included the 11 variables assessed in ENRICH, among them being communication, conflict resolution, role relationship, and sexual relationship. Family strengths included family pride and accord.

Couples and families possessing these strengths seemed to function more adequately across the life cycle. They also tended to be more satisfied with their marriages and family lives. These strengths seem to operate as major buffers or resistors to stressful life events. It could also be that having these strengths helped these families deal more effectively with the stress and changes that occur across the life cycle.

Marital and family satisfaction was higher at early and later stages of the family life cycle, when couples were living without children. Satisfaction was lowest at the adolescent stage, when family stress was the highest. There was a strong relationship among marital satisfaction, family satisfaction, and life satisfaction, and a strong association between these satisfaction measures and marital and family strengths. When family satisfaction was high, stress had minimal impact on the family. In other words, these families seem to have considerable resistance to stressful life events.

REFERENCES

Beavers, W. R. (1977). *Psychotherapy and growth: A family systems perspective.* New York: Brunner/Mazel.

Benjamin, L. (1974). Structural analysis of social behavior. *Psychological Review, 81,* 392–425.

Benjamin, L. (1977). Structural analysis of a family in therapy. *Journal of Counseling and Clinical Psychology, 45,* 391–406.

Burr, W. R., Leigh, G. K., Day, R. D., & Constantine, J. (1979). Symbolic interaction and the family. In W. R. Burr, R. Hill, F. I. Nye, & J. L. Reiss (Eds.), *Contemporary theories about the family* (pp. 42–111). New York: Free Press.

Campbell, A., Converse, P. E., & Rodgers, W. L. (1976). *The quality of life: Perceptions, evaluations and satisfactions.* New York: Russell Sage Foundation.

Constantine, L. (1983). Dysfunction and failure in open family systems: Application of a unified theory. *Journal of Marriage and the Family, 45,* 725–738.

Epstein, N. B., Bishop, D. S., & Levin, S. (1978). The McMaster model of family functioning. *Journal of Marriage and Family Counseling, 40,* 19–31.

Erikson, E. (1959). *Identity and the life cycle: Psychological issues.* New York: International Universities Press.

French, A. P., & Guidera, E. J. (1974). *The family as a system in four dimensions: A theoretical model.* Paper presented at the Academy of Child Psychiatry, San Francisco.

Glenn, N. D., & McLanahan, S. (1982). Children and marital happiness: A further specification of the relationship. *Journal of Marriage and the Family, 44,* 63–72.

Goetzel, V. (1973). Mental illness and cultural beliefs in a southern Italian immigrant family. *Canadian Psychiatric Association Journal, 18,* 219–222.

Haley, J. (1959). The family of the schizophrenic: A model system. *Journal of Nervous and Mental Disorders, 129,* 357-374.

Haley, J. (1962). Family experiments: A new type of experimentation. *Family Process, 1,* 265-293.

Haley, J. (1963). *Strategies of psychotherapy.* New York: Grune & Stratton.

Hawkins, J. L. (1968). Association between companionship, hostility and marital satisfaction. *Journal of Marriage and the Family, 30,* 647-650.

Hill, R. (1964). Methodological problems with the development approach to family study. *Family Process, 3,* 5-22.

Hill, R. (1970). *Family development in three generations.* Cambridge, MA: Schenkman Books.

Hill, R. (1971). Modern systems theory and the family: A confrontation. *Social Science Information, 10,* 7-26.

Hill, R., & Rodgers, R. (1964). The developmental approach. In H. T. Christensen (Ed.), *Handbook of marriage and the family* (pp. 238-274). Chicago: Rand McNally.

Kantor, D., & Lehr, W. (1975). *Inside the family.* San Francisco: Jossey-Bass.

Levinson, D., Darrow, C. N., Klein, E. B., Levinson, M. H., & McKee, B. (1978). *The seasons of a man's life.* New York: Alfred A. Knopf.

Lewis, J. M., Beavers, W. R., Gossert, J. T., & Philips, V. A. (1976). *No single thread: Psychological health in family systems.* New York: Brunner/Mazel.

Lewis, R. A., & Spanier, G. B. (1979). Theorizing about the quality and stability of marriage. In W. R. Burr, R. Hill, R. I. Nye, & I. L. Reiss (Eds.), *Contemporary theories about the family* (Vol. 1). New York: Free Press.

Locke, H. J., & Wallace, K. M. (1959). Short marital adjustment tests: Their reliability and validity. *Marriage and the Family, 21,* 251-255.

McCubbin, H. I., Patterson, J., & Wilson, L. (1980). *Family inventory of life events (FILE).* Madison, WI: University of Wisconsin.

Minuchin, S., Montalvo, B., Guerny, B. G., Rosman, B. L., & Schumer, S. (1967). *Families of the slums.* New York: Basic Books.

Olson, D. H. (1986). Circumplex model. VII: Validation studies and FACES III. *Family Process, 25,* 337-351.

Olson, D. H., Fournier, D. G., & Druckman, J. M. (1982). ENRICH Inventory. Minneapolis: PREPARE-ENRICH, Inc.

Olson, D. H., McCubbin, H. I., Barnes, H. L., Larsen, A. S., Muxen, M. J., & Wilson, M. A. (Eds.). (1982). *Family inventories.* St. Paul: Family Social Science, University of Minnesota.

Olson, D. H., McCubbin, H. I., Barnes, H. L., Larsen, A. S., Muxen, M. J., & Wilson, M. A. (1983). *Families: What makes them work.* Newbury Park, CA: Sage Publishing.

Olson, D. H., & Wilson, M. A. (1982). Family satisfaction scale. In D. H. Olson, H. I. McCubbin, H. L. Barnes, A. S. Larsen, M. J. Muxen, & M. A. Wilson (Eds.), *Family inventories.* St. Paul: Family Social Science, University of Minnesota.

Rollins, B. C., & Galligan, R. (1978). The developing child and marital satisfaction of parents. In R. M. Lerner & G. B. Spanier (Eds.), *Child influences on marital and family interaction: A life-span perspective.* New York: Academic Press.

Schram, R. W. (1979). Marital satisfaction over the life cycle: A critique and proposal. *Journal of Marriage and the Family, 40,* 7-12.

Schvaneveldt, J. D. (1973). Mormon adolescents: Likes and dislikes toward parents and home. *Adolescents, 8,* 171-178.

Sheehy, G. (1976). *Passages: Predictable crises of adult life.* New York: E. P. Dutton.

Spanier, G. B., & Lewis, R. A. (1980). Marital quality: A review of the seventies. *Journal of Marriage and the Family, 42,* 96-110.

Spanier, G. B., Lewis, R. A., & Cole, C. L. (1975). Marital adjustment over the family life cycle: The issue of curvilinearity. *Journal of Marriage and the Family, 36,* 263-275.

Speer, D. (1970). Family systems: Morphostasis and morphogenesis, or is homeostasis enough? *Family Process, 9,* 259-278.

Stein, H. F. (1978). The Slovak-American "swaddling ethos": Homeostat for family dynamics and cultural continuity. *Family Process, 17,* 31–45.

Stinnett, N., Chesser, B., DeFrain, J., & Knaub, P. (1980). *Family strengths: Positive models for family life.* Lincoln: University of Nebraska Press.

Waldron, H., & Routh, D. K. (1981). The effect of the first child on the marital relationship. *Journal of Marriage and the Family, 4,* 785–788.

Walsh, R. (1982). *Normal family processes.* New York: Guilford Press.

Wertheim, E. (1973). Family unit therapy and the science and typology of family systems. *Family Process, 12,* 361–376.

Wertheim, E. (1975). The science and typology of family systems. II: Further theoretical and practical considerations. *Family Process, 14,* 285–308.

Wittmer, J. (1973). Amish homogeneity of parental behavior characteristics. *Human Relations, 26,* 143–154.

3

An Epigenetic Model of Family Processes

LYMAN C. WYNNE
University of Rochester Medical Center

In an extensive literature in both family sociology (Duvall, 1962; Hill, 1964) and family therapy (Carter & McGoldrick, 1980; Grunebaum & Bryant, 1966; Haley, 1973; Solomon, 1973), family development has been studied in terms of the concept of the family life cycle. The most pivotal criterion for making transitions between stages in the family life cycle has been the exit and entry of family members, that is, changes in the formal structure or composition of the family, with births, deaths, marriage, divorce, and geographic moves. In a broad overview, the first stage of the family life cycle involves the separation of young adults from their families of origin and their entry into a new system. Normatively, the life cycle of American families has been divided into 4 to 24 stages (Rodgers, 1960). Thus, these stages vary considerably in the detail with which they are delineated. The partial departure of children from the family system, first entering into the school system and later into extrafamilial adolescent life, is followed by leaving home, with the family as a launching center. Each of these changes are marker points in the normatively defined family life cycle. In later life, we often see the reentry of the breadwinner into the home setting after retirement, and sometimes the reentry of aging, now dependent parents.

These gradually evolving events of the normative family life cycle are more drastically modified after premature deaths, during and after divorce, and with the formation of remarried families (Carter & McGoldrick, 1980). Much has been written about the problems for individuals who are not developmentally or experientially ready for such transitions. My concern here, however, is with the problems for the relational system when the quality of relating is inappropriate or when it provides a poor fit between persons at the time of these structural changes.

It is important to recognize that the exits and entries of the family life cycle often do not take place when the participants are psychologically or relationally ready. Therefore, conceptually, the family life cycle is not, except

Revised from a version in *Family Process, 23,* 297–318, 1984. I wish to acknowledge the collaboration of Adele R. Wynne in formulating the sections on mutuality and intimacy.

in terms of an idealized norm, a truly *epigenetic* process in which each stage builds upon the preceding stage in an expectable form.

What is crucial to my formulation here is the point that most of these life cycle changes in *family composition* proceed more or less inexorably, regardless of the *quality of relating* of the participants. The epigenesis of the quality of relational processes, I shall contend, proceeds at a rate and in a sequence that has its own inner "logic," sometimes unfolding smoothly and continuously, and sometimes destabilizing discontinuously as new ingredients are randomly introduced or created within each variety of relational process. This means that "structural" changes in family composition and the qualitative development of relational processes are expectably and frequently going to be out of synchrony. Thus the traditional approach to the family life cycle, defined primarily in terms of structural, compositional role change by exits and entries, is in a sense orthogonal to the unfolding of relational processes.

My epigenetic model builds upon the core hypothesis that relational processes within families and other enduring interpersonal systems follow one another in a certain developmental sequence. Do distortions of sequential patterning in the development of relational systems predictably lead to distress or to constrictions of growth? If so, what are the implications for assessment and intervention?

This formulation builds upon and revisits earlier hypotheses. My 1958 starting point for these ideas was the outline of a theory of relatedness. My colleagues and I postulated that a dilemma emerges in interpersonal systems because of the universal primary "striving for relatedness to other human beings" and the simultaneous striving "to develop a sense of personal identity" (Wynne, Ryckoff, Day, & Hirsch, 1958, p. 206). In enduring relational systems, such as families, two "solutions" were described, "genuine mutuality" and "pseudomutuality," the latter defined as "a predominant absorption in fitting together at the expense of the differentiation of the identities of the persons in the relation" (Wynne *et al.,* 1958, p. 207). Later, another pattern of intensely involved relatedness was labeled "pseudohostility," functionally equivalent to pseudomutuality from the standpoint of family system continuity (Wynne, 1961). Nonmutual complementarity was noted as a pattern that is characteristic of "institutionalized" roles in which there is not a strong emotional investment (Wynne *et al.,* 1958). In later writings, Singer and I turned to more specific details of the transactions, especially communicational, within both ongoing (cross-sectional) and developmental contexts of family relatedness (Singer & Wynne, 1965; Wynne, 1968).

THE CONCEPT OF EPIGENESIS

In 1965, Singer and I noted that our view of development was encompassed by the "epigenetic principle":

The interchanges or transactions of each developmental phase build upon the outcome of earlier transactions. This means that constitutional and experiential influences recombine in each developmental phase to create new biologic and behavioral potentialities which then help determine the next phase. If the transactions at any given developmental phase are distorted or omitted, all the subsequent developmental phases will be altered because they build upon a different substrate. We hypothesize that the family environment needs to provide certain kinds of influences in each maturational phase of the individual. What is appropriate and what may have psychopathological consequences thus varies over time and must always be considered in this developmental context. (Singer & Wynne, 1965, p. 208)

Our use of the concept of epigenesis was in accord with its most general meaning, referring to events of "becoming" ("genesis") that build "upon" ("epi") the immediately preceding events. There is now general agreement that epigenetic rules, even at the level of biologic systems, set limits on the *range* of variability but that within this range, random variation takes place. For example, the sociobiologists Lumsden and Wilson (1981, 1983) base their theory of gene–culture coevolution on a concept of biologic epigenesis. They contend that epigenetic rules are genetically transmitted for functions that have had evolutionary advantage, such as incest avoidance and the innate grammatical rules that Chomsky (1980) believes help shape language development. In the bidirectional causality of Lumsden and Wilson (1983), "culture is created and shaped by biological processes while the biological processes are simultaneously altered in response to cultural change" (p. 118). Critics (e.g., Alper & Lange, 1981) have cogently argued, and I agree, that Lumsden and Wilson exaggerate the degree to which *genetically* coded epigenesis can help explain *cultural* diversity. In any event, what I wish to emphasize here is that while epigenetic rules set limits on the range of stability, fluctuation within that range (Dell & Goolishian, 1981) is stochastic, that is, the "sequence of events combines a random component with a selective process" (Bateson, 1979, p. 230).

For psychologists, the most familiar reference to the epigenetic principle is by Erik H. Erikson (1968), who proposed a schema of stepwise, successive changes in ego formation out of a "ground plan" from which parts arise, "each part having its time of special ascendancy" (p. 92). He identified eight stages in the individual life cycle, beginning with basic trust, proceeding in adolescence to the consolidation of identity, and going on to generativity and integrity in the final developmental stages. Erikson (1968) argued that

the healthy child, given a reasonable amount of proper guidance, can be trusted to obey inner laws of development, laws which create a succession of potentialities for significant interaction with those persons who tend and respond to him and those institutions which are ready for him. While such interaction varies from culture to culture, it must remain within "the proper rate and the proper sequence" which governs all epigenesis. (p. 93)

In the past, such formulations have applied to personal/psychological and to biologic levels of systems organization. Neither I nor others have specifically applied the epigenetic principle at the level of *relational* systems. Even our 1965 transactional view (Singer & Wynne, 1965) was oriented to the person as the system level undergoing developmental change. Here I am proposing that the principles and processes of epigenetic development in relational systems, beyond the person or personality as a system, be explicitly considered. In doing so, it is helpful to remind ourselves of the concept of levels of organization in general systems theory. This principle has been emphasized by biologists such as Weiss (1925), by theoreticians such as Bertalanffy (1968) and Parsons (1951), and, more recently, by Engel in his biopsychosocial model (1980).

The key point here is that systems theory postulates that nature can be viewed in a hierarchically arranged continuum, with the more complex, larger units superordinate to the less complex, smaller units. Each level needs to be regarded as an organized whole, with distinctive properties and characteristics that are altered by interchange with other levels, but with no level reducible to simpler levels. Thus, organs are more than simple aggregates of cells, the person is more than an aggregate of organs, and the family is more than an aggregate of persons. In this hierarchy of organizations, each level has distinctive and unique qualities.

I take it as axiomatic that relatedness and relational systems of more than one person constitute system levels different from that of individual psychology. However, there is not a conceptually clear principle for differentiating marriages, families, communities, and societies. Stipulating the number of persons gives only a rough index as to the quality of these relational systems. Without proposing a comprehensive solution to this problem, I believe that a starting point is the distinction proposed by Charles H. Cooley who, in 1909, defined "primary groups": "those characterized by intimate face-to-face association and cooperation" with a unity not of "mere harmony," but always "a differentiated and usually a competitive unity, admitting of self-assertion and various appropriate passions; but these passions are socialized by sympathy and come, or tend to come, under the discipline of a common spirit" (p. 23). The principal example of a primary group is, of course, the family. In broad agreement with Cooley, I believe that the patterning and the quality of relatedness are more crucial issues than the specific number of persons or the name given to the primary group (family, marriage, intimate friendship, etc.).

THE PROCESSES OF RELATIONAL EPIGENESIS

In this overview, I shall not attempt to provide a full-scale critical exposition of my schema for the epigenesis of relational systems. Nor shall I justify at length my selection of terminology for the processes and compare in detail this terminology with that used by other authors for rather different purposes. Rather, my purpose here is primarily to introduce what I believe has been a neglected perspective, a developmental, epigenetic view of the *processes* of relational systems. This neglect is especially striking in view of the continuous and even strident insistence by family systems theorists that family systems are not adequately conceptualized in terms of the individual members or their disorders, such as schizophrenia.

Four processes appear to unfold epigenetically in relational systems:

1. *Attachment/caregiving,* complementary affectional bonding, prototypically manifest in parent–infant relatedness.
2. *Communicating,* beginning with the sharing of foci of attention and continuing in the exchange of meanings and messages.
3. *Joint problem solving* and renewable sharing of day-to-day tasks, interests, and recreational activities.
4. *Mutuality,* the flexible, selective integration of the preceding processes into an enduring, superordinate pattern of relatedness. There is a shared commitment to one another to shape the relationship as the life cycle unfolds, as unexpected events take place, as new interests and aspirations emerge. In mutuality, relatedness is reshaped multidimensionally, sometimes drastically reorganized, but with continuity of contributions from each person in the relationship. Mutuality incorporates both distancing or disengagement and constructive reengagement.

Relational Processes as Dimensionalized Systems

As Figure 3-1 suggests, each of these four processes can be regarded, from the vantage point of a relational system, as the "positive" pole of a dimension, or, more accurately, as the positive side of a domain. The corresponding "negative" pole, or side, for each is some form of relational distancing or difficulty. What

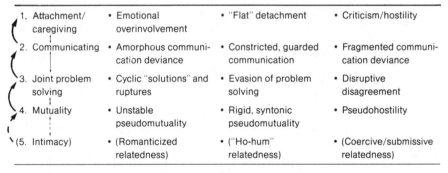

1. Attachment/ caregiving	• Emotional overinvolvement	• "Flat" detachment	• Criticism/hostility
2. Communicating	• Amorphous communication deviance	• Constricted, guarded communication	• Fragmented communication deviance
3. Joint problem solving	• Cyclic "solutions" and ruptures	• Evasion of problem solving	• Disruptive disagreement
4. Mutuality	• Unstable pseudomutuality	• Rigid, syntonic pseudomutuality	• Pseudohostility
(5. Intimacy)	• (Romanticized relatedness)	• ("Ho-hum" relatedness)	• (Coercive/submissive relatedness)

Figure 3-1. Major processes, and illustrative dysfunctions, in the epigenesis of enduring relational systems. The sequence may stop progressing at any stage. Intimacy is not essential for enduring relatedness, but if and when it becomes *reliably* available, intimacy is a subjective corollary of mutuality.

is "negative" at the relational system level may, of course, be "positive" for individual participants, for example, in achieving differentiation.

The positive poles can also be viewed as nodal points around which a range of fluctuations (first-order change) may occur that leave the relational system essentially unchanged (Ashby, 1952; Dell & Goolishian, 1981; Hoffman, 1981). Under certain circumstances, shifting to a different predominant form of relational functioning may constitute a discontinuous transformation (second-order change); this is not the case if such change is part of a cyclic, repeated pattern.

The positive side of each process, such as attachment/caregiving, implies the potentiality of a negative counterpart, such as separation. Indeed, the intensity of attachment/caregiving is strengthened by appropriately timed separation, whereas excessively prolonged and poorly timed separation can lead to detachment/rejection. Similarly, transient failure in sharing foci of attention sharpens attentional vigilance and the need to communicate, but sustained failures to share foci of attention and meaning may contribute to "transactional thought disorder" (Wynne & Singer, 1963). Also, temporary failures at joint problem solving may serve as challenges leading to mastery, but, if excessively repeated, they may lead to demoralized relational breakdown. Although prolonged, intense instability or divergence will surely impair or disrupt relatedness, divergence that is contextually and developmentally appropriate is necessary as a decisive stimulus for moving on to the next level or form of relating.

Analogously, in Erikson's (1968) epigenetic formulation, he described the need to consider the

> ratio between the positive and the negative which, if the balance is toward the positive, will help . . . to meet later crises. . . . One of the chief misuses of the schema [Erikson's] . . . is a dominant connotation given to the sense of trust, and to all other "positive" senses to be postulated, as *achievements* secured once and for all at a given stage. In fact, some writers are so intent on making an achievement scale out of these stages that they blithely omit all the "negative" potentials, basic mistrust, etc., which not only remain the dynamic counterpart of the positive potentials throughout life, but are equally necessary to psychosocial life. A person devoid of the capacity to mistrust would be as unable to live as one without trust. (p. 325)

Similarly, in relational systems, experiences of detachment/rejection, for example, are as essential to the further development of relatedness as are the experiences of attachment/caregiving.

The potentiality of impasse and disorder is implicit in the concept of a fluctuating range of functioning at each stage. But impasse also may be a precondition for creative new solutions. This point is reminiscent of what I once called the "anguish, and creative passions, of *not* escaping double binds" (Wynne, 1976) and also is relevant to recent discussions of those circumstances that generate change that is discontinuous, at least from an observer's viewpoint (Dell, 1982; Hoffman, 1981).

Relational Processes, Transactions, and Relationship Structures

Two terminological clarifications are needed. First, the relational processes that I shall be describing are primarily "transactional" rather than "interactional," applying the distinction first proposed by Dewey and Bentley in 1949. In transactional processes, persons undergo *internal* change during the course of interchange with one another. All parts of a transactional field are interdependent, each modifying the rest through recursive ("circular") feedback; the whole exhibits the functional relation between the parts, that is, the "whole and parts are complementary and indispensable to each other" (Spiegel, 1971, p. 41).

Nevertheless, not all components of a relational system can possibly change at the same time, to the same degree, or in the same qualitative manner. Therefore subsystems, especially persons and dyads, necessarily retain a degree of separateness, identity, and differentiation that varies over time. Indeed, the "dialectic" of fluctuations that I have described, for example, from attachment/caregiving to detachment/rejection, implies that persons may move to an extreme of symbiotic overinvolvement or emotional fusion, or, on the other hand, may become detached to the point of autism. Additionally, in the situation, for example, where a child has been removed from the primary parent and placed in a foster or adoptive home, the *initial* relational system can be regarded as dissolved or dead when the recursive elements of the system have disappeared from view.

ATTACHMENT/CAREGIVING

Bowlby's 1958 article "The Nature of the Child's Tie to His Mother" sparked a massive amount of research and speculation under the general heading of attachment theory. Some of these studies focused on unidirectional attachment behavior of the infant to the mother and did not refer to the mother--infant relational system. Other researchers (Klaus & Kennell, 1976; Leiderman & Seashore, 1975) observed what they call "bonding" in the direction of mother to infant, which takes place abruptly almost immediately after the birth of an infant, provided that conditions are optimal. The fully complementary "attachment" of infant to mother develops only gradually during the infant's first 6 months or so of life. There is also evidence (e.g., Peterson, Mehl, & Leiderman, 1979) that fathers may become affectively "bonded" to their infants.

Unidirectional models of attachment and bonding are being replaced by more systemic and transactional concepts (Svejda, Pannabecker, & Emde,

1982). Bowlby (1969, 1980) carefully noted that attachment behavior takes place in a feedback system in which the complementary function is caregiving. Some authors such as Svejda *et al.* (1982) have broadened their use of the term "attachment" to refer to both the parental growth of love for the infant and the reciprocal tie from infant to parent. Hinde (1982) uses the term "attachment behavior system" much as family system theorists would, to refer to the feedback processes that "incorporate sensitivity to and expectations about the other participant." Similarly, Sroufe, Fox, and Pancake (1983) note that the concept of a situationally "flexible *organization* of behavior" in the service of the "affective bond" between the prototypical infant and caregiver is now a central feature of attachment theory.

Present-day attachment theory also specifies that attachment/caregiving refers to the relatedness between an infant and a hierarchy of specific caregivers, in contrast to dependency and other behaviors of the child toward people in general (Ainsworth, 1982; Sroufe *et al.,* 1983). Interestingly, this specification that certain persons, rather than others, are emotionally involved is also a distinction made from an entirely different research starting point by Brown, Birley, and Wing (1972), by Vaughn and Leff (1976), and by other researchers working with the concept of expressed emotion. Expressed emotion is operationally defined in terms of the attitudes expressed by a relative about a *specific* family member (the patient) with whom there has been considerable face-to-face contact. The expressed emotion concept is nontransactional and unidirectional (from relative to patient), and does not measure feedback and multiperson processes, but the two major components of the concept, emotional overinvolvement and criticism, can be readily understood as special forms of attachment/caregiving that are likely to lead to dysfunctional communicating, problem solving, and intimacy (see Figure 3-1).

As Ainsworth (1982) notes in an excellent review, there is not yet full consensus concerning the terminology and criteria used in attachment theory, and further research is needed. Nevertheless, much animal and human research on the basic concept of attachment/caregiving has gone far in validating this construct as the starting point for what I am calling the epigenesis of relational systems (Ainsworth, Blehar, Walters, & Wall, 1978; Sroufe, 1979; Weiss, 1982).

To be relevant to a generalized model of relatedness, the concept of attachment/caregiving should be applicable throughout life, not just to parent-infant transactions. Weiss (1982) has written a valuable review of the unfolding of attachment/caregiving systems in adolescence and adulthood. He particularly identifies three criteria for attachment: the need for proximity to the attachment figure in situations of distress; heightened comfort and diminished anxiety in the company of the attachment figure; and a marked increase in discomfort and anxiety with the discovery that accessibility to the attachment figure is threatened. Weiss wonders whether these criteria characterize later-life, face-to-face, enduring relationships of the kind Cooley (1909) referred to as "primary." He concludes that "attachment in adults is an expression of the same emotional system, though one modified in the course of its development, as is attachment in children" (p. 175). He notes that these differences include, first, that "attachment in adults is not nearly so capable of overwhelming other behavioral systems as it is in infancy" (p. 173); second, that attachment after infancy draws increasingly upon affiliative relationships with peers; and third, that it is more often directed toward a figure with whom the adult has a sexual relationship. The concept of affiliative systems needs to be better understood in comparison with attachment/caregiving systems. Weiss (1982) has shown that friendship affiliations do not substitute for the loneliness that occurs, for example, after the ending of a marital attachment.

The most striking instance of attachment in later life, which actually may overwhelm other behavioral systems, is "falling in love," a relational change that is not unlike maternal bonding with the newborn infant in its intensity and abrupt onset. (This phenomenon should not be confused with "intimacy," in the sense in which I shall use that term later in the chapter.) Another form of intense attachment/caregiving emerges more gradually in long-standing marriages, again not necessarily in combination with "love" or intimacy. In later life, role reversals in terms of who is the caregiver and who is the recipient often occur if the relational system is organized in a situationally flexible manner. This point is relevant to Bowlby's (1975) definition of attachment behavior: "any form of behavior that results in a person obtaining or retaining proximity to some other differentiated and preferred individual, usually conceived as stronger and/or wiser" (p. 292). Ainsworth (1982) comments that "in a good marriage, each partner on occasion plays the role of stronger and wiser figure for the other, so that each derives security and comfort from the other, as well as wishing to be with the other and protesting actual or threatened separation" (p. 26).

In addition, the pattern of caregiving for one's children appears to be influenced by the pattern in which caregiving was received from one's parents. Research support for this hypothesis is found both in Harlow & Harlow's (1970) monkey experiments and in Engel's (1983) observations of Monica, the baby with esophageal atresia who is now a mother and who shows highly specific idiosyncrasies of caregiving.

COMMUNICATING

In 1968, in discussing the concept of epigenesis, I tentatively suggested a second stage of relatedness:

> There is a continuing series of transactions in which the "fit" between the person's innate and learned equipment and the kind of stimulation and responsiveness received from the environment are both critical to the development process. For example, in early infancy a reciprocal relatedness between mother and infant

on a nonverbal basis appears to influence the later development of communicative language. (Wynne, 1968, p. 187)

Singer and I have taken the position that a necessary precondition for communicating is the shared focusing of attention, leading to potentially shared meanings (Singer & Wynne, 1965; Singer, Wynne, & Toohey, 1978). This formulation is similar to what Blakar (1984) calls "the most basic precondition for successful communication," namely, "that the participants have established a 'shared social reality,' a common '*here-and-now*' within which exchange of messages can take place . . . *under the belief* that they are in the same situation" (p. 38).

A number of developmental psychologists have documented that separation distress decreases with increasing age among children aged 2 to 4 years when they are placed in strange situations in which attachment/caregiving is briefly interrupted. This decreased intensity of attachment appears to be directly associated with the emergence of the child's ability to understand something of the mother's perspective (Marvin, 1977) and "to reach or attempt to reach shared plans with his mother through verbal communication" (Ainsworth, 1982, p. 11).

These observations are relevant to another precondition for communicating proposed by Blakar (1984): "the individual's capacity to decenter and take the perspective of the other" (p. 44). Blakar (1984) and Lidz (1973), following Piaget (1926), appropriately label the negative pole of this ability as egocentrism. Lidz (1973) observes that "the egocentricities of the parent and child are reciprocal in many respects," may be confined within the family, and may contribute to the emergence of schizophrenic thought disorder (p. 74). In focusing on communicational disorders in the families of certain schizophrenics, Wynne and Singer (1963) noted that the sequences and patterns of family-wide transactions "cannot be adequately described by mechanically adding up the degree of disturbance of individuals out of context. As a loose analogy, [we spoke of] 'transactional thought disorder' in the family social system" (p. 194).

The distinction between attachment/caregiving and communicating has been blurred by overly broad and vague definitions of communication. I substantially agree with Blakar (1984) that "a major problem hindering progress in the field of family-interaction research is the application of too vague and extensive definitions of the concept of communication" (p. 17). For example, Watzlawick, Beavin, and Jackson (1967) used the terms "communication" and "behavior" "virtually synonymously" (p. 22). To be sure, there is a communicative component within attachment/caregiving. However, later in the development of relatedness, the learning of shared communicational codes and of skills in symbolic expression and in the use of language becomes the primary task. Analogously, in Erikson's (1968) formulation of the epigenesis of identity, the precursors of identity can be recognized long before consolidation of identity becomes the *central* developmental task of adolescence.

Singer and I (1966) have formulated the concept of "communication deviance," in which a "listener is unable to construct a consistent visual image or a consistent construct from the speaker's words" (Singer *et al.,* 1978, p. 500). We identified 32 categories of communication deviance that are significantly different in families with offspring diagnosed as having various forms and degrees of severe psychopathology (Singer & Wynne, 1965, 1966; Singer *et al.,* 1978; Wynne, Singer, Bartko, & Toohey, 1977). These categories mostly emphasize difficulties in sharing foci of attention and in conveying messages with shared meaning, that is, at the communicational level of relatedness as I am formulating it here. However, I now believe that our earlier concept of communication was, like that of Watzlawick *et al.* (1967), unduly expansive, because it incorporated behaviors that are better included under the heading of attachment/caregiving and its deviations. For example, the communication deviance category of "derogatory, disparaging, critical remarks" (Singer & Wynne, 1966) is essentially the same as the expressed emotion category of "critical comments," which I have identified as a deviant aspect of attachment/caregiving.

It is worth noting that despite a degree of ambiguity in both the communication deviance and expressed emotion concepts, their distinctiveness from one another has recently been supported by longitudinal data reported by Goldstein (1985). That is, communication deviance and affective style, the counterpart of expressed emotion when studied with direct observation of family interaction, were poorly correlated with each other, but both of these family measures contributed significantly to the prediction of outcome of schizophrenia and schizophrenia spectrum disorders at a 15-year follow-up. A broader conclusion that can be drawn is that attachment and communicating are indeed qualitatively different processes and are given priority at different times, both in the course of family development and in other situations, such as during the learning of a new technical language.

One gap of past research is highlighted by the present emphasis on "healthy" relating as the starting point, instead of on dysfunction, deviance, and psychopathology. The positive, integrative patterns of healthy communication are more than the *absence* of deviance. In recent research in Rochester, New York, on healthy family communication, we identified family patterns that can be positively defined and that, indeed, appear to be better predictors (statistically) of child competence than are the indices of deviance (Wynne, Jones, & Al-Khayyal, 1982). For example, positive parental recognition of the limited knowledge and affective state of the child is crucial for meaningful communication in family problem-solving tasks.

It can be argued that in adult situations, such as in the workplace, efforts at learning to communicate can take place without much evidence of a prior attachment/caregiving pattern. Obviously, communicational skills are used outside of the enduring relational systems or primary groups that are under consideration here. It is generally agreed that the family and its surrogates provide the basic framework for learning communicational and other relational skills that are used in contexts outside the family. When attachment/caregiving has not taken place, a shared cognitive and affective perspective cannot be well established. However, when communication processes build upon attachment/caregiving, the participants draw upon abundant information that can be taken for granted and no longer needs to be made explicit.

In Figure 3-1, I have indicated that through recursive, "circular" processes (a spiral, when viewed through time), the quality of communicating, for example, will modify subsequent attachment/caregiving. Certainly, this "feedback" occurs in enduring familial and marital relatedness. In addition, it should be noted that the sheer repetition of shared communicational (and problem-solving) patterns in the workplace (and in some cultures, in arranged marriages), may actually generate attachment/caregiving. Weiss (1982) comments that the "institution of marriage" tends to foster attachment, whatever the initial relationship of the couple.

JOINT PROBLEM SOLVING

In accord with my epigenetic schema, the effects of dysfunctional communication patterns emerge most vividly at the third stage, when joint problem solving becomes more primary. Although behavioral therapy has emphasized problem solving for some years, only more recently has the concept of *joint* problem solving as a task for healthy family relatedness been given much attention in family therapy. Individual problem-solving skills, industry, and task mastery surely constitute a major phase of psychological development. Erikson (1950) described "industry vs. inferiority" as the fourth stage in ego epigenesis. Some of the learning of such skills takes place through individual trial and error. What I wish to emphasize here is that *joint* problem solving and *shared* engagement in sustained and renewed tasks involve relational processes that create a potentiality for new relational growth. (For an earlier discussion of this point, see Wynne, 1970.)

Over time, shared task-related, problem-solving behavior becomes patterned into informal role relationships. These relationship patterns provide a bridge between what I have called the epigenesis of qualitative family processes and the "structural" role transitions of the family life cycle. Informal role structures may or may not be consonant with the norms and expectations associated with culturally provided, sociologically defined roles (such as husband or wife) and with family life cycle stages (such as the stage in which a family has adolescents chronologically ready for launching from home). Clearly, negotiation through these life cycle transitions requires joint problem-solving skills. But without a background of attachment/caregiving and communicational skills, joint problem solving is doomed to be muddled and dysfunctional. For example, if a family at the adolescent launching stage is still deeply enmeshed and emotionally overinvolved, or is still communicating in an amorphous, fragmented, or constricted manner (Singer & Wynne, 1965), problem solving will be difficult indeed. Most of the structural changes of the family life cycle move on inexorably as the "fallout" of gradual aging or of "random" events such as illness, death, divorce, and remarriage. In contrast, both the epigenetic processes of family relatedness and those of individual psychological growth and identity formation optimally march at the pace of their own drummers. Therefore, at any given time, the quality of functioning in family relational processes frequently does not fit with the more arbitrary progression of the family life cycle.

Ineffective, indecisive, and disorganized joint problem solving in a marriage or family is a "big" and obvious difficulty that frequently is the presenting complaint leading to therapy. In other clinical situations, the complaint may take another form; for example, a couple may request help with difficulties in communication or intimacy, but the therapist may see the problem-solving difficulty as a more definable, manageable focus for change. In current "schools" of family therapy, the emphasis on joint family problem solving (Epstein & Bishop, 1981; Falloon, Boyd, McGill, Strang, & Moos, 1981; Haley, 1976) has constituted a major focus for effective change.

A feature of Falloon *et al.'s* (1981) approach to behavioral family therapy is directly relevant to my epigenetic formulation. Falloon emphasizes the teaching of communicational skills as a prior and necessary step when efforts to help families with problem solving have failed. His assumption is that successful use of communicational skills is a basic task that must be accomplished before effective problem solving can proceed. Also, in any family therapy approach, family members must be sufficiently emotionally attached to one another so that they are willing to come together in order to learn communicational skills or anything else. With high levels of expressed emotion or communication deviance, family problem-solving difficulties will be inevitable. However, assisting couples or families in working on simple problems together may promote their becoming more comfortable affectively and their communicating more successfully. More complex and sustained problem solving, I believe, presupposes prior success in earlier developmental stages.

MUTUALITY

The final stage in my epigenetic schema centrally involves the processes of long-term relational renewal and reengagement. "Mutuality," the term that I am using in a special way to characterize this stage, begins with the recognition of difficulties that cannot be resolved within the framework of prior forms of relatedness and involves renegotiation and sometimes transformation to new patterns of relating. The possible new patterns include "ending" this relational system, which may actually be a shift to relatedness at a greater distance, as, for example, in divorce.

At each stage in the epigenesis of relatedness, difficulties are inevitable. In Figure 3-1, some of the possible adaptive "solutions" (forms of impasse) are outlined at each stage. The stage of mutuality builds most directly upon joint problem solving because, in a sense, the problem to be solved is whether the relationship should or will continue, and, if so, under what conditions. This implies a stocktaking of the current quality of relating and of the circumstances that are affecting it—illness, growth, and the aging of each family member; transitions in the family life cycle; and involvement in other systems (at work, with extended family, and with other persons). Mutuality differs from the other forms of relating considered thus far in that it requires that each person "observe," temporarily, the functioning of the system in which he or she has been participating, that is, take a "meta" position partially outside of the system.

Mutuality does not necessarily or automatically emerge after the sequence of attachment/caregiving, communicating, and joint problem solving has developed, but it does draw upon accrued relational experience and skill from each of these stages in order to return selectively to whatever form of relatedness is appropriate to changing internal and external contexts. Mutuality is a superordinate concept that is specifically oriented to the issue of relational change over time in the face of conflict and divergence. As formulated in 1958, the concept is defined as follows:

> With growth and situational changes, altered expectations inevitably come into any relation. Then at least transient nonfulfillment of expectations—that is, noncomplementarity—necessarily occurs. . . . Mutuality is experienced as having a larger context than a particular role. . . . Genuine mutuality, unlike pseudomutuality, not only tolerates divergence of self-interests, but thrives upon the recognition of such natural and inevitable divergence. (Wynne *et al.*, 1958, p. 207)

Enduring relatedness requires periodic stocktaking, with each person taking into account his or her own needs and preferences, those of each of the others, and the quality of what goes on between or among them. The result of such stocktaking may alter the previous relationship. It may move into "pathological" forms, what I have called "pseudomutuality" (Wynne *et al.*, 1958) and "pseudohostility" (Wynne, 1961), in which the preservation of a fixed pattern of relatedness takes priority at the expense of individual needs and despite changing circumstances. In other instances, change is not negotiated but simply asserted by one person, or a dyad, seemingly at the expense of the others. And finally, of course, without some degree of mutuality, the relation may break up quite abruptly (Weiss, 1982), with little genuine exploration of options, including whether there is any point to attempting a fresh start.

"Renegotiation" in mutuality may be quite explicit, for example, in the planning of a new life-style after retirement or in the reorganizing of household chores when a wife takes on a full-time job with children still at home. In other situations, the new pattern may be established without discussion or even awareness, for example, when an ailing parent or the workplace gradually becomes all-absorbing at the expense of the marriage or nuclear family.

The changes within the context of mutuality may involve not only expansion of relatedness but also narrowing of the range of involvement with one another. For example, when young adults leave the nuclear family to establish a new household of their own, a warm and diversified parent–offspring mutuality does not evaporate but changes into a new pattern. This changed pattern will include attachment/caregiving that is now more episodic, with less need for face-to-face accessibility. In later years, the attachment/caregiving will need to be reorganized again, perhaps with role reversal when circumstances change with aging and illness. Given a clear but flexible framework of attachment/caregiving, there can be a resumption of communicating and joint problem solving in an altered mutuality that is not so intense as in earlier years but that is still highly meaningful. Thus, the concept of mutuality does not imply that there is an optimal, necessary direction that relatedness must take. Instead, this concept involves repeated changes of direction and a high degree of flexible variation over time.

INTIMACY

The place of intimacy in a conceptualization of relational processes is extraordinarily difficult to delineate. Intimacy is often touted in today's popular (and family therapy) literature as the ideal type of highly valued relatedness. In earlier versions of this epigenetic schema, I located "intimacy" as a process between joint problem solving and mutuality. However, more sober reflection has led me to conclude that historically, across the full range of social class and cultural variations, intimacy has been more of a luxury than a developmental necessity in relational systems. For example, in the many cultures in which arranged marriages have been customary, attachment/caregiving slowly builds out of the realities of proximity, eventually leading to fine-tuned mutuality, but not necessarily with much intimacy.

As Schaefer and Olson (1981) point out, the research literature has "barely paused" to define, clearly conceptualize, or validate the nature of intimacy. In an attempt at definition, I believe that intimacy is best characterized as the inconstant, subjective side of relatedness, the sharing of personal feelings, fantasies, and affectively meaningful experience associated with each of the stages that have been described. These processes are relational, between persons, but are not necessarily symmetrical. They include emotionally charged verbal or nonverbal self-disclosures of a kind that connotes an acceptance of the listener, who could betray or exploit the speaker but who is trusted not to do so. This definition suggests that intimacy can be a deeply powerful, meaningful, and humanizing experience, subtly and emotionally complicated, seductive but frightening. At the same time, intimacy often seems incompatible with the actual life-styles and values of those in many economic and cultural groups, especially for many males.

The term "intimacy" is sometimes carelessly confused with—and sometimes difficult to distinguish from—the relatedness of attachment/caregiving. Erotic elements, joint inspiration, and reciprocal self-disclosures are some of the more obvious elements that contribute to intimacy beyond the elemental starting point of attachment/caregiving. I believe that the concept is best reserved for the multifaceted, elaborated relatedness of those who have grown beyond the basic stage of attachment/caregiving, however crucial this ground-plan stage is.

We also need to distinguish between intimacy and sexuality. Sexual passion within the context of enduring relatedness surely may arise out of experiences of intimacy and may greatly strengthen the motivation for future intimacy. Nevertheless, sober and nonromantic reflection leads me to conclude that passion all too often represents the attempt to conjure up intimacy willfully. "In willfulness, the will does the work of the imagination" (Farber, 1966, p. 103). If this occurs, relatedness will be diminished, or interrupted, rather than enhanced and sustained. This negative result often occurs with aggressive passions, but it also occurs with sexual passions more regularly than we generally assume.

Outside of enduring relatedness, the topic of this chapter, impassioned infatuations between near strangers are often erroneously described as episodes of intimacy. If the epigenetically earlier stages of relatedness have been bypassed, these infatuations are likely to collapse or to be transformed into what I have called pseudomutuality. Therapy that is preoccupied with encouraging "intimacy" without first assessing the quality of relational precursors is likely to flounder. These developmental precursors are less glamorous but nevertheless fundamental to establishing a true potentiality for intimacy. For a further discussion of issues concerning intimacy, see Wynne and Wynne (1986).

Whether gender differences are cultural or biologic in origin, there does seem to be a difference, over the life-span, between males and females in their readiness for intimacy. Perhaps over the course of evolution (genetic and cultural), the socioemotional components of all forms of relatedness have been emphasized more in female development, beginning with the maternal contribution to attachment/caregiving and continuing with the teaching of language and nonverbal communication. Not only in child rearing but also in female-to-female relatedness, females seem to have a greater readiness and aptitude for intimacy. In contrast, intimacy for males, if it occurs at all, seems to develop only after the urgent demands of joint problem solving have been met.

During the course of evolution, male pursuits, whether in hunting, combat, business, or sex, may have regularly aroused too much aggressive, competitive behavior to allow room for the consistent development of skills in intimacy. Even male recreation and socializing may involve more competitive boisterousness than truly intimate self-disclosure. Perhaps it is not surprising that reliable sharing of intimate experience between men and women is the exception, a current Western ideal that over the course of world history has seldom been sought and more rarely achieved. By contrast, in enduring marriages and in some friendships, especially in times of cultural stability, there may often be considerable mutuality in the sense in which I have used the term.

In my current version of an epigenetic schema, I locate recurrent intimacy as an inconstant stage beyond mutuality (see Figure 3-1). Intimacy is sometimes sought as a quality valued for itself. Persons with this goal as an ideal are overrepresented in the offices of marital therapists. A common difficulty of "modern" couples is that they are so preoccupied with maintaining intimacy that they fail to give adequate priority to the necessities of day-to-day problem solving. There may be much global talk about intimate "caring," but little attention may be paid to problem resolution or to the restructuring of attachment/caregiving and communication patterns.

When there is reciprocal respect between persons who have well-defined roles, a considerable degree of genuine mutuality can develop, even without much intimacy. However, when life circumstances change rapidly or drastically, intimate understanding of one another's needs and experiences can greatly facilitate the discovery of new ways of relating. Intimacy can infuse joint problem solving with new ingredients, and, at the same time, unfettered efforts at problem solving can set the stage for deepened experiences of intimacy.

This dialectic between the intersubjectivity of intimacy and the more observable aspects of relating was poetically characterized by Martin Buber (1955) in his "life of dialogue" and in his concept of movement between the world of I–It (especially, "joint problem solving," in my terms) and the world of I–Thou (of which "intimacy" is a part). Buber wrote:

> The particular *Thou,* after the relational event has run its course, *is bound* to become an *It.*
> The particular *It,* by entering the relational event, *may* become a *Thou.*
> These are the two basic privileges of the world of *It.* They move man to look on the world of *It* as the world in which he has to live, and in which it is comfortable to live, as the world, indeed, which offers him all manner of incitements and excitements, activity and knowledge. In this chronicle of solid benefits the moments of *Thou* appear as strange lyric and dramatic episodes, seductive and magical, but tearing us away to dangerous extremes, loosening the well-tried context, leaving more questions than satisfaction behind them, shattering security —in short, uncanny moments we can well dispense with. For since we are bound to leave them and go back into the world, why not remain in it? . . .

And in all the seriousness of truth, hear this: without *It* man cannot live. But he who lives with *It* alone is not a man. (Buber, 1937, pp. 33–34)

I suspect that a better present-day translation from the German would conclude, "But he who lives with *It* alone is not fully human." Buber accurately described, I believe, the inconstant quality of I–Thou relatedness and the conditions for its renewal. At the same time, he dramatically expressed a value judgment that is widely manifest today in the quest for more perfect intimacy. Paradoxically, preoccupation with intimacy as a goal, as with simultaneous orgasm, interferes with its attainment and also distracts, at the very least, from attention to other forms of relatedness.

A COMPARISON WITH OLSON'S CIRCUMPLEX MODEL

The concepts used here have similarities to, as well as differences from, concepts used by others in the literature on family development. Although I will not comprehensively review this literature, I will compare one other model for the study of family relationships—namely, the well-known Circumplex Model of Olson and his colleagues—with my formulation in order to help clarify it. In agreement with Bowlby (1969), Ainsworth (1982), Hinde (1982), and many others, I view attachment/caregiving systems as involving a basic biologic component of bonding, which has evolutionary origins. Olson, Russell, and Sprenkle (1983) do not mention attachment/caregiving among the 40 concepts they surveyed and from which they derived their concept of cohesion. Nevertheless, they define "cohesion" as "the emotional bonding which family members have toward one another" (p. 70). However, Olson and his colleagues go on to use the concept of cohesion more globally, as a central dimension with the extremes of "separateness–togetherness." In our view, this generalized feature fails to discriminate between the qualitatively and developmentally different forms of closeness and distance that characterize attachment/ caregiving versus mutuality.

Additionally, Schaefer and Olson (1981) acknowledge that cohesion and intimacy are "somewhat confused" and, in an effort at clarification, define cohesion as "a *resultant condition* of the dynamic processes within the group. Intimacy is actually part of the myriad of processes. A sharing of intimate experiences is a precondition for cohesion" (p. 50). I suggest that intimate experience flows out of and recursively strengthens *all* of the basic relational processes. Intimacy is the subjective corollary associated with the basic processes, but it is not necessarily a *precondition* for any of them.

Olson, McCubbin, Barnes, Larsen, Muxen, and Wilson (1983) describe communication as a "facilitatory" dimension in their model, but it is not clear just how communication relates to the primary dimensions of cohesion and adaptability. We suggest that a developmental framework helps "locate" communication in the unfolding of relational processes.

Joint problem solving is omitted from Olson's schema but perhaps can be encompassed within his other central dimension, "adaptability," a term that has been borrowed from theories of individual psychological systems and that has certain features in common with mutuality. The term "mutuality" may better imply the *reciprocal* adaptability that can take place within a relational system. Mutuality, as sketched out here, implies a balance between change and stability, between morphogenesis and morphostasis (Wertheim, 1973). The continuous reshaping and the discontinuous reorganization of relational patterns that are central to the concept of mutuality are qualitatively different from the negotiation over specific tasks that takes place distinctively in joint problem solving.

THERAPEUTIC IMPLICATIONS

A full discussion of the implications of my epigenetic model for therapeutic and enrichment programs, relevant to each stage in the development of relatedness, is beyond the scope of this chapter. Here I shall comment mainly on the distortion of mutuality and intimacy that, in 1958, my colleagues and I called pseudomutuality (Wynne *et al.*, 1958).

In pseudomutual relationships, there is a striving (willful or romantic) to create or to sustain intimacy (in Buber's terms, an I–Thou relatedness). The result will be the illusion of a close emotional tie—illusory in the sense that it does not have a substructure of shared tasks and communication in a role relationship, and perhaps not in an affective attachment, that can carry relatedness forward when divergence arises. Genuine mutuality, in the sense that I am using the term, obviously cannot emerge under these circumstances.

> In pseudomutuality, the subjective tension aroused by divergence or independence of expectations, including the open affirmation of a sense of personal identity, is experienced as not merely disrupting that particular transaction but as possibly demolishing the entire relation (with abandonment, death, or psychosis).
> The alternative outcome is overlooked or cannot be awaited: that the recognition and exploration of difference may lead to an expanded or deepened, although altered, basis for the relation. (Wynne *et al.*, 1958, p. 207)

A pseudomutual impasse occurs when people get stuck expecting and believing themselves to have unchanging, positive relatedness despite the actualities of developmental change. Subjectively, instead of being experienced as intimacy, such relatedness will have a "ho-hum" quality that is empty, boring, and barren, bereft of fun, humor, and creativity. Pseudomutuality takes place in many small ways in most of our lives, and we usually overlook them. Doing so no doubt facilitates ordinary social discourse, but there are families in which pseudomutuality becomes the overarching pattern of relating. If so, this pattern is usually preserved by the "creation of a pervasive familial subculture of myths, legends, and ideology which stress the catastrophic consequences of openly recognized divergence" (Wynne *et al.*, 1958, p. 211).

Relationships with qualities that we called pseudomutual impressed us soon after we began, in 1953, our long-term, intensive studies of the families of acute schizophrenics. Probably the early families who were willing to participate in prolonged meetings with us were those who, isomorphically, also were unusually stuck in their intrafamilial relationships. In these very early years, when family therapy was first being tried, the willingness of these families to be patiently reflective, hour after endless hour, in psychoanalytically guided efforts to grasp and share the "meanings" of the family, enabled us to empathize with their despair and anguish (Schaffer, Wynne, Day, Ryckoff, & Halperin, 1962; Wynne, 1965, 1976). We did become emotionally engaged on a limited experiential level. As I see it now, these "therapeutic" relationships often produced, over time, shared pseudomutual illusions between therapists and families. Little or no active problem solving, and little change in manifest behavioral patterns, took place with that approach to family treatment. These particular families earlier had evolved for themselves an enduring pseudomutual "solution" to their difficulties, a solution reached after desperate efforts to create a sense of relatedness. The interpretive treatment model at the level of communication and meanings that we offered to them attempted to move too directly to the level of empathy and intimacy; by neglecting the world of I-It, the structuring of tasks, and the solving of problems, we regrettably often perpetuated the pseudomutuality that these particular families brought to us. Current problem-oriented approaches to family and marital therapy are much less likely to result in such an impasse.

When divorce, death, and remarriage alter the family life cycle, difficulties in regaining developmental momentum are almost universal. The usual tendency is to expect a quick shift to a quality of relatedness that may or may not have existed before, but the development of relatedness cannot, in any event, be rushed without creating new difficulties. It is necessary to begin the epigenetic sequence again, to establish a new pattern of attachment/caregiving, to discover how to communicate empathically and elliptically, and to work out joint activities and means of problem solving. For example, the new stepparent and the child or adolescent need time and effort for some sort of affectional bond to grow and for new patterns of communication to emerge before negotiating the issues of complicated problem solving and intimacy. As a general principle, I hypothesize that relational processes need to be epigenetically repeated throughout life (see Figure 3-1), within the structure of each new enduring relationship, and at a pace that will depend upon the past experiences of each person and upon the "fit" that develops among them.

This sequence is set in motion with each new attachment and is reworked with each change in the family life cycle; it can usefully be assessed in every therapeutic and enrichment program.

RESEARCH IMPLICATIONS

I have mentioned above some of the research concepts that are related to an epigenetic schema, especially expressed emotion and communication deviance. The assessment methodologies appropriate for the different epigenetic levels are diverse and unevenly developed. In my research with Margaret Singer, we have emphasized communication studies (Singer *et al.,* 1978) and, to a lesser extent, joint problem-solving efforts, as, for example, in the task of the Family Consensus Rorschach Procedure (Loveland, Wynne, & Singer, 1963; Wynne, Jones, & Al-Khayyal, 1987). Joint problem solving has been examined extensively in many types of family research tasks (e.g., Reiss, 1981) and in the study of family interaction in family therapy (Morris & Wynne, 1965); much work in social psychology is relevant here but is beyond the scope of this overview.

Attachment/caregiving has been given a vast amount of attention in research in developmental psychology, but I believe this concept has not been adequately appreciated and used by family researchers. A useful distinction can be made between the "emotional bonding" found in attachment/caregiving and that found in mutuality and intimacy. The operational criteria for attachment and "bonding" in the literature on attachment theory are worthy of more attention by family researchers and therapists.

Intimacy is still more elusive as a subject for conceptualization and research, but fresh explorations in this area are now taking place (e.g., Schaefer & Olson, 1981; Stephen & Markham, 1983; Wynne & Wynne, 1986). I have noted that better conceptual distinctions are especially needed among attachment/caregiving, passion, and intimacy. Many adults in this culture flatter themselves with the notion that all of their interpersonal difficulties have to do with "communication" and/or "intimacy," but researchers might well pause before jumping on this bandwagon.

My attempt to formulate relational concepts developmentally leaves me, at this point, with heightened interest but no clear answers to many research questions. For example, more study needs to be devoted to understanding the developmental place of "intimacy" in adolescent and preadolescent "chumships." Sullivan (1953) believed that the experience of an intimate chumship in early adolescence would inoculate one against schizophrenia. Such friendships typically involve communication about complex secrets (kept apart from the adult world) and the taking on of intricate tasks and problems, communicated in special codes and private language.

I am especially interested in the potential applications of this developmental schema to research on family therapy processes and outcomes. It is not well recognized that the stage of the family life cycle should be routinely specified for each family in family therapy research. In addition, I believe that a classification of the quality of relational development and of the form of impasse may be helpful in such research. To do so will require sharpening the concepts outlined in Figure 3-1, so that they can be clearly identified at baseline in therapy studies, and so that changes can be recognized after therapy, or with the passage of time without therapy. I hope that this approach may contribute to improving our methods of family classification and typology, a problem about which there is widespread concern and little consensus among family researchers (Fisher, 1977). Also, this effort to conceptualize relational systems developmentally is intended to address another major pitfall in "relational diagnosis," namely, the tendency to revert to individual criteria rather than to use more fully and consistently relational concepts for relational problems (Fisher, 1982).

A fundamental proposition underlying the approach described in this chapter is that one cannot properly conceptualize the reciprocity of relatedness by using only the perspective of individual persons, even when one recognizes that persons are social beings. I have noted that life cycle changes in family structure usually proceed at a different pace than does the unfolding of relational processes during development. The interplay between the family life cycle model and the developmental unfolding of relational patterns remains to be explored in detail. Meanwhile, the epigenetic model has implications for identifying points of family impasse and for giving priorities to preventive and therapeutic interventions that are likely to be effective. For example, this formulation points specifically to the desirability of strengthening joint problem-solving skills in therapy before mutuality and intimacy can be expected to stabilize. In other instances, the focus of intervention must move farther back, to the behavioral building of communicational skills and to elemental experiences of affectional bonding. Many couples and families seek therapy, or engage in those encounters that serve as substitutes for therapy, with the misguided belief that they can create intimacy and mutuality directly by willful efforts rather than through the step-by-step growth of relatedness. Family therapy and marital enrichment programs have increasingly emphasized the strengthening of communication skills and problem-solving abilities. For the most part, such efforts are highly consistent with my conceptualization of an epigenetic sequence in the development of relatedness. Attachment/caregiving, intimacy, and mutuality are less amenable to structured therapeutic interventions and require renewed attention through dynamic and experiential approaches. I trust that the paradigm outlined here has both sobering and challenging implications for what remains to be done in achieving a comprehensive and integrated theory of family development and family therapy.

REFERENCES

Ainsworth, M. D. S. (1982). Attachment: Retrospect and prospect. In C. M. Parkes & J. Stevenson-Hinde (Eds.), *The place of attachment in human behavior* (pp. 3–30). New York: Basic Books.

Ainsworth, M. D. S., Blehar, M. C., Walters, E., & Wall, S. (1978). *Patterns of attachment: A psychological study of the strange situation.* Hillsdale, NJ: Erlbaum.

Alper, J. S., & Lange, R. V. (1981). Lumsden-Wilson theory of gene–culture coevolution. *Proceedings of the National Academy of Sciences USA, 70,* 3976–3979.

Ashby, W. R. (1952). *Design for a brain.* New York: Wiley.

Bateson, G. (1979). *Mind and nature: A necessary unity.* New York: E. P. Dutton.

Bertalanffy, L. V. (1968). *General systems theory: Foundations, development, applications.* New York: George Braziller.

Blakar, R. M. (1984). *Communication: A social perspective on clinical issues.* Oslo: Universitetsforlaget.

Bowlby, J. (1958). The nature of the child's tie to his mother. *International Journal of Psychoanalysis, 39,* 1–23.

Bowlby, J. (1969). *Attachment and loss: Vol. 1. Attachment.* New York: Basic Books.

Bowlby, J. (1975). Attachment theory, separation anxiety, and mourning. In D. A. Hamburg & H. K. M. Brodie (Eds.), *American handbook of psychiatry: Vol. 6. New psychiatric frontiers* (pp. 292–309). New York: Basic Books.

Bowlby, J. (1980). *Attachment and loss: Vol. III. Loss: Sadness and depression.* New York: Basic Books.

Brown, G. W., Birley, J. L. T., & Wing, J. K. (1972). Influence of family life on the course of schizophrenic disorders: A replication. *British Journal of Psychiatry, 121,* 241–258.

Buber, M. (1937). *I and thou,* (R. G. Smith, Trans.). Edinburgh: T. & T. Clark.

Buber, M. (1955). *Between man and man* (R. G. Smith, Trans.). Boston: Beacon Press. (Original work published 1947)

Carter, E. A., & McGoldrick, M. (Eds.). (1980). *The family life cycle: A framework for family therapy.* New York: Gardner Press.

Chomsky, N. (1980). *Rules and representations.* New York: Columbia University Press.

Cooley, C. H. (1909). *Social organization.* New York: Charles Scribner's Sons.

Dell, P. F. (1982). Beyond homeostasis: Toward a concept of coherence. *Family Process, 21,* 21–41.

Dell, P. F., & Goolishian, H. A. (1981). Ordnung durch Fluktuation: Eine evolutionare Epistemology fur menschliche Systeme. *Familiendynamik, 6,* 104–122.

Dewey, J., & Bentley, A. (1949). *Knowing and the known.* Boston: Beacon Press.

Duvall, E. M. (1962). *Family development* (rev. ed.). Chicago: J. B. Lippincott.

Engel, G. L. (1980). The clinical application of the biopsychosocial model. *American Journal of Psychiatry, 137,* 535–544.

Engel, G. L. (1983, April). *Trauma in infancy: Prospective validation of an early psychoanalytic concept.* Feldman Memorial Lecture, University of Rochester, NY.

Epstein, N. B., & Bishop, D. S. (1981). Problem-centered systems therapy of the family. In A. S. Gurman & D. P. Kniskern (Eds.), *Handbook of family therapy* (pp. 444–482). New York: Brunner/Mazel.

Erikson, E. H. (1950). *Childhood and society.* New York: W. W. Norton.

Erikson, E. H. (1956). The problem of ego identity. *Journal of the American Psychoanalytic Association, 4,* 56–121.

Erikson, E. H. (1968). *Identity: Youth and crisis.* New York: W. W. Norton.

Falloon, I. R. H., Boyd, J. L., McGill, C. W., Strang, J. S., & Moss, H. B. (1981). Family management training in the community care of schizophrenia. In M. J. Goldstein (Ed.), *New developments in interventions with families of schizophrenics* (pp. 61-77). San Francisco: Jossey-Bass.

Farber, L. H. (1966). *The ways of the will: Essays toward a psychology and psychopathology of will.* New York: Basic Books.

Fisher, L. (1977). On the classification of families: A progress report. *Archives of General Psychiatry, 34,* 424-433.

Fisher, L. (1982). Transactional theories but individual assessment: A frequent discrepancy in family research. *Family Process, 21,* 313-320.

Goldstein, M. J. (1985). Family factors that antedate the onset of schizophrenia and related disorders: The results of a 15-year prospective longitudinal study. *Acta Psychiatrica Scandinavica, 71* (Suppl. 319), 7-18.

Grunebaum, H. U., & Bryant, C. M. (1966). The theory and practice of the family diagnostic: Part II. Theoretical Aspects and Resident Education. In I. M. Cohen (Ed.), *Family structure, dynamics, and therapy* (Research Report No. 20, pp. 150-162). Washington, DC: American Psychiatric Association.

Haley, J. (1973). *Uncommon therapy: The psychiatric techniques of Milton H. Erickson.* New York: W. W. Norton.

Haley, J. (1976). *Problem-solving therapy.* San Francisco: Jossey-Bass.

Harlow, H. F., & Harlow, M. K. (1970). The Effect of Rearing Conditions on Behavior. *Bulletin of Menninger Clinic 26:* 213-224, 1962.

Hill, R. (1964). Methodological issues in family development research. *Family Process, 3,* 186-206.

Hinde, R. A. (1982). Attachment: Some conceptual and biological Issues. In C. M. Parkes & J. Stevenson-Hinde (Eds.), *The place of attachment in human behavior.* New York: Basic Books.

Hoffman, L. (1981). *Foundations of family therapy: A conceptual framework for systems change.* New York: Basic Books.

Klaus, M. H., & Kennell, J. H. (1976). *Maternal-infant bonding.* St. Louis: C. V. Mosby.

Leiderman, P. H., & Seashore, M. J. (1975). Mother-infant neonatal separation: Some delayed consequences. In *Parent-infant interaction* (Ciba Foundation Symposium 33). Amsterdam: Elsevier.

Lidz, T. (1973). *The origin and treatment of schizophrenic Disorders.* New York: Basic Books.

Loveland, N., Wynne, L. C., & Singer, M. T. (1963). The family Rorschach: A method for studying family interaction. *Family Process, 2,* 187-215.

Lumsden, C. J., & Wilson, E. O. (1981). *Genes, mind, and culture.* Cambridge, MA: Harvard University Press.

Lumsden, C. J., & Wilson, E. O. (1983). *Promethean fire: Reflections on the origin of mind.* Cambridge, MA: Harvard University Press.

Marvin, R. S. (1977). An ethological-cognitive model for the attenuation of mother-child attachment behavior. In T. M. Alloway, L. Krames, & P. Pliner (Eds.), *Advances in the study of communication and affect. Vol. 3: The development of social attachments.* New York: Plenum.

Morris, G., & Wynne, L. C. (1965). Schizophrenic offspring and styles of parental communication: A predictive study using family therapy excerpts. *Psychiatry, 28,* 19-44.

Olson, D. H., McCubbin, H. C. Barnes, H., Larsen, A., Muxen, M., & Wilson, M. (1983). *Families: What makes them work.* Beverly Hills, CA: Sage.

Olson, D. H., Russell, C. S., & Sprenkle, D. H. (1983). Circumplex model of marital and family systems: VI. Theoretical update. *Family Process, 22,* 69-83.

Olson, D. H., Sprenkle, D. H., & Russell, C. S. (1979). Circumplex model of marital and family systems: I. Cohesion and adaptability dimensions, family types, and clinical applications. *Family Process, 18,* 3-28.

Parsons, T. (1951). *The social system.* Glencoe, IL. The Free Press.

Peterson, G. H., Mehl, L. E., & Leiderman, P. H. (1979). The role of some birth related variables in father attachment. *American Journal of Orthopsychiatry, 49,* 330–338.

Piaget, J. (1926). *The language and thought of the child.* New York: Harcourt, Brace.

Reiss, D. (1981). *The family's construction of reality.* Cambridge, MA: Harvard University Press.

Rodgers, R. (1960, August). *Proposed modifications of Duvall's family life cycle stages.* Paper presented at the meeting of the American Sociological Association, New York.

Ryckoff, I., Day, J., & Wynne, L. C. (1959). Maintenance of stereotyped roles in the families of schizophrenics. *AMA Archives of Psychiatry, 1,* 93–98.

Schaefer, M. T., & Olson, D. H. (1981). Assessing intimacy: The PAIR Inventory. *Journal of Marital and Family Therapy, 7,* 47–60.

Schaffer, L., Wynne, L. C., Day, J., Ryckoff, I., & Halperin, A. (1962). On the nature and sources of the psychiatrist's experience with the family of the schizophrenic. *Psychiatry, 25,* 32–45.

Singer, M. T., & Wynne, L. C. (1965). Thought disorder and family relations of schizophrenics: IV. Results and implications. *Archives of General Psychiatry, 12,* 201–212.

Singer, M. T., & Wynne, L. C. (1966). Principles for scoring communication defects and deviances in parents of schizophrenics: Rorschach and TAT scoring manuals. *Psychiatry, 29,* 260–288.

Singer, M. T., Wynne, L. C., & Toohey, M. L. (1978). Communication disorders and the families of schizophrenics. In L. C. Wynne, R. Cromwell, & S. Matthysse (Eds.), *The nature of schizophrenia: New approaches to research and treatment* (pp. 499–511). New York: Wiley.

Solomon, M. A. (1973). A developmental, conceptual premise for family therapy. *Family Process, 12,* 179–196.

Spiegel, J. (1971). *Transactions: The interplay between individual, family, and society.* New York: Science House.

Sroufe, L. A. (1979). The coherence of individual development: Early care, attachment and subsequent developmental issues. *American Psychologist, 34,* 834–841.

Sroufe, L. A., Fox, N. E., & Pancake, V. R. (1983). Attachment and dependency in developmental perspective. *Child Development, 54,* 1615–1627.

Stephen, T. D., & Markham, H. J. (1983). Assessing the development of relationships: A new measure. *Family Process, 22,* 15–25.

Sullivan, H. S. (1953). *The interpersonal theory of psychiatry.* New York: W. W. Norton.

Svejda, M. J., Pannabecker, B. J., & Emde, R. N. (1982). Parent-to-infant attachment: A critique of the early "bonding" model. In R. N. Emde & R. J. Harmon (Eds.), *The development of attachment and affiliative systems* (pp. 83–93). New York: Plenum.

Vaughn, C. E., & Leff, J. P. (1976). The influence of family and social factors on the course of psychiatric illness: A comparison of schizophrenic and depressed neurotic patients. *British Journal of Psychiatry, 129,* 125–137.

Watzlawick, P., Beavin, J. H., & Jackson, D. D. (1967). Pragmatics of human communication: A study of interactional patterns, pathologies, and paradoxes. New York: W. W. Norton.

Weiss, P. (1925). Tierisches Verhalten als "Systemreaktion": Die Orientierung der Ruhestellungen von Schmetterdingen (Vanessa) gegen Licht und Schwerkraft. *Biologia Gen, 1,* 168–248.

Weiss, R. S. (1982). Attachment in adult life. In C. M. Parkes & J. Stevenson-Hinde (Eds.), *The place of attachment in human behavior* (pp. 171–184). New York: Basic Books.

Wertheim, E. S. (1973). Family unit therapy and the science and typology of family systems. *Family Process, 12,* 361–376.

Wynne, L. C. (1961). The study of intrafamilial alignments and splits in exploratory family therapy. In N. Ackerman, F. Beatman, & S. Sherman (Eds.), *Exploring the base for family therapy.* New York: Family Therapy Association of America.

Wynne, L. C. (1965). Some indications and contra-indications for exploratory family therapy. In I. Boszormenyi-Nagy & J. Framo (Eds.), *Intensive family therapy: Theoretical and practical aspects, with special reference to schizophrenia* (pp. 289–322). New York: Harper & Row.

Wynne, L. C. (1968). Methodologic and conceptual issues in the study of schizophrenics and their families. *Journal of Psychiatric Research, 6* (Suppl. 1), 185–199.

Wynne, L. C. (1970). Communication disorders and the quest for relatedness in families of schizophrenics. *American Journal of Psychoanalysis, 30,* 100–114.

Wynne, L. C. (1976). On the anguish and creative passions of not escaping double binds: A reformulation. In C. Sluzki & D. Ransom (Eds.), *Double bind: The foundation of the communicational approach to the family* (pp. 243–250). New York: Grune & Stratton.

Wynne, L. C., Jones, J. E., & Al-Khayyal, M. (1982). Healthy family communication patterns: Observations in families "at risk" for psychopathology. In F. Walsh (Ed.), *Normal family processes* (pp. 142–164). New York: Guilford Press.

Wynne, L. C., Ryckoff, I., Day, J., & Hirsch, S. (1958). Pseudo-mutuality in the family relations of schizophrenics. *Psychiatry, 21,* 205–220.

Wynne, L. C., & Singer, M. T. (1963). Thought disorder and family relations of schizophrenics: I. A research strategy. *Archives of General Psychiatry, 9,* 191–198.

Wynne, L. C., Singer, M. T., Bartko, J., & Toohey, M. L. (1977). Schizophrenics and their families: Recent research on parental communication. In J. M. Tanner (Ed.), *Developments in psychiatric research* (pp. 254–286). London: Hodder & Stoughton.

Wynne, L. C., & Wynne, A. R. The quest for intimacy. *Journal of Marital and Family Therapy. 12:*383–394, 1986.

4

Adolescent Sexuality in the Family Life Spiral

LEE COMBRINCK-GRAHAM
Institute for Juvenile Research, Chicago

Lucy was the first of three daughters. She was precocious and gifted, and her parents were challenged to keep her interests focused productively. Lucy's father worked long, hard hours at his profession. Her mother postponed her graduate education in order to oversee Lucy's early years. By the time Lucy was in school, her mother had become quite an expert in the education of exceptional children.

Lucy was often in trouble with her parents and with the school personnel. She quickly teamed up with the more adventurous youngsters in her class, with whom she continuously tested the limits of authority. When Lucy was 12, she was transferred to a private Friends school, in hopes that in this atmosphere she would settle down.

Lucy's parents often went out in the evening, leaving Lucy in charge of her younger sisters. When Lucy became curious about kissing, she paid her sisters to be quiet while she practiced kissing with the boy next door. Unfortunately, one of her sisters told their parents. Lucy was accused of being a lowlife, prostitute, and slut. She was forbidden to see any boys or to do anything unsupervised. And she was forced to spend several hours with the minister of their church reflecting on her behavior. Under this pressure, Lucy recalls, she finally "admitted" that she had been involved sexually with the boy. No one believed anything different, she pointed out. The pressure of moral judgments and intensive supervision was enormous. Lucy tried to be happy. She recalled dressing one time in the peasant-dress fashion of the times, feeling happy about the way she looked, going downstairs for breakfast, and encountering her mother, who told her, "Take off that dress!" Lucy protested, a quarrel started, and Lucy's father appeared with a pair of scissors. This usually mild-mannered man slit Lucy's dress right down the front as he said, "How dare you argue with your mother! Do as she says!"

I am indebted to Judy Shea, PhD, for a thorough literature search and précis of many of the articles reviewed in this chapter and to Jay Ann Jemail, PhD, and Madeline Nathanson, PhD, principal investigators of the study for which the materials were prepared.

Lucy ran away. When her parents found her, she ran away again. She was now 14. She went to another state and lived for 4 weeks as the companion of a man who picked her up. When he began to beat her, she ran away from him, contacted her parents, and arranged to come home. The family entered family therapy.

Lucy met a boy with whom she fell in love. She moved in with him when she was 16, and they married when she graduated from high school. She described their attachment as that of two lost and lonely "children" huddled together for comfort, creating their own fantasy of security. She felt that giving birth to her child, at 19, spelled the end of childhood for herself and her husband. The marriage could not bear the strain, and by 20 she had left her husband, because he was abusive to her and abused drugs and alcohol.

Lucy is now 28. Her daughter is beautiful, fanciful, gifted, and very savvy. Lucy appears to spend half of her energies in trying to break away, finally, from her parents, who supported her through the 4 or 5 years after she left her husband while she found a job. The other half of her energies seem spent on trying to reach a final understanding and restitution with them. Thus she will defiantly cohabitate with her current boyfriend, while her mother moralizes about the terrible effects of these liaisons on her granddaughter, but she will keep in close touch with her parents, remembering their birthdays and anniversaries, showing up for holiday celebrations, and calling to keep her mother company when her father is on a business trip. Lucy's mother wonders why she continues to be so provocative; Lucy wonders why her parents don't give her credit for her loyalty and attention to them.

Everyone in Lucy's family remembers the events of her sexual explorations in early adolescence as the most critical time of their lives. In many ways, these events crystallized relationships in the family, much the way some insects are preserved in lucite, preserving the same image, unmoving, forever.

This chapter will examine the interactions between events experienced by sexually developing adolescents and corresponding changes within their families, using a family life spiral model of development (Combrinck-Graham, 1983, 1985).

LEVELS OF INQUIRY AND UNDERSTANDING

The metaphor of a tapestry helps to create the picture of adolescent development in context. A tapestry is composed of threads, which, worked together, form a fabric. The fabric can be used for hanging, covering, or walking on. The particular way in which the threads are worked may form pictures. The Unicorn Tapestries are particularly rich examples of the layers of representation within tapestry, layers that emanate from the prosaic threads that have been worked to make the fabric. The Unicorn Tapestries are famous for their elaborate presentation of flora and fauna, the *mille fleurs* effect, which presents the natural or biologic context of the events being represented. In addition to the flowers and small animals, they show many wild beasts participating in the background of the events. They also show the servants, grooms, and dog handlers. And finally, they present the young nobleman, the human focus of the tapestries, surrounded by his retinue. As the seven tapestries are viewed in a series, a story is told, the story of the hunt of the unicorn: "The Start of the Hunt," "The Unicorn at the Fountain," "The Unicorn Crossing the Stream," "The Unicorn Defends Himself," "The Unicorn Is Tamed by the Maiden," "The Unicorn Is Killed and Brought to the Castle," "The Unicorn in Captivity." The story line emerges as successive tapestries are viewed. There are two more levels of abstraction to be found in the Unicorn Tapestries: the first is the secular meaning of the story, and the second is the religious significance. The story of the hunt of the unicorn has mythological and symbolic significance. In its secular interpretation, the story may represent the ceremony of courtship. In terms of its religious connotation, themes of purity, suffering, and redemption are represented.

Levels of meaning emerge from the working together of threads, to the elaboration of universal themes. In a similar way, one can take some threads, some lines of thinking about adolescent sexuality, and weave them together to develop a picture of the family context of adolescence and, consistent with the theme of the Unicorn Tapestries, to focus particularly on those areas leading to courtship and sexual intimacy.

THE FAMILY LIFE CYCLE AS THE CONTEXT OF INDIVIDUAL DEVELOPMENT

Classical developmental theories have viewed adolescence as the end of childhood and as the end of development. But the great interest in adult development over the past 20 years presses us to consider that development of the individual does not end with the end of adolescence and that the changes that take place in the individual after adulthood has begun are not just deteriorations, but continued adaptations and integrations.

Since the "discovery" of adult development, family systems thinkers have proposed models of development for the family. Initially, attempts were made to design developmental systems for the family that paralleled those for individuals. What resulted was a set of developmental issues of a given individual or of a single generation and observations about how the rest of the family accommodated to those issues. Stages of family development were given names such as "the family with adolescents." The early models (Minuchin & Fishman, 1981; Solomon, 1973), were simple and, like most developmental models, focused on the family with children, so that family development might arbitrarily begin at the time of marriage and end when the children left home—presumably to begin anew with a new marriage.[1] This is hardly a life cycle description. Instead, it describes a linear path from the beginning to the end of a particular nuclear family.

Carter and McGoldrick (1980) studied the intrafamilial process during different stages and proposed stage-appropriate family tasks and the "emotional process of transition" (p. 17) required for families to shift from one stage to the next. One such family task they proposed was the shifting of the parent–child relationship to permit the adolescent to move in and out of the system. This approach also recognized the kinds of tasks other family members were engaged in, so that during the children's adolescence, parents might be working on issues such as "refocus on mid-life marital and career issues" (p. 17). Identifying these stages of family development has led to an examination of the family processes in these periods. What is the relationship between the children's adolescence and the refocus on marital and career issues? Carter and McGoldrick described emotional processes of transition for each stage. For the stage they termed "the family with adolescents," they called the key emotional process "increasing flexibility of family boundaries to include children's independence" (p. 17).

The life of the family is not linear—it does not begin at one particular point, such as with a marriage or a birth, nor does it end with the departure of children or with a death. Rather, family movement through time is correctly described as cyclic, or, because things do not repeat themselves exactly, as a spiral. If one looks at the relationships between individual life issues of different generations, one can build a relational picture of the family life spiral (Combrinck-Graham, 1983, 1985). Figure 4-1 shows such a picture, where the life stages of each of three generations are lined up in a model that postulates about 25 years between generations. Obvious relationships are the coincidence of childbearing and birth and of the midlife reevaluation and adolescence. The frequent coincidence of the school-age years of childhood and the "settling in" period of a man's development (Levinson, 1978) would suggest some commonality between these developmental stages, too.

The distortion of the spiral in Figure 4-1 is deliberate. It illustrates that at certain times of family life, the family members are close and tightly involved with one another, and the primary forces in the family are centripetal. At other times, as at the bottom of the diagram, the family members are differentiated, and the forces in the family are centrifugal. Thus the family oscillates from a centripetal shape, where family members are primarily oriented inward, to a centrifugal shape, where family members are oriented more toward interests outside the family. This means that the individual moves from one generation to the next at a time when the family is held closely together and that he or she consolidates individual integrity at a time when the family is more molecular. For an individual whose life spans three generations, there will be three periods of centripetal family life and three of centrifugal family life. These different family atmospheres appear to provide

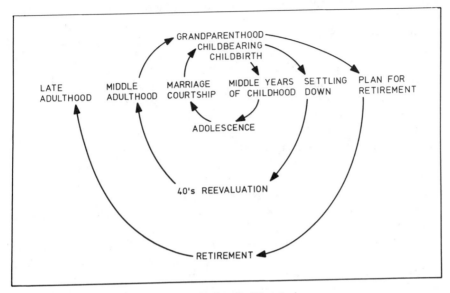

Figure 4-1. Family life spiral.

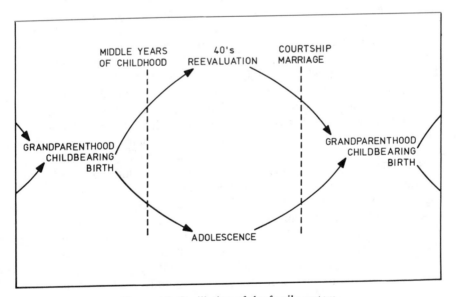

Figure 4-2. Oscillation of the family system.

opportunities, alternatively, for the individual to practice intimacy and involvement, and individuation and independence, as demonstrated in Figure 4-2.

Adolescence should generally occur when the family is passing through its more centrifugal period. Adolescent children do not necessarily create the centrifugal force, for, as Figure 4-1 shows, each generation at this point is involved in major reevaluations, with the older generation preparing for retirement, the middle generation entering the midlife transition, and the younger generation struggling with issues of personal identity. The major shaping forces in the family during this period are those that draw the attention and energies of its members to themselves as they differentiate from intrafamilial relationships and become more involved in activities outside the family. Events that normally occur in this centrifugal period include major changes in life-style, such as retirement, divorce, and remarriage; career changes; and leaving home. These pulls for an orientation away from family relationships are illustrated by adolescents' normal interest in their peers and in role models other than their parents. Such pulls are likewise illustrated by the parents' interests in reevaluating their commitments to work and their professional identities as well as their commitments to one another. Indeed, the whole family naturally shifts to a more individualized, differentiated system during this period.

ADOLESCENT DEVELOPMENT

Until the 14th century, children moved, sometime after the age of 7, when their strength and skills permitted it, in a rather uneventful fashion from the phase of apprenticeship to that of journeyman. Ceremonies which occur around the age of 13 previously marked the formal induction of the young person into adulthood and had much significance as *rites de passage* from childhood to adulthood. One such ceremony is illustrated in the Unicorn Tapestries. In contemporary Western society, these ceremonies do not usher in full adult status, but adolescence, a period that lasts nearly 10 years.

Adolescence, then, is a transition between childhood and adulthood. It can be distinguished at a variety of levels. Developmental scholars have described adolescence in terms of the individual preoccupation with emerging identity and the renegotiation of family relationships reflected in the concept of "the second separation/individuation process" (Blos, 1962). Of course, these issues of psychological development occur in the context of the youngster's physical development—with adolescence come the physical transformations in growth, body habitus, voice, strength, and secondary sexual characteristics that signal the change from child to young adult.

Increased attention to the family environment during these changes has led to studies attempting to characterize the family context of adolescent development. Many of these studies look for the family's influence on the youngster, as if the source of the youngster's healthy or unhealthy development is to be found in his or her parents. These studies take a linear view: that something about the parents causes a particular pattern of development in the youth. An example is provided by a study that examined the relationship of adolescent ego development to certain aspects of parental functioning (Hauser *et al.*, 1984). Although the results confirmed hypotheses about the parental influence on adolescent ego development, the study did not examine the reciprocal effects of adolescent behavior on parents. The authors found, for example, that youngsters whose parents ridiculed or limited their expression exhibited lower functioning on an ego development scale. The inference is that parents inhibit their children's ego functioning by this behavior. There is no speculation at all about how such behaviors of the parents could be responsive to the youngsters. For example, if a youngster takes himself too seriously, he may need to be teased; if another youngster is too grandiose, her parents may try to limit the amount of conversation. In short, the possibility that youngsters' ego development may also have an effect on how their parents communicate with them has not been considered.

Contrast this unidirectional hypothesis with some of the theoretical comments of Stierlin (1975) about the work of adolescents and their families: "Self-determination has always been part of the conflict of generations and of the separation drama of adolescence. . . . Along therewith, it has necessitated balancing moves—on the part of the adolescent and of the parents—of corresponding strength" (p. 199). Stierlin compares the relationship between an intensely rebellious, acting-out adolescent and her parents with Hegel's paradigm of the master (victimizer) and the servant (victim), where the more the master has to rely on the servant for making his life more comfortable, the more dependent upon the servant he becomes. And as the master becomes more dependent, the servant becomes more powerful: Thus in his power as victim, he becomes a kind of victimizer. Here Stierlin characterizes both the reciprocity of relationships and the recursive quality of interaction itself, which has a life of its own.

Asking adults to write a few words that describe how they were at 13 and at 18 illustrates the dramatic change of orientation that occurs in adolescence.[2] Some reflections on being 13 include "Frequent fights with parents," "Going from being the tallest in the class to the shortest," "I felt fat and ugly," "I was excited about growing up," "I had a crush on a boy who started dating my best friend," "I was competitive in school," and "I was getting very interested in sports." These statements reflect concerns with parents, physical changes, personal prowess in relation to others, and peer relationships. Contrast these with the same individuals' reflections on being 18: "How extremely serious I was about everything"; "Feeling that time didn't really have any meaning"; "I was very intelligent and a good student"; "It was quite a relief to get away from home"; "My self-confidence had improved, but I was still shy"; "I was feeling unfulfilled in high school, longing for new avenues to pursue, new people to meet"; "I was very idealistic, especially in my academic interests"; "I wanted to get away from home." These recollections at a later age emphasize a focus on the self as competent and reliable, as the young person moves away from family and peers and familiar childish objects and ways. In 5 short years, these individuals made a significant emotional move away from their families.

Adolescent Sexuality

Variously defined as sexual character, recognition of or emphasis on sexual matters, involvement in sexual activity, and preparedness for engagement in sexual activity, "sexuality" is a useful term for capturing a central movement in adolescent development. Sexuality develops in the youngster in three general areas: the physical, the psychological, and the social. In the physical area, secondary sex characteristics appear, preparing the individual to engage in the sexual act. Does the adolescent have sexuality if he or she does not yet have the physical equipment to engage in sex? Adolescents vary in their expression of sexuality, often not in relation to their physical maturity. A youngster whose puberty is late may have many sexual fantasies and attractions prior to physical changes, whereas a youngster who experiences puberty early may function emotionally like a child.

At the psychological level, adolescent sexuality is manifested in expressive and cognitive ways, including the individual's knowledge, intent, and curiosity about his or her sexuality. This level of expression of sexuality is crucially linked to developments in the adolescents' abilities to handle propositional thinking. It involves the mental activity of imagining oneself to be sexual, of developing plans and testing them out, of evaluating sexual objects and rejecting plans, if they are not feasible. Most of this activity occurs in the imagination of the adolescent. This same ability to carry out whole acts in imagination, to anticipate through fantasy, and to assess outcomes of mental experiments will affect how the adolescent will deal with his or her family members in relation to his or her sexuality.

The third level of sexuality is the social level, that is, actual sexual involvement with others—the orientation of self in the world outside the family. Of course, adolescents' choices of sexual objects reflect their work in this area. For example, some will relate first to older partners, some to members of their peer group, still others may begin with homosexual objects, while others begin with family members. Each choice can be understood as the adolescent's expression, through sexual activity, of work to be done in the social and interpersonal sphere. Each expression is a reflection of the youngster's contextual experience, the family being the adolescent's most immediate context.

FAMILY INFLUENCES ON ADOLESCENT SEXUALITY

A review of the literature on adolescent sexuality and the family reveals an extensive assessment of the influence of family factors on the development of adolescent sexual expression but almost nothing addressing the influence of adolescents' sexuality on the family. Banks and Kahn (1982) address some of the influences siblings may have on each other's sexual development. They explore the effects of one sibling's influence on another's sexual identification. Often the effect is of differentiation. For example, if an older sibling is sexually precocious, a younger one may concentrate on academic development. If an older sibling is macho, a younger one may be passive and effeminate. Other examples occur in sibling relationships in which the younger sibling may wait for the older one to lead the way in sexual exploration before the younger one will begin. This may be a cultural tradition, such as that directing the story line in *The Taming of the Shrew,* where the seductive younger sister, Bianca, could not marry until her older sister, Kate, had done so. A third kind of sibling interaction involves the older child's serving as a model for the younger. In fact, there are many possible interactions between siblings and no rules governing the outcomes. Though it can be said that siblings affect each other's sexuality, we must look at the larger family context in order to understand the patterns of these effects.

In general, the literature on adolescent sexuality and the family is limited to descriptions of parental influences on adolescent sexual expression, activity, and attitudes and to the family composition of adolescents who manifest sexual expression in troublesome ways, such as through sexual delinquency, pregnancy, or incest.

In fact, the influence of parents on the adolescent's sexual expression is indirect. Rarely, if ever, did adolescents report discussing sex, birth control, or pregnancy with their parents, especially after their own sexual development had begun. (That is, sex education by parents might have been direct before the child's puberty.) It was as if a door had slammed shut on the subject as the adolescent had moved beyond puberty. Adolescents reported more direct influence and information coming from siblings and peers than from parents.

I reviewed 23 articles describing the interaction of adolescents with families, peers, and the school system in matters relating to decision making, sexuality, contraception, and sex education.[3] Of the 23 articles, 13 dealt with college students, 11 dealt with high school students, and 2 included both populations. One article did not specify the ages of the population studied. In 8 studies (6 on college students and 5 on high school students), the teenagers specified that peers were a greater influence and source of information than their parents. Interestingly, several studies indicated that most adolescents felt that their parents should be more available. Another interesting finding was that in the five studies involving mothers and daughters, the mothers thought they should be or had been important resources to their daughters; a smaller proportion of the daughters agreed with their mothers; an even smaller proportion of daughters acknowledged that their mothers had actually been resources in this area. Three studies noted an influence of the family on the expression of sexuality, especially among college students. These studies showed, however, that the direct influence of the family on daughters was greater if the daughters were not sexually active, and less, if they were. One study demonstrated that even when youngsters reported that their families were a greater source of information about the ovulation cycle and contraception than were sex education courses at school, the information they had was largely incorrect!

AN ALMOST IMPENETRABLE BOUNDARY

It is difficult to compare these studies, which involve different populations and different age groups, use different methodologies, and ask different questions. Yet it is tempting to conclude what I have mentioned before, that when an adolescent begins to experience his or her own sexuality—either by exploring it in discussions with peers, by relating personally to a sex education course in school, or by actually engaging in sexual activity—a door closes on the interchange between the adolescent and the family.

At each level of expression of adolescent sexuality, we can see the figurative closing of the door, from the modesty that accompanies physical changes, to the privacy of plans and fantasies at the cognitive level, to the conduct of experimentation and exploration outside the family. The youth may close the door, but it also happens that other family members, too, increase the privacy boundaries. Mothers will intercede on behalf of their adolescent's modesty with younger children. Parents will become less relaxed about nudity in the face of their children's sexual maturity.

The metaphoric door that closes represents an interpersonal boundary between the youth and his or her family. The defining of this boundary, also called "separation and individuation," has been a gradual process in the family as it has evolved since the birth of the children. As sexuality becomes an issue, however, the boundary becomes almost impermeable. This development very much enhances the process of differentiation within the family, coinciding with the increasing centrifugal familial forces. Such differentiation is the major task for the family in this phase of the life cycle.

FAMILY RESPONSES TO ADOLESCENT SEXUALITY

As stated previously, there is little information on the effect of the adolescent's sexual development on the family. Some have proposed that the adolescent's emerging sexuality is actually stimulating to his or her parents, thus explaining extramarital affairs or parents' seeking younger lovers. A model for the effect of adolescent sexuality on the parents may be extracted from Johnson and Szurek's (1952) observations about the "genesis of antisocial acting-out." These authors observed that a particular youngster's acting-out was covertly encouraged by the intense interest of one of the parents, whose own comportment was a paradigm of propriety. Johnson and Szurek explored one parent--child dyad; they did not make observations about the parent-to-parent relationship, nor about the family triad. Looking into these areas of family functioning, we might guess that the involved parent's interest in the child occurred in the context of a marital relationship strained by the drive for increased differentiation between the parents. The child's sexuality may have been stimulating, whereas sex between the husband and the wife may not have been.

Working from the hypothesis of structural change, it is obvious that when a new boundary is formed, that is, when the door closes around the adolescent's sexuality, there are repercussions throughout the family system. Ackerman (1980) has described a three-generational perspective on the family with adolescents. He presents an example in which an adolescent daughter who has had a cuddly relationship with her father begins to push him away as her own sexuality develops. In his example, the mother has been preoccupied with her own family, reflecting at her generational level what was going on in her family of origin. The daughter's pulling away from the father leads him to require more from his wife. This, in turn, requires the mother to pull away from her family of origin. We might add that the father may also push his daughter away as she develops—that the pulling apart is often a mutual effort. Figure 4-3 illustrates these changes.

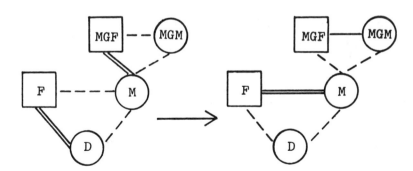

Figure 4-3. Three-generational effects of adolescent sexuality (D = daughter, F = father, M = mother, MGF = maternal grand father, MGM = maternal grandmother; double solid lines indicate a strong relationship, and broken lines indicate a weak relationship).

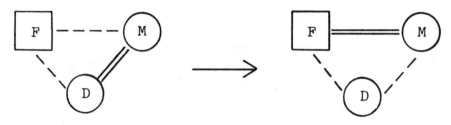

Figure 4-4. Reorganization in the nuclear family (D = daughter, F = father, M = mother; double solid lines indicate a strong relationship, and broken lines indicate a weak relationship).

There are numerous examples of these repercussions and changes just within the nuclear family. The conflict between adolescent daughters and their mothers is legendary. Traditionally, it has been thought that the mother wants to hold the daughter close and that the daughter has to push the mother away—that the developmental push is in the daughter. Our family model would suggest, however, that the mother contributes to the distancing herself. As a woman approaching menopause, she may respond to the daughter's maturation by experiencing stimulation of her own sexuality and by consequent rivalry with her daughter. Thus a mother and daughter who may have been very close will draw apart as the daughter seeks the company of peers and as the mother redefines her own roles. The mother may then turn to her husband, requiring more of him than she had in past years. Or, she may turn away from the nuclear family, seeking productivity in other relationships or in other work. Figure 4-4 illustrates these changes.

Corresponding changes in structure could be hypothesized with adolescent boys, as well. In addition, the closing of the door may shift a sibling subsystem, sometimes differentiating between the sexually mature and those who are not, or separating the sexually mature siblings from each other and from the other, younger siblings. Figures 4-5 and 4-6 illustrate these rippling effects through the family structure.

All of these adjustments depend upon a certain degree of adaptability in the family's organization, for the overall requirement of the family in this period of the life spiral is to increase the differentiation and individuation of all its members. The development of sexuality in the offspring can be seen as a stimulus for this process.

THREE PROBLEM "SOLUTIONS" TO FAMILY STRESS

Although many families negotiate the change and readjustment of the centrifugal period without major problems, there are some who do not. It is helpful to view the difficulties experienced by families of adolescents in

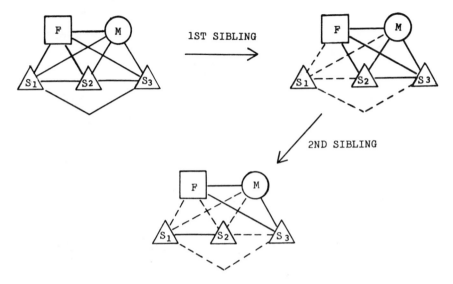

Figure 4-5. Example of shifting sibling subsystem, an effect of adolescent sexuality (F = father; M = mother; S_1, S_2, S_3 = siblings 1, 2, and 3, respectively; solid lines indicate a good relationship, and broken lines indicate a weak relationship).

terms of the overall family movement. In discussing three common and troublesome problems stemming from adolescent sexuality—sexual delinquency, incest, and pregnancy—I will illustrate the application of a model weaving together the strands of individual adolescent development within particular families.

Sexual Delinquency

"Sexual delinquency" is defined as the sexually active behavior of an unmarried adolescent that is in flagrant disregard of societal norms or family rules. Often the behavior will occur with multiple partners.

Jungreis's 1969 study of 24 families with a sexually acting-out daughter found several interesting relationships. Of the 24 families, 19 had other serious problems in the family, such as psychosis, alcoholism, or serious failure in development of another child, yet the parents appeared to be undisturbed about these problems in contrast to their concern about the sexual acting-out. Twenty-two of the families showed little family unity or common purpose beyond their interest in the identified patient. In most of the families, the fathers, who were otherwise peripheral, became involved through their great concern about the daughter's behavior. Of all the wives, 21 reported that their husbands were adequate both as husbands and fathers, yet 42% of the fathers worked such long hours that they were out of the house during times that the

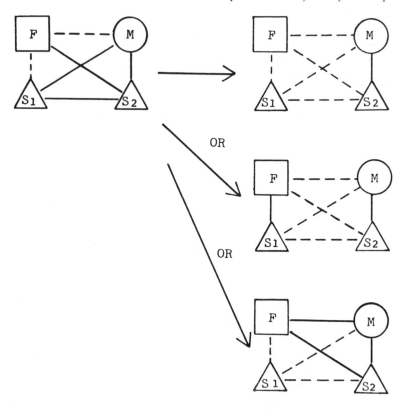

Figure 4-6. Examples of shifting sibling subsystem, an effect of adolescent sexuality
(F = father; M = mother; S_1, S_2 = siblings 1 and 2, respectively; solid lines indicate a
good relationship, and broken lines indicate a weak relationship).

family was normally assembled. Of the 24 families, 17 were very involved with
their families of origin. Of the 24 sets of parents, 20 sets were more concerned
about the social indiscretion of the behavior rather than the inherent meaning
of the behavior for them or their daughters. Most of the parents showed an
exaggerated interest in their youngsters' dating habits. Most of the sexually
acting-out daughters were immature, had poor school records despite adequate abilities, and experienced poor peer relationships. They were seen as
pseudoseductive and not really very sexual.

    In summary, Jungreis (1969) observed that one effect of the sexually
delinquent behavior on the family was to convert the father from being a
distant person into an authoritarian, critical, and totally involved person

who frequently displayed rages about his daughter's behavior. The mother, in most cases, showed no concern for the daughter personally, but only for the social stigma of her behavior. These issues were enacted in the parent-child–parent triad, with other children in the family not being included or affected.

Assessing these findings leads to some hypotheses about the structure of families with sexually delinquent adolescents. In many of the families described, one or more family members had severe dysfunction, yet the family functioned in a protective way about them. This same protectiveness was reflected in the families' embarrassment about the daughters' sexual delinquency, in that it called negative attention to the families. The fathers in these families had long or unusual work hours, keeping them away during much of the time that the rest of the family was together. There was close involvement with at least one family of origin. Thus the mothers, to whom most of the parenting had fallen, may have turned to their own parents or parents-in-law for support with the children.

In the context of this sort of family, the adolescent's developing sexuality threatens the integrity and stability of family habits. The family system does not move with the centrifugal forces of the "adolescent" system. It reacts to the adolescent's behaviors by scapegoating the youngster. The child, for her part, selects a demonstration of emerging sexuality that holds the family together—that in fact brings in the peripheral father. Thus the family effectively remains a closed, relatively centripetal system, in which the daughter is traded with the father to become the extruded, peripheral, but still captive, family member. Instead of increasing the impermeability of the boundary between the youth and the family, and instead of pushing family members more toward outside interests, the effect of sexual delinquency in these cases was to increase centripetal movement.

Incest

"Incest" is defined as sexual activity between unmarried members of a marital cohort. Though the most common form of incest is thought to be between siblings, this is not usually held to be as dysfunctional or as damaging as those forms of incest that occur across generations. Of the latter, the most common form is between the father (or the mother's boyfriend or mate) and the daughter, and this form has received the most attention. A classification of incest differentiates between cases of child rape, single episodes involving a psychotic adult, and cases involving an ongoing incestuous relationship, often lasting more than a year. Of the latter cases, endogamous incest, defined as that which occurs on an ongoing basis without apparent disturbance of the family functioning, is the most common. The average length of time for endogamous incest has been reported to be 3 years.

Exploration of relationships in families where endogamous father–daughter incest occurs has yielded an enormous amount of data on the personality characteristics of the fathers, mothers, and daughters in these systems. More recently, researchers have looked at interpersonal characteristics, the dyadic relationships, and the larger family contexts in which the various observed personality types are embedded. Gutheil and Avery (1977) described four family concerns that they observed in treating a family with multiple incest:

1. A preoccupation with separation and loss
2. Allegiance and obedience, rather than emotional ties, binding the family together
3. A perceived chasm between inside and outside the family
4. A perception that the world outside the family is a pleasurable temptation that must be resisted

Other observations about the conditions in families in which endogamous incest occurred were that the sexual relationship between the parents was often curtailed as a result of the unavailability of the mother through illness, absence, or, often, her preoccupation with her own mother. In this kind of situation, the daughter is left to fulfill many of the roles of her mother, including housekeeper, caregiver of the children, and caregiver of her father. Furthermore, the family's preoccupation with fears of loss and separation, or the strong morality and loyalty to the family group described by many of these families, would interfere with the father's seeking sexual relationships outside of the marital cohort. If the forces holding the family together are so strong, then it may be equally difficult for the maturing daughter in the family to seek sexual relationships outside of the family.

The onset of the daughter's adolescent sexuality may result in one of two scenarios in these types of families. First, if the incest has been going on before her adolescence, the awakening sexuality will induce the daughter to put a stop to it. A functional solution is for the father and daughter to agree to stop. Another functional solution is for the adolescent to make herself unavailable to her father by dating and becoming involved with her peer group. Early marriage, providing an acceptable way to leave home, is a common solution. Some daughters try to blow the whistle on their fathers by first telling their mothers and then by involving other authorities, such as school and legal personnel. Often, even the intervention of such authorities does not ensure the daughter's freedom from the father's advances. The daughter, not wanting to break up the family, may recant under inquiry. Her main defense then may be to run away. Thus her drive to separate may be enacted by breaking powerful family rules of closeness and loyalty, which almost inevitably leads to the continued alienation of the daughter from her family. What can be seen in terms of the family system's developmental task of separating is that other intrafamilial issues are often so powerful that the adolescent separation, if it can take place, does so at tremendous cost to the strongly protected family security.

The second scenario in father–daughter incest is when the incest begins after the daughter has attained sexual maturity. This might be understood as an intrafamilial response to the emerging sexuality of the adolescent, and it represents a greater degree of dysfunction than in those cases in which the incest ends at the child's adolescence. It appears that the entire family system pulls together to resist the strong developmental centrifugal forces that are normally expressed through the adolescent's sexual explorations outside of the family. As with sexual delinquency, if incest begins or continues in adolescence, the boundary does not form; the door does not close.

Pregnancy

The family contexts within which an unmarried adolescent pregnancy occurs are different, depending on the conditions and outcome of the pregnancy. The three possible outcomes of pregnancy, over which the mother has some control, are abortion, adoption, and keeping the child. It is to be expected that each of these outcomes would reflect different family patterns. In fact, though this is so, the differences are slighter than might be expected.

Several studies of adolescent pregnancy have examined characteristics of the families. One study (Boyce & Benoit, 1975) found few differences between pregnant adolescents who chose to abort and those who chose to deliver in age, contraceptive use, and sexual history but found a striking difference in educational level, with twice as many deliverers as aborters not having progressed beyond eighth grade.

A second study (Miller, 1974) compared unmarried adolescent mothers with a control group of girl scouts and attempted to characterize differences in family interactions in these two groups. They discovered that the girl scouts were generally the first-born children or the oldest girls in their families, whereas the unmarried mothers were later-born children in their families. The unmarried mothers made poorer grades in school. Mothers of the unmarried mothers were significantly more powerful in family discussions than were mothers of the girl scouts, while the fathers of the unmarried mothers had significantly less power. Clinical reports described the unmarried mothers to be in a conflicted, dependent relationship with their mothers and to be relatively out of contact with their fathers, talking more to their mothers and less to their fathers than did the girl scouts.

A third study, done in Israel (Hertz, 1977), assessed the families of 12 pregnant adolescents between the ages of 15 and 17. Of these 12, 75% came from broken homes, though in only three of the families had the parents actually divorced. In the case of the "intact" families, the atmosphere was reportedly strained, according to the daughters, with the fathers involved in affairs outside of the marriage. The girls reported that their fathers' infidelities had been repeatedly discussed with them by their mothers. Most daughters reported that they had been frequently warned by their mothers not to become involved with men and not to repeat the mistakes of their mothers.

They also reported that they had become involved sexually more out of a desire to be held than out of a desire for sexual relations. Finally, most reported that the pregnancy was discovered first by the mother, who, in many cases, kept track of her daughter's menstrual cycle.

A number of studies of unmarried mothers have observed that the vast majority of them live in at home with their parents. In one study (Furstenberg, 1980), 77% were still with a relative after 1 year, while 50% were still at home after 5 years. This study found that families offered more help if the adolescent remained single. This finding highlights the competing pressures on the adolescent from her family and from her partner in her decisions about caring for the child and herself. The frequent choice of the adolescent to remain with her family can be understood in light of this conflict. Other studies (Presser, 1980; Young, 1975) found a similarly high proportion of adolescent mothers living with their own mothers. Young (1975) found that mothers had a clearer—and what proved at follow-up to be a more accurate—view than did their daughters of how the infants would be cared for and whether the daughters would return to school.

This review of some studies of the families of adolescents who carry pregnancies to term leads to several conclusions:

1. Many of these families are headed by a single parent, with the mother being the single parent. In those families in which there are two parents, the father is reported to be quite uninvolved with his daughter.

2. The mother and the adolescent are overinvolved with one another. The mother almost substitutes the daughter for the absent or distant mate, while the daughter yields personal information, such as the dates of her menstrual cycle, to her mother.

3. The pregnant adolescents who carry to term have a poorer educational history than their peers. They have less education and have done less well in school. This suggests that the role of the adolescent as a companion to the parent at home may have long preceded the pregnancy.

4. The incidence of unmarried pregnancy in adolescents is higher if the adolescent's mother had also had an unmarried pregnancy.

How, then, does producing a child in adolescence serve the family? It is likely that the family of the unmarried adolescent mother is not at all able to move into the centrifugal stage of the family life cycle. Bringing an infant into the home can forestall the normal movement of all family members into the more differentiated relationship that would be normal in the centrifugal period. In some cases, it is reported that a girl may buy her freedom by leaving her child with her own mother, seemingly as a substitute. Though this may be a solution for some, in most cases the adolescent who leaves her child at home leaves to pursue promiscuity, drugs, or some other self-destructive course. The family pattern of overinvolved mother and daughter with a peripheral father will tend to be repeated in future generations. Thus adolescent pregnancy is another situation in which the door does not close in order to structure the strong generational boundary that should be built in the centripetal family.

ADOLESCENT SEXUALITY AND FAMILY THERAPY

The preceding problems have obviously provoked a great deal of study and concern, but they do not define the largest proportion of youngsters whose families seek treatment during their adolescence. For this reason, other and more ordinary situations are presented in order to demonstrate how the family interaction around the adolescents' emerging sexuality and sexual expression can be assessed and worked into a treatment plan.

Sean: A Boy in a Too Centrifugal Family

Sean was 16 years old, the oldest of three children of an achieving Irish-Catholic family. Both of his parents were professionals, though his mother had only recently completed her doctoral work. His two younger siblings were successful in school. Sean was brilliant, but he had not achieved up to his potential. Troubles leading to treatment had begun during summer camp when he was 15, when he had his first girlfriend. He was deliriously happy, as he reported in his letters home, but when the summer came to an end, he and his girlfriend had broken up. Sean was depressed upon his return from camp. He withdrew more from his family and appeared to have even greater difficulties in school, which he attributed to difficulties in concentrating. Sean confided to his father that he felt he needed help, and his father arranged for Sean to begin treatment with a friend of the family, who agreed to treat Sean individually. Sean went for six sessions, then decided that it was doing no good, so he stopped. He selected his next therapist himself, after doing some reading, and saw this therapist for about 3 months, but he left, once again, when he felt he was not making any progress. Finally, the parents sought family therapy. The third therapist made the observation that the "door had been slammed" between Sean and the other members of his family, leaving Sean isolated and struggling fearfully with his own inadequate assessment of himself.

Treatment began by developing family resources for Sean. His parents were encouraged to protest the episodes where he would suddenly emerge from his isolated contemplation of himself and demand something from them. They began to insist that he explain himself better. In return, they demanded less from him than he expected. For example, Sean was to spend the summer with a group of young people in Ireland. He had already steeled himself to expect that his parents would hassle him about letters home. In fact, they laughingly indicated that a postcard now and then, to let them know he was alive, would be fine. The change in Sean's demeanor and outlook in a matter of 4 or 5 weeks was striking. In addition, his parents had developed a position of involvement with him that could be genuinely helpful without being intrusive, whereas previously they had held themselves back, fearing to intrude.

In this instance, it appeared that the door had closed tightly apparently out of his parents' respect for his privacy in his first romance. Sean had been prematurely isolated from sources of assurance and confirmation from his family.

Sean's parents had met and decided to marry when they were 14. They had received no emotional or financial support from their own families, and they had struggled on their own through the father's graduate schooling, then three children, and finally the mother's schooling. Sean was born while the father was still in graduate school. His mother stopped working and studying to take care of him, so that her husband could continue his studies without distraction. Needless to say, Sean was a difficult baby, and his mother had to involve his father, so that Sean's early years were difficult for both of them. They attributed these hardships to Sean; they did not acknowledge disappointment in or resentment of each other. When Sean reached his adolescence, his mother was finishing her doctorate. Her work on this demanded that his father be more involved with day-to-day home life, tasks that he did without complaint. They went through these adjustments with a determination to remain committed to each other, declaring that their only concern was for their difficult son.

When Sean returned from Ireland, he was contemplating becoming a theologian. Though both of his parents were well versed in theology, Sean took the arrogant position that they knew nothing, and once again retreated to his room. Family therapy resumed. A trial of antidepressants offered no improvement. The therapist worked with Sean, alone, *and* involved his parents. As Sean was applying to colleges, the parents were encouraged to let Sean work on the applications on his own—which is what he was requesting. As the parents had actually withdrawn in the face of Sean's first love, it was important that they be kept involved without increasing his confusion about what they expected from him and how he could please them while still knowing and respecting himself. Their tendency was to drop the boy off with the therapist and throw up their hands, thus removing themselves, as their families had done with them, in the face of their first love. The therapist functioned as a gateway between the parents and Sean, monitoring access while keeping it open. Other help for Sean came from school, where he had relationships that did not involve his parents. With parents involved, but at a greater distance, Sean was freer to act. He was accepted by all of the colleges to which he applied. When last contacted, he had completed the first semester, was doing well academically, and was participating in numerous student activities. He even grudgingly declared himself to be pleased with his life and said something nice to his mother.

Jane and Ellen: Girls in a Too Centripetal Family

Jane and Ellen were sisters who, at the time of the first therapy contact, were 15 and 13, respectively. They lived in a close Jewish family, a nuclear family ambivalently, but very much involved with both families of origin. The initial presenting problem was Jane, the older sister, who was overweight, irritable, and doing poorly in school. She was obviously unhappy, and her parents, in addition to being irritated with her sloppiness and laziness about schoolwork, were very concerned about her mood. However, unlike Sean's parents, Jane's parents responded to their concerns by becoming more involved with her. They monitored her homework and her social life closely. Of course, Jane responded to this with even more irritation and moodiness.

In contrast to Jane, Ellen was seen by her parents as an easy child, who managed her schoolwork independently, was attractive, and generally had an easier time of it than her chunky sister.

The initial intervention, with Jane and her parents present, was to point out that Jane was an intelligent, aware young woman who could plan her own time and could foresee the consequences of her actions or inactions. This was a prelude to encouraging the parents to pull back and let Jane manage her own time, to fail on her own, if necessary. This process was dragged out over more than a year, with Jane wavering back and forth between autonomous action and giving in, while her parents had bursts of confidence in her and then would rush in to take over for her.

A crisis arose when Ellen, the easy child, became involved with a boy, at age 14. Her parents objected to her seeing just one boy. They said she was too young, that she could not spend time with him alone, that she could not go out with him on consecutive weekend nights, and so on. Ellen became angry, then depressed, and her parents brought her to therapy. In fact, the issues of parent overinvolvement were highlighted, as they had been with Jane, but Ellen was able to confront her parents more directly and in a personally less self-destructive fashion than had Jane.

The therapy began to focus on the parents' relationship with their own parents and on the observation that a door had never closed between the mother and her own parents, so that her husband always had a sense that his parents-in-law were in bed with him. In fact, in their early married life, the mother's parents would telephone frequently, around 11 or 12 at night, to see if she was all right. This practice, then, of being intimately involved in the sexuality of succeeding generations, had a precedent. Work in therapy focused on the couple's getting the mother's parents out of their bedroom and on closing the door between the mother and her mother, redirecting her to her husband. As this progressed, the couple's sex life improved, and both daughters were able to negotiate their own privacy. Follow-up found that Jane had completed high school, not without difficulties, and had gone on to college, where she continues to struggle, but she continues to struggle with her own determination, observed by her respectful parents.

SUMMARY

Adolescence is a family matter. It has been proposed that the families of adolescents are in a period of development when the family system opens up and the families disassemble, reevaluate relationships, and release the offspring to find new relationships and form new families. In this context, the emergence of sexuality appears to close a door between the adolescent and his or her family. What this means is that the youngster becomes modest and ordinarily cannot talk about sexual matters with his or her parents, often turning for information to peers or adults outside the family, if they are available. The adolescent usually continues to need support from his or her parents in other matters, so that a door sealing off access between the parents and the child may result in great disturbance and unhappiness, as has been seen in the case of sexual delinquency. In other cases, the door does not close, either because the family situation does not permit it or because the child remains more attached and loyal to those within. The cases of incest and unmarried pregnancy illustrate the instance of the unclosed door. In each case described, although the situation appeared to be a problem for the adolescent, it also appeared to offer a solution to a family system unprepared for dismantling itself and fostering developmentally appropriate individuation among all its members. Though the problem for the adolescent is great, the youngster's continued problem behavior could be seen to be contributing to the integrity of the family functioning and therefore helpful to the family. Keeping these configurations in mind can be most helpful in treating troubled families in the centripetal period.

Lucy Revisited

Lucy was a difficult child from birth, being exceptionally bright. Her mother had postponed her own graduate education, while her father was a busy professional. By the time Lucy was well into her school years, her mother was well into a "career" of managing Lucy's education. When Lucy began to express her own sexual curiosity, at age 13, the door slammed between herself and her parents. They viewed her as if she were a stranger, and labeled her accordingly.

Lucy's mother consulted me for herself when her efforts to complete her 20-year study for a doctoral degree ended with such anxiety that she was unable to take her qualifying exams. Working with Lucy's mother, I learned about the events of Lucy's life from her point of view, and my impression was sustained that Lucy's unfortunate adolescence had fixed the family in a way that had a larger function. One meeting with Lucy's busy father confirmed that the close-knit, centripetal triangle of mother, father, and Lucy worked best for them, despite the personal pain experienced by all three. Lucy is not free to pursue intimate relationships outside the family, her mother is not free to pursue her professional identity and academic dream, and her father, while advancing in his profession, is unchanging in his life-style.

Lucy has struggled to survive, to preserve her separateness, and to keep her family involvement, three tasks that were often contradictory. Surviving and separateness often meant defiance, while keeping involved with the family often meant failure and capitulation. It is an exhausting process for Lucy and her family, even as she approaches 30. Her sisters have managed to leave the area, but Lucy still lives several miles away from her family home, by this time twice married and twice divorced, without having completed college, and still trying to decide what she will do when she grows up, but desperately preventing that from happening.

NOTES

1. Solomon (1973) suggested five stages: marriage, the birth of the first child and of subsequent children, individuation of family members, departure of the children, and integration of loss.

2. I am indebted to L. D. Tashjian, MD, for this idea.

3. Bell and Buerkle, 1961; Bennet and Dickenson, 1980; Brittain, 1963; Darling and Hicks, 1982; Elias, 1978; Finkel and Finkel, 1975; Fox and Inazu, 1980; Garfield and Morganthau, 1976; Gehard, 1977; Hansson, 1979; Herold and Goodwin, 1981; Inazu and Fox, 1980; Jessor and Jessor, 1975; Jorgensen, 1981; Kelly, 1979; Lewis, 1973; Libby, *et al.,* 1978; Miller and Simon, 1974; Miller, 1976; Sebald and White, 1980; Shipman, 1968; Thompson and Spanier, 1978; Zelnik, 1979.

REFERENCES

Ackerman, N. D. (1980). The family with adolescents. In E. A. Carter & M. McGoldrick (Eds.), *The family life cycle: A framework for family therapy* (pp. 147-169). New York: Gardner Press.

Banks, S. P., & Kahn, M. D. (1982). *The sibling bond.* New York: Basic Books.

Bell, R. R., & Buerkle, J. V. (1961). Mother and daughter attitudes to premarital sexual behavior. *Marriage and Family Living, 23,* 390-392.

Bennett, S. M., & Dickenson, W. B. (1980). Student-parent rapport and parent involvement in sex, birth control, and venereal disease education. *Journal of Sex Research, 16,* 114-130.

Blos, P. (1962). *On adolescence: A psychoanalytic interpretation.* New York: Free Press of Glencoe.

Boyce, J., & Benoit, C. (1975). Adolescent pregnancy. *New York State Journal of Medicine, 75*(6), 872-874.

Brittain, C. V. (1963). Adolescent choices and parent–peer cross pressures. *American Sociological Review, 28,* 385–391.

Carter, E. A., & McGoldrick, M. (1980). The family life cycle and family therapy: An overview. In E. A. Carter & M. McGoldrick (Eds.), *The family life cycle: A framework for family therapy* (pp. 3–20). New York: Gardner Press.

Combrinck-Graham, L. (1983). The family life cycle and families with young children. In H. Liddle (Ed.), *Clinical implications of the family life cycle* (pp. 35–53). Rockville, MD: Aspen.

Combrinck-Graham, L. (1985). A model for family development. *Family Process, 24,* 139–150.

Darling, C. A., & Hicks, M. W. (1982). Parental influences on adolescent sexuality: Implications for parents as educators. *Journal of Youth and Adolescence, 14,* 231–245.

Elias, J. E. (1978). Adolescents and sex. *The Humanist,* March/April: 29–31.

Finkel, M. L., & Finkel, D. J. (1975). Sexual and contraceptive knowledge, attitudes and behavior of male adolescents. *Family Planning Perspectives, 7,* 256–260.

Fox, G. L., & Inazu, J. K. (1980). Mother–daughter communication about sex. *Family Relations, 29,* 347–352.

Furstenberg, F. F., Jr. (1980). Burdens and benefits: The impact of early childbearing on the family. *Journal of Social Issues, 36,* 64–87.

Garfield, M. G., & Morgenthau, J. E. (1976). Sex talks between mothers and daughters. *Medical Aspects of Human Sexuality,* November, 6–18.

Gebhard, P. H. (1977). The acquisition of basic sex information. *Journal of Sex Research, 13,* 148–169.

Gutheil, T. G., & Avery, N. C. (1977). Multiple overt incest as family defense against loss. *Family Process, 16,* 105–116.

Hansson, R. O., Jones, W. H., & Charnovetz, M. E. (1979). Contraceptive knowledge: Antecedents and implications. *The Family Coordinator, 28,* 29–34.

Hauser, S. T., Powers, S. I., Noam, G. G., Jacobson, A. M., Weiss, B., & Follansbee, D. J. (1984). Familial contexts of adolescent ego development. *Child Development, 55,* 195–213.

Herold, E. S., & Goodwin, M. S. (1981). Reasons given by female virgins for not having premarital intercourse. *Journal of School Health, 51,* 496–500.

Hertz, D. G. (1977). Psychological implications of adolescent pregnancy: Patterns of family interaction in adolescent mothers-to-be. *Psychosomatics, 18,* 13–16.

Inazu, J. K., & Fox, S. L. (1980). Maternal influence on the sexual behavior of teenage daughters: Direct and indirect sources. *Journal of Family Issues, 1,* 81–102.

Jessor, S. L., & Jessor, R. (1975). Transition from virginity to nonvirginity among youth: A social-psychological study over time. *Developmental Psychology, 11,* 473–484.

Johnson, A. M., & Szurek, S. A. (1952). The genesis of antisocial acting out in children and adults. *Psychoanalytic Quarterly, 21,* 323–343.

Jorgensen, S. R. (1981). Sex education and the reduction of adolescent pregnancies: Prospects for the 1980's. *Journal of Early Adolescence, 1*(1) 38–52.

Jungreis, J. E. (1969). The sexually delinquent female. In O. Pollak & A. S. Friedman, (Eds.), *Family dynamics and female sexual delinquency* (pp. 198–204). Palo Alto, CA: Science & Behavior Books.

Kelly, K. (1979). Socialization factors in contraceptive attitudes: Roles of affective responses, parental attitudes, and sexual experience. *Journal of Sex Research, 15,* 6–20.

Levinson, D. J., Darrow, C. N., Klein, E. B., Levinson, M. H., & McKee, B. (1978). *The seasons of a man's life.* New York: Alfred A. Knopf.

Lewis, R. A. (1973). Parents and peers: Socialization agents in the coital behavior of young adults. *Journal of Sex Research, 9,* 156–170.

Libby, W., Gray, L., & White, M. (1978). A test and reformulation of reference group and role correlates of premarital and sexual permissiveness theory. *Journal of Marriage and the Family, 40,* 79–82.

Miller, A. G. (1974). The relationship between family interaction and sexual behavior in adolescence. *Journal of Community Psychology, 2,* 285–288.

Miller, P. Y., & Simon, W. (1974). Adolescent sexual behavior: Content and change. *Social Problems, 22,* 58–75.

Miller, W. B. (1976). Sexual and contraceptive behavior in young unmarried women. *Primary Care, 3,* 427–453.

Minuchin, S., & Fishman, H. C. (1981). *Family therapy techniques.* Cambridge, MA: Harvard University Press.

Presser, H. B. (1980). Sally's corner: Coping with unmarried motherhood. *Journal of Social Issues, 36,* 107–129.

Rosen, R. H. (1980). Adolescent pregnancy decision-making: Are parents important? *Adolescence, 15,* 43–54.

Sebald, H., & White, B. (1980). Teenagers' divided reference groups: Uneven alignment with parents and peers. *Adolescence, 15,* 979–984.

Shipman, G. (1968). The psychodynamics of sex education. *The Family Coordinator, 17,* 3–12.

Solomon, M. A. (1973). A developmental, conceptual premise for family therapy. *Family Process, 12,* 179–188.

Stierlin, H. (1975). Family therapy with adolescents and the process of intergenerational reconciliation. In M. Sugar (Ed.), *The adolescent in group and family therapy* (pp. 194–204). New York: Brunner/Mazel.

Thompson, L., & Spanier, R. B. (1978). The influence of parents, peers, and partners on the contraceptive use of college men and women. *Journal of Marriage and the Family, 40,* 481–492.

Young, A. T., Berkman, B., & Rehr, H. (1975). Parental influence on pregnant adolescents. *Social Work,* Sept. 387–391.

Zelnik, M. (1979). Sex education and knowledge of pregnancy risk among U.S. teenage women. *Family Planning Perspectives, 11,* 335–357.

5

Oscillation Theory and Family Development

DOUGLAS C. BREUNLIN
Institute for Juvenile Research, Chicago

Ideas, like families, have a life cycle. They are born, sometimes of the most unlikely parents; develop and mature by increasing in complexity; and then decline, often giving birth to new ideas before disappearing. Born of the conceptual wizardry of Milton Erickson (Haley, 1973) and the sociological concept of family development (Duvall, 1977), the family life cycle (FLC) was welcomed as a breath of fresh air in a field that was still somewhat constricted by a pathological and deficit-based view of families' functioning. Subsequently, almost every model of family therapy adopted this developmental view of the family. The life cycle became a central idea providing support for the positive stance adopted by most family therapists, who argued for the capacity of a family to change. Clearly, symptoms, even serious ones, generated by a family's inability to negotiate the transitions of the life cycle, were more easily and hopefully resolved than those produced by double binding (Bateson, Jackson, Haley, & Weakland, 1956), contagious affect (Ackerman, 1966), triangulation (Minuchin, 1974), or any of the other deficit-oriented concepts that first explained symptoms as a function of family context.

Unfortunately, the FLC model is currently viewed by many as developmentally delayed and possibly terminal. For example, Fisch (1983) noted that the FLC, once closely linked to the MRI model of brief therapy, is no longer viewed as central to this group's thinking, and Hoffman (1981) provided strong statements detailing her dislike of the FLC model.

Just how the FLC concept reached this state of decline is not entirely clear. One explanation is that while many writers have acknowledged the concept, few have adopted it and nurtured its growth. Rather, in the decade following the birth of the FLC, most of the writing in the family therapy field has focused on the conceptual and technical development of the major models of family therapy, and few writers have attempted to refine the FLC. Like a neglected child, the FLC now lacks the complexity required to compete with its more sophisticated siblings, the major models of family therapy. Liddle and Saba (1983), describing the clinical limitations of the FLC, noted

133

that for many, its only value arises as a framing device or, at best, as a transparency to be placed over the conceptual framework of a preferred model of therapy, which complements but does not lead the therapist's thinking and action regarding a family. In short, the FLC's life cycle is in grave danger of being truncated prematurely.

In my opinion, the realities of family development are compelling and vital data for the family therapist if they can be ordered with sufficient clarity and detail so as to become clinically relevant. The FLC should be, as Carter and McGoldrick (1980) intended, a framework for family therapy. To achieve this position, however, the FLC must advance in two significant ways. First, the conceptual underpinnings of the FLC must be refined to the point where they can accurately map highly complex family data. Second, the theory must translate directly into meaningful interventions. In this chapter, I will attempt to initiate these advances by introducing the concept of oscillation (Breunlin, 1981, 1982; Liddle & Saba, 1983). This concept will afford additional complexity and pave the way for the FLC to be linked to therapeutic interventions.

CONCEPTUAL WEAKNESSES OF THE FAMILY LIFE CYCLE

The currently accepted model of the FLC is most easily described through reference to the pie diagram shown in Figure 5-1. This diagram, based on the work of Evelyn Duvall (1977), depicts a stage–transition model of the FLC, where the pieces of the pie represent the stages, and the lines separating them, the transitions. The model argues that for each stage (Stage I, beginning family; Stage II, childbearing family; etc.), families must master a set of tasks that are specific for that stage. A transition signals the need for change in the family, enabling it to leave a previous stage and to begin negotiating the tasks of the next stage. Transitions correspond to the points of nodal change, largely involving changes in family composition, such as birth, marriage, leaving home, and death, but also involving major shifts in autonomy, such as going to school, entering adolescence, and retiring from the work force. Henceforth I will refer to such transitions as "nodal transitions." Failure to accomplish a nodal transition leaves the family functioning in the wrong stage.

The pie diagram is a deceptively simple representation of the FLC, masking many of its conceptual flaws. By juxtaposing two related, but essentially discrete, views of family development—the sociological view of stages and their associated tasks, and the clinical view of family transitions—the FLC tells us something about each but very little about the relationship between the two and how they combine to form a total pattern of family development. Moreover, what is in reality a fluid process—that is, family development— has, like the diagram, been reified into a discrete sequencing of stages separated by arbitrary transitions. This reification has produced a stereotypic and oversimplified view of family development that is not borne out under careful

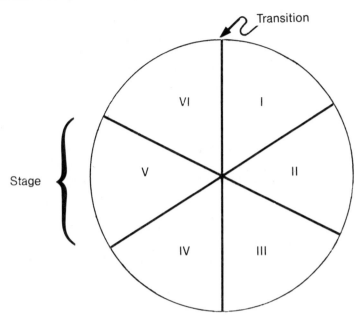

Figure 5-1. Pie diagram depicting the stage–transition model of the FLC.

scrutiny. Falicov (1984), for example, questioned the stage concept of the FLC, noting that families rarely follow stage expectations in an orderly and prescribed manner. Nor has the concept of a transition been adequately defined. The current view of the FLC begs two questions: What actually changes in a transition, and how does the transition process actually work? Further, by equating transitions with events such as birth, marriage, and death, the current model ignores other transitions that may also be important to a family's development. Finally, the model also ignores the reality that development in most families involves multiple simultaneous transitions. In short, the FLC, in its current form, raises more questions than it answers.

The following vignette is but one clinical example highlighting the conceptual weakness of the FLC model:

A 30-year-old woman was referred for family therapy, having been hospitalized for severe compulsive behavior and anorexia. Prior to her hospitalization, she lived at home with her parents and helped with the care of her wheelchair-bound mother, who had developed multiple sclerosis when the daughter was 14. Her three older brothers had all grown up and left home, while she had become progressively more isolated, dropping out of school and losing all of her friends. As an adolescent, she was described as immature and unable to meet the demands of school, but, at the same time, she provided daily care for her mother and ran the household.

Her symptoms intensified when her father, who had always worked two jobs, retired and started to help with the mother. The daughter, now more free to consider her own life, would stand for hours at the front door, swinging it open and then closed, metaphorically leaving but not leaving.

The current FLC model offers two hypotheses about this case: first, that the onset of problems corresponded to the transition to adolescence, and second, that the problems corresponded to the transition of retirement. The first hypothesis would suggest that the family was arrested in the latency stage for 16 years! If this were the case, how, then, did the three sons successfully negotiate adolescence and leave home, or, for that matter, how did the woman grow up and learn to competently care for her mother? Acceptance of the hypothesis of retirement begs the question that the woman functioned very poorly in many areas of her life prior to the father's retirement. The retirement exacerbated, but did not cause, the symptoms. Moreover, were the transition to retirement completed, it is unlikely that the woman would suddenly experience a discontinuous leap and begin to function as a competent 30-year-old. Finally, neither hypothesis explains how the woman functioned so competently in some areas of her life but yet so incompetently in others.

This vignette illustrates that despite problems at two nodal transitions, many aspects of the family continued to develop, albeit the gains were more beneficial for some members than for others. Either the failure to make a transition or an arrest in a particular stage is an impossibility. A family cannot *not* make a transition, because, if nothing else, time never stands still and children in a family do grow up. The only relevant questions are, how is a transition made, and how can that process become problematic?

The relationship between family development and time becomes more apparent if we cut the pie diagram, unwind it, and attempt to express the FLC graphically, as suggested in Figure 5-2. With such a graph, it is possible to express family development as a function of time. This graph raises three questions that further expose the conceptual weakness of the FLC model: (1) What is the relationship between the FLC and time? (2) Over time, what aspects of a family change? (3) What is the shape of the curve that emerges when family development is plotted as a function of time?

What Is the Relationship of the FLC to Time?

By representing the FLC as a circle, the pie diagram creates the deception that the FLC is circular. It is circular only insofar as each generation passes through similar stages and transitions. Expressing development as a function of time, as in Figure 5-2, exposes the inherent linearity of any developmental model. This linearity has led many family therapists to pay lip service to the

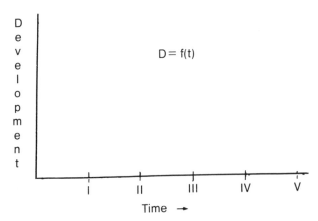

Figure 5-2. The FLC expressed graphically, showing family development (D) as a function of time (t).

FLC but not to embrace it fully, lest they be accused of linear causal thinking. Attributing symptoms to the difficulties involved in negotiating the relatively infrequent nodal transitions further implies an atemporal approach but, in the process, ignores the time that passes prior to and after the transition. This restricted focus also denies the cumulative effects of development. In the vignette, for instance, what are the cumulative effects of 16 years of social isolation?

For the FLC to survive in a field dominated by systemic thought, it must propose ways to think about time systemically. In other words, the FLC must be able to acknowledge the temporal relationship existing among events throughout a family's development while still proposing a model where current functioning can explain behavior and where interventions drawn from the systemic family therapies can be used.

What Family Aspects Change?

This question can be posed at two levels: First, what variables of family life change over the life cycle such that a family develops? Second, how can these variables be operationalized such that they become observable and accessible in therapy? The literature about the life cycle has typically included a preferred conceptual framework drawn from one of the models of family therapy. Hence, when the question "What changes?" is asked, the answer is framed within one of these therapy models. The structural therapist would say the structure changes (Minuchin, 1974; Minuchin & Fishman, 1981), the MRI therapist would say the rules change (Watzlawick, Weakland, & Fisch, 1974), a Bowen therapist may say that the level of anxiety changes (Carter & McGoldrick, 1980), and Wynne (1985) argues that the relational system must change. By attempting to be all things to all therapy models, the answer to the question (What changes) has emerged as a hodgepodge of variables that, taken together, mean virtually nothing because they amount to everything. The result is that it is impossible to specify an operationalized variable to be measured on the vertical axis of Figure 5-2. To be a useful model of family development, the FLC must specify such variables not just at nodal transitions but throughout the course of development.

What Is the Shape of the Curve?

Figure 5-2 shows an equation suggesting that the FLC can express family development as a function of time. This equation specifies the shape of the curve; the FLC itself does not hypothesize the shape. In the mid-1970s, however, the shape was hypothesized when the theory of change proposed by the MRI group (Watzlawick *et al.,* 1974) was applied to the FLC (Hughes, Berger, & Wright, 1978; Weeks & Wright, 1979). The MRI group argued that there are two types of change: first-order change, which is gradual, continuous, and within the current rules of a system; and second-order change, which is abrupt and discontinuous and involves a change in the rules of the system. They argued that first-order change is quantitative, and second-order change, qualitative. Take the example of making a car move. If you push the accelerator, you can make the car go faster. That's more of the same, or first-order change. If you shift the gears, you're actually changing the rules of operation of the engine. That's second-order change (Watzlawick *et al.,* 1974).

The marriage between the MRI concept of change and the FLC seemed ideal. Hughes *et al.* (1978) argued that during a stage, when specific tasks are being mastered, first-order change is involved, whereas during a transition, necessitating fundamental change in the family (in terms of rules, organization patterns, etc.), second-order change is involved.

The shape of the curve derived from the MRI theory of change is depicted in Figure 5-3. This curve, although not always depicted graphically, became the organizing metaphor not only for how change takes place over the course of the life cycle but also for how most family therapists view change in general. Again, its simplicity was deceptive. It is easy to forget that this step-function curve derives from an application of the MRI theory of change to the FLC and not from empirical study of family development. Upon further scrutiny, we might ask two questions: First, what is actually meant by a discontinuous leap at the time of a nodal transition? In the vignette, for instance, how would the transition of retirement constitute a discontinuous leap that would suddenly free the woman to lead a normal life after 16 years of

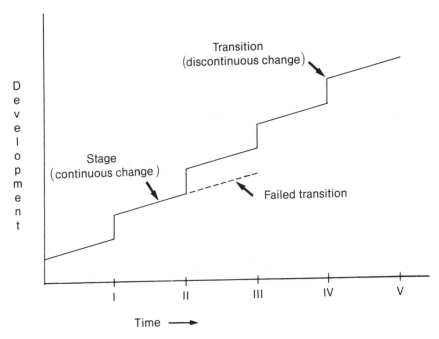

Figure 5-3. The MRI theory of change applied to the stage–transition model of the FLC.

social isolation? Second, what is the significance of changes that occur during the stages? In the vignette, the woman did learn to function competently in some areas despite the family's arrest in a particular stage.

The distinction between first- and second-order change is now being challenged in the field of family therapy (Breunlin, 1983; Fishman, Chapter 16, this volume; Liddle & Saba, 1983) as an artificial and overly constraining way to view the process of change. Applied to the life cycle, the MRI theory introduces a distinction that relegates change during a stage to a position of secondary importance. As discussed later, this simply isn't the case. I believe, therefore, that the step-function curve is not appropriate for depicting the complexities of family development.

In summary, the FLC is seriously handicapped by its failure to propose systemic ways to think about time, to specify what changes occur as families develop, and to propose a curve that accurately reflects family development as a function of time. The theory of oscillation posed in the next section answers these questions and provides some of the conceptual vigor needed for the FLC to be relevant in today's rapidly evolving field of family therapy.

OSCILLATION THEORY

In the vignette described in the preceding section, the woman's obsessive behavior of standing for hours swinging the front door open and closed serves as a metaphor for her family's specific life cycle dilemma, and, more generally, for oscillation theory. The woman was both the most competent and the least competent of the siblings. On the one hand, she ran the family and cared for her invalid mother, while on the other, at 30, she had no education, few social skills, and the appearance of a teenager. Her obsessive behavior metaphorically expressed an extreme oscillation between highly competent and highly incompetent behavior. This oscillation had developed early in her adolescence, roughly at the onset of her mother's illness, and had persisted for 16 years. The oscillations were intensified but not caused by her father's retirement.

Oscillation theory hypothesizes that transitions occur not as step functions, where discontinuous leaps are made from one level of functioning to another, but rather through an oscillation between levels of functioning, as shown in Figure 5-4. Such oscillations are an inevitable feature of all transitions. In normal families, the oscillations dampen when the higher level functioning predominates and replaces a previous level of functioning. Symptoms emerge and are maintained when a family negotiates a transition by stabilizing an oscillation, which then persists over time, as in the vignette.

An oscillation, although set in motion by a developmental change at a particular time, is observable in the present and is therefore sufficient for explaining the maintenance of symptoms without reference to linear causality.

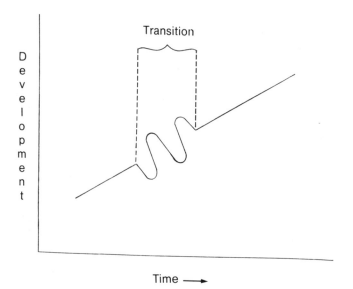

Figure 5-4. An oscillation in the developmental process.

Once an oscillation becomes stable, it passes through time as part of the family's total pattern of interaction. Like a wave, its basic form is preserved while it evolves with each developmental issue. Oscillation theory thus affords a systemic way to think about time.

Oscillation theory proposes that it is the *competence* of each family member that changes over the course of the life cycle, thus enabling a family to develop. When oscillations occur, they are expressed in terms of this competence and can be observed as a swing between overly competent and overly incompetent behavior. Such oscillations are always characteristic of the behavior of the identified patient, but they may also be observed in other family members. The oscillation may occur for just a brief period and hence may be observable within a session, or it may extend over a much longer period of time.

The following vignette illustrates how an oscillation can emerge and persist in a family's development:

A 12-year-old boy, who lived alone with his mother, was referred to me for repeatedly running away from home. He would disappear for several days and would usually be returned home by the police, having been caught sleeping on a subway train. His mother suffered from multiple sclerosis. From the age of 6, she had taught her son to use public transportation, because she wanted him to be able to handle himself should anything ever happen to her. Other greater-than-competent behaviors also appeared whenever the mother experienced an exacerbation of her illness. During these times, the boy would run the house quite competently and would not run away. When the mother recovered, the boy would fall apart, his competence giving way to immaturity as he refused to help around the house and did very poorly in school. Frustrated by this collapse, the mother would attempt to control her son, which resulted in his running away again. The oscillation between greater-than-competent and less-than-competent behavior occurred in relationship to the mother's illness.

To complicate matters further, when the boy was born, the mother was just 16 years old; now, some 12 years later, she was attending nursing school and stated bluntly that she would not allow his behavior to interfere with her plans to have a career. Accordingly, the mother acted competently as a student but incompetently in the context of the family, wherein she neglected her responsibilities as a parent. She oscillated between the extremes of wanting to be a teenager finishing school and being an adult raising a family. By running away, the boy periodically tried to solve his mother's dilemma, again making himself more competent than his years.

To arrive at a working model of oscillation theory, it is essential, first, to establish competence as an operational variable for "what changes." Second, it is essential to establish how oscillations are initiated and maintained, that is, how I arrive at the shape of the curve. Third, I must establish how the model translates into clinical practice.

Behavioral Competence

The variable selected to measure what changes as a family develops must satisfy two criteria: First, it must be observable and operational, and second, it must provide relevant information about the family as a system. Behavioral competence can be operationalized and hence satisfies the first criterion. Regarding the second, just as the presenting problem is often used as a point of entry to obtain information about and leverage in a complex family system, so can the level of behavioral competence of the identified patient be used to serve the same function with regard to family development. The relationship between a specific behavior and the family is defined by family sequences that regulate the behaviors of family members (Haley, 1976). The total pattern of a family is composed of myriad sequences, many of which regulate levels of behavioral competence (Breunlin & Schwartz, 1986). For example, in the first vignette, if the woman began to spend too much time outside the home, her mother would become upset, and the woman would then stay at home and intensify her care. This sequence limited her competence outside the home and increased it inside.

Such variables as structure and rules are nothing more than midlevel constructs (Sluzki, 1983) that are inferred from sequences. They cannot, of themselves, be operationalized, except through observations of behavior. I believe, therefore, that it is preferable to use behavioral competence as the operational variable for what changes in family development, recognizing that all aspects of competence are regulated by sequences and that from these sequences we can infer midlevel constructs such as structure and rules.

Developmental changes necessitate that the total pattern of a family constantly evolve. This evolution is in the direction of increased complexity and differentiation of the family system, which emerges as higher levels of competence are manifested among all family members. For this to happen, sequences regulating existing competence must change, and new sequences regulating newly required competence must also emerge. For instance, when a teenager begins to drive, parents and teenager must change the sequences that regulate time away from home but also must generate new sequences that regulate the use of the family car.

What Is the Shape of the Curve?

How do we move from the step-function curve of Figure 5-3 to the oscillation curve of Figure 5-4? The step-function curve arises from the juxtaposition of the MRI theory of change with the stage–transition model of the FLC, a model that punctuates transitions only at points of nodal change. If, however, we operationalize competence as the variable to measure family development, we are left with the question, does competence change only at nodal transitions? Development necessitates that competence change throughout the life cycle and not only at nodal transitions. Such changes in competence occur whenever a sequence changes in order to regulate behavior to higher levels of functioning. Terkelson (1980) noted that "even very small incremental developments can produce surprisingly widespread perturbations in family structure" (p. 35). For example, he notes that a small child learns to be apart from his or her parents when they progressively leave the child for longer periods of time. This allows the parents more time to relate to each other and to do other things. I refer to the process by which competence is regulated to a different level through change in a sequence as a "microtransition."

With oscillation theory, the distinction between a stage and a transition is dropped in favor of the concept of a microtransition. Family development is viewed as relentless, with significant microtransitions always taking place. At points of nodal transition, the process is similar but intensified, because the number of microtransitions clustered at a given time is greatly increased. These microtransitions involve sequences that regulate existing competence to higher levels and those that generate newly required competence. When a child starts school, for instance, sequences that regulate existing behaviors, such as getting up, going to bed, dressing, and leaving a parent, must all change in the direction of higher levels of competence. New sequences must also emerge that regulate behaviors newly acquired for school, such as going to and coming from a strange place.

The shape of the curve when viewed microscopically is a series of microtransitions, as shown in Figure 5-5a. From calculus, we know that the step-function curve approximates a smooth curve in the limit as the number of microtransitions is increased, as shown in Figure 5-5b. The distinction between the step-function curve, symbolizing discontinuous change, and the smooth curve, symbolizing continuous change, thus can be said to originate from the frame of reference of the observer (Dell, 1982). The larger the time frame of punctuation, the more likely the curve will be a step function, as is the case when development is punctuated by a small number of nodal transitions. As the time frame becomes increasingly smaller, the curve as a whole approximates smoothness, as is the case when development is punctuated by every microtransition. I would suggest, therefore, that development as a function of time over the life cycle could just as well be expressed as a continuous curve, as shown in Figure 5-5b.

Two considerations make it necessary to further modify this curve. First, development is a function of context; hence behavior that is developmentally appropriate in one context may not be in another. Second, development is an aggregate of many behaviors; consequently, we must find a way to plot all competence behaviors while still being able to detect the developmental curve.

We can account for development as a function of context if we use an analogy drawn from a standard pediatric growth chart. The chart suggests that there exist acceptable upper and lower limits for competence at any given

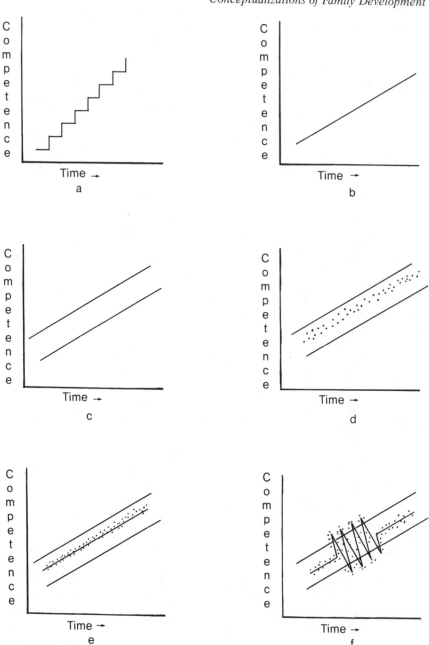

Figure 5-5. How an oscillation develops from microtransitions: (a) microtransitions as a step function; (b) microtransitions as a smooth curve; (c) range of acceptable competence; (d) plotting competence behaviors; (e) applying the curve-fitting analogy; (f) detectable pattern of oscillation.

age. These limits are set by the context of each family, including cultural background, resources, and life circumstances, and by the physical and intellectual potential of an individual. The expected range of competence for an attractive child with a high IQ living in a middle-class family of educated parents would be greater than it would be for a handicapped child with a low IQ living in poverty. For any given family, its context, and individual potential, one could predict an expected range of competence that would be normal for that situation (see Figure 5-5c). Behaviors that fall above that range are defined as greater than competent, and those below, as less than competent for that situation.

The second consideration, that development is an aggregate of competence behaviors, can be handled using a curve-fitting analogy. Theoretically, one could measure each competence behavior and plot it on the graph. The plotting of all competence behaviors over time would produce a set of data points, as shown in Figure 5-5d. The curve-fitting analogy suggests that it is possible to "fit" a curve to these data. If the majority of data cluster closely together, the fit will produce a smooth curve, as shown in Figure 5-5e. If one or two data points fall outside of the clustering of data, they would be ignored by the curve-fitting process. The curve-fitting analogy suggests that isolated instances involving less-than-competent or greater-than-competent behavior do not have an impact on overall development. When substantial numbers of behaviors fall in these ranges, however, the curve-fitting process would take them into account, and a detectable oscillation would appear in the curve, as depicted in Figure 5-5f.

The next question is, how does an oscillation arise in such a curve? The answer can be found by examining how microtransitions occur.

Microtransitions

At any particular time, the level of complexity in a family is defined by a pattern of interlocking sequences that regulates the competence of all family members. Developmental demands dictated by biology, demands of socialization, and other events such as illness constantly necessitate changes in these sequences such that competence is regulated from an existing level to a higher level (Terkelson, 1980). A discontinuous model suggests that microtransitions occur when one sequence abruptly replaces another with an associated higher level of competence. In reality, this rarely occurs. Instead, a microtransition consists of a period during which both sequences and their associated levels of competence exist simultaneously—in other words, an oscillation exists between the two sequences and the two levels of competence. For instance, when a child first walks, walking does not abruptly replace crawling in a discontinuous fashion. Rather, sometimes the child walks (and frequently falls), and sometimes the child crawls. Likewise, during the microtransition, family sequences that regulate crawling and walking exist simultaneously.

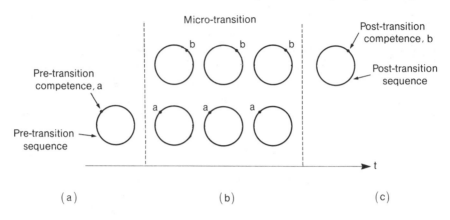

Figure 5-6. The process of a microtransition. At left, (a) Pre-transition competence, a, regulated by pre-transition sequence. (b) Pre-transition competence, a, and post-transition competence, b, exist during the micro-transition. (c) Post-transition competence, b, regulated by post-transition sequence replaces pre-transition competence and sequence.

Sometimes the parents offer a hand or encourage and praise the child for walking, while at other times, it is more convenient for the parents if the child crawls. The oscillation persists until sequences that regulate walking predominate and crawling is abandoned. The process of this crawling-to-walking microtransition is very similar to the three phases of developmental change described by Terkelson (1980). Figure 5-6 depicts the overall process of a microtransition. The following vignette describes a microtransition in detail and illustrates how it contributes to the increased complexity of the family system:

In my family, the children drink juice that can always be found in a plastic pitcher in the refrigerator. A pretransition sequence involved my daughter's asking for juice; we would agree, decline, or say "Wait a minute," and she would respond, etc. Below a certain age, this sequence had only one outcome: My daughter relied upon one of us to pour the juice. Hence she was not competent to pour the juice herself.

At some point in time, a variation in the sequence became possible: My daughter decided to pour juice herself. This option greatly increased the complexity of the sequence, because the juice could now be accessed in a new way, and, as parents, we had to respond to both the request and our daughter's getting her own juice. Of course, at this point, getting the juice in all likelihood also meant spilling some of it, in which case we may have been angered not only by her attempt to pour but also by the mess.

Pouring juice is a simple competence behavior. Child developmentalists may even say she is mastering eye–hand coordination. But, as parents, we had to decide whether she was ready to achieve such competence. If she were too young and we didn't say "no," the outcome would consistently have been spilled juice and angry parents. If we said "no" but she was able, then competence was frustrated. When my daughter first initiated juice pouring, we were inconsistent, sometimes saying "no" and sometimes "yes," and were frequently annoyed by the spilled juice. This period of "Don't pour the juice" and "I'll pour the juice" constituted a period of oscillation. In our family, this oscillation dampened until she could successfully pour the juice herself.

The microtransition involving juice pouring may seem insignificant, but it isn't. Not only is juice pouring an area of competence in its own right, but it serves as a gateway to additional competence. Once my daughter had mastered juice pouring, her access to the kitchen was expanded, and she began to fix her own cereal. She also did so for her younger brother and felt competent about that, too. Before long, on the weekends, the parents would provide cereal, bowls, and spoons the night before, and the kids would provide breakfast for themselves in the morning, while the parents enjoyed some additional sleep. This exercise of competence was always greatly appreciated by the parents, and both children were insulted if a parent happened to stumble upon their early morning ritual uninvited. In this manner, the juice-pouring microtransition increased the complexity of our family.

In every family, there are myriad competent behaviors that must change as various family members grow and develop. As development necessitates higher levels of competence, the sequences regulating these behaviors change, creating microtransitions. These behaviors, however, are not automatically regulated at an appropriate level of competence. The microtransition may involve one of three outcomes: (1) The sequence may continue to regulate behavior at a pretransition level of competence, so that what may once have been an appropriate level becomes, with time, inappropriate; (2) the sequence may regulate behavior at a level of competence that exceeds what is appropriate; or (3) the sequence may regulate behavior at an appropriate level of competence. A microtransition, therefore, may result in a less than, greater than, or an appropriate level of competence for a particular behavior.

For example, as a child grows older, his or her competence with regard to safety should become increasingly complex. For a small child who has little competence, the parents rightly make most decisions, to the point of child-proofing the house. A 7-year-old, possessing more competence, should be allowed more decisions, for instance, deciding when it is safe to cross a street. Older adolescents should possess the competence to make complex decisions about safety in social situations, such as driving when dating. If a child is 7, and the parents continue to make all decisions about safety, the outcome of microtransitions regarding safety will produce less-than-competent behavior; on the other hand, if the parents allow the 7-year-old to enter into situations where an adolescent's level of competence about safety is required, the outcome is likely to be greater-than-competent behavior. As a third alternative, parents may correctly assess what safety decisions a 7-year-old can handle and thus regulate competence at an appropriate level.

When a microtransition results in a sequence that regulates competence behavior at a less-than-competent or a greater-than-competent level, the potential for an oscillation emerges. This potential is realized when a significant number of microtransitions produce a similar outcome and the oscillation becomes detectable. Detectable oscillations are most likely to occur at nodal transitions because of the large number of microtransitions clustered at such times, but they may also arise in response to other stresses such as chronic illness or evolve gradually over time as microtransitions fail to regulate behavior at the age-appropriate level of competence. The mother's multiple sclerosis in one of the earlier vignettes served as a trigger for sequences to regulate greater-than-competent behavior in her 12-year-old son.

An oscillation in the developmental curve dampens when sufficient microtransitions have outcomes that regulate competence at an appropriate level. This dampening process can occur over a long period. For example, early adolescence is marked by dramatic oscillations between the adolescent's acting like a young adult and his or her acting like a child. This oscillation may not dampen until well into adolescence.

The oscillation fails to dampen when the family stabilizes around it. In the first vignette, for example, the onset of the mother's illness, which occurred as the girl entered adolescence, resulted in an oscillation between the extremes of greater-than-competent caregiving and less-than-competent involvement with peers and school. This oscillation proved functional for the family and hence stabilized as part of the family's total pattern of interaction. It persisted through time, modified but not dampened, as successive microtransitions and nodal transitions occurred.

Although the terms "less-than-competent" and "greater-than-competent" are not commonly used in the literature and are a bit awkward, I have selected them because they are neutral and do not reflect a deficit-based view of behavior. Moreover, the terms, connected as they are to sequences, are context specific and therefore are not to be viewed as traits. If the sequences change, the level of competence will change.

Such terms as "immature," "developmentally delayed," or "regressed" suggest less-than-competent behavior, but they are not synonymous with this latter term because they generally refer to a presentation of self that is pervasive and not easily changed, whereas "less-than-competent behavior" refers to a context-specific act wherein an individual at a given age behaves as if he or she is less than competent because such a behavior is the logical outcome of the sequence by which it is regulated.

Although it is easy to see how a microtransition that results in less-than-competent behavior will adversely affect family development, one may rightfully question whether an outcome of greater-than-competent behavior is problematic. One may argue that there is no such thing as too much competence. Reading three grades above level is better than reading at grade level. I believe, however, that in symptomatic families, the identified patient almost always exhibits some behaviors that are too competent for his or her age. For example, a latchkey child who, at the age of 6, lets himself or herself into the house after school in order to allow a single parent to work longer hours is acting in a greater-than-competent way. Patricia Minuchin (1985) provides a useful example of how a behavior can be viewed as greater than competent:

> Developmental psychologists have documented the growth of empathy, altruism, and the ability to take another person's perspective with an implicit assumption that more is better. While this is an understandable assumption, the experience of family therapists (like that of Freudians) calls attention to the balance between concern for others and an awareness of one's own needs. The developmental psychologist sees an 11-year-old whose empathy and ability to take another perspective tests at a high level—and considers the child's development to be proceeding very well. The family therapist sees an 11-year-old who has a handkerchief in her mother's hand before the mother's first tear falls—and considers it important to move the child out of situations that should not be her concern, both for the good of her own development and the health of the husband–wife subsystem that has generated the tears and must settle its own issues. (p. 297)

In the field of family therapy, a number of concepts describe greater-than-competent behavior. The term "incongruous hierarchy" (Madanes, 1981) suggests that at one level a child is higher in the hierarchy than the parents. The "violation of a generational boundary" (Minuchin, 1974) suggests that a child is allowed to share inappropriately in the world of adults. Finally, the "function of a symptom" suggests that a behavior somehow serves to protect the family. Any time a child behaves in a symptomatic way in order to protect his or her family, that child is acting in a greater-than-competent manner.

Of course, in any pattern of oscillation, appropriate levels of competence can also be detected. These behaviors are quite important because they signal the potential for a family to negotiate microtransitions in a manner that does not produce permanent oscillations. These areas of appropriate competence point toward individual and family strengths and often serve as a starting point for dampening the oscillation.

Theoretically, it is possible that microtransitions result only in sequences regulating competence at one extreme or the other; however, my clinical experience suggests that this rarely happens. Even when a child presents with an apparently pervasive set of less-than-competent behaviors, the family has usually organized around these behaviors in a way that produces an incongruous hierarchy or that results in symptoms that serve a protective function. Hence greater-than-competent behavior is present.

When microtransitions consistently regulate behavior in the direction of greater-than-competent behavior, the individual usually compensates by finding ways in which to act less than competently or will exhibit a symptom that metaphorically expresses less-than-competent behavior. For instance, an adolescent who acts much older than her age may be enuretic. The following clinical vignette is a typical example of oscillation between extremes of less-than-competent and greater-than-competent behavior.

An 8-year-old boy, the eldest of three male siblings, was referred for evaluation to determine whether his aggressive behavior merited placement in a behavior disorders classroom. During an initial interview, his mother reported that she was unable to get any of the boys to act their ages. At home, she functioned like a slave to them, picking up their toys, tying their shoes, brushing their teeth, and sometimes dressing them. She also walked the 8-year-old to school and accompanied him to the park one block from home. Needless to say, these were all less-than-competent behaviors.

The mother also reported that the boy was very nosy and would always be found eavesdropping on parental conversations. Moreover, since the father worked two jobs and often arrived home late at night, the boy could usually be found sitting up, keeping his mother company. These were greater-than-competent behaviors. There existed, therefore, a clear oscillation, with the boy unable to put on his own shoes but able to share an adult world, where he protected his mother.

Clinical Application

It is beyond the scope of a theoretical chapter to address fully the clinical applications of oscillation theory. Nevertheless, to illustrate this vital component of the model, I will discuss briefly how oscillation theory translates into clinical practice. A more complete statement of clinical applications can be found elsewhere (Breunlin, 1989).

For any theory to be clinically applicable, it should guide the therapeutic process in three ways. It should (1) define the relevant information to be gathered in the assessment process, (2) provide a redefinition of the problem in interactional and solvable terms, and (3) suggest a plan of action for producing change.

Oscillation theory hypothesizes that a symptom arises as a result of the family's inability to regulate behavior at an appropriate level of competence. Instead, through the microtransition processes, sequences also regulate significant numbers of less-than-competent and greater-than-competent behaviors. The symptom may appear as a metaphor for the oscillation, as an attempted solution, or as a manifestation of one of its extremes.

The basic clinical hypothesis is quite simple: *Since a symptom is maintained by an oscillation, interventions must be targeted to dampen and eliminate the oscillation, thus restoring normal development and eliminating the symptom.*

The goal of assessment is to detect an oscillation in the developmental process. In my clinical experience, oscillations in families have been easily detected. The data consist of competence behaviors that, taken together, form a "clinical curve fit" equivalent to that shown in Figure 5-5f. At the therapist's disposal is an enormous wealth of immediate data obtained from observations made during sessions and from reports by family members on behaviors occurring outside of sessions. In the session, the therapist looks for short sequences regulating competence, behavioral indicators of competence, and metaphoric expressions of oscillations. Perhaps the most powerful and succinct evidence of an oscillation is conveyed through metaphor. For instance, a 10-year-old may be dressed like a teenager yet answer the therapist in a whining and insecure voice.

Information about the time of onset and the persistence of an oscillation is useful because it can orient the therapist to the severity of the problem and guide the choice of intervention. If the oscillation is of recent origin and is caused by the sequence-generating events of a nodal transition, or if it appears to involve a small number of competence-regulating sequences, the interventions may be quite straightforward. If, however, an oscillation has lasted for a number of years and has persisted through several nodal transitions as it did for 16 years for the woman in the first vignette, or if the number of competence-regulating sequences at the greater-than-competent and less-than-competent levels are many, then the problem is more severe and interventions must be carefully selected. Moreover, in such cases, the oscillations, having persisted for some time, give rise to real deficiencies in behavior competencies such as social skills and academic performance. For instance, an adolescent whose presenting problem is school related may have been placed in a behavior disorders class for so many years that language skills are several grades below level. Such an adolescent is often terrified at the prospect of having to function in a regular class. In such a case, the interventions must take into account that this child can't read and that he or she therefore fears having to function in a regular class.

Having detected an oscillation, the therapist confirms its existence by using the language of the family and then reframes the symptom as a manifestation of an oscillation. This type of developmental reframing has often been used by family therapists (Coppersmith, 1981; Minuchin & Fishman, 1981) and is now afforded theoretical backing by oscillation theory. The basic message is as follows: Your child's problem arises because he or she sometimes acts too old and sometimes too young. When he or she learns to act his or her age, the problem will be solved.

Once parents accept the problem redefinition, that the symptom is nothing more than their child's not acting his or her age, they can be included as part of the solution—therapy will help them find ways for their child to act his or her age (Breunlin & Cimmarusti, 1983). The therapist next targets interventions that will dampen the oscillation. Theoretically, the oscillations can be dampened by arresting either one of the extremes of competency behavior. Arresting one extreme sometimes eliminates the other, but in more severe oscillations, interventions must be targeted for both extremes. This is particularly the case when interventions target greater-than-competent behavior that serves a protective function—the identified patient may give up the primary symptom only to remain handicapped by less-than-competent behaviors. In the case of the 30-year-old woman who spent 16 years caring for her invalid mother, a systemic prescription may help the woman give up her 16-year task of caregiving only for her to face the reality that she dropped out of school years ago and lost all peer contact. Any treatment that does not address the associated less-than-competent behavior in this context is likely to fail. In fact, most treatment failures occur in cases in which chronic oscillations of this sort exist but are ignored.

Once the severity of the problem has been assessed in terms of the chronicity and intensity of the oscillation, four treatment options exist:

1. Increase the number of sequences that regulate competence at an appropriate level.
2. Make direct requests to the family to change sequences that regulate less-than-competent or greater-than-competent behavior.
3. Paradoxically encourage less-than-competent behaviors and/or their associated sequences.
4. Paradoxically encourage greater-than-competent behaviors and/or their associated sequences.

The option chosen depends somewhat on the initial assessment and on the preference of the therapist. Interventions selected from the models of family therapy may be appropriately used for a given option. Straightforward education and behavior modification work well for Option 1. Interventions drawn from structural family therapy (Minuchin, 1974; Minuchin & Fishman, 1981) and direct strategic interventions (Haley, 1976; Madanes, 1981) can be used for Option 2. Indirect techniques and paradoxical interventions are used for Option 3; defiance-based strategies (Rohrbaugh, Tennen, Press, & White, 1981) directed at less-than-competent behavior are particularly powerful. Finally, positive connotations and systemic prescriptions (Selvini-Palazzoli, Cecchin, Prata, & Boscolo, 1978) are effective interventions for use with Option 4.

Oscillation theory has several strengths that commend it for clinical application. First, it is derived from direct observation of family development and does not require, therefore, the juxtaposition of a separate theory to account for change. Second, oscillation theory possesses the flexibility to analyze development at the level of detail essential to formulating a useful clinical picture. Sometimes a simple metaphor is sufficient for defining the oscillation, whereas in other cases, considerable detail may be needed in order to obtain a clear clinical picture. Third, oscillation theory affords a coherent explanation for many of the inconsistencies often apparent in clinical families: They derive from oscillations between less-than-competent and greater-than-competent behavior. Fourth, oscillation theory draws a distinction between acute and chronic problems. Acute problems are associated with the recent onset of a detectable oscillation. Chronic problems are maintained by oscillations that have persisted for some time and generally through more than one nodal transition. Finally, oscillation theory can explain failure and relapse. Unless an oscillation is dampened successfully, symptoms may not remit, or they may remit only temporarily and return as a function of a recurrent oscillation.

CONCLUSIONS

At the outset of this chapter, I raised concerns that the concept of the FLC may never complete its own life cycle. By stagnating in the form of an underdeveloped stage–transition model, it was increasingly being bypassed in favor of the major therapy models. In this chapter, I have attempted to introduce conceptual refinement in order to add complexity to the FLC and to enhance its clinical relevance. Oscillation theory provides a pathway for this endeavor.

As with any developing theory, oscillation theory still requires further conceptual refinement. At this point in the development of the theory, I am expressing family development as a function of individual competence. Oscillation theory, when applied to the identified patient, is clinically relevant because it provides a blueprint for devising interventions to address symptoms. But family development includes the competence of all family members. As an intermediate step, one could plot a curve for each family member and examine the relationship of the curves to each other. The complementarity of relating at specific moments in time and across time may become more apparent. Synchronous and dissynchronous oscillations may reveal patterns of symptom formation and maintenance. For example, during their early years of marriage, a couple may exhibit curves wherein one spouse shows greater-than-competent behavior and the other, less-than-competent behavior. In the final analysis, it would be desirable to translate the individual curves into one curve that expresses family competence. But we are a long way from an outcome in which family competence can be operationalized.

Another concern is how oscillation theory applies to later life. In this chapter, I have used examples of family development during the child-rearing years, a time when the development curve is positive and competence is becoming increasingly complex. The question may be raised, what shape does the developmental curve take in later life? How are we to define competence? What constitutes an oscillation? Oscillation theory still applies but may require a different framing. Whereas in the early years, societal values are such that younger is bad and older is good, in the later years, these values are reversed, and younger is good and older is bad.

Senior citizens have to develop the competence to be old, but when competence-regulating sequences fail to allow for this, oscillations may occur, only in reverse. For example, a grandmother who continues to function as a mother may be viewed as being engaged in less-than-competent behavior. Or in another family, some members may be unable to accept the illness of an elderly person. When this occurs, family sequences prevent that elderly person from developing the competence needed to face illness and ultimately death.

REFERENCES

Ackerman, N. W. (1966). *Treating the troubled family.* New York: Basic Books.

Bateson, G., Jackson, D., Haley, J., & Weakland, J. (1956). Toward a theory of schizophrenia. *Behavioral Science, 1,* 251–264.

Breunlin, D. C. (1981, March). *The family life cycle.* With C. Falicov, D. Schnitman, L. Hoffman, C. Sluzki, D. Breunlin, & M. McGoldrick. Panel conducted at the meeting of the American Orthopsychiatry Association, New York.

Breunlin, D. C. (1982). *Clinical dimensions of the family life cycle.* Paper presented at the meeting of the American Association for Marriage and Family Therapy, Dallas.

Breunlin, D. C. (1983). Therapy in stages: A life cycle view. In H. A. Liddle (Ed.), *Clinical implications of the family life cycle.* (pp. 2–11). Rockville, MD: Aspen.

Breunlin, D. C. (1989). Clinical applications of oscillation theory. In C. Ramsey (Ed.), *The science of family medicine.* New York: Guilford Press.

Breunlin, D. C., & Cimmarusti, R. (1983). Seven opportunities for brief therapy: A recipe for rapid change. In M. Aronson & L. Wolberg (Eds.), *Group and family therapy, 1983.* New York: Brunner/Mazel.

Breunlin, D. C., & Schwartz, R. C. (1986). Sequences: Toward a common denominator of family therapy. *Family Process, 25,* 67–87.

Carter, E. A., & McGoldrick, M. (Eds.). (1980). *The family life cycle: A framework for family therapy.* New York: Gardner Press.

Coppersmith, E. I. (1981). Developmental reframing: He's not bad, he's not mad, he's just young. *Journal of Strategic and Systemic Therapies. 1,* 1–7.

Dell, P. (1982). Beyond homeostasis: Toward a concept of coherence. *Family Process, 21,* 21–41.

Duvall, E. (1977). *Marriage and family development* (5th ed.). Philadelphia: J. B. Lippincott.

Falicov, C. (1984). Commentary: Focus on stages. *Family Process, 23,* 329–333.

Fisch, R. (1983). Commentary to contrasting strategic and Milan therapies. *Family Process, 22,* 438–440.

Haley, J. (1973). *Uncommon therapy: The psychiatric techniques of Milton H. Erickson, M.D.* New York: W. W. Norton.

Haley, J. (1976). *Problem-solving therapy.* San Francisco: Jossey-Bass.

Hoffman, L. (1981, March). *The family life cycle.* With C. Falicov, D. Schnitman, L. Hoffman, C. Sluzki, D. Breunlin, & M. McGoldrick. Panel conducted at the meeting of the American Orthopsychiatry Association, New York.

Hughes, S., Berger, M., & Wright, L. (1978). The family life cycle and clinical intervention. *Journal of Marriage and Family Counseling, 4,* 33–40.

Liddle, H. A., & Saba, G. (1983). Clinical uses of the family life cycle: Some cautionary guidelines. In H. A. Liddle (Ed.), *Clinical implications of the family life cycle* (pp. 161–176). Rockville, MD: Aspen.

Madanes, C. (1981). *Strategic family therapy.* San Francisco: Jossey-Bass.

Minuchin, P. (1985). Families and individual development: Provocations from the field of family therapy. *Child Development, 56,* 289–302.

Minuchin, S. (1974). *Families and family therapy.* Cambridge, MA: Harvard University Press.

Minuchin, S., & Fishman, C. (1981). *Family therapy techniques.* Cambridge, MA: Harvard University Press.

Rohrbaugh, M., Tennen, H., Press, S., & White, L. (1981). Compliance, defiance and therapeutic paradox: Guidelines for strategic use of paradoxical interventions. *American Journal of Orthopsychiatry, 51,* 454–467.

Selvini-Palazzoli, M., Cecchin, G., Prata, G., & Boscolo, L. (1978). *Paradox and counterparadox.* New York: Jason Aronson.

Sluzki, C. (1983). Process, structure and world views: Toward an integrated view of systemic models in family therapy. *Family Process, 22,* 469–476.

Terkelson, K. (1980). Toward a theory of the family life cycle. In E. A. Carter & M. McGoldrick (Eds.), *The family life cycle: A framework for family therapy* (pp. 21–52). New York: Gardner Press.

Watzlawick, P., Weakland, J., & Fisch, R. (1974). *Change: Principles of problem formation and problem resolution.* New York: W. W. Norton.

Weeks, G. R., & Wright, L. (1979). Dialectics of the family life cycle. *American Journal of Family Therapy, 7,* 85–91.

Wynne, L. C. (1985). The epigenesis of relational systems: A model for understanding family development. *Family Process, 23,* 297–318.

PART TWO

PERSPECTIVES ON FAMILY DEVELOPMENT

6

Individual Change and Family Development: Individuation as a Family Process

ESTER R. SHAPIRO
Cambridge Hospital, Harvard Medical School

The study of family development requires theory capable of articulating and choreographing four kinds of motion in the developmental history of the family: (1) the movement of each individual—adult and child—through his or her unique life cycle; (2) the interaction of these life cycles at a given moment of the family history; (3) the developmental motion of this interacting family organization through the family life cycle; and (4) the interweaving of intergenerational family life cycles, since the young parent in a family of procreation is at the same time an offspring in a maturing family of origin. At all times in the course of family development, there is an interrelationship between individual, systemic, and intergenerational lines of development.

In this chapter, an integrative theory of family development will be proposed that expands existing family sociology and family systems theories primarily based on stages of the family life cycle (Carter & McGoldrick, 1980; Duvall, 1977; Haley, 1973; Hill, 1970; Rodgers, 1973). It will be argued that both stage and process concepts are required for the full study of family development as the interrelationship of multiple individual and family life cycles. The concept of individuation will be discussed as a means of integrating individual life-span, interpersonal, and systemic theories in the study of family development. The usefulness of family life cycle stages can be expanded by studying the developmental process of individuation during family life cycle transitions.

INTEGRATING STAGE AND PROCESS IN FAMILY DEVELOPMENT

The study of family development can be advanced by the use of both stage and process theories of development. (For a discussion of stage and process theories of individual and family development, see Chapter 1.)

159

The study of the stages of development in the family life cycle has provided the major organizational scheme for understanding family development. The family therapy and life-span psychoanalytic writings on individuation can provide a crucial process concept with which transitions in the family life cycle can be more closely examined.

In the psychoanalytic developmental literature (Blos, 1962; Jung, 1933; Loevinger, 1976; Mahler, Pine, & Bergman, 1975; Searles, 1979), "individuation" describes the evolving definition of self in relation to others, from the infant's first recognition of body boundaries in relation to the mother's body, through the adolescent's initial definition of identity in relation to the parents, through adult experiences requiring reassessment of identity within relationships. Psychoanalytic theory of individuation emphasizes the individual's increasing separation of self from others and tends to equate successful individuation with separation. However, recent psychoanalytic writings emphasize the balance between autonomy and intimacy in development throughout life (Lewis, 1974).

Family systems theories of individuation (Boszormenyi-Nagy and Spark, 1973; Bowen, 1972; Karpel, 1976; Stierlin, 1969) also focus on the boundary between self and others but view individuation as an interpersonal process involving the family as a unit. The family systems literature has emphasized the contrast between differentiated families, with good boundaries between self and others, and undifferentiated, or "enmeshed," families, with diffuse boundaries and confusion between self and others.

Individuation theory is most useful in the study of family development when it is applied as a life-span developmental and systemic concept. Individuation theory as applied in this chapter assumes that all persons exist in relationships and that the self is interpersonally established, maintained, developmentally modified, and reorganized through transactions in family relationships throughout the family life cycle.

Family life cycle transitions, by their very definition, involve reciprocal, interdependent changes in close others. From the family developmental point of view, individual identity is delineated within close relationships, so that changes in relationships require reorganization of the self. In turn, the interpersonal self will be redefined and reintegrated in the process of adapting to family changes during family life cycle transitions. As suggested by Werner's organismic developmental theory (1948), the view of self within relationships will become increasingly more articulated and organized with maturation and with the integration of new information from new situations.

Riegel's dialectical developmental theory (1976) further suggests, in agreement with clinical theories of individuation, that the impetus for growth is provided by discordant information that has to be organized into meaningful patterns. Systems theory adds the important perspective that these individual transformations take place in mutual exchange within the family system, so that change in self requires change in others, and change in others requires change in self.

Although theories of normal development are useful in understanding individuation and family development, it is important for clinicians to know what developmental processes lead to pathological individuation. That is, what circumstances lead family members to respond to shared change with defensive or growth-restricting responses, and what family circumstances facilitate growth-expanding responses? With these questions in mind, let us turn to those theories of individuation in child and adult development that address the cognitive and emotional processes involved in families' responses to developmental challenges.

INDIVIDUATION AS A FAMILY PROCESS

To integrate family life cycle and individuation theories in family development, it is helpful to explore the concept of individuation as it appears in the life-span developmental literature. The organization of this section of the chapter follows Werner's organismic theory. At this early point in our understanding of family development, it is necessary to articulate the functioning of component parts within the whole family system. Toward this end of articulation and hierarchical integration, I will review selected theories of individuation in childhood, in adulthood, in parenthood, and in the family system. In each section, I will explore the systemic implications of the individual theories and the interrelationship among individual, interpersonal, and systemic components of family development.

Individuation in Childhood

Family therapists have most often treated and studied families in which the family process of defining autonomous individual identities within intimate relationships has gone wrong. An individual's attempts at spontaneous, independent action are experienced as threats to the family's cohesive self-definition and thus are systematically restricted.

Child development theories of the self–other differentiation process, especially the psychoanalytic work of Mahler (1979; Mahler *et al.,* 1975) and the cognitive developmental research of Piaget (1954; Piaget & Inhelder, 1969), can deepen the understanding of individuation in the family system. According to both Mahler and Piaget, we are born with an undifferentiated sense of the physical boundaries between self and others. Mahler and her co-workers (1975) have used the phrase "the psychological birth of the infant" to describe the gradual emergence, during the first year of life, of the awareness of self and others as having separate physical boundaries. In a complementary work on infant development, Piaget (1954) used the phrase "the child's construction of reality" to describe the cognitive process by which the infant discovers the principles of science in the real world: that people and physical objects have constancy beyond the infant's perception or action, that objects are governed by laws of causal, temporal, and spatial organization.

It is interesting to note that while cognitive and psychoanalytic descriptions of infant development are clearly describing the same developmental time period for the same infant, the emphases are quite distinct. Piaget describes the infant as creative scientist, systematically and enthusiastically investigating, through complex hypothesis testing, the laws of the physical world. Mahler and her colleagues tend to focus on the anguish of the infant's realization (at the developmental point when the cognitive realization of separate body boundaries becomes possible) that mother is a separate being and therefore capable of abandonment. The child's elation at cognitive exploration and mastery is accompanied by the painful loss of the illusion of omnipotent control from earlier infancy.

What are the implications of these analyses of early child development for the understanding of family development? The awareness of body boundary seems to be a fundamental and profound learning of infancy, which takes place in the developmental context of both excitement in the discovery of new perceptions and anguish in the awareness of interpersonal vulnerabilities. If finding new truths means facing the possibility of abandonment, it requires a love of new truths to face the anxiety of separation accompanying learning.

That growth simultaneously involves the gain of the new along with the loss of the old is an extremely important dimension of the process of development. From the time that the child first becomes capable of distinguishing self and other, she or he begins a process of negotiating a balance between the need for autonomous exploration and mastery of the environment and the need for reassurance that the safety of close relationships will be sustained. Mahler (1979) observes that the mother's own developmental capacity for responsiveness to the toddler's complex balance of needs is crucial for the child's integration of self as separate from, yet connected to, the mother. Typical of the psychoanalytic developmental literature, the mother is seen as providing a context or holding environment for the child's growth that is either good enough or not good enough. In expanding this point of view to a systemic developmental theory, it becomes necessary to understand the developmental experience of the caregiver and the transactions in the family that best support mutual learning and mutually responsive change.

Piaget (1954) offers another concept in cognitive development that can be applied to understanding family development. According to Piaget, the progression from the stages of sensorimotor development in infancy to the fully developed capacity for abstract reasoning of adulthood is fueled by the processes of assimilation and accommodation. In assimilation, the child perceives information and fits it in with an already existing "schema," or concept. That is, the information is matched to and made to fit an already explored and familiar category of action or thought. In accommodation, the child encounters new information that does not fit any existing categories and modifies an existing "schema" so that a new category of thought is created.

The recognition and integration of new information causes a change in the child's existing categories of cognitive organization. For example, in early infancy, the child develops the schema "things to be sucked" and applies that schema to a diverse range of objects he or she encounters in the environment. With cognitive and motoric development, the child will encounter objects that will not readily fit the schema for sucking but that will best be handled as "things to be banged on the floor." According to Piaget, children will ignore objects that are too novel or complex for them to integrate into an existing schema. Rather, children are most curious about objects that are at the same time somewhat familiar and somewhat novel, in this way gravitating toward opportunities to expand their cognitive development.

Although Piaget did not intend the concepts of assimilation and accommodation to be applied beyond the understanding of childhood cognition, they provide a useful model for understanding family reactions to change. As was noted earlier, the definition of the self is an interpersonal one, so that changes in any member of the family require reorganization of the self for all family members. Within the family, the constantly changing adults and children will relentlessly present to each other new information, new ways of understanding the self or of being with others, which require response from others. Family members can respond with an "accommodating" change in their schema for self-with-other or with an "assimilating" change in the new information, to make it fit already existing, familiar categories of thought and response.

There is one important difference between the process of cognitive learning as described by Piaget and the process of interpersonal learning experienced in family development: Whereas exploration of the physical world lends itself to a great deal of control over the information encountered, the interpersonal world presents fewer opportunities for control over the environment. When the new information is provided by the differentiating moves of a family member, the other family members are forced to respond, either with accommodating changes in self or with assimilating attempts to change the other, so that these disquieting differentiating moves will cease.

For example, the mothers described in Mahler *et al.*'s (1975) infant observations were viewed critically when they failed to respond flexibly to their toddlers' increasing independence. Yet these mothers had just established a hard-won sense of competence during the difficult period of learning to care for a totally dependent infant, and they may not have been altogether ready to change their schema "self-as-mother-to-dependent-child" to the new "self-as-mother-to-a-still-dependent-child-who-wants-to-be-master-of-his-own-universe." The mother, too, was balancing the familiar with the novel in her development of self-as-mother. Gradually, with adequate support from others, a mother will shift from "assimilation" of her child's behavior and of her own response as self-as-mother-of-newborn to "accommodation," with the creation of a new view of the child's increasing independence and of a corresponding definition of self-as-mother-of-toddler.

As can be seen in the preceding example, the response of accommodation requires a redefinition of the individual's sense of self and a full perception of difference in others. The response of assimilation can be developmentally appropriate in circumstances involving relatively little family change. However, in circumstances involving rapid family change, such as when a child enters nursery school or reaches puberty, the response of assimilation can be problematic, since it involves denial of change in others. A climate of safety, a sense of personal competence, and the experience of some control over one's environment are necessary in order for individuals to learn from their experiences. When family members feel fragile or overwhelmed, they are more likely to distort their perceptions of other family members and are less likely to respond flexibly to changes in others with corresponding changes in themselves.

Over the course of family development, it is largely the parent's responsibility to integrate new information about a changing child into a new definition of self as parent who responds to the child in novel and appropriate ways. It becomes important, then, to understand the process of individuation of self in the adult years.

Individuation in Adulthood

The process of individuation in adulthood has been discussed by Jung (1933). His clinical description of adult growth has been supported by much of the recent research and writing on adult development (Levinson, 1978; Lowenthal, Thurnher, & Chiriboga, 1975; Neugarten, 1968). Jung articulated a few provocative themes in the development of consciousness from childhood through youth to middle and old age. According to Jung, the adolescent takes the crucial step from childhood to youth by giving up "monarchic," or self-centered, consciousness for a dualistic consciousness. Children experience external limitations that oppose their subjective impulses, but these conflicts are viewed by the child as being exclusively between self and others. In attaining dualistic consciousness, the youth becomes aware not only of the division of self from others but also of the divisions within the self. In Jung's view, the inner tension experienced when one desire or impulse internally opposes another is possible only with the advanced consciousness of youth.

The dualistic consciousness of youth results in self-doubts as well as expanded horizons. Jung describes the wish to avoid the consciousness of the divided self and the realities of one's own limitations as a major problem during youth. Jung adds that the process of fully exploring and integrating internal opposing forces is extremely difficult and is unrewarded by society, so that the typical young person makes socially prescribed choices at the expense of the potential expansion of the self. He believes that in midlife, these ignored aspects of the self, often consisting of opposite-sex characteristics, are once again available for exploration.

According to Jung, then, the turbulence of adolescence is resolved by the constriction of potential avenues of development through which personal equilibrium is gained. The adult's greater feeling of security and greater tolerance of complexity will permit the reemergence and the more complete exploration of previously denied aspects of the self, which can then be more fully integrated into the adult personality.

Jung's theory of adult development can be usefully expanded through a family developmental perspective. The young adult's resolution of internal conflict through the acquisition of socially stereotyped roles takes place within the family developmental context of the launching from the family of origin and the establishment of a new family. Typically, limitations are placed on aspects of the self as a result of making a choice about one's life's work, getting married, and having children.

Research in adult development has supported Jung's theory of individuation in that researchers have found that opposite-sex characteristics increase in midlife (Lowenthal *et al.,* 1975; Livson, 1976; Neugarten, 1968). Guttman (1975) suggests that the key to this process of sex-role change in adulthood lies in the closer study of parenting. Guttman (1975) and other researchers propose that sex-role stereotyping in adulthood varies with the stage of the family life cycle rather than with chronological age (Abrahams, Feldman, & Nash, 1978; Feldman, Bivingen, & Nash, 1981). From a family systems point of view, relationships with developing children in the family challenge adults' established self-definitions and evoke changing responses in the adults over the family life cycle.

Individuation in Parenthood

The study of parenting as an adult developmental process is a neglected area that could greatly benefit from the influence of a family interactional point of view. Rossi (1968) noted that the study of mother–infant relationships has focused entirely on the needs of the child and has not addressed the changes that women experience when they take on the maternal role. With some exceptions (Falicov, 1971; Shapiro, 1985), it is difficult for most theorists and researchers to suspend a focus on the child and examine family experience from the point of view of adult needs and adult adjustment.

The choice of parenting is made at a time when young adults make a commitment to settle down, limit choices, and focus awareness on restricted aspects of the self. Yet paradoxically, after the birth of children, adults confront unacknowledged aspects of themselves in their developing children. From earliest infancy, children present their parents with intensely emotional situations. If the emotions are overwhelming for the adults, they may recruit their children to help them cope with family living and relating.

A child's new behavior may arouse conflict in a parent because it reflects an unresolved conflict in the parent's own life. For example, a parent who was a dependent or an obedient child while growing up may easily identify with a compliant latency-age child and then have terrible difficulty dealing with the emergence of the child's rebellious independence in early adolescence. Under these developmental circumstances, the parent, in order to respond to the child's growing independence, must honestly self-examine his or her own growing-up experience and life choices.

At certain developmental stages, the child is less aware of or less concerned with parental distortions of the child's character or behavior, as long as these distortions are not severe. Of course, every clinician has observed families—even those with very young children—in which the child's development is affected by parental projections (Fraiberg, 1980). For most families, though, these parental projections do not lead to either conscious protest or unconscious symptom formation on the part of the children. In adolescence, when a child is developing a more articulated sense of self-as-separate-from-parents and is preparing to function in the world independently of parents, even minor parental distortions and projections are experienced by the adolescent as compromising the integrity of an emerging personal identity.

The negotiation of change during family life cycle transitions requires that adults confront the discrepancies between themselves in the past, as children with their parents, and themselves in the present, as parents to their children. The adult's successful confrontation of the differences between historical, internalized family-of-origin relationships and present family relationships furthers the development of a more autonomous adult self, which is more highly differentiated within family-of-origin relationships.

Family development provides adults with the opportunity to accomplish in living what is attempted in both individual and family therapy: differentiation of self within three generations of ongoing family relationships. Most adults are aware that their childhood perceptions of their own parents change and become more complex as they experience life with their own children. The grandparents, in turn, have typically matured through the course of their own family life cycle, so that they are often capable of greater self-awareness and responsiveness as their children become adults and as they are relieved of the more acute pressures of family responsibility. Individuated adults are capable of recognizing these changes in their own parents and of relating to their parents flexibly in a way that differentiates past from present. The maturation of family-of-origin relationships enhances, in turn, the adult's capacity to relate flexibly to his or her spouse and children.

However, family life seldom takes place under the best of circumstances, and parents may, for a variety of reasons, feel too stressed to respond to changes in the family with flexible change in self. Identification with the family of origin, especially at a time of stressful family change, provides some of the continuity and stability that is prerequisite for flexible change. Confronting too much discrepancy between self-as-child in the family of origin and self-as-parent-with-child in the family of procreation may prove too disequilibrating under stress. The adult may then attempt to restrict directions of development in the child, because acknowledging and responding to the child's changes will bring into awareness aspects of the adult's self in relation to the family of origin that cannot be acknowledged or examined.

In undifferentiated families, the child is seen not as himself or herself but as an extension of parental self-definitions established in the parent's family of origin and elaborated in the early stages of the couple's courtship and marriage. In fact, the main goal of family therapy with a symptomatic family often is to extricate the parents from their focus on a symptomatic child and to explore those difficulties in the marital relationship and in family-of-origin relationships that are defensively avoided by this focus on the child. The confusion of the child's needs and the parent's needs protects the parent from painful self-awareness but restricts the parent's awareness of his or her current reality as an adult with a child.

New parents realistically find the work of caring for children extremely self-sacrificing, yet experienced parents will report that the more they are able to take care of themselves and be fully aware of their own needs and limits, the more capable they are of responding to their children (Shapiro, 1985). The simultaneous examination of parents' and childrens' needs and experiences can add enormously to an understanding of family development.

Individuation in the Family System

Development from childhood to adulthood involves a recurring process of individuation. "Individuation" means the definition of self in relation to others, from the infant's first recognition of body boundaries in relation to the mother's body, through the adolescent's initial definition of identity in relation to the parents, and through the major and minor adult experiences that require reassessment of identity within relationships. Family intimacy requires readiness and generosity on the part of family members, who will willingly or reluctantly have to grow as other family members move towards growth. Clearly, the simultaneous readiness to respond fully to changes in self and in others that is required by family development is often difficult to achieve.

While the maturation of children is a major source of family change, it is not the sole source of family development. The developmental stage of the parents in relation to their families of origin, their personal formation of identity, and their marriage will interact with the child's developmental stage in determining the family's readiness to experience the stressful, disorienting nature of family transitions. External and social circumstances may also present family members with situations that require changes in relationships. Most families experience changes to which the entire family must adapt—for example, illness, an untimely death, changes in economic circumstances, or moves to another community.

Individuation theory, applied in this chapter as an interdisciplinary, interpersonal, life-span developmental theory, helps us to examine the processes of family transition. Individuation theory implicitly describes two fundamental dualities in family development: the simultaneous need for both continuity and change, and the simultaneous need for both intimacy and independence. The belief that autonomy and mastery require the loss of close relationships holds power both in families and, too often, in the disciplines that study families. There seems to be an optimal balance between exploration of the novel and preservation of the securely familiar—a balance that is age and situation appropriate and that is more likely to lead to a growth-producing rather than a growth-restricting response to new interpersonal situations.

The line between a growth-producing and a growth-restricting response to change is not always clear. Responses to new situations may be adaptively focusing or inflexibly restrictive, and a previously adaptive response that has been maintained can become inappropriate in a new situation. In Piaget's model of cognitive growth through assimilation and accommodation, the child elaborates a schema by taking interest in objects that are discrepant enough from existing schemas to attract attention and by avoiding objects that are so discrepant that they cannot be processed or integrated.

The adult's recognition of internal conflict is often controlled by reliance on reassuring, if limiting, personal and cultural stereotypes. Family life cycle transitions are challenging because they create discontinuity of identity within relationships. The greater the stress experienced in a developmental transition, the more desperate the need for a reassuring solution to cling to.

Choosing traditional roles and familiar rules for living can protect the adult from confrontation only for a while; eventually, these roles and rules must be gradually adjusted, so that new experience can be incorporated into a new definition of self. Situations involving high anxiety or overwhelming emotion will often produce a defensive response. This implies that in periods of very high stress, persons will more likely use older, more familiar responses, even if these previously learned responses are not appropriate to the present situation.

In normal family development, growth involves both the loss of old patterns of relating and the gain of new learning. In most families, there is more promise of gain than of loss in the process of development, and for each family member, there is enough differentiation between self and other family members that the growth of the others is not experienced as a threat to the organization of the self. When the growth of others is experienced as a threat to the self, such growth must then be controlled so that the personal self can survive.

Dysfunctional families, such as the "enmeshed" or "schizophrenogenic" families, have failed in their shared process of individuation. The healthy, necessary balance between exploring the new and maintaining the safety of the familiar has been lost, with a shift to maintaining the familiar at all costs. Paradoxically, family patterns that were once meant to preserve equilibrium now make growth impossible through rigid maintenance of the existing state.

Most often, families are able to tolerate the ordinary transitions in the family life cycle and to negotiate the periods of discontinuity with at least some flexibility and mutual responsiveness. If parents find their children out of control, or if children find their parents rigid, the generations within the family can support and sympathize with each other. For example, parents can turn to one another in the difficult job of raising their child, or grandparents might remind parents that they, too, passed through a phase when they were difficult; siblings can commiserate about being children of these particular parents. Further, most families have access to a community network of social resources, which can provide the means for regaining perspective and gaining support for the continuing process of change.

Families require intervention by mental health professionals when the mutual learning from changing relationships has failed. In such cases, response that was initially meant to maintain equilibrium so that growth could continue has become inappropriate to a changing situation. Children, especially adolescents, are notorious for their capacity to challenge adult rigidity with sometimes escalating interactional confrontations.

Clearly, families provide simultaneously the opportunity for dramatic creativity and growth and the opportunity for equally dramatic constriction and psychopathology. A family developmental theory can provide a comprehensive framework for understanding the developmental experiences of ordinary families as well as the experiences of families who enter therapy. Such a theory can also enable therapists to formulate therapeutic interventions that allow families to resume their development in a growth-expanding rather than a growth-constricting way.

SEIZING THE DEVELOPMENTAL MOMENT: THE CASE OF THE CLARK FAMILY

The Clarks can provide an illustration of a family and couples therapy in which a family developmental view provided the crucial framework for understanding the case and formulating the interventions.

The Clarks were a family of eight: Ed, 46, a laboratory technician; Lynn, 44, an intensive care nurse; Ted, 23, who was diagnosed as schizophrenic and was living in a nearby halfway house; Susan, 22, who had just completed nursing school and was living in a nearby city; Peter, 20, Jeff, 18, Steve, 15, and Joan, 10, all of whom were living at home.

The Clarks had made extensive rounds of the mental health system in their community because of problems with Ted and Jeff. When Ed scheduled their first interview at our community clinic, requesting family therapy, they were making a return visit to the clinic where 8 years earlier they had brought Ted, then 15, and Jeff, then 10, for individual child therapy. By the time I met the Clarks, Ted had been diagnosed as schizophrenic and was a veteran of numerous inpatient hospitalizations and of life in local halfway houses.

Mr. and Mrs. Clark appeared for the first family therapy session with Ted, Jeff, and Joan. Ed explained the absence of the three other children: Susan had just graduated from nursing school and was living away from home, or else she probably would have attended; Peter and Steve were irresponsible, out-of-control teenagers, and they would never do anything for the family at all.

The dramatic division of the Clark family along gender lines was apparent immediately: The two girls were seen as helpful, successful members of the family, whereas the four boys were described as showing a variety of serious symptoms. Ted entered adolescence with rebellious anger, which he initially expressed through delinquency, although later in adolescence, he became increasingly bizarre and delusional in his thinking. At the same time that Ted was having serious problems in early adolescence, Jeff was also showing serious trouble. From the age of 5, he would sneak into his mother's or sister's bedrooms and put on their clothes. He was a withdrawn boy who preferred isolative games, especially feminine ones. Peter and Steve were described as having problems with delinquency, and they had had school and occasional police problems as well as constant feuds with their father.

Ed explained that Ted, Jeff, Peter, and Steve were very angry with their parents, that you couldn't rub any of them very hard before they would explode. The trigger that got Ed very angry was money and work; Jeff and Peter had finally gotten jobs, but that didn't make any difference to him; the problems were still the same. In talking about his sons, Ed demonstrated the derisive, combative style that characterized his treatment of them since early childhood. After Ed's impassioned statement, Lynn, the mother, commented flatly that she thought they were coming in for couple's therapy, that there were severe problems in the marriage, and that they had already focused on the children's problems far too much and perhaps destructively. Ted offered that he was already in therapy elsewhere, although he did spend a great deal of time at home. Jeff said he had no desire to work on family problems at this point in his life. The family agreed that since the children were so reluctant to come for family sessions, and since the marriage was clearly in trouble, they would continue in couple's therapy and call the family in as needed. It emerged at the end of the first session that the couple had already agreed that they needed couple's therapy, but that Ed had made one final attempt to place his sons between him and his wife.

From the initial family session, it seemed that the Clarks were at a point of greater developmental readiness for therapeutic work than they had been in their earlier attempts to get help. That their youngest son was entering early adolescence and was showing the same problems their oldest son had shown prior to the onset of severe disturbance made the couple realize that their family tragedy could potentially be repeated. At this point in the family life cycle, the youngest child, Joan, was now 10 and was becoming far more independent. Ed and Lynn were entering middle age and were feeling discouraged that their marital and personal lives were so unrewarding. Because in reality they had fewer childcare burdens, and because they had reached a point of greater emotional maturity, the Clarks engaged in a family developmental therapeutic process in a surprisingly productive way.

The Clarks initially presented as an extremely fused and communications-disordered pair. They immediately identified their main marital problem as one of dominance, establishing who is boss. Yet it was agonizingly difficult for them to proceed further. Whenever either brought up a direct complaint about the other, the other would typically agree and then withdraw, in this way disqualifying the attempt at confrontation. Whenever one of them seemed at all available for a genuine, emotional discussion of an event, the other distanced by disappearing or else shifting the discussion to a problem with a child so that they could fight. If all else failed, one or the other would interrupt the discussion by turning to me and complaining that the therapy couldn't possibly get them anywhere.

The couple's communication disorder, designed to enable them to avoid conflict, maintained their perceptions of themselves and of one another in static, undifferentiated ways which were impervious to change. As unhappy as they were with the state of their lives, they so feared what they might learn about themselves that they colluded in failing to listen to any messages from each other that might force them to see themselves within the relationship in a new light. Frequent confrontation with their communicational evasions enabled Ed and Lynn to engage directly in previously avoided conflict. They were able for the first time to listen to the other's point of view in ways that enhanced their sense of a unique, articulated self responding sympathetically to the other.

Ed did a great deal of the talking in the initial sessions. He complained that Lynn had forced him to have the six children; after Ted was born, he wanted to go back to school to get a doctorate in biology. He accused Lynn of getting pregnant with Susan behind his back and then following with the four other unwanted pregnancies. The youngest child, Joan, was born when Ed was awarded a prestigious fellowship to fund his doctoral dissertation research; shortly after that, Ted and Jeff began to show serious psychological problems. Ed never completed his degree and continued to work as a lab technician in the same laboratory where he had been an outstanding doctoral student 7 years earlier. Ed described his work as essentially janitorial and was self-derisive about this decline in his career aspirations.

Ed complained that Lynn had conceived this brood of children and had then avoided him and them by working the night shift at the intensive care unit, so that he had had to bring them up instead of concentrating on his work. He felt like a middle-aged housewife whose children were growing up and who had nothing to show for her work. Surprisingly, Lynn accepted the blame for conceiving the children against Ed's wishes and his criticism of her as an inadequate mother.

Lynn assumed that Ed couldn't respond to her needs and insisted on maintaining her family position of Rock of Gibraltar. Her mother, too, had been an extremely strong woman married to a weak man, and neither parent had ever been responsive to her needs. She was an only child and described her experience of growing up in her family as intensely lonely. At the beginning of their marriage, she had hoped that married life would provide her with some of the sense of loving intimacy she had longed for, but after Ted was born and Ed began having problems handling family life and career, she assumed that these wishes were not to be satisfied. She became resigned to the care of her babies and the care of her extremely sick patients in the intensive care unit. Over time, it became clearer just how vigorously she fended off any attempts at sympathetic relating to her needs because she became furious at me for encouraging her to talk more about herself.

Lynn's unwillingness to confront Ed about his attacks of her, which she saw as protective, was eventually redefined as her unwillingness to give up the role of martyr and acknowledge her own confusions and needs. So much did she need to keep the disturbances located in her husband that she even stood by in silence while he acted in painfully destructive ways toward their sons. At a time in his life when Ed was feeling inadequate about his own abilities as a man, he constantly criticized their sons, whom he saw as extensions of himself. Although Lynn saw his criticism undermining the boys' self-esteem, she did not challenge Ed directly.

As the couple's work proceeded, Ted and Steve began to have escalating difficulties, and a series of family sessions were called. For the first of these, the couple came with five of the six children: Ted, Susan, Peter, Jeff, and Joan. Ed entered complaining that they had waited for Steve as long as possible but that Steve, as usual, could not be depended on for anything and had failed to show up. The other children proposed that maybe Steve had simply been late and might make his way there on his own, but Ed denied that any such thing was possible with the irresponsible Steve. The family then started to talk about the father's focus on the children's, especially the boys', problems and failings. Ed responded by stating that he had carried the brunt of the family burden over the years, and he asked the children to tell him who had cared more for them, he or their mother. Susan stated that the family burden had been her father's job failure; Jeff added that the family burden had been his father's focus on him and his brothers and their problems; Ted, for the first time, talked psychotically and said he was thinking about suicide, or what if his father died.

At that point in the session, Steve made a dramatic entry into the therapy room, flushed and out of breath. He had gotten the appointment time confused and had arrived at the house after his parents had left. As soon as he had realized his error, he had hitchhiked over to the clinic. His siblings cheered him, while his father was shocked by the visible enactment of the interaction his older children had been in the process of confronting him with. Steve's action enabled us to process in very concrete terms the interactional process in which Ed projected his feelings of inadequacy as a man onto his sons, as a means of avoiding this painful self-awareness of his own failures.

This incident in particular seemed to illustrate the enormous power of a developmental moment in which a parent was capable of seeing a child's behavior in a new way, different from the parent's distorting, self-protective projections about the child. Ed's moment of real "accommodation" to the reality of Steve's capacity for responsible behavior, rather than his insistent focus on Steve's irresponsibility, enabled him to proceed much further in his own exploration of self. The couple's work on differentiation of self in the marriage had helped lay the groundwork for Ed's moment of insight in relation to Steve. Yet Ed's ability to see and acknowledge the self-protective ways he made use of his sons enabled him to separate his own identity from that of his sons and to greatly expand his own insights into himself.

These family consultations with the adolescent children enabled Ed and Lynn to continue in couple's therapy at a new and productive level of direct engagement with one another. Ed began to explore his problems as a father in the light of his family-of-origin experience. In his family of origin, he had been the youngest child, with three older sisters and two older brothers, and felt that he had few memories of his father except those as filtered through the resentment of his older siblings. They described their father to him as a brutal, critical, vindictive man, who was always verbally abusive and sometimes physically abusive. Ed, for himself, had much more positive memories of his father, who, as an aging father, had moderated his temper and been more nurturant, or at least less destructive, toward Ed. His father died when he was an early adolescent, and his mother died when he was first married, so that he no longer had anyone in the family with whom to discuss these discrepant, confusing views of his father. Ed felt that this very limited connection to his father alienated him from the rest of the family, especially his mother and sisters. He began to make connections between the acrimonious, mutually critical experience of his family of origin and the unexamined critical style he had adopted as a father.

Ed also began to wonder what internal limitations he had placed on his own career. He talked about his memories of his own father's frustrated career ambitions. His father had been the janitor at a local college and had always been disappointed that he had not been able to use his talents in a more fulfilling job. Ed was able to make the connection between his career failings and the loyalty to his father that he was expressing by rising no higher in his career than his father had. Ed was at that time offered a promotion to a prestigious supervisory job in research, which was much more appropriate to his level of training.

As Ed began to take responsibility for his own contribution to the family problems, Lynn was afforded greater freedom to focus on her own difficulties. Lynn more clearly realized how much she had saved herself from self-awareness by focusing on the children's problems, blaming Ed for them, and then "protecting" Ed from the realization that he had caused their problems. Lynn began to wonder just what she was avoiding in herself by focusing so much on the care of other people, especially in holding on to her very draining job in the intensive care unit far longer than most nurses lasted in such a unit. She realized that in working in such close proximity to life-and-death situations, she had to numb her feelings in order to continue functioning. Although she wasn't ready to let the job go, she started to wonder what her life might be like if she were to work in a setting that allowed her greater freedom to be aware of her own emotional reactions. In one poignant realization, Lynn remembered that when Ted was still in high school, she came home one day and found him smashing full beer bottles against the cellar wall. She asked him, "What are you on?," meaning what drugs. She remembered that Ted responded, "Just myself." She had found his response mystifying at the time but had remembered it, because after a lifetime of rigid emotional controls, she finally understood for herself what it felt like to be that agitated and upset with inner confusion and conflict.

Although Steve ceased to be a serious problem after the first year of therapy, Ted was too deeply embarked on his life course as a schizophrenic to benefit very much from his parents' progress. In fact, at times when the couple were engaging in greater intimacy and stirring up painful memories and feelings in themselves, Ted would repeatedly become symptomatic or generate a crisis in which the couple would attempt to become embroiled. At a point when Lynn and Ed began to take better care of their own lives, including setting some limits on how responsible they would continue to be for Ted, they learned that Ted had a girlfriend, another patient from his halfway house, and that she had become pregnant.

This family developmental transition generated a crisis for the Clarks in that they were forced by the painful circumstances of the birth of their first grandchild to make a decision about the kind of support they should offer their son. The therapeutic exploration of this decision enabled the couple to explore their own family developmental history in a new light. The Clarks reviewed their own early stages of family development. They remembered together their high hopes for the marriage during their courtship. When the couple first met, they both felt, for the first time in their lives, that they had found the loving relationship they had lacked in their own families. Shortly after they married, though, several stressful family changes coincided: Their first child, Ted, was conceived; Ed's mother died; and Ed was drafted into the army and had to go on a tour of duty in Korea. Ed was gone for only a year, because he entered near the close of the war, but his absence, Ted's birth, and the death of his mother all seriously disrupted the development of their marital intimacy.

Lynn felt abandoned by Ed and found Ted a very difficult baby to take care of. She began to work as a nurse to help support the family while Ed started graduate school, and Ed found himself taking care of the baby more while Lynn worked. At the same time, Lynn felt lonely and wanted to have a second child as a means of feeling more like she was part of a close family. Although Ed objected to the idea of the pregnancy, he went along with her decision. In reviewing this period of their family life, Ed finally acknowledged that he found taking care of the children an important and satisfying aspect of his life. Lynn remembered that she had always liked the children as infants, when they were very responsive and close to her, much more than she liked them as they grew older and more independent. Yet it seemed that every time Ed's career development absorbed him with thoughts outside the family, they conceived another baby as a means of keeping him more involved with the family. They were able to acknowledge that they both had arrived at the solution of having a large family for reasons that satisfied their own developmental conflicts and needs.

This review of their own early stages of family development took place in a context of enormous immediacy because of the impending birth of their first grandchild under such complex circumstances. They agreed that the halfway house was no place for a new family but disagreed about how involved they should become in Ted's life at this juncture. The couple shared strong worry about whether Ted and his wife were capable of taking care of an infant, and they felt pressured to decide whether they should invite Ted and his wife and baby to move in with them. They were able to decide together that they needed to concentrate on each other at this phase of their family life, and were able to help provide Ted and his wife with the support they needed to establish their own household nearby.

At the end of the therapy, the couple felt they were enjoying being married for the first time in many years. They began participating in shared activities that both enjoyed, and they established a renewed sense of intimacy with each other and with their children.

The Clarks began their marriage and their early parenting almost simultaneously, under circumstances that severely stressed their psychological resources. In response to the demands of early parenting and early career development, Ed and Lynn found themselves confused by their own complex reactions. As a man, Ed's primary focus was expected to be his career development, but he found the care of young children a secretly satisfying experience. He was further blocked by an unconscious or invisible loyalty to his father, so that he could not let himself advance in his work. As a woman, Lynn's primary focus was expected to be the nurturance of her children, but she found mothering disappointing and preferred the caretaking of her very sick patients. Although she loved taking care of the children when they were dependent infants, she found it difficult to nurture them after they became toddlers and began to assert their independence. The couple arrived at a nontraditional distribution of labor as a solution to these internal and logistical family problems.

However, both Ed and Lynn experienced enormous unexamined internal conflict. Neither one felt comfortable with a nontraditional division of labor. To establish a necessary sense of personal equilibrium, they found the explanation for their own disappointments and compromises in the failings of the other, while secretly fearing a confrontation with their own painful choices and limitations. To protect this equilibrium, the couple developed a communicational style within the marriage that avoided conflict at all costs, so that they became unable to learn from new family experiences in growth-producing ways.

The couple were able to make excellent use of therapy, productively exploring their family-of-origin and marital conflicts, and resuming their family development in more expansive ways. It was probably very important to their learning that they had reached the midlife stage of development, where acknowledgment of opposite-sex needs or characteristics did not arouse enormous personal anxiety. Over the course of the therapy, they were able to review their individual and family histories and to make peace with their limitations and decisions, so as to establish a different course for their family's future.

Elements of a Family Developmental Therapy

The case of the Clarks illustrates the following four elements of a therapy formulated from a family developmental perspective:

1. *Awareness of the current stage of the family life cycle with which the family presents.* At different points in the family life cycle, the family's readiness for change may differ. The approach used with a family of inexperienced parents and young children will have to be different from that used with a family of more mature parents and older children. The Clarks were more ready to change their family organization at a later stage of the family life cycle, when they weren't preoccupied with the overwhelming demands of caring for a large family with still-dependent children.

The therapist should become aware of special family life cycle circumstances, or of especially difficult periods in the family's developmental history, as the context for the family's current difficulties. Just as a family genogram is useful in highlighting intergenerational family events and repetitions, a review of important events in the family life cycle offers invaluable information about the context of the family's difficulties. The timing and circumstances of births, deaths, career changes and relocations, and other frequently occurring life cycle events illuminate the family's developmental struggles. This review of the family's own history can initiate a process of examining shared family experience with more sympathy and less blame for what was endured together.

For the Clarks, the coincidence of the birth of their first child with the death of Ed's mother and with Ed's departure for the army created an overwhelmingly stressful situation in their early family development. As families recount and recollect the concurrence of difficult family life cycle events, and as they explore their emotional responses to these events, they are better able to see their current difficulties in a less mutually recriminating light.

2. *Awareness of the family's current balance of continuity and change in the process of individuation.* From a family developmental point of view,

unconscious identifications with the family of origin, or rigid views of other family members, can be understood as mechanisms meant to provide family members with much-needed stability and continuity. Over the course of the family life cycle, however, these methods of maintaining personal equilibrium restrict one's capacity to learn creatively from changing family experience.

It is usually necessary to help families establish a sense of continuity and competence before they are ready to let go of these problematic means of arriving at a sense of personal stability. The more rigidly symptomatic a family, the more support family members require before they can begin to face this challenge. A family developmental perspective, as compared to a family pathology perspective, in fact aids the therapist in maintaining the sympathetic view of family difficulties that provides the best climate for this kind of family learning.

3. *Intervention in family mechanisms that reduce awareness of conflict.* The awareness and exploration of conflict between views of self and views of others is a crucial generator of family change. In the Clark family, the therapeutic confrontation of conflict avoidance in the marriage was the crucial first step toward family developmental progress. Also, family sessions were used as opportunities to generate small doses of manageable conflict between the rigid views of parent–child relationships and alternative views, which take in new information. For example, Ed was able to see that Steve was more responsible than he gave him credit for. This new insight was made possible by the groundwork established in the marital therapy.

Ed's confrontation with the conflict between his self-protective view of Steve and the reality of Steve's behavior enabled him to explore his unacknowledged identification with his own overcritical but much-missed father, which had obscured his ability to see his own son objectively. It also enabled Ed to explore his personal conflicts with work, which he had been projecting onto his sons rather than confronting directly. The powerful shift from assimilation to accommodation that occurred in that situation precipitated a greater differentiation of self from other, and of past from present. This case example illustrates the simultaneous family structural and inner organizational change that occurs at a moment of family development.

4. *Anticipation of upcoming stages of family development, as opportunities to try out new ways of responding to family change.* Changes in the family life cycle that occur during therapy present opportunities to review the family history with more immediacy, as happened with the Clarks when they were about to become grandparents. Families may choose to return to therapy during family life cycle transitions, as did the Clarks when the last of their sons reached adolescence. The exploration of the family's developmental future should leave family members with a feeling that they have rediscovered their own developmental strengths and have reestablished access to the growth-producing resources in their family relationships outside of therapy.

INTEGRATING FAMILY DEVELOPMENT
WITH FAMILY THERAPY TECHNIQUES

It is important to acknowledge that families have their own normal developmental mechanisms for negotiating family life cycle transitions. Family therapy interventions provide the family with the opportunity to redirect their energies toward more effective, growth-enhancing responses to one another. The reality that many different family therapy interventions turn out to be helpful may be explained by the resilience of these ordinary family developmental processes, even in extremely disturbed families. Some existing successful techniques in family therapy may in fact be formulated from a family developmental perspective. For example, Hoffman (1981) suggests that paradoxical techniques enhance the awareness of conflict. From a family developmental point of view, any technique that promotes the awareness of contradiction and conflict will enhance the process of differentiation and integration.

The family therapy techniques of reframing the meaning or purpose of symptomatic behavior, which are often used with paradoxical intent, can also be understood as enhancing normal family development. For example, a mother who is destructively overprotective of her child may be congratulated for her caring vigilance on behalf of her child. The great majority of parents do not intend to do their children harm. Rather, most parents attempt to remedy a problematic family situation as they understand it, but personal pain or anxiety restricts their capacity to respond in creative ways to others. A supportive acknowledgment of their genuine attempts to be good, competent parents will reduce defensive externalizations and enhance the process of responsible self-examination, which will more likely lead to a new view of self-within-family relationships.

A family developmental model based on individuation theory clearly draws on the family therapy techniques based on differentiation theory, such as the work of Bowen (1972, 1978) and Boszormenyi-Nagy (1965, Boszormenyi-Nagy and Spark, 1973.). The contextual therapy of Boszormenyi-Nagy is especially helpful in formulating a family developmental therapeutic approach. Boszormenyi-Nagy described invisible loyalties as unacknowledged, self-destructive attempts to fulfill family obligations and to affirm parental identifications. As an example, in the Clark family, Ed Clark expressed invisible loyalty to his father by not exceeding his father's limited career accomplishments.

The developmental context of invisible loyalties can be seen as the unconscious attempt to provide growth-enhancing continuity, a need that becomes more intense for adults in developmental transition. The idea that current relationships with extended family are an integral part of family living is very easily communicated to families from many diverse ethnic backgrounds, such as Hispanic families, whose cultural values already emphasize family connections. However, most adults find that understanding family relationships in terms of loyalty, reciprocity, and fairness, and acknowledging what is genuinely owed to one's own parents, will greatly enhance their freedom to function autonomously within relationships in both the family of origin and the family of procreation.

In a recent work, Boszormenyi-Nagy and Krasnow (1987) emphasize the establishment of relational resources as an alternative to a psychopathology model. Family members often participate in growth-constricting and potentially destructive interactions; the empathic support of any family's strengths facilitates their self-reliance and more successful adaptation in new situations. The emphasis on family members' creative resourcefulness in solving their own problems enhances the developmental strength they will bring to their next developmental challenge.

As psychotherapists, we have relied heavily on the study of psychopathology in our attempts to understand individuals and families. With illness as a starting point, we have tried to piece together the full course of human experience. It is far more powerful to begin with an understanding of ordinary human events as a basis for determining what enables people to learn from relationships. As family therapists, we need to study these developmental techniques from real life so that we may make use of family developmental processes more systematically in our therapeutic work.

REFERENCES

Abrahams, B., Feldman, S., and Nash, S. (1978). Sex role self-concept and sex-role attitudes: Enduring personality characteristics or adaptations to changing life situations. *Developmental Psychology, 14,* pp. 393–400.

Blos, P. (1962). *On adolescence: A psychoanalytic interpretation.* New York: Free Press of Glencoe.

Boszormenyi-Nagy, I. (1965). A theory of relationships: Experience and transaction. In I. Boszormenyi-Nagy & J. Framo (Eds.), *Intensive family therapy* (pp. 33–86). New York: Harper & Row.

Boszormenyi-Nagy, I., & Spark, G. (1973). *Invisible loyalties.* New York: Harper & Row.

Boszormenyi-Nagy, I., & Krasner, B. (1987). *Between give and take: An introduction to contextual therapy.* New York: Brunner/Mazel.

Bowen, M. (1972). Toward the differentiation of a self in one's own family. In J. Framo (Ed.), *Family interaction* (pp. 111–173). New York: Springer.

Bowen, M. (1978). *Family therapy in clinical practice.* New York: Jason Aaronson.

Carter, E., & McGoldrick, M. (1980). *The family life cycle: A framework for family therapy.* New York: Gardner Press.

Duvall, E. (1977). *Family development* (5th ed.). Philadelphia: Lippincott.

Falicov, C. (1971). *Interpersonal reorganizations during pregnancy and parenthood.* Unpublished doctoral dissertation, University of Chicago.

Feldman, S., Biringer, Z., & Nash, S. (1981). Fluctuations of sex-related self-attributions as a function of stage of family life cycle. *Developmental Psychology, 17,* 24–35.

Fraiberg, S. (1980). *Clinical studies in infant mental health.* New York: Basic Books.

Framo, J. (1970). Symptoms from a family transactional viewpoint. In N. Ackerman, J. Lieb, & J. Pearce (Eds.), *Family therapy in transition.* Boston: Little, Brown.

Guttman, D. (1975). Parenthood: Key to the comparative psychology of the life cycle. In N. Datan & L. Ginsberg (Eds.), *Life span developmental psychology.* New York: Academic Press.

Haley, J. (1973). *Uncommon therapy.* New York: W. W. Norton.

Hill, R. (1970). *Family development in three generations.* Cambridge, MA: Schenckman Books.

Hoffman, L. (1981). *Foundations of family therapy.* New York: Basic Books.

Jung, C. (1933). The stages of life. In *Modern man in search of a soul* (pp. 95-114). New York: Harcourt Brace.

Karpel, M. (1976). Individuation: From fusion to dialogue. *Family Process, 15,* 65-82.

Levinson, D. (1978). *The seasons of a man's life.* New York: Knopf.

Lewis, H. B. (1974). *Psychic war in men and women.* New York: New York University Press.

Livson, F. (1976). Patterns of personality development in middle aged women. *International Journal of Aging and Human Development, 7*(2), 107-115.

Loevinger, J. (1976). *Ego development: Conceptions and theories.* San Francisco: Jossey Bass.

Lowenthal, M., Thurnher, M., & Chiriboga, D. (1975). *Four stages of life: A comparative study of men and women facing transitions.* San Francisco: Jossey Bass.

Mahler, M. (1979). *The selected papers of Margaret Mahler* (Vols. 1 & 2). New York: Jason Aaronson.

Mahler, M., Pine, F., & Bergman, A. (1975). *The psychological birth of the human infant.* New York: Basic Books.

Neugarten, B. (1968). *Middle age and aging.* Chicago: University of Chicago Press.

Piaget, J. (1954). *The construction of reality in the child.* New York: Basic Books.

Piaget, J., & Inhelder, B. (1969). *The psychology of the child.* New York: Basic Books.

Riegel, K. (1976). The dialectics of human development. *American Psychologist, 31,* 689-700.

Rodgers, R. (1973). *Family interaction and transaction.* Englewood Cliffs, NJ: Prentice-Hall.

Rossi, A. (1968). Transition to parenthood. *Journal of Marriage and the Family, 30,* 26-39.

Searles, H. (1979). *Countertransference and related subjects.* New York: International Universities Press.

Shapiro, E. R. (1985). *Transition to parenthood as a phase of family development.* Manuscript submitted for publication.

Stierlin, H. (1969). *Conflict and reconciliation.* New York: Anchor Books.

Werner, H. (1948). *Comparative psychology of mental development.* Chicago: Wilcox & Follett.

7

The Emphasis on Cultural Identity: A Developmental-Ecological Constraint

BRAULIO MONTALVO
The Family Institute of New Mexico

MANUEL GUTIERREZ
Aspira Inc. of Pennsylvania

During the last two decades, there has been an emphasis in the United States on the discovery of one's roots and on the development and expression of the cultural identity of ethnic groups. By means of this emphasis, some members of our society hope to bring about equality and justice for minority ethnic groups and solve a basic dilemma—how to create a cohesive society while protecting cultural differences. Positive consequences of this emphasis have been obvious: increased respect for different cultural backgrounds, visible attempts to have different groups share the best of their ethnic legacy, and growth, in legal terms, in protection of the rights of minorities.

Still, for significant institutions in the Puerto Rican ecology—the hospital, the mental health clinic, the courts, and the school—the goal of bringing effective relief to Puerto Rican families has proven difficult. The most common operating principle of these institutions has been to ignore cultural identity issues. When they have chosen to become responsive to these issues, their problem has been how to implement that responsiveness usefully. An emphasis on cultural identity brought us such commendable efforts as totally bilingual and bicultural juvenile court diversion projects, which rely more on familial resources than on custodial institutions (Rivera de Buchanan, 1975). But such an emphasis also brought unfortunate situations, like that of the judge who sent an abused boy back home against a social worker's recommendation. According to the judge, the recommendation showed no appreciation for the cultural identity of Puerto Ricans, particularly for the father's tough, disciplinary ways, which the judge saw as an integral feature of the patriarchal system. A few weeks later that boy was killed by his father.

Case studies reported in this chapter, except where otherwise indicated, are drawn from the authors' direct clinical or supervisory experiences.

181

Unfortunate situations also have been shaped when a concept of cultural identity has worked as a powerful and unconscious determinant in creating sentence disparities in the judicial system. Among drug offenders, for example, Puerto Ricans have received longer sentences than blacks or whites for similar offenses (Sissons, 1979). The concept may also be at work in the problems of interpreters in the court. An interpreter can be encouraged to feel that only he or she knows what a Puerto Rican really means. The interpreter winds up doing advocacy work instead of effective interpreting, and obstructs justice in the process. Doing nothing to relieve the overcrowded housing conditions of Hispanics can also be justified as a response to their "cultural preference."

The trend to support cultural identity brought us the programs that provided a greater appreciation of cultural heritage, thus meeting the special learning problems of the Hispanic child. But it also brought the teachers who dealt poorly with such notions as "enhancing Latino awareness." It became possible for schools to teach about great men and women in the youngsters' glorious past without the youngsters' discovering how that past could help them deal with deteriorating neighborhoods, unemployment, and their own catastrophe—a national dropout rate for Puerto Ricans twice as great as the national average (Gutierrez & Montalvo, 1980; U.S. Commission on Civil Rights, 1976).

This chapter offers comments on the misuse of the cultural identity emphasis. The concept of cultural identity has extraordinary impact and scope. The idea permeates the ecology of the Puerto Rican working-class family in ways that constrain individual and family development. It has had influence in the fields of health and mental health, in the explanations given for the failures of Puerto Ricans, in community and educational programs for youth, and in attempts to understand the behavior of the Puerto Rican woman interacting with outside institutions. A summary of trends, misuses, and alternative uses of cultural identity notions appears in Table 7-1.

HEALTH AND CULTURAL IDENTITY

For the family to fulfill its basic function of socializing and caring for the young, facilitating the transition from infancy to childhood, more than psychological equipment is required on the part of the adults. In the urban setting, the adults must rely on some minimal access to appropriate health facilities.

There are enough facilities in most cities on the eastern seaboard to take care of the health needs of Puerto Rican families, but there is still the problem of not having enough bilingual and bicultural personnel in strategic service positions. Most hospital emergency services inside the *barrios* still lack the minimal services of qualified translators on a reliable 24-hour basis, especially at night, when they are most needed. Families continue to report that they have been refused services at hospital emergency rooms because they did not bring a translator: "Why didn't you bring someone with you who can speak English? Come back tomorrow with someone." Some hospitals claim that they have adequate translation services available, meaning that they have a clerk or a security guard who is called away from his or her job to translate for the family. These employees are usually untrained for medical translation. Families complain that unless they come during certain daytime hours, they are at the mercy of well-meaning translators who distort their communication with the professionals. This is usually part of a broader institutional dynamic in which hospital staff are protected from dealing with Puerto Rican families by giving the cases to Puerto Ricans in the name of support for cultural identity. Presumably, only those initiated into the mysteries of Puerto Rican folklore, those with the language and the culture, should touch this population. This notion is often supported by Hispanics on the staff, and it damages the delivery of services:

- It complicates the logistics of coordinating availability of medical personnel, translators, and families in need. Families who need immediate help cannot receive it. They must wait for a translator from another department to be free.
- Hispanic families who cannot speak English have to wait longer and accommodate to the internal needs of the hospital instead of the hospital's accommodating to the family's needs.
- In the long run, this breeds a system of subtle role exchange in which hospital administration and medical staff shift their responsibility for the proper care of Hispanic patients over to the available Hispanic employees.

Since this system of exchange of roles is usually presented as a way of being culturally responsive, not as a discriminatory practice, it is hard to identify and resolve. It offers short-term relief for some families and is readily endorsed by well-meaning Hispanic employees, who resist any long-term policy-seeking interplay between *all* staff (Hispanic and non-Hispanic) and patients. To these employees, such a policy appears unfair and threatens their jobs and their control over "their" population. In this atmosphere, both the administration and the Hispanic service providers shortchange the patient population. The right to proper treatment, independent of ethnic affiliation, is superseded by the idea that proper treatment is possible only within that affiliation. The families are trapped. Restricted by language, poor transportation, lack of information, and genuine desire for resources in their neighborhood, they do not seek competitive services elsewhere in the city. Their range of choice is limited to unresponsive, segregated, or inadequate hospital services and to individual practitioners in the *barrio,* some of whom provide unnecessary services.

When services are organized so that they offer real accessibility to the population, with bilingual personnel in a familiar and culturally syntonic setting, the scope of real needs quickly surfaces. A case in point is what

Table 7-1. Summary of Trends, Misuses, and Alternative Uses of Puerto Rican Cultural Identity Notions

Trend	Misuse	Alternative use
	Mental health training	
Cultivation of cultural and ethnic sensitivity becomes a central training concern.	Problem-solving emphasis is trivialized. The focus of accomplishment shifts to understanding the culture instead of helping the family from within the culture and overcome the problem. Understanding based on the outside struggle between the two cultures—the family's and the host society's—is neglected. Understanding based on family coping with surrounding institutions is neglected. Therapists erroneously explain the family's work in defining and redefining boundaries to the outside institutions as cultural idiosyncracies or externalizations. They fail to support and use this area as essential to competent problem solving within the family.	Demonstrate effective clinical skills with an exploratory and respectful attitude toward a group's cultural identity. The integration of openness to culture with clinical skills entails not allowing ethnicity to become an ascendent and overriding consideration. Underlying philosophy should be: People are more similar than they are different. Rapport does not depend on cultural attunement only. Theory must suggest how change proceeds not only from within the family to the outside but from the outside to the interior of the family. The concept of interfaces must be substantiated. Develop clinical theory and evidence on the extent to which firming up of boundaries between family and the outside facilitates changes between generations and/or between spouses.
	Misleading training ideas prevail, such as the colonial effect on personality producing passive-aggressive traits and requiring specialized purification and remediation experience for Puerto Rican therapists. Countertransference potential must be worked through in own therapy before you can deal with Puerto Ricans.	
	Popular explanations for failure	
Psychoanalytically derived stereotypes. Attempts to understand dynamic reasons for Puerto Ricans' developmental adjustment difficulties. Most Puerto Rican problems explained according to political history: colonial effect, producing or amplifying passive-aggressive personality.	Colonial mentality perceived as an unchangeable inherent trait, which waits for change in island status, and then time to recover from its effects.	Rejection of simplistic explanations. Understanding of frustrating interpersonal context, of neighborhood, of unemployment, etc. Reject explanations applying analogue of relationships between countries to relationships between people. Resist efforts to purify, "therapize," or reeducate. Macrosystem effects from historical context cannot be assumed to have an impact on microsystem events in family without first establishing complex intervening variables. Resist false parsimony.

Child-rearing practices assumed to foster arrested, dependent ego development.	Puerto Rican child-rearing practices promote defective ego development. Mothers cause extreme dependency in children.	Understanding of cultural differences and environmental pressures on child-rearing practices.
Overemphasis on sex roles: *machismo*; the compulsion to prove or prevail through aggressive display of "virility" at all costs; a negative patriarchal derivative.	Counterreaction to *machismo*. Rationalization of its "good side;" thus a positive virtue, a display of responsibility, assertiveness, and heterosexual vitality sorely lacking in the host culture. This excuses arbitrary associations of aggressiveness and manliness.	Emphasis on understanding relationships in context with skeptical attitude toward presumed cultural blueprints of expression. Examine *machismo* at least from a dyadic perspective. Establish the extent to which power asymmetry between man and woman is really only man induced or reciprocally held in place by the couple. Be careful in use of term since it is used to explain all phenomena.

Education

Emphasis on bilingual programs as the commanding teaching approach and remediation technique to deal with language as a primary barrier to mainstreaming and development.	Neglect of substantive curriculum and qualitative dimensions; educational objectives become secondary to job maintenance among teachers and to political control of program; segregated tracks develop; no mainstreaming; original goals for broadening of intellectual skills and cultural enrichment forgotten. Bilingualism is made an all-encompassing rallying point. Equating bilingual programs with all Hispanic needs (housing, education, employment, health). Family numb to the child's poor educational outcome. Distracted by the cause of bilingualism.	High standards on quality education; emphasis on outcome. Diversified approaches. Immersion-based English as second language and other methods should be given systematic opportunities to prove effectiveness and to show applicability to different student needs. Development of new and diverse rallying points around employment, housing, health, political participation, and voter registration, and representation. Diverse rallying points require separate political processes. These needs cannot obtain differentiated attention when a single rallying point like education is used to satisfy all needs.

(continued)

185

Table 7-1. (*Continued*)

Trend	Misuse	Alternative use
	Cultural expressions	
Display and endorse cultural legacy to enhance ethnic pride.	Eagerness to display cultural identity products. Rush to expose materials compromises excellence and fosters development of fake materials. Emphasis on product being culturally syntonic overcomes idea of functional or esthetic excellence and reinforces, instead, a negative identity.	Programs to orient parents as to how to protect the best cultural expressions (art, music, dance, theatre). Community programs to develop leadership, with standards of excellence uppermost. Increased parental alertness to pseudocultural products. Community request of authenticity in cultural events from schools, media, recreation centers. Youngsters' efforts to differentiate phony products from real ones should be actively supported.
	Family and outside institutions	
Woman's increasing assertiveness explained as shedding of patriarchal tradition and acceptance of women's liberation in host culture. Outside institutions deal with her as the pivotal figure in the family. The school, the hospital, the churches, etc., attempt to assist her and centralize her, while the husband, if available, struggles to keep or find a job.	Devaluation of the formative contribution of her original background to her increasing assertiveness; subtle undermining of her ethnic pride; agencies acting as if she must be always rescued from her husband, and as if her busy role in dealing with institutions was only one more exploitation of her time and energy by the jobless husband.	Highlight the flexible features within patriarchal arrangements; credit the formative experiences in which the patriarch allowed himself to be modified by the wife or daughter. Display the matriarchal elements in the pre-Colombian history of the Puerto Ricans. Generate long-term changes in economic opportunity and socioeconomic mobility. Address issues of chronic unemployment for fathers and young adult males, which continues to skew the heterosexual relationship by detracting from the man's relative power in the family.

186

happened when a front-line social service agency in Philadelphia, in liaison with a local hospital, opened a well baby clinic for routine physical examinations and immunizations. The first 53 babies turned out to be not well at all. They were sick babies, facing serious developmental impasses, and they required more involved intervention than the clinic was set up to handle. In spite of its usefulness to and support by the community, this clinic was headed for inevitable collapse because of its funding pattern, which was temporary. It provided for hiring a few Spanish-speaking doctors and nurses to service poor Puerto Rican families exclusively. What emerged was an indigent, low-prestige clinic, which could be amputated at the end of the fiscal allocation period. This is the familiar fate of clinics that do not develop mechanisms for integrating federal and state funds into the actual service operation. They need procedures to guarantee that funds leave behind a lasting improvement in the quality of the services for families.

Attempts to better organize and improve the quality of health services to Hispanics need not lead to a single model; different models may suit different communities.[1] As service providers and consumer families search for an appropriate model, they need to identify at least the following harmful personnel practices:

- Compliance with equal opportunity employment guidelines, which provide for hiring Hispanics in low-prestige jobs only. Although these jobs provide an entry level for many Hispanics in the *barrio*, more qualified Hispanics are not considered for middle-management positions.
- Cursory recruitment of Hispanic professionals, with no advertising done in areas of greater Hispanic concentration.
- No concern with solving long-term needs by discouraging aggressive policies for multiplying the cooperation between universities and hospitals by not setting up systematic health career development programs, and by not providing scholarships or work–study arrangements for Hispanic students.

Despite current antiregulatory policies, guidelines for what should constitute adequate staffing and an adequate manner of providing services for non-English-speaking families—as well as federal penalties for noncompliance at this level—must be sought. Strong grass-roots participation may not be enough to influence the bodies legally responsible for hospital administration, the boards of trustees and the accreditation boards, towards endorsing Alers's (1978) recommendation for "Puerto Rican representation, in proportion to their use of the services dispensed." Even more difficult for families to influence is the fragmentation of services, which still urgently requires organizational creativity with a family medicine orientation. By now it is no discovery that the family overutilizing the pediatric services for psychosomatic abdominal pains in a child can turn out to be the same family underutilizing the adult alcoholic services for an abusive father out of work.

MENTAL HEALTH AND CULTURAL IDENTITY

The discovery of cultural identity has also had uneven effects on mental health practices. Some families are no longer as grossly manipulated by mental health workers as they once were. They are now treated with new "respect," but they are not expected to deliver much. To confront a poor Puerto Rican family and hold them accountable for delinquent or manipulative behavior becomes unusual. It is a rare clinician who dares to become indignant and blame the "victim"—even when that is tactically necessary, to mobilize responsibility.

For fledgling Puerto Rican clinicians, the emphasis on cultural identity sometimes means exposure to strange teaching ideas. Some are taught that they accrued a special countertransference potential because in growing up they were targets of racism and identity devaluation. They are advised to take up with their resistant ethnic clients the meaning of their "Puertorican-ness" and, if they are also black, the meaning of both their Puertorican-ness and their blackness. Those who try this with their clients and fall into an apologetic "I am guilty" stance seem to be as numerous as those who fall into a "You are guilty" stance. Not finding this useful, they turn to the graduate schools and the family institutes for the "right" way of doing it. But in these settings, scholarly discussions of racism and ethnicity continue to serve the faculties as a way to hide from teaching basic problem-solving and interview skills to students. As problem-solving concerns become secondary to seeking deliberate frameworks for enhancing sensitivity and openness to ethnicity, it becomes necessary for the clinician to stumble on new ways to enlightenment. Enlightenment comes from watching, since colleagues who are not from the client's culture often prove more effective than those coming from the culture itself. It comes from observing someone helping a Puerto Rican family without ever using role playing, which, for Puerto Ricans, is often deemed effective because they are an "expressive, dramatic people." It also comes from watching someone earn a Puerto Rican family's respect while using the forked tongue, the confrontative insult, and the paradox, all of which are supposed to be culturally nonsyntonic.

The focus on cultural identity was often seen in work with a distressed family in a struggle with an adolescent making a difficult developmental transition. In these families, particularly if the adolescent was female and at risk of dropping out of school, there was a strong possibility that the mother was seeking support from out-of-the-mainstream indigenous healers like the *espiritista*. Superstitiousness and cult practices provide new points of contact for professionals dealing with Puerto Rican families. This continues a trend from the 1960s, when mental health professionals were set on discovering strengths in the ethnic populations. Many Puerto Rican families, however, are still puzzled by the mental health workers' unconcealed admiration for the *espiritista*. We see a new development, disappointed clients, who complain bitterly that they go to the mental health worker expecting him or her to be different from the *espiritista*. For those Puerto Ricans, going to the *espiritista* is still a partial abandonment of rational means, an appeal to a measure that is reserved as a last resort. The professional's fascination with *Espiritismo* implies for them a condescending communication, an endorsement of an inferior alternative service. They feel they are being told that they cannot recognize differences in skills or levels of professional competence. Among Puerto Ricans of all socioeconomic classes, it is still believed that the doctor can handle some things better than the *espiritista*.[2] The professionals were suspected of needing to transform this population—so difficult to work with—into something exotic in order to be able to stick with it. Their readiness to glorify healers among the poor, and even to make referrals to them, was seen by some families as an admission of professional impotence or as another way to avoid providing quality services while claiming sensitivity to cultural needs.

Reactions such as these were not altogether unrealistic, given the tradition of less-than-careful evaluation and follow-up in mental health services. The woman who ministered to a cancer patient with herbs prescribed by the *espiritista* or the severely asthmatic child who received delayed pediatric care because the mother was following the *espiritista*'s recommendations were not likely to become the center of research attention in that climate. Finding the common ground between the *espiritista*'s ways of working and the mental health worker's methods was more interesting, more ethnically "with it," than comparing outcomes.

By emphasizing the interchangeable functions of the mental health worker and the *espiritista,* it was possible to sound anthropologically sophisticated and to avoid the disappointing discovery of the family as a chagrined consumer, exploited and restricted by inadequate choices. Since offering choices became the salient issue, the adequacy of these choices mattered less. Among mental health professionals who saw the *espiritista* as a competent choice in the Puerto Rican ecology, limitations developed. Preferring to wait for the culture's indigenous resource to solve the problems, they did not move to employ *espiritista*-like practices to sequester family pathology.

A brief illustration can be given of one such practice:

A single-parent family, a mother and her four children, was "spooked" by the spirit of an older daughter. The daughter's recent overdosing suicide had been followed by suicide attempts on the part of the three other siblings, who had heard her "calling them." A therapist was contacted to see the family. After gently mourning with the depressed mother and scared youngsters over the loss of the sister, the therapist firmly requested that the mother immediately clear all medicine cabinets and lock everything. He told the family they were also to get ready to do something special for their sister the next time they met. The mother and the youngsters were instructed to bring special kinds of candles that would be needed. A simple ceremonial session followed, with the mother, her youngsters, and the therapist joining in solemnly, lighting the candles to soothe the girl's spirit. Toward the end of the ritual, after ensuring that each youngster had participated, the therapist expressed gladness at the love that the sister had had for them and they for the sister. The light from the candles would be a way of being with her, of calming her without going with her. Everyone was visibly relieved. Help was given to this family by quickly assisting the mother in recovering enough executive control to protect her children in spite of her depression and by providing alternative means of reconnecting with a lost member. The alternative means were clearly culturally syntonic, yet available to any sensitive therapist—and not just the *espiritista.*

The fascination with *Espiritismo* as an outstanding element of Puerto Rican cultural identity has had some fortunate consequences, particularly for indigenous resources in other sectors of the community.[3] It saved from meddling research, at least for a while, the prolific Evangelical churches, which were packed with cured alcoholics and drug addicts who found no effective help in mental health centers or at the hands of the *espiritistas.* It left alone such developments as the Aspira Clubs, where thousands of young-sters improved their chances of school survival while strengthening their sense of Puertorican-ness. It left untouched the emerging Puerto Rican Fam-ily Institutes, indigenous professional agencies free of the belief that Latins are especially protective and loving of children. These institutes are able to deal honestly with the many families that attempt to relieve all stress by seeking quick placement of children. It also left unbothered the few programs that try to relieve the exploited elderly, who live under virtual house arrest because of language barriers, fear of moving around in the unsafe neighbor-hoods, and the unceasing housekeeping demands they must fulfill for the working couple and grandchildren. The situation of this captive group was not explored because the population presumably does not exist, since Puerto Ricans are supposed to have "supportive extended families."

As those supportive extended families diminish, and as their sense of vulnerability increases, their involvement with *Espiritismo* can be expected to continue growing. It helps the families and those who serve them to keep the illusion of control over the uncontrollable. This illusion has become even more necessary in the face of increased oil prices and unmanageable housing problems. During 1979, out of 6,000 family visits to a front-line agency[4] in the Philadelphia *barrio,* at least 80% were estimated to be directly related to heating problems or some other housing-related complaint, such as leaky plumbing, inadequate insulation, delays in obtaining repairs, and conflicts with the landlord. These concrete problems require relevant and practical solutions. For example, local crews made from a consortium of companies could meet emergency oil needs on a 24-hour basis, working in close liaison with the agencies to which people turn first when in need of food or shelter. Other assistance could be provided by house and roofing repair crews capable of meeting emergency needs under the supervision of trained professionals, and by a housing and law center, patterned after the education and law centers that actively moved the courts in this country to protect the educational rights of children.[5]

Because *Espiritismo* is as much related to pressures in the social environment as it is to cultural identity, it will continue to be invoked in an effort to cope with the effects of irregular heating on the health of families. Innumerable mysterious respiratory ailments, "asthmas" in the pediatric and adult population, particularly in geriatric emergencies, have been easily linked to housing problems. Less easy to link to health problems but even more devastating in their long-range impact are the demoralizing shortage of housing and the absence of construction activities to give jobs and hope to the people. Equally depressing are the inflationary mortgage rate and the fast deterioration of buildings and homes, which continue unabated while families in the *barrios* see construction and progress taking place only outside their area. Even more discouraging is the dirt and ugliness that accumulates around a rare block where families have managed to do something with help from federal urban development programs. Though these programs seldom rally community participation in such a way as to make a big difference, they do raise just enough hope to intensify the sense of frustration and depression, which grabs family members when they see that the rest of the environment remains unchangeable. *Espiritismo* can be expected to flourish, while houses, streets, and buildings in need of cleaning and repair continue to sit right alongside the 40% estimated unemployed in the *barrios,* the general awareness of dead-end training programs, and the cynicism and skepticism toward the idea that sizable tax breaks for companies and businesses will definitely trickle down in the form of employment for minorities. By clinging to *Espiritismo,* the families can hold on to the very belief that change and transition are still possible, coping with their stagnant situation in a selective economic recovery that does not select them.

EXPLANATIONS FOR FAILURES

Crippling personality limitations such as passivity, hyperactivity, or simply not being smart enough are not as popular as they used to be in explaining the failure of Puerto Ricans to make certain developmental transitions.

The "colonial effect" is a popular explanation now. This shift from intrapsychic to more externally based determinants still makes definite and negative assumptions about cultural identity and does little to improve the psychological profile of Puerto Ricans. The colonial effect explanation agrees with the core clinical stereotype that Puerto Ricans are inherently passive-aggressive, dependent, and docile (Rothenberg, 1964), but it emphasizes that this is the unfortunate natural development of the historical context, the many years of feudal colonization by Spain and the United States (Marques, 1977).

By using the colonial effect, it is possible to hold that Puerto Ricans are generally inadequate, softening that message at the same time by arguing in scholarly and compassionate style that it is not their fault but the fault of the colonizers. Of course, the accusation of inactivity, of crippling passive dependency, remains there. Informed Puerto Ricans who question these psychoanalytically derived labels try to counter these accusations by defensively pointing to Puerto Ricans who do come out to vote in the elections, who do not drop out, and who are productive in their professions, in their trades, in the arts and entertainment. When that does not work, they mention the lootings, bombings, and riots in which Puerto Ricans have participated.

For the sensitive adolescent caught in the Puerto Rican slum in the United States, it is less easy to counter the accusation of passive dependence, of being *doblegado* (subservient). He hears too much about the effects of food stamps and welfare checks and of the island as an enslaved captive market. His dependence, and that of the island, become for him one and the same. His parents may be accommodating and gentle amidst the ferocious, militant talk of ethnic groups erupting around him. They may be reactionary, making their own contributions to interethnic strife. In either case, the contrast between the relative calm of his group and the clamor of all the protesting ethnics eventually gets to him. It must be wrong for him to feel peaceful. It must be the colonial effect working on him! If he becomes exasperated to the point of having a typical Puerto Rican *ataque*[6] and becomes curious as to its social significance, he could be in more trouble. Even his dramatic paroxysms would be explained away as merely explosive outlets of tension and rage from a dependent personality (Fernandez-Marina, 1961). This underemphasizing of the rich intercultural and intrafamilial functions of the syndrome would leave him only purely personal failure in coping with aggressive feelings as the reason for his developmental impasse.

The colonial effect explanation was useful to graduate school faculties attempting to rationalize why the Puerto Rican students they saw graduate were now failures—the students failed because of the deep effect that long colonization had on their parents and, through them, on the students themselves. Evidence of those effects was obvious in the students' lack of intellectual assertiveness; their dependent, expectant attitude toward the faculty; and their masking of aggressive feelings toward them with an outward show of friendliness. For smart minority students, those explanations were only slightly insulting. They knew that incompetent peers were allowed to pass because the well-meaning faculty lacked the aggressiveness to flunk minority students and defend some standards. The faculty was dependent on the belief that students really should not expect skills; they would pick them up in the field. To empower the poor, the faculty felt, it was necessary to provide only access and opportunity for them to get to the right position.

Recently, the colonial effect has been employed by clients themselves to explain male–female relationships in the family. An example comes from a more advantaged third-generation couple.

She had some college education, and he had small but successful business interests. She showed up in a clinic because of their 3-year-old boy's clinging behavior but soon presented herself as a typical case of a "colonized" woman in search of liberation. She complained that her tyrannical husband forced her to leave her outside job, where she was doing well. However, when her husband came in, she was scared and less combative, and joined him against the mental health worker. It looked as if she had, indeed, an intimidating "colonizing" husband. The session continued, and it was learned that as the man cooperated with childcare and household duties in obvious support of her wish for an outside job, she became neglectful in child rearing and more interested in her outside world. She had reached new heights of neglect when complementarity prevailed, and he became transformed into the full-fledged, dictatorial "colonizer"—"Mind your duties around here or get out." The colonizing tyrant versus the colonized woman was not then, in this third generation, as fixed a cultural drama as was first apparent. Rather, it had become an optional way of being, collaboratively summoned into action by the couple in order to reorganize responsibilities in the new culture without losing their traditions. After the reorganization occurred, the arrangement between them became more symmetrical. The wife obtained a part-time job and became more mindful of the child, who, in turn, became less clinging.

Some variations of the colonial effect explanation, when utilized by service providers, can be so handicapping as to warrant separate discussion. One of these variations is seen in the following example of a family's failure to connect on an initial casework contact.

Jose, a second-grader, was depressed and looked phobic. He constantly refused to go to school. His mother was urged by the school to get in touch with the mental health clinic. She made an appointment but failed to keep it. Even after a home visit, Jose's mother still did not show up. All efforts were unsuccessful, and the case was then transferred to a second worker. This one managed to get them in because he had a different perception of the family's cultural identity.

During his initial home visit, the first worker had been impressed by the family's lack of assertiveness in social situations. They were on their way out when he arrived, but they changed plans and stayed because of him. They offered him coffee. To the offer of coffee, he responded by politely insisting on leaving. To their request for a signed note to take to the welfare department to change their monthly check, he responded that he would be glad to take care of the matter when they went to the office. Their behavior impressed him as manipulative, passive, and dependent. He saw typical colonized behavior, by which the family was attempting to reestablish in the States the system of "It is who you know that counts" so prevalent on the island. The family never went to his office.

The second worker handled things differently. He, too, arrived when they were about to go out, but when he felt they were staying for him, he saw a culture asserting its hospitality. He did not insist on leaving. He insisted on more coffee. When mother and son cheerfully worked on him for a note to take to the welfare department, he took this as an opportunity to develop a relationship. He did not feel so manipulated, since he figured out that in the States, too, you are dependent on "who you know" in coping with the bureaucratic maze of the welfare system. This worker signed the note, asking the welfare worker to give him a call. A week later, the family went to his office at the mental health clinic.

Variations of the colonial effect explanation, such as the "typical colonized manner" or "lack of social assertiveness," which, in this case, almost prevented delivery of services to Jose's family, will continue to work against helping Puerto Rican families. These explanations, however, may suffer the fate of the *machismo* concept. *Machismo* has been used so widely to explain everything, good or bad, about Hispanics that it may be about to die from overuse. Hastening its departure is the current idea that *machismo* is the real explanation for relationship failures between Puerto Rican men and women by means of the colonial effect. The argument goes, as noted by Steiner (1974), that only cultures socioeconomically and governmentally castrated by colonizers compensate by developing a stereotyped system in which men inevitably become exploitative machos, pushing down on obliging, passive virgins. This explanation, of course, does not consider cross-cultural evidence or whether *machismo,* as a derivative of twisted patriarchal arrangements, exists in cultures that were never colonized. By conveniently turning problematic relationships between people into analogues of such relationships between countries, the colonial effect becomes a serviceable, all-encompassing explanation of Puerto Rican failure. The idea is versatile. It can be employed destructively, that is, by those who need little excuse to maintain the status quo and who do not think about how to improve the ecological situation of Puerto Ricans (Jose's first worker). It can be used constructively, when criticizing the stylish hospitality that always favors the Anglo professionals and artists who are brought to the island beaches for workshops, consultations, and research studies at the expense of Puerto Rican talent. It is also richly applied when deploring the constant *homenajes* that plague the culture—the endless hypocritical parties, given in honor of some undeserving person with political, educational, or economic clout.

COMMUNITY AND EDUCATIONAL PROGRAMS FOR YOUTH

The cultural identity concept has also played a role in community and educational programs for youth, imposing additional worries on Puerto Rican families in the big cities. When the youngsters developed anything in art, music, theater, or any professional endeavor, it was rushed to exposure— whether ready or not—in order to provide representation. Some youngsters faced actual developmental arrest because they were rushed into academic and artistic performances nowhere near their best potential. In school performances, in community center plays, and on radio and television, a growing number of Puerto Rican young people felt embarrassed by what they saw out there representing them, but they could not have it stopped. The well-meaning adults involved in the activity were insistent upon accepting or reinforcing anything ethnic that young people produced. When youngsters were ashamed of the performance, the adults did not take it as an indirect call for excellence or as a natural reaction against mediocrity but as more evidence of self-devaluation. Thus one heard, "They don't cherish the little they have—they must be encouraged; it's the way to help them."

Youngsters in Philadelphia, for instance, expectantly watched a Puerto Rican dance group performing a *jibaro* (Puerto Rican peasant) folk dance on television. The brighter ones soon made an embarrassing discovery. The Puerto Rican peasants were wearing Venezuelan costumes. Embittered youngsters, moaning at the grownups that the show had no class, were immediately silenced: "Well, it might not be perfect, but it's yours. Be proud of it."

Fortunately, this pressure to bring forth evidence of cultural identity, no matter what, had one good consequence. It sharpened youngsters' skills in distinguishing fake identity material from the real thing. Many now protect themselves from the risk of accepting a manufactured past and erecting on that a false pride. Recently, several girls walked out fuming from a fundraising dinner for a Puerto Rican social service organization. When asked what made them leave so suddenly, they pointed to the innumerable Puerto Rican Taino masks that adorned the tables. Their number far exceeded anything resembling the actual number of tribes they represented. These discriminating youngsters were resisting society's latest request that the ethnic group become even more ethnic, parodying itself to fit a presumably more accepting atmosphere for differentiated cultural minorities.

Aware parents of such youngsters have feared not only the development of a fake past but also that youngsters would grow up feeling like fakes. They have worried about the demoralizing effects of unemployment and welfare rolls on the children. Parents sensed what recent studies verify—that the feelings of insignificance and the familial disorganization that accompany long-lasting joblessness in Puerto Rican men have systemic effects on the third generation.[7] In a Philadelphia sample, the most vulnerable year for making a transition in the school system is the 10th grade. Most youngsters who drop out do so in that year, and the fathers of those 10th-grade dropouts are usually chronically unemployed. It appears that just as the father cannot make his transition from being jobless to being employed, the youngster is discouraged from making his own transition from the 10th to the 11th grade.

EDUCATION

The emphasis on cultural identity was nowhere more evident than in the controversial bilingual programs. Problems arose as families questioned whether these programs were helping or hindering youngsters in making the transition from the subculture into the host culture. The programs attempted to introduce a language–culture component into education while creating jobs for Puerto Rican parents. They were a significant source of employment in *barrios* where jobs were scarce. In this context, parents continued to be sold the idea that these kinds of programs were better because they were in Spanish, had a cultural emphasis, and would better prepare their children to succeed in school. A study (in Philadelphia; Gutierrez & Montalvo, 1984), however, has shown that proportionately more school dropouts than stay-ins are likely to come from bilingual, rather than regular, programs. And national studies have documented the shortcomings of bilingual education as delivered in the public school system (Carnegie Foundation, 1979; Twentieth Century Fund Independent Task Force on Federal Education Policy, 1983). The original agenda, to employ the bilingual programs to facilitate the migrant family's transition and assimilation into the mainstream of the host culture, began to erode.

Moving into the 1980s under the threat of massive federal cuts in education, bilingual programs—and their rescue—again became a rallying point of cultural identity. A coalition of politicians, jobholders, parents, and other Hispanics was mobilized to prevail on the government to restore their funding. Since more fundamental and painful cuts into programs serving the vital needs of poor families were planned (food stamps, welfare, Medicaid, Medicare, school lunch programs, maternal nutrition, legal aid in education, and housing), it proved politically useful for the government to yield on the bilingual education front. In that process, evidence as to the quality and effectiveness of most bilingual programs was not important. What was significant was that the programs were highly visible, tended to co-opt the representation of all Hispanic needs, and could distract attention from assaults that would be made on basic family necessities in the areas of health, housing, and employment.

WOMEN AND OUTSIDE INSTITUTIONS

The cultural identity emphasis is displayed in efforts on the part of the school to assist the Puerto Rican woman. It is also displayed in the mental health clinic's attempts to understand her relationship to her children and husband as well as the contribution of her culture to her development. We discuss these efforts here in terms of helpful, but asystemic, attempts to assist her and to understand the sources of stress in her immediate family relationships. We also consider her response to her unsafe ecology, the drawing of a tight circle of safety; her perceived mandate to take care of aged family members; and her need to break the chain of familial events shaping subordinate females.

To institutions in the ecology of the Puerto Rican working-class family, the woman appears to be the perfect vehicle through which to track changes in the family and to be of help to the culture. Change in the family could also be tracked through shifts in the man's position, but usually the woman is chosen because she is the one with the pivotal position in dealing with the school, the hospital, the community center, and other institutions.

Asystemic School Help

As mother, the woman is central to the socialization of the second generation and to the process of passing on the cultural identity. As spouse, she is seen as having an unascendant position in the family, inviting outside intervention that seeks to strengthen her neglected position. Too often, that intervention deals with her strictly as an individual attempting a developmental leap and not as a member of a social network.

For example, schools try to strengthen the young woman's identity by teaching her that getting a job is the road to liberation. The youngster observes that her mother has a job but also sees that her mother's burden of chores in the home remains as unchanged as the father's expectations of her. In high schools and small colleges, operating under the belief that Puerto Rican parents do not push their children academically, staff try aggressively to prevent the Puerto Rican girls from dropping out. They use special tutoring, offer flexible classroom demands, and give supportive counseling to keep the girl in school, only to see her leave after having prolonged her misery. The counselor discovers later that her boyfriend was not likely to go to college and hence was factory bound. Her dropping out was not just to protect herself but to protect her boyfriend from feeling that she had outdone him. Her parents were not altogether displeased. If those parents had found a sense of belonging and identity in one of the spreading Evangelical sects, they were often positively relieved. In exchange for that sense of belonging and identity, they had committed themselves to actualizing a set of life-denying rules they thought protective of the daughter—no dating, no dancing, no singing (except for hymns), and no flashy dressing. Dropping out was another instance of a family recalling one of its members from an offending world. That member was seen as someone dragging them forcefully into a developmental transition, toward a world they were not ready for.

Stress in the Family

The emphasis on cultural identity also reveals itself in the reaction of human-service workers to the change in the Puerto Rican woman as she attempts to deal with her husband. This is best seen when she considers moving out, or when she shows a sense of urgency and combativeness toward the use of alcohol and drugs by her husband and children. Alcohol and drugs have always impaired a large segment of the Puerto Rican young adult population. What is new is that more women are less able to stand passively by. It is now easier to find the woman who works on discrediting the notion that experimentation with drugs and alcohol, particularly alcohol, is a necessary masculine "rite of passage." She no longer takes drinking as a badge of cultural identity. She sometimes threatens to leave the family if the alcoholism or the addiction continues. Much too often, she cannot do this, but will try to prevent shifts in the situation of the alcoholic or drug-addicted family member, depleting herself as she tries to hold the family together. She cannot leave—not just because she wants to keep the family intact at all costs but because she has no supportive ecology and no place to go and is seldom ready for the job market. Yet these ecological restraints are only cursorily addressed when planning how to assist her. Her decision to leave the extended family is seldom sufficiently supported; among the reasons for this is the mental health professional's insistence that her extended family offers her a refuge and a resource.

In reality, that "extended family" cannot be prejudged, since it may amount to a unsupportive network of disapproving people impeding her drive to change. This is seen when the network neutralizes her courage to leave and her unwillingness to be abused, delaying her reaching out for help. This situation often resolves itself through violence. As pointed out by Alers (1978), almost 20% of all deaths of Puerto Ricans aged 15–44 years are due to homicide. The rate is twice that of the total population in the same age group. It is reasonable to infer that the rate reflects cumulative tensions preceding and following attempts to leave the family. The attempt to leave is frequently a thwarted or delayed change, which entails life stresses and increases the probability of the appearance of aggressive explosions or specific illnesses in the near future following the stress. This should not be surprising, since statistically significant relationships have been found in the general population between the stresses of life change and subsequent heart attacks, accidents, leukemia, diabetes, and mental and emotional disturbances (Holmes & Rahe, 1967).

It is easy for the helping professional to be misled as to how stressful the intrafamilial situations can be because of what Puerto Ricans themselves want to believe about their cultural identity. Puerto Ricans generally tend to find the conditions involved in spouse or child abuse too embarrassing and guilt producing to acknowledge. The community invests so much in its image of the family as a unit of friendly adults and child-loving people that shame and denial ensues whenever an attempt is made to look at the scope of this negative reality. Many still insist that the problem is less widespread than it is, while secretly fearing that it reaches epidemic proportions. The most unfortunate situation develops when the belief among Puerto Ricans that the family is a friendly, intact unit merges with the belief of the helping agencies that the family constitutes a resourceful extended network. The community is thereby prevented from complaining openly, from acknowledging the problems, and from planning coping strategies to reshape its inadequate ecological resources— strategies that might bring relief to the family.

The Circle of Safety

Without relief from ecological resources, the Puerto Rican woman has to resist—almost alone—the influence of neighborhood women who are burnt out by the size of their families, household obligations, and absent or unsupportive husbands. These women are out to discourage her from using, for relief, the rarely available day-care center. These burnt-out women have lost much and feed their own spirals of escalating tension, increasing the likelihood of physical and psychosomatic illness and also of child abuse. They react by trying to hold back the more assertive and exploratory women, and by rejecting those who do not readily join the traditionally admired club of complaining martyrs.

What these women have lost is the culture's enduring capacity for *relajo* —that readiness for bantering and good-natured teasing that makes burdens easier to carry, allows people to bounce back, and makes a great festive occasion out of a friend's stopping over for coffee or a neighbor's planning for a wedding or a child's baptism. Instead, these women dwell incessantly on how dangerous it is to open the "circle of safety"—the few restricted areas and activities that they allow their youngsters. This dwelling on the theme of "how narrow is the circle of safety" is not taken as a serious plea for help by the helping institutions. They still tend to respond with a secondary prevention emphasis, with a one-to-one approach now refueled with concepts from individual biochemistry and genetic counseling (Eisenberg, 1975), which are totally unrelated to the stressful ecology. Soft psychosociological concepts like the "circle of safety" are avoided. Such concepts may draw attention to the family's culture in its dealings with neighborhood institutions and could get the staff involved in the uncertainties of working out a resourceful community ecology and perhaps a community psychiatry. Those uncertainties involve dealing with the tasks of primary prevention left unresolved by the social psychiatry of the 1960s as it struggled with, and then failed to answer, the overwhelming findings relating mental disturbance and crime to the social circumstances of poverty. Somewhere around that time, unemployment stopped being seen as a source of stress that could really be solved once and for all. Ideas such as Striner's (1976) plan, aiming at the elimination of joblessness by giving national priority to investment in human resources, fell out of currency. Unemployment, instead of being considered a fundamental force, became, once again, just one more associated, aggravating factor of mental health troubles in difficult neighborhoods.

For most mothers, being vigilant of their youngsters' neighborhood is like watching over their selection of peers. It is a way of preventing sons from becoming delinquent and of facilitating adequate social development (Gutierrez & Montalvo, 1984). For other mothers, being vigilant becomes an all-encompassing, excessive occupation, which blocks their youngsters' development as the youngsters respond to dangers outside. The core problem remains: For mothers in these families, to disengage from the youngsters is to betray their idea of what a good mother should be. Any attempt to expand their youngsters' limited jurisdiction elicits from them honest justifications—such as the realistic occurrences of frequent crime or the unreliability of the safety corridors on the way to school. The ecology validates and justifies their protectiveness, even as it reaches crippling dimensions and facilitates a phobic outlook towards life.

Unfortunately, the insistence of these mothers on drawing a tight circle of safety is increasingly warranted, since, as Alers (1978) describes, Puerto Ricans have a high accident mortality in all age groups under 65, and particularly in the age group under 16, when compared with the total population. Ironically, implementing the circle could itself be one of the forces helping to create such a high mortality rate for youngsters (with 28% of all deaths due to accidents). The overprotected child does not handle well the developmental task of self-protection and becomes vulnerable to accidents. The "tight circle of safety" mentality has even more elusive and devastating effects on development when the family allows itself to be manipulated and divided by one of its own—in order to protect him or her. This extreme situation is evident in the cases of addiction, alcoholism, and abuse in which the family remains forever willing to "forgive," sheltering the symptomatic member from the consequences of his or her actions until actively preventing or sabotaging change.[8]

Until recently, if their circle of safety eroded, overstressed mothers would retrieve the child and send him or her to Puerto Rico. Nowadays they live in a "no exit" situation where that solution cannot be applied. They brew much longer in chronic tension: "I sent him to Cidra, my small hometown, but there, too, drugs were all over the school. I have to bring him back."[9] The Puerto Rican woman who refuses to join in the shared obsession of "how the circle of safety keeps getting smaller" is almost always able to show her strength in her dealings with institutions such as the school or the hospital. She is increasingly capable of readjusting and redefining the boundaries of the circle rather than reacting protectively in a generalized way to perceived outside threats. She no longer shares with the teacher, for instance, those incidents when the child is "bad" with her. She has readjusted the old patterns, which she used in Puerto Rico, of deference to, and collaboration with, school authorities. She keeps to herself problems of control over her child. She does this because she has finally discovered that the teacher is no longer an extension of the family and that she cannot assume that what she tells the people in the school will be used only to her child's benefit. For her, the school often proves to be *outside* the circle of safety.

An angry involvement in redefining the boundaries to the outside also alienates this woman from therapists who insist on seeing her anger as a displaced marital fight. It is easier for therapists to understand her disturbance as being caused by problems in establishing boundaries within the family than in terms of problems in establishing boundaries between her family and external institutions. The behaviors and expectations of school, hospital, place of employment, and agencies concerned with support for the aged are not understood as being an integral part of a primary problem.

Taking Care of Their Own

A 75-year-old woman, drowned in guilt, asks, "What am I supposed to do with my 90-year-old mother if my arthritis keeps getting worse?" An overstressed younger woman complains, "In Puerto Rico my 87-year-old father would go out, get lost, and urinate in public. But it was a small town and everyone knew us, so someone would always find him and bring him back. Here, it took me 6 hours to find him after a call from a police station. By the time I got home, my husband was overwhelmed by the children and was angry at me for not being there earlier."

One can now find the Puerto Rican woman who resists the popular belief that aged parents can always be sustained in the family and in the community through senior citizens' clubs and the English-speaking hospital, with occassional visits from relatives and maybe an assigned Hispanic ombudsman to supply some contact. For the new Puerto Rican woman, the idea of the extended, self-sufficient Hispanic family remains a middle-class myth of cultural identity, a myth that is conveniently shared by the staffs of the service agencies who want to believe that most older citizens will remain forever in their Hispanic families because the families will "always take care of their own." Since this myth fits the current policy of deinstitutionalization, it works to prevent the development of necessary services for the growing group of dependent elderly. The net result is that they have to stay in their families, overtaxing the emotional resources of already stressed people and increasing their chances of being abused.

Breaking Chains

The emphasis on cultural identity has also handicapped the education and mental health professionals' understanding of the Puerto Rican woman's transition toward a more demanding, assertive stance. The woman's development toward assertiveness tends to be seen by mainstream institutions, such as the school or the clinic, as due mainly to the influence of the host culture. Particularly, the women's liberation movement is seen as working against legacies of female subordination in the rigidly patriarchal subcultures. This notion, by underestimating the formative contribution of the girl's original background to her increasing assertiveness, subtracts from the foundations of her self-esteem and ethnic pride. To see her change only as a result of events occurring in the host culture is to ignore many events within her own culture that contribute to her liberation.

For instance, we have observed that for a girl to be liberated, the girl's mother must have the strength to break out of her own subservience, surprisingly not from her father or her husband, but from her *own* mother. The woman-to-woman struggle has finally surfaced as one that is crucial to family development. To erode one of the original culture's primary mechanisms for making females subservient and for facilitating the assimilation of the family into the host culture, many a second-generation woman actively protects her daughter from her own mother. This mechanism is obvious in mildly problematic families who are working to lessen the natural alliance between grandparents and grandchild. A brief example follows:

As a little girl in New Jersey, Carmen had to come home to her grandmother, who would tell her repeatedly to clean up, do the dishes, do the rooms, and so forth. She was not allowed to play with other children. She was always pressed into service by the grandmother—until one day when the mother was home from work ill. The mother saw quite clearly that her daughter was carrying a heavy burden, and she finally mustered the courage to confront the grandmother: "I do not want her doing any of these chores. Ever." By removing Carmen from her grandmother's influence, the mother quickly precipitated the grandmother's decision to leave the home and go back to Puerto Rico. We later learned that she had recruited there an orphaned grandniece, who, in the mother's own words, "is almost becoming her new slave." In the meantime, Carmen's sadness left her.

When the second-generation woman breaks the chain of events perpetuating the role of subservient Puerto Rican females, she prevents developmental stagnation in the family. She does this by relying on more than the host culture's liberation movement. She relies mainly on the fact that the imbalance in the situation is in her favor. In this country, grandmothers have less support from the vestiges of the patriarchal tradition. They are away from their home turf.[10] If the mother can rely on female relatives—aunts or cousins—who will not be as likely to use her child, she sends the child to them frequently and fosters that contact in lieu of the tie to the grandmother. The mother keeps the grandmother away from the child by offering herself, deflecting the grandmother's demands by fielding and interrupting them, often at quite an emotional cost. If she is not a single parent—and statistically she often is—she can rely on a husband or a companion to help her regain dignity and strength. She can have this male figure step in as she defends her rights, preventing her mother from taking over completely.

Finally, the mother relies on the daughter herself. The daughter usually has extraordinary power in these circumstances, because she brings new relationship models from the outside, from peer groups and school. These new models give the mother a sharp sense of contrast and courage. When she sees that her daughter's peers do not seem to get the treatment at home that her daughter is getting, she is all the more encouraged to rescue her from the grandmother. This rescuing step is almost always experienced as a long overdue character-building event. Its delay is understandable, since, almost invariably, by rescuing herself in her daughter, the mother risks losing her own mother. She also risks being labeled "cruel" by the Anglo people outside the family. When she steps out into her immediate environment and speaks, for instance, to a counselor or a teacher about conflict in the family with her own mother, she is perceived as being harsh, irreverent, and "rejecting" of the grandmother. She is not seen as being respectful of the aged, as the stereotype of Puerto Rican identity dictates that she should be.

Families that manage to change these kinds of interpersonal arrangements around the grandmother are usually able to facilitate most developmental transitions. They not only have prevented potential pathology in the third generation but also have curtailed the perpetuation of an anachronistic pattern. The grandmother's behavior would have seemed perfectly reasonable in the 18th or 19th century, when her stance simply would have mirrored the patriarchal, vertical arrangement in which she was placed in relation to her husband. In feudal Puerto Rico, she worked the land and the household, and it was necessary to have obedient children helping out under the orders of a woman who was, in turn, obedient to the patriarchal *señor*. Family members were, first and foremost, members of an economic unit in a difficult environment.

The chances of a Puerto Rican girl's becoming a subservient female are, of course, lessened immensely if her family lives in a particular ecology, that is, in a *barrio* where the grandmother can get around, where she knows other people who speak her language, and where activities such as playing the lottery, joining senior citizen clubs, or other informal groups (such as TV soap-watchers) allow some target of control—other than the grandchildren. Families lacking that ecology and forced to carry a tyrannical grandmother with no outlet are now more numerous than ever. She cannot be sent back because of the high price of the plane ticket and the deteriorated economic resources of family members living on the island.

The notion that the subordinate stance of the Puerto Rican woman results mostly from an original patriarchal culture that suppressed her fails to acknowledge the loopholes in the patriarchal system. These loopholes can be found in the early experiences of many women from the second generation who today defend their daughters from the grandmothers. These are usually experiences that occurred at the beginning of the century. The patriarch lived then in a Caribbean context, far removed from the women's liberation movement. Yet he was tested in some way by the women in his family, and he was not allowed to prevail. These were usually occasions when, because of his love for his daughter and/or his wife's hidden influence in buffering his power, the patriarch would allow the daughter to "win."

One such daughter, Doña Petra, remembers her father with fear and admiration: She credits her experiences with him as a motivational source for her ability to help her current family cope with the host culture. She recalls vividly how, as a little girl, she had a duel of wills with her patriarch. He boasted out loud that he could kill anyone in his family who flunked—and she knew he meant it. The threat grew in her as a kind of strange and personal challenge, a test of power, yet a test of love. It kept working on her mind until she started deliberately and slowly to let herself flunk, looking forward with fear and fascination to her father's reaction. "Will he go ahead and kill me? Hurt me?" Doña Petra remembers that finally he got the news, and "I won!" After that, she could do many more things. Her flunking in school was insignificant in comparison to her interpersonal gains. "Today I have two daughters, and they both are going to college."

The changes we see in the situations of Doña Petra and Carmen mark shifts in the marital arrangement of the Puerto Rican family. These shifts are associated with a new image of the man as a benevolent tyrant, a powerful force that can be stopped or influenced directly by women. Eventually, the increasing ability of wife or daughter to modify the patriarch will lead to a flexible and open family system evolving toward an increasingly symmetrical arrangement between spouses and between daughters and mothers.

Of course, these shifts are more conspicuous among the stable rather than the unstable poor. Few helping institutions deal with the families that present the more flexible evolving patterns, with some equality between the spouses beginning to show. By their very nature, the helping agencies draw their stereotyped ideas of the subculture's identity from their dealings with the more impoverished and unstable families, who usually present the more extreme pathological instances—such as the most primitive of the incest situations. These cases usually involve the exploitative use of a daughter, which is sanctioned by an extremely subordinate mother. Such a mother sees herself as a hungry rival for the scarce favors of the patriarch. The following situation typifies this:

Norma fled from her rural family because her stepfather was about to abuse her sexually. Announcing that he had already abused her older sister, he threatened, "Before a boy can do it, I . . . ," as if the patriarchal male could perform the function of initiating all females of his clan. Norma ran off to another city, where she took refuge with an older man who later married her. She remembers calling home 2 days after running away and finding out that her mother betrayed her and betrayed her sister. The mother blamed them, not the stepfather, for what happened.

It remains important to broaden mental health professionals' concept of Puerto Rican family heterogeneity. This entails helping them achieve a more varied normative framework. To do this, it will help to systematically expose professionals to families with less extreme problems, such as those in turmoil because of an adolescent daughter's having an unwanted pregnancy. Until recently, this common situation was often thought to be a result of the daughter's having a possessive, forbidding, overstrict father and a helpless, though supportive, mother in the background. A new development is the daughter's suggesting that the pregnancy might have been prevented if she had been able to talk to her mother, if she had felt that her mother "understood." Lack of friendship between mother and daughter—and not just the strictness of the father—is increasingly brought out as a key determinant in the girl's actions. This, too, suggests that simple curtailment of the patriarchal influence is overemphasized as an explanation for the growth of assertiveness in the Puerto Rican woman. A more likely explanation for these complex changes is that they involve a blending of two forces: (1) the drive for liberation on the part of the American woman within the Anglo culture at large and (2) the Puerto Rican woman's own independent urge to test the patriarch—a development much more contained within her own tradition and probably having roots far back in pre-Columbian family life.

CONCLUSIONS

Human services agencies are currently making attempts to solve problems created by their having ignored the ethnic diversity of families in need. One of these attempts has been the development of a basic idea—the setting in motion of a corrective trend to support each group's cultural identity. Our comments have dealt with inadequate applications of this notion and with some of the perplexing situations they have created for Puerto Rican families. Since support for cultural identity is fundamental to American democracy and its commitment to fairness and pluralism, it is important to recover the original intent underlying the concept. One way of working on its behalf is not to allow poor applications to go unexamined and uncorrected. Because of socioeconomic and cultural reasons, families are already restricted to a limited range of choices in their dealings with the court, the hospital, the school, and the mental health clinic. They do not need the added burdens imposed by misapplications of the cultural identity concept or by levels of intervention that take into account family dynamics *without* considering the interaction of families with the outside institutions (Montalvo & Gutierrez, 1983). Families need a thoughtful implementation of ideas, balancing the demands of the ethnic group and those of society at large without unduly sacrificing either.

The unchanged circumstances of Puerto Rican families—their unemployment, poor housing, inadequate health services, and educational blockage—remain impressive. Yet, within this picture, scattered signs of productive entropy exist.[11] We see parents' dissatisfaction with, and resistance to, the decay of bilingual programs. They call for program review, and they flee to other public or parochial schools. We see the docile parent giving way to the combative parent, who now sets boundaries between the family and the school or who is unwilling to accept the hospital's imposition of second-class service or the institutional view of the older person's "special" position in the Puerto Rican family. There are families who question the mental health professional's reliance on *Espiritismo,* and youngsters who can discriminate between real and fake cultural identity materials. Changes are also evident when students see through the condescending use of the colonial effect as an explanation for Puerto Rican failure, when women attempt to discredit excessive drinking as a Puerto Rican virtue, or when certain new intergenerational dynamics alter the subservience of women. Such changes reflect a more heterogeneous population than is usually presented in the literature. These changes are not statistically documented, widespread, or stable enough to delude us into thinking that Puerto Rican families as a whole are undergoing a remarkable transformation. However, these changes seem to be the precursors of an emerging readiness for community organization and the development of politically aware pressure groups, which will, in turn, enrich the host culture.

NOTES

1. See Alers (1978) and Trevino (1979) for thoughtful discussion on health services models. Also noteworthy is the comprehensive model developed by Dr. Patricio Vives at the Children's Hospital Medical Center, Harvard Medical School.

2. Lower-class Latins (primarily Puerto Ricans) in East Harlem expressed a definite preference for the services of a psychiatrist over those of an *espiritista,* and for prescription drugs over home remedies (unpublished study conducted in New York City by Louis Johnson and reported by Alers, 1978). In our clinical experience, the tendency among Puerto Ricans to prefer the professional over the *espiritista* increases with higher socioeconomic status. In a Philadelphia sample of 400 working-class families, only 25% claimed they would use an *espiritista.* However, 68% said they had friends who would (Gutierrez & Montalvo, 1980). This large group may gather many who use one and need to deny it. In this sample, use of the *espiritista* was prevalent among mothers of female dropouts and not among mothers of male dropouts. This reflects the culture's view that the girl is in need of special protection but not the boy. It also displays that the legacy of using the *espiritista* is passed on mainly through female lines. Since the *espiritista* is usually used at times of crisis rather than for routine problems, the finding also suggests that mothers of female dropouts and their daughters represent a population of distressed families.

3. The importance of such community resources cannot be exaggerated. According to a careful survey of mental health needs and services for the general population in Boston, the non-mental-health sectors are the chief providers of service. Social agencies, neighborhood centers, settlement houses, casework agencies, welfare

departments, churches, temples, and various youth service agencies were seeing as many young people as *all* of the mental health settings combined. In this city, the best equipped with psychiatric clinics in the world, clergymen were counseling twice as many Bostonians as were in psychotherapy with private psychiatrists. Casework agencies were treating twice as many emotionally disturbed patients as were psychiatric clinics (Ryan, 1979).

4. Casa del Carmen, a Catholic Charities storefront agency.

5. Even this level of intervention is beset by difficulties. Families need to be prepared, reassured, and protected by these advocacy institutions. Often, families are intimidated by the complexity and formality of the process and are afraid of the potential reprisals from landlords, neighbors, schools, hospitals, and so forth. Their fears are well founded and adaptive. When the legal action ends, they remain in the slums, and previous promises of safety by the advocacy agencies prove insufficient.

6. This is a state of high excitability often presenting with seizure-like phenomena and rampant anxiety. *Ataque* can reach incapacitating levels and usually results from being caught in severe interpersonal conflict and having to choose one side or the other. The *ataque* "resolves" a situation for the person who felt to assert himself or herself would cause a painful loss of approval from family, friends, or both. For a case example emphasizing the syndrome's intercultural function, see "Maria Should Look Different" in Montalvo (1974).

7. A survey research study on Puerto Rican youngsters in Philadelphia revealed that male dropouts were much more likely to come from families where both parents were present but the father was unemployed than from single-parent families or two-parent families with the father employed. These findings give further evidence as to how the world of work affects family functioning and emphasize the permeability of boundaries between these systems (Gutierrez & Montalvo, 1980).

8. Stanton and Todd (1979) describe a promising way of working with the addict and his or her family, which starts with the assumption that families and addicts will routinely try to sabotage each other's efforts to change by being interprotective. In the Stanton and Todd project, the addict's and the family's capacity to outmaneuver each other has been observed in different ethnic groups; thus these processes of reciprocal sabotage cannot be regarded as a special feature of Puerto Rican cultural identity. Various ethnic groups seem to display similar intrafamilial determinants (i.e., cohesion, inclination toward forgiveness, primacy of blood ties), which produce similar behavioral patterns. These patterns interact with poverty, alienation, drug accessibility, and other external dimensions to shape the treatment-failure statistics. The projected population growth among Hispanics and their increased drug addiction require experimentation with different preventive and therapeutic measures designed to have an impact on the family, for instance, (1) stronger ecological controls at the source, cutting drug suppliers by means of honest and effective law enforcement; (2) well-conceived, theatrically appealing materials for popular media (radio, TV soaps, etc.), showing the role of the "helpful" family in the maintenance of the addiction and highlighting the everyday heroics displayed by the family when it actually helps the addict disengage from his or her habit; and (3) a new breed of bilingual drug counselors, with special skills in detecting and countering the family's indulgence and fragmentation when dealing with the addict's guile.

9. Not being able to send the youngster to Puerto Rico has major consequences. For some families, there is an increase in problematic behavior in the youngster and in

symptoms of stress in the caretaking adults. This is associated with increased requests for institutionalization of youngsters. Many families react by dealing differently with the child, by forcing internal modifications. Of special interest are those few families who *also* change their way of dealing with institutions. They make up for the closed exit by better utilizing extrafamilial resources and also facilitate change for the community by becoming politically conscious.

10. Situations in which grandmother's being away from her turf encourages the second generation to exploit or abuse her, remain underreported. The no-win situation for the grandmother is that she recovers a measure of compensatory control and support only through activities in the home. This usually means that she is trapped and turns even more to the children, unwittingly exploiting the third generation because she cannot cope with the environment outside the home.

11. Ilya Prigogine offers an explanation, complete with mathematical proofs, as to how order and complexity may emerge in a universe of ever-increasing disorder. Order emerges *because* of entropy, not *despite* it (see Jentsch and Waddington, 1976).

REFERENCES

Alers, J. A. (1978). *Puerto Ricans and health: Findings from New York City.* New York: Hispanic Research Center.

Carnegie Foundation. (1979). *Bilingual education and the Hispanic challenge* (Annual Report). New York: Author.

Eisenberg, L. (1975). Primary prevention and early detection in mental illness. *Bulletin of the New York Academy of Medicine, 51,* 118-129.

Fernandez-Marina, R. (1961). Puerto Rican syndrome: Its dynamics and cultural determinants. *Psychiatry, 24,* 79-82.

Gutierrez, M. J., & Montalvo, B. (1980). *Choice of non-delinquent and delinquent careers among Puerto Rican dropouts* (Interim Report No. 1). Philadelphia, PA: Office of Juvenile Justice and Delinquency Prevention.

Gutierrez, M. J., & Montalvo, B. (1984). *Dropping out and delinquency among Puerto Rican youths: A longitudinal study* (Final Report). Philadelphia, PA: Office of Juvenile Justice and Delinquency Prevention.

Holmes, T. H., & Rahe, R. H. (1967). The Social Readjustment Rating Scale. *Journal of Psychosomatic Research, 11,* 213-228.

Jentsch, E., & Waddington, C. (Eds.). (1976). *Evolution and consciousness: Human systems in transition.* Reading, MA: Addison-Wesley.

Marques, R. (1977). *El Puertorriqueno Docil y otros ensayos.* San Juan, Puerto Rico: Editorial Antillana.

Montalvo, B. (1974). Home-school conflict and the Puerto Rican child. *Social Casework, 55,* 100-110.

Montalvo, B., & Gutierrez, M. J. (1983). A perspective for the use of the cultural dimension in family therapy. In C. Falicov (Ed.), *Cultural perspectives in family therapy.* Rockville, MD: Aspen Systems Corporation.

Rivera de Buchanan, M. (1975). Community mental health and the juvenile justice system. In D. J. Curren (Ed.), *Proceedings of Puerto Rican Conferences on Human Services* (pp. 125-131). Washington, DC: National Coalition of Spanish-Speaking Mental Health Organizations.

Rothenberg, A. (1964). Puerto Rico and aggression. *American Journal of Psychiatry, 120,* 962-970.

Ryan, W. (Ed.). (1979). *Distress in the city.* Cleveland: The Press of Case Western Reserve University.

Sissons, P. L. (1979). *The Hispanic experience of criminal justice.* New York: Hispanic Research Center.

Stanton, M. D., & Todd, T. C. (1979). Structural family therapy with drug addicts. In E. Kaufman & P. Kaufman (Eds.), *The family therapy of drug abuse and alcohol abusers.* New York: Halsted Press.

Steiner, S. (1974). *The Islands: The worlds of the Puerto Ricans.* New York: Harper & Row.

Striner, R. (1976). *Regaining the lead: Policies for economic growth.* New York: Praeger.

Trevino, M. C. (1979) *The sociocultural influences on health services research and health services delivery for Hispanics.* Presented at the meeting of the American Public Health Association. Albuquerque, NM.

Twentieth Century Fund Independent Task Force on Federal Education Policy. (1983). *Making the grade.* New York: Author.

U. S. Commission on Civil Rights. (1976). *Puerto Ricans in the United States: An uncertain future.* Washington, DC: Author.

8

Family Identity, Ritual, and Myth:
A Cultural Perspective on Life Cycle Transitions

LINDA A. BENNETT
Memphis State University

STEVEN J. WOLIN
George Washington University Medical Center

KATHARINE J. MCAVITY
Washington Psychological Center, Washington, DC

Why do families vary so much in terms of the continuity of family culture from one generation to the next? Our understanding of this phenomenon is limited. Sociocultural studies of family characteristics that influence generational continuity are rare. Although clinicians recognize the impact of prior generations on current family attitudes and behavior, family specialists do not have an adequate vocabulary, let alone a carefully constructed paradigm, to explain how the process of cultural transmission does—or does not—take place.

Because the evolution of family culture is a dynamic process, the study of intergenerational continuity requires a flexible and holistic approach. Thus we view families from a broad and systemic perspective in order to clarify the ways in which they negotiate the maintenance or loss of various aspects of their cultural legacies. At the same time, we focus on a particular vehicle for this transmission, which we call "family identity," a composite construct of what the family represents in the minds of its members.

In this chapter, we explore family identity and its various components. First, we define family identity and demonstrate how rituals and myths both represent and perpetuate family identity over time. Next, we examine the interrelationship between family identity processes and generational transitions in two very different family groups—the ethnic family and the alcoholic family. Finally, we suggest the clinical implications of family ritual maintenance and change. We hope the concept will ring true to family researchers and clinicians alike and will provide a tool for assessing and redirecting the process of family transitions over generations.

FAMILY IDENTITY: THE ROLE OF RITUAL AND MYTH

Definition of Family Identity

Family identity is the family's subjective sense of its own continuity over time, its present situation, and its character. It is the gestalt of qualities and attributes that make it a particular family and that differentiate it from other families. As a family-level construct, family identity is analogous to the individual-level construct of ego identity conceptualized by Erikson (1959). Like ego identity, it is subjective and reflexive: By definition, it must resonate within the family whose identity it is.

In defining identity for the individual, Goffman (1963) suggests a three-part typology that helps to distinguish "felt" identity from its more objective counterparts. "Objective social identity" consists of the characteristics that we (the external world) impute to a person and comes in two versions: "virtual," or in the eye of the beholder, and "actual," meaning the attributes that the person could in fact be proved to possess. "Felt," or personal, identity, in Goffman's thinking, has one basic form derived from two sources: "identity pegs"—the image of the individual in the minds of others, or their knowledge of the individual's niche in the world—and the unique life history that is attached to this one person. For the individual, identity encompasses, but surpasses, the mere facts of existence. In Erikson's (1959) formulation, there is a merging of the individual's core and the inner coherence of the group or groups with which he or she is identified: "The term identity expresses ... a mutual relation in that it connotes both a persistent sameness within oneself and a persistent sharing of some kind of essential character with others" (p. 102).

Family identity is similarly characterized by subjectivity. However, our notion of family identity goes beyond the supposition that family is one determinant—albeit a powerful one—of individual identity. It is, instead, a group psychological phenomenon, which has as its foundation a shared system of beliefs. Shared belief systems are the implicit assumptions about roles, relationships, and values that govern interaction in families and other groups. The existence of shared belief systems in families is supported by the work of Handel (1967) on family themes; by Jackson (1965), Riskin (1963), and Ford and Herrick (1974) on family rules; by Ferreira (1966) on family myths; and by Reiss (1971, 1981) on family constructs.

Handel (1967) describes a "family theme" as "a pattern of feelings, motives, fantasies and conventionalized understandings" which organizes the family's view of reality. Themes are found in the family's implicit directions, its notions of 'who we are' and 'what we do about it' " (p. 18). A family theme may have both adaptive and dysfunctional features, affecting behavior in a variety of areas and activities. The theme can regulate interaction with the external world and can influence interpersonal involvement within the family.

Whereas Handel states that a theme is an organizing principle, Ford and

Herrick posit that "family rules" are binding directives concerning the ways in which family members should relate to one another and to the outside world. "Smaller" rules help to regulate behavior, while "larger" rules "express a philosophy, contain a definition, and refer to a theoretical ideal or goal. They have character and style" (Ford & Herrick, 1974, p. 62).

Ferreira's (1966) notion of family myth emphasizes the extent to which this kind of shared belief system supports pathology. "Family myth" refers to "a number of well-systematized beliefs, shared by all family members, about their mutual roles in the family and the nature of their relationship" (Ferreira, 1966, p. 86). Although the myth may serve as the family group's defense against reality, "at the same time, it constitutes, by its very existence, a fragment of life, a piece of the reality that faces, and thus shapes, the children born into it and the outsiders that brush by."

Another form of shared belief system is the "family construct." Through a series of experimental studies, Reiss (1971) has demonstrated that "the family's shared view of its environment may be partly a product—directly or indirectly—of the perceptual and cognitive response dispositions of its members and the influence of these dispositions on one another." Reiss describes the way in which each family creates its own paradigm, a system of shared assumptions to make sense of the world and coordinate the actions of the members.

Family identity—like family theme, rule, myth, or paradigm—is largely unarticulated. Themes, rules, and myths are perhaps most accurately described as metaphors inferred by an outside observer to account for redundant patterns of behavior that are perpetuated in families. The family paradigm, while systematically deduced from laboratory observations and procedures, is similarly a descriptive label affixed by someone outside the family. By contrast, each expression of family identity is unique. There are as many family identities as there are families, making a typology a contradiction in terms.

What attitudes and assumptions constitute this "system of shared beliefs"? What are the components of family identity? First and most fundamentally, it incorporates certain beliefs about family membership, that is, who is in and who is out, both now and in the past. For example, in some families, second cousins are members; in others, they are not. Second, family identity is made up of certain "temperamental qualities" of day-to-day life in the family. These include (1) the degree to which individual family members are differentiated from each other—whether differences between members are tolerated; (2) the intensity of life in the family—the degree of detachment versus intimacy; (3) the breadth of family experience—both literally, in terms of geographic dispersion and social interaction, and less literally, in respect to the degree to which the family can comprehend or envision the world beyond its doors; (4) the degree to which the family is inclined to evaluate its own experience— its self-reflection; and (5) the relative rigidity or flexibility of the family toward the moral aspects of its experience—its sense of right and wrong.

In addition to possessing attributes having to do with membership and temperament, family identity is greatly influenced by the family's beliefs and recollections about past history. An elusive historical aspect shapes family identity and the extent to which the family understands its present condition as part of a continuum over time. For most families, the past motivates the family to preserve its identity from one generation to the next.

Phases of Family Identity Development

Most people are part of and influenced by two family identities: that of the family in which they are reared, and that of the family they form through marriage and procreation. To the extent that elements of the family-of-origin experience—attitudes, values, patterns of behavior—carry over into the nuclear family, we can say that this "new" family has or has not adopted that particular heritage. Heritage is the measure of continuity. Thus at marriage, two individuals, newly joined, have two established family identities to draw from in the elaboration of their own.

The new family identity will somehow integrate and reflect these two pasts. Berger and Kellner (1974) refer to this process as an active attempt "to match two individual definitions of reality" in the service of constructing a shared identity that preserves continuity with the past.

> The two distinct biographies, as subjectively apprehended by the two individuals who have lived through them, are overruled and reinterpreted in the course of their conversation.... The couple thus construct not only their present reality but reconstruct past reality as well, fabricating a common memory that integrates the recollections of the two individual pasts. (p. 167)

Thus the creation of a single family identity—"this is who we are as a couple and as a family, distinct in important ways from all others"—is the critical goal for newlyweds during the early phase of their union. Whether it is a first or a later marriage, this mission applies. Couples who do not successfully establish a sense of shared family identity at this time may encounter serious developmental setbacks in later phases of their career; some may dissolve the marriage out of disappointment caused by unsynthesized differences between them.

During the family's middle phase—the child-rearing years—conditions are at their best for the consolidation of family identity. Although identity is shaped by the decision making of the first phase, it ripens in the course of the family's experiences during these years. The family at this point cannot *not* be a family, a fact that is demonstrated unintentionally in the myriad of everyday routines and interactions that take place in every household. This is the long stretch of time in which "the way we do things" gets acted out with relatively little interference from the outside world and in which there is as much internal constancy as the family will ever achieve.

During this phase, families will invoke the past as precedent in determining their behavior, whether consciously or not. Some will be more didactic ("Your grandmother said to use these dishes only on special occasions"); some will be more authoritarian ("You'll do just as I did when I was a child"). Styles that are repeated can vary widely, from the formality of the family that continues to demand the attendance of all members at Sunday dinner to the casualness of the family that duplicates the drifting of its members through the kitchen as they make their own sandwiches.

The late phase of the family is a period of transition and loss. Each instance of change might be a universal and even an expectable crisis, but the net effect on the family is instability of identity. Boundaries shift as children leave home, as they establish families of their own, as health fails in the older generation, and as members are lost through death. On many fronts, the certainties of family life in midphase are being challenged. Roles must be reviewed and revised as the children become more self-sufficient outside the home and more capable within it, as parents make midlife career adjustments, and as retirement looms.

During transitional periods, identity becomes more explicit. As the oldest family members age, for example, issues of heritage and inheritance become increasingly relevant. Even those families least predisposed toward self-analysis are given to retrospection in this phase, and what has long been simply assumed—the whole sense of who they are as a group—receives more conscious recognition.

Ritual

Rituals enact the family identity. As a symbolic form of communication repeated in a stereotypic fashion, rituals provide meaning and satisfaction to participants. Family rituals, as defined by Bossard and Boll (1950), are primarily centered in the home, away from public scrutiny and away from the direct intervention of religious institutions. Rituals are condensed versions of family life as a whole. Their performance clarifies roles, delineates boundaries, and defines rules. With repetition, they serve to stabilize the family and affirm its shared belief system.

In practice, family rituals fit into three groupings: celebrations, traditions, and patterned routines. Whatever the family's socioeconomic background, ethnic orientation, or religious beliefs, rituals from all three categories are part of its life experience (Wolin & Bennett, 1984).

Family celebrations are the holidays and occasions widely practiced throughout the culture and deemed special by a particular family. To this category belong rites of passage such as weddings, funerals, baptisms, and bar mitzvahs; annual religious celebrations such as Christmas, Easter, and the Passover seder; and secular holiday observances such as Thanksgiving or the Fourth of July. These rituals are characterized by their relative standardization across most families in American society by the fact that they are usually specific to the subculture that chooses to celebrate them, and by the universality of the symbols that pertain to each of them. It is the atypical family that would not list a series of such occasions as part of its ritual legacy.

Such holidays and occasions offer members the opportunity to clarify their status within the family and to assert their group identity *as* a family. Celebration rituals have another unique function: They denote the family's perceived identification with a wider ethnic, cultural, or religious community. The rites of passage have other important functions for the family: They help to define membership, and they signify developmental milestones. As will be seen in the Klipa family celebration of the Serbian-American *krsna slava* holiday described later, holiday rituals have the power to convey ethnic identity over generations.

Family traditions are less culture-specific than celebrations and more idiosyncratic to particular families. They do not have the annual periodicity of holidays or the standardization of rites of passage, though they recur with regularity in most families. In terms of the extent of preparation and the specificity with which events unfold, they are only moderately well-organized in comparison with celebration rituals.

Each family describes its own set of traditions, commonly naming summer vacations, visits to and from extended family members, anniversary and birthday customs, parties of various kinds, and special meals. Participation in annual community events may constitute a family tradition, as does attendance at family reunions. Although the culture influences the form of these rituals (e.g., with birthday cards or birthday cake), the family itself chooses the occasions it will embrace or emphasize as traditions. Perhaps this element of choice contributes to the high degree of meaning family members generally attribute to their traditions, and to the attachment they exhibit to their continuing observance.

The least-often acknowledged family rituals are *patterned routines.* Among rituals, these are the ones most frequently enacted but least consciously planned by the participants. To this category belong the family's regular dinner time, bedtime routines with children, the customary treatment of guests in the home, or leisure-time activities on weekends or evenings. In some families, the discipline of children or everyday greetings and good-byes are considered rituals. Whatever the patterns, these interactions help to define the members' roles and responsibilities; they are a means of organizing daily life.

All of these rituals in family life have characteristics that help to distinguish them from mere routines. They are bounded, in that the family conducts them at certain times and places with as little interruption as possible. They follow a sequence that entails a period of preparation and clearly defined beginnings and endings, and they allow for recollection or reminiscence at a later date. They are compelling: They have the power to preempt. They are symbolic: "This is the way we do it."

Because ritual behavior itself is patterned, ordered, and predictable, it has a pervasive power to organize the family. And though there are some exceptions, rituals involve all members of the family, who must coordinate their individual activities in order for the ritual to be realized. Family rituals therefore demand cooperation in planning and in implementation. Through repetition of the familiar, they reinforce and sustain the particular attitudes or assumptions on which they are built.

Most germane to our theory of the maintenance of family identity over time is the role of ritual in transmitting family culture from one generation to the next. Rituals are, above all else, memorable. Though each nuclear family creates its own celebrations, traditions, and patterned routines, frequently they contain elements of rituals performed in previous generations. By the same token, the rituals of the present will persist in some form into the future.

Family ritual development follows a course paralleling the stages of the family career and has the potential to advance or retard it. Rituals evolve in the early phase as the couple selects the occasions and events it will mark and settles on meaningful domestic routines. The birth of the first child is an important impetus to the process. Suddenly there are many more "problems" that require "solutions," and in many instances, rituals will be devised to satisfy these needs.

Rituals reach their fullest expression in midphase. During this period, we can discern variations in family ritual life most clearly. Orthodox or rigid families tolerate few, if any, deviations in their ritual practices. Role relationships in these families tend to be hierarchical, with parents in command, expecting all family members to follow the script scrupulously. In the least conventional families, by contrast, rituals are subject to modification or revision, even for inconsequential reasons. Role relationships tend to be egalitarian, and any member can make changes in the preparations for, or the carrying out of, a ritual; rituals deemed important in earlier years may be abandoned for simple lack of interest. A third type of family has a more flexible stance toward its ritual life. In these families, the parental hierarchy is supported, but children gain power in the family as they mature. Rituals are valued, but variations on old themes are permitted, and even encouraged, to the extent that they reflect or capitalize on changes in the family.

As the family makes its transition to the late phase, we see the implications of these differing styles in the transmission of family heritage. In more rigid families, the unyielding adherence to ritual performance may result in foreclosure of the identity issue. Codified beliefs and unchallenged parental authority limit the children's late-phase options, since the transmission of family identity has a take-it-or-leave-it quality. We see this kind of rigidity illustrated when strict limits are imposed on participation in a ritual: "only members of our household" or "we only invite Dad's family for Christmas." When children in such families grow up and leave home, they feel pressured to return for family celebrations and traditional events, a demand often in conflict with profound changes in their own growth and development. This orthodoxy takes yet another form when a grown child brings close friends or potential marital partners into the family, and the newcomers are made to feel like unwelcome foreigners. Such a family cannot accommodate itself to late-phase realities.

In contrast are those families whose ritual performances are casual and infrequent. These families also limit the options for passing on their heritage in the late phase, since they have conveyed relatively little in the way of traditions and values to their children. When the children face their own task of selecting mates and starting the family cycle anew, they may legitimately ask of their family of origin, "What were you people all about anyway?"

Myth

Whereas ritual transmits family identity via behavior, myth conveys it in narrative form. In creating its myths, the family draws upon its factual history and its folktales. The myths that emerge are a blend of fact and fantasy, incorporating crucial events, important people (the heroes and the rogues), and major themes in the family's history.

Like societal myths, family myths do not have one "true" or definitive version. There will be considerable variation in the way they are recounted by different members of the family, particularly with regard to the meaning ascribed to events and the relative importance of people. But when all the members' stories are considered as a whole, certain similarities will reflect the family's shared beliefs.

Family myths and rituals are mutually reinforcing. Myths include information about the performance of rituals in previous generations, and rituals concretely illustrate the attitudes inherent in the myths. Leach (1954) proposes that "myth is the counterpart of ritual . . . myth regarded as a statement in words 'says' the same thing as ritual regarded as a statement in action" (p. 13). Their function is essentially the same: to inform or remind all family members who they are, what they are to believe, and how they are to behave, and to promote the continuity of family identity from one generation to another.

Like rituals, myths are subject to change over time. In the early phase of family life, the newly married couple engages in myth construction, a process of drawing on material from the two families of origin (which is naturally subject to reinterpretation in the course of marital interaction) and adding details from their own experience as a couple. During the middle years, these myths will be elaborated upon, but they are seldom challenged. The late phase is the time when children are most apt to question the myths they have grown up with. They seek clarification and may obtain new information that permits—or demands—a new perspective on familiar material. If family myths are validated in this phase, they may endure into the next generation in essentially the same form. If not, the grown offspring will reject them, and they will not survive.

Just as they demonstrate different styles of ritual adherence, families exhibit different degrees of attachment to their myths. In the most orthodox families, myths may be very elaborate. At the other end of the spectrum, the family stories are insubstantial and contradictory, hardly sufficient to inspire belief. Most families fall in between, with a stock of descriptive stories about themselves that are part history and part imagination. Whether the family memory tends toward the benevolent or the suspicious, family members accept and value these tales. In the late phase, they may be taken with a cautionary grain of salt.

RITUAL CELEBRATION IN THE ETHNIC FAMILY

To illustrate the relationship between maintenance of ritual and transmission of family identity, we present a case of the ethnic family in the United States. Although we are well aware of the many examples of intergenerational loss of ethnicity, many orthodox families of various ethnic groups and religious denominations cherish and preserve the traditions of the past. The Klipa[1] family and its celebration of the Serbian *krsna slava,* or patron saint's day ritual, is a case in point. The ritual combines ethnic, religious, and family symbols and is transmitted patrilineally over the generations. For most Serbian families, it is one of the most meaningful occasions of the annual holiday cycle, if not the most valued (Bennett, 1981). By reviewing the details of this family's patron saint's day celebration, we can see the relationship between the annual ritual enactment and its transition in family identity across three generations.

Steve (48) and Georgeann (44) have lived their entire lives in the Pittsburgh area; both are Serbian. They have four children: George (21), Judith (18), Nicholas (15), and Paula (11). Steve's mother, however, was born in Russia and adopted Serbian customs upon marriage to his father, including the family tradition of *krsna slava* celebration, which she learned from her husband. At 73, she is the only remaining grandparent in the family. The other three grandparents came from an area of Yugoslavia known as Kordun, a region of Croatia where many Serbs settled during the Turkish occupation and from which many early 20th-century Serbian *émigrés* to the United States originated.

Steve is next to the youngest child in a family of several siblings, and Georgeann is one of the two youngest (twins), also from a large family. Born in a coal-mining community outside Pittsburgh, Steve and his family moved to the Monroeville area when he was a young teenager; they were parishioners in St. Nicholas Serbian Orthodox Church. After graduating from college and getting a master's degree in secondary education, Steve became a high school math teacher and a football coach.

Georgeann was born and raised in the McKeesport area of Pittsburgh; her family belonged to St. Sava Serbian Orthodox Church. A high school graduate, Georgeann worked as a secretary before marriage, and since then she has been a housewife. She and Steve moved upstairs in his mother's home upon marrying and to their present house 8 years later. Most of their siblings live in the area, and some reside in the immediate neighborhood. The family has always belonged to the St. Nicholas parish and is an active leader in the church.

The four children are recognized as being unusually involved in Serbian activities, generally. For example, they have all learned to play Tamburitzan instruments and to perform ethnic dances. Although the Serbian language is not the primary language of the home, it is widely used. Steve and George are fluent, and Georgeann and Judy, moderately fluent speakers. Serbian phrases are often used, and native terminology for food is regularly employed. Serbian dishes are regularly prepared and served in the home.

Two years ago, Steve and George went to Yugoslavia, the first trip anyone in the immediate family had made. They visited family members remaining in Kordun and toured the monastery area of Serbia. The entire family would very much like to go again in the near future, and such a trip is seen as a family goal.

The celebration of *krsna slava* in the present generation of the family is highly valued. In both families of origin, the patron saint's day celebration was a major event; Steve's family celebrated Saint George (*Sveti Djurdje*) on May 6, and Georgeann's celebrated Saint Nicholas (*Sveti Nikola*) on December 19. Following the traditional patrilineal custom of the Serbs, they continued to celebrate St. George as their *krsna slava* upon marriage, but they also perpetuated the observance of St. Nicholas, mainly as a day of fasting and piety. In recognition of both family-of-origin legacies, they named their first son after the husband's family's patron saint, George, and their second son after the patron saint of Georgeann's family, Nicholas. They observe both St. George and St. Nicholas days at the present time, closely emulating the customs from the parents' growing-up years.

When Steve was a boy, the immediate family and close relatives on his father's side of the family came for *krsna slava,* which was held in his father's home. Asked if they celebrated it every year, Steve exclaimed: "Every year, every year. My father left the strongest sense for perpetuating it." The following is a digest of Steve's description of his family's patron saint's day celebration during those years:

It would be a whole day affair. No matter how early I'd get up, father would have gone out and cut green branches. And he would adorn the doors with them. He'd go to the woods nearby and get the green branches. So you knew that this was Saint George.

The spiritual part came first. And the reason they cut the green branches is that during the Turkish oppression, over the winter the Serbs would more or less lay low. But now [May 6] the foliage is starting to come out in the mountains, and they would leave the villages and go cut the branches. They'd go to the mountains and be ready to give their lives, not knowing if they were coming back.

As we got older, we'd do it with my father. When I bought this property, that was one of the first things I thought of, how blessed I am that I have the foliage, and then my kids can do the same thing. We go out early in the morning. After you get the branches and spread them around the house, all the family members go outside and wash their faces in the dew.

Then we'd take the *kolac* (bread) to church and have it blessed. When people began coming to the house, you'd have a spontaneous warm feeling. Hospitable. It's festive from the start. You'd come in and eat and drink. The *kolac* was in the middle of the table, with a candle; it stays there. That's what adorns the table, at any Serbian holiday. And you know, bread, bread is very much . . . we were always taught reverence for bread. If it would fall on the ground, you would kiss it. Before you cut the bread, you'd make the sign of the cross on it.

Inside the house you have put boughs around the icon on the wall [picture of St. George]. During the *slava* you're always thinking about your forefathers. And naturally on *slava* you're always talking about the relatives and your favorite stories are going to come up again. You look forward to hearing them. You could have heard it a hundred times, it sounds just as good.

My father would make sure that everyone's happy and that everything's in order. If there is anybody who is going to be last, he wants to make sure he is it. Right off the bat he would offer drinks. And the food would come later on, and then continuous, you know. It would go on up 'til 11:00.

Another unique thing about my family is my mother. My mother being Russian, the Orthodox was first. But my mother learned Serbian and speaks it. She did all the cooking; she says my father taught her a lot. There were many unique simple tricks about the exotic part of cooking which my father would do. He taught her what she didn't already know about the cooking for *slava*.

Music is a big part of the festive occasion. You come, you're happy to see each other, and the occasion is ever-present on your mind. Drink, eat, and be as merry as you can the rest of the night. And my father loved group singing when I was growing up, but because his hand was mangled and he lost it, he didn't play any instruments. But they all sang so beautifully, so we'd sing. We love the instruments, that part of it, but if there's no instrument, that doesn't stop you either. You sing. And then that was that much richer, as our kids started getting older and learning the instruments.

The most spiritual, meaningful things were always and still are the same. But you know, when they first came over here, some inconveniences deterred them from doing things exactly as they would have earlier. You have instruments now; you can afford things that we couldn't then. So things just got richer. And then when your family's younger, you'd have more close relatives come, but now as they get older, it starts reaching out. So it's clustered now in several homes. That's the one change among my family. My kids have a very close *slava,* and they'll always be part of it. As they get older, they'll still have our *slava,* but the first cousins will be starting on their own. When the kids were younger, we even had all my wife's family, besides my family. Then it became so big that it became impractical.

You have to give my dad the credit; my father's spirit was so strong. But at the same time, my mother being Orthodox, that helps us to be stronger in the way we observe it.

The shift in verb tense from the past to the present and back again throughout Steve's interview reflects similarities in the way his family observed *slava* when he was a child and in the way he celebrates it now with his nuclear family. The important central elements remain: the *kolac* and the blessing of the *kolac* in church on the day of the *slava;* the candle; the green boughs over the doorways and on the icon; traditional drinks, such as plum brandy and wine; traditional foods, such as lamb, bread, *sarma;* the presence of certain people; washing their faces in the dew (a family custom); music and dancing; father at the head of the table and oldest son to his left. The very elements that were described as having occurred when Steve was a boy were either described to us by the children as still occurring or observed by us during the course of our being part of their *slava.* The family follows the same religious practices for proper *slava* observance, the most vital being the blessing of the *kolac* in the church, with all family members present. An elaborate turning, cutting, and pouring of wine on the *kolac* ritual is conducted by the parish priest, with all family members taking turns kissing the *kolac* and helping to turn it.

Spiritually, the emotions that the father felt as a child as *his* father led their *slava* observance and that *he* now feels as he directs his family's celebration are deeply felt and dramatically expressed by everyone in the family, particularly by George. The family myth paralleling the ritual is firmly maintained. Being outwardly emotional about these feelings is an acceptable style to the family; in fact, it seems to be encouraged. Such emotions are conveyed mainly by the men. The women concur with the positive value placed on expressing such feelings openly but seem less inclined to be the ones to express them. Instead, they tend to be the workers behind the scene, handling the preparations for *slava.* In adopting the husband's family's *slava* through marriage, it is clearly an advantage if the wife comes from a family in which it is observed, so that she understands the basic traditions and how they are carried out (as does Georgeann), or if she is receptive to learning the appropriate customs (as was Steve's mother).

St. Nicholas day also has potent religious connotations for Serbs; therefore it is not surprising that the Klipas would observe it even if it had not been the *slava* celebrated by Georgeann's family-of-origin. However, as family members discussed St. Nicholas day, they associated its importance, in part, with the fact that it was the maternal family's patron saint day. They communicated a strong sense of its continuation in the family, especially the emphasis placed upon fasting (following certain rules about what food was acceptable to eat during this period). Georgeann described St. Nicholas day as it was when she was a child:

Daddy always said it was a big, big fast day, no matter what. And everybody would come. We'd always eat in the dining room. That was such a special day. It was a traditional fast day, which meant you could have your beans and sauerkraut, and then naturally you have your fish and your bread and your *pogaca* (flat breads); that's *posno* (food with no fat).

He used to always tell us, "Whatever you do, always hold your *slava.*" Once the girls get married, we inherit our husband's, which is for me St. George. But we keep St. Nicholas. Some people figure, "It's not my *slava:* I'm going to eat meat." But it is still mine, and we keep it.

We definitely took St. Nicholas day off from school, and daddy didn't work. And to this day the children, I just tell them [the school] they're observing a religious holiday.

My father always had the cross on the *kolac,* and my aunt would make the braid for it. [Georgeann's mother died when she was 11.] For our *slava* you would always have the candle, and the church calendar, and it is always decorated in red, blue, and white, the Serbian flag, and a beautiful cross in the middle. We had a beautiful big icon [of St. Nicholas]. He'd take it down from my brothers' bedroom.

And then, when Steve and I were going together, he was at my house for St. Nicholas. And when my dad brought the icon down and he lit the candle, Steve . . . it's super. When he saw that, he said, well he didn't say it was then but he asks it now, "Is that why you fell in love with me?" No, but little things like that are important.

To Steve and Georgeann, those considerations were very important in deciding to marry. They talk now about how much they agreed about keeping the Serbian customs and having a family. They explicitly concurred that they wanted to marry soon (within a year), to hold the wedding immediately after Lent and Easter, and to begin having children right away. The priests from St. Nicholas and St. Sava parishes performed the wedding ceremony in St. Nicholas Church. Since their marriage, it appears that they have had little trouble agreeing about issues such as how much money to donate to the church, how many children to have, what to name the children, ties to the extended family, and how to observe holidays. They clearly see their family as strongly connected to both the paternal and maternal lineages. In a general way, Steve and Georgeann have similar heritages, which facilitated development of a shared family identity drawing upon traditions from both sides of the family, with somewhat more emphasis placed upon Steve's heritage, especially with respect to the *slava* celebration and to living above his mother's home for years. The myths that they recount about their family history are similarly congruent.

Being the ages that they are, George and Judy think about whether they will "marry Serbian" and about what kind of families they will have.

George: I always watch myself, because I want to marry a Serbian. That's important to me, because it makes life easier. For me, as deep as I am into this, I want somebody who could cook for me, my food. I want somebody who could celebrate my *slava* with me, know what's going on, have respect. You know, you marry an Orthodox Christian; that's most important to me, but my first preference would be a Serbian Orthodox. But if I fell in love with a Greek girl or a Russian girl, I wouldn't feel any great loss about it.

Judy: I would always be wary to get real involved with somebody who wasn't Serbian. They used to ask me in civics class, "Are your parents making you marry a Serb?" I said, "No, but they would really want me to." The older I get, the more I see; it's so much easier when you marry Serbian.

George and Judy have met many Serbs—American and Yugoslav born—at Serbian events in Pittsburgh and other cities; in the course of those contacts, they have learned new ideas about how *krsna slava* can be celebrated and have introduced those new perspectives to their family.

Judy: I saw people up in Chicago. They have the same *slava* as us, but do even different things than we did. Like they save an egg from Easter and put it with all kinds of greens on the table.

George: Good things, constructive things, not to make you seem any less Serbian. I think it's more beautiful to incorporate them. If you see somebody else doing something really nice, bring it home, and you do it. Like my dad, we always washed our face in the dew [on St. George day]: That's generations of tradition. But this other Serb over in West Wilmerding, he never knew it. And my dad told him about that, and they love it. They can't seem to wait to do that every year.

The combination of adherence to the family customs around *slava* and openness to incorporating new traditions seems to reflect a flexibility within the overall design of the Klipa patron saint's day celebration. Answers on the Slava Inventory[2] indicate a strong inclination for maintaining the *slava* intergenerationally. All six family members strongly agreed with the following statements:

- The *slava* is an important family event.
- It is good that *slava* has been handed down over the generations.
- During times of financial hardship, the family should still celebrate *slava.*
- Children should know the history of the *slava* in their family.
- Celebration of *slava* makes me particularly aware that I am Serbian.
- When Serbian families do not observe *slava,* they seem less Serbian.
- I would like to see our *slava* continued into the next generation.

There is evidence of some flexibility regarding the rules of *slava* observance in that everyone disagreed or strongly disagreed with the statements "Only family members and godparents should be invited to *slava*" and "I prefer that we invite only Serbian guests for *slava.*" Interestingly, all family members agreed or strongly agreed that "when Serbian women marry non-Serbian men, I approve of their continuing the *slava* into their own families." This may be an indication of the family's flexibility regarding strict patrilineal inheritance of the patron saint and a realization that with intermarriage being as common as it is, the *slava* would be lost in many families if women were not permitted to continue it themselves. Evidence of their firm adherence to the traditions is found in the following statements:

- It is essential that a priest come to the house for *slava*.
- It is necessary for the oldest male on the father's side to be present.
- It is necessary to prepare food and drink in the traditional way.
- It is necessary to take the *kolac* to church to be blessed.

This synopsis of *krsna slava* continuity in the Klipa family portrays a family in which tremendous value is placed on preservation of the patron saint's day celebration as well as other aspects of the Serbian ritual traditions. The Klipas do not constitute the "typical" Serbian family. "We're different, I tell you, this family," George said. "We're very traditional about how we do things, but we are also very liberal about how other people do things." As such, they represent a family that has successfully made the transitions in family identity across the generations. They accomplish this, we assert, through their adherence to family rituals and their espousing of family myths.

THE STRUGGLE TO CHANGE A FAMILY IDENTITY

In the Klipa family's construction of its ethnic heritage, the successful transmission of family identity takes on a positive value from the point of view of its members. However, continuity of family identity is not so advantageous in all families. Children from family environments characterized by severe, chronic stress may adapt better if they can modify—or lose entirely—the identity of their family of origin. For them, the passage into a new generation offers the main opportunity for escape and the hope that their past can be altered in the future.

Grown children of alcoholic parents are an especially vivid example of this struggle to modify one's family identity. Among the familial psychopathologies, alcoholism is distinctive for its pervasiveness and its destructive consequences. No family member, regardless of age, is left untouched. Few family activities are spared from the effects of alcoholic interactions. Grown children will look backward (often as patients in psychotherapy) and describe how they knew that their family was unusual and how they planned a different life for themselves once they were free and on their own. They looked forward to these days of independence. Yet many remain scarred by the childhood experience, with persistent sequelae such as difficulties in intimate relations and low self-esteem. Regarding the establishment of a new and healthier family, these victims of alcohol abuse often say, "I didn't know how to make one; I didn't know what was normal."

The case of Paul T is a classic example of this dilemma. Paul typifies many such children of alcoholic parents in that the final outcome of his attempt to separate from the past remains uncertain. The family identity in his parent's generation was definitely alcoholic. In his own generation, it is unclear whether he has maintained an alcoholic family identity or not. Perhaps it will not be completely resolved until the next generation.

When Paul T was a young boy, he observed his playmates in their homes and longed to be taken away, to be adopted by another family. Perhaps he could just live with a distant relative, he thought, to get far away from the frightening and painful confusion of family life with his hard-drinking father and his seemingly helpless mother. He daydreamed about life on his own, about the peaceful routine with imaginary parents. But most of all, Paul silently vowed he would be a different father to his children and a different husband to his wife. He would, he swore, make a different family, one that reflected what he was about, and one that was quite different from the home he lived in as a boy.

Dreams and daydreams are often a means of escape for some children who are captive in the chaos of life in an alcoholic family. Such wishes for escape are not limited to flights of imagination. Some young boys and girls make plans to run away, which range from Huck Finn fantasies to somewhat more plausible schemes, such as finding a friendly relative who will offer the child a new home and replace the parent. Another kind of defense against the reality of the family's disrupted life is to spend an unusual amount of time at the house of a friend or neighbor. Ironically, so much familiarity with the healthier, happier family atmosphere may only serve to increase the child's unhappiness by making the return to home a dreaded and difficult event. Daydreams are safer, since they protect against this kind of overinvolvement.

At an early age, Paul began a long and intense process of emotional disengagement from his biologic family. This was not simply the rejection of a parent or the general disaffection with the family that we usually associate with adolescence. Rather, it was an intentional process of taking stock and distancing himself from the family as a whole.

But as he grew older, Paul increasingly kept these feelings of alienation and disappointment deep inside himself. His accepting, responsible behavior disguised his real emotions. In marked contrast, Paul's older sister and younger brother appeared to be more obviously affected by the drinking problems in the family. Elizabeth, Paul's senior, bolted the house at 16. She ran away with her first real boyfriend, an Irish Catholic boy of 19. Unfortunately, it was not a lucky match. Elizabeth's husband proved to be an alcoholic himself, and although they raised three children together, it was not until Elizabeth divorced him 10 years later that she actually escaped an alcoholic home environment.

Paul's brother William provides an even more dramatic example of one option open to the children of an alcoholic parent. As the youngest child, William got caught in the web of alcoholic family behavior to a greater extent than either Paul or Elizabeth. After Elizabeth had left home and as Paul was preparing for college, their father's drinking grew worse, precipitated largely by their mother's developing what proved to be fatal breast cancer. Paul cut short his plans for full-time college and switched to night school and a daytime job to help support the family. With Elizabeth gone and his father barely managing to hold any regular employment because of his drinking, William, 10 at the time, was forced to take care of both his mother and father. By the time he was 13, he was failing in school. He dropped out entirely at 15, the year his mother died. Like his father, William began drinking heavily at that time and proceeded on a downhill course. By the time he was 20, he had almost no contact with Paul, and except for requesting money in occasional calls from a distant city, William has not been heard from in 15 years.

Children in this situation rarely blame the parent. They have not yet become confident in the growing awareness that theirs is not a normal way of life; there is still some uncertainty about the right way to behave, along with considerable doubt about what they deserve. Add to this the child's worry that he or she is responsible for the situation that is so out of control—a responsibility that is all too often attributed to them by the parents. With so many doubts and too little experience to realize that he or she is simply a victim of these circumstances, it is no wonder that the child's imagination turns to thoughts of rescue rather than revenge.

The death of Paul's mother tore his family apart. Even though battered by alcohol abuse, the family retained some sense of cohesion while she remained alive and drew together more closely during her illness. With her death, however, Paul's father gave up all attempts at sobriety. Within several months, Paul left the family home, ready to make his long-planned escape. He enrolled in college full time. While a student, he began dating Monica, and he was introduced to her family soon thereafter.

Paul clearly recalls his attraction to Monica, a secretary in the city. "I loved her organized life, the planning that went into everything she did, which showed up especially in the way she took care of me!" She had acquired these abilities in her own family, Paul told us in an interview much later, and he recognized it as an atmosphere very different from the one he grew up in. "They went on regular vacations," he recalled. "I was very impressed by that."

Paul's relationship with Monica has had a major impact on his life. It was an event we understand as a crucial step for some children with alcoholic parents. Paul's wish to disengage from the family he grew up in, which he had felt from early childhood, was dormant in his adolescence. As he left home to begin a new family, it reemerged as an objective to be realized. He could now take advantage of his early deliberateness—the distancing and the urge to disown his family-of-origin identity. His sister Elizabeth had also attempted an escape, but without much awareness of what she was running from or any clarity in respect to her choice of a new partner. William, the least deliberate of the three siblings, never knew what hit him, and he lost control over his life.

Entering the late adolescent/young adult phase, the child who has already set a course for escape may act more slowly and cautiously than the sibling who is enmeshed as part of the problem. The unaware child will begin several possible scenarios at this transition point, each related to the child's uncritical stance toward the family. In the simplest version, the child takes no issue with the way family members act or think, since he or she is too well integrated into the system to reflect upon it. It is not surprising that these children are apt to repeat the alcohol abuse patterns of their parents. A variation on this theme is the child who makes sporadic, unplanned, or impulsive acting-out attempts to flee the alcoholic environment—the "problem child" who runs away, gets involved with drugs or alcohol, drops out of school. Finally, some children who are closely allied with the family may attempt to control the alcoholism— and their vulnerability to it—by exhibiting overly responsible, hypermature behavior. Some signs of this particular scenario include a constricted personality, rigid control in the use of alcohol (and a fixed negative attitude toward its misuse by others), and, very often, marriage to an alcoholic spouse.

Paul's marriage, on the other hand, provided a framework for establishing a new family identity. He adapted easily to the patterns and rituals of Monica's family, while occasionally complaining about its overcontrol of him. In the course of the next 9 years, three children were born, two daughters and a son. Professionally, Paul pursued a successful career as a lawyer in corporate practice.

But after Paul had been in the law firm for a few years, boredom got the best of him. He was about 30 when he had the first of several affairs. His drinking got heavier at about the same time. Monica discovered the extramarital activities, confronted Paul, and demanded a decision regarding his plans for their marriage. Paul decided that he wouldn't risk the family life he essentially loved. He dropped the casual liaisons, cut back on his drinking, and left the law firm, which had demanded more than its fair share of Paul's energies. The family—a powerful force in Paul's maintenance of equilibrium— had won its case, for the time being.

Tragically, Monica developed an incurable illness soon thereafter. Paul had just taken an exciting and exhausting position as legal counsel for a southern city government. This required that the family move. Monica's sickness, a form of lupus erythematosus, added a burden that this young family could hardly withstand. Paul would interrupt most days for medical appointments and watched helplessly as his wife became progressively more ill and then gradually, inexorably, died.

Left with three children to raise and a demanding job in a strange city, Paul was under his severest stress. He began to drink heavily. Soon it was out of control, with morning hangovers, regular blackouts, and weekend binges. On two occasions, a sympathetic colleague encouraged Paul to dry out in week-long hospital stays. But without the safety of Monica's strong influence, Paul's vulnerability surfaced.

The next 2 years were Paul's worst since his mother's illness. Daily alcoholic drinking, with typical physical and social consequences, were ruling the family life, subsuming all that had been built by Paul and Monica.

About a year after Monica's death, Paul met Judy. He saw in her some of the same characteristics he had been attracted to in Monica: a strength of conviction, an organized and stable life, and a strongly ritualized, nonalcoholic family of origin. Judy was 12 years younger than Paul when she moved into his house, replacing Monica.

The alcohol problem did not go away overnight. Judy had to persistently display her commitment to a nonalcoholic way of life, and she finally insisted that Paul stop drinking altogether. Paul went cold turkey, a painful experience as they reflect on it today, but a turning point in their relationship as well as in Paul's drinking behavior. They were married within several months; Paul quit his job in the city government, agreed to support Judy in her attempt to complete graduate school, and vowed to change his abusive alcohol patterns.

Amazingly, it has worked. Paul and Judy have been married for 5 years now. Judy has completed social work school. Paul's children have grown up and left home. He has attempted social drinking for almost 6 years, and with the exception of an occasional party where he becomes mildly intoxicated, he feels confident about his ability to use alcohol moderately.

The case of Paul T illustrates the struggle to alter a family identity for the children coming from an alcoholic family. Deliberate children use their awareness of their past as a tool for decision making in the present. Although they may not specifically confront the potential vulnerability to alcoholism, the care that they exercise in marital choices marks them as different from their nondeliberate siblings. Paul's selection of Monica, then Judy, vividly documents a constructive wish to protect himself from the past.

Families defined by such chronic psychopathology as alcoholism often focus their family identity upon the pathology. Other, healthier family self-concepts are usually overruled. The normal family rituals, such as dinner times, holidays, and vacations, frequently revolve around the drinking or the drinking interferes in their regular observance. (Wolin, Bennett, Noonan, & Teitelbaum, 1980) Thus children growing up in such a cultural context have fewer nonalcoholic rituals to draw upon for modeling their own nuclear families. Similarly, the family mythology is most likely burdened by alcohol-related tales, some horror stories, and some "amusing" anecdotes, such as the time the Christmas tree was knocked over. We recognize that there are many exceptions to this highly negative depiction of the impact of parental alcoholism upon family identity, rituals, and myths. However, most offspring of alcoholics seem to have at least some experiences akin to those recounted by Paul T. Without some constructive, non-alcohol-laden rituals and myths to draw on, it is an awesome challenge for grown children of alcoholics to develop successfully a nonalcoholic family identity in their own generation. Spouse selection and deliberate action help in making that struggle work. In such instances, the transition over the generation gap becomes one predominantly of change rather than of continuity.

CONCLUSIONS AND CLINICAL IMPLICATIONS

In this section, we discuss three issues pertaining to family identity that are relevant to the family therapist. First, we review the concept of family identity. Second, we examine what the concept suggests about family and individual development. Third, we address how the family therapist can use the family ritual concept in the clinical situation.

A Review of the Family Identity Concept

The shared beliefs of a family are carried and transmitted by its rituals and myths. These family-level beliefs encompass more conspicuous aspects, such as ethnicity, religiosity, and work ethic, as well as more subtle components of the family's gestalt. They take into account the family legacy from prior generations and represent the family's sense of its current place in the world.

During the years when they are being launched into a family of their own, offspring are not typically preoccupied with maintaining continuity with their family-of-origin culture (Bengston & Kuypers, 1977). In fact, as part of the message to their parents that they have grown up and are now independent, children characteristically question their attachment to their family identity. Nevertheless, family identity does play an important role in the life of the young adult leaving home and an even greater role in the experience of the young couple beginning to create its own family.

Family identity issues are powerful forces, for example, in the child's selection of a mate. Some children try to disengage from their family heritage by choosing a particular spouse; it is as though they are attempting to make an explicit statement to members of their family of origin about their determination to escape. As such couples develop their own family identity, they may emulate the spouse's family culture and/or may rely upon very novel rituals drawn mainly from their general cultural environment. As we have noted in the case of Paul T, the sources of family identity are especially important when the child has grown up in a family with severe problems.

In contrast, other children automatically accept and repeat the cultural patterns of their family of origin without much critical review. When this new generation later includes children, and when the annual cycle of family activities requires the young couple to select certain rituals upon which to anchor the new family identity, the legacy of their two families of origin will present a more restricted set of options. In such instances, they tend to repeat the past.

Some children, like those in the Klipa family, act quite deliberately to maintain their family identity. They have been deeply instilled with values, often reflecting their ethnic and/or religious heritage, which they know will be severely compromised if they "leave the faith." Parental influences are strong for such children; they expect to have frequent contact with their extended family and count on those ties for many family functions. By contrast, children in families like Paul T's may take similarly deliberate care to disengage from the past and adopt the family identity of a very different family. Or they may create a novel family identity, one that is attached to a contemporary institution, such as a cult or unusual religious sect, which provides a substitute "family." In our study of couples with alcoholic families of origin, those offspring who employed this strategy—that is, careful planning regarding the heritage development of their generation—were relatively protected from transmitting alcoholism across generations (Bennett, Wolin, Reiss, & Teitelbaum, 1987; Steinglass, Bennett, Wolin & Reiss, 1987).

Family Identity and Developmental Change

As individuals grow up and undergo transitions over the family life cycle, family identity represents a strong force mitigating change and encouraging cultural continuity. In the face of uprooting life events, such as when the family moves to a new neighborhood, family identity can serve to tie the family to old routines and traditions, such that members feel a comfortable *esprit de corps* regardless of their strange new setting. This stability is extremely important for the health of the family, collectively and individually, especially as they encounter situations where they can maintain little control over the external world. Family therapists are well aware of the feelings of insecurity created in some families when they undergo a change in location, jobs, and so forth. Such changes are less stressful, we suggest, in families with a strong cultural identity, in that the family identity serves as a port in the storm of uncertainty in the external world.

Changes in family identity are often brought about by the addition of new members and by wider social developments such as the women's movement and social mobility. We see the tension between change and continuity as being healthy and productive for most families. It promotes a continuous dialogue, requiring the family to keep the past relevant.

Family identity is not only a force against change, however. In adaptable families, as opposed to those that are either excessively rigid or so chaotic that they lack sufficient ritual structure, identity evolves gradually over time (Wolin & Bennett, 1984). More adaptable families allow members to develop over life cycle transitions. These changes are symbolized in current ritual practice and myths, which reinforce new roles and new relationships. Annual ceremonies, for example, provide an opportunity for young couples to demonstrate newly acquired rituals and for their ability to successfully pass over life cycle transitions to be underscored. Family identity, therefore, is not like an immovable anchor in such adaptable families; rather, it is like a rudder, which the family uses to direct its course.

Family Therapy: The Power of Rituals

As one of the mechanisms of family identity continuity, family rituals can play a highly positive role in crossing the juncture between generations. When this transition gets mired in conflict over family identity formation, ritual can be used in clinical contexts to make sense out of the painful confusion. In the therapy situation, rituals provide an excellent entry to exploring difficulties couples have encountered in making the transition from their families of origin to their own generation. Furthermore, they can become a useful focus of therapeutic strategies. Ritual is readily understood by both therapist and family and can easily be discussed in concrete, yet relatively unpersonalized, terms.

We recommend that clinicians working with families consider rituals in planning the course of therapy. Depending on the specific problems of the family, we see five ritual-related therapeutic strategies. First, the therapist can help the couple *construct* a ritual that has never been there. Similar to Schwartzman's (1984) idea of developing a ritual to demarcate a difficult rite of passage, the therapist can work with the couple to create an entirely new ritual, which will serve to resolve a particular family problem. Second, the family that has lost its rituals—perhaps as a result of the intrusive effect of familial alcoholism—can *reinstate* those that it sees as being most meaningful. The particular form and timing of the performance may vary from that of earlier years, since the ritual must make sense to the family in its current developmental stage.

Third, the therapist may encounter families at a time when its rituals are undergoing destructive changes. This is an ideal point to *redirect* a ritual back to an earlier, yet currently relevant, form. Fourth, when a couple represent two highly divergent family-of-origin cultures, they often use family ritual as a battlefield upon which to negotiate indirectly their family identity formation. A therapist may urge such couples to *modify* their current practice of the ritual in order to make it acceptable and meaningful to the family. If they can reach consensus on the elements that are absolutely critical to the ritual and can agree to try it out in its newly constructed form, the family members may very well discover that they can perform the ritual to everyone's satisfaction. Finally, some families develop rituals seemingly for the sake of developing them, with relatively little attention paid to the overall pattern of ritual observation in the home. Early in marriage, some couples struggle futilely in deciding which rituals to maintain, leading to a hodgepodge of ritual assemblage. Such rituals seem hollow and without context, and probably provide little benefit for family members. A therapist might recommend that such families reconsider which rituals are the really important ones for them and urge them to *integrate* those rituals into a coherent whole.

NOTES

1. Real names are used in this case study. The family has been described in an earlier publication (Bennett, 1981) and was accurately identified with the family's permission. Interviews were conducted in 1978-1979, and the data reported here are written as of that time.

2. The Slava Inventory is available from Dr. Bennett at the Department of Anthropology, Memphis State University, Memphis, TN 38152.

REFERENCES

Bengston, V. L., & Kuypers, J. A. (1977). Generational difference and the "developmental stake." *Aging and Human Development, 2,* 245-266.

Bennett, L. A. (1981). The Steve Klipa family: The intergenerational preservation of *Krsna Slava. Serb World, 2* (5), 20-29.

Bennett, L. A., Wolin, S. J., Reiss, D., & Teitelbaum, M. A. (1987). *Couples at risk for alcoholism transmission: Protective influences. Family Process 26,* 111-129.

Berger, P., & Kellner, H. (1974). Marriage and the construction of reality. In R. L. Coser (Ed.), *The family: Its structures and functions.* New York: St. Martin's Press.

Bossard, J., & Boll, E. (1950). *Rituals in family living.* Philadelphia: University of Pennsylvania Press.

Erikson, E. (1959). *Identity and the life cycle* (Psychological Issues, Monograph 1). New York: International Universities Press.

Ferreira, A. (1966). Family myths. *Psychiatric Research Reports, 20,* 85-90.

Ford, F., & Herrick, J. (1974). Family rules: Family life styles. *American Journal of Orthopsychiatry, 44* (1).

Goffman, E. (1963). *Stigma: Notes on the management of spoiled identity.* Englewood Cliffs, NJ: Prentice-Hall.

Handel, G. (1967). *The psychosocial interior of the family.* Chicago: University of Chicago Press.

Jackson, D. (1965). Family rules: Marital quid pro quo. *Archives of General Psychiatry, 12,* 589-594.

Leach, E. (1954). *Political systems of highland Burma.* Boston: Beacon Press.

Reiss, D. (1971). Perceptual and cognitive resources of family members. *Archives of General Psychiatry, 24,* 121-133.

Reiss, D. (1981). *The family's construction of reality.* Cambridge, MA: Harvard University Press.

Riskin, J. (1963). Methodology for studying family interaction. *Archives of General Psychiatry, 8,* 343-348.

Schwartzman, J. (1984). Ritual, change and psychotherapy. *Australian Journal of Family Therapy, 4,* 159-163.

Steinglass, P., L. A. Bennett, S. J. Wolin, and D. Reiss, (1987) *The alcoholic family.* New York: Basic Books.

Wolin, S. J., & Bennett, L. A. (1984). Family rituals. *Family Process, 23,* 401–420.

Wolin, S. J., Bennett, L. A., Noonan, D. L., & Teitelbaum, M. A. (1980). Disrupted family rituals: A factor in the intergenerational transmission of alcoholism. *Journal of Studies of Alcohol, 41,* 199–214.

9

Rethinking Assumptions about Women's Development and Family Therapy

PAULINE BOSS
J. PAMELA WEINER
University of Minnesota, St. Paul

As our field of family therapy is in the process of paradigmatic change, we struggle with the shift from reliance on the precepts of a faltering paradigm to integration of new assumptions from the incoming epistemology. This transitional stage creates conflict and tension in the field of family therapy, but also excitement. There are emotional arguments at conferences and heated letters to the editors of professional newsletters. Traditional academic journals have their share of rejoinders and responses to responses of published articles. Epistemology is discussed at length in journals and at conferences, even to the point of excess that some call "epistobabble." And finally, we see the rare publication of a collective statement by 47 of the nation's senior female family therapists stating their beliefs about women in families in challenge to others who see family reality more traditionally.[1] Change is in the air. We are struggling with ways to do family therapy and must look both forward and backward to chart our course.

As a contribution to this transitional period in family therapy, we offer this chapter on women's development in order to critique existing assumptions and to explore new assumptions for a new, more flexible systemic paradigm. Specifically, we believe it is time for family therapists, both male and female, to reconsider the standard assumptions about women's development on which we have based both our interpretations of and interventions in family relationships.

DEVELOPMENT AND FEMALE VULNERABILITY

The evidence in psychology and sociology is now fairly substantial that developmental pressures after childhood are greater for females than for males in Western culture. In addition, anthropological studies have shown that puberty rites for boys are more supportive for entering the adult world than are the rites for pubescent girls, which focus more on "cleansing" than on "maturing." If, indeed, there is an emergence of female vulnerability during adolescence, one could ask whether this sets a pattern for the female's adult life, with more pressure on her than is necessary if we take just maturational changes into account. In a context of negative sanction (as exemplified by a community telling a girl she needs to cleanse herself, a media and fashion industry telling her she must be thin and flat-chested to be attractive, or men's magazines telling her a flat-chested girl is *not* attractive), are not young girls and women at developmental risk? In addition, females are vulnerable to incest, rape, and domestic violence in a culture where violence is evident.

Because of evidence of female vulnerability, both generally and in the context of therapy, we challenge existing assumptions about female development. To begin, we enumerate the traditional assumptions about women that we consider most pernicious and unfounded, and attempt to identify their sources and explain their popularity among developmental thinkers and clinicians. These are the assumptions we have traditionally held in our field about women's development, and we submit that they have not been supportive of women's development.

TRADITIONAL ASSUMPTIONS ABOUT WOMEN'S DEVELOPMENT

The Primacy of Nurturance

A good woman never says "no" to her family's request for her nurturance. Her role is to "smooth emotional waters" for the family—as well as for others. If there is emotional turmoil in her family, it is her fault for not having succeeded as peacemaker and caretaker. She should gain fulfillment through her husband and children. (German women say their role traditionally was to do *Kinder, Kirche, und Küche,* or "children, church, and kitchen.") A woman without a husband and children thus cannot be fulfilled or sufficiently developed. Accordingly, she should be more invested in the happiness, satisfaction, and so forth, of others than in her own personal condition.

From this traditional perspective, then, if a woman focuses on her own development, she is viewed as selfish and narcissistic. Her total devotion and attention to the needs of others (especially husband and children) are what is societally admired, even if her nurturing is given at high cost to herself. (We think of the wife of an Alzheimer patient who died before her demented husband did simply because she believed it was her duty to care for him at all costs. She stopped taking her own blood pressure medication because it made her too tired to care for her sick husband.)

Based on this assumption, the establishment of boundaries between a woman and her family is unacceptable, as is the notion of setting limits on what she owes to others or may be called upon to give up or sacrifice. She is socialized and reinforced to be other-centered as opposed to self-centered. But at the same time, she is criticized for being dependent on her husband or children for her identity as a woman.

Women as Inferior

A second assumption that has traditionally supported the thinking of family therapists is that women are the weaker sex, the second sex, the "other" sex, and thus are less fully and completely equipped than are men for a full range of human abilities and accomplishments. Accordingly, women need special help. This assumes that they are less competent than males, and it implies that if women do succeed, their success is due to the help they received from a male. So, the men are still in charge.

If a woman therefore does something well or receives notice for an accomplishment, her womanhood, femininity, or integrity may be questioned by her colleagues, especially if she behaved in an assertive, ambitious, or competitive manner. Men as well as women tend to attribute a woman's successful performance more to luck than to skill as compared with attributions about a male's success. This is because of our assumption that females are less capable than males.

Women as Asexual

The traditional assumption that women should be asexual reflects the belief that a healthy woman cannot vary from the prescription of "virgin mother." That is, she should attract a man and conceive a child but do it all without revealing an interest in being sexual. If she shows open interest in sexuality, she is cast as oversexed. (The cruel term of "nymphomaniac" has been used for women, with no pejorative counterpart for males.) On the other hand, if she shows no interest, she is cast as undersexed (with the equally cruel terms of "frigid" or "butch"). Within marriage, she should meet her mate's sexual needs willingly and may, in private, be an interested and active partner, provided that her sexuality is hidden from everyone else. The double standard punishes her harshly for extramarital affairs and, in many situations, for visible premarital sexual activity with other than a committed partner or fiancé.

Women as Total Mothers

Motherhood is a woman's absolute role, and she should become strongly child centered in order to secure her child's well-being, according to this traditional assumption. Behavior of the child is attributed primarily to her behavior.

Fathers are not considered a critical part of the parent–child system. That is, they are considered transient and are functional primarily outside the family, in the world of work. It is noteworthy here that even in animal studies, monkey mothers are written about less negatively than are human mothers. Ethologists do not exhibit the harshness of words that therapists have traditionally used to describe mothers: for example, schizophrenogenic, engulfing, enmeshing, smothering, or castrating.

Women as Rigidly Differentiated from Men in All Roles

This traditional assumption is based on the belief that rigidly defined and mutually exclusive sex roles help male and female children develop more healthy personalities. Parental roles are prescribed to be rigidly differentiated— the husband/father being instrumental, and the wife/mother being expressive. According to traditional structure functionalists, not only is there a biologic basis for this differentiation, but it is pragmatically the most efficient family structure for freeing the man to enter the workplace, unencumbered with responsibilities for children, housekeeping, and the emotional climate of the home. (These assumptions are based on ideas from Talcott Parsons and Robert Bales [1955] and are perpetuated by many therapists today.)

SOURCES OF TRADITIONAL ASSUMPTIONS ABOUT WOMEN'S DEVELOPMENT

These assumptions about women's development and families are difficult to trace in a simplistic, linear fashion; they are woven so deeply into our associations and expectations that we find it hard to locate their beginnings, historically and socially. Several themes *do* recur consistently and clearly, however. First, the focus of these ideas about women's development is not on women at all but on women's functions in relation to males and children, as nurturer, caretaker, and helper. Second, her "nature" is described in relative and comparative terms; for example, she is *not* sexual (compared to men) and *not* equal (compared to men). Moreover, when her value is highlighted, it is never freestanding or self-contained, as is a man's potential for achievement or a child's ability to grow and develop. Historically, her greatest function has always been to contribute to the well-being of others and to "accomplish something" only through them, vicariously and once removed.

We suggest that these views of women do not tell us much about women at all, because they have evolved without a woman-centered perspective and depend largely on male attitudes, values, and priorities. They are therefore more instructive about men's experiences and development. Unfortunately, this lack of a view from female reality in popular knowledge and common cultural assumptions parallels the deficit status of formal knowledge from social and psychological research about women's development. Historically, we simply have not studied women's experiences and researched women's developmental issues from a woman-centered perspective.[2]

The androcentrism of dominant developmental premises should not surprise the serious student of family therapy or psychology. Virtually all of the theory, research, and scholarly literature about human growth and development that appeared during the first 70 years of this century has been specific to the lives of men and boys. Most experimental and observation-based research has been conducted by men, with explicit or implicit focus on male subjects. Evidence of this focus has recently been pointed out by Gilligan (1982) in her critique of male-based moral development theory applied inappropriately to girls and women.

If you are a mental health professional who studied at an American graduate school during the last 20 years, you were most likely taught male-derived developmental theories as straight lecture material, largely without the benefit of interpretive treatment or contextual assessment. At the universities that we and our students attended, the concepts of development and psychosocial maturation proposed by Erik Erikson were very popular in several departments; rarely, if ever, were the psychoanalytic roots of Erikson's ideas identified or clarified. Frequently, Freudian explanations of relationship conflicts, sexuality, and, most important, women's development were offered as fact, without reference to their scientifically speculative and historically Victorian origin. It seems that since the 1940s and 1950s, the social sciences, education, and human services in American institutions of higher learning have been permeated with psychoanalytic "theories" about human development.

There are several possible explanations for this phenomenon. The high status of postgraduate psychoanalytic training in the mental health professions and the hyperelevation of medicine as the foremost American profession in the middle of the century have certainly been instrumental in the proliferation of Freud's ideas. Social and economic values during the post-World War II era were suddenly rigidified as women left the factories and returned to the traditional hearth to produce the baby boom. Culturally, the American people were ripe for the dualistic psychosexual dynamics of psychoanalytic ideas in which the notion of "opposite sexes" was grounded in genital differences in order to explain passivity and masochism as central to female sexuality.

We suggest that these developmental theories were, and are, at the very core of education and, more significantly, of the process of professional self-creation. Family therapists are to some extent the products of the course work, training, and supervision they absorbed: A majority of mental health practitioners have been working within the meanings of predominantly male-derived, male-focused ideas about behavior and relationships. They have diagnosed, labeled, and, in a clinical sense, seen their clients through these lenses, these versions of truth. And women, through these metaphoric glasses, are relegated to the peripheral function of a lens focused on men. In other words, the dominant theoretical concepts and assumptions underlying beliefs about mental health and therapeutic interventions should be applied primarily to male experience, male psychology, and male development because the research, theory building, and cultural grounding have been male focused to the extent that women are "the other" (what men are not) or are an added-on afterthought to male reality.

Perhaps no documentation of the orientation to exclusively male reality among therapists is clearer or more striking than the results of the well-known study of male and female psychologists, social workers, and psychiatrists undertaken by Broverman, Broverman, Clarkson, Rosenkrantz, and Vogel (1970). Therapists were asked to choose the qualities that they believed characterized (1) the healthy adult, (2) the adult man, and (3) the adult woman. The clinicians' perceptions of the healthy adult and the adult man were almost identical; however, the adult woman was described in terms of opposite, unhealthy traits. Specifically, adult women differed from adult men and healthy adults in general by being more submissive and emotional and less independent, objective, and competitive. For these therapists, the authors concluded, a "normal" woman was a mentally unhealthy adult.

The idea that women's development is not adequately addressed by prevailing theory is not a new one. In 1924, challenging the Freudian notions of "penis envy" and female inferiority, Horney wrote of gender-biased assumptions:

> Like all sciences and all valuations, the psychology of women has hitherto been considered only from the point of view of men. It is inevitable that the man's position of advantage should cause objective validity to be attributed to his subjective, affective relations to the women—the psychology of women hitherto actually represents a deposit of the desires and disappointments of men. . . . If we are clear about the extent to which all our being, thinking, and doing conform to these masculine standards, we can see how difficult it is for the individual man and also for the individual woman really to shake off this mode of thought. The question then is how far analytical psychology also, when its researches have women for their object, is under the spell of this way of thinking, insofar as it has not yet wholly left behind the stage in which, frankly and as a matter of course, masculine development only was considered. (p. 37)

Horney's hypothesis cannot be nullified or overlooked even today as family therapists work with women in the context of couple or family relationships. One trend that emerges in current commentary on therapy with women is the appearance of more female clients who display and express great competence in their professional and creative activities but who have profound dependency needs on the personal level and who manifest deep feelings of inferiority and helplessness in conjunction with their femaleness (Hare-Mustin & Marecek, 1986; Kjervik, 1979; Lerner, 1980; Symonds, 1976). Often, these female clients base their self-esteem on a husband or lover, valuing themselves solely on approval from external, primarily male sources.

When asked to share their inner needs, desires, or core beliefs, their responses reflect a lack of self-concept, or, as one of our clients stated, "an empty sense of self, which makes me feel like I deserve to be ignored." Upon closer scrutiny, we find that these women are fulfilling powerful maintenance functions in their relationships and families, keeping others strong through their understanding.

The popular press today refers to something called the "Cinderella complex," which explains woman's lack of self-development as a wish to not grow up and a desire to remain childlike, passive, and unindividuated indefinitely. We suggest that this kind of labeling ("Cinderella") smacks of woman blaming and misogyny (i.e., a return to the notion of female masochism so popular with classical psychoanalytic clinicians) and is a reification of the myth of female helplessness. Because severe dependency needs and lack of self-development in women reflect traditional gender-role socialization, the superficial and circular explanations for these phenomena reflect the absence of appropriate, female-focused models of development and mental health.

RETHINKING WOMEN'S DEVELOPMENT

A rethinking of women's development—a kind of conceptual affirmative action—based on research and theory about women over the life cycle has begun, and early contributors are starting to influence family therapists. We offer several examples from the literature to illustrate emerging shifts in assumptions about women's psychosocial development and to encourage the reader's own questioning and exploration of old and new assumptions about women's development in the context of her family.

Chodorow's *The Reproduction of Mothering* (1978) is a reframing of object relations theory and of notions of early gender-role formation, with an emphasis on the mother–infant processes and differential patterning effects on female and male children. Drawing on psychoanalytic concepts, social learning theory, and social psychological precepts, Chodorow suggests that the psychological identification of the female infant with the caretaking mother generates the concept of a female capacity for empathy, attachment, and interpersonal sensitivity. Another important contribution is Dorothy Dinnerstein's *The Mermaid and the Minotaur* (1976), which explores the effects of traditional gender roles and parenting functions on beliefs about female and male power. She hypothesizes that early maternal dominance in child rearing inculcates deep-seated fears about the engulfing and irrational power of women compared with a more logical and measurable male power associated with fathers and the world outside the home. Dinnerstein calls, as do we, for a critical look at the structure-functional dichotomy (Parsons & Bales, 1955) of instrumental–expressive gender roles in families. The influence of traditional "structural" thinkers on marriage and family therapy cannot be overlooked, especially among well-known and influential clinicians such as Minuchin, Bowen, and Haley. The reader is referred to Goldner (1985), Hare-Mustin (1978), Layton (1984), and Weiner and Boss (1985) for a thorough discussion of gender issues, mother blaming, dependency, and autonomy in family therapy.

Clearly, the development and strengthening of woman-focused, woman-based conceptual frameworks and theories of family therapy will depend upon the contributions of researchers and clinicians in building on these and many other works. The generation of such substantive work can be furthered by (1) clarifying the sociocultural and historical components of family therapy theory; (2) establishing criteria sensitive to gender roles for guiding supervision, training, and consultation practices, including special attention to the identification and prevention of sexual harassment; (3) updating and correcting negative and unsubstantiated information about female development in courses, textbooks, lectures, and journals; and (4) acquiring empirical evidence about women's psychosocial development through sound but varied research approaches. But above all, the traditional theoretical assumptions about women's development upon which all such work would be based must be changed to reflect the reality of family life and of women's development today.

Underlying the new assumptions we present in this chapter is our belief that women and men are equal. Indeed, they are different, but those differences result more from social reinforcement than from biology. We believe, therefore, that our efforts as marriage and family therapists must be tempered by what Norman Paul has called "gender empathy" (Paul & Paul, 1976). We need to be attentive to the reality base of our clients and to the larger societal context. The following are facts to consider in our reconceptualization of assumptions:

1. Women make up the majority of people who seek therapy, for themselves as well as for the family.

2. Women develop differently than do men, and they report different experiences. We assume that biologic and sociocultural factors interact to produce significant differences in female and male experiences.

3. The power of socialization cannot be overlooked when assessing gender issues generically and women's experiences specifically. Girls and boys are socialized differently (Block, 1979). Thus this process is amenable to some intervention and change through education and/or therapy.

4. Families as well as the individuals within them differ over time. Getting older matters both physically and psychologically. Older women have a different view of the world, a different physiology, and a different economics in comparison with younger women. This fact must be taken into account by therapists.

5. Family relationships and gender role socialization are affected by powerful economic, political, and, above all, cultural factors (Carter & McGoldrick, 1980). A woman's development cannot be assessed apart from the contexts in which she has lived. In family therapy, socioeconomic and ethnic

aspects of family-of-origin issues must be explored with women as well as with men. How the role of women was defined when a woman was growing up as well as now is a critical area to explore if we are to understand her behavior.

Based on these realities, we present new assumptions for family therapists to consider in their support of women's development.

NEW ASSUMPTIONS ABOUT WOMEN'S DEVELOPMENT

Women and Nurturance

It is healthy for a woman to refuse to be nurturant at times. There is no reason why a woman should be solely responsible for the emotional well-being of children and of aging parents, hers as well as her husband's. Beyond an adherence to an old paradigm, there is no reason why men and boys cannot perform nurturant, caregiving jobs as well.

Rather than a rigid sex-role differentiation, what is needed now is a new flexibility in the attitudes of both men and women about limit setting in nurturant behavior and the healthy use of boundaries in relationships. Women have traditionally not been good in setting limits around their nurturant role. Therapists need to give them permission to say "no" at times.

Using the old Parsonian paradigm of a healthy family, women and girls are supposed to be the emotional fixers in the family; they are not to refuse emotionally needy men and boys. Based on this assumption, the wife cannot refuse to tend to her husband's needs after a hard day at work, regardless of the difficulty of her own day; a sister can be told to wait on her brother, but not vice versa; and, carrying it to the extreme, the little girl cannot refuse her father when he comes into her bed. Women in such families will have trouble saying "no" to demands for nurturance even when they are extreme. This is not resistance or seduction; it is simply a rigid socialization for women to be passive and nurturant at all costs.

Using these traditional beliefs, a woman more than a man will have difficulty setting boundaries with her own family-of-origin (as well as with her husband's). Since women are assumed to have the job of tending to connections with relatives, they may see any breach or friction as their fault—or at least as something they should be able to fix if they are "good" wives or "good" daughters-in-law. They may therefore tend the elderly to the point of exhaustion, without asking a brother or a husband to share the burden. Research indicates that although adult male children help frail elderly parents with financial support, the female relatives, primarily daughters, are left with the physical care. This family structure simply replicates the younger family in which the father provides the money and the mother takes care of the children. Regarding gender and roles, nothing has changed since Parsons and Bales (1955) in the care of aging families. Women remain the nurturers.

Women and Inferiority

Many women are physically smaller, less muscled, and shorter than most males, but because of technology and other such equalizers, such differentials have much less relevance now for married couples in terms of problem solving, earning income, caring for children, and doing the mundane jobs of family living. A woman can be smaller than her husband but be equally powerful given, for example, automation that helps her lift a heavy load. Individual differences across gender and subculture and during certain life cycle events must also be recognized. Indeed, women's endurance in child-bearing and in other rigorous activities may more than equalize male strength in the long view. In fact, negative attitudes about women's reproductive functions have always been employed to justify limits imposed on women in the arenas of intellect and achievement and to reinforce notions of female inferiority. Mortality and morbidity statistics favor females overall from the fetal stage to old age and death. This may be due to some protective hormonal factors, which remain unexplored because of the relative paucity of studies focused on women's physiology and health.

Rather than viewing women as the "weaker sex," therefore, we assume that *both* males and females in families, old and young, will need help at times and should be able to ask for it and accept it from the opposite sex without negative sanction, shame, ridicule, or conditions. We all need help at times; periodic dependence is not solely a female condition.

Women and Sexuality

A woman's healthy sexual development is based on the assumption that both biology and environment matter. From our perspective, the latter (environment) gets more weight over the long run, and the former (biology) receives more weight situationally (especially pregnancy and lactation). We assume that females as well as males are interested in sex but recognize that socialization and reinforcement can influence that interest either positively or negatively for *both* genders. For women, however, especially in our American culture, social reinforcement has been guilt producing and inhibiting.

A woman's level of education or class may not have changed this puritanical socialization, so marital and family therapists must begin with the assumption that a woman or a girl may feel more ashamed and guilty about an interest in sex than will a male. Therapists must also be aware of their own feelings about female sexuality. It is sometimes a shock to find that traditional and limiting assumptions are woven deeply into our own assessments of what we hear as we listen to our clients' discuss their behaviors. We may all too often agree at some level with a client that a wife has indeed done something wrong if she has not met her husband's sexual needs. If she has deviated from the rigid expectations of our society's double standard by having had an extramarital affair, we may be challenged to avoid a punitive and shaming response.

Motherhood and Sex-Role Rigidity

The idealization of motherhood, pervasive pronatalism, and the assumption that the mother is solely responsible for the child's well-being are crippling myths for women's development.

A child's personality development is deeply influenced by what parents do, but strict sex-role delineation can lead to negative development outcomes. A family with rigid sex-role delineation (mother as expressive, father as instrumental) is a fragile system, since it is totally dependent upon two parents *always* being present. If either one is absent because of illness, work demands, death, or divorce, we then have a deficit family structure or a broken family. Instead, when we assume that there are two parents, both should interact in the family, physically as well as emotionally. Old assumptions normalized the absence of the father if it was for work reasons but filled mothers with guilt for being absent for the same reasons. Our new assumption is that families can function well as long as it is clear to all members "who is in and who is out of the family" (see Boss, 1977, 1980, 1986b, 1987, 1988). This more flexible systems criterion will better predict whether a single-parent family as well as a two-parent family can function or not in the care and socialization of children.

The development of a woman's independence and self-sufficiency will, therefore, improve rather than threaten family functioning. Her interest in being nurturant, complemented by her development of self-sufficiency, will support balanced and respectful interaction among family members. A mother also has a chance to get out of the historical double-bind this way. It is less likely that she will be accused of overfunctioning, hovering, or clinging if she is also connected to the world outside of home and children.

IMPLICATIONS OF NEW ASSUMPTIONS ABOUT WOMEN'S DEVELOPMENT FOR PRACTICING FAMILY THERAPISTS

Praxis and Application

For the therapist, male or female, the following questions[3] should be asked whenever families or individuals come for therapy:

1. What are the gender issues in this case? Consult with cotherapists or colleagues, male and female, to get other opinions. (We find that we often miss gender issues with clients who are not of our own gender, so we can seek opinions from a peer of the opposite sex. We support Norman Paul in his call for "gender empathy"; see Paul & Paul, 1976.)

2. How do you think your gender as a therapist will influence these issues for the family?

3. What are possible countertransference issues for you as a therapist in this case? Do gender issues play a part in this countertransference?

4. What would be your goal for the family? Is this goal related to the gender issues you have identified? Do the goals for family members conflict? If so, do you always go with what favors the father (his work schedule, his career demands, etc.)?

5. What is the family's collective goal? Is this collective goal related to individual gender issues in the family? Is a synthesis possible?

In support of these questions and the newly recommended assumptions, we now offer a case study as an illustration of gender-empathic clinical work.

Empowerment: A Major Gender Developmental Issue in Family Therapy

THE CASE OF MOLLY

When I first saw this 34-year-old woman in my office, she looked to me like a 4-year-old. I could hardly hear her tiny voice, and she spoke to me with bent head, only occasionally lifting her head to make eye contact. She was clearly a little girl. At age 6 she had been held down at knife point by one brother while the other brother sexually abused her. The brothers took turns doing this until Molly was 12 and finally able to get away. The parents were focusing on their own trouble (Dad was alcoholic and Mom was trying to cope with that), so no one ever intervened. She had also been sexually abused by her grandfather.

We worked slowly. Trust had to be developed. She expected to be overpowered again. She was puzzled when I would ask her to decide something ("Do you want to come at 4:00 or at 5:00?"), but gradually she developed her strength and regained some of her power. She went back to art school. Months later, she brought with her to therapy a sketch and unfolded it for me, a wonderful smile on her face and looking strong. It was a charcoal sketch of a nude male. I looked at her. She said, "I finally did it; I finally did it." I think it was her way of saying that she had mastered the male figure, including the genitals (which she had discreetly presented in her drawing). She confessed she had struggled for weeks over this drawing, and her teacher had not understood why she was having so much trouble with this sketch since she had done so well with the others.

I saw the sketch as a wonderful overcoming of the helplessness she had learned to feel with males—and male genitalia. She had taken back her power. She looked now like about 18. We still had a way to go, but she was no longer 4.

Although this is an extreme case about a woman who was overpowered as a little girl, we assume that all women in this culture are less empowered than are men. We start from that premise. Indeed, we are sometimes wrong, and the power balance lies in the other direction. But it is a case of Type I or

Type II error, and we find that we are most often closer to reality if we simply assume women are less powerful than men.

Our task as family therapists, then, is to empower without patronizing, so that optimal development is possible. Power cannot be handed to women who were overpowered as children. We cannot *insist* they take control. Neither can we use a strategy that will manipulate them into using it—unless it is to abuse them further so that they finally fire us, a behavior that we have labeled pejoratively as "resistance."[4] Indeed it is resistance, but it may be a positive developmental sign in such clients.

So what do we do? There must be a respect for and reinforcement of any move for change. As the woman takes charge of her own destiny, even if it means she refuses to come at a certain hour or insists that she is not ready to face her abusive or incestuous father yet, we believe and support her. We do not believe that resistance is pathology, especially in people who have previously been abused. They are resisting for a good reason; they may even try to manipulate us. This is how they have survived. They do not trust people, and for good reason. They have been abused. They are often stuck developmentally at the age when they were first abused.

Given this background of deceit and abuse, we feel it is important to develop a therapeutic relationship based on trust rather than on manipulation, simulation, or strategy. Thus transference becomes for us the primary tool of therapy (and sometimes countertransference) as we work with women who, because of early abuse, are stuck at earlier stages of development. As we proceed, there comes a time when the client becomes very angry at the therapist—like a teenager who needs to break away from the parent. This, too, is as it should be. It is not resistance, to be labeled pejoratively. The client wants to be who she is, to grow up. This is what she is saying in a clumsy but essential rebellion.

Too often, rebellion in female clients has been defined as resistance, whereas compliance and submission have been defined as health. For a woman who has been in a powerless position and whose development has been stymied, exactly the opposite is true.

What such women need from a family therapist in order to move forward developmentally is to experience a relationship that is based on trust; to experience a relationship that has limits and boundaries; to learn how to take care of themselves (get locks on doors, finish high school, have emergency phone numbers by the phone in case someone tries to harm them); and to become aware of the high-risk quality of their own intrusion into their children's lives, their own lack of boundaries, and their own behavior as victims. Knowledge is power; resources are power; once they feel empowered and supported, they will move quickly through the remedial developmental stages.

We often see a victimized woman come into therapy like a child and walk out, finally, like an adult. Family-of-origin work is primary. Facing her parents when she is ready is critical to her empowerment. Having her children there, if she has any, is also important, in order to break the cycle of victimization. Having her mate along, if there is one, for joint and family sessions is also critical, but not all the time. We found that women often do not see themselves apart from their roles as wife and mother. If this is true, we see such women alone at times, to work on their development as individuals so that they may balance their familial roles. Often we may see adult sisters together for this kind of work. We recall two adult sisters who came in to change their marital and family relationships so as to avoid replicating the way their mother became a martyr with her alcoholic husband. We invited the mother as well. She sent word that she would talk with her priest instead but that she was glad her "girls" were coming. With this one message, this mother clearly indicated that "her girls" could be different than she was and that this was okay. The young women did indeed change in their personal development as well as in their marital and parenting behaviors.

For women to develop fully, such family-of-origin work will provide a better basis for growth than will an overdependence on an all-too-helpful therapist. It is also more respectful of a woman's capacity to help herself, given a context free of double binds.

CONCLUSION

We have discussed the assumptions, old and new, about women's development as applied to family therapy. Ultimately, we have to consider how family connectedness is programmed into the minds of women and men. There are developmental differences between men and women in families, which are due less to biology than to socialization and cultural context. We have not, in this chapter, presented a clean set of clinical techniques or rules with which to secure gender empathy, nor do we think that researchers have enough knowledge yet about women's development for us to do so. Rather, we have suggested new assumptions under which we can conduct family therapy with women's development in mind. Indeed, in family therapy at this time, we need to be wary of new rules. The pioneers of family therapy had no rules; that was the nature of the first paradigmatic shift. Old rules gave way, and for a period we had experimentation, disagreement, discourse, and creativity rather than hard-and-fast rules. Because we are in another such transition now, we believe that compiling a list of rules for conducting therapy with women would, at this time, be premature.

Instead, we have focused on assumptions, the traditional as well as those that we believe better reflect women's reality today. Each of us must become aware of the assumptions made in the course of our own work and then reassess them. Only then can we develop rules for ourselves, for our situation, and for the families with whom we work.

To this day, family scholars and therapists cannot agree on what a normal family is. It is not even guaranteed that the same reality can be shared by Catholic families who go to a Catholic family therapist, Jewish families who go to a Jewish family therapist, or black families who go to a black family therapist. Families and individuals present themselves with their own perception of reality, and it is often not the same as ours. A time of groundlessness (or normlessness) may be useful during this paradigmatic transition period in the field of family therapy. There may therefore be a current meshing of ideas from Maturana, Varela, and Dell with those of feminist theory in family therapy. The thesis of the former group, especially regarding groundlessness, appears to agree with the feminist challenge to cybernetic theory and is congruent with feminist critiques of traditional structure functionalism as it applies to the family (F. Varela, personal communication, April, 1986).

In this chapter, we have presented an alternative set of developmental premises that we believe can serve to guide our work with women in families today. Clearly, an ongoing refinement of assumptions about women and families that takes women's development into account should concern us at this time of change in the field of family therapy. We present our ideas toward that end.

NOTES

1. From *The Family Therapy Networker,* November–December, 1985, page 17:

COMMUNICATION TO THE FAMILY THERAPY COMMUNITY

In September 1984, almost fifty women family therapy clinicians, trainers, theorists and researchers assembled at a colloquium at Stonehenge in Connecticut to address the role of women in families and in family therapy. This meeting gave structure and support to the attempts of individuals and small groups in our field to focus attention on an examination of gender issues in our theory, in our practice, in our research, and in our collegial associations.

We were concerned and now, a year later, we are still concerned that the family therapy field has ignored gender in conceptualizations of family life. Under the rubric of systemic thinking, family therapists have come to assume that the interior of the family is the source of all dysfunction of its members. Such thinking results too often in holding women ultimately responsible for family functioning and penalizing them for their centrality in domestic life. Colloquium participants expressed concern about the lack of theory (and therefore practice) which connects family functioning to the gender inequalities in the social system which forms the family context.

The massive demographic changes in contemporary family life require a critical appreciation of sex-related issues in marriage, child rearing, work, separation and divorce. The feminization of poverty, the lack of resources for the rearing and maintenance of children, and the rise in domestic violence, all should move family therapists beyond the systemic myths that husbands and wives hold equal power in families, or that families can be treated apart from this context.

We are resolved to challenge sexist theory and practice within family therapy in our work settings, workshops, and conferences—wherever it appears.

We are committed to supporting women's professional development in our field.

We offer the suggestion that colleagues form study groups to develop nonsexist theory and clinical interventions, and then share this work in public forums in our field. [47 names follow.]

2. An exemplary exception to this deficit is the field of home economics, where the mundane tasks of homemaking have been researched in detail for decades. For a review of this literature, see Thorne and Yalom's *Re-Thinking the Family* (1982).

3. These questions are adapted from those used by Carol Anderson, Peggy Papp, Monica McGoldrick, and Olga Silverstein in their presentation at the meeting of the editorial board of *Family Process* in the spring of 1986.

4. The question might be raised, is behavioral marital therapy or strategic family therapy safe for women? These approaches encourage skills rather than insight; they encourage a cognitive reprogramming where the therapist remains the teacher, guide, or strategist. These approaches may therefore merely reinforce a female's dependency. Strategic and behavioral marital therapists, for example, do nothing to promote equality in the family; they are less likely to emphasize the sources of inequity because they do not focus on the larger context in which the family is embedded. Finally, as with most other therapies, these approaches do not appear to recognize the fact that women constitute the majority who seek treatment and that an approach that emphasizes dependency may affect many women differently than it does males.

REFERENCES

Block, J. H. (1979). Another look at sex differentiation in the socialization behaviors of mothers and fathers. In J. Sherman & F. Denmark (Eds.), *The psychology of women: Future directions in research* (pp. 174-191). New York: Psychological Dimensions.

Boss, P. G. (1977). A clarification of the concept of psychological father presence in families experiencing ambiguity of boundary. *Journal of Marriage and the Family, 39* (1), 141-151.

Boss, P. G. (1980). Normative family stress: Family boundary changes across the lifespan. *Family Relations, 29* (4), 445-450.

Boss, P. G. (1986a). The process of gatekeeping in scientific publications. In M. Sussman (Ed.), The charybdis complex [Special issue of *Marriage and Family Review, 10* (1), 33-39]. New York: Haworth Press.

Boss, P. G. (1986b). Psychological absence in intact families: A systems approach to a study on fathering. In M. Sussman (Ed.) The charybdis complex [Special issue of *Marriage and Family Review, 10* (1), 11-32]. New York: Haworth Press.

Boss, P. G. (1987). Family stress: Perception and context. In M. Sussman & S. Steinmetz (Eds.), *Handbook of marriage and the family,* pp. 695-723. New York: Plenum.

Boss, P. G. (1988). *Family stress management.* Newbury Park, CA: Sage Publications.

Broverman, I., Broverman, D., Clarkson, F., Rosenkrantz, P., & Vogel, F. (1970). Sex-role stereotypes and clinical judgments of mental health. *Journal of Consulting and Clinical Psychology, 34* (1), 1-7.

Carter, E. A., & McGoldrick, M. (1980). *The family life cycle.* New York: Gardner Press.

Chodorow, N. (1978). *The reproduction of mothering, psychoanalysis, and the sociology of gender.* Berkeley: University of California Press.

Dinnerstein, D. (1976). *The mermaid and the minotaur: Sexual arrangements and human malaise.* New York: Harper & Row.

Gilligan, C. (1982). *In a different voice.* Cambridge: Harvard University Press.

Goldner, V. (1985). Feminism and family therapy. *Family Process, 24* (1), 31-47.

Hare-Mustin, R. (1978). A feminist approach to family therapy. *Family Process, 17,* 181-194.

Hare-Mustin, R., & Marecek, J. (1986). Autonomy and gender: Some questions for therapists. *Psychotherapy, 23,* 205-212.

Horney, K. (1924). On the genesis of the castration complex in women. *International Journal of Psycho-Analysis, 5,* 37.

Kjervik, D. (1979). The stress of sexism on the mental health of women. In D. Kjervik & I. Martinson (Eds.), *Women in stress: A nursing perspective* (pp. 144-156). New York: Appleton-Century-Crofts.

Layton, M. (1984). Tipping the therapeutic scales: Masculine, feminine, or neuter? *Family Therapy Networker, 8 (3),* 20-27.

Lerner, M. J. (1980). *The belief in a just world: A fundamental delusion.* New York: Plenum.

Parsons, T. & Bales, R. (Eds.). (1955). *Family, socialization, and interaction process.* New York: Free Press.

Paul, N. L., & Paul, B. B. (1976). *A marital puzzle: Transgenerational analysis in marriage counseling.* New York: W. W. Norton.

Symonds, A. (1976). Neurotic dependency in successful women. *Journal of American Academy of Psychoanalysis, 4* (1), 96-102.

Thorne, B. & Yalom, M. (Eds.). (1982). *Re-thinking the family.* New York: Longman.

Weiner, J. P. & Boss, P. (1985). Exploring gender bias against women: Ethics for marriage and family therapy [Special issue of *Counseling and Values, 30* (1), 9-23.]

PART THREE

DEVELOPMENTAL DISRUPTIONS AND THE FAMILY LIFE CYCLE

10

Family Crises: Expectable and Unexpectable

FRANK S. PITTMAN, III
Emory University and Georgia State University

"Crisis" is, simply, the state of things at a time of impending change, the point at which things could get better or worse but at which things will inevitably change. Rumor has it that the Chinese word for crisis is made up of the characters for "danger" and for "opportunity." Whether that is true or not, crisis is indeed a dangerous opportunity. People in crisis, undergoing inexorable change, may react in a variety of ways. They may lie back and wait for the changes to occur, they may attempt to direct the change, they may find someone to blame for the crisis state, or they may call for help in preventing unwanted change. "Emergency," a term often confused with "crisis," is the subjective sense that outside help is needed to protect one from undesired change. Emergency is an awareness of danger, of impending disaster. Certainly many people are terrified of change and want to prevent it; therefore they experience the crisis state as an emergency in which someone must be called in to stop the process of change, thereby enabling them to avoid the danger but also avoid the opportunity.

Our theories about crisis owe much to Erich Lindemann's classic 1944 study of the survivors of a natural disaster, the Coconut Grove fire. Entrenched in psychoanalytic theory, Lindemann attributed the variations in survivors' reactions to each individual's unresolved childhood conflicts. Gerald Caplan (1956, 1964) extended the study of crisis by identifying the typical stages in crisis resolution and the typical sequence of events during the 6 weeks of postcrisis disequilibrium, before the crisis state becomes a way of life. According to Caplan, crises are much the same, whatever the precipitating stress. Reuben Hill looked at families under stress from 1949. David Kaplan (1960, 1962) began our focus on the specific nature of the specific crisis. By the 1960s, Caplan, Kaplan, Hill, and many others were looking at the family system as the unit of crisis response and resolution and were applying the name "crisis" to any experience that required people to do things that were previously outside their comfortable repertoire. Even then, the concept of crisis was much influenced by theories derived from individual response to natural disasters. Most of the experiences we now consider crises are not of that sort and don't quite follow the pattern discovered by Lindemann and described extensively by Caplan.

In the mid-1960s, Kaplan and his co-workers (Langsley, Pittman, Machotka, Flomenhaft, and DeYoung) on the Denver project studied crises that had led to requests for psychiatric hospitalization. The clinical team—Kal Flomenhaft, Carol DeYoung, and I—treated about 200 families in crisis by offering family therapy as an alternative to psychiatric hospitalization. We would see the families for an average of six visits, and we kept virtually all of them out of the hospital and returned them to functioning quite quickly. The advantages of family crisis therapy were initially impressive when the families we treated were compared with matched hospitalized controls: Our families experienced less chronicity, fewer subsequent hospitalizations, and more efficient crisis management.

The Denver project defined four general types of crises, only one of which, "the bolt from the blue," resembled the crises described by Lindemann and Caplan. The other three were "developmental crises," in which a relatively normal and expectable stage of development requires changes that are uncomfortable for the family; "structural crises," in which the family's structure is inherently crisis prone and produces recurrent exacerbations of conflict; and "caretaker crises," in which the family becomes dependent on outside helpers who have the power to offhandedly disrupt the family.

A crisis therapist must understand all four types of crises in order not to confuse one with another. The treatment of each type is, as will be seen, somewhat different. One familiar crisis that can occur in any of the four patterns is that of infidelity, which will be used to illustrate the range of family crises. First, the crisis must be defined.

DEFINING THE CRISIS

The Bolt-from-the-Blue Crisis

The "bolt from the blue" is a crisis in which the precipitating stress is real, unique, overt, and unexpectable, and arises from forces outside the individual and the family system. Such stresses as a fire, a war, an illness, an accident, a damaged baby, and unearned wealth or poverty fit into this category. Families often adapt fairly well to the tremendous effects of such a crisis, perhaps because they feel little guilt, assign little blame, and receive support from one another and all around as the survivors pull together and adapt to the changed circumstances. Whatever sort of emergency such crises produce, they don't usually require the attention of mental health professionals. It is often surprising how well even the sickest families respond to external stresses and real, obvious crises. If, however, the source of the stress is unclear, and the crisis poorly defined, guilt and blame can occur, and response to the immediate external stress can get lost in the family's own favorite crisis pattern. Some families will respond to any crisis in their usual nonfunctional manner. For example, alcoholics will throw a drunk when the lottery ticket wins or when the plumbing overflows, and violent people will scream and yell and hit someone when the tire goes flat or the business fails. The characteristic response is familiar and unrelated to the situation at hand, but after the familiar pathological response, the family may settle down and adapt.

Those crises that arise most clearly from forces outside the family seem, in my experience, less threatening to the family's most cherished idiosyncrasies and therefore become easier to deal with without therapeutic intervention. Most bolts from the blue do not come to the attention of therapists. It is the other kinds of crises, no less real, but far more personal, that attract therapists— the developmental, structural, and caretaker crises.

Developmental Crises

Developmental crises are those that occur in response to the normal stages of development—the sorts of things that everyone should expect and prepare for. Such stresses are universal and usually overt, and they should be expectable, but in certain families they are resisted as if they could be prevented at will rather than adapted to.

The nature of the human animal is such that we do not suffer change gladly. We do not develop emotionally over a lifetime by gentle, imperceptible progress toward maturity. We are dragged kicking and screaming into it. The process is one of fits and starts, surges and shrivels, ebbs and flows. Between the plateaus there are crises, and without those crises life would be flat indeed. Yet many people seek a life without crisis, a life without challenge and stimulation, and therefore without opportunity to discover the richness of the human experience.

Most of life's crises are universal, are part of being human, and are therefore predictable and expectable; they move the individual to a different level of maturity. Ideally, they should be prepared for, celebrated, and shared as part of the process of life, part of what forces us into maturity. Life's personal ceremonies surround such events—a baby's birth, his or her first step, first word, first tooth, first day at school, first date, driver's license, graduation, marriage, retirement, death, and all the birthdays and anniversaries and discoveries in between. A few of life's crisis points are celebrated more privately, but celebrated nonetheless—puberty, the first sexual experience, the first encounter with various drugs and substances, and adventures. Those postpubertal experiences that are kept secret from the parents are regaled over, are exaggerated and bragged about with peers, and mark graduation from the status of child in the family to membership in an age group of semi-independent semiadults.

There are some developmental crises that are universal, or nearly so, but that are insufficiently discussed, so the person experiencing them feels isolated, confused, or guilty, thinking there is something amiss that may even be abnormal. There are any number of these, but a few are particularly traumatic for the individual who assumes they are personal or unique. Some occur as early as childhood, and the classic Freudian oedipal triangle may be the prototype of this group—the fantasies and feelings that are normal, but frightening, easily misunderstood, and overreacted to. Essentially all children at a certain age have the fantasy of replacing the parent of the same sex and of incest with parents and siblings. Most have fantasies of being of the opposite gender at one time or another. Most cross-dress a little and are preoccupied with genitals, their own and those of others. Most children also have fantasies of being adopted, of being the lost child of someone rich and famous.

Most children have sexual experiences, ranging from mutual exploration between peers to forced molestation by adults, even parents. The child who considers this experience unique may see it as a confirmation of wickedness or worthlessness, and fail to report it. Or adults may react to it by increasing the shame and guilt and thereby produce even greater damage to the child. At puberty, the secret crises begin in full force. Early adolescents may be naive enough to consider masturbation unique. The early adolescent homosexual experiences (perhaps not universal, but certainly common) may be considered unique. Sexual doubts are universal among boys, with fears of homosexuality continuing until the first successful heterosexual experiences, and sometimes even after. Many suffer a major or minor disaster with their first heterosexual experience.

Almost all adolescents doubt their attractiveness, and most doubt their "popularity" or social acceptability, at that point when they first notice the social pecking order around them and begin social competitiveness in earnest. Fortunately, most parents remember the horrors of the 8th-grade popularity struggles and can give support, but parents who don't recall them, or who didn't notice them at the time, can be singularly unhelpful, increasing the social anxiety and self-consciousness that spells social death.

All children have other failures, disappointments, and fears—they may not let one another know about them and may therefore feel isolated by their unrevealed normality. At a later age, when courtships begin in earnest, there is a crisis in most courtship relationships when one partner begins to think favorably of marriage before the other does. As one pursues more ardently, the other will back off, permanently or temporarily. Typically, the female pursues and the male backs off a bit. If the female panics at that point and clutches the man too tightly, she will lose him, since his fears will be confirmed that he cannot maintain both himself and the relationship. Yet her impulse to clutch tightly is as natural as slamming on the brakes when skidding on the ice, and as potentially disastrous. Increasingly, it is the female who feels a need to back off briefly to consider the proposed marriage, but that is still not nearly as universal as the male response to the impending talk of marriage.

One of the more painful universal, but undiscussed, crises is the end of romance. This is likely to occur about 6 months into the marriage, but it can occur as early as the honeymoon or even before the wedding, in the form of prewedding jitters. There is a sudden, often shocking realization that the loved one is merely another human being. Idiosyncrasies become irritants, differences become conflicts, and one or both may feel "out of love" and trapped. The end of romance marks the end of the adolescent fantasy and the beginning of the real marriage. But some people can't tolerate that much reality since it requires adult commitment rather than the less mature romantic haze. Some people have to go through several marriages before they catch on to this.

In marriage, after a while, people will begin to notice they are sexually attracted to others. If they act on this and have an affair, they may blame it on a failure in the spouse or in the institution of marriage and proceed to absolve themselves of responsibility for their actions by sabotaging their marriage. Even if they don't act on it, there may be guilt and therefore distance in the marriage, and the arousal of concern and jealousy in the spouse. People may not know the universal truth that marriage does not protect one from sexual attractions, that love does not ensure fidelity.

An even less understood crisis occurs when men reach the age of 30 or so. At about the age when men suddenly sprout hairs on their ears, a change takes place in them sexually. Although sex had previously been a powerful drive, and the deprivation of sex aroused even stronger desire, it suddenly turns into a habit. If a man over this age is deprived of sex for whatever reason, he loses interest in it, even forgets about it. It isn't lost, merely mislaid, and it can be easily restored by a partner who seeks and finds it. But without the outside stimulus, no sex may take place. Sex becomes a habit that, once broken, may be conquered forever. The sexual drive will return if the habit is reestablished. The wife may feel she has become unattractive and undesirable and therefore may hesitate to force herself upon the seemingly unwilling partner. Sex may leave the marriage forever, until either the wife, or some third party, provides the stimulus lacking in the husband.

All of these are among the lifetime supply of developmental crises. As we study the normal human life cycle, we discover more and more such normal transitions, each of which may be harmless when it is understood, but hazardous when it is taken personally. For instance, it is normal to desire to have an affair, it is hazardous to do so, and it is potentially disastrous to keep it secret.

Structural Crises

Most of the family literature seems to focus on structural crises, in which there is a defect in the family structure that makes it resistant to change and prone to intermittent exacerbations of some inherent conflict. Perhaps all family crises are to some extent structural, since all occur when a stress threatens some sensitive aspect of the family structure. A purely structural crisis is one in which the stress arises from the family structure itself rather than from forces extrinsic to the family or from developmental stages, which are more or less inevitable in all families. Though the stress arises from within the system, it may appear to coincide with a stage of development or even be a bolt from the blue. The diagnosis is made through the family history, which may show that the same crisis has occurred over and over again, whatever the stress. The prototype might be the alcoholic family in which the drinker drinks because the rent came due, the transmission went out, the shirt wasn't folded right, the kid made bad grades, he turned 40, it was the anniversary of his mother's death, or it was Friday. It doesn't help much to understand the specific stress or the stage of someone's development if the pattern of behavior is the same no matter what the stage or what the stress. Violence, philandering, suicide attempting, job jumping, and other obnoxious acts occur within a specific family structure rather than in response to a specific stress and are responded to in ways that guarantee their recurrence and tolerance of them rather than their cessation. Such families have a recurrent series of emergencies, in which outside help is requested. But they rarely seem to see the recurrent episodes as related to one another in a pattern that could be defined as the problem. By their treating each episode as unique, the habitual structural problem remains undefined and therefore untreated.

Certainly, there are specific family structures that make specific developmental stages particularly hazardous. Families terrified of sex have more trouble during their children's adolescence than during their children's starting school or leaving home. Families afraid of closeness may have more difficulty at Christmas, those afraid of disorder may dread family vacations, and those uncomfortable with authority may dread April 15. Decisions about having children may disrupt cautious, pessimistic, controlling families. Retirement, empty nests, and deaths of parents are quite different crises in close marriages than in more distant and formal ones, and they are something else again in stormy and insecure ones.

There may be no family structure that can insulate a family against all the developmental crises, but some structures are so unstable that almost any change can be devastating. These are the true crisis-prone families, those that are structured around inflexibility. Some families contain an unstable member—an alcoholic, an adulterer, a schizophrenic, a violent member—and yet must protect that unstable member from change. Others have a secret or a historical defect, which means that openness and honesty are impossible. Others contain an unwieldy power structure—those in which the power must always be excruciatingly equal or in which everyone must be satisfied, those in which someone must always have the final say, or those in which all decisions must be approved by one of the in-laws.

Families with a structural defect have recurrent crises, and it may take very little to exacerbate them. But each crisis is just an emergency, just a cry for someone to come in and protect the family one more time from having to change its obvious defect.

Caretaker Crises

Such families may, in time, develop a network of caretakers who perform certain services for the family, which protect it from changing. The caretakers, who are not members of the family but relatives, friends, therapists, or social agencies, get into the role through a desire to be helpful, rescuing, and even powerful, so the caretaker needs the family at first as much as the family needs the caretaker. In time, the family grows more dependent, the caretaker loses interest or patience, and the relationship becomes unbalanced. The caretaker crisis occurs when the caretaker backs off, is unavailable for a family crisis, or shifts direction and attempts to cure the family rather than protect it. Perhaps the caretaker has a crisis of his or her own, or changes jobs, policies, or location. Perhaps the family loses insurance coverage or eligibility for a low-cost agency. The caretaker may not even realize the importance to the family of his or her services.

In the Denver project, throughout the period of follow-up, both index and control families were sent postcards monthly just to maintain contact. When the project ended, they were sent postcards informing them, in effect, that we were no longer available. Immediately, there was a rash of hospitalizations of patients with whom we'd had no contact for years, other than through the postcards. We had completely overlooked the caretaking function of those postcards. Our availability had enabled the families to manage their inevitable crises without having to escalate them and have anyone hospitalized. When we were no longer available, the families had to produce horrendous crises in order to find new caretakers-in-waiting. Families who have someone available to help them in case all hell breaks loose have an advantage over families who don't. It's like a psychiatric savings account.

Caretakers perform some function for families that the families don't perform for themselves. Sometimes it is a function they realistically can't perform for themselves. But often the caretaker protects the family from developing the ability to perform that function. I recall a cartoon showing a woman pushing a full-grown man in a wheelchair. She was speaking to a passerby, saying, "Of course my son can walk, but thank God, he'll never have to." Trust funds, generous parents, and disability incomes are helpful for the severely, permanently, and totally disabled but can be crippling for the merely uncomfortable. Affairs can relieve sexual tension in marriages between sexually incompatible persons, but they can make resolution of the sexual incompatibility impossible and can severely restrict marital communication and trust. Similarly, parents-in-law and therapists can offer useful wisdom and reality testing, but they can produce stifling dependency and prevent the development of marital communication skills. Generally, caretakers who stay past the state of emergency do more harm than good. Therapists who make themselves indispensable are dangerous. It is hard for a therapist to know when it is time to bow out—there are no clear guidelines in the matter—but the therapist must keep the question in mind and may want to raise it from time to time. There are exceptional families, perhaps those with child abusers, conceivably those with alcoholics or schizophrenics, who may need long-term therapeutic caretakers, but in most families, it is safer for therapists to be available than for therapists to be in residence.

DIAGNOSING THE CRISIS

People typically come into therapy at a time of crisis with a sense of emergency and a hope of preventing some dreaded change. They may present themselves as suffering from some bolt from the blue, a unique and unexpectable set of circumstances. That, rarely, is indeed the case. Most often, there is a structural defect apparent to the astute therapist. Overcoming that structural defect can then be redefined as an overdue developmental crisis, in which family members learn to do something for themselves that they have not been willing to learn previously. If the therapist instead conspires with the family to avoid that change in the family's development, the therapist is in danger of becoming a caretaker and thereby stifling the family's development.

The four types of crises require somewhat different therapeutic approaches, and though the four types may intersect or merge, it is important, if not always easy, to differentiate them. For example, a crisis of infidelity may take any of the four forms, having the features of a bolt from the blue, a developmental crisis, a structural crisis, or a caretaker crisis.

The Typical Crisis: Four Kinds of Infidelity

Few problems create as much havoc, disruption, and even disaster as infidelity. A Holocaust survivor once told me something that has haunted me ever after. She said that the Holocaust, in which she lost every member of her family and barely escaped the ovens herself, was far easier to survive than an infidelity because "what the Nazis did was not so personal." To compare an infidelity with the Holocaust struck me as outrageous. In time, though, I understood something of what she meant—that she could live with the expectation of being tortured by her enemies better than she could face being betrayed by her only surviving loved one.

Certainly, infidelity is the major direct and indirect cause of divorce, and it is a major cause of homicide and suicide. In theory, and in the family therapy literature, it seems almost trivial and rather innocent. In reality, it is devastating and disorienting. Perhaps it is confusing because it can take several forms, and its meaning can therefore be easily misunderstood. The involvement of a third person in a monogamous relationship can cover a range from rape to bigamy, and the meaning of each is, of course, quite different.

Accidental Infidelity: Bolts from the Blue

Rape could not be considered an infidelity of course, but it is the purest example of a bolt-from-the-blue sexual crisis. Rape is a unique, unpredictable, situational event. The event itself is brief, and the visible effects are usually quickly over. The impact, however, may be profound and long lasting. There is posttraumatic anxiety after a rape just as there is after an automobile accident or a mugging or any other assault, with a continuing sense that it might happen again at any moment and that life is no longer as safe and secure as it seemed before. But rape is the most personal of assaults. Even if the motivation is not sexual, the act is. The victim may be unjustly seen as an accomplice. There may be blame, there may even be guilt, and there is certainly shame as well as a continuing sense of having been damaged. Other forms of assault produce increased distance between the perpetrator and the victim, but rape narrows that distance and somehow unites the rapist and the raped, not in their minds, but in the minds of others. Rape trials seem to focus on the degree to which the object of the assault encouraged it, and great damage can be done to a rape victim if she (or he) is considered to be in some way responsible for the act. It is the misdiagnosis of the bolt-from-the-blue crisis of rape—the effort to blame the victim and make her take responsibility for something that she didn't do but that was done to her—that causes the most damage.

Frequently, sexual misadventures of a voluntary nature have many of the characteristics of a bolt from the blue. Someone may fall into an act of infidelity out of drunkenness, politeness, or social pressure and awaken a short time later, reacting as if he or she had just emerged from an attack of temporary insanity and was determined not to repeat the event, but feeling guilty, isolated, and afraid of discovery. The unfaithful one, to protect himself or herself from acknowledgment of a misstep, may consider it appropriate and as "something people just do," as if it were developmental, or may consider it proof that the marriage is faulty, as if it were structural. The seducer may even be blamed, as if a caretaker had done a bad job. It would probably work better if such unique sexual dalliances were treated as embarrassing accidents—as events that have consequences, often severe and unpleasant ones, but that were not really caused by anything significant. Of course, people who carry their flirtations to a danger point and are then too embarrassed to back out are placing the responsibility for their fidelity in the hands of passing strangers and are not taking total responsibility for their own behavior.

However, immature drivers often need to bend a fender or two before they learn that the world is not going to conspire to clear a safe path for careless people. To learn from one's mistakes, either in traffic or in flirtations, one must take responsibility for one's actions and try not to blame what one does on the stars or bolts from the blue.

Situational Infidelity: A Developmental Crisis

Infidelities are most often serial rather than unique, perhaps because the first one is justified either as normal behavior ("Everybody does it") or as an appropriate reaction to some defect in the marriage ("If I did it, then he or she must have made me do it"). This common belief—that fidelity is impossible or unnatural and that infidelity is universal and appropriate, and that the spouse, because he or she has some deficiency, should take responsibility for causing it—is not just illogical but dangerous. Each person must take responsibility for his or her own fidelity, since no one else can do so. One may, for a variety of reasons, decide not to be faithful, but it does seem absurd to make that choice and blame it on someone else who isn't being given a voice in the matter. To blame a victim of adultery would be as heartless as blaming a victim of rape; during most acts of infidelity, the spouse isn't even present, much less in control of who does what to whom. A victim's being responsible for infidelity strikes me as being comparable to a victim of marital violence being responsible for it—such a victim could take partial responsibility for the relationship, the atmosphere, the failure to establish more healthy patterns of problem solving, or even the reactions that escalate the offending behavior, but he or she could not take responsibility for the act itself. Finding that delicate balance between individual responsibility and systemic amplification of behavior becomes a major focus of systemic therapies.

Adulterers often have a characterological lacuna in which their sexual choices are left in the hands of the opposite sex, either the spouse, the partner in adultery, or both. It has traditionally been taught that the woman should be the one to determine whether sex will take place or not and that men do not have to take responsibility for such choices themselves. An alternate view is that all men are adulterous and that therefore women should have affairs to protect themselves from male dominance. Either view is obviously irresponsible and paints members of either gender as victims of the other.

Most people enter marriage pledging fidelity and fully expecting it from themselves and their partners. Most of those who attempt fidelity actually come close to achieving it. A significant minority do not. In the course of the life cycle, many developmental crises directly or indirectly impinge upon this initial pledge of fidelity. There are crisis points at which infidelity is most likely to occur. Some of these crisis points are temporal—the seven-year itch, the forties syndrome, the last fling. Others are related to specific problems in the family or in the life of the prospective adulterer.

It is commonplace for men about to marry to have a bachelor party at which they may experience their farewell to extramarital sex. Some grooms and brides are so alarmed by the vow of fidelity that they rebel and begin their infidelities on their honeymoon. Most manage to wait a few months or years, until they experience the almost universal crisis of the end of the romance, when it becomes apparent that the magic is impermanent, that fidelity is not automatic and instinctive, and that marriage requires effort and attention. This may be the point at which people recognize an inherent defect in the human animal, that romance doesn't last but jealousy does, that they desire others sexually but fear losing their mate to a rival. It requires a fair amount of maturity to recognize that each spouse must accept owner-ship of the marriage rather than feel possessed and controlled by it. In a society that does not value and protect marriage, it requires two rather mature and farsighted people to maintain one. Some experience the loss of the compelling tingle as a defect in the spouse or in marriage in general, unless someone helps them see that loss as universal and as the beginning of the real intimacy between imperfect people tied together as they run the same obstacle course.

Some maintain their fidelity for many years, understanding that it is no more automatic to be faithful than to stop for traffic lights or get up for work on time, and they turn the marriage into a working partnership rather than a magical entrancement. But then others of life's inevitable crises come along and weaken the attachment. The birth of children is a hazard for some men, who feel displaced. A parent's death or infirmity can be a time of danger. One's own career failures and one's spouse's career successes can tip the balance. A particularly dangerous period occurs when the children become pubertal, sexy, and independent, while the parents feel less and less so. Midlife is difficult, with its sense of life, power, and attractiveness passing by. Women who have relied on their seductive beauty may panic at this point. Whatever the developmental crisis, the individual may long for a moment of excitement and adventure or nurturance and reassurance that seems unattainable at home, and he or she may work up enough anger at this deprivation to embark upon an affair.

Structural Infidelity: A Crisis of Exacerbation

Each marriage requires an agreement about whether, and if so, under what circumstances, extramarital sex will be allowed or encouraged. Structural crises occur when one partner breaks that agreement, whatever it is.

Extramarital sex may be built into the structure of the marriage, and in such marriages it is not an infidelity. Those who expect to have affairs themselves or who expect that their spouses will may keep the marriage at a level of distance that will permit it. Actually, though the sacrifice in intimacy is enormous, such arrangements can work, but they are prone to crises when one partner desires greater intimacy that seems to intrude upon the other's desire for greater distance. Open marriage was a concept that was briefly popular a decade ago, but it didn't seem to work well enough to catch on, and most of those who tried it and still stayed together abandoned it for either open fidelity or secret infidelities. The human animal seems to have difficulty being unfaithful without some element of anger and blame, and the continuing affairs seemed a form of punishment. I'm sure some couples still try open marriage, but it seems to be on the decline.

Other couples are far less civilized about it. They don't even try to get or give permission for infidelities. Instead, they use infidelity as a threat or a punishment and may compete over how crazy they can drive one another with their affairs and the ensuing battles over those affairs. The storminess of the marriage seems an insurance against intimacy.

There are sexually dead marriages and emotionally dead ones, in which the bad marriage can be kept just barely afloat with supplements of sex and emotion from the outside. In all of these structurally defective marriages, the partners protect themselves from intimacy through recurrent infidelities. Couples may protect themselves from change, intimacy, or divorce by turning the marriage into a cat-and-mouse game in which the affairs are implicitly known, but the burden is on the couple to discover and prove them. In that way, the couple can enjoy playing hide and seek against one another, both being careful never to quite win or lose, so that the game goes on for a lifetime without either partner having to do anything honest that might solve problems or risk intimacy.

Romantic Infidelity: A Caretaker Crisis

Adulterers, particularly amateur ones or those fearing advancing age, may experience the intensity of an affair as "love" and may enter into an excruciatingly intense romance from which escape seems impossible. The greater the secretiveness of the affair, the greater the dishonesty in the marriage. The more distant the marriage becomes, the more intense the affair seems. Some seem to deliberately choose a partner for an affair who is unpredictable, dependent, and even insane. Whereas most affairs stop once they are discovered, if not before, romantic affairs seem buoyed by disaster and disapproval. They become true caretaker relationships as the affair becomes the only sanctuary from a world that disapproves of the affair. Occasionally, the affair is actually a sane sanctuary from an awful marriage and serves to hold the awful marriage together for months or years. These more stable, long-term affairs resemble parent–child relationships and may develop from close working or social relationships. In either case, the affair and the marriage may both be inescapable. When either ends, the other may end too. Marriages sometimes result from these affairs, but not often; without the marriage, the affair is unnecessary. They are really just caretaker relationships.

TREATMENT OF FAMILY CRISES

A crisis of infidelity may thus have features typical of any of the four types of crises. A unique, or bolt-from-the-blue, dalliance is quite different from a permanent, or caretaker, romance. A marriage in which someone has an affair at a time of developmental crisis is totally unlike a marriage whose structure is based on the hide-and-seek farce of chronic adultery. Resolution of the crisis depends upon the therapist's clarity in diagnosing it. If the therapist is stuck with a theory that assumes that all behavior is dictated by the structure of the family system, or that any symptom points to a developmental failure, the current crisis may be badly, even disastrously, misinterpreted. There is no safe, neutral assumption that will fit all cases, so accuracy of diagnosis is crucial. Such accuracy is difficult to achieve, however, since the adulterer will often be lying, and the victim carrying on in ways that exaggerate the situation. In unraveling a crisis that involves infidelity, it is important to know the secrets, the reality of the affair, whether it has happened before, how long it has been going on, and what the situation was before it began. Those issues are important, but the information is not always accurate. There is probably no area of human endeavor in which a greater premium is put on dishonesty. Honesty is, of course, the enemy of infidelity. People don't often realize that a crisis of infidelity dealt with honestly can lead to a renaissance of the marriage. Marriages routinely rise like phoenixes from the ashes of an affair, but only if it is dealt with openly. By contrast, a secret affair leads to a slow withering of the relationship. People think there is safety in lying. They are almost always wrong.

There are two vital questions that must be answered in dealing with any crisis: "Why now?" and "What change, above all, is being prevented by this crisis?" The answers may be sufficient to differentiate or even define the crisis. In a bolt from the blue, the answers may be something like "I don't know what happened—I guess I had too much to drink and just woke up in bed with her" and "I don't want anything to change—I sure don't want to ruin my marriage, and I don't want this to happen again." In a developmental crisis, the answers might be as follows: "I've just wanted something different in life. Ever since the children left home, I haven't been happy with him"; and "I want everything to change. I just can't go on the way I always have, and if I have to get a divorce to have somebody to talk to, I'll do it." In a structural crisis, the answers might be "He's always had his women, but he's never taken one of them out in public before" and "We've been through this over and over again. She might want me to be faithful, but she's always known I never would. I can get rid of this woman if she forces it, but there'll just be another one. There's no adventure at home." A caretaker crisis might involve the following answers: "I'm in love. I can't give him up, whether my husband or his wife like it or not"; and "I don't want to make a decision—just leave me alone and give me time to think."

The treatment of families in crisis was described by the Denver project as involving seven steps. These are:

1. *Emergency response*—quickly intervene to reduce the sense of emergency and focus attention on the specific crisis and on the particular changes the crisis requires.

2. *Involve the family*—make sure all those who might have to change are involved in understanding the change.

3. *Define the crisis*—answer the questions "Why now?" and "What, above all, is being protected from change?"; determine whether the situation is a unique bolt from the blue, an expectable developmental crisis, a recurrent structural crisis or crisis of exacerbation, or a permanent caretaker crisis.

4. *General prescription*—relieve the subjective sense of emergency in order to make possible the more subtle process of change.

5. *Specific prescription*—outline the changes that most people would make in response to this situation and assign symbolic or actual tasks for moving toward resolution.

6. *Negotiate resistance to change*—diagnose the underlying family problems by determining who is preventing change, how it is being prevented, and why it is being prevented; determine precisely what is being protected, at all costs, from change.

7. *Termination*—avoid becoming a barrier to change by taking on a caretaking function for the family.

This process of crisis intervention is quite simple and flexible, and centers on Steps 3, 5, and 6. Yet many therapists attempt to treat crises by using only Steps 1, 2, and 4. They simply get the family together and try to calm everyone down, and then find themselves unable to terminate at the end. They have provided emergency intervention rather than crisis intervention, they have produced dependency rather than change, and they have emerged as caretakers. Successful crisis intervention depends on a clear definition of the problem and of what reasonable people do to solve that problem, followed by efforts to permit change without sacrificing the uniqueness of the family.

Crisis therapists are advised to emphasize the developmental aspects of every crisis, that is, its connection to the universals of the human experience. The human comedy seems tragic when experienced in isolation and shame. Likewise, it is important to keep people from seeing themselves as innocent victims of a uniquely bad fate—life as an unrelenting series of bolts from the blue. However attractive the sense of blamelessness may be, it produces helplessness. It is also dangerous to be too structural, making people take responsibility for others' behavior, over which they have no control; anything that relieves anyone of responsibility for his or her own behavior is a setup for disaster. It is probably safe to assume that families are not encouraging the things they complain about—they just don't know how to stop maladaptive patterns once they have gotten started.

There is much hope and relief to be gained in diagnosing a developmental crisis. It relieves the isolation that comes from believing that one's problems are unique and shameful. It restores the sense of normality and of just being partakers of the human condition. When life is seen as a series of crises, an obstacle course, in which there are many hurdles, many spills, and a pie in the face from time to time, the crisis process can be another of life's adventures, and at heart a lot of fun.

Crisis therapists must be directive. They must tell people what they are doing wrong and what they can do about it. Most of the problems in the world are caused by sheer ignorance of what works and what doesn't, and therapists should have or develop expertise at just that. A useful metaphor for the therapist is the series of little metal discs that mark the dividing lines between the lanes on a highway. When a car goes out of its lane, the discs bump and whir, not to prevent the changing of lanes but to warn of the danger. Another warning signal in life is the noisy old metal zipper, which, unfortunately, has been replaced by a silent plastic one, so that the sound of impending adultery is muffled. This most dangerous of common crises thus can be entered without warning.

Crisis therapists encourage people to take responsibility for their own behavior. The distinction between the mature and the immature, the adult and the child, the successful and the unsuccessful may center on the tendency to accept or to deny responsibility for one's actions. A childlike or legalistic approach to problem solving seeks to place the blame outside one's own actions and to find some way in which the world could provide sufficient sanctuary that people would not have to change their own actions in order to achieve security and success. The effort to get everyone else to change so that the individual won't have to do so, the effort to subdivide responsibility for consequences, and the effort to go through life blameless protect one from changing in the direction of maturity.

The opposite extreme is reached by extending maturity to absurd limits, by accepting responsibility not only for one's own actions but for everyone else's also, and by assuming that everything that happens is somehow earned or deserved. Therapists, particularly those with an inflexibly systemic orientation, can believe that the alcoholic's spouse is as major a contributor as the alcoholic, that the homeowner is as much to blame as the burglar, or that the rape victim is as responsible as the rapist. The end result of such an approach can only be the hypermaturity, anxiety, and obsessive-compulsiveness of a martyred caretaker who protects everyone else from maturing during the crisis process.

Family therapy, a uniquely optimistic approach to mental health, problem solving, and human development, has been under the sway of a philosophy of nonblaming. Perhaps it is the humanistic holiday from guilt of the 1960s. Perhaps it is a sociological perspective that prefers to see the individual as a helpless victim of an imperfect society. Perhaps it is a rejection of psychiatry's tendency to frame everything in terms of pathology. Certainly, it is related to therapists' determination not to be guilt producing and parental. The effort to help people realize that all emotion and thought is acceptable and part of the universal human experience has been distorted into the idea that all behavior must be declared acceptable and all interaction noble. Therapists have strained to become able to place a positive connotation on just about anything, from cruelty to adultery. Perhaps therapists should not make people feel guilty or even ashamed of what they do; certainly many people believe that. I don't. I prefer a more conservative approach—that people should be encouraged to feel anything but to behave in a way that helps them achieve their long-range goals.

Therapists, in my view, should not be purveyors of pardons but teachers of reality, of cause and effect, of the way the human and societal machinery operates, of what works and what doesn't work and why. Therapists are the repairmen of human relationships and therefore should transmit accurate reality testing about the world and the human condition. To do so, therapists must be able, which many are, and also willing, which many are not, to point out to people what they are doing that does not work for them. If therapists don't know what works and what doesn't, they should try to find out. Crisis therapists, especially, must be experts in reality and knowledgeable about the range of possible ways of dealing with it.

POSTSCRIPT

I learned something as a boy in rural southern Alabama. We lived in the middle of a state game preserve. The nearest civilization was Buck Shellnut's filling station and store up on the highway, a short bicycle ride away. I used to ride up there to watch the cars go by and to get a piece of Zelma Shellnut's special pecan pie. There was nothing better to eat in all of southern Alabama. One summer, they were rerouting the highway and the traffic was a mess, and it wasn't at all clear which was the road to Birmingham and which the road to Selma. Actually, poor Buck and Zelma were no longer on the road to anywhere much, but the cars still came by and stopped and got gas, and the people asked whether they were on the right road. Buck always assured them they were on the right road and then sold them some of Zelma's wonderful pecan pie, and they drove off happy and full on the road to nowhere. I finally got up the curiosity and then the courage to ask Buck why he told people they were on the right road when they weren't. He said, "When you tell folks they're doing something wrong, they don't like it and they won't buy any pecan pie, and they're not gonna find any better pecan pie on the right road than they can get right here." As therapists, we have to decide whether the important product we're selling is our directions or our pecan pie, whether we're trying to make people feel loved or whether we're trying to get them oriented and on the right road. With skill, we may even be able to do both.

Of course, if neither the family nor the therapist knows the way, the adventure of therapy becomes a crisis for both—a caretaker crisis for the family, a developmental crisis for the therapist. Life at its richest is a series of crises, ideally crises of development, in which each new stress becomes an opportunity for learning more about the nature of ourselves and our world.

REFERENCES

Caplan, G. (1956). *An approach to the study of family mental health* (U.S. Public Health Reports, 71, No. 10). Washington, DC: US Government Printing Office.

Caplan, G. (1964). *Principles of preventive psychiatry.* New York: Basic Books.

Hill, R. (1958). Generic features of families under stress. *Social Casework, 39,* 2-3.

Kaplan, D. (1962). A concept of acute situational disorder. *Social Casework, 7* (2), 15-23.

Kaplan, D., & Mason, E. (1960). Maternal reactions to premature birth viewed as an acute emotional disorder. *American Journal of Orthopsychiatry, 30*(3), 539-547.

Langsley, D., Kaplan, D., Pittman, F., Machotka, P., Flomenhaft, K., and DeYoung, C. (1968). *The treatment of families in crisis.* New York: Grune and Stratton.

Langsley, D., Pittman, F., Machotka, P., and Flomenhaft, K. (1968). Crisis family therapy: Results and implications. *Family Process, 7* (2), 145-168.

Lindemann, E. (1944). Symptomatology and management of acute grief. *American Journal of Psychiatry, 101,* 141-148.

Pittman, F. (1973). Managing acute psychiatric emergencies: defining the family crisis. In D. Bloch (Ed.), *Seminars in Psychiatry, 5* (2). New York: Grune and Stratton.

Pittman, F. (1985). Evaluating the family in crisis. In S. Henao and N. Grose (Eds.), *Principles of family systems in family medicine* (pp. 347-371). New York: Brunner/Mazel.

Pittman, F. (1987). *Turning points: Treating families in transition and crisis.* New York: W. W. Norton.

Pittman, F., Flomenhaft, K., DeYoung, C., Kaplan, D., and Langsley, D. (1966). Crisis family therapy. In J. Masserman (Ed.), *Current psychiatric therapies.* New York: Grune and Stratton.

Pittman, F., Langsley, D., Flomenhaft, K., DeYoung, C., Machotka, P., and Kaplan, D. (1971). Therapy techniques of the family treatment unit. In J. Haley (Ed.), *Changing families: A family therapy reader.* New York: Grune and Stratton.

11

Family Transitions, Cumulative Stress, and Crises

ESTRELLA JOSELEVICH
Buenos Aires

CRISIS: EXPECTABLE AND UNEXPECTABLE

Some changes in the family are triggered by sudden, dramatic events. Picture the following catastrophic scenario: The father is dying of cancer. The mother receives a call from school: Their two boys are to be expelled because the Parents' Committee has discovered her secret lesbian relationship. This is a critical family transition that includes sufficient cumulative stress to make the family's world explode and cause the family to enter into a state of crisis. It is of critical importance to understand the structure of the relationship between catastrophic events and the family crises they can engender.

The term "family crisis" denotes disruption in the family social system (Burr, 1973; McCubbin & Patterson, 1983). A family in crisis has lost the ability to reinstate equilibrium and, instead, suffers from the continual need to accommodate by changing the patterns of interaction among its members. Stress need not produce a crisis. Crisis occurs when the family can no longer access and utilize its resources in a way that controls and contains the forces of change. Once a crisis is under way, the family responds to at least five different types of stressors: "(a) the initial stressor and its hardships; (b) normative transitions; (c) prior strains; (d) the consequences of family efforts to cope; and (e) ambiguity, both intrafamily and social" (McCubbin & Patterson, 1983).

Many family transitions that become crises include a combination of cumulative stress and evolution, such as it happens with common turning points in the life cycle and in other processes of developmental change. We must distinguish between "expectable," predictable crises and "unexpectable" crises that follow a sudden event. A family evolution that has been anticipated, desired, and prepared for with care (e.g., a child's leaving home, a mother's going to work) is in some sense a predictable crisis, and therefore certain basic family paradigms, including rules, beliefs, and values, remain untouched. There are also unexpectable crises, often triggered by an unanticipated occurrence, internal or external to the family, such as an accident. During a process of discontinuous change, family members exhibit learning and creativity that feed on the random rather than on the repetitive (Bateson, 1979).

The normative processes of development, present concurrently with the family's immediate response to stimulation, subject the family to cumulative stress and may lead to the onset of a true crisis. In such cases, the system goes through a protracted period of imbalance, with one or several acute peaks.

We must also distinguish between an "emergency" and a "crisis." An emergency is an abrupt occurrence that requires quick relief. In general, families going through an emergency (e.g., a suicide attempt), feeling overwhelmed and unable to change the situation, require immediate outside help from policemen, firemen, physicians, psychotherapists, or relatives. Almost by definition, an emergency is unpredictable. Although an emergency can be a starting point for a crisis, as is sometimes the case with a psychotic episode, a *true* crisis involves a relatively slow process. Crises are felt by family members as periods of intense instability and impending change because of the loss of previous relational patterns and the lack of new ones to replace them. What we are considering here is a system in an unstable situation, in the process of transition between order and disorder. When a system has been suddenly catapulted into disorganization, chaos takes hold.

Although a true crisis will, indeed, touch all members of a family, it affects each one differently. Until the true crisis is resolved, family members cannot proceed to new stages of development. Because the basic organization of the family is shaken, emotional intensity runs high, and there is deep suffering. The severe pain is related to a loss of context and territorial definition. Family members are no longer what they used to be, but they have not yet achieved a new identity. This feeling of incoherence, in both the existential and the situational sense, is managed variously by members of any group.

Bateson (1972) referred to the transition from one context to another as the "transcontextual syndrome." Readers of James Michener's magnificent description, in his book *Hawaii,* of the birth or the appearance of volcanic islands may feel equally moved by the grandeur of the transformational aspect of human life. Basic scenery components and their interrelationships are restructured to permit the establishment of the new and the different.

A satisfactory conceptual and clinical paradigm is not yet available for describing and handling such high-intensity change—change that may build up to mutation (Lent, 1984). Therefore, at present it is possible to present only an outline of a preliminary model based on concepts of the family life cycle and the theory of crisis and on concepts that arise within clinical practice. The outline also borrows ideas from Morin (1973, 1977) about the processes of change and movement in living systems.

The S-matrix developed by Heisenberg (1962) and used nowadays in other fields incorporates a graphical concept of change that, in some ways, bears a strong similarity to the point of view generally adopted in work with families as systems. Capra (1976) provides a framework for the discussion of both physical and social systems in his discussion of such subjects as "velocity of change," "directions of movements," "complexity of reactions," "sequence of reactions," "tendency to react," "channel of reactions," and "reaction possibilities" because he considers the role of movements in a pattern of change rather than what takes place in each element. Capra also establishes certain similarities between Eastern and Western notions of order and change in a manner reminiscent of the work of Watzlawick, Weakland, and Fisch (1974), who also adopted many Oriental ideas in their description of change and movement.

What follows in this chapter integrates general concepts of change into the development of a frame of reference for examining aspects of particular transition periods.

A CASE EXAMPLE

In this case example, the transition, the various stressors, and the crisis can be clearly illustrated because the therapist saw the family in preventive consultation first, and then later again. The family lived in Bahia Blanca, a big city about 400 miles from Buenos Aires, Argentina, and was planning to move to the capital city 6 months later. The family was going through a planned transition, coincidental with an important period in their life cycle. They were getting ready for a trip, the same way an airplane crew does, or the way Carlos Castaneda did with Don Juan in preparing for his "jump" (Castaneda, 1972). They were preparing for the new, while still adhering firmly to their present set of values.

Pablo Martinez, 37, was an engineer, and his wife, Juana, 35, was a child psychologist, both working successfully in their own fields. The couple had three children, two girls, Maria and Ana, 12 and 9 years old, and a 5-year-old boy, Daniel. They were all very affectionate towards each other, and closely bound. The mother was the central love-and-help axis, the father, the loving authority and economic axis. Both parents were slightly demanding, very respectful towards each other, and perhaps a little overzealous in trying to do the best for everybody. It would not have hurt to relax a little and have more fun, but basically it was a healthy family. Various stages of a period in their life journey are discussed in the paragraphs that follow.

Decision and Preparation: The Uprooting Period

Pablo and Juana consulted with the therapist twice on their own, and then the whole family did twice, to deal with the "relocation project," both as a family unit and as individual members. A whole range of issues arose: what life in

Buenos Aires would be like; what changes it would imply for one and all; where they would like their house to be located; what kind of work the father would be doing, and what opportunities there were for self-employment. They also discussed economic and financial issues, changes in Juana's work, schools for the children and other activities for them, and relations with their extended family in Buenos Aires, including grandparents, aunts, uncles, and cousins.

A variety of treatment issues converge in this situation. First, it is legitimate to ask whether the relocation project was truly a self-organizing process growing toward a new evolutionary state. Second, it is worth asking whether the consultations actually functioned as a way of helping the family cope better with the increasing pressures for a favorable change. Third, it is necessary to consider the possibility that members of this family, specifically the mother and the father, were in "hypostress"[1] and that this, because of their higher expectations, helped trigger a "push forward" and a decision to relocate. In other words, their resources actually exceeded the demands of their situation (McCubbin & Patterson, 1983).

All of the members of the family, except the small boy, who did not understand very well what was happening, knew that they were moving because the parents wanted to improve the family's life-style, enjoy better cultural and educational opportunities, and generally enrich their life. This move was actively set in motion by the parent's decision to make a structural-contextual change.

At the time, the family was going through a significant period in their life cycle. The elder daughter was reaching adolescence and starting high school, and the youngest child was just entering elementary school, which meant that the family was already out of the kindergarten stage. Furthermore, Pablo and Juana were especially concerned with the quality of their relationship with the extended family. They had already had some trouble with them. For example, Juana's parents had insisted that since her father had retired, he should be in charge of building a house for them in Buenos Aires. This was not at all what Pablo and Juana desired. They also described Pablo's side of the family as unloving, detached, selfish, and psychologically sick.

Being good people and caring parents, the Martinezes tried to be well prepared for the great change and, if possible, to handle many problems in advance. They wanted to have the children's schools and extracurricular activities chosen, Pablo's work options listed, and the family home already bought or rented before the actual move. In sessions with their therapist, Pablo and Juana made jokes about being overprotective parents, good parents, and good-enough parents, and also about the problem of being "extra good."

The whole family wanted to have a good farewell from Bahia Blanca. They had spent an important part of their lives there and had many close friends. The place was "in their blood," and the children, especially, had deep roots in that city and in their own neighborhood. Photographs could be taken as mementos. Of course, the children also wanted a farewell party for their schoolmates.

Buenos Aires: Preparation versus Reality

The children started out well. They missed Bahia Blanca, but were feeling interested and having fun in a summer day-camp. Pablo had some trouble starting to work on his own. Although he had clear, workable ideas, he was unable, at first, to put them into practice in starting a business. He felt overwhelmed and confused. After attending two fortnightly individual sessions, however, he overcame the problem and was soon doing well. He worked his problems out when the therapist asked him directly how he was blocking himself. He felt he was apt to forget details. The therapist suggested he write down in a notebook all the items and actions essential for his daily work and underline those he anticipated forgetting. As Winnicott (1971) might have said, he just "got unstuck" and went forward.

Around that time, the boy started complaining of pain in his groin. It turned out to be a hernia, and his physician decided he had to undergo surgery, although not necessarily right away. The parents were anxious about this, as neither had had surgery before. They felt it was a burden for the boy and them to bear, so soon after the relocation. Also, they would have to wait for almost a month, as their doctor would be on vacation. This waiting period gave them a breathing space in one way, but also increased their anxiety.

Pablo and Juana arranged for two psychotherapeutic sessions for themselves as part of their strategy for dealing with the child's surgery. Since he was doing quite well, it did not seem necessary to make any more fuss by bringing the boy in for extra consultation. It was the therapist's opinion that the parents could handle the new situation alone. It would probably strengthen their self-confidence and increase their ability to cope with new stressful events.

The surgeon also thought it was a good idea not to bring Daniel in for psychotherapy, because too much attention could lead to an exaggeration of a young boy's negative genital fantasies, such as fear of castration. Acting on the therapist's advice, Pablo and Juana obtained from the surgeon all the information available on the operation in advance—the hospital chosen, the type of anesthesia, the surgical procedure itself, postoperative care, recovery and convalescent period. Starting 6 days before the surgery, the mother and father took turns explaining the whole operation through play acting, and they practiced everything, such as anesthesia and bandage changing, with the boy for about 10 minutes every day. The boy did well in surgery, but the parents found the convalescent period longer and harder to bear than they had anticipated. It was the therapist's impression that they were anxious for the boy to "get better" or "be all right" promptly.

Soon after the surgery and convalescence, two more stressful events occurred. The time came for the elder daughter to start secondary school and for the younger daughter to start elementary school. Juana's plan seemed to be that she would have everybody settled and functioning before she started with her own projects. She had, therefore, postponed her own relocation process.

One day in April, Juana asked for a session because everybody else was more or less settled in, but she really did not feel good about herself and could not do the things she wanted to do. She saw herself as a little lost, and now she felt it was her turn to get involved in a life in Buenos Aires. Juana's involvement became, in fact, the focus of therapy at that point. When Pablo and Juana analyzed their feelings about what they wanted from life in Buenos Aires, her goals appeared to be much more vague than his.

Juana's possibilities and desires were explored through a fantasy-exploration procedure. With the therapist's guidance, Juana was encouraged to express her wishes and ideas while she practiced physical relaxation techniques. As a result of two sessions of that type, Juana decided that, aside from continuing her work, which was adequate and enriching, she would start doing sculpture [she has a strong artistic side] and also would take part in a physical expressiveness course.

Movement toward a Crisis

So far, we have discussed several important events. There was a turning point in the family life cycle and a wished-for transition in the family, including a decision to move, an uprooting, and a relocation. There were several sources of stress operating in the family, such as the management of extended family relationships, the father's being "blocked" in his work, the boy's surgery, and the mother's dissatisfaction, a feeling of postponement in her adjustment to the new city.

None of these events, however, precipitated a serious crisis. The event that actually plunged the family, specifically the parents, into crisis, was the father's serious illness, a stressor that acted as a catastrophic event for them. Here we find that the stimulus struck the hierarchy of the family, deeply affecting both the father and the mother. The children were "protected" for a time by not being informed about what was happening to their father, that is, until the prognosis and treatment were clearly understood.

The family's life situation thus far can be summarized as shown in Table 11-1. Pablo had probably had a tumor for a long time, and it had passed unnoticed. It is interesting to distinguish several phenomena occurring almost simultaneously, all closely related to his illness and diagnosis.

Illness, disablement, and death fantasies centered around the father's surgery and its outcome. Since he had a tumor in the hypophysis, and even though the prognosis was good, both husband and wife were afraid of cancer and of the delicate surgery itself. They tried hard to keep calm, and both made a great effort to be reasonable.

The elder daughter, Maria, was affected early on and started having "day

Table 11-1. Summary of Events in the Life Cycle of the Martinez Family

Type of transition	Crisis	Type of stress
Expectable family transitions	Natural, normative (Beginning of adolescence) (End of kindergarten)	Stress–crisis Hypostress
	Crisis—awaited, wished for (Decision to relocate) (Father's decision to become self-employed)	
Unexpectable family transitions	Emergency (Father becomes seriously ill)	Catastrophic event (stressor)
	Crisis—Unexpected (Whole process of migration) (Illness in the family) (Financial difficulties)	Hyperstress Crisis

accidents" (wetting herself), something that had never happened to her before and that made her feel embarrassed, because she considered herself too grown up for these episodes. So, in the belief that these symptoms were connected with the tension over the father's tumor, of which the children were still "unaware," Pablo and Juana spoke to her about it. The "accidents" never happened again. It was fascinating to observe how they timed the information they gave the eldest and the younger children. This differentiated timing of information also constituted a certain departure from the way they normally handled things, since before this illness, they would have chosen to tell all the children at once, right from the beginning, experiencing "everything together." As it was, they felt surer in their roles as "holders" of part of the process, instead of "spilling over" the information on the children.

Because of the illness and the father's increased dependency on his wife for such activities as going to his physician, the grandparents entered the nuclear family system much more easily. The family's borders became weaker and dependency increased. For instance, the grandmother came in to take care of the children; the grandfather went with the father for a 20-day business trip. There were other qualitative differences, such as the children's being invited by other relatives on weekends, whereas the family had functioned in a totally independent way before. The grandmother kept saying, "Everything is all right," "Everything will soon be over," and clearly expected and demanded from Juana that she behave as if nothing were happening.

To develop his work, the father had to go on a 20-day trip abroad. It was the first time that the couple had separated during a difficult situation and for such a long time. The wife, who was seeing the therapist at the time, felt a great burden, as if the husband were not taking the illness and impending surgery with him, but rather leaving it behind to be "taken over" by her. Besides, they experienced time differently, since he was much more distracted with his trip than she was with her everyday life in Buenos Aires.

Juana and Pablo had difficulty in accepting their inability to live up to their previous expectations. Since they could not carry out their plan of keeping and improving their standard of living, it was the first time Juana and Pablo could actually not live up to their own hopes in their "grown-up" lives. The belief that "everything has to be OK, perfect, the best" and that "everything will be OK for us together" colored the way in which they responded to life. He came from a family whose members were uninvolved and self-centered. However, he himself was devoted to his nuclear family, striving to develop a close relationship. For that reason, Juana and Pablo tried, without even realizing it, to diminish the negative effects of this illness. They resisted the grandmother's dictums, the "nothing bad is happening" idea or myth, but they unwittingly played along with them, and, in fact, tended to reenact this. For example, when Juana felt frightened or depressed, she always tried to "press the brakes" and block those feelings.

As a result, Juana couldn't take Pablo's behavior as an irritable, demanding patient in stride. She couldn't see it as a natural consequence of an exceptionally tense period and was unable to give his behavior a value other than the one she would attribute to an everyday situation. His reactions towards her were categorized as aggressions or dissatisfactions. She took them as an expression of his "true negative feelings" towards her.

In fact, she clung to her parents' lifelong message to her, that "everything is all right, and has to be all right." When Pablo appeared depressed to her, she felt overburdened by having to help him or give him her support. Juana was becoming frightened and anxious. Pablo was too preoccupied with himself to notice the complexity of Juana's reactions, something he normally would have done at other times. This could have developed further, into a new repetitive pattern: She would feel unloved and mistreated, would get frustrated and resentful, would start losing confidence, and would reject him. He would react negatively and, feeling rejected himself, take a bigger distance.

From the therapist's point of view, these phenomena might have established themselves in a new dysfunctional relational pattern rather than remaining aspects of a simple situational reaction. The therapist intervened because sets of interactions were taking place in a context that gave them a strongly negative meaning.

Preventive Therapeutic Intervention

Transformation of the interactional significance of a small but deep wound prevents the development of a new dysfunctional pattern of organization. Failure to detect an important vulnerability can render therapy iatrogenic.

The first stage of the therapeutic intervention during Pablo's illness involved discussing with both husband and wife the ways that sick people interact with those around them. Since so many things were happening to them, both physical and emotional, they were encouraged by the therapist to perceive clearly the extraordinary circumstances of their present situation.

A second stage was carried out with Juana in a sort of humorous, teasing way, bordering on the absurd. Florence Nightingale was mentioned, as well as the reasons why she was a good nurse. The extreme postures of being completely devoted to the other or of not being in the least a good "Florence Nightingale" were tossed back and forth, as well as the mistaken idea that a sick person was the same as a healthy one and that his behavior should be considered as such.

The last stage of the intervention focused on the couple's tendency to take everything that happened between them too seriously. They were then able to distinguish between really crucial issues and those that could be taken more in stride.

The possibility of sharing their problems with their friends arose. They had an excellent group of caring and helpful friends, some of whom had, in fact, already teased them affectionately about the "pleasure of adding complications" to their present circumstances and had mentioned their incredulity at seeing them pick at each other for unimportant things at such a time.

The Waiting Period between Diagnosis and Surgery: More Stress

Surgery had to be postponed for 2 months, because the surgeon would be absent from the country and he was the only appropriate specialist in Argentina. That meant that 4 months intervened between the first consultation and the actual surgery. Since the survival of the family system depended on it, the surgery was a stimulus that could hardly be placed in a drawer and let out as desired. It weighed heavily upon the family, disturbing and disordering every instant of their lives as an unavoidable threat. They now felt trapped in a very hard and traumatic situation. Waiting for the surgery was a stressor with a catastrophic impact.

During this period, fluctuations between the old context and a blurred new one were at their climax, and *hyperstress* appeared to be at its highest. Peaks of tension developed into small "stampedes" and momentarily threatened the system. The school reported two of the children as being distracted and nervous. The third child had a stormy episode with the mother and father, during which she cried desperately and shouted that she wanted to go back to Bahia Blanca. Their "old world" was secure and defined. The pain of their present situation was unbearable.

We may describe this family's circumstances using the concepts involved in Morin's (1977) scheme of interrelation. During the first part of the family's transition (the turning point in the family life cycle, the decision, and the relocation), the family oscillated between order and disorder throughout everyday life. During the more profound crisis period, they had to face real survival issues. There was the organic side of survival—illness, surgery, and its outcome—and a psychological side, since a fundamental belief of this couple—that with love and hard work, they could conquer any obstacles and achieve all their goals—was in danger of being destroyed. This idea, that had guided them and protected them like the Great Wall of China, was being shattered and rendered obsolete. It had been meaningful in their old world but was useless in their new world. They were caught in the middle, and the earth trembled beneath them.

The Surgery is Over

After Pablo's successful surgery, the therapist saw the couple at the hospital. They were managing the situation quite well, with the support of their friends and extended family. Nevertheless, after the first crucial weeks of convalescence, Juana again felt burdened with Pablo's anxiety over his work. Hers was going fine. Pablo's export business was complicated by two external circumstances—a sudden lack of raw materials and an unexpected change in export regulations. These two factors affected his anticipated progress.

Also, the increased interaction with Juana's family of origin seemed to create some problems. She suffered two attacks of asthma—an old somatic symptom from her adolescence—following a disagreeable exchange with her parents. For the first time, her parents spoke to Juana about her hard times. They themselves were quite well-to-do and wished to give her a "nice present." Her mother took her shopping so she might choose whatever she wished, but they went to a bargain store. Juana was cheerfully invited to select a blouse from the cheapest rack, but she asked for one of better quality, and her mother reluctantly purchased it. On the way back home, her mother felt generous and pleased with herself, and Juana started having breathing problems.

Later on, her father lectured Juana on the need for a summer vacation. Although Juana's parents owned several holiday homes at different resorts, they suggested that Juana go away with her family in December, since it was the least expensive month of the summer season, without ever offering her one of their own houses to stay in. On the other hand, both Juana and Pablo worked in December, so it was not a feasible vacation time for them. Right after this conversation, Juana had another asthma episode.

As far as the couple was concerned, Juana's asthma had particular connotations in husband-wife relations. When Juana's asthma developed, Pablo's health improved. He was also strongly motivated to recover and keep fit, probably as a reaction to his own family background and relatives, some of whom he perceived as psychologically sick. Juana was, for her part, quite satisfied with her husband's postsurgery recovery, since she could fall back on her parents' old paradigm, "Everything has to be all right," while trying to ignore her own asthmatic episodes.

The reappearance at this stage of an old symptom, after so many years, gives rise to many questions. Did the asthma reemerge because Juana was at such a critical moment in her life (being much more vulnerable than at any other time in the previous 15 years) and hence more liable to fall back into a discarded communicative pattern with her parents? Does the appearance of the old system, having been overcome for so many years—what we could consider a real change—imply that an irreversible change had not really occurred? If we follow this line of thought, then the possibility must be considered that the old pattern was "latent" in her, an easier road to take as a reaction than others (in S-matrix language, the "tendency to react"). Her response suggests that although certain symptoms had been overcome, they could reappear, even after many years, under circumstances of exceptional stress. Moreover, we might conclude that in important crises, old surmounted symptoms must be sought out during the evaluation process, in the context of the existing interrelations, in order to prevent their reappearance. We need not, however, go so far as to include such a search process as a major feature of the present model of crisis and crisis therapy.

Things Change

Juana realized that the children did not need her as much as before and that it was also better to leave Pablo more on his own at times. So, for the first time in many years, she stayed in bed instead of serving breakfast to him, feeling it was agreeable to everyone. Once, when she was very tired, she left a note for the eldest daughter to tell her she would not accompany her to lunch.

In addition, Pablo remarked during a joint session that perhaps Juana was in a worse spot than he was, since she was the "filter" for everything that happened to them. Although the stressors—his health and his work—had a direct impact on him, they also had a catastrophic effect on her because of their importance for both of them. He therefore changed somewhat in his demanding attitude and started helping out a bit with the children. For instance, he intervened to stop or distract a child who was putting too much pressure on Juana, since this was her "weak point." He thought that Juana was always at her children's disposal and that the children were in the habit of being too demanding, so he decided to "do something about it." He stated that he was quite capable of taking matters into his own hands, and in fact he did. Furthermore, on that same weekend, he diminished the "pouring over" of his work anxiety on her. She was quite pleased with this, appearing more relaxed later on.

It is difficult to determine exactly which part of the change can be attributed to the therapeutic process and which to the crisis itself. It is the therapist's impression that these changes were made possible by the crisis itself but were facilitated by the ripple effect of the therapeutic work. Whatever its cause, the period of change was a crucial moment, and the quality of the resolution of the crisis had to be carefully assessed. During the process of change, the therapist sometimes is, in a certain sense, an active observer of a transformation, of the foundation of a new interrelational pattern that gives rise to new values. Given the right sort of awareness, such a moment might be regarded with the same awe that a birth inspires. The therapist must, however, remain alert to signals that the new pattern or belief is dysfunctional for the family members.

Forward Progress

A chain of beneficial reactions took place. For Pablo's birthday, they were planning a small party for their friends. To their surprise, Pablo and Juana found they were thinking of serving the familiar "good old spicy rice" and the special "cozy fruit salad" Juana normally prepared. This was a clear departure from their old way of doing things. They stated that before, they would have thought up some superb food requiring a lot of extra-special work for which they did not have either the energy or the money at the moment. They were happy about this change, which indicated a clear break with the past.

Indeed, it represented inward and outward harmony. In this sense, preparations for the birthday party turned out to be not only a rite of passage but also a rite of transition: from one life-style to another, and from a discarded paradigm to a new and invigorating one. The couple and the children had agreed that Juana would not be an ever-present figure, and they no longer expected Pablo to be "a winner" but rather, a common mortal with ups and downs.

Another important change was a reappraisal of their essential needs and material expectations. They felt strengthened in their mutual love, and, during the last follow-up family session, the couple briefly smiled at each other, held hands for a moment, and said, "Hey, we *are* different people in a certain sense now!" Going back to the relocation process, they found themselves remembering Bahia Blanca, their beautiful house there, and all the troubles they had overcome since they had relocated. They grieved over their old town but did not question the move to Buenos Aires.

Summary of the Therapeutic Process

Since therapy involved working with different subsystems at different stages, the format of the therapeutic process can be summarized as shown in Table 11-2. The therapeutic process took 33 sessions over a period of at least a year and a half, quite long compared with other crisis cases in which cumulative stress combines with a transitional development. The therapist enjoyed a significant degree of flexibility in the formal structure of the therapeutic process, taking into account the frequency and number of sessions, the choice of family members present, and the type of interventions employed.

Table 11-2. Format of the Therapeutic Process Used with the Martinez Family

Participants	Number of sessions	Type of event
Parents and children.	4 (widely spaced)	Anticipation of uprooting and relocation; hypostress and stress
Parents and then the father alone for work-related problems.	3	Stress during relocation period
Parents alone.	2	Preparation for child's surgery
Parents alone and then the mother alone for "her turn."	4	Stress during relocation period
Parents together alternating with the mother alone during the father's illness, surgery, and recovery. Hospital visits.	12 (higher frequency of visits)	True crisis; hyperstress
The mother alone, once a week.	4	Out of the crisis
The parents alone.	3 (includes 1 follow-up session)	Out of the crisis
The whole family.	1 (follow-up session)	Out of the crisis

A CLINICAL MODEL FOR THE THERAPY OF FAMILIES IN CRISIS WITH CUMULATIVE STRESS

A clinical model to be used with families undergoing a crisis with cumulative stress must include four basic aspects: the evaluative, the preventive, the therapeutic, and the informational.

Evaluation continues throughout therapy. Crises and emergencies are distinguished from the beginning, because they require different psychological assistance. The therapist clearly establishes the focus, defines the stressors, and determines the internal and external resources available to the family. The differentiation of the critical and dysfunctional aspects of the situation is important, as is establishing whether the major critical stressor is truly life threatening or attacks the survival of the family. If the therapist is dealing with a crisis, its phase or moment of development must be pinpointed. Finally, the therapist must determine which aspects of the family system should not be tampered with and which parts of the therapeutic process are simply not advisable or necessary.

Regarding the preventive aspects of a clinical model, we may consider several factors. One is early and anticipatory care of the family when a potentially catastrophic stressor is present. Another is being permanently alert to the establishment of new dysfunctional interactional patterns. Yet another factor is making sure that the family members determine in a timely way what resources they can count on in themselves and in their environment during an exceptional period.

The therapeutic aspect involves the therapist's position and function, witnessing and perhaps distinguishing the green, yellow, and red signals of systemic change. The therapist needs to be ready to trigger, with one or two "touches" of intervention, the unblocking of certain areas and to act as an agent of change when dysfunction is present. On the other hand, throughout a period of change, it is often necessary to support family members emotionally in an atmosphere of freedom that includes taking a step sideways so that they can "go on with their own dance." "In all transitions, the major difficulty lies in knowing what should be discarded and what is to be preserved and kept" (author's translation; Terragno, 1985, p. 84).

Considerable subtlety is required in treating family crises, since mistakes and iatrogenic effects are ever-present dangers. The therapist's limits and "blind areas" should not be neglected, and crisis must be differentiated from pathology. Perhaps one of the most delicate balances to maintain involves respect for the family's change and for their new construction of reality. What not to touch is a subtle side of this type of therapeutic process, as well as what to touch minimally. It is vital to let people carry on with their own resources.[2]

Even if we partially agree with Kantor and Neal's (1985) distinction of a "formed structure" (the family) and a "forming structure" (the therapeutic system), we are nevertheless, in crisis cases, facing a "transformation of a destructured structure" (p. 17). In contrast with other therapeutic processes, where instability needs to be provoked, here it is already present, and we do not have to help produce it.

The therapist must be able to take the intensely emotional situation in stride and tolerate the intense pain that is felt during the process, since the whole therapeutic system is shaken for a long period of time. Just as those therapists working with families with terminal illnesses must be prepared to endure situations involving death and the anxieties related to it, those working with families in crisis (not just emergencies, it must be stressed) have to be able to deal with intense human pain and suffering. Crisis therapy sometimes means bearing the family's anxiety when all their basic beliefs are shaken, making the therapeutic bond serve an anesthetic function (Whitaker, 1975).

In connection with the informational aspect, it is important at certain times in the treatment of a family crisis to encourage the use of resources available in the community and to fill in gaps when family members demonstrate a lack of knowledge in certain areas related to their own problems. For example, they might not realize that they are going through a crisis with cumulative stress and what this implies.

FURTHER CASES OF DEVELOPMENTAL TRANSITION: CUMULATIVE STRESS AND CRISIS

Let us look at an entirely different case example, that of a family system undergoing a crisis that seemed to threaten the very existence of that family. The couple in question approached therapy as "the last resort," without either great motivation or great interest. The deterioration of their relationship was serious and covered almost all areas of the couple's life; they were full of bitterness, frustration, and rage. Nevertheless, both preferred to remain married.

The couple reported the presence of dissatisfaction with each other from the beginning. Their marriage was brought about by external influences they accepted—a well-known astrologer had told her that it was her only chance to get married! A few months earlier, her brother had committed suicide, and she was feeling desperate. She decided to get married, and he assented. Both of their families of origin accepted the union.

Against this background of basic dysfunction, they started their life as a couple and later as a family, when they became the parents of a baby boy. The boy, whose birth proved to be a serious stressor, was described by them as always being very difficult. The wife then tightened her close bond with her own mother, and the husband traveled more often since he worked in the country and they lived in the city. Later they had a baby girl, who became sick soon after birth. The infant's illness increased the stress in the family and took the husband and wife almost to the fracture point, at which time they sought advice. It is clear that the cumulative stress was more than they could cope with as a couple. Let us look at what happened.

When the baby girl had to be hospitalized at one juncture, the husband took his wife and the baby to the clinic and left them there but only went to visit them once. A short time later, the baby was taken home without a definite diagnosis, only to be readmitted a week later. This time, the father neither accompanied them to the hospital nor visited them during the fortnight the baby was hospitalized, diagnosed, and treated. When the mother and baby returned home, and the child still slept badly at night, the mother took care of her alone. Overburdened, she turned to her own mother for help. The father was irritable and did not take care of either of the children at all. The grandmother on the father's side helped out by taking care of the boy, who at the time attended kindergarten. He had become tense and nervous, behaved "badly," and refused to eat.

The couple, who could not function together nor truly help one another in the crisis, intended to handle it as disengaged members of a system. They could not bear the necessary changes, feeling that they did not have the "right stuff" to pull through the crisis. In this sense, it may be true that "it is not those who want but those who can, who make a crisis possible" (Lent, 1984, p. 96).

Because there was no emotional resonance between them, they handled the situation by not being there for each other. For example, the father was absent during the baby's illness, and the mother brought the grandmother into the family picture. In this way, they were trying to avoid the crisis through bypassing the breakup limit.

The couple reviewed their relationship and renegotiated their basic bond during 9 sessions of psychotherapy. Both grandmothers were called in together and were actively present with the couple during three sessions, so the whole process took 12 sessions, held fortnightly.

It is instructive to compare this case with that of the Martinez family. The two families differ on one critical dimension. The first family was growing, happy, and changing, with normal conflicts and difficulties, whereas the second was dysfunctional, frustrated, unloving, and dependent even before the developmental changes occurred. Although the events that precipitated a true crisis in each family were similar—sudden, life-threatening illnesses—the two families drew on vastly different levels of emotional resources. Since the second couple had less cohesion and strength than the first, they were hardly able to cope with serious stress. A couple's immaturity often leads to unsatisfactory family relationships and unsatisfactory parenthood (Barragan, 1976). Although both families had difficulties involving the children, only the second family had a clearly symptomatic child, the boy. Another obvious distinction is that the illness was located in the upper hierarchy of the first family (the father) and in the lower one of the second family (the baby).

In another case of family crisis with different characteristics, the family consisted of the father, the mother, and two young school-age boys. They asked for consultation to help the family in a moment of crisis, since the father was dying of cancer. A week after the first consultation, the mother phoned, anxiously asking for an urgent individual session. Because of the exceptional terminal situation, and since she said it mainly concerned the boys and herself, it was arranged. She revealed during the interview that by "an unlucky coincidence," one of the members of the very powerful Parents' Committee at the boys' school had learned that she had established a lesbian relationship and, for that reason, wanted to have her children immediately expelled from the school.

The mother said that she did have such a secret liaison but that she was reluctant to tell the family and that it would be terrible for the children to have to change schools then, especially with the father dying. She said that she would tell her children later on, which she in fact did, about 6 months after her husband's death. She had already spoken to the members of the committee but to no avail, so she felt particularly desperate and at a loss as to how to manage this urgent problem, and asked the therapist for help. Thus the family faced an extremely stressful situation: the father's impending death, to which not only one extra emergency stressor was added (the children's expulsion from school) but a second (the mother's feelings about her lesbian relationship). It was a bit too much for the children.

Surely this was a catastrophic juncture. In this instance, the therapist tried to help resolve the immediate problem by dealing directly with the different aspects of the crisis. The therapist held a meeting with the mother and the board of the Parents' Committee in order to consider the issue. It was a long, difficult encounter, since the school had a very strict tradition. It is clear that in this case the therapist's management involved the school as part of the therapeutic system, and therefore therapy actively included the school context. Afterward, a second session was conducted with the family, regarding the father's imminent death, which happened a week later. At that point, the process had lasted 5 weeks in all.

During this time, the following happened: (1) a crisis, owing to the father's imminent death; (2) an emergency—sudden knowledge of the mother's lesbianism reentering the system as a menace to the relationship, beliefs, and identity of its members, and to the children's schooling and stability—a potentially catastrophic stressor; and (3) a deeper crisis, resulting from the emergency. The therapist had to show a great deal of flexibility when confronted with the coherence–incoherence of the family values, their choices, and their actions (a strict school for the children, a lesbian mother, but still a traditional marriage). A decision had to be taken about this sensitive information. Was it the right time to work with the family on its communicative style, that is, to tell or not to tell the "truth" about sexual identification when the father was on the brink of death? Should the therapist refuse to be the mother's accomplice in her secrecy or make a separate alliance with her only for the sake of avoiding further grief at such a critical time?

Considering the father's imminent death, the therapist decided to accept the mother's proposal temporarily. With the mother taking into consideration the therapist's construction of reality, and with the therapist respecting the family's own construction of reality, a coconstruction of reality emerged whereby the matter of the mother's homosexuality was postponed to a more appropriate time in the future.

CONCLUSION

In all three cases that I have described, situations of cumulative stress coincided with a developmental transition. These situations stem from very different kinds of external and internal stimuli, all of which can plunge a family system into a crisis.

Regrettably, a particular kind of external stressor has been quite frequent in Argentina during the last decade. Total violation of human rights and extreme repression were the norm of the day. Many families suffered intolerable pressure because of the political violence. Sometimes one or both parents were abducted ("disappeared") and tortured beyond human endurance. Sometimes their bodies were found in mass graves; some were never seen again. These families are finally receiving close attention.

The surviving family members have suffered immensely from an absolute lack of official response to their pleas for legal remedy, from government "ignorance" about their loved ones' whereabouts, and even from continuing threats against their own lives. All this has resulted in deep-seated feelings of utter helplessness. This state of affairs lasted several years and provoked a pervasive and widespread emotional as well as political crisis hitherto unknown in Argentina.

Perhaps our studies in family transition, cumulative stress, and crisis will help us gain an understanding of the relationship between extreme stress and family development. We can hope that such knowledge will be of assistance in dealing with the tragedies that occur in nations as well as in families.

NOTES

1. "Family stress" (as distinct from "stressor") is defined as a state arising from an actual or a perceived imbalance between demand (e.g., challenge, threat) and capability (e.g., resources, coping) in the family's functioning. When the imbalance is due to demands exceeding resources, this is a state of hyperstress; conversely, when the imbalance is due to resources exceeding demands, the family experiences hypostress (McCubbin & Patterson, 1983).

2. For this approach, two excellent models of clinical attitude from a psychoanalytic school of thought are available: Balint's (Balint, Balint, & Ornstein, 1972) "focal psychotherapy" task force group and his insistence on "thoughts thought by the therapist but not to be worked upon"; and Winnicott's (1971) "one and only" consultation using the "squiggle game" with children, as an example of his position regarding development. Several specialists dealing with loss and grief also advocate respecting the spontaneous resolution of these processes.

REFERENCES

Balint, M., Balint, E., & Ornstein, P. (1972). *Focal psychotherapy.* London: Tavistock Publications.
Barragan, M. (1976). The child-centered family. In P. Guerin (Ed.), *Family therapy.* New York: Gardner Press.
Bateson, G. (1972). *Steps to an ecology of mind.* New York: Ballantine Books.
Bateson, G. (1979). *Mind and nature.* New York: E. P. Dutton.
Burr, W. (1973). *Theory construction in the sociology of the family.* New York: Wiley.
Capra, F. (1976). *The Tao of physics.* New York: Bantam Books.
Castaneda, C. (1972). *Journey to Ixtlan: The lessons of Don Juan.* New York: Pocket Books.
Heisenberg, W. (1962). *Physics and philosophy.* New York: Harper & Row.

Kantor, D., & Neal, J. (1985). Integrative shifts for the theory and practice of family systems therapy. *Family Process, 24,* 1, 13–30.

Lent, C. (1984). Entre a primeriera e a segunda fundacao: A migracao psiquica; uma visao de crise em Psicologia. In M. Bursztyn, A. Chain, & P. Leita (Eds.), *Crises* (pp. 65–101). Concilio Nacional de Pesquise. Rio de Janeiro, Brasil: Editorial Brasiliense.

McCubbin, H., & Patterson, J. (1983). Family transitions: adaptation to stress. In H. McCubbin & C. Figley (Eds.), *Stress and the family* (Vol. 1). New York: Brunner/Mazel.

Morin, E. (1973). *Le paradigme perdu.* Paris: Editions du Seuil.

Morin, E. (1977). *La methode: 1. La nature de la nature; 2. La vie de la vie.* Paris: Editions du Seuil.

Terragno, R. (1985). *La Argentina del Siglo XXI.* Buenos Aires: Sudamericana-Planeta.

Watzlawick, P., Weakland, J., & Fisch, R. (1974). *Change: Principles of problem formation and problem resolution.* New York: W. W. Norton.

Whitaker, C. (1975). Psychotherapy of the absurd, with a special emphasis on the psychotherapy of aggression. *Family Process, 14,* 1–16.

Winnicott, D. (1971). *Therapeutic consultations in child psychiatry.* London: Hogarth Press.

12

Family Development and the Impact of A Child's Chronic Illness

BERNICE L. ROSMAN
Philadelphia Child Guidance Clinic

Most people think of an illness or a debilitating injury as confined to the body of the affected individual. But an illness also has an impact on the family of the sick person, and the family can, at the same time, have an impact on the course of the disease or disorder of one of its members. Previous studies have focused on the patterns of interaction within the family that maintain symptoms longer than the normal course of the disease or disorder would predict and that can even make those symptoms worse (Minuchin *et al.,* 1975; Minuchin, Rosman, & Baker, 1978), but they did not elaborate on developmental issues. In this chapter, the significance of a child's chronic illness on family development and on the family life cycle will be discussed from the point of view of structural family therapy.

Three aspects will be considered—the impact of the onset of the illness on the organization of the family and its adaptational response in maintaining stability and the capacity to change; the implications of the illness for the developmental process of the family system through the life cycle; and the effects of therapeutic interventions on the family developmental process when family dysfunction around a child's illness is treated.

FAMILY DEVELOPMENT: STRUCTURAL MODELS

The development of the family over time through the life cycle may be schematized utilizing structural concepts. Two models of family development basic to the subsequent discussion of the impact of illness will be briefly summarized here. Minuchin and Fishman (1981) have described a child-focused developmental model of the family encompassing four stages: couple formation, family with young children, family with school-age and/or adolescent children, and family with grown children. Each of these stages is initiated by a period of instability and disequilibrium resulting from demands for change, coming from within and without, that challenge the structure of the family. As these demands increase beyond the capacity of the family organization to accommodate to them, a reorganization or restructuring occurs, reflected in a more differentiated, more complex family structure. As new rules, tasks, accommodations, and skills associated with the reorganization are developed and mastered, a period of balance, stability, and adaptation is experienced.

Stage 1. In the stage of couple formation, the two members of the newly forming spousal system must accommodate their differing expectations, values, and mode of relating learned in their family of origin to the development of a new transactional system composed of his, hers, and ultimately theirs. They need to develop a boundary, or set of rules, that will protect the integrity of the subsystem and give them the privacy, space, and freedom from intrusions necessary for the development of spousal intimacy, support, and regard. At the same time, this boundary must also permit maintenance of contact with important extrafamilial others and respect for each other as individuals.

Stage 2. The birth of the first child plunges the spousal system into a state of disequilibrium and rapid reorganization of the family structure, with the creation of new transactional units, the parental (coparent) and parent–child subsystems. The spousal unit needs to maintain subsystem integrity and continue to carry out spousal functions. This system is stressed since the same participants also need to function in a different way, together as parents sharing responsibilities for their offspring, and also in mother–child or father–child subsystems. In the new subsystems, the major tasks to be mastered are nurturance, socialization, and, somewhat later, protective support of the young child's autonomy. With the birth of more children, a sibling subsystem is created, again increasing the complexity of the family structure and further differentiating the parent–child subsystems. Over time, with the increasing growth and individuation of the children, an internal hierarchical structuring of the sibling subsystem, organized around age and sex distinctions, develops through the differential competencies and interests of the siblings. This process may just begin in this period and probably is more typical of the next stage of development.

Stage 3. The disequilibrium of the third stage is initiated when the children begin to go to school. The family system is opened up to new inputs and influences from extrafamilial sources such as the school system, families of their children's friends, and peer groups. No new subsystems are formed, but the relations between existing ones are transformed, with increased distancing within the parent–child subsystems and an associated increase in autonomy for the children. The how of the adolescent's participation in the parent–child system may change considerably as increasing competence enables him or her to negotiate with the parent, from a more powerful position, new issues of control and autonomy. The culmination of this stage is the separation phase, when the former adolescent, now a young adult, leaves home for college, work, or marriage, precipitating a new disequilibrium period for those who are still at home.

At this point, I will diverge from the Minuchin family-developmental model and not discuss the fourth stage, the family with grown children. First, it is beyond the focus of this chapter on families with sick children not yet fully grown or independent. More important, however, it should be noted that the fourth stage overlaps completely with Stage 1, couple formation, except that it views the couple from a different vantage point. Instead of focusing on the tasks of the new couple in both separating from and maintaining relationships with the families of origin, Stage 4 defines the tasks and relationships from both sides of the generational boundaries and delineates the new tasks for the older (parental) generation.

A multilayered and continuous flow of family members (organized in individual, age-graded, or generational subsystems) through the family life cycle has been very clearly conceptualized by Combrinck-Graham (1985) as a spiral with no first or last stages. This model expands the more traditional model describing a linear series of changes in family structure organized around children's stages of development. Within her model, Combrinck-Graham examines the connections and reciprocities between the developmental tasks for individual family members at each generational level (grandparent, parent, child, adolescent) in relation to the others; even more interestingly, she describes the synchrony of movement of these generational subsystems, coming closer together at significant developmental stages for each generation (a centripetal period) and moving further apart at other stages (a centrifugal period). Generational change ushers in the closeness phase (childbirth, couple becoming parents, parents becoming grandparents), while individual differentiation is associated with greater distancing (adolescence, midlife transition of parents, retirement of grandparents). Looked at from the point of view of family organization, "in the centrifugal period the family dismantles old family structures" (Combrinck-Graham, 1985, p. 144), whereas in the centripetal period there is rebuilding—"a renegotiation of relationships begins between family members and the reforming of structures" (p. 145).

At this point, the interface (interaction) between family organization and chronic illness in a child will be considered. Later on in the discussion, these relationships will be examined within the context of this more complex family developmental model.

CHRONIC ILLNESS AND FAMILY ORGANIZATION

Any family system is subject to considerable stress when one of its members, particularly a child, is diagnosed as having a chronic illness such as diabetes, hemophilia, or, rheumatoid arthritis. Emotional arousal in the form of anxiety and guilt and the potential threat of loss or disability of a family member place heavy demands on family members for mutual support, reassurance, and information sharing. Subsequent needs of the child for long-term care and management, which involve changes in family routines, pose additional challenges to family stability. Although these are givens in this situation, there is considerable variation in the adaptational outcomes for different families, with many, or even most, managing to recover a reasonably normal balance while providing adequate care. Others remain in a state of disequilibrium, stabilize into a dysfunctional structure, or stabilize but provide inadequate care.

Certain family structural characteristics may serve to amplify the stress experience. These include families with an already unbalanced parental subsystem in which one parent is carrying out most of the parental responsibility even prior to the onset of the illness. The addition of the new stress may overburden this system. Iatrogenic stress may contribute to the burden when the pediatrician deals exclusively with this parent, adding to the skew of the system. In the other direction, members of a previously disengaged spousal system lose the opportunity to support each other and probably are less able to reassure or even take care of their children appropriately. A system in which the spousal functions are overly submerged in the parental function, as is often the case in families with a young diabetic child, is similarly handicapped. Some families are isolated, with too rigid boundaries around the entire system, cutting them off from extrafamilial sources of support, such as extended kin, for respite care. Others may be too open to intrusion by well-meaning, but disruptive and poorly informed, "helpers."

Optimal Adaptation

The coping responses of the family can be very revealing and important in determining the adaptational success around the illness. Generally speaking, the least amount of family structural change consistent with providing good medical management leads to the better adaptation in terms of stabilizing the system at a functional level. First-order change involves increasing emotional support and flexibility in carrying out subsystem tasks, broadening the range of skills within all the subsystems (sharing medical management information competencies and responsibilities), and normalizing the medical regimen by incorporating it into normal routines where possible. Caretaking tasks may be distributed differently in different families; the key factors are parental coresponsibility and backup support systems that work. This is particularly important for single-parent families or those with two working parents. *While family members may be doing some things differently than they did before, the basic family structure need not change.*

Dysfunctional Adaptations

Other adaptations may be seen which lead to dysfunctional consequences, both for the family's capacity to carry out nurturant and socialization functions and for achieving a balance between stability and change.

Some families overrespond, reorganizing around the management of the illness to an excessive degree. Second-order change in family structure involving unnecessarily large accommodations to the medical routines usually results in less differentiation of subsystems (e.g., the development of enmeshed parent–child subsystems, the diminished status of the patient in the sibling hierarchy as a weakling or scapegoat, or the submersion of the spousal subsystem in the parental subsystem).

In a preliminary analysis of a prospective study of newly diagnosed juvenile diabetics and their families conducted in 1979–1984 at the Philadelphia Child Guidance Clinic and the Children's Hospital of Philadelphia, we did indeed find that families that were assessed as generally more poorly functioning at the time of diagnosis were more likely subsequently to make major changes in family life routines, organizing around the diabetes, and that both of these stages of family assessments were associated with poorer diabetic control at a later follow-up (Rosman & Baker, 1986).

Paradoxically, the families that overrespond to the perceived medical demands and "change" the most are often the ones least able to negotiate the changes associated with the normal developmental progression. The "changes" that occur do not indicate flexibility but, rather, a rigid commitment to a limited pattern of functioning, with fewer alternatives for role flexibility and sharing of responsibilities and greater expectations of severe medical consequences if changes are made. Sometimes the larger system (i.e., pediatric inputs and physician–family relationships) may intensify these problems, by fostering excessive dependency on the medical system and preoccupation with caretaking, thus contributing to the family's inability to move along to more appropriate levels of organization, with consequent limitations on the development of the patient's competence and psychosocial development.

On the other hand, disengaged families may be unwilling or unable to accommodate appropriately in order to provide adequate care for the patient. They will display a too speedy developmental progression, with unrealistic expectations for family members' autonomy, when increased cooperation and flexibility in sharing tasks may be required. Here, for example, the young patient may be presented with the whole responsibility for self-care, with little or no supervision or guidance. Little or no emotional support may be given, and the whole issue may be treated like another routine task, such as cleaning the closet or doing homework. Some physicians, again, may inadvertently reinforce these patterns in their efforts to support child or adolescent autonomy for example, so that parents may not get to hear about adverse reports of their child's checkups or feel entitled to intervene. In such families, the disengaged structure may also be reflected in distant spousal or parental relationships, so that parents may miscommunicate about their expectations and be unable to support each other or the child either emotionally or in providing appropriate care.

Families exhibiting these two types of dysfunctional adaptations usually intensify their commitment to their preferred transactional patterns or develop an even more rigid one. Children with somatic problems in these families are at high risk for the development of psychosomatic or behavioral symptoms, which become part of the dysfunctional family system. A precarious stability is achieved at a high cost to the individual family members. In avoiding potential new stressors and challenges, the family members also reduce their opportunities to diversify interactions with the environment, learn from others' experiences, and try out new patterns of behavior. Families such as these, who depend heavily on less flexible, less stage-appropriate family structures, are vulnerable at life cycle transition points.

The discussion thus far has been concerned exclusively with children who have a chronic illness. Similar considerations, of course, may apply in the case of a severe handicap or injury with long-term effects. The observations also seem to apply fairly consistently to somatic problems of psychogenic (nonorganic) origin, such as anorexia or bulimia. Often, the pattern of overorganization around the illness may be seen (with the patients cast as "victims of a disease"), leading to rigidification of family patterns and an impairment of the individual and family developmental processes.

IMPLICATIONS OF THE ILLNESS FOR THE DEVELOPMENTAL PROCESS

The effects on the family developmental process of a child's illness are related to age of onset. Issues relating to two stages may be differentiated—first, the development of illness in infancy or young childhood, and second, the problems of families with school-age or adolescent offspring. In this section and in the later case examples, the more expanded concepts of family development proposed by Combrinck-Graham are utilized in the discussion.

Families with Infants or Young Children

Some of the most difficult problems for families arise when a child is born with a somatic disorder or develops one in early childhood. The couple or young family reorganizing to include a new member is plunged into an even greater disequilibrium as new and more demanding caretaking and emotional-supportive tasks need to be assigned and mastered. Young children cannot report on their condition or symptoms adequately, or participate in self-care. The parent(s) must become more vigilant and instrumentally competent. The diabetic child may become hypoglycemic and convulse without previous warning; the exploring hemophiliac child may fall while climbing and hemorrhage. The parents need to learn to give insulin injections or transfusions, run to the hospital for emergency visits or checkups, keep charts and diaries, and comfort each other and the child(ren). As nurturance tasks expand, socialization problems can also develop. Parents may fear disciplining a vulnerable child; they may feel the need to inhibit or check the normal rough-and-tumble play of siblings and not to expect the same standards of behavior (thou shalt not hit thy sibling) from the patient.

Even in healthy families, the new challenges to the structure of the family system during early child rearing are the differentiation of the spouse and the parental subsystems as well as the "regression" of the parent–child subsystem patterns to the influence of the families of origin. This is one of the centripetal periods described by Combrinck-Graham (1985), reflecting the change of generations.

Maintenance of Differentiation of Spousal and Parental Subsystems

During the prechildren phase, spouses create together a viable relationship of mutual regard, support, and intimacy. The development of the parental subsystem may overshadow, at times, the spousal system in the early child-rearing years. With a chronically ill child in the forefront, the spousal subsystem may disappear or be frustrated to a dangerous degree.

Complaints from parents of diabetic children, severely asthmatic children, and hemophiliac children from both functional and dysfunctional families seen in our clinical and research work were very similar: the difficulty of finding babysitters or competent caretakers; the fears of separating, even for brief periods, from the children or of trusting their care to others who might be less vigilant; the fatigue and stress of dealing with crises; the couple's need to renegotiate or their inability to agree on equitable labor distribution or responsibility for decision making. All of these concerns impinged on the time, energy, and affect available for the spousal relationship and sometimes taxed the parental alliance as well. Families in which the spousal system was not well consolidated in the prechildren phase could be in even worse difficulty unless the couple shared a value system emphasizing a parental union as the primary goal of the marriage. One well-functioning couple with a lively 4-year-old diabetic child actually had been on the verge of divorce at the time of diagnosis at the age of 2, but they decided to stay together to share in his care. Through a successful adaptation to parenting a diabetic child, they seemed to have resolved or subordinated their marital difficulties. Although these adaptations may work adequately or even well in the early stages of the family, the question remains, what do these couples do later, when parenting activities need to diminish or cease? Too often they do not diminish but are clung to in lieu of a spousal relationship, often at the expense of maintaining infantile behavior in the child and amplifying the somatic problems.

Mutual Influences of Nuclear Family and Family of Origin

The second major vulnerable aspect of the transition into this stage is the change in proximity between the nuclear family and the families of origin of the parents. During the prechildren stage, the couple and their parents were somewhat more distant than prior to the marriage, while maintaining contact under normal conditions. When children (grandchildren) are born, the proximity between the systems increases again, the centripetal process described by Combrinck-Graham (1985). Under normal circumstances, grandparents provide support, assistance, and advice, which may or may not be utilized. Under adverse conditions, proximity may not increase or it may increase too much. Extended kin may be disengaged and unavailable or intrusive and enmeshed.

The presence of two families of origin (two sets of grandparents) may pose additional problems if their child-rearing attitudes or their relationships with the nuclear family differ in proximity, power, affect, and supportiveness. These conflicts may also extend to the siblings of the parents or to other significant relatives. To the extent that the spousal or parental subsystem is weak, there may be additional pulls and tugs on the family system from these extrafamilial sources. This becomes critical when the nuclear family is most vulnerable, coping with the problems of a chronically ill child. Couples with slightly differing attitudes about protectiveness, autonomy, and other common aspects of child rearing, probably deriving from their own developmental experiences, might find their differences amplified when faced with the day-to-day challenges presented by their sick children.

To find out more about some of these issues, a couples group consisting of parents of very young children with hemophilia was conducted for 12 sessions, to discuss common problems they experienced and to share their coping behaviors.[1] Some of these parents experienced their own parents, their spouse's parents, or their siblings as helpful; others found them to be critical, intrusive, misinformed, and nonsupportive. During the course of these group sessions, it became apparent that two of the couples experienced considerable difficulty in their spousal relationships and some difficulty in their management of the child's illness. These problems seemed to be clearly related to conflicting affiliations with their extended kin. Other couples reported similar negative input from extended kin, but their own spousal subsystems were strongly differentiated and withstood the negative influences through the marital partners' support of each other.

Moderately well functioning and well-functioning families with young children who have a chronic illness or disability often seek and can find support in groups composed of parents in similar situations. In our experience, these associations serve best when they are advocacy oriented or devoted to supporting, coping, and competence. Groups organized around catharsis and the sharing of difficult and painful experiences and feelings only usually do not retain members over any useful period of time. Couples groups or groups composed of single parents with supporters are preferable to groups of "mothers only" in that they avoid further splitting of the natural supportive units.

Families with School-Age and Adolescent Children

The school years mark the "opening up" of the family and the beginning of increasing distance between the parental and child/sibling subsystems. Children are in contact with authoritative and informational sources other than the parents and have a wider variety of peer contacts than they experienced with their siblings alone. The parents can invest more time in spousal interests or in individual personal development. Grandparents also may become less involved with the child-rearing generation at this time. In short, this is the transitional period, in Combrinck-Graham's terms, between the centripetal and centrifugal stages. For the family with a chronically ill child, these trends may be fraught with dangers and difficulties.

For those whose children may have been ill for years prior to this period, the disequilibrium of the transition may be extraordinarily heightened. Relinquishment of the nurturant–protective functions by the parent–child subsystem to "strangers," and the encounters between the child and new peers, who have not been socialized, as the siblings may have been, in dealing with a sick child, may pose critical problems for the family. Although psychosocial problems experienced by some chronically ill children in school or peer settings are typically ascribed to the "infantilization" of that child, careful assessment of the family may reveal more widespread problems, reflecting the family's difficulty to make a family-system-wide transition to the next developmental level. For example, the parents themselves may still be more involved in parental functions than is age appropriate for the child(ren) and less involved in spousal activities than they could be; they may not be pursuing their own interests (i.e., mothers wishing to resume careers); sibling hierarchies may be still inappropriately arranged; and sibling interests or peer group activities that might be expected may be curtailed or discouraged.

For those children whose illness is diagnosed during the school years, a somewhat different pattern may emerge, depending on the prior levels and course of development accomplished by the family. Families who have made successful developmental transitions prior to the onset of the illness tend to adapt successfully and flexibly. Some families whose organization is borderline in some areas of subsystem functioning or who are clearly dysfunctional prior to diagnosis become more vulnerable to the stress of a crisis event such as a child's illness. Behavior or management problems and psychosomatic symptoms may emerge in these dysfunctional contexts. Families may revert to earlier developmental patterns of family behavior, or they may be unable to shift flexibly into new patterns of behavior, which, while developmentally appropriate, will still guarantee adequate care and protection for the sick child.

Newly diagnosed adolescents, who may be fairly autonomous, competent, and self-sufficient in other areas of their lives, will need to accept training, supervision, and monitoring of self-care in the early stages of the illness, to ensure appropriate treatment until competence is achieved. The parental relationship needs to be strong enough to withstand the increasing distance of the adolescent as he or she strives for independence while acting responsibly. In dysfunctional families with adolescents, instead of negotiating around increased autonomy and self-control, the parent–child subsystems may become involved in a battle over a degree of nurturance/protectiveness and instrumental control appropriate to an earlier stage, or they may not make the transitional attempt at all if symptom exacerbation precludes any negotiations or battles whatsoever. Limited experience with peers and poor training in the sibling subsystem may have left the diabetic child or adolescent ill prepared to attempt separation from the family when this would be appropriate. The child's parents may also be stuck in an earlier phase of development, in which parents and children were much closer and more involved. Thus the adults miss the opportunity to develop or redevelop the spousal ties and the individuated self subsystems that become available as the children mature, begin to distance, and become more involved in extrafamilial activities.

An additional set of relationships may be redefined at this time—those between the parents and the grandparents. As described previously, for the children, the middle school-age years, and, more especially, the adolescent years, are a period of individuation and preparation for separation; for the parents, these years are a period for reworking the spousal relationship and enjoying the opportunity for further growth and individuation of each spouse. For the grandparents, these are the years of later adulthood, of planning for retirement, and perhaps of coping with illness or the death of a spouse.

For families with a sick child, the illness may become a transactional element in detouring the natural distancing and separating process (the centrifugal trend) appropriate to this period. Grandparents may stay overinvolved and intrusive, or become so, in a style more appropriate to the earlier developmental stages. Plans for retirement or geographic relocation may be postponed, especially if separation and differentiation of the parent–grandparent generations had not been clearly established at earlier stages. Conversely, overinvolvement of parents with their child's medical problems may not only preclude their own possibilities of individual development while they struggle with their maturing children's needs for autonomy but also make them less available or even overburdened if they need to assist their own aging parents through various life crises. While engaged in the tasks of separating from parents, older children and adolescents may often approach and engage their grandparents as a means of maintaining nurturant family connections without involvement in struggles over control. Grandparent–parent relationships, however, may not be completely free from struggle in this area; the grandparents and grandchildren may form alliances that significantly impinge on the management of the illness as defined by the parents. Clarification of executive responsibilities may need to take place on several levels—with children, between spouses, with grandparents, or with other involved extended kin. These problems can be magnified if the disease has a known genetic component, establishing one side of the family as "the cause" or the "experts."

CLINICAL WORK WITH FAMILIES WITH A CHRONICALLY ILL CHILD

When one works for a time with dysfunctional families with a child suffering from a somatic disorder, one can observe a process in which (1) the development of the family has been significantly shaped by the presence of the illness and (2) the course of the illness and the psychosocial development of the patient (and other family members) have been influenced by the family organization. In our earlier work (Minuchin *et al.*, 1975), we focused primary attention on the family organization connections. In a more recent study (Rosman & Baker, 1986), however, we attempted to examine longitudinally some of the developmental processes. In reconsidering some of the cases treated during the course of the earlier study, the full-blown family developmental issues became apparent. Some of these case illustrations will be shared in this section of the chapter.[2]

The Good and Bad Monsters of Developmental Change

P was a 14-year-old boy with severe asthma who was referred to treatment with his mother and stepfather halfway through the first year of their marriage. They were seen in the context of the "psychosomatic families" research project; their interactions, in response to the assessment protocols, were typical of the enmeshed and conflict-avoiding patterns we had been seeing. For example, in response to a request for the family to discuss a family argument, the stepfather replied that they had been so busy with P's asthma attacks, they had no time or opportunity to argue.

P had been diagnosed as an asthmatic during his first year of life. He lived with his mother and maternal grandparents. Mother had been married twice before her present marriage but had never succeeded in separating from her parental household before. At night, P had slept most of the time with grandparents or mother in the same room, to monitor his breathing and to be available in case of severe asthma attacks. This new marriage, which finally took mother out of her parental home, was thus a dramatic step forward in separation for her and her son. Adding to the stresses of this newly blending family were the weekend visits of the stepfather's own teenage son by a previous marriage, whose healthy physique and athletic interests (similar to his father's) were in considerable contrast to P's limited scope of activities and a body stunted by long periods of steroid medication for his illness. His asthma attacks escalated, and the family was referred for treatment.

I will not discuss here the treatment for the asthma *per se* or describe the early stages of treatment, which dealt with issues of the blending family, conflict detouring, disengagement of enmeshed subsystems, and so forth, concepts which have been described at length elsewhere (Minuchin, *et al.*, 1975). I will pick up the story at the point at which the asthma had been brought under some degree of control and some significant changes had been made in the family organization, primarily in the direction of strengthening the marital alliance and increasing the parental expectations for greater autonomy and individuation on the part of P.

P was now sleeping alone at night in his own room. At this point, he developed a new symptom! Each night before falling asleep, he was plagued by seeing a monster (based on a TV image) that frightened him so that he couldn't sleep and would call for his mother. This sleep disorder affected father also, who then needed medication so that he could go to work the next day.

The therapist addressed the problem seriously with P in the presence of the parents, stating that P needed to "own" his own fear and could no longer be helped by mother. P and the parents agreed. A very detailed description of the monster was elicited (color of scary eyes, size of horns, etc.) from P, which then formed the basis of a guided fantasy through which he was led by the therapist. P was encouraged to change the monster's image in all aspects, making it both more and less scary. Finally, a "good" monster was established. The final instruction by the therapist to P (still in the presence of his parents) was that each night P should collect all his own supportive resources (stuffed animals, etc.) in bed and then evoke both the "good" and "bad" monster images *now under his control* at the foot of his bed *while his mother "will stay in her bed with her husband."*

The family therapy continued for a while and then ceased during the summer; upon resuming in the fall, it was revealed that P had chosen, with the agreement of his parents, to go back to live with his grandparents so that he could rejoin his friends and peers at school. His asthma had greatly improved, and medication requirements were considerably diminished. A follow-up 3 years later (Rosman, Minuchin, Liebman, & Baker, 1978) indicated consolidation of both physical and psychosocial improvements. P had become manager of one of his high school's athletic teams!

This case illustrates, in almost exaggerated form, the degree to which a threatening chronic disorder can become intertwined with a family's developmental history. To what extent the child's illness increased the difficulties for the mother, already apparent, in separating from her family of origin, or to what extent those difficulties exacerbated the illness, cannot be determined.

We can look upon these factors as the two aspects of a single process. We must admire, with such a history, the willingness of the new family to engage, with all the complexities of a blended family, chronic illness, developmental lag, and the rest, in making the great and precarious leap forward. The value of the therapy lay not only in helping the family members relinquish the illness and other symptoms as solutions but also in turning them to their own new tasks of individuation and of negotiating new relationships. The ingenious solution of family "restructuring" developed by the family members themselves furthered these goals. By the residential separation, the mother and stepfather could more readily move on to work out their issues of couple formation (some of which were totally new experiences for the mother). P, by returning to his school and his friends while still based in a familiar and nurturant environment, could face the new adolescent challenges fortified with better health, more self-esteem, and more age-appropriate psychosocial skills. He had removed himself, at least for the while, from the additional complications of dealing with the blended-family issues from too close a vantage point. Everyone could now finally "own" his or her own developmental tasks.

Who's in Charge Here? The Case of the Weeping Diabetic

M was 17 at the time she and her family were referred for therapy, but she looked and acted about 12½ at the time. The oldest of ten children living in a semirural setting with their parents, M had been diagnosed as having juvenile diabetes when she was 10 years old. She had a brief fling with anorexia during the early period of the illness, in an apparent effort to reduce her insulin needs, but gave this up when confronted by a pediatric resident during a checkup. Subsequently, she settled into an unsatisfactory diabetic adjustment, with frequent episodes of acetonuria, several hospitalizations to evaluate poor diabetic control, a lot of school absence, and very little acceptance of responsibility for her own care.

During the assessment sessions, family members interacted in a concerned, close-knit, and lively way, with some humor, except for M. She seemed depressed, anxious, and given to outbursts, weeping easily at the drop of a pin or at a hint of conflict. This turned out to be a characteristic transactional style for her and was considered by the therapy team to be a good indicator of the family's emotional weather. For M, this weepy and emotionally labile behavior was at one and the same time her greatest source of power and weakness.

As the sessions continued, a picture developed of a family with poor subsystem boundaries and confused hierarchies. At the older end, there were unresolved conflicts between the parents and the grandparents, which occasionally disrupted family life. M complained and cried about that. M's father did some additional work to support his large family, which involved traveling

306 Developmental Disruptions and the Family Life Cycle

away from home. M's mother worried about that and also felt overburdened. M was her confidante and also worried a lot. (Later, mother recognized how intrusive M was when mother wanted to communicate privately or spend time with father alone.) Both of M's parents could refuse her little because, as the therapist noted, the parents were "exploited by fear." When M threw tantrums or overreacted to "every little thing," they were afraid she would go into shock or get sick. (She occasionally did.) While she seemed to have much power, it was the power of a baby. Despite her age, M's place in the sibling hierarchy was very low, since she was scapegoated and rejected by siblings who were angry and hurt by her favored status with the parents and disgusted by her babyish behavior.

During the early stages of therapy, the parents were encouraged to make age-appropriate demands of M. The psychosomatic symptoms were characterized to some extent as behaviors that M could control. While she got angry during these sessions, she began to perceive different possibilities for herself, better sources of power.

The success of this therapy, as with much of the work with chronic illness, depended heavily on a strong alliance between the therapist and the diabetologist. This physician could provide reassurance and a safety net for the patient and family in case of medical crises during stressful therapeutic periods. Broader goals in the family sessions (some with parents alone, some including other children with M) were to clarify and define better boundaries between generations and within the sibling group.

Following the series of family sessions, M was engaged in a sequence of individual sessions. A goal of going away to college, hitherto an unlikely possibility, was worked on successfully. This was a developmental achievement not only for this young woman but also for the rest of her family. It represented the beginning, for this exceedingly centripetal family, of their transition into a new family stage in the cycle—the family with children who are leaving home.

The family was seen for a follow-up about a year after they had begun therapy. M looked and acted so differently that it was hard to recognize her; the sickly and preadolescent-looking girl had been transformed into a self-possessed and assertive young woman. As the family talked about their changes, it became clear that M was functioning as an assistant to her mother with some of the younger children. She had clearly risen in the sibling hierarchy to her appropriate status. Her immediately younger sister was now able to verbalize her own previous jealous and current good relationship with M. Now she felt free to weep a little and have *her* feelings taken account of. M replied with sensitive awareness of her impact on her siblings; it was clear things had changed. Mother proudly spoke of M's total competence in self-care; M also had developed some behavioral techniques to deal with blood-sugar changes when anxious about school.

This family was able to launch successfully the first of their large brood;

they had many more to go before moving on. As the enormous power of the scary illness subsided, the individual needs and problems of the other children became apparent, as did some of the unresolved issues for the parents. They might, at some later time, request some further assistance, or they might not need to. The lessons learned in dealing with the interaction of developmental and medical crises might stand them in good stead on other occasions.

The Case of "The Puppet" Reconsidered: Three Women in Transition

This final example illustrates the developmental issues that arise when a somatic symptom of nonorganic origin organizes and is organized by the family. This family was seen with their therapist in a consultation, so that the discussion will not pursue the entire ongoing process of therapy. However, since the case provides such a clear example of how multiple individual developmental issues can be interwoven in a family developmental crisis, I have chosen to present it here.

Q, the 16-year-old bulimic patient, her parents, grandmother, and younger brother were brought to consultation by their family therapist. They had made some modest progress in dealing with the symptoms but were still in turmoil and unable to move on in the therapy. As is often the case with bulimic/vomiting disorders, in contrast to anorexia, there was much more open conflict in the family—in this instance, between daughter and mother in particular. The parents were unable to deal with Q's eating disorder, and there were bitter complaints about her generally rebellious and obnoxious behavior at home, her use of abusive language, and her manipulative threatened or actual self-injurious activities.

The consultant turned to the maternal grandmother and solicited her opinion as an elder "sage," a fellow consultant who knew the family well, as to her view of the problem. Her comments were of little direct assistance, consisting mostly of banalities about how sad it was they couldn't get along better, that it was too bad that Q, to whom she was much attached and with whom she got along well, had these problems, and so forth. However, in the course of this discussion, important information about the family structure emerged. Grandmother, who was divorced, had come to live with her own daughter's (Q's mother's) nuclear family. Grandmother described her relationships with the other family members as very cordial and herself as making scrupulous efforts to be helpful without being intrusive, to be a good mother-in-law (which her son-in-law confirmed). When the family members had a conflict, she withdrew to her own domain.

During a series of heated interactions between Q and her mother, further important information was obtained. Mother had recently returned to work, to a professional occupation identical to father's. Some of Q's behavior, to which mother most objected, was Q's constant critique of mother's performance as a homemaker. She would leave notes for her mother about supermarket specials and about chores that mother was not, according to Q, carrying out with super efficiency, not cleaning or cooking satisfactorily, and so on. Mother replied defensively to these critiques and complained to the consultant that Q was attempting to take her place. The consultant disagreed, commenting that as he heard it, Q was not taking on mother's role but mother's mother's (grandmother's) role. As he put it, having one mother living in might be complicated, but having two mothers was impossible. Q was lecturing her own mother as if she were a mother criticizing a daughter. The consultant elicited from grandmother some of the mutual concerns she and Q shared. Characterizing the strange behavior of Q as similar to that of a "ventriloquist's puppet," he requested that Q sit on grandmother's lap and voice all of their joint criticisms. In this dramatic enactment, this up-until-then resistant and outspoken girl complied, sitting on grandmother's lap, and in a tiny voice, repeating all her criticizing remarks to mother.

In other poignant segments of this session, the parents described their continuous vacillation between their frequently stimulated fears for Q's well-being and their wishes to protect her and, on the other hand, their anger, even rage, at her out-of-control behavior. Q's adolescent ambivalence took classic horrific–comic forms. For instance, she would lock herself in her room and not reply to her parents' knocks on the door. When they anxiously broke in (with some justification, based on past history) to see if she was alive and well, she complained of their intrusiveness, which she had elicited.

As this information-gathering and consultative session concluded, some new goals had become apparent: to restructure the alliances more appropriately, reducing the power of the patient, and to block the undermining of the parental coalition. Unspoken, but lurking in the background, was the consciousness of a conjunction of critical transitions for the three women in this family (involving their relationships to each other and with the males as well, although this was less clear).

The most obvious out-front issue was the stormy passage into adolescence of the identified patient, whose symptoms represented both her attempt to separate and individuate from the family and her demand to be taken care of by the family. This was occurring in a context where the most important caretaker, the mother, was herself separating and individuating from the family. (We can only speculate about how her occupational role affected her husband's response to this change in the family organization.) The mother's defensiveness indicated some of her own possible concerns about the relinquishment of her traditional role and about the conflicts and guilt stimulated by her daughter's "sick" behavior. The grandmother's return, to live as a dependent in relation to her own daughter's family, certainly represented a retrogressive transition. This was not only a movement in a direction contrary to that of the others (increased closeness instead of distance) but a reversal of an earlier hierarchical status. Furthermore, no particular role or status had been established in the family organization that was congruent with any earlier family history. She was everyone's peer and could not carve out a meaningful identity within the family. The consultant's invocation of her as the experienced elder seemed to surprise her, and as the session revealed, her sense of efficacy was implemented only indirectly.

If we consider all of these patterns within the family spiral model, we would diagnose this family system to be at the height of the centrifugal stage, in which the women, who are making the most sharply defined transitions, are at cross-purposes with each other, and where alliances that should facilitate growth are not supportive. A treatment plan reorganizing and coordinating the developmental tasks for all the generations and genders in this family might prove more useful over time than a schema conceptualized only in relation to the family crisis organized around the adolescent patient.

To sum up, this chapter has examined some of the ways in which family organization and the individual and family developmental processes interact with the impact and demands of chronic illness (or a psychosomatic disorder) in a family member. To the extent that these complex patterns can be understood based on information derived from research and clinical observations, we can hope to develop early identification and prevention strategies to best promote the growth and development of all family members.

NOTES

1. The leaders of the group were Kenneth Covelman, PhD, Sam Scott, BA, and Bruce Buchanan, MA, MS, from the Philadelphia Child Guidance Clinic, in collaboration with Regina Butler, RN, Children's Hospital of Philadelphia.

2. Salvador Minuchin, MD, was the therapist and consultant in these cases.

REFERENCES

Combrinck-Graham, L. (1985). A developmental model for family systems. *Family Process, 24,* 139-150.

Minuchin, S. (1974). *Families and family therapy.* Cambridge, MA: Harvard University Press.

Minuchin, S., Baker, L., Rosman, B., Liebman, R., Milman, L., & Todd, T. (1975). A conceptual model of psychosomatic illness in children. *Archives of General Psychiatry, 32,* 1031-1038.

Minuchin, S., & Fishman, H. C. (1981). *Family therapy techniques.* Cambridge, MA: Harvard University Press.

Minuchin, S., Rosman, B., & Baker, L. (1978). *Psychosomatic families.* Cambridge, MA: Harvard University Press.

Rosman, B., & Baker, L. (1986, June). *Multimodal family assessment of juvenile diabetics: A prospective study.* Paper presented at meetings of the American Family Therapy Association, Washington, D.C.

Rosman, B., Minuchin, S., Liebman, R., & Baker, L. (1978, November). *Family therapy for psychosomatic diabetic and asthmatic children: Follow-up and outcome.* Paper presented at the meeting of the Academy of Psychosomatic Medicine, Atlanta.

13

Loss and the Family Life Cycle

FROMA WALSH
University of Chicago

MONICA McGOLDRICK
University of Medicine and Dentistry of New Jersey

There is no love without loss. And there is no moving beyond loss without some experience of mourning. To be unable to mourn is to be unable to enter into the great human life cycle of death and rebirth—to be unable, that is, to live again (Lifton, 1975). In this chapter, we wish to present such a life cycle perspective on loss. From an evolutionary family systems perspective, death can be viewed as a transactional process involving the deceased and the survivors in a shared life cycle that acknowledges both the finality of death and the continuity of life. Coming to terms with this process is the most difficult adaptational task we confront in life. In our view, the tendency of many in the family therapy field to discount family history goes hand in hand with our culture's denial of death, and both create a significant problem for families in dealing with loss.

In whatever different forms, mourning must be experienced. Throughout history and in every culture, mourning rituals have involved not only integrating the death of another but also changes in self-concept and the transition to a new stage of identity (Osterweis, Solomon, & Green, 1984). In ancient Mesopotamia, tear vials, like miniature bud vases, were found buried with the deceased in tombs. This simple act acknowledged the emotional significance of loss, the value of grieving, and, in burying those tears with the deceased, the importance of moving on with life.

The family life cycle has always been profoundly influenced by death, just as, reciprocally, a family's life cycle development influences its response to death. In the past, death was a social and public fact (Aries, 1974). Before the present century, no matter what conditions families faced or what family arrangements they preferred, they all, in one way or another, had to confront the uncertainty of life. Death was a common experience to all families. People died at home, and death was a natural occurrence that they were helpless to control.

In 17-century America, for example, life expectancy at birth for both males and females was just over 35 years. Only about half of all children survived to adulthood. Those who survived to the age of 25 could expect to live only to their early 50s. With the high rate of mortality of women in childbirth, and with one out of two men and women dying before 50, families lived with the uncertainty whether either parent would survive to raise all children to maturity. No more than a third of families had a single marriage last over 10 years. The frequent remarriage of widowed spouses was typically followed by the repeated experience of widowhood. The death of young children occurred before that of a parent in one out of every two cases. Half of the surviving children saw a parent die before they reached majority. Parental death commonly disrupted families and shifted them into other forms. This often produced families with a highly dense and complex network of full, half, and step relationships and a vast extended kinship network (Scott & Wishy, 1982).

Thus the ideal image of the traditional normal family as intact is a myth in our society (Walsh, 1983a); our denial of death contributes to the maintenance of that myth. In our times, we have come to hide death, making the process of adapting to loss all the more difficult. In contrast to traditional cultures, our society lacks cultural supports to assist families in integrating the fact of death with ongoing life (Aries, 1974; Becker, 1973; Mitford, 1978). Medical practice and technology have increased the problems of adaptation by removing death from everyday reality while at the same time confronting families with unprecedented decisions to prolong or to end life.

Every year, an estimated 8 million Americans experience the death of an immediate family member. About 800,000 spouses die each year, as do about 400,000 children under 25. Although death of a child used to be a common experience in family life (and still is in much of the world), deaths of children aged 1 to 14 now account for less than 5% of the mortality in the United States (Osterweis *et al.,* 1984). Yet poor families in our society suffer traumatic losses disproportionately. One alarming trend is the rising infant mortality among poor, unwed teenage parents. The high rate of violent deaths of black youths is another problem receiving insufficient attention.

Epidemiologic studies now confirm what has long been suspected: The death of a close family member increases vulnerability to premature illness and death for the survivors (Osterweis *et al.,* 1984). In view of the profound connections among members of a family system, it is not surprising that families have more difficulty adjusting to death than to any other life transition (Holmes & Rahe, 1967). Most clinical and research attention to the impact of loss on the family has limited its focus to the direct dyadic relationship between the individual bearing symptoms and the deceased relative, with nonsymptomatic members presumed to be adjusting normally.

The mental health field has not given sufficient attention to the *family* impact of loss, neglecting the immediate and long-term effects on siblings, parents, children, extended family, and others, including those who may never have even known the deceased but who are touched by the survivors. Life cycle theory and research, which have tended to focus predominantly on the effects of childhood loss for individual development, have not appreciated the differential impact of loss at different stages in family development and for various members and the family as a functional unit.

A SYSTEMS PERSPECTIVE ON LOSS

Family systems theory introduced a new paradigm for understanding the network of relationships in families. The particular significance of loss, however, has been addressed by only a few systems theorists. Bowen (1978) outlined the disruptive impact of death or threatened loss on a family's functional equilibrium, describing the emotional shock wave that may reverberate throughout an entire family system long after the loss of an important family member. Paul (Paul & Grosser, 1965; Paul & Paul, 1982) has described the impact of unresolved mourning for an individual's other relationships, especially in marital and sexual dysfunction. Both Bowen and Paul, in different therapeutic approaches, emphasized the importance of coming to terms with loss and the changing relationship patterns associated with it.

Despite these pioneering efforts and a few recent contributions to the literature (e.g., Herz, 1980, 1988), the field of family therapy has not attended to the systemic processes surrounding loss (McGoldrick & Walsh, 1983). One reason for the neglect of the topic has been the split that has occurred in the field regarding the importance of "content" versus "process," and of history versus the here and now, for the understanding and treatment of families in distress. Loss is regarded by some as purely a "content" issue, involving individual feelings and reactions to events in time, particularly in the past. However, loss is also a structural modifier, requiring systemic reorganization. Unfortunately, the subject of loss is dismissed as either insignificant or irrelevant to system change by many structural and strategic therapists, who prefer to limit attention to family "process" operations that can be observed in current behavior. When the focus is limited to the pattern of interaction between members present in a family interview, out of view is the relationship that has been lost (past) or a threatened impending loss (future), which may bear directly on the family's current distress.

Although a family cannot change its past, changes in the present and future occur in relation to that past. Systemic change involves a transformation of that relationship. Indeed, as Hoffman (1981) comments, "A problem may remain frozen until patterns connected with the original laying down of the problem are changed. But let it be understood that one is still dealing with an addiction in the present. Bowen's use of history suggests strongly that it is not the revisiting of the past, but the redoing of the present that counts" (p. 249). Just as Bowen (1978) maintains that an individual cannot change others but only one's relationship to others, so a family cannot change its past but only its relationship to it. We propose that families need to be in balance or harmony with their past, not in a struggle with it, whether to recapture it or to forget it. Because a family's sense of motion may become stuck or distorted following a loss, therapy involves regaining a sense of life as passage through time from the past and into the future.

FAMILY ADAPTATION TO LOSS

The family life cycle model of Carter and McGoldrick (1980) offers a framework for taking into account the reciprocal influences of several generations as they move forward over time. From a systemic perspective, loss is viewed as a major transition that disrupts life cycle patterns of interaction, requires family reorganization, and poses shared adaptational challenges.

Family Tasks in Adaptation to Loss

The family, operating as a system, both approaches and reacts to loss through a circular process of influence in which all members participate in mutually reinforcing ways. The death of a family member disrupts the family equilibrium. Adaptation to the loss involves both immediate and long-term reorganization of the system. Just as individual tasks in the process of mourning have been delineated (Kubler-Ross, 1969; Worden, 1982), family tasks of mourning can be identified that facilitate adaptation and further life cycle development of all family members and the family as a whole. These can be viewed as normative transitional tasks involving both separation and reentry (Golan, 1981). It would be a mistake to impose expectations of fixed "stages" or schedules on such a complex process as grief, given the diversity of family and individual coping styles; nevertheless, four family tasks can be specified, which are typically—although not necessarily—sequential and overlapping:

  1. *Shared acknowledgment of the reality of the death.* This task is facilitated by clear information and open communication about the death and by direct confrontation with the reality of death, especially through the funeral rite and visits to the gravesite. Attempts to protect children or vulnerable members from such shared experiences are more likely to block resolution of the loss and lead to dysfunction.

  2. *Shared experience of the pain of grief.* This requires mutual understanding and acceptance of the expression of complicated and mixed feelings, including anger, disappointment, helplessness, relief, and guilt, which are present to some degree in most family relationships. Where family loyalty disallows certain feelings, or where unacceptable aspects are assumed piecemeal by different family members, expression in symptomatic behavior may occur (Reilly, 1978).

3. *Reorganization of the family system.* This process involves a realignment of relationships to delegate role functions needed to compensate for the loss in order to carry on with life. The turmoil of disorganization during the transition period may lead families to try to hold onto old patterns that are no longer functional or to prematurely seek replacements in order to regain stability.

4. *Reinvestment in other relationships and life pursuits.* The process of mourning is likely to take at least 1 to 2 years, with each new season, holiday, and anniversary reevoking the loss. Idealization of the deceased, a sense of disloyalty, or the catastrophic fear of another loss may block the formation of other attachments and commitments. The risk of suicide is highest at this stage.

A number of variables influence both a family's ability to adapt to the death of a member and the strategies the family employs (Herz, 1980, 1988; McGoldrick & Walsh, 1983). The impact and response depends largely on the role and functioning of the deceased member in the family system. The general flexibility and openness of the system and the level of differentiation and functioning of other members are crucial. The availability of social support (Anderson, 1982) and varying ethnic/cultural rituals for dealing with death (McGoldrick, Pearce, & Giordano, 1982) are no less important. The manner of death has differential impact: Sudden, unexpected death or lingering, painful deterioration are especially stressful and require different family coping mechanisms. Violent deaths, and suicides in particular, are the most difficult to come to terms with (Cain & Fast, 1966, 1972). Each of these variables should be carefully assessed.

Adaptational Factors: The Timing of Loss

Here we would like to call attention to factors in adaptation that concern the timing of loss in the three-generational family life cycle and that hold particularly high risk for dysfunction (McGoldrick & Gerson, 1985; Walsh, 1983b). The following linkages should not be overlooked:

1. *Loss and concurrent symptom onset.* A wide range of mental and physical disorders have been found to be associated with the occurrence of major stress events, especially loss. Family developmental crises of loss of members have been found to be correlated with symptom onset (Hadley, Jacob, Miliones, Caplan, & Spitz, 1974). The onset of symptoms in a child may be connected to the bereavement of parents at the recent or anticipated loss of one of their parents or another significant member (Walsh, 1975). Because the mental health field has tended to focus narrowly on the nuclear family and to consider the family of origin primarily in terms of formative influences in early childhood development, clinicians have failed to appreciate the impact of current relationships and losses in the extended family throughout the life cycle.

2. *Loss and concurrent stresses.* The temporal coincidence of major life

cycle events produces a cumulative stress effect that is likely to overwhelm families and to complicate and confound tasks of mourning and other simultaneous adaptational tasks. In some cases, significant loss triggers other relationship changes, such as divorce or the cutting off of other important relationships, or precipitous replacement through marriage or conception of a child, without experiencing the process of mourning. Clinicians need to be alert to the concurrence of multiple losses and to the coincidence of loss with other developmental milestones, particularly the birth of a child. Studies by Walsh (1978) and Mueller and McGoldrick Orfanidis (1976) suggest that the concurrence of the death of a grandparent and the birth of a child places that child at risk for later emotional disorder. In families of schizophrenics, more than 40% had experienced such concurrence, with mourning apparently unresolved and the child serving a special replacement function in the family system. In families of young adults with other severe disorders, especially affective disturbances, more than 20% had lost a grandparent around the birth of the patient, with mourning preoccupation tending to interfere with parenting tasks. Of note, only 8% of "normal" families with no disorders had experienced concurrent grandparent death and childbirth, and in those cases, spousal and extended-family support for grieving and parenting were more available.

3. *Previous traumatic loss and unresolved mourning.* Families with prior traumatic loss and unresolved mourning are likely to be more vulnerable to subsequent losses. We pay particular attention to losses where recall is blocked or distorted and where feelings are cut off or still intense. Past losses can intersect with current life cycle passage in many ways. A family may experience a transitional crisis when a child who has been serving a replacement function attempts to leave home at launching, thereby disrupting the family's homeostatic pattern. The first schizophrenic breakdown typically occurs at launching, with family separation concerns focusing even more on the well-being of parents than on that of the vulnerable child (Walsh, 1987). Although there is clear evidence of a biologic component in schizophrenia, family stress factors, such as unresolved mourning, also need to be taken into account. Research on families of substance abusers also has found a connection between the self-destructive behavior of the addict, family separation issues, and unresolved mourning of previous traumatic losses in the family (Coleman, 1981; Coleman & Stanton, 1978; Stanton, 1977). Where separation issues are prominent in presenting problems, the possible relevance of past losses should be assessed. Of particular importance are (1) losses that coincide with the birth of the symptomatic child and (2) transgenerational anniversaries, the age or life cycle stage at symptom onset coinciding with the point in the life cycle at which a parent died or lost a parent (Walsh, 1983b).

4. *Untimely deaths.* Premature losses that are "off-time" in terms of normative expectations, such as early widowhood and early parent loss, tend to be more difficult for families to come to terms with. The death of a child,

reversing generational expectations, can be the most painful loss for a family. Prolonged mourning, often for many years, is a normal occurrence, as is long-term survival guilt for siblings and parents.

In the following section, these timing factors will be examined as we explore the impact of loss at each successive phase of the family life cycle.

LOSS AT DIFFERENT LIFE CYCLE STAGES

Knowledge of the normative developmental tasks and issues for families at each successive stage in the family life cycle informs our understanding of the impact that loss is likely to have for a family. We recognize that there is great cultural diversity in patterns of dealing with all life cycle transitions, especially loss (McGoldrick, 1986). Nevertheless, certain systemic regularities tend to characterize a family's adaptation to loss at different life cycle phases. Some patterns may also be more functional at one life cycle phase than at another.

The following discussion examines the salient issues of loss at each phase in the family life cycle. We have organized our presentation around family life cycle phases in order to frame the reader's construction of the experience of loss of any individual member of a family, be it child, parent, or grandparent, in terms of the three-generational systemic ramifications. In understanding any death, we explore the individual's and the family's short-term pattern of response and their coevolution over time following the death. The impact of loss can be seen to vary with the particular life cycle stage of the family and with the nature of the relationship that is lost. This is not to reify the punctuation of the stream of interaction over time into life cycle stages. Rather, the framework enables us to highlight typical family patterns at different points in time. We find spurious the tendency of some clinicians to argue about whether the life cycle should be thought of in stages or in micro and macro oscillations. A life cycle framework is, in our view, an extremely useful way of organizing the overwhelming complexity of family life into meaningful patterns for the purpose of developing maps to guide intervention.

We oppose any stereotyping of families that imposes certain "correct" or "ideal" patterns, that incorrectly labels deviant patterns as necessarily pathological, or that limits clinicians' ability to appreciate each family's uniqueness. As noted previously, we appreciate fully the well-documented variability in the predictable patterns of adaptation of families in our culture to various life cycle transitions (Carter & McGoldrick, 1980, 1988; Walsh, 1982). However, because of the general neglect of this crucial subject, we have considered it useful to lay out a framework describing patterns that are typical at each life cycle phase, and in this sense "normal" (Walsh, 1982). We hope that this framework may serve as a guide to further research on this topic.

From the perspective of the family, death involves multiple losses—of a child, a sibling, a parent, a spouse, or a grandparent. In each family, the unique constellation of these relationships affects the impact of loss for each family member, each generation, and the family as a whole. While recognizing this diversity among families, we have also observed that the meaning and consequences of loss vary, depending on the particular phase of life cycle development the family is negotiating at the time of the loss. It is useful to identify salient developmental tasks at each phase in the family life cycle because they are likely to have a bearing on adaptation to loss. To examine these common issues, we will consider the impact of loss at each successive stage in the cycle, following the framework of Carter and McGoldrick (1980, 1986).

Between Families: The Unattached Young Adult

In the vast literature on loss, it is remarkable that so little attention has been given to the impact of loss in young adulthood. Clinical theory has been strongly influenced by a prevailing myth in our culture that once children have grown up and left home, their relationships with their families are no longer significant (Walsh, 1983a). The hallmark of young adulthood is regarded as complete emotional, physical, and financial independence from one's family of origin. Our culture has defined certain tasks as age appropriate: Young adults are expected to become self-sufficient and to direct their energies away from the family toward the establishment of careers and intimate peer relationships. Such normative expectations encourage a pushing away from the family and a denial of the importance of family relationships. In fact, there is ample research (e.g., Cohler & Geyer, 1982) that normal (i.e., typical) parent–child relationships remain intimate and interdependent throughout adulthood. However, before members of the younger generation become established on their own and a rapprochement occurs, most often at their own transition to parenthood, unattached young adults accept the myth as the reality and tend to minimize the importance of ties with parents.

Moreover, at launching, the family system is involved in reorganizing and renegotiating intergenerational relationships, from the dependency and controls of childhood and adolescence to a more equal balance as adults to adults. The new rules and terms of the relationship are at first tenuous, as are the young adult ventures into the adult social world. Young adults are commonly concerned—as are their parents—that they could slide back into a previous dependency. In families where relationships have been especially close or characterized by intense conflict, young adults may cut off entirely in order to gain physical or emotional distance. Such cutoffs generally produce only a pseudoautonomy, which cannot be maintained in contact with the family. However, because this pattern fits with the normative stereotype of independence, its risk for dysfunction may not be recognized.

Given the developmental tasks of young adulthood and the culturally sanctioned tendency to deny the importance of family ties at this time, loss can hold unanticipated complications. The impact of loss of a parent for young adults is likely to be seriously underestimated by them and by families, friends, and even therapists. Because our culture regards leaving home as a ritual proof of achieving adult autonomy, we may fail to appreciate the significant emotional bonds that are maintained in adulthood.

The terminal illness of a parent may be particularly difficult for young adult children who have moved away and are invested in launching a career and in new relationship commitments (Walsh, 1980, 1988.) The children are likely to be torn between their own immediate pursuits and premature filial caretaking obligations. Here, the developmental imperatives of a dying parent may conflict with the priorities of young adulthood. At the end of life, parents are attempting to come to terms with their lives as they have been lived in order to accept impending death (Erikson, 1959). Especially for women, this life review centers largely on parenting accomplishments and the relationships with one's children. In addition to heightened physical dependency, there is a need to draw the children in, to affirm that one has been successful in parenting, and to enjoy a final closeness together. The young adult children, however, are turning—or even pushing—away from their parents and may be threatened by closeness and dependence when not yet secure on their own. As Erikson (1950, 1959) has noted, young adults are emerging from the search for identity into issues of commitment. The fear of loss of self in such a situation may lead to isolation and self-absorption in the normative tasks involved in finding one's place in the adult world. The impact of the loss may not be acknowledged, and the young adult may distance still further from the family.

Another common source of distancing is the fear that one will be forced to abandon newly initiated adult life pursuits out of obligation to care for the surviving parent and other family members. This expectation tends to weigh most heavily on the eldest, or parentified, child. The eldest son may be expected to become the head of the family with the death of his father, whereas daughters are typically expected to assume major caretaking functions for either surviving parent, younger siblings, and grandparents. It is not uncommon for an adult child to move back home to assist in the immediate adjustment of a widowed parent, putting tasks of young adulthood temporarily on hold. Where such caretaking obligation becomes prolonged, it may block forward movement in the life cycle for the young adult.

The death of a young adult is a tragedy for the entire family and may produce the most distressing and long-lasting grief (Gorer, 1965). We previously noted the difficulty of "off-time" premature deaths for families, particularly when a child dies before parents, reversing the normal course of life cycle passage. When the death occurs in young adulthood, the family experiences a sense of cruel injustice in the ending of a life they have nurtured to adulthood before it has reached its prime. The young adult is full of potential, on the brink of life commitments and achievements, which death prevents from realization. Parents and siblings may find themselves blocked from continuing their own pursuits in the pain of loss and in the guilt common to survivors. In cases where the young adult had cut off in conflict, or where he or she dies by suicide or drug-involved accident, mourning is likely to be complicated by the unresolved state of the relationship.

The Young Couple: The Joining of Families through Marriage

The death of a spouse at this phase in the life cycle is relatively uncommon, and in its untimeliness, the resolution for the spouse is made more difficult. Not surprisingly, sudden death has been found to be more traumatic at this phase (Parkes 1972, 1975) than in later life, where lingering deaths were found to produce the greatest strain (Gerber, Rusalem, Hannon, Battin, & Arkin, 1975). Not only does the widowed spouse have to cope with the loss itself and the loss of status (especially women), but he or she is often shunned by siblings and peers to avoid confronting their own mortality. There is also a tendency for the family to expect the widowed spouse to move on quickly to a new relationship, denying the significance of the experience because of the pain it creates. Relationships between the surviving spouse and in-laws often become complicated because they are often somewhat strained at this phase, without the mellowing that comes with years and with grandchildren. If the surviving spouse goes along with the pressure not to grieve too publicly or too long, or tries to avoid the pain of the loss by running to a new relationship, the unresolved mourning will most likely be carried along, to surface later. It is noteworthy that women have greater difficulty than men in moving into a new relationship; women tend to feel guilty and as if it represents a betrayal of the former spouse, which in-laws may imply. Men tend to move on more rapidly, expecting a new partner to be sympathetic toward their continued mourning (Glick, Parkes, & Weiss, 1975).

The death of a parent that occurs as young adults are focusing on their own lives may not be mourned as directly as at other phases. In fact, parental illness or death may be a precipitating factor for many marriages, without the partners' realizing the emotional issues behind their decision to marry (McGoldrick, 1980). Parental loss may not be as difficult after marriage as it might have been during the independent young adult phase if the person has come to terms with the parent. A spouse may help the person to move toward a dying parent and provide comfort and support, facilitating the mourning process.

An issue that receives scant clinical attention is the change in adult sibling relationships brought on by the death of a parent—and in sibling-spouse relationships, which will also require renegotiation. Sisters will likely be more stressed in this process than brothers because of the expectation in our culture that daughters will be parental caretakers. This sense of responsibility may generate triangular conflicts between the loyalty to one's parent and that to one's spouse. Increased expectations for attention or caretaking of the surviving parent may stress the marital relationship, especially if the spouse feels that he or she no longer "comes first." The death of a parent at this phase, when couples are shifting their primary allegiance to the marital relationship, may push them back to family-of-origin obligations, complicating their adaptation to the new system. If it is the second parent who dies, the young adult prematurely becomes the last surviving generation, which may increase the pressure to have children.

The loss of grandparents at this phase may be easier, because the young adult has had the advantage of knowing them throughout childhood and into adulthood. If the grandparent was a favorite, the loss will be upsetting, of course, but emotional ramifications are more likely to flow down the system if the parent and grandparent had an unresolved relationship.

Other significant losses at this phase include miscarriages, stillbirths, and abortions. Infertility, which also represents the loss of a desired child, is currently affecting an unprecedented number of couples. These losses are typically seen by others as nonevents, making the loss more painful because of its disconfirmation by the outside world. Often, women feel the pain more deeply, especially when the child has grown in their bodies, whereas their husbands may feel less attachment to the fetus and be more inclined to think about future children. Women are also more likely to blame themselves, fearing that the loss resulted from their own deficiency or harmful actions, such as contraception, diet, smoking, or drugs. These experiences will also depend on the families' cultural beliefs about the meaning of the death of an infant or an abortion. Support for the wife from her friends and from the other women in her family will be important in her ability to move past the loss. The trauma will challenge the equilibrium of the new couple, requiring a loosening of the boundary around it to absorb the stress. If these resources are not available and/or the couple turns in on itself, the risk is either of fusion in a "two against the world" stance or of blaming each other for their not being able to fill each other's sense of loss and emptiness.

The Family with Young Children

The death of a child is likely to be more distressing to a family than any other loss. It can have a devastating effect on the parents' health and marriage. Distress tends to persist for at least 1 or 2 years, and grief may even intensify with the passage of time (Rando, 1985). A number of studies have documented the high distress of bereaved parents on such mental health indicators as depression, anxiety, somatic symptoms, self-esteem, and sense of control in life. Videka-Sherman and Lieberman (1985) found that the marital relationship is particularly vulnerable after a child dies, with high levels of distress on several measures of marital quality, and further deterioration of marital satisfaction over time. Divorce rates as high as 80% have been reported for bereaved parents (Kaplan, Grobstein, & Smith, 1976; Schiff, 1977; Strauss, 1975).

The death of a child is probably the most difficult loss for families to deal with psychologically since it is the most untimely and incomprehensible. Because small children are so utterly dependent on parents for their well-being, safety, and survival, guilt feelings tend to be especially strong. Also, of all deaths, that of a deceased child is the hardest not to idealize. The loss of a child involves the loss of parents' hopes and dreams. It has been said, "When your parent dies, you have lost your past. When your child dies, you have lost your future" (Schiff, 1977).

Furthermore, men and women tend to experience their grief differently and to utilize different coping strategies. Such differences increase marital strain, even for couples with previously strong and stable relationships (Sherman, 1982). For example, in a study of parents' reactions to sudden infant death syndrome (SIDS), fathers reported anger, fear, and a loss of control, along with a desire to keep their grieving private, whereas mothers responded more with sorrow and depression (DeFrain, Taylor, & Ernst, 1982). Fathers are more likely to withdraw, to take refuge in their work, and to be uncomfortable with their wives' expressions of grief, not knowing how to respond and fearful of losing control of their own feelings. Mothers are likely to perceive their husbands' emotional unavailability as abandonment just when they need comfort most, and thereby they experience a double loss. In contrast, husbands' expressiveness of feelings and their active involvement in the child's illness and death lead to better marital quality as assessed by wives.

Specific factors regarding the child who dies will affect the outcome for the family. Distress is greater in losing a child who is over the age of one. Particularly difficult may be the death of the firstborn, an only child, the only child of one sex, a gifted child, a difficult child for whom parents' feelings have been particularly ambivalent, or a child who dies in an accident for which the parents blame themselves.

There is some indication that bereavement is less problematic when both parents participate in taking care of a sick child prior to death (Mulhern, Laurer, & Hoffman, 1983) and when they have a consistent philosophy of life (Spinetta, Swarner, & Sheposh, 1981) or strong religious beliefs (Martinson, Moldow, & Henry, 1980). Self-help groups are extremely valuable for bereaved parents, providing a supportive network to facilitate dealing with the pain of the experience (Videka-Sherman & Lieberman, 1985).

What is too often neglected, however, is attention to siblings and other family members for whom the loss will also be devastating. The death of a sibling has been shown to be followed by prolonged grieving in children, with a high percentage of anniversary reactions for years afterward (Cain, Fast, & Erickson, 1964). Normal sibling rivalry may contribute to intense feelings of survival guilt that can block developmental strivings into adulthood. For children, a sibling's death is likely to mean also the loss of the parents to a significant extent, since they will be preoccupied with caretaking or grieving, and may even withdraw from their other children out of fear of ever being so vulnerable to loss again. Siblings may also have had to cope with a lack of attention to their own needs if the child who died was ill for a long time and required prolonged parental attention. In many cases, parents become overly protective and vigilant of surviving children and have later difficulty with normative transitions involving separation in adolescence and at launching. A sibling may also be inducted into a replacement role for the family. In fact, it is quite common for bereaved parents, and parents of a dying child, to conceive another child as soon as possible. Studies suggest that such replacement response is not necessarily pathogenic. Having a new child or investing energy in surviving children has been found to facilitate positive adjustment over time for parents (Vidaka-Sherman, 1982). However, the long-term consequences for the replacement child have not yet been well investigated (Cain & Cain, 1964). Our own clinical experience suggests that while such a system response may be functional for the parents, it can be dysfunctional for the child if he or she is treated as an undifferentiated replacement and if his or her own needs and unique qualities are not acknowledged or valued. In such cases, normative attempts at separation and individuation are likely to become problematic, to disrupt the family equilibrium, and to elicit delayed grief responses in other family members.

Children who lose a parent may suffer profound short- and long-term consequences (Furman, 1974; Osterweis *et al.,* 1984), and the impact may continue for generations. There are many findings of illness, depression, and other emotional disturbance in subsequent adult life. Later functioning may be impaired, specifically in the formation of other intimate attachments and in catastrophic fears of separation and abandonment. Our clinical experience suggests that marital commitments are more likely to be problematic when the opposite-sexed parent has been lost. Later difficulty in parenting is common, especially if it is the same-sexed parent who has died. A parent may function normally until a child reaches the same age at which the parent had been bereaved. At that point, the relationship may become blocked, the parent may distance, or the child may become symptomatic.

Children's reactions to death will depend on their stage of cognitive development, on the way adults deal with them about the loss, and on the degree to which they lose a caretaker as well as a parent. First, it is important for adults to recognize the limitations of a child's ability to understand what is happening and not to be alarmed by seemingly unemotional or inappropriate responses. For instance, a small child may approach strangers saying "My mother died" as a way of seeking support and understanding through observing the reactions of others (Osterweis *et al.,* 1984). Second, it is crucial for parents and other adults not to exclude children from the experience of loss, hoping thus to spare them pain. Bowen's (1976) account of coaching a father to help his children deal with the death of their mother is a powerful description of a way to help minimize potentially long-term devastating effects of the trauma of parental death. Third, it is important that the role functions of the lost parent and of the bereaved spouse be recognized and carried out by others in the system. If, in addition to coping with the loss of a mother or father, the child must cope with a vacuum in caretaking because the surviving parent is depressed or preoccupied, there may be severe consequences over a long period of time. There are indications that a child's handling of the loss of a parent will in fact depend on the emotional state of the surviving parent (Rutter, 1966; Van Eerdewegh, Bieri, Parilla, & Clayton, 1982). The loss for the surviving spouse at this phase is complicated by financial and caretaking obligations for the children, which are likely to interfere with the tasks of mourning. Children are likely to distract the bereaved parent from grieving in order to maintain the functioning of their only surviving parent (Fulmer, 1983). Symptoms in a child may serve such a function of distraction. Other siblings may cover over their own grief in order not to further burden the surviving parent. It is important for other adult family members and friends to contribute with caretaking, meals, and other concrete supports, to permit the widow or widower to withdraw to grieve. Generally, widowers receive much more support than do widows in this situation.

The loss of a grandparent at this phase is likely to be the first experience for a child in learning how to deal with death. Children will probably be most helped if included in their parents' experience of mourning and at the same time will be reassured by seeing that the parents can cope with the loss. If the grandparent suffers a prolonged illness for which a parent has major caretaking responsibility, it will stress the parent, who now is pulled in two directions: toward the normal heavy responsibility involved in caring for young children and toward the filial responsibilities regarding the dying parent and the surviving parent. As in dealing with any death, the fewer the family resources in terms of available extended family, friends, and financial supports, the more the system will be stressed by this experience.

The Family with Adolescents

Death at this phase in the life cycle may be particularly traumatic because the primary developmental task of separation conflicts with the experience of loss, which requires the family to move closer in support of its members. The most common adolescent deaths are from accidents (often complicated by risky behavior, such as drug and alcohol abuse and careless driving), suicide, homicide, and cancer. Younger children with cancer usually comply with treatment and remain close to their parents; for adolescents, however, the trauma of the disease and its treatment becomes interwoven with adolescent rebelliousness and moodiness, compounding the difficulty for parents. Children may resist medications or required treatments as attempts to control them by parents or medical authorities, thereby taking severe risks with their health. Parents, more conscious of the long-term consequences, may end up struggling with the present-focused adolescent, who refuses to consider the long-run implications of his or her impulsive behavior, and helping agencies may become caught in between. Where the death is associated with risk-taking behavior, both parents and siblings may have conflicting feelings in the form of anger at the dead child, frustration about the impulsive behavior, and sadness at the senseless loss.

Siblings frequently retreat from family and friends following an adolescent sibling's death. They often talk to no one at all about the experience, never even clarifying the nature of the death. The differences in coping styles of different family members may compound the problems following loss: Adolescents may become sulky, their mothers may seek to share feelings and their fathers may withdraw into angry silence or bury themselves in work. The different responses of family members will often grate on each other's nerves, making grieving even more difficult.

For the adolescent, whose developmental tasks involve a pushing away from parental influence and control, the death of a parent will be complicated by negative and conflictual feelings toward the parent. If other family members idealize the deceased parent, the adolescent's experience of disqualification may lead to an increased sense of being cut off and isolated from family members and of not being understood. The wish to be rid of a parent's control may generate considerable guilt. The death of a parent at this phase is also complicated by the availability of peer models of acting-out behavior to escape the pain. Boys who lose a parent often turn to stealing, drugs, or fighting, or they withdraw socially, whereas girls are likely to sexualize relationships, seeking closeness in order to comfort themselves and replace their loss (Osterweis *et al.,* 1984). Adolescent acting-out behavior is always stressful for the family, and the experience of parental loss at the same time may stretch the adaptive abilities of the system. Outside agencies may become involved, particularly school or juvenile authorities. Such larger systems tend to focus narrowly on the child's problem behavior and thus may only exacerbate the situation. It is crucial to assess routinely the context of behavior problems and, where recent losses have occurred, to assist the family, not only the child, in resolution.

In our experience, the death of a grandparent is often an underlying precipitant bringing parents and an adolescent into treatment, to focus on problems in the adolescent's behavior. An adolescent is often the barometer of family feelings, one who expresses the unexpressible and who draws needed attention to family problems. If the parents cannot deal with their own feelings about a loss, the adolescent often will pick up the parental feelings and, not knowing a better way to help the parents, will draw fire by misbehavior. The adolescent is often less ambivalent and more able to openly express sadness about the loss of a grandparent. Such situations usually reflect long-standing triangles in which problems between parent and grandparent a generation ago have led to a natural alliance between grandparent and grandchild, with the parent in the outside position. Naturally, the parent feels squeezed when having to cope simultaneously with the grandparent's death and the adolescent's pulling away, and this experience will be intensified if the parent's own adolescence was troublesome.

Launching Children and Moving On

The family at launching experiences a major transitional upheaval as the two-generational household unit reorganizes as a marital dyad and as the couple renegotiate their relationship, which no longer centers on child rearing. Couples at this stage are typically confronting losses on both sides: As their children are leaving home, their aging parents are declining in health and dying. The impact of the death of a young adult child on parents and that of the death of a parent on the young adult have already been discussed. The death of a grandparent and of a spouse will be considered here.

Research with normal, well-functioning families indicates that most adults in their middle years are prepared to assume increased caretaking responsibilities for aging parents and to accept their deaths as a natural, inevitable occurrence in the life cycle (Lewis, 1976; Neugarten, 1970). Nevertheless, adjustment to loss is frequently complicated by concerns about caretaker burden, neglect, or abandonment; the surviving children may feel that their efforts were unappreciated, or they may feel guilty that they didn't do more.

In our society, as in most, caring for the dying parent and for the surviving parent is typically the burden of women, both daughters and daughters-in-law. Men tend to remain emotionally and physically more peripheral, with involvement limited to financial and property arrangements. Interventions need to be aimed at decreasing the sex-role split so that all family members can both experience their own grief and become supportive to one another in adapting to the loss.

Caretaking and mourning processes are likely to be more complicated for the entire family in cases where intergenerational tensions or cutoffs have been long standing. Here we move, wherever possible, to bridge cutoffs and promote intergenerational connectedness, to strengthen the family in coping with its loss. A conjoint family life review (Walsh, 1980, 1988) can be valuable in structuring the sharing of memories over the course of the family life cycle in order to gain a more balanced, evolutionary perspective on family relationships. Because growth and change take place continually, members may find that issues that were painful at an earlier stage in the life cycle are currently viewed differently, with new opportunity for resolution, or at least empathic understanding of differences and disappointments.

With the death of aging parents, adult children typically begin to confront their own mortality and to think increasingly about the time that remains ahead of them. The death of the last surviving member of the older generation(s) makes them especially aware that they are now the oldest generation and the next to die. Because the existence of grandchildren commonly eases the acceptance of mortality, there may be pressure on the recently launched generation to marry and start a family.

At this time, concerns about widowhood also become prominent for women, who know that they can expect to outlive their husbands. With this expectation, women who have been centered and financially dependent on their husbands become even more concerned about the health of their husbands than about their own well-being (Neugarten, 1970). We encourage women to put their own lives in perspective—to consider how they will manage and to build a supportive social network for the years they are likely to spend alone.

Widowhood at midlife is much more difficult than in later life, when it is socially anticipated and experienced by peers. Early widowhood tends to be a shocking and isolating experience, without emotional preparation or essential social supports. At launching, the couple reinvest energy in the marriage and make plans for their future together, with the anticipation of sharing activities that have been postponed while child rearing consumed attention and financial resources. With the death of a partner, these plans and dreams of a shared future are lost. Other couples and friends who are not yet ready to confront their own mortality and survivorship are likely to distance. The surviving spouse may be reluctant to burden recently launched children who are not yet established or aging parents who have diminished resources and increased needs for caretaking. It should be noted that the suicide rate for men widowed at midlife is exceptionally high (Butler & Lewis, 1983).

The Family in Later Life

With increasing life expectancy, four- and five-generation families are becoming more common, and postretirement couples with declining resources may be called upon to care for their very elderly parents through illness and death. The central life cycle task of old age, that of accepting one's own mortality, becomes quite real as siblings, spouses, and peers die around one. Surviving the death of an adult child can be especially painful. Multiple concurrent losses, though common at this time, are nevertheless a shock. In reaction, some elderly withdraw from closeness and dependency on other elders so as not to have to experience yet another painful loss. Intergenerational family conflicts may erupt over issues of caretaking, dependency, and loss of functioning and control as health declines and death approaches (Walsh, 1980, 1988).

For couples, it is inevitable that one partner will die before the other. As noted previously, women are likely to outlive their husbands; the average is 7 years. Women begin in middle age to become concerned about the prospect of widowhood (Neugarten, 1970): They are four times more likely than men to be widowed, they are more likely to become widows at an earlier age, and they are more likely to remain widows with many years of life remaining. More than three fourths of men over 65 are married, in contrast to only around one third of women of this age (Butler & Lewis, 1983). Butler and Lewis note that this gender imbalance is one of the most poignant problems of the elderly. Older men have greater options maritally; the odds are against women remarrying because there are fewer men in their age group and because relationships with younger men are less socially acceptable.

Widowers, however, are at especially high risk of death and suicide in the first year of bereavement because of the initial sense of loss, disorientation, and loneliness, and because of the loss of a wife's caretaking functions. Perhaps husbands' vulnerability to loss is greater because men are socialized to minimize their awareness of dependency on their spouses and, because men are less likely to be widowed, they are less prepared for the adjustment. Deaths of widowers during the first 6 months of bereavement have been found to be 40% above the expected rate for married men of the same age, with, astonishingly, 22% of the causes of death of the widowers being from the same diagnostic group as those of the wives (Butler & Lewis, 1983).

The process of adjustment to widowhood has been well studied (Lopata, 1973). The psychosocial tasks for this transition are twofold: to grieve the loss of the spouse and to reinvest in future functioning. Lopata has identified three phases in this adjustment process for women. The first is to loosen bonds to the spouse and to acknowledge the fact of the death, transforming shared daily experiences into memories; the encouragement of open expression of grief and loss is paramount at this time. Second, typically within a year, attention turns to the demands of daily functioning, of self-support, and of household management, with adjustment to being physically as well as emotionally alone. Within 2 years, women begin the third phase of adjustment, involving a shift to new activities and interest in others. Loss in widowhood is often compounded by other dislocations, for example, when the family home and social community are given up, or when financial problems or illness reduce independent functioning. It is interesting that widows are the one class of mourners given a specific title defining their status. Yet, that identity is also a constant reminder of the loss and may impede the process of reentry, particularly when family and friends have not themselves faced their loss or come to terms with their own mortality.

THE SOCIAL CONTEXT OF LOSS

Gender Impact of Societal Change

Although our society has been changing rapidly over the past two decades, normative expectations for men and women in families have lagged behind emerging realities of family life (Walsh, 1982). Women have been socialized to assume the major role in handling the social and emotional tasks of bereavement, from the expression of grief to the caretaking of the terminally ill as well as of the surviving family members. Elderly widows whose husbands had handled all instrumental tasks find themselves ill equipped to assume financial responsibilities. Now that most women are combining work and family responsibilities, they are increasingly likely to become overburdened, until men assume their share of socio-emotional tasks. For men, society's prohibition against emotional responsiveness has greatly restricted their ability to handle any but the instrumental tasks of bereavement, such as funeral, burial, and financial arrangements. Society's denial of male dependency needs and its prohibition of male emotional expressiveness undoubtedly contribute to marital distress after the loss of a family member and to the high rate of illness and suicide for men following the death of a spouse. In the future, a greater flexibility of allowable roles for both men and women will permit both to experience the full range of human functioning in bereavement as in other areas of family life.

A different sort of gender issue concerns family and societal attitudes toward homosexual relationships. The loss of a homosexual partner may be grieved in isolation when the relationship has been a secret or has been disapproved of by the family. The terrifying epidemic of acquired immune deficiency syndrome (AIDS) has involved a distancing of families and others from victims and potential victims, so that family and social supports are not there in most cases. Such cutoffs not only make impending death more lonely and painful for victims but also complicate the family's mourning process.

Cultural Influences

Family adaptation to loss is strongly influenced by culture in two major ways: (1) by guidelines for behavior and coping and (2) through patterns of community support. Western culture has been moving toward the minimization of all rituals for dealing with death. Through legislation, custom, and public health and work regulations, there is considerable social control over the process. Funeral rituals have been taken over and commercialized by the funeral industry. The allowable time for bereavement leave in the workplace (usually 1–3 days) severely constrains cultural groups from retaining their traditional attitudes and practices toward death and mourning.

Nevertheless, values regarding bereavement continue to vary in profound ways, and clinicians should be careful about definitions of "normality" in assessing families' responses to a death. In certain Mediterranean cultures, such as Greek and Italian, a woman traditionally was supposed to mourn, and wear the outward signs of mourning, from the time of her husband's death through the rest of her life. At the opposite extreme, Americans of British ancestry tend to value a rational handling of death that involves "no mess, no fuss," with minimal expression of feeling, carried out in the most pragmatic way. As one friend put it, when explaining why he had not attended the funeral of his twin sister, "What would have been the point of spending money on the airfare to get there? She was already dead." They tend to prefer death in hospitals, where they are out of the way and not an inconvenience to the family or incurring any unnecessary obligations because of their dependence. (In hospitals, care is provided on the rational basis of fee for service.) For other ethnic groups, to die away from the family, which provides support in one's own environment, is a double tragedy. Italians, Greeks, Indians, and many other groups consider human interdependence to be natural to life and would consider it unnatural and a deprivation not to care for a family member in time of such need.

For black and Irish families, death is generally considered the most significant life cycle transition, and family members will go to great lengths not to miss a wake or a funeral. Black families in the South often went to great expense to have a band play and to have flowers and singing and other accompaniments for their funerals. Funerals may be delayed for days to ensure that all family members can get there. The Irish will make it a point to attend all wakes and funerals of family members and friends, sparing no expense for drink and arrangements, even if they have very little money. Such customs undoubtedly relate to the belief in these two cultural groups that life in this world is generally full of suffering and that death brings a release to a better world in the afterlife.

These two groups differ greatly, however, in their handling of emotional experience. Black families tend to express emotions freely, whereas the Irish are much more likely to get drunk, tell jokes, and treat the wake as a kind of party, with little or no overt expression of grief, a custom that would be perceived by many as incomprehensible and unfeeling. In the Puerto Rican culture, for example, women in particular "are expected to express their sorrow dramatically through displays of seizure-like attacks and uncontrollable emotions" (Osterweis *et al.*, 1984, p. 209). In contrast, various Southeast Asian groups are expected to participate in public displays of emotion but to retain composure and be stoic about their feelings in private (Osterweis *et al.*, 1984).

Jewish culture has a prescribed pattern of rituals to help family members deal with death, including, generally, burial within 24 hours; a week of "shiva," during which family members are in mourning and friends and family bring food and visit; certain prayers called "Kaddish," which are said for 11 months; and a memorial service, referred to as the "unveiling," which marks the end of the mourning period (Herz & Rosen, 1982). In traditional Eastern European Jewish culture, the belief was that the worst life is better than the best death (Zborowski & Herzog, 1952), a belief in obvious contrast to beliefs held in the black and Irish cultures. Another striking feature of Jewish culture is the prescription of guidelines for reentry into normal life after loss, including resumption of normal dress and activities.

It is important for clinicians to appreciate that cultural groups have specific beliefs about forms of mourning and to learn from each family what its members believe about the nature of death, the required rituals that should surround it, and the afterlife. For various reasons, a failure to carry out death rituals is often an important component of a family's lack of resolution of a loss over time. In fact, because of the dominant culture's tendency to minimize the need for rituals, and because of the influences of hospital and funeral systems in the death process, family members may have lost control of their traditions and may have ignored the meaning of death for them, perceiving it as a sign of weakness or of being "uncultivated" or superstitious. We encourage family members to have great respect for the traditions of their heritage and to be most active in determining what cultural forms will help them deal with their losses. Clinicians can also facilitate the creation of new rituals that will have personal meaning for a family and assist them in honoring the dead, sharing grief, and moving on together with life.

CONCLUSION

In our view, it is important to track patterns of adaptation to loss as a routine part of family assessment, even when loss is not initially presented as relevant to chief complaints. We find it most useful to construct a three-generational genogram and a family chronology, or time line, of major stress events as part of each family evaluation (McGoldrick & Gerson, 1985). These tools allow us to organize quickly and easily information gathered in an interview without the necessity of taking elaborate family histories. We can note all losses and track their timing, circumstances, and impact. We can then scan for patterns relevant to presenting problems as well as for family coping strategies and resources for adapting to current stresses.

As discussed previously, knowledge of the normative developmental tasks at each stage in the family life cycle can help clinicians be aware of and respond to the particular ways in which loss is likely to intersect with salient family life cycle issues. Early intervention that is sensitive to such normative complications can have important preventive effects.

In many cases, especially where presenting problems involve separation issues, movement forward in the life cycle may be blocked by unresolved mourning issues from the past. Most families have experienced numerous losses; extensive family histories are not required, nor is it necessary to delve into every past loss. This chapter has identified a number of factors that adversely affect family mourning processes; where such factors are present, those losses should be more closely examined. As discussed before, particular attention should be given to the following:

1. Losses at the same point in the family life cycle a generation earlier. For example, where launching difficulties are presented, focused inquiry on critical loss experiences of parents around the time they were attempting to

leave home may reveal a transgenerational replication pattern at the same developmental transition, and even at the same exact age.

2. Losses at a major developmental transition involving the identified patient, which posed concurrent and conflictual adaptational challenges for the family. For example, the death of an important family member around the birth of a child poses inherent difficulties in simultaneously attending to tasks of mourning and tasks of parenting, and a confounding of the two relationships may occur. Where mourning is blocked and the child assumes a replacement function for the family, problems may not arise until that pattern is later disrupted by the child's normative separation attempts.

3. Significant or traumatic losses where recall is blocked or distorted and where feelings remain intense or cut off. Violent deaths, suicides, sudden deaths, deaths after prolonged illness, and deaths that were "off-time" in the expectable life cycle are most likely to present long-term complications.

Where a recent death has occurred, or where past loss appears relevant to current dysfunction, the family's progress in accomplishing tasks of adaptation to the loss should be assessed. Inquiry should be directed toward learning to what extent and in what ways the family has attempted to (1) share acknowledgment of the reality of the death, (2) share the experience of the pain of grief, (3) reorganize the family system, and (4) reinvest in other relationships and life pursuits. At the point where a family is blocked, a major objective of therapy is to help the family move forward on these tasks in ways that are not dysfunctional for members.

A range of interventions can be effective in facilitating family adaptation to loss. It would be an error to assume that intensive, individual psychotherapy is required for the family member who reveals signs or symptoms of unresolved mourning. When an important family member is dying or has been lost, the entire family is affected, and each member affects all others; thus all should be involved in therapy when possible. Because the marital unit is at risk for dysfunction and dissolution, husbands and wives need help in sharing the grief process together, thereby strengthening the family unit. Intervention efforts should also assist parents in taking leadership in the family in order to accomplish the tasks of family adaptation.

While it is generally helpful to promote more open communication about the loss and its impact, it is also crucial to respect each family's timing for dealing with their feelings and the diverse family patterns of adaptation. We encourage families to take charge of their death rituals so that they reflect their own values and customs. Where mourning is blocked, we will attempt to work with at least one member of the family toward opening up the painful issues around the loss (see also Herz, 1988).

When we meet a family at a later point in the life cycle, after they have closed down around an earlier death we encourage them to visit the grave, carry out such rituals as sorting out old family pictures and other memorabilia, plan memorial tributes to the deceased, and other concrete actions that unblock the process of mourning and adaptation. Where past losses and the family interaction patterns set into motion by those losses contribute to current dysfunction, it is important to help families recognize covert connections between the past and the present so that they can differentiate the present and negotiate current life cycle transitions in a more adaptive way. The value in making such connections explicit is not in producing some curative insight into "origins" of current distress, but rather, in helping each family gain an evolutionary perspective on their immediate situation in the context of their own family life cycle.

A final point, which cannot be overstressed, is the importance of normalizing the complete range of feelings about death in working with families. For this reason, we frequently encourage those who have experienced a traumatizing, untimely death to become involved in the growing self-help network, where their feelings will be confirmed in a nonclinical setting. Compassionate Friends, a self-help network for families who have lost a child, serves just this function. Widows' groups and groups for families following a suicide are also important resources. In the aftermath of a traumatic loss, family members will frequently lose their perspective and feel that their reactions are pathological. Normalizing their responses of anger, grief, and an inability to "snap out of it," as well as helping family members tolerate each other's different coping styles, may be very important in enabling them to persevere through the painful stages of grieving and change in family relationships that follow a death.

Loss can also lead to growth. Despite the distress of loss, half of the parents in a self-help project reported some positive changes as a result of the grief experience Videka-Sherman & Lieberman, 1985). They reported a clearer sense of life priorities, specifically, an increased valuing of interpersonal relationships and a heightened capacity for intimacy and empathy, especially among family members. They also gained a recognition of formerly unrealized adaptive potential: that they were stronger than they realized and that they could now survive anything. Whatever our therapeutic approach with families, a life cycle perspective on loss can enable us to facilitate adaptation to loss in ways that strengthen the family in their future passage.

REFERENCES

Anderson, C. (1982). The community connection: The impact of social network on family and individual functioning. In F. Walsh (Ed.), *Normal family processes.* New York: Guilford Press.

Aries, P. (1974). *Western attitudes toward death.* Baltimore: Johns Hopkins University Press.

Becker, E. (1973). *The denial of death.* New York: Free Press.

Bowen, M. (1976). Family reaction to death. In P. Guerin (Ed.), *Family therapy.* New York: Gardner Press.

Bowen, M. (1978). *Family therapy in clinical practice.* New York: Jason Aronson.

Butler, R., & Lewis, M. (1983). *Aging and mental health.* St. Louis: C. V. Mosby.

Cain, A., & Cain, B. (1964). On replacing a child. *Journal of the American Academy of Child Psychiatry, 3,* 443–456.

Cain, A., & Fast, I. (1966). The legacy of suicide: Observations on the pathogenic impact of suicide upon marital partners. *Psychiatry, 29,* 406–411.

Cain, A., & Fast, I. (1972). The legacy of suicide: Observations on the pathogenic impact of suicide upon marital partners. In A. Cain (Ed.), *Survivors of suicide.* Springfield, IL: Charles C. Thomas.

Cain, A., Fast, I., & Erickson, M. (1964). Children's disturbed reactions to the death of a sibling. *American Journal of Orthopsychiatry, 34,* 741–752.

Carter, E., & McGoldrick, M. (1980). *The family life cycle: A framework for family therapy.* New York: Gardner Press.

Carter, E., & McGoldrick, M. (1988). *The family life cycle: A framework for family therapy* (2nd ed.). New York: Gardner Press.

Cohler, B. J., & Geyer, S. (1982). Autonomy and interdependence within the family. In F. Walsh (Ed.), *Normal family processes.* New York: Guilford Press.

Coleman, S. B. (1981). Incomplete mourning in substance-abusing families: Theory, research and practice. In M. Aronson (Ed.), *Group and family therapy 1981.* New York: Brunner/ Mazel.

Coleman, S. B., & Stanton, D. M. (1978). The role of death in the addict family. *Journal of Marriage and Family Counseling, 4,* 79–91.

DeFrain, J., Taylor, J., Ernst, L. (1982). *Coping with sudden infant death.* Lexington, MA: D. C. Heath.

Erikson, E. (1950). *Childhood and society.* New York: W. W. Norton.

Erikson, E. H. (1959). *Identity and the life cycle.* New York: International Universities Press.

Fulmer, R. (1983). A structural approach to unresolved mourning in single parent family systems. *Journal of Marital and Family Therapy, 9*(3), 259–270.

Furman, E. (1974). *A child's parent dies.* New Haven, CT: Yale University Press.

Gerber, I., Rusalem, R., Hannon, N., Battin, D., & Arkin, A. (1975). Anticipatory grief and aged widows and widowers. *Journal of Gerontology, 30,* 225–229.

Glick, I. O., Parkes, C. M., & Weiss, R. (1975). *The first year of bereavement.* New York: Basic Books.

Golan, N. (1981). *Passing through transitions.* New York: Free Press.

Gorer, G. (1965). *Death, grief and mourning.* New York: Doubleday.

Hadley, T., Jacob, T., Miliones, J., Caplan, J., & Spitz, D. (1974). The relationship between family developmental crises and the appearance of symptoms in a family member. *Family Process, 13,* 207–214.

Herz, F. (1980). The impact of death and serious illness on the family life cycle. In E. A. Carter & M. McGoldrick (Eds.), *The family life cycle: A framework for family therapy.* New York: Gardner Press.

Herz, F. (1988). The impact of death and serious illness on the family life cycle. In E. A. Carter & M. McGoldrick (Eds.), *The family life cycle: A framework for family therapy* (2nd ed.). New York: Gardner Press.

Herz, F. M., & Rosen, E. J.(1982). Jewish families. In M. McGoldrick, J. K. Pearce, & J. Giordano (Eds.), *Ethnicity and family therapy.* New York: Guilford Press.

Hoffman, L. (1981). *Foundations of family therapy.* New York: Basic Books.

Holmes, T., & Rahe, R. H. (1967). The Social Adjustment Rating Scale. *Journal of Psychosomatic Research, 11,* 213–218.

Kaplan, D., Grobstein, R., & Smith, A. (1976). Predicting the impact of severe illness in families. *Health and Social Work, 1,* 71–82.

Kubler-Ross, E. (1969). *On death and dying.* New York: Macmillan.

Lewis, E. (1976). The management of stillbirth—Coping with an unreality. *Lancet, 2,* 619–620.

Lifton, R. J. (1975). Preface. In A. Mitscherlich & M. Mitscherlich (Eds.), *The inability to mourn.* New York: Grove Press.

Lopata, H. (1973). *Widowhood in an American city.* Cambridge, MA: Schenckman Books.

Martinson, I., Moldow, D., & Henry, W. (1980). *Home care for the child with cancer* (Final report of Grant No. CA 19490). Washington, DC: National Cancer Institute.

McGoldrick, M. (1980). The young couple: The joining of families in marriage. In E. A. Carter & M. McGoldrick (Eds.), *The family life cycle: A framework for family therapy.* New York: Gardner Press.

McGoldrick, M. (1986). Ethnicity and the family life cycle. In E. A. Carter & M. McGoldrick (Eds.), *The family life cycle: A framework for family therapy* (2nd ed.). New York: Gardner Press.

McGoldrick, M., & Gerson, R. (1985). *Genograms in family assessment.* New York: W. W. Norton.

McGoldrick, M., Pearce, J. K., & Giordano, J. (1982). *Ethnicity and family therapy.* New York: Guilford Press.

McGoldrick, M., & Walsh, F. (1983). A systemic view of family history and loss. In M. Aronson (Ed.), *Group and family therapy 1983.* New York: Brunner/Mazel.

Mitford, J. (1978). *The American way of death.* New York: Touchstone Books.

Mueller, P. S., & McGoldrick Orfanidis, M. (1976). A method of co-therapy for schizophrenic families. *Family Process, 15,* 179-192.

Mulhern, R., Laurer, M., & Hoffmann, R. (1983). Death of a child at home or in the hospital: Subsequent psychological adjustment of the family. *Pediatrics, 71,* 743-747.

Neugarten, B. (1970). Dynamics of transition of middle age to old age: Adaptation and the life cycle. *Journal of Geriatric Psychiatry, 4,* 71-87.

Osterweis, M., Solomon, F., & Green, M. (Eds.). (1984). *Bereavement: Reactions, consequences, and care.* Washington, DC: National Academy Press.

Parkes, C. M. (1972). *Bereavement: Studies of grief in adult life.* New York: International Universities Press.

Parkes, C. M. (1975). Determinents of outcome following bereavement. *Omega, 6,* 303-323.

Paul, N., & Grosser, G. (1965). Operational mourning and its role in conjoint family therapy. *Community Mental Health Journal, 1,* 339-345.

Paul, N. L., & Paul, B. B. (1982). Death and changes in sexual behavior. In F. Walsh (Ed.), *Normal family processes.* New York: Guilford Press.

Rando, T. (1985). Bereaved parents: Particular difficulties, unique factors, and treatment issues. *Social Work, 30,* 20.

Reilly, D. M. (1978). Death propensity, dying, and bereavement: A family systems perspective. *Family Therapy, 5,* 35-55.

Rutter, M. (1966). *Children of sick parents.* London: Oxford University Press.

Schiff, H. S. (1977). *The bereaved parent.* New York: Penguin Books.

Scott, D., & Wishy, B. (Eds.). (1982). *America's families: A documentary history.* New York: Harper & Row.

Sherman, B. (1982). *Parental bereavement and marriage.* Unpublished doctoral dissertation, University of Chicago.

Spinetta, J., Swarner, J., & Sheposh, J. (1981). Effective parental coping following the death of a child from cancer. *Journal of Pediatric Psychology, 6,* 251-263.

Stanton, D. M. (1977). The addict as savior: Heroin, death and the family. *Family Process, 16,* 191-197.

Strauss, A. (1975). *Chronic illness and the quality of life.* St. Louis: C. V. Mosby.

Van Eerdewegh, M., Bieri, M., Parilla, R., & Clayton, P. (1982). The bereaved child. *British Journal of Psychiatry, 140,* 23-29.

Videka-Sherman, L. (1982). Coping with the death of a child: A study over time. *American Journal of Orthopsychiatry, 52,* 688-98.

Videka-Sherman, L., & Lieberman, M. (1985). Effects of self-help groups and psychotherapy after a child dies: The limits of recovery. *American Journal of Orthopsychiatry, 55,* 70–82.

Walsh, F. (1975). *Living for the dead? Schizophrenia and three-generational family relations.* Paper presented at the meeting of the American Psychological Association, Chicago.

Walsh, F. (1978). Concurrent grandparent death and birth of schizophrenic offspring: An intriguing finding. *Family Process, 17,* 457–463.

Walsh, F. (1980). The family in later life. In E. A. Carter & M. McGoldrick (Eds.), *The family life cycle: A framework for family therapy.* New York: Gardner Press.

Walsh, F. (1982). Conceptualization of normal family functioning. In F. Walsh (Ed.), *Normal family processes.* New York: Guilford Press.

Walsh, F. (1983a). Normal family ideologies: Myths and realities. In C. Falicov (Ed.), *Cultural dimensions in family therapy.* Rockville, MD: Aspen.

Walsh, F. (1983b). The timing of symptoms and critical events in the family life cycle. In H. Liddle (Ed.), *Clinical implications of the family life cycle.* Rockville, MD: Aspen.

Walsh, F. (1987). Family relationship patterns in schizophrenia. In R. Grinker & M. Harrow (Eds.), *Clinical research in schizophrenia.* Springfield, IL: Thomas.

Walsh, F. (1988). The family in later life. In E. A. Carter & M. McGoldrick (Eds.), *The family life cycle: A framework for family therapy* (2nd ed.). New York: Gardner Press.

Worden, J. W. (1982). *Grief counseling and grief therapy: A handbook for the mental health practitioner.* New York: Springer.

Zborowski, M., & Herzog, E. (1952). *Life is with people.* New York: International Universities Press.

14

Developmental Cycles and Substance Abuse

THOMAS C. TODD
Illinois School of Professional Psychology
Center for Family Studies/Family Institute of Chicago

The link between substance abuse and the stages of individual and family development has been clearly demonstrated, particularly in the work of Stanton, Todd, and Associates (1982) and Haley (1980).[1] Many of the basic concepts in this chapter were initially developed during the Addicts and Families Project at the Philadelphia Child Guidance Clinic, for which Jay Haley served as a consultant. Since the basic approach has been described in *The Family Therapy of Drug Abuse and Addiction* (Stanton *et al.*, 1982), it will be only briefly summarized here. This chapter expands on that work to include (1) life cycle stages in addition to the "leaving-home" stage, (2) the subtleties of clinical application of life cycle concepts to assessment and treatment, and (3) the relationship between stages of addiction and stages of treatment and recovery.

THE CONCEPTUAL MODEL

Symptom Function

In an early article stemming from the Stanton and Todd research project (Stanton *et al.*, 1978), substance abuse was viewed as a "paradoxical resolution" to several developmental dilemmas facing the addict and his family.[2] Drugs allow the addict to be close but distant, to be aggressive and powerful without taking responsibility for his actions, to have a quasi-sexual experience yet remain loyal to his mother—in short, to become an independent adult through a form of pseudoindividuation.

337

The Addiction Cycle and the Family

The Stanton *et al.* (1978) conceptual model proposed that drug addiction could be thought of as part of a cyclic process involving three or more individuals, commonly the addict and his two parents or parent surrogates. When the equilibrium of this interpersonal system is threatened, such as through threats of separation by the parents or other marital crises, the addict behaves in a way that dramatically focuses attention upon himself. Typically, after the marital crisis has been successfully avoided, the addict begins to behave more competently. As the addict demonstrates increased competence and starts to function independently of the family, the parents are left to deal with their previously unresolved conflicts. At this point in the cycle, marital tensions increase and the threat of separation arises again. The addict then behaves in an attention-getting or self-destructive way, and the dysfunctional triadic cycle continues.

Life Cycle Stages and Drug Addiction

In contrast to purely static notions of family patterns and structure, Stanton and Todd (1982) were impressed with the utility of the family life cycle as a paradigm for identifying variables surrounding the drug abuser's problem and for dictating the direction for treatment. In this respect, they were heavily influenced by Haley, who in turn had analyzed the role of these concepts in Erickson's work (Haley, 1973).

Stanton and Todd (1982) viewed two life cycle stages as particularly salient in the development of addiction in a young person. The first is the point at which he or she reaches adolescence. The second one of importance is the stage of leaving home emphasized by Haley (1980). In this section, I will discuss the clinical handling of these two developmental stages and will conclude with a discussion of adulthood-onset substance abuse. This appears to be a particularly critical stage for many alcoholics, who may have been, at worst, only problem drinkers prior to this stage. There is increasing evidence, however, that the developmental hurdles of adult life can also signal the onset of exacerbation of drug abuse, particularly the abuse of prescription drugs and cocaine.

Adolescence

Fishman, Stanton, and Rosman (1982) have noted several ways in which adolescent substance abusers differ from young adult addicts. Adolescent abusers are less likely to be physiologically addicted, and, since their drug usage is generally of a shorter duration, the pattern is typically less entrenched. Although peers are important to the adolescent user, he or she is less likely than an adult addict to be immersed in the drug subculture, and the family typically is a more potent influence. Similarly, adolescent users are less likely to be deeply involved in criminal activity.

As with adult addiction, adolescent drug abuse is seen partly as a response to a developmental crisis facing the whole family. Adolescence is typically a time in which the young person begins to assume adult-like responsibilities and to move toward the peer group, especially toward heterosexual relationships. Family structures and rules that were sufficient when the drug abuser was more involved in the family and more amenable to its influence begin to break down, and drug abuse is one possible form the symptoms may take.

In treating adolescent substance abusers, therapists need to take into account the stage of family development. In particular, this means that the goal of the therapy should be the transformation of the family within its existing structure, in contrast to treatment that is given when the young person is attempting to leave home, where physical separation is an appropriate goal. Some support for parental control is usually in order, although the parents may also need to relax their authority to some extent.

Fishman, *et al.* (1982) present a detailed discussion of technical issues in the family treatment of adolescent substance abuse. For the purposes of the discussion here, I will focus primarily upon issues of boundary making and appropriate parental control, since these issues relate so directly to the family life cycle.

Boundary issues tend to be crucial in the family therapy of adolescent substance abuse. As is the case with young adult addicts, there is often a dysfunctional cross-generational coalition between one parent and the adolescent abuser against the other parent. In such cases, one of the obvious structural goals is to create a "united front" between the parents, yet one that is not overly harsh. Similarly, it is appropriate for the teenager to have a stronger boundary around himself or herself and the peer group. This can be enhanced by giving the young person some "private time" in therapy, either individually or with siblings, or even with a friend. Parents can be encouraged to give the teenager more space and to spend more time together as a couple.

Therapeutic strategies to deal with control issues vary, depending on whether the parents are attempting to be overcontrolling or whether they have lost control or been underreactive. When one or both parents attempt to overcontrol the activities of the teenager, any evidence of drug use, even of modest drug experimentation, is taken as proof that constant surveillance is required. The therapist should not regard this parental involvement purely as a response to the drug use — it is more helpful to view it developmentally, as a response to parental anxiety about the diminished importance of the family, the increased importance of peers, and the child's eventual departure from home.

Faced with this developmental difficulty, the therapist may try straightforward attempts to establish appropriate boundaries and to get the overinvolved parent(s) to back off. This may include having the less involved parent reassure the overinvolved one or making rules and consequences clearer and more automatic. Often, the therapist can join with the parents by validating their wishes for the teenager yet having them recognize that there are limits to what they can do. More entrenched situations may require interventions with a strategic flavor, such as overloading the parents by pushing them to double their efforts at surveillance until they begin to rebel, or by using "strategic compression" (Stanton, 1984) until they back off "spontaneously."

At the other extreme, the therapist working with families of adolescent substance abusers may encounter parents who have lost control over the teenager's actions. First, the therapist needs to help the parents agree upon enforceable "house rules," which will help them regain authority. The therapist may initially need to lend his or her authority to the parents until some semblance of control is achieved. Later, after the teenager begins to conform, the therapist can take a less rigid stance and ensure that the teenager also gets some of his or her issues on the agenda. (Since the parental authority is weak at first, it is usually a mistake to reverse these steps and start with the teenager's agenda.)

The Leaving-Home Stage

Haley (1980) has placed particular emphasis on the stage of leaving home in the etiology of disturbed behavior in young people. He based his theoretical work on his observations of young heroin abusers and their families in the Stanton and Todd project, of the families of psychotic adolescents and young adults, and of other extremely symptomatic young people, such as anorectics. All of these observations led him to conclude that the stage of leaving home presents the greatest risk of symptom development of all the developmental stages.

When it is clear that the family has been unsuccessful at negotiating the leaving-home stage, it becomes critical for the family to be brought together for treatment, even though the identified patient may be living apart from the parents. By bringing them together, the goal of therapy is for the parents to help the young person to leave the "right way," with the parents' blessing. This movement may be underscored by having the parents participate in such activities as helping the young person manage a budget and find a suitable place to live, thereby showing their support for this move. (Other features of this approach, with clinical details, can be found in the case "Heroin My Baby" [Haley, 1982].)

When the leaving-home stage is at issue, the involvement of the parents and other members of the family of origin in therapy is critically important, even if the patient is a young adult with a spouse and children. Often, at least in the experience of the Stanton and Todd project, the drug abuser will attempt to create a "smoke screen" by offering to bring in his spouse or girlfriend and emphasizing his need for help in that area of his life. One addict even begged for family therapy with his family of procreation so that he could be a better father. It is a reflection of the vital importance of this developmental stage that it proved to be extremely difficult to stabilize the addict's marriage or other heterosexual relationships without first going back to the family of origin, at least to obtain the parents' blessing for the success of the relationship. This was not surprising, considering that the message from the family had been that the patient had not left home satisfactorily and could not be expected to succeed as a competent adult.

When, on the other hand, the family has given its blessing to the former substance abuser and has indicated its belief that he or she is ready to move on, clinical work with the married couple or the new family can be quite productive. (To judge the potential for such a relationship, it is usually critically important to ascertain whether the marital relationship was initially "drug free" or whether it has been based almost exclusively on periods of drug involvement. If both parties are heavily drug dependent, the chances for stabilizing the relationship without drugs are extremely bleak.)

Adulthood Onset

It is comparatively rare to find an adult substance abuser who was not involved with drugs or alcohol as an adolescent or a young adult. One of the best predictors of addiction or abuse as an adult is the age at which substance use began. There is also good evidence of a progression from soft to harder drugs and from legal to illegal drugs. In addition to these factors, however, consideration of stages of adult individual and family development can add considerable explanatory power to considerations of why substance abuse is a problem now.

In modern industrialized society, the stages of adult life stretch over a considerable time, from independence and marriage to old age. Any of the developmental tasks of adult life can contribute to the initiation or exacerbation of substance abuse, or to the return to a previous pattern of abuse. (To take a depressing extreme example of the latter, in many of the retirement and "leisure" communities, an unexpectedly high relapse rate has been informally noted among alcoholics, including recovering alcoholics with many years of previous sobriety.)

When substance abuse has begun or escalated at some point following marriage, it is usually important to involve the spouse (rather than the family of origin) in therapy. In addition to looking at the stage of development of the marriage and family, it is also important to consider the individual life of each spouse. Changes in job or career of one or both spouses may be just as significant as changes with the children, and such changes can definitely add to the impact of family changes, such as having the children less available.

Although work on the marital relationship is usually critical, it is often developmentally inappropriate and therapeutically unwise to place the sole focus on the marriage. Often, there is too great a dependency on the marriage already, and it is therefore important for the therapist to help both spouses have a balanced involvement in the marital relationship and in extrafamilial systems such as work, peers, and community.

Unless the marital system has broken down or the patient's spouse has died, it is usually not necessary to involve the family of origin. There are, however, subpopulations for which this may be crucial. Most notably, there is a much greater tendency for female alcoholics and drug addicts than for males to be divorced or abandoned by their spouses. Often, they have no alternative financial or emotional supports other than the family of origin, although mobilization of this system may require considerable effort from the therapist.

THE BASIC THERAPY MODEL

When a family is seen as "stuck" at a particular life cycle stage, with the symptom of substance abuse having acquired a functional role in the family's dealing with this impasse, a variety of clinical approaches are used to help the family resolve the impasse. The spectrum of interventions includes (1) structural interventions, such as boundary making, to reinforce the appropriate developmental shifts and reduce the need for the symptom; (2) the use of reframing and other more strategic interventions, which block the function of the symptom; (3) more paradoxical interventions, which promote a "recoil" from previous patterns of behavior.

Briefly stated, the structural–strategic model developed by Stanton and Todd (1982) is a goal-oriented and relatively short-term therapy that focuses on the concrete behavior of the addict and the family members. Successful therapy almost invariably involves helping the family weather crises involving drugs and drug-related behavior as well as interpersonal crises, especially between the parents, not involving drugs. More recently, the therapy has involved creating a deliberate therapeutic crisis in the form of detoxification at home (see Scott & Van Deusen, 1982, and Stanton, Steier, Cook, & Todd, 1984).

For the purposes of this chapter, I will focus, in the next section, on incorporating life cycle issues in the therapy model. A scheme for arriving at a life cycle diagnosis is presented first, followed by a presentation of four strategies for incorporating life cycle issues in treatment.

LIFE CYCLE ASPECTS OF THE THERAPY MODEL

Life Cycle Diagnosis

By now, one of the major implications of this chapter should be clear—that a comprehensive treatment plan in any case of substance abuse should include an explicit component of life cycle "diagnosis." This section will focus upon the diagnostic process itself.

Current Life Cycle Stage

Most family therapists are already somewhat attuned to consideration of the current life cycle stage. This is the simplest aspect of life cycle diagnosis, since it is obvious from the family composition and the ages of family members what life cycle stage is currently operative and what developmental demands this stage places upon the family. For example, many adult addicts in the Stanton and Todd project had failed to negotiate the leaving-home stage successfully. Since most of the addicts were in their early 30s and many had spouses and children, they were immediately faced with many demands to form or consolidate their new families, as soon as the leaving-home stage could be left behind. This obviously presents a very different situation for a therapist than working with a family with a much younger patient who is having difficulty leaving home at the age when that might typically be expected.

Earlier Life Cycle Stages

Although more "detective work" is involved, it is important for the therapist to verify that the family has successfully negotiated previous life cycle stages that have been passed chronologically but perhaps not psychologically. This may be comparatively simple when the physical evidence is straightforward, such as when an addict has never left home and is unmarried and unemployed.

Often, however, the evidence is not so clear-cut. In many cases, the literal evidence might seem to indicate a higher stage of functioning than is, in fact, the case when the qualitative aspects of the adjustment are considered. A substance abuser may have served in the army or gotten married, yet may never have been treated as a competent adult by his parents or siblings. In many of the cases in the Stanton and Todd project, close analysis revealed that the addict had never been engaged in appropriate adolescent rebellion. This meant that some assertiveness and independence needed to be established before genuine leaving home could be accomplished.

To arrive at an accurate diagnosis, the therapist needs to consider more than the behavior of the substance abuser and how this person is viewed and treated within the family. In addition to changes in how this member is treated over time, there are corollary changes in other relationships that need to take place.

Without these changes, it is questionable whether the stage has been successfully negotiated and whether the potential for regression is definitely present.

The leaving-home stage, for example, requires more than an acceptance of the maturity of the offspring who is leaving. It also requires a renegotiation of the marital system as a dyad and the realignment of the family system to include potential new members. Often, realignments are also occurring with respect to the older, grandparent generation. When any of these elements are missing, the therapist should at least regard this as a danger sign and as a clue that closer examination is warranted.

Complicating Factors

After the therapist has done a careful life cycle analysis, including ascertaining the life cycle stage during which the substance abuse began or became significantly worse, there may still be other factors present that may complicate the diagnostic picture and have important treatment implications. One of these concerns is the occupational status of the abuser's parents—particularly that of the breadwinner(s). If a parent loses a job or experiences a dramatic loss of status, the effect can be catastrophic on the family. This may be manifest through symptoms of the parent or through marital conflict. In either event, the drug abuser may become increasingly incompetent and problematic, which may function to increase the status of the parent or even to keep him or her "employed."

Other events that may be related to the onset of drug abuse include death or illness in the family. Their impact is most obvious when a parent is involved, but the indirect impact from the death or illness of a grandparent or even a seemingly distant relative should not be overlooked.

Incorporating Life Cycle Issues in Treatment

A number of specific treatment principles and strategies have been mentioned in the discussion of particular life cycle stages. Lengthy case examples can also be found in Stanton, *et al.* (1982). This section offers a more abstract and schematic presentation of how life cycle considerations can be incorporated in treatment once an accurate assessment has been made. There are four basic strategies, which are based on whether the life cycle stage is used explicitly or only implicitly, and whether the basic therapeutic stance is straightforward as opposed to strategic and provocative or paradoxical. Most cases are not "pure," and it is usually important for the therapist to be prepared to shift back and forth, in line with the general principles of an integrated structural–strategic approach (Stanton, 1981a, 1981b; Todd, 1986).

1. *Straightforward and implicit.* Though it is important for the therapist

to analyze life cycle factors carefully and to include them in the treatment plan, it is by no means necessary to make these issues explicit to the family. One of the cardinal principles in the Stanton and Todd model is the avoidance of placing blame, especially upon the parents. It is, unfortunately, all too easy for the parents to feel attacked and blamed when the therapist makes a connection between the substance abuse and the parents' failure to let go of their child and begin to treat the child as a young adult.

Our preferred approach is to begin with straightforward tasks that relate to the life cycle issues, but without making the connection explicit. If, for example, the parents successfully negotiate new "house rules," they are also changing the rules of their relationship and beginning to interact more directly with each other. If they begin to succeed, they may be given credit as a couple and asked to go out for an evening together as a reward.

2. *Straightforward and explicit.* In some cases, it may be useful to make life cycle considerations explicit, if this can be done without increasing resistance and if this increases compliance with straightforward tasks. To accomplish this, it is usually necessary to find a positive framework within which to present the connection. For example Kirschner, the therapist in "Heroin My Baby" (Haley, 1982), used a parental move to a new house as providing an opportunity for a "fresh beginning," rather than focusing on the parents' failure to let go of their son (Haley, 1982, p. 174).

It is difficult to draw a neat distinction between straightforward and strategic interventions. In a further example from "Heroin My Baby," Kirschner deliberately misquotes the father: "If he was straightened out, then you would get closer to your wife, is that what you're saying?" (Haley, 1982, p. 177). He knows that this is not quite what the father has said, but he counts on the fact that the father will not deny the statement, so that it can become an explicit link and an explicit goal.

3. *Strategic and indirect.* Strategic interventions are warranted only when more straightforward approaches are temporarily or chronically met with resistance (Stanton, 1981a, 1981b; Todd, 1986). In such circumstances, the therapist may utilize seemingly "regressive" tasks to propel the family forward in the family life cycle. Techniques include the "compression" techniques of Stanton (1984) and deliberate parental overloading, as described by Fishman *et al.* (1982). A classic example is a case in which Paul Riley was the therapist. Faced with a single mother holding on tightly to her only son, Riley verbally regressed them to an infantile stage, asking her to describe her son as a baby, including a graphic description of nursing him. Such a focus, which resulted in considerable squirming on the son's part, began to loosen their symbiotic relationship and allowed Riley to get them to focus on more appropriate mother–son interaction.

4. *Strategic and explicit.* There are at least two major circumstances in which life cycle issues may be explicitly invoked within a more strategic

approach. The first is when these issues are used as part of a strategic reframing, in order to block patterns of interaction that are keeping the family developmentally "stuck." In "Heroin My Baby" (Haley, 1982), for example, Kirschner met considerable resistance to the notion that the son would eventually have to move out. The behavior of the parents shifted radically, however, when this was reframed as the son's need to take care of them, which was unacceptable.

Life cycle issues can also be used as part of a strategic or provocative challenge by the therapist. A typical gambit in leaving-home situations is to claim that the child does not believe that the parents can tolerate having the child leave (while the therapist may or may not indicate agreement). A more direct strategic challenge is the use of "restraining" (Todd, 1981), where the therapist argues that it would be premature for the child to leave, since the parents might rediscover each other "and nobody is ready for that."

CASE EXAMPLE

A case example from my practice should give a realistic picture of the actual complexities involved in using the family life cycle in the assessment and treatment of drug abuse.

The identified patient, who will be called Jim, was a 34-year-old heroin abuser who was currently living with his retired parents. He had been using drugs to a significant extent since his first year of high school, but this had not been considered a major problem by the parents. Conflict with his father during his teenage years had been high, and his mother had interceded frequently. After graduating from high school and holding several jobs, he moved out and became quite successful financially. He began to live with a woman and eventually purchased an apartment house. He maintained this level of independence for several years, but he lost his job and ultimately the relationship foundered because of his increasing drug abuse.

While the evidence of Jim's independence was definitely a favorable prognostic sign, there were two early clues to the therapist that Jim was not really independent and that involvement of the family was definitely crucial for treatment. All of the inquiries about treatment were made by Jim's older sister, Susan, who was a social worker. While some of her investment in finding appropriate treatment may have been explainable on the basis of her profession, she appeared to be overinvolved and had already located several programs that Jim had failed to finish.

The father was clearly involved in infantilizing "Jimmie," as he called his son, with drug abuse providing the opportunity. Jim would purchase heroin every 2 or 3 days. He would give the envelopes to his father, who would then dole them out to him, almost like a daily allowance to a child who could not manage his money. Since Jim could not be trusted with money either, his father would go with Jim to make purchases. After Jim had selected an item, such as tires for his car, his father would write out the check (Jim's money) and hand the check to Jim. The therapist did not feel that it was wise to point out the father's "enabling" behavior, particularly since he was already feeling like a failure.

Given this behavior on the father's part, it was not surprising to find that his behavior was linked to life cycle difficulties he was experiencing. He had been forced to retire early from his civil service job and was left with a small pension and no sense of pride or accomplishment from his work. His wife was eagerly awaiting the birth of a grandchild by their youngest child, a daughter, but he was uninterested in this and could see himself as nothing but a "has-been."

From a life cycle perspective, therefore, it is easy to see that Jim's drug behavior might well have a component of "helpfulness" for his father, giving him a renewed sense of purpose. Indeed, helping Jim had become virtually a full-time job for the father. A reasonable strategy would be to have him help Jim to leave home again, this time for good. Since Jim had been seemingly independent and successful already, it was anticipated that he would resist any need for parental help.

As expected, Jim did question the need for his parents to be involved in treatment, feeling that he should not still be at home and that he was already imposing on them. The therapist noted that Jim's attempts to "do it himself" had failed, since he had been in and out of two detoxification programs in 6 weeks.

The parents and Jim were involved in the initial goal setting for therapy. While all agreed that Jim ultimately needed to be drug free, they felt that employment and financial stability should be the first priority, since Jim found financial dependence so humiliating. Jim's father was encouraged to help Jim make choices about vocational training and a job. Since Jim had been stabilized on a fairly high dose of methadone, there was not much "action" in the family sessions, and the therapist decided to hold them on a biweekly basis, seeing Jim occasionally on the off weeks for individual sessions.

At times Jim made the expected threats to move out prematurely but was restrained by the parents, with considerable encouragement from the therapist. The mother's role in the triangle became clear in a session held with only the father and son. (The mother was off helping her daughter with her new baby.) Things became heated between the two men in the session, and Jim walked out rather than get violent toward his father. The father was afraid Jim would shoot up again and was tempted to kick him out of the house, but he knew that his wife would never forgive him. The therapist supported his self-restraint and reiterated that it was crucial for Jim to leave with the blessing of both parents.

Jim went through a successful and comparatively uneventful detoxification at home from a low dose of methadone. This was the final symbolic stage of the parents' involvement in his recovery. He remains drug free several years later, although he needed the support of Alcoholics Anonymous [AA] to maintain his sobriety. Later Jim was instrumental in starting two local Narcotics Anonymous [NA] chapters. The parents appear to have a happy life together, and the father no longer seems to feel such a sense of failure.

THE STAGES OF ADDICTION AND RECOVERY

Although, as we have seen, it is crucial for treatment that the therapist consider the point at which the family life cycle has been disrupted, this is not the only developmental process that must be taken into account. In this section, we will see that the process of addiction, as well as the process of recovery, can be viewed as a developmental continuum, with each point on the continuum dictating modifications in the treatment plan.

Preaddiction

It is important to remember that a stage of drug use exists that precedes addiction and that is not addiction, contrary to the assertions of some zealots in the treatment community who seem to equate all drug use with addiction. Similarly, the therapist may need to resist and counteract overzealousness on the part of the parents or a spouse if drug use is still in the preaddiction stage.

In this early stage, three of the characteristics of later stages are missing: (1) physical addiction and increased tolerance, (2) pronounced reliance on the use of drugs as a coping mechanism, and (3) negative consequences of substance use.

Effective marital and family treatment during this stage involves helping the family members to recognize this stage for what it is and to react appropriately. Especially with adolescents, it is a mistake to ignore the drug use completely, particularly if there is a heavy component of rebelliousness, since this may lead to escalated levels of use. More commonly, however, the greater danger is an exaggerated response equating drug experimentation with hard-core addiction. This extreme stance creates several problems:

1. Psychologically, there is the possibility of creating a self-fulfilling prophecy.

2. Overreaction tends to destroy the credibility of the parent or spouse concerning the topic of drug use.

3. When the reaction to moderate levels of use is extreme and highly punitive, there is no room left for a stronger response to more serious levels of drug involvement.

Early Addiction

In the early addiction stage, some or all of the previously listed characteristics are present, but there is usually widespread denial by all parties, especially the abuser. Usually, there are also characteristics of hard-core drug use that are lacking, particularly having to do with the pattern of use. Absence of these characteristics can cloud the diagnostic picture and make denial easier for the substance abuser and the family. Because use is not constant and withdrawal symptoms are not present, the abuser is able to argue that the substance use is not a problem; this argument often is persuasive to some of those around the abuser.

Obviously, it is important to distinguish this stage from the preceding one. This is particularly critical because the appropriate treatment is almost the opposite of that used in the previous stage. In the early addiction stage, the therapist needs to break through the denial system of the spouse or family in order to help them confront the abuser.

In the early addiction stage, there are two major traps. At one extreme are those family members who maintain that there is nothing they can do that will make a difference. This feeling is often reinforced by those who emphasize that the abuser must want to be helped and may need to "bottom out" before help is possible. Such a position ignores the actions of family members and others that help to protect the abuser from the consequences of the substance abuse and that tend to prolong the usage. Discontinuing such "enabling" behavior and confronting the abuser with the consequences of his or her drug use can often have considerable impact long before the abuser has "bottomed out" on his or her own.

At the other extreme are family members (and professional helpers) who take too much responsibility for "curing" the addict. This is a particular danger at this stage, because the addict has generally not acknowledged his or her addiction. The parent or spouse often expends considerable effort researching treatment resources, going to meetings, and reading about the problem, only to have all of these helpful efforts fall on deaf ears. In such instances, the therapist will need to show the helper that this form of "help" is counterproductive. Rather than having the helper continue such efforts to be directly helpful, it is more useful to have such a person acknowledge the limits of what can be done for the drug abuser at this time and to get the helper to focus more on taking care of himself or herself.

Bottoming Out

Although we have seen that the stage of extreme "bottoming out" is not a necessary stage when there is appropriate early intervention, many cases reach this stage nevertheless. In such cases, the addiction has reached a point where it can no longer be ignored. Often the abuser is brought into treatment as a result of medical complications or legal difficulties, such as a drunk-driving conviction or a drug-related arrest. Other harsh realities may also have propelled the abuser into treatment, such as the loss of a job or the threat of divorce.

At times, the impact of these events may be sufficiently extreme to break through the abuser's denial system. Patients (and families) in this stage are often more receptive to more extreme treatment measures, such as inpatient detoxification and rehabilitation, and to involvement in AA and Al-Anon. It is well, however, to examine this motivation carefully, since often the major motivator is avoiding external consequences, such as jail or the loss of a driver's license. While the consequences have increased dramatically, so has the degree of physical and psychological drug dependence, so it is not surprising that abuse can continue despite severe consequences.

Even when genuine motivation to be helped can be mobilized, extreme problems remain. Often the support system has been "burned out," so that one of the major tasks for the therapist may be instilling appropriate levels of hope in family members and other supports. In addition, there may have been other relatively irreversible consequences in physical functioning, vocational history, and so forth, which may place real limits on the degree of recovery that is possible.

Pretreatment

The marital or family therapist often encounters cases in the "pretreatment" phase. This phase, which characterizes a significant percentage of drug-related cases, refers to those cases in which the "customer" is not the abuser but instead is a parent, spouse, girlfriend, or other interested person. The therapist can help such a person analyze his or her helping efforts along the lines indicated previously.

Beyond that, the most useful approach is to encourage the primary helper to enlist others in the effort in order to have them participate in a family intervention, along the lines developed by the Johnson Institute (Maxwell, 1976, pp. 95-104). In such an intervention, an attempt is made to mobilize as many significant members of the abuser's network as possible. Members of this network initially meet with the therapist, without the abuser present, to outline the goals of the intervention and to make sure that they will all abide by the ground rules. When the intervention is conducted with the abuser, each person describes to the abuser in a nonblaming and nonattacking manner exactly what the impact of the drug abuse has been on him or her personally. Although the ultimate goal is, certainly, to get the substance abuser to enter treatment, no direct pressure is applied; instead, all of those present reiterate their willingness to help and their faith that the abuse can stop.

Early Treatment

The early treatment phase begins when the abuser accepts the need for treatment and actually enters treatment. Naturally, there are many variations at this stage—whether treatment is carried out on an inpatient or outpatient basis, the degree to which participation is voluntary or coerced, whether medications such as methadone or Antabuse are used, and so forth. For the purposes of this discussion, we will pay little attention to such variations and focus primarily on the role of the family in treatment.

There is little question that this is a crucial stage for engaging the family in treatment, or for maintaining their involvement in treatment if they are already involved. At times, this goes against the emphasis of the drug treatment program, either implicitly or explicitly. This is particularly true of inpatient or residential programs, which reinforce the idea that the patient is the problem and bears sole responsibility for recovery, and of programs emphasizing chemical substitution or chemical antagonists, which tend to de-emphasize all psychosocial factors. There is good evidence, however, that family involvement can have a significant impact on the success of any program, regardless of the primary modality used (Todd & Stanton, 1983). Family members can increase treatment compliance, whether treatment consists of taking Antabuse, attending AA, or remaining in a residential program rather than signing out "against medical advice." In addition, the family can serve as a valuable "early warning" system, breaking through the abuser's denial or alerting treatment professionals of a slip or other danger signs.

By contrast, when a treatment program ignores or even antagonizes family members, it is inviting disaster. Under such circumstances, an abuser's complaints or distortions about the treatment program often fall on receptive ears, and the family cooperates in undermining treatment. Similarly, the uninvolved family members often continue or even escalate their previous enabling behavior, typically at times when the treatment program is beginning to show signs of success.

Although there is no clear consensus in the treatment community about how to involve the family in the early treatment stage, there are a few major guidelines that should be considered:

1. When the treatment is moderately long inpatient or residential treatment, and the patient is an adult with an extensive history of substance abuse, there is general agreement that the abuser and other family members should be seen separately, especially at first.

2. At the other extreme, if treatment is on an outpatient or brief inpatient basis, or if the patient is an adolescent or young adult living at home, it is imperative that the family be involved in treatment with the abuser as quickly as possible.

3. Many programs attempt to promote the notion of substance abuse as a "family disease" and seek to get family members to acknowledge that they are coming to treatment for themselves rather than for the benefit of the substance abuser. When this approach is successful, it undoubtedly enhances the depth and intensity of therapy.

4. When, on the other hand, resistance is high or the abuse pattern is well entrenched or severe, a "soft-sell" approach is probably preferable. Many programs begin with a family education approach. Rather than emphasizing the "family disease," similar content can be conveyed by talking about patterns of adaptation to a chronic situation. (For example, the therapist might argue that although no one likes the symptoms, each family member has made some modifications in his or her behavior in response to the symptoms. Such

adaptations are often unwitting forms of "enabling" and will probably interfere with recovery from chemical dependency.)

5. Common to all of these approaches is the assumption that the family should be made fully knowledgeable about the treatment program and should have a major voice in goal setting. Although this point is most obvious when the substance abuser is an adolescent, it is universally true that agreement on explicit goals will be extremely helpful to the treatment and need not represent any loss of autonomy for the substance abuser.

6. Another foolproof ingredient for treatment at this stage is to prepare the family (and the substance abuser) for what to expect at later stages of treatment. Advance preparation is especially critical for any factors that could undermine the success of treatment. Such factors include complacency regarding the difficulty of remaining abstinent, possible jealousy and resentment of family members toward the addict's ongoing involvement in treatment (especially toward programs based on the AA model, which require such intense involvement of the addict that family members can experience them as excluding the family), and unrealistic expectations concerning improvement in other areas (see Posttreatment section).

Posttreatment

Perhaps a less confusing label for this stage would be "early sobriety" or "early aftercare," since such labels indicate more clearly that treatment is far from over. Even though inpatient or residential treatment may have been completed, much more remains to be done. Even when such treatment has been highly successful, this is clearly the stage in which the chances of relapse are greatest. During this period, which can last from 3 months to 2 years or more, family members and therapists typically report a feeling of "walking on eggs" because of their concerns about relapse.

Continued abstinence should be the primary goal of treatment at this stage, and all other goals should be distinctly secondary. Unfortunately, marital and family therapists often help to promote relapse by ignoring this priority and encouraging spouses and family members to make heavy demands on the recovering person rather than helping the spouse or family members to slow down and moderate their expectations.

It is important to acknowledge that working in this fashion can be extremely frustrating for both family and therapist. Consistent with this, it may be useful to schedule sessions less frequently than once a week, in order to scale down the therapist's expectations and minimize frustration. For the family, it is helpful to acknowledge their unmet needs to have a fully functioning spouse, parent, or child, and to reiterate that full recovery is the ultimate goal. In the meantime, family members will usually find it helpful to participate in self-help support groups such as Al-Anon and Alateen, to realize that they are not alone and that they are making progress.

"True Sobriety"

As most recovering persons will tell you, "true sobriety" often seems to be an elusive goal. Nevertheless, there are some distinguishing characteristics. Often, the addict has gone through a period of intense involvement in a program based on the AA model, including becoming a sponsor and proceeding through the 12-step program. After this period of intense involvement, many addicts begin to feel a diminished need to be involved to this extent and become significantly less rigid about "The Program." When this is a healthy development, it is usually characterized by a broadening in perspective rather than by a disenchantment or radical break with the program.

From the family's point of view, they can clearly sense a major change in the abuser and no longer feel that they need to tiptoe around. In response to this sense of strength and connectedness on the part of the addicted family member, they now feel that it is safe to make more direct demands for family involvement and emotional support and expression.

In a very real sense, this is the first stage in which genuine marital and family therapy is possible. It often occurs in response to the family's own sense of timing, which may be 5 to 7 years into sobriety. (Such a lengthy delay has not occurred in situations where there was consistent family involvement earlier in treatment.) Even when the time seems ripe for conjoint treatment, the therapist should not underestimate the magnitude of the task. As recovering persons will readily admit, they often feel ill equipped to deal with emotional and interpersonal issues, because of gaps in their development as well as childhood experiences. Similarly, one should not underestimate the difficulty in helping spouses and others reared in an alcoholic or abusive environment to learn to trust and depend on others, put their own needs first, and abandon control strategies.

CONCLUSION

The family life cycle has provided an important conceptual framework for the marital and family therapy of substance abuse, particularly for the structural-strategic approach of Stanton and Todd. We are, however, only beginning to appreciate the complex interaction between life cycle stages and other developmental processes, such as the developmental stages of addiction and recovery. Furthermore, though there has been a very useful emphasis on the leaving-home stage in the etiology and treatment of substance abuse, there has been, to date, insufficient exploration of substance abuse that begins or escalates at a later stage. The life cycle framework can continue to be useful for further work in this field.

NOTES

1. Although the bulk of the early clinical work involved heroin and alcohol, the model has been extended to deal with other drugs, including, most recently, cocaine (Todd, Stanton, & Carway, 1986).

2. In this research project, only male addicts were studied. The results obtained can not automatically be generalized to include female addicts; the use of only the male pronoun in parts of the chapter is intended to alert the reader to this.

REFERENCES

Fishman, H. C., Stanton, M. D., & Rosman, B. L. (1982). Treating families of adolescent drug abusers. In M. D. Stanton, T. C. Todd, & Associates, *The family therapy of drug abuse and addiction* (pp. 335-357). New York: Guilford Press.

Haley, J. (1973). *Uncommon therapy.* New York: W. W. Norton.

Haley, J. (1980). *Leaving home.* San Francisco: Jossey-Bass.

Haley, J. (1982). Heroin my baby: A clinical model. In M. D. Stanton, T. C. Todd, & Associates, *The family therapy of drug abuse and addiction* (pp. 154-189). New York: Guilford Press.

Maxwell, R. (1976). *The booze battle.* New York: Ballantine Books.

Scher, J. (1966). Patterns and profiles of addiction and drug abuse. *Archives of General Psychiatry, 15,* 539-551.

Scott, S. M., & Van Deusen, J. M. (1982). Detoxification at home: A family approach. In M. D. Stanton, T. C. Todd, & Associates, *The family therapy of drug abuse and addiction* (pp. 310-334). New York: Guilford Press.

Stanton, M. D. (1981a). An integrated structural/strategic approach to family therapy. *Journal of Marital and Family Therapy, 7,* 427-439.

Stanton, M. D. (1981b). Marital therapy from a structural/strategic viewpoint. In G. P. Sholevar (Ed.), *Handbook of marriage and marital therapy* (pp. 303-334). Jamaica, NY: S. P. Medical & Scientific Books.

Stanton, M. D. (1984). Fusion, compression, diversion and the workings of paradox: A theory of therapeutic/systemic change. *Family Process, 23,* 135-167.

Stanton, M. D., Steier, F., Cook, L., & Todd, T. C. (1984). *Narcotic detoxification in a family and home context* (Final Report 1980-1983, NIDA Grant No. 5 R01 DA 03097).

Stanton, M. D., & Todd, T. C. (1982). The therapy model. In M. D. Stanton, T. C. Todd, & Associates, *The family therapy of drug abuse and addiction* (pp. 109-153). New York: Guilford Press.

Stanton, M. D., Todd, T. C., & Associates. (1982). *The family therapy of drug abuse and addiction.* New York: Guilford Press.

Stanton, M. D., Todd, T. C., Heard, D. B., Kirschner, S., Kleiman, J. I., Mowatt, D. T., Riley, P., Scott, S. M., & VanDeusen, J. M. (1978). Heroin addiction as a family phenomenon: A new conceptual model. *American Journal of Drug and Alcohol Abuse, 5,* 125-150.

Todd, T. C. (1981). Paradoxical prescriptions: Applications of consistent paradox using a strategic team. *Journal of Strategic and Systemic Therapies, 1* (1), 28-44.

Todd, T. C., (1986). Structural-strategic marital therapy. In N. S. Jacobson & A. S. Gurman (Eds.), *Clinical handbook of marital therapy* (pp. 71-105). New York: Guilford Press.

Todd, T. C., & Stanton, M. D. (1983). Research on marital and family therapy: Answers, issues and recommendations for the future. In B. B. Wolman & G. Stricker (Eds.), *Handbook of family and marital therapy* (pp. 91-115). New York: Plenum.

Todd, T. C., Stanton, M. D., & Carway, J. (1986). *Treatment manual for structural-strategic family therapy of cocaine abuse.* Unpublished manuscript.

PART FOUR

THE FAMILY LIFE CYCLE IN FAMILY THERAPY PRACTICE AND CLINICAL TRAINING

15

Family Development and Change across the Generations: An Intergenerational Perspective

DONALD S. WILLIAMSON
Baylor College of Medicine

JAMES H. BRAY
Texas Woman's University, Houston Center

A multigenerational approach to families and family therapy provides a useful and rich theoretical viewpoint for understanding individual and family development. There are several different theoretical and therapeutic systems within the intergenerational, or transgenerational, orientations that share certain commonalities in understanding families across multiple generations of family evolution (Boszormenyi-Nagy & Spark, 1973; Bowen, 1978; Framo, 1981; Paul, 1976; Williamson, 1981). In this chapter, we first provide a brief overview of these theories and then present a detailed description of one theoretical and therapeutic system, developed originally by Williamson (1981, 1982a, 1982b), that focuses on an intergenerational model of family development and change. This model is a synthesis and an extension of previous multigenerational models and is proving useful for understanding individual and family development in a variety of social, psychological, and health-related contexts.

Given a multigenerational focus, an immediate question is, how many generations is it necessary to evaluate? This reflects an ongoing debate in the family theory and therapy fields. It is also important to make a distinction between explaining or describing family development and intervening for change. Although the various theoretical positions differ on the exact number, at least three generations are considered a minimum for understanding any given family system. This three-generational perspective usually includes the adult generation (second), their parents (first), and their children (third), or an adult generation (third), their parents (second), and their grandparents (first).

In terms of intervening for change, a multigenerational perspective usu-

Dr. Bray's contribution was supported by NIH grant 1 RO1 HD18025-01 from the National Institute of Child Health and Human Development.

ally focuses on the adults in the second or third generation as the point of therapeutic entry into a system. This is not to say that children and older adults are unimportant or irrelevant. Rather, developmental tasks and changes are usually best dealt with at this point in the family system. As Framo (1981) concludes, "the best way to help children is to help their parents. The greatest gift parents can give their children is a viable marriage relationship based on each parent having a strong sense of self" (p. 134). Children generally do not have either the power or the interest to make changes in the family. Much older adults in the first generation usually no longer have the motivation for these changes. As with all systems-oriented approaches, it is assumed that individual behavior is interconnected and mutually influenced by the behavior of all other family members. Thus, all are involved in the process in some manner, directly or indirectly.

FAMILY DEVELOPMENT

Family and individual development are basic building blocks within a multi-generational theoretical perspective. There are at least two distinct processes that influence family development: multigenerational family patterns and family life cycle events and processes. The major focus of this chapter is on the *ongoing process* of development and change across the generations and on how various interactional and emotional patterns are transmitted within a particular family and on through the generations. These multigenerational patterns determine the ways in which individuals and families grow and develop, or stagnate and disintegrate.

Multigenerational Family Patterning

Multigenerational family theorists have developed several explanatory concepts for understanding family functioning and development. These concepts are employed to describe how interactional patterns develop and are passed on across the generations. Although these concepts have been valuable in clinical practice, there is a distinct dearth of empirical research in the area. In particular, there is no detailed explanation of the actual process of transmission of family patterns. Bowen (1978) indicates that family patterns are developed through a process of projection both within the nuclear family's emotional system and across the generations. Likewise, Boszormenyi-Nagy and Ulrich (1981) state that "issues of entitlement and indebtedness vis-à-vis others are existentially given, whether acknowledged or not" (p. 160). Similarly, Framo (1981) and Paul (1981) view the transmission of family patterns as occurring through a projection or transferential process, often at an unconscious level. In pathological cases, it is argued that family members have an extreme interpersonal sensitivity to other family members (Friedrich & Pollack, 1982) and that the transmission of family patterns occurs through analogic modes of communication that are inherently affective and relational (Watzlawick, Beavin, & Jackson, 1967).

An alternative explanation is that these processes occur through a combination of overt and covert expectations and attributions about given family members. These are translated into behavior patterns through reinforcement of specific behaviors and through social learning and modeling (Bandura, 1977). However, the specifics of this projection process are not fully defined and need further exploration and explanation.

Differentiation of Self

Differentiation of self (Bowen, 1978; Kerr, 1981, 1984) is a key concept for evaluating individual and family functioning and how family members will respond to life cycle and environmental changes. The concept refers to processes that occur (1) in individuals and (2) in their relationships with others. In terms of the individual, "differentiation" refers to the degree to which one is able to have control over one's own thoughts and feelings, to discriminate between thoughts and emotions, to respect one's judgments as adequate bases for actions, and to take responsibility for the consequences of these actions. Bowen and Kerr distinguish between "basic" and "functional" levels of differentiation. The basic level is relatively "fixed" and is determined both genetically and experientially as a child develops in the family of origin. It is that portion of the self that is stable and nonnegotiable in relationships or in response to environmental influences. By contrast, the functional level of differentiation is that part of the self that changes with the current environment and in various relationships. With the functional self, one may operate at a higher or lower level, depending on the relationship and the environment. It is assumed that this basic level of differentiation will greatly influence how the individual and his or her given family deals with stress and anxiety.

In terms of relationships, "differentiation" refers to the degree to which a person or a family operates in an autonomous and self-directed manner. A differentiated person is able to function optimally around significant others without feeling responsible for them, controlled by them, or impaired by them. A differentiated family is one that allows its members to function independently and autonomously and that can maintain this level of functioning in the face of stress and anxiety. Differentiated families promote the health and growth of *each* member in a manner that is not at the expense of other family members. The basic level of differentiation observed in adults reflects the level that they inherited and learned in their family of origin (Kerr, 1984). This level is "set" unless an adult actively works on increasing his or her level of differentiation, and even then the result is modest (Kerr, 1981).

At a more practical level, Bowen and Kerr have not completely specified how one distinguishes between basic and functional levels of self. What the distinction does provide is a way of accounting for situationally specific behavior while at the same time offering an explanation for some form of consistency (in personality or traits) in the self. This argues against a purely systemic explanation of behavior as something that is entirely contextually specific.

Fusion

Fusion (Bowen, 1978) is the opposite pole of differentiation. "Fusion" refers to how "emotionally stuck together" persons are in relationships. People who have a high level of fusion do not have a clear sense of self, operate from a more "emotionally reactive" basis, and are more likely to develop symptoms in the face of stress. The level of fusion reflects the degree of unresolved emotional attachment to the parental family.

Fusion can also be assessed at two levels. A fused, or undifferentiated, person functions in a dependent, emotionally reflexive, semiautomatic, or irrational manner in relationships. In terms of the family, fusion is indicated when family members think for each other, feel for each other, and/or function for each other. High levels of family fusion usually result in one or more members being impaired or symptomatic in some manner.

At the other extreme is the individual who emotionally cuts off contact with the family of origin as a means of dealing with fusion. The emotional cutoff can be expressed through limited visits with the family of origin (such as only obligatory holiday visits once a year or one or two phone calls annually) or by emotionally distancing one's self psychologically (e.g., through withdrawal into the self, books, or fantasy, or by being preoccupied with health concerns; Kerr, 1981, 1984). At first glance, this may appear to constitute a differentiated position. However, individuals who emotionally cut off from their families of origin suffer the same kinds of problems as other undifferentiated persons. There is also a tendency for these people to overinvest in other relationships, which puts added pressure on these to succeed.

It is assumed that the basic level of differentiation or fusion in a family is reflected by individual family members and vice versa. Thus, although one family member may appear very differentiated, if other family members are symptomatic, one's basic level of differentiation is assumed to be that of the overall family. Given enough stress, any family may develop symptomatic behavior, no matter how differentiated the members. However, the more differentiated a person or family is, the more they will be able to cope with stress and anxiety *without* developing symptoms.

Triangles

Bowen (1978) proposed that the two-person system is inherently unstable because of the inevitable fusion between individuals in relationships. The way people deal with this is to "triangle in a third person," to decrease the anxiety or stress in the dyad. Triangling is a common process that operates in all human relationships, familial, work, social, and so forth. There is a certain amount of tension in any triangled relationship because invariably two members are "in" and the third person is "out." In most triangles, this is a dynamic process, which is constantly changing. When the interactions among the three people get stuck, the triangle frequently becomes pathological. Because triangles are formed in response to stress and fusion, they are not always easily observable.

Invisible (Covert) Loyalties

The concept of transgenerational loyalties and mandates is an important one for understanding the continuation of patterns across the generations and the development of dysfunctional behavior in families. Loyalty and fairness to the parents and the family of origin are basic premises in relational behavior. Loyalty implies a certain amount of trust and commitment to a relationship. "Invisible loyalties" (Boszormenyi-Nagy & Spark, 1973) are therefore mandates operating at an unconscious, or "underground," level that mold and direct individual behavior. The loyalties reflect the attempt to pay back some indebtedness to the family. However, because they operate in a covert manner, these actions are prime candidates for producing dysfunction in families. The debt cannot be repaid because the child "may 'buy into' the expectation that the debt to the parents is endless and that its payment takes priority over every other human concern" (Boszormenyi-Nagy & Ulrich, 1981, p. 166). A related concept is that of "split loyalties." These occur where an individual becomes involved in a conflicted relational triangle in which being loyal to one person comes at the expense of not being loyal to another. The most common case is when a child (of any age) has a split in loyalty to the parents.

Relational Ethics

Relational ethics (Boszormenyi-Nagy & Ulrich, 1981) is the opposite pole of invisible loyalties. "Relational ethics" implies a balance and fairness between people, not in a moral or "right-versus-wrong" sense, but in the sense of a long-term overall balance among family members. Relational ethics is the bedrock assumption of Boszormenyi-Nagy's viewpoint of family development. Fairness is determined not through an individual criterion, but rather by evaluating the interests and needs of all family members. In this regard, Boszormenyi-Nagy suggests that therapists should adopt a posture of "multidirectional partiality" in their dealings with families in order to maintain the balance in therapy.

Unmourned Grief Reactions

Paul (1981) hypothesizes that if significant loss experiences occur in one generation and are not mourned by that generation, then the unmourned loss and unexpressed grief will be transmitted to and absorbed by subsequent generations. These toxic energies are likely to result in individual and relational dysfunction in the new generation, as is illustrated in *The Marital Puzzle* (Paul & Paul, 1975).

The two dimensions of differentiation of self/fusion and relational ethics/invisible loyalties speak to similar patterns in family development (Williamson, 1982a). Differentiation and balancing the ledger (or paying off indebtedness) reflect similar processes of dealing with the unresolved emotional attachments to the parental family and hence the transgenerational patterns and mandates. Boszormenyi-Nagy and Ulrich (1981) acknowledge this connection when they state that "it is the claim of the contextual approach that there is a dynamic linkage between steps toward differentiation and an engagement in the process of balancing one's debts and entitlements" (p. 171). Likewise, fusion, invisible loyalties, and transmitted grief reactions are expressions of the unending payment of multigenerational debts and ongoing emotional attachments to the family, which result in a sacrifice of autonomy and selfhood. In this regard, emotional cutoffs within a family will not work satisfactorily because they represent a breakdown in trustworthiness and equitability in relationships. Some research is beginning to support this conceptualization empirically (Bray, Williamson, & Malone, 1984).

Triangulation and split loyalties also reflect a similar pattern of relational behavior. The split loyalty indicates that "the child is charged with being loyal to one parent at the cost of his or her loyalty to the other" (Boszormenyi-Nagy & Ulrich, 1981, p. 165). While triangulation is considered a basic way in which individuals relate in any emotional system, split loyalties generally lead to dysfunctional behavior in families. However, as Bowen (1978) indicates, one of the most common triangles is that between a child and his or her mother and father. Triangulation is a way of dealing with fusion and anxiety in a two-person relationship and was initially conceptualized as the same process as fusion (Williamson, 1982a). However, our research indicates that triangulation, and hence split loyalties, represents a dimension that is distinct from differentiation/fusion (Bray *et al.*, 1984).

Personal Authority in the Family System

It is argued here that differentiation of self and relational ethics are in a Hegelian dialectic with intimacy (Williamson, 1982a). "Intimacy" is defined as the ability to be close but at the same time maintain clear boundaries to the self (Lewis, Beavers, Gossett, & Phillips, 1976; Williamson, 1982a). Intimacy comprises four components: trust, love–fondness, self-disclosure, and commitment (Bray *et al.,* 1984). It is viewed as a type of "voluntary fusion," which can be initiated or terminated at the discretion of the individual. Closeness without voluntariness or boundaries is synonymous with fusion and therefore is not in the same domain as intimacy.

Personal authority in the family system (PAFS; Williamson, 1982a) is offered as a synthesizing construct in the inherent tension between differentiation and intimacy, since this occurs in the biologic family and is then recreated in other significant personal relationships. This construct is a continuum, with personal authority at one pole and intergenerational intimidation at the other. The PAFS construct implies the behavioral patterns characteristic of an integrated and differentiated self (Bowen, 1978) exercising increased control over individual destiny in life and choosing personal health and well-being in a systemic sense. This can be observed behaviorally through the resolution of intrapsychic conflicts as well as through the resolution of relational intimacy issues. However, on the other hand, and at the same time, it includes an individual's reconnection and intimacy with the family of origin, while he or she *simultaneously* acts from a differentiated position *within* the family of origin. This dual and simultaneous consciousness of "differentness from" and "belongingness with" the family of origin is the essence of PAFS. This dual consciousness creates a sense of belonging to, and having a purpose in, the human experience (Williamson, 1982a; Bray *et al.,* 1984).

Family Life Cycle Progression

In addition to the multigenerational family patterning, there is a second process in family development—the predictable and unpredictable changes and events that occur throughout the family life cycle (Carter & McGoldrick, 1980). The predictable family life cycle events reflect common stages and sequences that families encounter across time. Carter and McGoldrick (1980) have provided a useful and clinically relevant discussion of these stages. It is hypothesized that the transition from one stage to the next can be a stressful period for families because it requires changes in old behavior patterns and the development of new coping skills and behaviors. The unpredictable events occurring across the life cycle reflect environmental influences usually out of the family's control, such as wars, economic recessions, illnesses, divorces, and unexpected deaths. It should be emphasized that although somewhat discrete stages or time periods have been identified, most families will not progress through these in a standard or similar fashion. The more important point is that this is a *continuous process* that evolves over time.

Family systems theory (Bowen, 1978; Kerr, 1981) and contextual family theory (Boszormenyi-Nagy & Ulrich, 1981) do not explicitly focus on family life cycle stages. However, this information is certainly incorporated in these theories and in the clinical practices related to them. This incorporation reflects the emphasis of these theories on the ongoing process of family development and change rather than on discrete stages or time periods. In the viewpoint of these theories, there are important "windows," or time periods, for change in families that offer discrete opportunities for change. If change is attempted before or after the appropriate time frame, families are less likely to be willing or able to complete the change successfully.

There is an *interaction* between family life cycle events and multi-generational family patterns, and both are necessary to fully understanding a family's functioning at any given point in time. These processes can operate in distinct ways and do not always go hand in hand. For example, the ongoing process of differentiation of self can occur at any life cycle stage, although we argue that it is more likely to occur at particular times rather than others. In a similar fashion, when transitions are difficult from one stage to another, it is more likely to be because these issues were not dealt with in previous generations. From this point of view, the multigenerational patterns constitute the *primary* influence on the ways in which families cope with predictable and unpredictable stresses and changes encountered throughout the life cycle. This is the central process. For example, Bowen (1978) argues that more differentiated people are *less* likely to develop symptoms in the face of environmental stresses and that they will recover from any symptoms quicker than less differentiated people. A study we discuss later provides some empirical support for this position. Although it is assumed that families are constantly changing and evolving, there are particular periods or stages in which certain changes usually occur or can be created for therapeutic gains. The development of PAFS is one example of such a stage. It is assumed that *all* families make some kind of adjustment during these periods if they continue to exist and that their basic responses are largely governed by patterns learned from their families of origin.

Harvey and Bray (1985) evaluated an intergenerational model of family functioning as a means of predicting current psychological and physical health functioning in college students. The methodology employed to test the model was structural equation modeling using the LISREL program (Jöreskog & Sörbom, 1978). The LISREL program provides a methodology for testing the direct and indirect effects of factors (unobserved variables) defined by multiple indicators (observed variables) to test the "fit" of a given theoretical model empirically with a set of data. Subjects were assessed twice, at a 2-month interval, on their relationships with parents, current peer relationships, life stress, current psychological adjustment, and physical health status, using several self-report measures of these concepts. The model that best fit the data in this study is presented in Figure 15-1. The model is based on the intergenerational approach proposed by Williamson (1982a), with appropriate modifications based on the differences that were expected as a result of the ages of the subjects. The arrows, or "path diagrams," indicate the direction of proposed causal influences. A single-directed path indicates a direct or indirect inferred causal connection between two factors, while a two-sided path

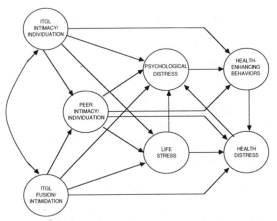

Figure 15-1. Intergenerational model of family functioning (from Harvey & Bray, 1985).

indicates a correlation between factors without a specification of direction of causality. The way to follow the direct and indirect paths is to trace the direction of the paths from one factor through the others.

The model predicts that Intergenerational Individuation/Intimacy and Intergenerational Intimidation are primary direct and indirect causal constructs that influence the functioning of Peer Individuation/Intimacy, Life Stress, Psychological Adjustment, and Health Enhancing Behaviors. For example, Intergenerational Individuation/ Intimacy has direct effects on Psychological Adjustment and Health Enhancing Behaviors but operates indirectly through Life Stress, Peer Individuation/Intimacy, and Psychological Adjustment on Health Distress. Peer Individuation/Intimacy is a direct cause of Psychological Adjustment and Health Enhancing Behaviors and operates indirectly through Life Stress on Health Distress. The model indicates that family and other relationships are important factors not only in psychological functioning but also in physical health. This supports Bowen (1978) and Williamson and Bray's (1985) hypotheses about the relationship between family relationship patterns and health. Overall, the study generally confirmed the proposed model and adds empirical support for this intergenerational perspective on family development.

Personal Authority in the Family System

Two important unanswered questions remain from this review of multigenerational family theory. The first concerns the impact on family development of the process of change. This question will be addressed in the next section. The second question relates to the predominant issues that need to be addressed by adults in the ongoing process of development.

We argue that there are two dominant psychosocial issues of adulthood. The first of these is how to leave the parental home *psychologically*. This implies getting control over one's own destiny and getting clear title to one's own life. Effective solutions result in recovery of aspects of the self that have been "loaned" in various significant relationships within the three-generational individual/family life cycle. This recovery of self will offer a way of dealing with fusion and triangulation (Bowen, 1978), of renegotiating invisible loyalties and mandates (Boszormenyi-Nagy & Spark, 1973), and of transcending the transgenerational (and mostly unconscious) transmission of the family heritage, especially that stemming from unmourned loss experiences (Paul, 1976).

The second dominant issue of adulthood is how to leave the parental home psychologically *and at the same time* stay connected to and intimate with the "former parents" (Williamson, 1981). The goal is to be able to take a "strong I position" (Bowen, 1978) and at the same time weave an intimate relational "pattern that connects" (Bateson, 1972). How does one terminate transgenerational loyalties when they are crippling the new self and *simultaneously* embrace one's own roots and biopsychosocial heritage?

These difficult questions are complicated further by the fact that every human being begins life in total dependency upon the parents. The infant's life is in their hands; if they turn away, the infant dies. Given this, how can one ever subsequently stand alone emotionally? Second, the adult cannot deny the persisting power of the biologic connection or "fire the family." Family members must reciprocate fully, both backward and forward in time, if they are to experience well-being.

The overall dilemma, then, is how to embrace and assimilate one's history and heritage in an explicit way and simultaneously be able to transcend the emotionality of the family. This is necessary in order to create a pleasing and productive personal reality in life, of a kind that can generate something distinctively new, free from the dominating indwelling of any foreign body from a previous generation.

The response to this dilemma is the development of PAFS, which has three dominant characteristics (Williamson, 1982a). The first of these is the ability to order and direct one's own thoughts and feelings, to choose to express or not express them, to respect one's judgments as an adequate basis for action, and to take full responsibility for the consequences of these actions. Second is the ability to voluntarily initiate, receive, or decline to receive intimacy (and to tolerate the same freedom in significant others) while simultaneously maintaining clear boundaries to the self. Third, PAFS includes the ability to relate to *all* other human beings, including the parents, as peers in the fundamental experience of being human.

The PAFS construct is understood systemically from quite different perspectives. That is, it is seen as both an individual and a family life cycle stage, and simultaneously as a unifying principle between individual and family theory, between differentiation and intimacy, between thinking and feeling, between "inner" and "outer." It is viewed as a set of relational skills and interactional behavior patterns, and not as a personality construct.

From the point of view of this chapter, PAFS—the family stage—occurs in the fourth and early fifth decade of life, with the majority of individuals clustering between 35 and 45 years of age (Williamson, 1981; Bray *et al.,* 1984). This is not axiomatic but grows out of observation as to when people seem to be able and willing to do (and not to do) this work of developing personal authority within the family of origin. Speculations as to why the timing may be so have been advanced elsewhere (Erikson, 1968; Levinson, Darrow, Klein, Levinson, & McKee, 1978; Williamson, 1981).

We propose that the termination of the intergenerational hierarchical power boundary with the parents is the necessary and sufficient condition of PAFS. This is the primary psychosocial task of this family developmental stage. The negotiation itself is a systemic event. There must be a clear hierarchical boundary in the family, with the parental relationship as the dominating power relationship, if young children are to mature and be able to leave home physically (Minuchin, 1974; Haley, 1980). On the other hand, this hierarchical boundary must be terminated in favor of psychosocial peerhood between the first and second generations if the adult is to be adult and leave home emotionally. Power can be redistributed across the generational boundary through a renegotiation of relational politics. There will be a subsequent rebalancing of positions within the family through changing relational patterns and cognitive structures. This is the prototype of power politics.

Against this background, the essence of PAFS is the giving up of the *need to be parented.* No further parenting of any sort is needed, expected, or demanded. The adult in the second generation no longer has need for a parent in the social psychological sense of the term. The parents themselves are viewed as being A-OK just as they are, as human beings. Simultaneously, the adult son or daughter can and will be different in ways unique to the new self. Parents may stay the same, and the son or daughter *can* become different. For most adults, this is a radically new realization. The persons who were formerly "the parents" are now available (some more than others) for new intimate relationships as peers. The most important fact about the past at this point is that it is past.

We propose that PAFS addresses the two key intergenerational psychosocial tasks, which are specific expressions of the two dominant psychological issues of adulthood. The first of these is the continuing emotional dependency upon parents (fusion). The second is the drama of the family romance (or triangulation into the parental marriage, which results in split loyalties). All of this prepares the way for a mature intimacy between the generations by building toward peerhood. Intimacy is possible only between peers. Intimacy requires relational trust via assurance that it is now safe for the parent to reveal the private inner self. A child is not safe in this regard, since he or she (of whatever chronological age) is constantly judging the parenting (and so the parent). The emerging adult becomes compassionate toward, and nonjudgmental of, the parents' humanness. There also has to be "otherness" for intimacy to occur. As the adult adopts a peer stance, and as the older parent reveals the self, the adult son or daughter develops an awareness of the "otherness" of the older parent. This sets the scene for the creation of a new sense of the "otherness," that is, differentiation of the self.

Overall, this process is a gradual one, occurring informally over a period of 10 years or more. However, there are discrete events and historical watershed moments that can be planned in advance and completed "on schedule." This planning is the role of the consultation sequences to be described later. For example, the family romance may have been cooling for some time, but this ending can be acknowledged in a moment of closure in a planned sequence on a historical occasion in the therapist's office.

Subsequently, after the formal therapeutic consultation has ended, the personal authority work continues informally through a continuing discovery by the adult not only of his or her belongingness within the family of origin but also, and most important, his or her differentness from either parent. This differentness is declared and celebrated within the relational experience. There is a continuing and reciprocal coevolution within individuals and between the generations. The therapy process is time limited, but the informal process continues throughout life.

Finally, the effects of renegotiating intergenerational politics within the family of origin are likely to generalize to all parental figures, such as spouses (and other lovers), children (by projection and by the transposing of the generations), clergy, bosses, teachers, former supervisors, and former therapists. The effects will also bring increased satisfaction with one's occupation and work (Bray, Williamson, & Malone, 1986).

CHANGE PROCESSES

The processes of change within families revolve around the basic theoretical principles discussed previously. Change in certain behavior patterns and expressions of multigenerational family processes, such as differentiation of self and personal authority in the family, is assumed to be occurring constantly throughout the family life cycle.

The aspects of family life that change represent expressions of these basic multigenerational family patterns interacting with predictable and unpredictable life cycle events. Functional aspects of the self are always in flux, depending on the relational and environmental context (Kerr, 1981, 1984). Triangulation in emotional systems is ongoing and occurs in various forms, depending on the stresses on the system. The expression of covert and split loyalties also operates in a similar manner. There is a constant oscillating of the balance of the ledger of indebtedness, preferably in the direction of relational balance and trust.

According to Bowen (1978), individuals tend to attract and marry others who are at a similar level of differentiation. Thus more differentiated families tend to produce more differentiated children, who select more differentiated mates, who produce more differentiated children, and so on. A similar process occurs in the case of less differentiated families. This process can take a turn in the opposite direction, however, when a particular child is "selected" to receive the unresolved projections within a family and becomes the "scapegoat" and hence a dysfunctional child. This child will emerge with a significantly lower level of differentiation and therefore start a downward spiral, perhaps eventually resulting in later generations being caught in schizophrenic transactions, the ultimate sign of fusion. On the other hand, if individuals maintain trustworthiness in their relationships and continue to pay back indebtedness by balancing the ledger, families will continue to evolve and grow in a positive manner throughout the life cycle (Boszormenyi-Nagy & Ulrich, 1981).

However, without some concerted, conscious effort on the part of one or more individuals in a family, multigenerational patterns do not change greatly. More specifically, Bowen (1978) and Kerr (1981) indicate that the *basic* level of differentiation of self that an individual emerges with from his or her family of origin remains constant throughout the family life cycle. Likewise, Boszormenyi-Nagy and Ulrich (1981) argue that individuals spend their lifetimes paying back acquired indebtedness by fulfilling multigenerational mandates and legacies. This process often involves a "revolving slate," in which patterns are constantly repeated again and again across the generations. Framo (1981) also indicates that certain internalized object representations gained through the projective identification process as a child remain generally unchanged throughout adulthood.

Symptom Development

When a certain level of stress and anxiety develops in a family (this level is determined uniquely for each family), it activates the fusion and unresolved emotional issues for families, and symptoms will probably develop. The stress arises from interactions among family members, external life stressors, and family life cycle changes. Since transitions between stages can be particularly stressful, symptoms are more likely to develop during these periods.

Bowen (1978) states that symptoms are usually expressed in three ways: (1) through marital conflict, which tends to appear in symmetrical marital relationships; (2) through dysfunction in a spouse, which tends to happen in complementary marital relationships and may involve physical illness, psychological dysfunction, and/or social dysfunction; and (3) through dysfunction in one or more children, which results from triangling the child through the family projection process. The child's dysfunction may follow any one of the three patterns described for dysfunction in a spouse. It is important to note that one or all of these symtoms may develop in a family over time. The symptoms are simply expressions of the way a family responds to stress, given their basic level of differentiation. The higher the level of differentiation, the more stress is required before a family will develop symptoms. In addition, a more differentiated family will "bounce back" quicker following a stressful event than a less differentiated family.

Boszormenyi-Nagy and Ulrich (1981) state that symptom development is probable when there is a breakdown of trustworthiness in relationships because of a lack of balanced or multilateral care and accountability of actions. This may occur because of invisible loyalty payments, stagnation in the payment of debts, and/or the revolving slate of repeated dysfunctional behavior patterns. The particular symptoms that develop depend on a number of biopsychosocial factors and family developmental issues.

In our view, symptoms may develop because the reasons outlined frequently represent repeated attempts at solutions to problems that simply do not work (Watzlawick, Weakland, & Fisch, 1974). While symptoms may represent obedience to transgenerational or multigenerational family mandates, loyalties, fusion, or projections, the problems and "solutions" are played out in the contemporary intergenerational relationships in the three-generational family context. If these relationships are changed in the present generation, it is assumed that they are resolved and that an upward shift will occur in future generations.

There is a particular period during which this type of change is most appropriate and available—when an individual has reached adulthood. When an adult has entered the fourth or fifth decade of life and has not terminated the intergenerational hierarchical boundary with the first generation, there is an incongruous (and therefore dysfunctional) hierarchical organization within the family. The adult in the second generation will not experience the self as adult in the presence of the parents (or other authority figures). The adult's consciousness may become so incongruent that if too much of the self is forfeited, only brief, obligatory visits to the parental home can be tolerated. The intergenerational relational pattern no longer flows, because it is politically frozen at an earlier developmental stage, which is no longer psychologically appropriate or emotionally authentic. This is likely to produce problems in both the nuclear family and the work setting, as discussed previously. When this political freeze occurs, it is due primarily to *intergenerational intimidation.* This intimidation finds its source in the protectiveness of parents, in the fear of punishment by parents, or in both.

Change in Therapy

The degree of change possible in therapy is viewed very differently by various multigenerational theorists. Family systems theory (Bowen, 1978; Kerr, 1981) and contextual family therapy (Boszormenyi-Nagy & Ulrich, 1981) are surprisingly pessimistic about the possibility of change in therapy. Kerr (1981) indicates that changes in the basic level of differentiation occur very slowly, in small increments, through a systematic effort that takes many years. Framo (1976, 1981), Paul (1976; Paul & Paul, 1975), and Williamson (1982a, 1982b), on the other hand, are much more optimistic about, and encouraged by, the possibility of change in therapy. The pessimism has been the source of a general critique of the transgenerational viewpoint. Although the theory is useful for understanding family processes, it leaves little room for hope and change in the current family context. In this regard, the pessimism concerning change may betray its Bowen theory's psychoanalytic origins. The intellectual family of origin work of family of origin theories may not yet be complete.

In our view, *change is possible,* and sometimes to a great degree; there is some empirical evidence to support this view (Bray *et al.,* 1986). All responsibility for change rests with the new adult. When he or she changes, then the intergenerational, and hence multigenerational, relational patterns inevitably change. In the important act of illuminating the circularity and recursiveness in all human behavior, "systems thinking" can readily obscure the equally important matter of personal responsibility for change and problem resolution. The desired change first occurs in the way in which the adult internally holds or perceives himself or herself to be, that is, as fully adult or as less than adult. This changed internal posture then becomes evident in actual changes in relational behavior. The responsibility for initiating such changes can lie only with the younger adult.

Therapeutically, the change process works from three fundamental assumptions: (1) that benevolent and desirable change in the client's life is involuntary, inescapable, and already under way; (2) that this inevitable change occurs naturally, with exquisite timing, so as to be in perfect consort with the personal rhythm of the client's life; and (3) that the client comes for consultation simply to ensure that he or she will not inadvertently force the pace of change or get unduly ahead of himself or herself. There is no thought, language, or behavior from the client that cannot, with a little imagination, be framed or reframed to fit with these assumptions.

THE CONSULTATION PROCESS

The consultation method, developed in tandem with the theoretical point of view that we have summarized, may be described as short-term, strategic, experiential intergenerational family therapy. It is *short term* in that most people do the work in 9 to 12 months, which is relatively short term for transgenerational therapy. This period covers time spent working with the consultant and does not necessarily include time spent before and after consultation in the normal processes of development and change. The method is *strategic* in that the preparation carefully identifies the nuances of strategic language to use for initiative and response as the client later moves carefully to explore the family emotional system. It is *experiential* in that the consultation in the very small group is first and foremost engaging theater and live drama. The family story is enacted, not reported. It is contemporary, not remembered. Finally, the method is *intergenerational* in that the focus is restricted primarily to the business of the "self with parents" as the drama is being played out today. The focus does not travel extensively across several generations; the relevant and important issues are here and now. Siblings are often consulted, but invariably in an ancillary role—unless one of them has been "parent" to the client. Other members of the extended family may offer information or support, but the basic work revolves around the high-voltage relationship of self with parents. This is the arena for the intergenerational power issues and the biologic conduit to the multigenerational family emotional system.

Careful self-preparation by the client is essential for the work. Many necessary preconditions must be met beforehand (c.f. Williamson, 1981). For example, whatever rage, grief, confusion, and/or denial may be present needs to be resolved before opening direct political negotiations with "former parents." The therapeutic consultations will work to reduce the intergenerational intimidation. The client needs to be able to speak calmly and from an adult posture, since any intense emotionality will get in the way. The client also needs to move beyond demanding or blaming, or any other such "childish" stance. The therapist is there as guarantor that the renegotiation *can* happen. It is assumed that if it has happened to one person, then, in principle, it can happen to anybody. The very small group provides opportunity for ventilation and catharsis for as long as it is needed. It also makes explicit and then escalates the absurdity of any continuing intense feelings about events that are so far past. There is no shortcut for this critical work of emotional preparation.

At times, parents may be invited in for an early consultation before all of the preliminary work is completed. This usually occurs for one or two reasons. First, the parents may provide some useful information to help the client move past an impasse or get "unstuck" around some particular issues. Second, the consultant may not have been able to clearly "read" the client and the family as to their joint readiness. In this case, it soon becomes apparent during the in-office consultation that the client is not yet ready to terminate the intergenerational hierarchical boundary. In both cases, it is important that the consultant provide some protection and support for both generations during the consultation; that is, it is usually not productive to allow the client to use the session as an opportunity to publicly harass, blame, or yell at the parents. In addition, it is useful to view this type of session as an assessment of the client's progress and as practice for the "real thing" when the client and his or her family are finally ready.

The goal of this general preparation (including preliminary visits with parents) is for the client to move to a position from which it is possible to know *directly* the persons behind the roles of the parents. This is quite different from knowing about them or from the reassuring "closeness" experienced by children. Essentially, it means that the client experiences directly with and from the parent the inner private meanings of the parent's historical life experiences and significant life events. Knowing the parents in this reciprocal sense demystifies and humanizes them. It is, par excellence, the experience that creates the road to peerhood between the generations.

This "knowing" occurs through direct conversations and, especially, through eye-to-eye contact. As the subtle nuances of private meanings are conveyed in this way, and as the parent is humanized, power is redistributed and rebalanced, as eye engages eye and as the client probes, challenges, answers, and, in general, discovers who this "former parent" really is today.

Ambience of the Consultation Process

The consultant adopts a particular stance toward the processes of change. This stance is taken in order to promote therapeutic change, and, as noted previously, the assumptions are not necessarily believed to be "really true." For example, it is assumed that change has long since been under way, since the client is in the office. Change is inevitable and involuntary, even preordained. Everything that happens now in the client's life, at least everything that is worth reporting, is evidence of this change in some form. If it can be talked about, then it is "change," since "no change" is not anything and so cannot be talked about. It is further assumed that the client is always in exactly the right place at any given time, ready and poised for further change. Everything the client thinks, says, or does is a fruitful step in the right direction, whether that step be forward, backward, sideways, or just an elegant pirouette. It takes just a little extra imagination from the consultant to bring this frame into focus. We assert that this "frame" is as "true" as any other and that it is particularly more *useful* than most for helping the client change. The most intense feelings of "stuckness" are themselves compelling evidence of the energy and commitment available for change. Indeed, it can now be acknowledged openly that the client comes for consultation in order to get help in controlling structuring, and slowing down a change process that is threatening to break away and head toward an impulsive, and perhaps rash, transformation.

It is not that the client necessarily "believes" this pattern of meanings offered by the consultant. But as a result, the client does invariably experience more space, a greater freedom of movement, and a more playful stance toward his or her life—all of which serves to reduce, and hence confirm, the very change already alleged to have been taking place. The nimble therapist jumps on and off the carousel of the client's behavior at will, so as to increase or decrease client momentum when it seems most useful to do so at a given moment. The only serious threat to the client's otherwise inevitable progress toward resolution is the universal temptation to get there ahead of one's self. If the consultant gets lucky, he or she can slow things down. (Of course, the consultant will also have to cope with his or her own impulse to arrive early.) Occasionally, a client will practice developing a skill at bringing change to a complete standstill temporarily and *voluntarily*. Once the client can *stop* change voluntarily, it is an easy next step to *make change happen* voluntarily. Stopping change is difficult, but once it is mastered, learning to create change becomes relatively easy.

The following are examples of clinical dialogue in which the therapist takes the stance just described. The first example is taken from an initial session, where the presenting problem is "stuckness" with parents.

Therapist: What brings you here at this time?

Client: I feel like I am in a bad place with my parents, especially my father. I'd like to do something about it before either of them dies.

Therapist: So a lot of things are changing right now and that's unsettling.

Client: No, not at all. It's just the opposite. Nothing is changing. I feel stuck with them.

Therapist: And you can't help feeling less patient with that than before.

Client: That's right.

Therapist: So your head is full of all these pictures about how things might be different . . . if you're not careful.

Client: But it won't happen.

Therapist: Good, I hope not. So the problem is that you do have all these different pictures about change in your mind.

Client: No, the problem is I don't do anything about it.

Therapist: Yet these pictures won't go away. You find you are thinking about them more and more and more.

Client: True . . .

Therapist: I'm afraid that means that there's a lot of change threatening on the horizon. It is probably too late to stop it now. You may need help keeping it at bay . . . or at least under control.

Client: Well, I do think about it a lot.

Therapist: That's what worries me. Maybe you could just start by thinking about maybe soon thinking less about it. You don't have to think less about it just yet. But begin to think now about maybe thinking less about it later. It won't be easy.

The second example is also from a session in which the client is complaining of being chronically stuck with parents and unable to change. This example illustrates the use of absurdity in reframing the "stuckness" as actually being part of the change process itself.

Client: I haven't talked to my parents in over a year.

Therapist: That's good.

Client: It could be another year before I do.

Therapist: Perfect!

Client: What's so good about that?

Therapist: Well, through a great team effort between you and Mom and Dad, you have now prepared the ground for a very fruitful contact and conversation.

Client: I don't follow that at all.

Therapist: Well, think of it this way. Some folks talk with their parents every few days. It gets not to mean much and not much gets said. But you have now intuitively and very patiently prepared the way for a real summit conference, with an agenda that really matters. You are poised, ready for dramatic change.

Client: So what should I do?

Therapist: You could do what you've already thought about doing.

Client: Yes, but why would I say I was calling?

Therapist: Because you know they are missing you.

Client: I couldn't say that.

Therapist: True. But you could mention it as something you had just realized that you couldn't possibly say.

Client: I'm not sure I could even say that.

Therapist: Right. But you could think about it even in that very moment when you're not saying it and they would sense it anyway.

Client: How would they sense it?

Therapist: I've never figured that out.

Client: How would I know if they did?

Therapist: By the way they wouldn't respond to it. So you should concentrate on what they are careful not to respond to as you are thinking about not being able to say it.

Client: This is beginning to sound a bit silly.

Therapist: That's how you know it's important. But it doesn't mean you have to change it yet.

Client: Well, I'll try it.

Therapist: Just as long as you know you don't have to do it.

Client: I might do it.

Therapist: Well, either do that or something different which ever happens. The nice thing is it will work either way. For the time has probably come.

There are four presumptions underlying the consultation process illustrated above (and below). First, *all change is considered benevolent,* or at least potentially benevolent. Of course, the client is always close to creating that benevolent meaning. This attitude toward "change" creates a context in which it is easy for clients to engage in autohypnotic experiences, in which they can transform their own consciousness about self-in-the-world and self-in-the-family, and self-talking-to-self and changing self (Erickson & Rossi, 1979).

Second, the therapy process is *noncoercive.* The client's authority, rhythm, and personal timing are of the essence. The consultation conversations probe and test, promote and encourage, but the determining condition for change is the client's personal timetable. The client is continually checking with and reading the older generation. Consequently, the rhythm of the client will assimilate and reflect the readiness of the parents as well. Clients learn to decode the family's language and to know which parental behavior means "wait" and which means "ready." The important restructuring of intergenerational relationships does not occur (obviously, it cannot occur) until both generations are "ready."

The concepts of circularity and recursiveness have called into question hard polarities like "either/or" in favor of "both/and" (Taggart, 1983). An outcome characterized as "both/and" is the desirable goal in intergenerational consultation. Ideally, neither generation ultimately emerges with greater well-being at the expense of the other. For this reason, the consultant takes a stance of "multidirectional partiality" (Boszormenyi-Nagy & Ulrich, 1981), although the underlying bias is in favor of individual freedom, and clearly the new hope lies with the new generation.

Third, the psychological tone of the consultation process is one of *playfulness and absurdity* throughout. This helps to create distance and to increase emotional objectivity and therefore the thinking (and reframing) response. In this way, the client can construct a more flexible and playful, and therefore more useful, "personal reality," especially with regard to personal history. Many people acquire this skill spontaneously; clients have to be taught. So there is a repeated use of a role-playing style in which the client plays the parent and the consultant plays the client. Outlandish conversations follow, in which the consultant thinks the unthinkable and speaks the unspeakable. This apparently cavalier boundary crossing sabotages intergenerational intimidation and teaches clients new skills in the strategic use of language, nuance, and humor.

Following are illustrations of role playing in which clients deal with considerable intergenerational intimidation by playing the role of a parent, with the consultant in the role of the client. The following role play of a phone conversation occurs when a daughter (Joan) calls her father (Ned). The consultant plays the daughter, and the client plays the father. This conversation begins to make explicit the covert process of the family romance.

Father: Hello.
Daughter: Hi Ned, is that yourself?
Father: Who is this?
Daughter: Your little ray of sunshine.
Father: Is this Joan?
Daughter: I knew you'd recognize me.
Father: You're talking a bit strange, aren't you? Did you want to talk to your mother?

Daughter: No, no, keep your wife out of this, Ned. Just you and me, Dad.

Father: Well, what do you want?

Daughter: Oh, I just want you, Ned. You know how it is. Nothing has changed.

Father: Honey, are you feeling alright? You don't sound like yourself at all.

Daughter: Just to hear you call me honey makes it alright. That makes my day. Think about it. I'll call again soon.

In the second example, a client (Jack) plays his mother (Nona), while the consultant plays Jack. Jack places the call, and Dad answers the phone.

Father: Hello.

Son: Hi Dad, this is Jack. Is your wife there?

Father: You want to talk to your mother?

Son: Yeah, or your wife. Whichever one is handy.

Father: Hold on.

Mother: Hello son, how nice to hear from you.

Son: Hi, Nona. How's he treating you?

Mother: What?

Son: That old boy you are living with, is he treating you alright, or do you need me to talk to him?

Mother: John, what do you mean? Your father is wonderful to me.

Son: Okay Nona, just checking up. I'm always worrying about you. Looking out for you, you know. I mean, you're number one with me, and I'm going to see that the world treats you right, beginning with that old fellow you married.

Mother: Jack, you sound crazy!

Son: Yeah, about time, isn't it Nona?

Fourth the consultant's feedback is *affectively low-key* and is addressed simultaneously to multiple levels of awareness. Interpretations and reframing are offered primarily through disclaimer, or in the form of "denial" or at least nagging doubt as to their relevance, and only as "truth" to be accepted when the consultant gets caught in it. He or she frequently escalates the inherent absurdity and natural paradox prevalent in every life and in most intimate relational patterns. Since the therapeutic goal is the development of the personal authority of the client, the consultant maintains a low emotional profile throughout. Most of the impact of the consultation comes through the use of the language chosen and the circular ideation employed. An example of such a clinical dialogue follows:

Client: My boss was really rude today. Sometimes I can't stand his incompetence.

Therapist: Okay, but I don't see how you connect that to your father.

Client: I didn't connect it to my father.

Therapist: Oh, I must have missed something.

Client: Well, does it have something to do with my father?

Therapist: I don't see myself that it has to. I mean it is not as if your father didn't acknowledge your person in the way you wanted.

Client: Well, often he didn't.

Therapist: And even that doesn't necessarily mean that he still is the number one man in your life today.

Client: I'd hate to think that were true.

Therapist: You don't have to. Even if we knew it to be true . . . which you don't yet. That's one of the reasons I mentioned it as not being necessarily true.

Client: You mean you think it is true?

Therapist: I'm not sure what I meant for you to think. I simply mean that this might not be a good time for you to think of it as true. If you wanted, you could save it as something to consider being true at another time.

Client: I'll have to think about that.

Therapist: I'm concerned that you think that you "have to." You don't have to. Which, of course, doesn't mean that you can't.

Client: I'm getting confused now.

Therapist: Yes, but have you noticed that it's a clearer kind of confusion?

Client: Yes, in a way it is.

Therapist: That is a good first step.

Client: Can you explain that?

Therapist: If you will remember to come back to it later.

Client: I do want to separate my boss from my father.

Therapist: I think you've started.

Obviously, in none of these instances of role playing are the clients expected to carry on conversations as they are played in the office. But playing it like this in fantasy does produce a new freedom for the client, who does subsequently talk in some different and more useful ways to his or her parents.

Assessment

Formal and informal assessment of clients is an ongoing procedure during the consultation process. The assessment includes an evaluation of the client's current psychological and social functioning and of his or her physical health status as well (Williamson & Bray, 1985), all of which is essential for a complete understanding of family functioning. There are several methods of assessment. The first is to take a family history that focuses on family relationships and patterns of development over time. A second method is to have the client write a history of growing up in the family of origin, which is then read to the consultant during the session. Third, the genogram is a useful way to summarize the client's family relationships (Guerin & Pendagast, 1976). The genogram includes a list of important life events (e.g., divorces, significant illnesses) and life changes (moves, new jobs), providing a concise social and psychological record of the client and his or her family.

When gathering the family history and compiling the genogram, it is important to assess the current life cycle stage for the individual and the family. Since the transition from one family life cycle stage to another is usually a highly stressful time that may result in symptom development (Carter & McGoldrick, 1980), attention to these life cycle changes further clarifies the context for the problems and may have important implications for treatment. When evaluating the family's life cycle stage, three issues are important: (1) the current problems and symptoms associated with this stage, (2) how the family has coped with previous life cycle transitions, and (3) how the adult's family of origin coped with similar life cycle stages.

Observing the way in which the client describes his or her family, rather than focusing only on content, also provides important data. A clinical assessment of level of fusion, differentiation, or personal authority can be made by listening to the "music," that is, the way in which the client presents information. Less differentiated individuals tend to blame others for their actions, do not take responsibility for their lives and their health, and/or are frequently "stuck" in indecision. Low personal authority is indicated by the client's being intimidated by significant hierarchical figures in his or her life, especially parents. Such individuals are inhibited and in general function at a lower level, particularly around authority figures. They also have difficulty forming close, intimate relationships. On the other hand, more differentiated individuals express their opinions through "I statements," such as, "I think, I believe, I want, I prefer," rather than through "we statements." Individuals behaving with personal authority also take responsibility and make decisions for their lives and are not intimidated by authority figures. These processes can also be observed in homework assignments involving letters that are written to or taped for parents during the very small group sessions.

More formal assessment is useful in certain circumstances. The Personal Authority in the Family System Questionnaire (PAFS-Q; Bray *et al.,* 1984) is one such instrument that is designed to assess intergenerational processes in the three-generational family system. The PAFS-Q is a self-report measure that clients can complete on their own. It is easily hand scored and provides eight scale scores that measure these behaviors and processes (individuation, intimacy, intimidation, personal authority, and triangulation). The PAFS-Q is useful not only as an assessment device but also as an intervention tool to help clients begin to think about the current status of their intergenerational family relationships (Bray & Williamson, 1987).

Consultation Method

The social context for the consultation is a very small group of four persons (Williamson, 1982b; Williamson & Malone, 1983). The group is a Greek chorus for the consultant. There is seldom a focus upon intragroup relationships, since each person is going *directly* to the source in the family of origin. There is also little perceived transference, since each person is consistently being pointed back to the personal family system for resolution and connection (Bray *et al.,* 1986). The small group itself becomes like a primary family of siblings. There is a remarkable mirroring effect between the clients and an even more remarkable reciprocal feedback and support for each other's work. The preparation experience in the group allows for an adequate emotional catharsis over time and for detoxification of the self from intensely negative feelings of disappointment, grief, and rage. It is crucial that this catharsis and detoxification occur *before* beginning significant political renegotiation with "former parents."

The small-group experience consists of various sequences and rituals (Williamson, 1982a, 1982b; Williamson & Malone, 1983). It begins with a written autobiography, followed by audiotaped letters to parents; next come audiotaped phone conversations, followed by informal conversations at the parental home. These visits are mostly to observe, in order to begin to identify questions and issues for the direct work with parents that is to follow. Consultation with siblings, with members of the extended family, and with older friends of the parents may also occur at this time.

From all of this, the client produces an agenda of items for discussion (and renegotiation) with "former parents." The sequence concludes with the in-office consultation with the parents and the subsequent debriefing (Williamson, 1982b). The purpose of these in-office conversations is to provide an opportunity for the client explicitly (1) to give up the little boy or girl role; (2) to terminate the family romance; (3) to face the aging and approaching deaths of parents, and therefore, by implication, of the self; (4) to express appreciation for the lives of the parents and for what they have contributed to the client's self that he or she particularly values; and (5) to declare and celebrate the differentness of the new self of the client from either the mother or the father. It is not that either one is right or better; each expression of differentness is perfect for each at this time. Together, the family learns that "differentness" can coexist with belongingness and that neither of these aspects needs to deny the other. Finally, special rituals may be used for termination with a deceased parent (Williamson, 1978).

CASE EXAMPLE

A woman in her mid-30s, herself a member of the helping professions, came in for consultation. She had been married for several years, had two children, and had developed a successful private practice. She told the consultant that she and her family had moved back a year earlier to the city where her parents lived in order to be closer to them as they got older and ready to die. However, she felt very burdened and saddened by her feelings of intense responsibility and guilt toward her parents, not much of which she really understood.

She spent a few months in weekly consultation in preparation for the 3-day in-office visit with her parents (Williamson, 1982b). The preparation began with reflections upon her autobiography, followed by the playing of imaginary audiotaped conversations with her parents. Next came taped phone conversations and, finally, live conversations in the parental home. All of these interactions were brought to the consultation office for reflection and catharsis and, ultimately, for the identification of items from which she constructed her agenda for the in-office visit with her parents.

During the in-office conversations within the primary triangle, the client gave up her father as the "number one love" in her life while confirming his lifelong position as the number two man. She explained that her husband was now moving into the top spot and acknowledged the loss and sadness for both parties involved in this transition. Her father observed that he had not been the number one man for many years now and that therefore this was unnecessary and he didn't really understand it as he looked away to hide the silent tears. Second, the client explained to her mother, who behaved generally in a helpless and dependent fashion, about several important ways in which she already was or intended to be different as a woman from her mother. This included both her sexuality and the ways in which she had divided her energy between homemaking and an outside profession. She also acknowledged explicitly, with regret and compassion, mother's deeper and persisting attitude of disappointment and despair in her own life. And while doing this with compassion, the daughter further declared her own sense of excitement and purpose in her own life.

Third, she gave up her role once and for all as both the dependent and the protective child, congratulated her father and mother on the superb job they had done, and took them off the hook now and forever as "parents." Finally, she listed the particular ways in which she admired her parents, each in turn, and described in detail what she valued in her life that she had learned and incorporated from them. The session concluded with some conversation about mutual hopes and expectations for the future relationship between these two generations. The sadness at the explicit acknowledgment of the dying and approaching deaths of the parents was tempered by the new sense of authenticity and intimacy between these people connected by both blood and love.

The client later described herself as having "more space in her life and in her head." She felt well connected to her parents but no longer responsible for their happiness or survival. Her father died about a year after these conversations. The client grieved appropriately and was pleased that most of what she had wanted to say and negotiate with her father had been completed prior to his death. A weeping mother, repeatedly and insatiably seeking solace, declared, "We have all suffered this terrible loss and must pull together." In a nonrejecting, but firm, way the client replied, "Yes, but this loss is quite different for you than for me. You have just lost your husband, whereas I still have my husband. I miss my father, but it's not the same as the loss for you." In this way, she expressed and celebrated her own new sense of differentiation within the family of origin. While remaining supportive of her mother, she also relieved herself of carrying a burden of grief and sadness for her father's wife at the loss of her husband.

Evaluation of the Consultation Method

Bray *et al.* (1986) evaluated the effects of this consultation process on marital and family functioning. Seventy former clients who completed the intergenerational family therapy (IFT) process with and as described by Williamson (1982a) were compared to 25 former clients (controls) who participated in systems-oriented marital therapy that did not include work on their families of origin. Clients completed a therapy evaluation questionnaire, the PAFS-Q (Bray *et al.*, 1984), and the Dyadic Adjustment Scale (DAS; Spanier, 1976) after therapy and also retrospectively as they perceived themselves and families before therapy.

A number of significant differences were found between the groups and among the IFT clients. Clients who participated in IFT reported a significant decrease in intergenerational triangulation and intimidation and an increase in personal authority as compared to clients who participated in marital therapy alone. The IFT clients also reported significantly more change in satisfaction with peer relationships and with their occupation than did the control subjects. Compared to a normative sample of adults aged 30–50, former clients in the IFT group reported significantly more individuation and personal authority and less triangulation and intergenerational intimidation following therapy. There were no significant differences between the normative sample and the control subjects following therapy. An interesting finding was that IFT clients who brought one or both parents into the office for consultation reported significantly more positive change in their level of individuation and personal authority and simultaneously less intergenerational intimidation than those IFT clients who did not have their parents come into the office for consultation.

Further controlled research is needed in order to investigate which aspects of the consultation process are most effective in creating change. However, the findings of this study lend some initial empirical support to the effectiveness of this type of family consultation. In addition, the other studies reviewed (Bray *et al.*, 1984; Bray, Harvey, & Williamson, 1987; Harvey & Bray, 1985; Williamson & Bray, 1985) provide empirical support for this theory of intergenerational family development.

CONCLUSIONS

We believe that the intergenerational family perspective provides a rich and powerful way of understanding family development and change across the generations. Although previous multigenerational perspectives (Boszormenyi-Nagy & Ulrich, 1981; Bowen, 1978; Kerr, 1981) have presented models for understanding family development, these models have not identified the *critical* developmental issues for adults in the middle generation. The development of PAFS is offered as the critical process for this family life cycle stage (Williamson, 1981). The multigenerational theorists have also been criticized for the long duration of therapy and for their general pessimism concerning the possibility of change in families. We have argued here that change *is* possible, often to a great degree. The use of strategic "technology" and interventions provides a context and a means with which to accomplish these goals. We believe that the application of these types of interventions within an intergenerational family framework offers a systemic and cybernetic perspective for family development and an effective means for helping families and individuals change.

REFERENCES

Bandura, A. (1977). *Social-learning theory.* Englewood Cliffs, NJ: Prentice-Hall.

Bateson, G. (1972). *Steps to an ecology of mind.* New York: Ballantine Books.

Boszormenyi-Nagy, I. & Spark, G. (1973). *Invisible loyalties.* New York: Harper & Row.

Boszormenyi-Nagy, I., & Ulrich, D. (1981). Contextual family therapy. In A. Gurman & D. Kniskern (Eds.), *Handbook of family therapy* (pp. 159–186). New York: Brunner/Mazel.

Bowen, M. (1978). *Family therapy in clinical practice.* New York: Jason Aronson.

Bray, J. H., Harvey, D. M., & Williamson, D. S. (1987). Intergenerational family relationships: An evaluation of theory and measurement. *Psychotherapy, 24,* 516–528.

Bray, J. H., & Williamson, D. S., (1987). Assessment of intergenerational family relationships. In A. J. Hovestadt & M. Fine (Eds.), *Family of origin therapy: Application in clinical practice* (pp. 31–43) [Family Therapy Collections]. Rockville, MD: Apsen Press.

Bray, J. H., Williamson, D. S., & Malone, P. E. (1984). Personal authority in the family system: Development of a questionnaire to measure personal authority in intergenerational family processes. *Journal of Marital and Family Therapy, 10,* 167–178.

Bray, J. H., Williamson, D. S., & Malone, P. E. (1986). An evaluation of an intergenerational consultation process to increase personal authority in the family system. *Family Process, 25,* 423–436.

Carter, E. A., & McGoldrick, M. (Eds.). (1980). *The family life cycle: A framework for family therapy.* New York: Gardner Press.

Erickson, M. H., & Rossi, E. L. (1979). *Hypotherapy: An exploratory casebook.* New York: Halsted Press.

Erikson, E. H. (1968). *Identity: Youth and crisis.* New York: W. W. Norton.

Framo, J. (1976). Family of origin as a therapeutic resource for adults in marital and family therapy: You can and should go home again. *Family Process, 15,* 193–210.

Framo, J. (1981). The integration of marital therapy with sessions with family of origin. In A. Gurman & D. Kniskern (Eds.), *Handbook of family therapy* (pp. 133–158). New York: Brunner/Mazel.

Friedrich, W., & Pollack, S. (1982). Extreme interpersonal sensitivity in family members. *American Journal of Family Therapy, 10,* 27–34.

Guerin, P. J., & Pendagast, E. G. (1976). Evaluation of a family system and genogram. In P. J. Guerin (Ed.), *Family therapy: Theory and practice.* New York: Gardner Press.

Haley, J. (1980). *Leaving home: Therapy with disturbed young people.* New York: McGraw-Hill.

Harvey, D., & Bray, J. H. (1985, August). *Family process determinants of psychological and health distress: A structural equation analysis.* Paper presented at the American Psychological Association annual convention, Los Angeles, CA.

Jöreskog, K. G., & Sörbom, D. (1978). *LISREL: Analysis of linear structural relationships by the method of maximum likelihood.* Chicago, IL: National Educational Resources.

Kerr, M. E. (1981). Family systems theory and therapy. In A. Gurman & D. Kniskern (Eds.), *Handbook of family therapy* (pp. 226–264). New York: Brunner/Mazel.

Kerr, M. E. (1984). Theoretical base for differentiation of self in one's family of origin. *The Clinical Supervisor, 2,* 3–36.

Levinson, D. J., Darrow, C. N., Klein, E. B., Levinson, M. H., & McKee, B. (1978). *The seasons of a man's life.* New York: Ballantine Books.

Lewis, J. M., Beavers, W. R., Gossett, J. T., & Phillips, V. A. (1976). *No single thread.* New York: Brunner/Mazel.

Minuchin, S. (1974). *Families and family therapy.* Cambridge, MA: Harvard University Press.

Paul, N. (1976). Cross confrontation. In P. Guerin (Ed.), *Family therapy: Therapy and practice* (pp. 520–548). New York: Gardner Press.

Paul, N. (1981, October). *The unconscious transmission of hidden images and the schizophrenic process.* Paper presented at the 7th International Symposium on the Psychotherapy of Schizophrenia, University of Heidelberg, West Germany.

Paul, N. L., & Paul, B. B. (1975). *A marital puzzle.* New York: W. W. Norton.

Spanier, G. B. (1976). Measuring dyadic adjustment: New scales for assessing the quality of marriage and similar dyads. *Journal of Marriage and the Family, 36,* 15–28.

Taggart, M. (1983). *Clinical epistemology and questions of context: The aesthetics/pragmatics debate.* Unpublished manuscript.

Watzlawick, P., Beavin, J., & Jackson, D. (1967). *Pragmatics of human communication.* New York: W. W. Norton.

Watzlawick, P., Weakland, J., & Fisch, R. (1974). *Change.* New York: W. W. Norton.

Williamson, D. S. (1978). New life at the graveyard: A method of therapy for individuation from a dead former parent. *Journal of Marital and Family Counseling, 4,* 93–101.

Williamson, D. S. (1981). Personal authority via termination of the intergenerational hierarchical boundary: A "new" stage in the family life cycle. *Journal of Marital and Family Therapy, 7,* 441–452.

Williamson, D. S. (1982a). Personal authority in family experience via termination of the intergenerational hierarchical boundary: Part III—Personal authority defined and the power of play in the change process. *Journal of Marital and Family Therapy, 8,* 309–323.

Williamson, D. S. (1982b). Personal authority via termination of the intergenerational hierarchical boundary: Part II—The consultation process and the therapeutic method. *Journal of Marital and Family Therapy, 8,* 25–37.

Williamson, D. S., & Bray, J. H. (1985). The intergenerational point of view. In S. Henoa & N. Gross (Eds.), *Family systems medicine* (pp. 90–107). New York: Brunner/Mazel.

Williamson, D. S., & Malone, P. E. (1983). Systems-oriented, small group, family-of-origin family therapy: A comparison with traditional group psychotherapy. *Journal of Group Psychotherapy, Psychodrama and Sociometry, 35,* 165–177.

16

Structural Family Therapy and the Family Life Cycle: A Four-Dimensional Model for Family Assessment

H. CHARLES FISHMAN
DHS Mental Healthcare, Inc.

Three umpires were having an argument about which of them was the best umpire. The first said, "I am the best because I calls 'em as I sees 'em." The second retorted, "I'm the best because I calls 'em the way they are." The third umpire, stepping back slightly from the other two, cried, "I'm the best umpire because the balls, they ain't nothin' 'til I calls 'em. —MacKay (1977)

The concept of the family life cycle is fundamental to structural family therapy. To assess family problems fully and to generate appropriate goals for therapeutic change, structural therapists view the family in the context of its life cycle. We look at the family in relation to predictable family crises and to the developmental history of that particular family. This chapter deals with the use of the life cycle in assessment, presents an example of life cycle concepts in a clinical session, and discusses concepts of change—continuous and discontinuous.

Concepts of family development, at the cornerstone of structural family therapy, are based on the notion that social contexts change with the passage of time (Haley, 1973) and that these changes tend to follow regular patterns (Minuchin, 1974). Indeed, the usefulness of structure as a tool for assessing the functionality of a system hinges on the use of a family developmental perspective. The structural therapist assesses a family system on the basis of the *appropriateness* of the distance between its members at a given point in the family's development. The appropriateness is determined by using the developmental perspective implicit in the family life cycle. The therapist then examines how a particular relationship corresponds to the organization of the entire system.

SEEKING A FOUR-DIMENSIONAL MODEL FOR ASSESSMENT

To employ the life cycle in assessment, I use a tool that I call the "four-dimensional model" of unfolding family phenomena. I use this conceptualization both to assess the family initially and to evaluate the likelihood that the changes will be maintained after termination of treatment. This model incorporates concepts of the life cycle as well as concepts of structuralism and systems theory.

The concept of four-dimensional space has been used in other fields for a long time. In mathematics, the principles of four-dimensional, non-Euclidean space were initially formulated in the 1820s. During the first decades of the 20th century, when Hinton and others suggested that space might possess a fourth dimension, the idea of higher, unseen dimensions became a dominant influence in much intellectual discourse in science and the arts (Henderson, 1983). Integration of non-Euclidean geometry with the fourth dimension in contemporary physics happened at exactly the same time at which cubism developed in painting. Marcel Duchamp's painting "Nude Descending the Staircase," in which a female figure is portrayed from different angles, is considered a classic demonstration of four-dimensional space.

The emergence of the relativity proposition made possible Einstein's historic theory and Picasso's cubism. The synchroneity of these major events attests to the profound importance of these ideas, which were sufficiently powerful to influence our own infant field half a century later.

In many ways, family therapy depends on the relativity proposition because the constructionist viewpoint underlies much of our thinking as well as the mode of our interventions. A family therapist operates in four dimensions. Like Duchamp, with a kaleidoscopic view of his figure, the family therapist looks at a dynamic system from different perspectives by moving in and out of that system. The therapist is at one point an observer, at another, a protagonist supporting a family member; at yet another, the therapist finds himself or herself being controlled by the family. Once it is recognized, such objective and subjective experience with the system provides invaluable data to the clinician.

THE FOUR PARAMETERS OF THE MODEL

These parameters are presented separately for the sake of clarity *only*, since they are obviously recursively bound so that no single one takes precedence. The four dimensions are presented diagrammatically in Figure 16-1.

Parameter 1: Development

The ordinate (horizontal line) in Figure 16-1 represents the developmental dimension of either an individual or a family. Every patient who presents with

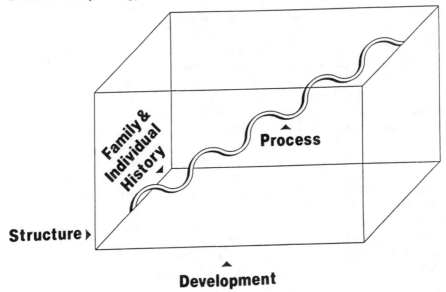

Figure 16-1. The therapeutic system as a four dimensional organism.

a medical or psychological problem is living in a system that is in a state of developmental instability. Research by Holmes and Rahe (Beck, 1974) has shown that the chances of a medical illness are greatly increased when an individual's life stress is high. Stress can also lead to psychological symptoms at points where the stress is high and the system decompensates. To use Prigogine's term, such decompensation is a "dissipative state", a point of flux where the customary rules do not hold (Minuchin & Fishman, 1981).

Increased stress results in symptoms that every family system handles differently. Some respond with transformation—when the rules change, they allow expression of new, more functional facets of the family members. Other systems get stuck instead of growing to a new level of organization. In such systems, the emergence of the symptom is the mechanism that *maintains* the system's status quo and stabilizes the family, reinforcing the homeostasis.

Structural therapists take a developmental view, consistent with that of Carter and McGoldrick (1980), that the family system is more than the concurrent development of children and adults. There is also a developmental progression of the family itself. Thus we see a moiré-like pattern, the overlapping of individual child development, individual adult development, and the development of the family. Observation of this convergence leads to a view of the family as "more than the sum of its parts."

When looking at intake information, the therapist should be able to make a preliminary assessment of the developmental stage of a family by examining what developmental forces led to the instability that brought the family to the consulting room. There are certain key transition points that seem to be universal (though they await refinement by cross-cultural research). In this culture, as in most Western cultures, these include being newly married, having young children, having adolescent children, having children who are leaving home, and being responsible for the care of elderly parents. Certain predictable adult crises occur with the same regularity as do developmental stages in children: breaking away from parents, the crisis at age 40 (which tends to occur in the 30s in blue-collar families), middle age, and retirement (Levinson, Darrow, Klein, Levinson, & McKee, 1978). Passages evolve in adults, and emergence into a particular stage does not occur in a vacuum. The adult does not negotiate transitions outside of a context, nor does the evolving child hatch and grow in a static field—with the adults forming just a gray backdrop—as some child development literature seems to indicate.

In reality, every family member lives in an ever-changing context. The 40-year-old executive, reassessing the existential meaning of being a sales representative for a toiletries importer, may happen to have an adolescent boy who has just entered high school and a daughter in her early 20s who cannot find a job. His wife could also be resonating with the changes in her larger context. She may, for example, have just returned to a career. For such a family, the "when" and "how" of a career, and of family economics, will loom large as broad contextual factors influencing the family life cycle.

Parameter 2: Organization and Structure

This parameter includes not only relationships within the family but also those important relationships outside the family that should be considered in therapy. The therapist must ascertain what the "family" is, that is, what system should be treated. Like the third umpire, in the epigraph to this chapter, who "defines" the balls, the therapist defines who the important people are to try to bring into therapy. The system, as Varela (1976) says, is like a set of Chinese boxes: a box within a box within a box. It is the responsibility of the therapist, in his or her role as observer, to put brackets, even at times arbitrarily, around certain segments of the system and deem that unit the therapeutic system.

In the creation of the therapeutic system, the therapist not only defines the family as a unit (an organization) but goes even further: He or she distinguishes certain repetitive behaviors considered to be representative of the family structure. G. Spencer-Brown (1969) has suggested that the fundamental information is difference: "Draw a distinction! This is the fundamental command and, whether it is obeyed consciously or unconsciously, it is the starting point for any action, decision, thought, description, theory and epistemology" (Keeney, 1983). The process of drawing distinctions among patterns creates structure.

The structural therapist, like the third umpire, looks at relationships among people and makes a distinction. Every family has similar developmental transitions, but the life cycle concept, although extremely important, is insufficient by itself to explain why *this* particular family has a problem. What is keeping the family from addressing the developmental pressures, metabolizing them, and going on? For this, the clinician must also go beyond developmental instabilities and look at the relationships in the family system as evaluated against the developmental backdrop.

In Humberto Maturana's (1984) terminology, there are two lenses of different resolutions that the observer can use to observe—and thus create—a system. A low-power lens presents the system as a unitary entity, but it does not have the power to discriminate among the various parts within the system. Maturana calls this unity an "organization." If we adopt his terms, the family *qua* family is an organization. The structural therapist, however, is not satisfied with looking only from afar. Instead, the therapist looks beyond the system *qua* organization to examine the relationships among the parts. Maturana calls the distinctions that result from observing through a high-power lens the "structure" of the system. The structural family therapist observes and distinguishes the relationships among the actual components of the system— in this case, the family members.

One key factor that the therapist scans for is the *distance* between people in the system. In observing the unfolding of the life cycle, it is useful to watch very specifically for the shifts in the proximity of family members. These shifts reflect the family structure, and knowledge of them is essential to evaluating the family. Keeping in mind that the family members are in dynamic flux, the therapist perceives the parts that make up the unit called the family system. The system moves through time in unfolding cycles that contain shifts in distance among its parts. It is essential not only to ascertain the distance between specific members of the system but also to look at the larger picture. How does the state of a given relationship reflect the organizational functioning of the system?

Parameter 3: History

History runs back from the surface of the page in Figure 16-1. It is only an inference from the other three parameters, which are contemporary. History, then, is considered to be contextually influenced. Which aspects of a person's or a family's history are most relevant are influenced by present contingencies. History itself is called forth and maintained by the demands of the current context. In this recursive game, however, the dependence of past upon present does not mean that the history of a system has not also had a role in influencing the evolution of that system.

On the basis of the present context, the individual and the family scan the past and deem certain things important and others unimportant. For example, every generation has a different history of the Roman Empire. Like all other dimensions, history operates recursively to effect the other parameters. Of course, history also involves the story that the family and each of its members presents with.

Parameter 4: Process

A description of a family by a clinician is different from descriptions by an anthropologist or a novelist. Unlike our colleagues in other disciplines, we do not maintain a fixed distance from the family. At times, we become part of the system, and even become protagonists in the family drama through techniques such as unbalancing (Minuchin & Fishman, 1981). Since the use of the therapist self is applicable in both assessment and therapy, our tools must go beyond linear assessment to an attempt at describing the *process* of assessing a system. It is this process of assessment that I call the *fourth dimension.*

The fourth dimension, or process parameter, has two facets, objective and subjective. The objective facet is the assessment of observed transactional patterns in the system, such as enmeshment and conflict diffusion through the participation of a third party. The subjective facet is the therapist's use, within the system, of his or her capacity to participate in ongoing activities. The independence of the therapist serves to vary the input into the family system. When he or she enters the system and joins in its process, the therapist is utilizing information he or she abstracted from the system as part of objective disengagement. Thus the therapist has a Janus-like position in the therapeutic system, being both inside of it and outside of it. Although joined in the process, the therapist remains free from systemic pressures. In this way, the therapist first assumes the position assigned by the family, and then withdraws. The therapist's awareness of this position provides important information about the system.

Another aspect of the process parameter is the therapist's own context, both the professional and the personal. In addition to our being affected by our professional context, our capacity to evaluate and change a particular system (our perceptions and intervention) is affected to some extent by our own particular family context—our family of origin, our contemporary family system, and our spouse, children, and extended family.

In this fourth dimension, all of these factors come into play as one moves in to diagnose and repair the system. By resisting the pressures of his or her own context, as well as those of the family, the therapist is able to recognize essential information about the differences in context. The therapist must do what is necessary according to the dictates of higher values. Ultimately, the therapist's cognitive independence and sensitivity to the family should prevail.

APPLICATION OF THE FOUR-DIMENSIONAL MODEL

PARAMETER 1: DEVELOPMENT

Dorothy's family had potentially destabilizing developmental pressures on every level.

The presence of an adolescent in the home pressures the family to change. The rules are challenged, the values are challenged, and at times, the parent's hierarchical power seems more like an illusion than a reality. And in this family both children were adolescents!

Dorothy and her husband both had many midlife issues. Both were in their early 40s. Dorothy was examining all aspects of her life: her marriage, her occupation. Now that the children needed her less, she wanted to find something more for herself, but her quest was being blocked by her husband, who did not want her to work. Her husband, Herb, felt stuck in his present position at work. He felt that he was just marking time, 9 hours a day.

Dorothy's parents had been floundering since her father's retirement. Their already shaky marriage was tottering.

Within the larger context, the women's movement had awakened Dorothy's ambitions to be more seriously involved in activities outside the home.

Therapy with this family required a slightly broadened definition of "family." When Dorothy called to set up an initial appointment, I asked who else was close to the family. She answered, "My parents. In fact they are driving me crazy. I talk to them at least once a day. They visit every Sunday—welcome or not—and I worry about them constantly." I decided to include Dorothy's parents at the onset of therapy.

PARAMETER 2: ORGANIZATION AND STRUCTURE

Analysis of the family's structure revealed inappropriate closeness between the children and Dorothy. The children spent a goodly portion of their free hours watchfully caring for their mother. Another enmeshed subsystem included Dorothy and her parents. She was apparently involved with them her every waking hour, either actually or in her thoughts. The marital relationships of both couples were extremely distant. The younger couple were engaged in a cold war, while the elders were engaged in a heated conflagration.

Another significant aspect of the system was Herb's attachment to his job. Significant in the children's lives was the paucity of their relationships with peers. This was a very troublesome sign for their future development.

PARAMETER 3: HISTORY

Dorothy had been anorectic for more than 20 years. She gorged herself with laxatives, often a box at a time. The laxative abuse had caused five bouts of metabolic disturbance leading to coma. During these episodes, Dorothy would be rushed to the hospital, often on the verge of dying.

My work with this family was a therapy in stages. The first stage involved Dorothy and her husband, together with Dorothy's parents; the second involved Dorothy and Herb and their two adolescent children; the third included only Dorothy and Herb as a couple.

It was remarkable that any time this family described past generations, they talked about what a close family it was. Dorothy's mother described spending Sundays with her own parents. Dorothy and Herb were, in turn, visited by Dorothy's mother and father every Sunday, but her parents never told Dorothy and Herb what time they were arriving. Dorothy, Herb, and their two children would simply hold breakfast until they arrived. At no point prior to therapy did Dorothy and Herb think to challenge this pattern.

Herb's family of origin was quite the opposite. He was not at all close to his siblings, and his parents were deceased.

PARAMETER 4: PROCESS

The most important process information about this system was that this was a classically psychosomatic family. The characteristics of a psychosomatic family, as described by Minuchin, Rosman, and Baker (1978), were pervasive: enmeshment, overprotectiveness, lack of conflict resolution, diffusion, and conflict caused by the participation of a third party.

Subjectively, during my work with this family, I experienced the desire to protect Dorothy and to be angry with Herb. The sense of Dorothy's vulnerability organized both her family and her physician. The children, Greg and Jenny, experienced this same desire to protect their mother to such an extent that they spent much of their time at home watching over her. Because of her fragility, no one would challenge Dorothy, nor would she challenge anyone.

In a therapy where one works to facilitate controlled crises among family members, I had to struggle to recognize that my perception of Dorothy was only a partial reality maintained by the system she was living in and that she could certainly withstand challenge. Indeed, anyone who has fasted for 20 years has got to have Herculean mettle!

My own context was supportive to a point. I worked in contact with Dorothy's internist, but there was some skepticism from him regarding the family therapy. At one time during the course of treatment, Dorothy took many laxatives and was hospitalized. I had to fight with myself to maintain the current direction of the therapy in the face of the internist's skepticism.

Therapeutic and Developmental Goals

The goal with this family was to transform the extreme psychosomatic system. This goal was addressed hand in hand with the developmental goals. The first issue to be addressed was the intrusiveness of Dorothy's parents. The developmental goal that followed from this structural change was to build a boundary between generations such that each generation was free to effectively address its own needs and at the same time develop a better relationship with the other generation.

Second, I addressed the developmentally crippling situation of the children, Jenny, age 12, and Greg, age 16. These youngsters needed to be freed from the pattern of overprotectiveness in which they felt responsible for taking care of their mother. This caretaking role was impeding their social development. Rather than being out with their friends, they were at home tending their mother.

The third developmental goal involved the marriage. Dorothy and Herb needed to reassess the significance of their marriage on the basis of their new position as middle-aged individuals whose children needed them increasingly less.

Case Example: Releasing Developmental Change

Structural therapy seeks to reorganize the family system based on certain developmental norms—what is developmentally desirable for these children and parents?

In the first session with Greg and Jenny, it was clear that the children were living lives of fear. They were frightened that their mother would again go into a coma but that they would not be there to rush her to the hospital. Thus one or the other of the children was always with her, like a private duty nurse, quietly observing. This preoccupation, and the ensuing isolation from peers, inevitably stunted their development.

Work to free these children from their mother could occur, of course, only in the family context. I needed the other parent, the father, to be there as the cotherapist while the mother and children distanced. The father had to be available not only because of the need to watch his wife but also because his very presence reassured the children that their mother was taken care of, allowing them to feel more free.

In the ensuing segment, the family is seated around the therapy room, with Dorothy and Herb seated to the therapist's left, and with Greg and Jenny completing the circle.

> Dr. Fishman: You're there to keep an eye on your mom.
> Jenny: To keep her company.
> Dorothy: I didn't know that.

Jenny: You know I always ask you, "Do you want me to keep you company?"

Dorothy: I always tell you, "No—go. I don't want any company."

Dr. Fishman: (*To Jenny.*) But you know she doesn't really mean it.

Jenny: I know, I don't want you to be alone . . .

Dorothy: No, I really do mean it. You don't understand that doesn't bother me at all. I'd rather see you with your friends. I keep telling you, Jenny, I'd always rather see you with your friends.

Jenny: Well, I don't always want to be with my friends. Sometimes I just feel like staying home.

Dorothy: As long as you feel like staying home just to stay home because you feel like it—not so . . .

Jenny: I didn't feel like going anywhere. I felt like staying home.

Dorothy: But I don't want you to stay home because you think you have to stay home with me. Because I'm always doing something and . . .

Jenny: I know that, but . . .

Dr. Fishman: Really, she needs you there to take care of her, doesn't she?

Jenny: Yeah.

Dorothy: No I don't.

Greg: I always feel guilty about the time she got real sick and I was out—the first time . . .

Jenny: I was there.

Greg: You were there and I wasn't.

Dorothy: You feel guilty about that!?

Greg: Yes, because Jenny was there and I wasn't and you got really sick and then—I don't know if you went to the hospital or not . . .

Jenny: Um mm.

Greg: Chances are if you came to our house at any time one of us would be there.

Jenny: Or both of us.

Dr. Fishman: But you kind of want to keep an eye on her. (*To Jenny.*) How old are you?

Jenny: Twelve.

Dr. Fishman: Twelve. (*To Greg.*) And you're 16?

Jenny: Like I walked through the door from school and I see Mom on the sofa screaming her lungs out. She says, "Call Mrs. Jones! Get her over here!" I called her up and all—if I wasn't home, I don't know what she would have done.

Greg: She couldn't get up or anything.

Jenny: She couldn't move.

Greg: If one of us wasn't there, you might have died.

Dorothy: Oh no. But that happened so long ago, I mean they're talking 6 years ago.

Jenny: Six years!? It wasn't that long.

Greg: It was a long time ago. Not 6 years though—maybe 5.

Dorothy: No—it was a long time ago.

Greg: There's been five of them [five laxative-induced comas]—so I don't know . . .

Dorothy: It was a long time ago and I made you a promise when I was in here—I said that'll never happen again, and I told you it would never happen again.

Dr. Fishman: (*To Greg and Jenny.*) You don't believe it, do you?

Dorothy: They don't and they have no reason to believe it yet.

Dr. Fishman: You see that—your mother just disqualified herself.

Jenny: I believe it.

Focusing on small interactions, and even ballooning their significance, helped to prove the case that the youngsters were hooked into the role of caretaker. That this role had detrimental effects on the childrens' growth and development was compelling to these child-oriented, upper-middle-class parents.

From the therapist's point of view, it is important to have concrete developmental markers in order to determine if the therapy is being effective. Freeing the children is one such marker. If the therapy gets the children out of the house and relieves them of their nursemaid role, it has been truly effective—it has facilitated the children's development.

Had I tried, in this segment, just to bring Dorothy to an awareness of her relationship with her children, I would have been working with only one facet of the system. To expedite true developmental change, one must work to restructure the entire system. I restructured it by encouraging the uninvolved father to function as a cotherapist. By building in a cotherapist, I could have two forces working on one vector. Indeed, all these years, Herb had been a brother to Dorothy, a nonchallenger of the system. This intervention, bringing him in, was developmentally appropriate because getting the son and daughter out was a *parental* task.

Dr. Fishman: So at age 12, instead of being out with your friends . . .

Dorothy: She's watching her mother.

Jenny: I want to make sure she eats. I mean, I don't watch her. Like a lot of times I'll see that she's eaten. Like when we eat pork chops, like I'll see her eat one, and I'll just go like, "Why can't you take two?"

Dr. Fishman: So, Jenny, how much time a week do you spend doing this?

Jenny: I might say—a lot—fair—three quarters of the time.

Dr. Fishman: Three quarters. If you get a chance, do you go out with your girlfriends?

Jenny: Oh, yeah.

Dr. Fishman: Yes? How much?

Jenny: Whenever I want.

Dr. Fishman: How much is that?

Jenny: (*To Dorothy.*) How much?

Dorothy: It's however much *you* want. In other words, it's always a choice. [Dorothy is about to derail the purpose of my query. I go back.]

Dr. Fishman: So you can't even remember, you have to ask your mother. When was the last time you went out with a girlfriend?

Jenny: Out? Like out somewhere?

Dr. Fishman: Went to the mall? I mean 12-year-old girls like to go to the mall.

Dorothy: Were you at Maureen's yesterday?

Jenny: Yeah.

Dr. Fishman: Who was home with your mother?

Jenny and Dorothy: Dad.

Herb: And her mother and father.

Dorothy: (*Laughing.*) That's another story.

Jenny: (*To Greg.*) Where were you yesterday?

Greg: I was out.

Dorothy: Greg played golf yesterday.

Dr. Fishman: What can you do for these kids to stop this?

Dorothy: I would like to know . . .

Dr. Fishman: Because this is all upside down.

When Herb accepts the captain's role, I insist that change begin immediately.

Dorothy: I would like to know how I can get them out of the house. I really mean that. I don't want to get rid of them but I want them out.

Herb: If you would have something to eat.

Dr. Fishman: No, the question now is how to get the kids out of the house. You have tried for 20 years to get Dorothy to eat; don't try it here.

The session is working to redirect the family forces so that Herb will fulfill his parental function toward the youngsters, which is to pluck them away from their mother. Also significant here is the diagnostic hunch that it would be easier to help the children fly from their mother than to make her eat. This acknowledges her power to defeat everyone who tries to change her directly. Greg and Jenny also have fallen for this. When the context is changed, then she will eat.

Herb: Yeah, but isn't that why the kids won't leave the house?

Dr. Fishman: No. The kids are in the house because there is somehow an inappropriate job in your house.

Greg: (*To Jenny.*) What do you want to do?

Jenny: I'm having fun with what I'm doing.

Dr. Fishman: See, they don't even know what fun they are missing.

Herb: Well . . .

Jenny: I'm not missing anything.

Herb: Well, they're not in any trouble. (*Laughs.*)

Herb sees the children as not being in any trouble because they do not make any disturbances and do not challenge the rules. In this psychosomatic and rigid family, they are not in any "trouble" because there is no expression of conflict. They are difficult to diagnose as having problems because there are few overt signs of disruption. But, from a developmentalist's vantage point, they *are* in trouble.

Adolescents who are prevented from having their own lives and their own fun by having to fit into the perfect roles a psychosomatic family demands are going to be very troubled young adults because someone missed the correct diagnosis of their existential situation. The preventive task is to analyze their existential situation and discover whether they are too constrained to move on to the next developmental stage. These youngsters are living in a family in which there is never any challenge; thus it is a family that cannot serve as a laboratory where they can learn negotiation skills.

Dr. Fishman: Yes, they are, because they are missing a lot of important experiences in adolescence that will help them to grow up. In other words, there are a lot of important types of growth experiences that will help them grow, like the times a 12-year-old girl has with her girlfriends and things like that, that they are not having. (*Pointing to the children.*) Instead you have a couple of practical nurses. When we started therapy, I brought in your mother and father. I think I may have brought in the wrong ones—Greg is your father and Jenny is your mother.

Dorothy: How can I get them to stop doing this? By not being an adolescent myself. By taking some control over my life.

Dr. Fishman: Umm. But that's probably unlikely.

Dorothy: You know, I tried last year and I pooped out. But not in that respect; I tried to go to work and it wasn't fitting in with everybody's schedule and it just kind of faded by and I . . .

Dr. Fishman: I don't want to know about that. Do something with the kids right now. Because they shouldn't be there to be your mother and father. It's just not right. Do you agree with me?

Dorothy: Yes, but I just don't know what to do.

Dr. Fishman: (*To Herb.*) Because right now your family is upside down. The kids are mothering mother—and I don't see Dorothy as changing it. I don't think she wants to. I think she likes having the kids like this.

Dorothy: I don't like to!

Dr. Fishman: Otherwise she wouldn't do it. (*To Herb.*) So I'm going to look to you to change it. You are the only one who can.

Herb: Yeah, but I don't know how to arrange that.

Dr. Fishman: I don't know either but I think you need to, because Dorothy says all the time, "Well you know, I'm just a poor, poor wet noodle and I can't be responsible." And you're a man of the world. So, in other words, it's you that needs to change that. I'm certain of that.

Herb: (*Shrugs and laughs.*) Well, I guess I'll have to take the kids out of the house myself.

Dr. Fishman: All right. Or order them out. I see it as real serious, and I see Dorothy as absolutely not motivated to change it. I mean she talks about eating as if it's the second coming—and it isn't. All she has to do is eat. And so she's not motivated at all. You're the only one who is. Your kids are bright kids, and really nice kids, but they don't have the maturity of judgment. So you're the only one who can. I mean I'm telling it to you as straight as I can.

Herb: Yeah, I'm hearing you but I'm trying to think about what I can do about it—but I . . .

Dr. Fishman: You are the father.

This segment demonstrates how developmental concerns are utilized as a powerful therapeutic wedge to mobilize the family. Of course, there is a flip side to this—to the extent that the children are no longer there, it puts more pressure on the parents. Suddenly, they are now relatively alone. What is left of their marriage after all these years is a common midlife question. But in this family, where there has been so much emotional distance between the spouses, the question is all the more terrifying. Of course, this new intimacy also opens a great many doors for the couple. They could experience some of the intimacy that has been absent from their marriage.

MAINTENANCE OF CHANGE: WHEN TO STOP THERAPY

This section of the chapter will deal with concepts of change and with how the four-dimensional model is used as a tool to help the therapist determine when change, be it continuous or discontinuous, will sustain itself.

The first definition of "change" that is useful for our purposes is Ashby's, cited in the book *Change: Principles of Problem Formulation and Problem Resolution* (Watzlawick, Weakland, & Fisch, 1974). Ashby talks about two different kinds of change. The first is a change from state to state. The second is a change from transformation to transformation, a change in the way of behaving that occurs at the whim of an experimenter or of some outside factor. The latter kind is important because it leads us to the concept of transformation in the therapy room, which is where a different organization emerges in a session.

Discontinuous Change

Another important concept to be considered is discontinuous (catastrophic) change, which is the subject of work by Rene Thom and others on "catastrophe theory" (Hampden-Turner, 1982). Catastrophe theory is a useful way of describing situations in which the interaction of two or more forces in combination influences some behavior in a way that leads to discontinuous, often sudden, change. In structural therapy, the goal is to have discontinuous change emerge in the therapy room, as illustrated in the segment that appears later in this section.

Learning how to harness discontinuous change for the purpose of furthering the growth of the whole family system has been one of the key advances of the past 50 years. The structural family therapist works very much as if he or she were the director of a play in which he or she sometimes takes the role of protagonist. In an effort to help the family change, the therapist can consciously utilize the concept of discontinuous change to reorder the proximity of family members and to free the family from a developmentally stunting situation.

Continuity and Change

A different way of assessing change derives from the model presented here. The attitudes of the therapist regarding continuity and change have a profound effect on the therapeutic process. Like the third umpire in the exchange that opened this chapter, the therapist defines the phenomena.

Both continuous change and discontinuous change represent transformation in the organization of a system. The difference between the two is in the rate of change. Whereas discontinuous change is a sudden reorganization, continuous change is gradual. The therapist, acting like an umpire, distinguishes what the rate of change is in the therapeutic environment—not always a simple judgment. An earthquake is certainly discontinuous change, and the growth of a flower is continuous change, but classifying change within a therapeutic system is not always an easy task.

What is more important here is that the therapist be aware of making the observation that some change is continuous and other change, discontinuous. If one expects that there will be only continuous change, then it is likely that self-fulfilling prophecies will obviate sudden reorganization. On the other hand, if one uses a model that focuses on discontinuous change only and that ignores longer term continuous change, then one has a blind spot.

Following is a segment of a marital therapy session with Dorothy and Herb. The session has been analyzed, on the basis of a 2½-year follow-up session, in terms of both types of change—continuous and discontinuous— and, more important, in terms of how the therapist is aided in ascertaining change in a system by the use of the four-dimensional model.

The following exchange, which occurred two thirds of the way into the session, characterizes the stage of bringing out a couple's accumulated grievances in such a way that the hurt and the plea for change are clearly heard. In this process, Dorothy and Herb are editing their shared past.[1]

Dorothy: Before I got sick I was never really good enough, and I knew it. I was never enough for you.

Herb: That's all in your mind.

Dr. Fishman: He's doing it to you. There go the gaslights.

Dorothy: No, it isn't. It is not all in my mind. It absolutely isn't. You used to get very angry with me. When I was at parties—oh, my god—you would get so mad at me and drag me home. And I would say, "How come you're making me go home, just when I'm starting to have a good time?"

Herb: Yeah—well, when you have a lampshade on your head.

Dorothy: No. I never did have a lampshade on my head—ever. I mean, I've seen people in really bad shape at a lot of those things.

Herb: Yeah, well, I saved you from all that.

Dorothy: That's what you were doing—"I'm getting her out of here." I never really felt I was doing anything bad. I was just with all of your friends.

Herb: Yeah, well, isn't 3 o'clock in the morning time to go home from something?

Dorothy: Not when everybody else is there and I'm having a good time.

Herb: Didn't it ever occur to you that sometimes we were the only ones left?

Dorothy: But you know what—you loved me when I had to go to bed at 10:00 every night and couldn't even walk—when we were on the cruise . . .

Herb: I had to be kind to you.

Dorothy: That's why I'm indebted to you. I really am. Because you hung in there. But every time I get to be my own self again, I feel that I'm losing you.

Herb: No. That's all in your mind.

Dorothy: I know it is.

The repair of the "gaslighting" entails a process of reciprocal expiation. Through a process of atonement, the participants are liberated to move to new levels of demanding of each other. This, then, is not just a therapy to render Dorothy assertive; it is also a therapy to render Herb free of guilt. When Herb comes to feel that he does not owe Dorothy anything and that he has a right to leave, there comes a legitimate moment of reappraisal and recontracting. Thus this session is a carefully calibrated sequence arranged to unbalance the system in such a way that both spouses can become free.

Dr. Fishman: No, it's not. He just did it to you again. There goes the gaslight.

Herb: What? "It's all in your mind?"

Dr. Fishman: Yes, by saying, "It's all in your mind."

Dorothy: But isn't it in my mind?

Dr. Fishman: (*To Dorothy.*) You see what you did? You accepted it.

Dorothy: I know. I know.

Dr. Fishman: Change him. The question is, can you be you—a full, robust person?

Dorothy: You know, unfortunately, that's what I basically was.

Dr. Fishman: Can you be a full person and have him love you?

In essence, I am asking, "Can you be a person who is more than just a one-down invalid in this family? Can you be strong so that there can be symmetry in your marriage?" A functional relationship must include both complementary and symmetrical interactions.

In this family, there is a fixed complementary pattern that stabilizes the system: Dorothy's being sick. In the functional family, however, both the complementary (nurturing, reciprocal) and the symmetrical (competitive, challenging) behaviors are present. The goal of the session is to work toward the emergence of the missing pattern, symmetry. The aim is for discontinuous change to occur and for the pattern of symmetrical challenge to emerge—for Dorothy to be able to challenge her husband, and for her husband to challenge back.

Dorothy: I decided purposely to get thin like this, and I told him 10 years ago when it happened.

Dr. Fishman: Talk to him.

Dorothy: (*Turning to Herb.*) And you wouldn't listen to me. Do you remember?

Herb: You said it a few times, yeah.

Dorothy: Well, I did tell you at the time. But I had to. I really had to. You never paid any attention to me. You really never did.

Herb: Well, if you die, I can't pay attention to you either.

Here we see a quintessential developmental issue emerging. This is Dorothy's existential dilemma, her midlife crisis. It took quite some courage for Dorothy to get better!

Herb: Anybody that has gone through all this crap would have left you long ago. (*Laughs.*)

Dorothy: But maybe there's nothing there any more. Maybe you're going to stay, but maybe there won't be anything left for *us* any more. Of course you will stay. It's too convenient for you to leave. Who else is going to be as good a cook? And who else is going to iron all those shirts real nice, and make sure the collars are starched? The laundry will, I know—eventually. But I'm comfortable. I am comfortable. I'm home every night. We have that big sofa, you can sleep on it at 9:00 if you want to and I never say anything. You get home at 7:00, you go to sleep at 9:00. But I never tell you anything about it. You say, "Do you mind if I close my eyes?" No, I don't mind if you close your eyes. At one time I told you I was going to drink too much because then at least I would go to sleep. I couldn't even do that. Because that was doing something. I can only deprive myself.

Family therapy, in its focus upon systemic events, sometimes loses sight of the fact that the component parts—the family members—enter into a contractual arrangement that makes them into a system. But they remain free individuals as well as coexisting members of a system. Thus the individuals in a system must be addressed as free agents who could dismantle the system of which they are a part. With this couple, I raised the possibility of high-risk atomizing—the breaking up of the system, the destruction of the family—as I emphasized the degree of freedom. They have to change to be married. To understand human systems, we must speak to the issue of the freedom *not* to be a member of the system. Living systems have the dual quality that the participants are simultaneously free *and* chained.

In life cycle terms, Dorothy and Herb are facing the midlife reassessment involving the acceptance of exits from and entries into the family system (Carter & McGoldrick, 1980). They realize that there are not many people in their lives at this point who have both entered and left, but they themselves have that freedom in their marriage. Dorothy is also going through the midlife reassessment of her marriage; it may be like what Gertrude Stein said about Los Angeles: "There's no *there* there."

Follow-up Session

Dorothy and Herb changed from being stuck in a pattern of being only complementary. A symmetrical interaction emerged, and they could still be complementary. The follow-up session, at 2½ years, sheds more light on what change is.

The following segment occurred midway through the session. I was seeing the parents and Jenny—Greg was too busy at college to come in. Things are greatly improved. Dorothy is no longer symptomatic. She no longer takes laxatives, and her weight is normal. She and Herb are happy together; they are talking about the last time Dorothy dosed herself with laxatives (which was during the course of therapy).

Herb: (*To therapist.*) I don't think you were forceful enough in getting Dorothy to change her ways. (*Dorothy laughs.*)

Herb: It took a couple of bangs from her problems for her to finally wake up. Now, is this the culmination of the therapy that caused her to change her mind, or ... ?

Dr. Fishman: After the therapy there were a couple of bangs?

Dorothy: No.

Herb: Like, remember the last electrolyte imbalance, where she went to the hospital?

Dorothy: It was during the therapy though.

Herb: Was it the culmination of therapy that made her realize this after that bang—or was it—what I thought was maybe if somebody said, "Goddamn it, Dorothy, you've got to stop all this stuff. You've got to stop indulging, taking laxatives and all that stuff ... "

Dorothy: (*To therapist.*) That's what you used to try to get him to do. You used to say, "How can you be so patient? Why don't you just tell her to knock it off?"

Herb: Yeah, but you were going around saying, "You're picking on me," or, "You and Greg are picking on me." I don't know. The only thing is, I don't know what finally woke her up—whether it was the therapy or being scared from the bang or a combination of it all or . . .

Dr. Fishman: I think you contributed to waking Dorothy up.

Dorothy: No, I tried to . . .

Dr. Fishman: (*To Dorothy.*) What do you think?

Dorothy: Oh, definitely.

Dr. Fishman: Because I kept saying, "You need to be there for your wife."

Dorothy: But I can tell you another thing from my point of view. The last time I was in the hospital, Herb came to see me, and I've never seen him so completely disgusted with me. There was no sympathy at all. He said, "I am so sick of you. I'm sick of what you're doing. I can't take it any more." I really got scared I was going to lose him. I felt at that moment—here you are, 80 pounds, with your face twisted. And I couldn't move my face anymore—I mean it was just over to the side. My hands were like claws. And I thought—who would ever bed you? And I felt he was going to go. I think I got scared.

Herb: I thought you were going, too, but not that way—not through the divorce court.

It was not merely a personal insight that Dorothy was desperate and had to change direction: If she did not change her ways, her husband would leave her.

These, indeed, are the contextual reinforcers of the existential crisis. Herb was able to challenge his wife because Dorothy, in therapy, was able to challenge him. The creation of a new interactional template could then be generalized outside of therapy. In this case, the new paradigm for behavior was the challenge—the direct confrontation and the ultimatum. Herb utilized the exact same template to challenge his wife by saying, "Listen, if you don't shape up, I'm going to evaporate."

Dorothy talks about having left some sessions while still in therapy and going into a rut, becoming very sick, being hospitalized, and getting a reaction from her husband that was not previously there. This time, Herb reacts with open anger, frustration, and disgust to such an extent that Dorothy thinks, "This time, I may actually lose him." The anger is a new reaction that has become possible because of a variety of sequences engineered and sponsored during therapy. Dorothy was supported and pushed to attack Herb thoroughly, to get out all her complaints about him. This was carried to such an extreme that the unbalancing event finally was allowed to happen. That is, Herb felt thrashed enough that now it was his turn to make complaints and he was free to leave. With the assistance and backing of the therapist, Dorothy was finally able to administer a thrashing to her husband.

CONCLUSION

What is most significant for the therapist is not whether discontinuous or continuous change has emerged but whether the context in which the change has occurred will *maintain* the change. In the case of Herb and Dorothy, the discontinuous change that occurred in the marital therapy session was carried over into the different context of the husband's visit to the hospital, which marked the last time that Dorothy has abused laxatives to date. What maintained the change after Herb's significant blowup at the hospital? In fact, even before the confrontation at the hospital, major changes were going on in the family system.

The four-dimensional model provides a useful tool for examining what has changed in the system. The presumption is that if enough of the parameters have changed, the therapist can be more confident that the changes, whether continuous or discontinuous, will be maintained. Thus the therapist can be more sanguine about terminating therapy.

Parameter 1: Development. Dorothy addressed the midlife issue of readjusting from being the mother of younger children, who are relatively dependent, to being the mother of adolescents, who are much more autonomous. She had a full-time job for the first time in her adult life, teaching aerobics. As Dorothy said in the follow-up interview, "My work makes me feel good about myself. In fact, I couldn't go back to the old behavior because I need the food for energy."

Her children were very involved in outside activities. The previous summer, Jenny had gone away to camp, and Greg had traveled to Europe with a group from school. They were no longer trapped at home caring for their mother. Jenny said in the follow-up session, "I can go out, because I no longer have to worry about my mother."

Dorothy's parents addressed retirement as their new stage in life by being very busy. Dorothy's mother took a job at a day-care center, and her father worked weekends for a caterer.

Parameter 2: Organization and structure. To quote Dorothy, "I got my mother a job at the same day-care center where I teach aerobics. She is very happy taking care of the little kids. I see her daily, but it's mostly through the glass." There was a very new structure to the system. Dorothy was able to maintain a distance from her parents.

What about the marriage? When I asked Dorothy if Herb still sided with the children against her, she said, "Herb is my biggest supporter. And Herb will say nice things about me in front of other people. . . . We spend a lot of time together."

Parameter 3: History. Dorothy reported feeling better than she has felt since she was 30. She relinquished her guilt over eating and has given up the purging, even though it took months for her physiological balance to return after she stopped taking the laxatives. Her weight went from 80 to 115 pounds, and she enjoys feeling well at that weight. When she came into therapy, she had lost all capacity for fun, but during the follow-up, she said she could "think of a million things that are fun."

Parameter 4: Process. Has the pattern of conflict avoidance changed? To quote Dorothy, "I don't think that my parents just bugged off. I had to finally say, 'You may not come up anymore. You may not come on Sundays, you may not come on Saturday. We'll have to see one another on an occasional basis. If I invite you to come on up or you invite me to come down, that's alright. But it just can't be constant.'" This quote typifies a signal change in the process parameter. The pattern of conflict avoidance has changed. Conflicts are resolved, boundaries maintained.

Through the use of the four-dimensional model, the important parameters of the system were changed. Information about change reassures the therapist that the *system* is in a different orbit and that the change instituted in therapy has a likelihood of being maintained.

In conclusion, the therapist, as the umpire, is responsible for the "creation" of the therapeutic system. Within this creation, the therapist, using the four-dimensional model, assesses the system's most salient parameters. Therapy is then based on structural and developmental goals elucidated by the model. Using the four-dimensional model, the therapist arrives at the answer to a very important clinical concern: when to *stop* therapy.

NOTE

1. Reference is made, in this exchange, to the movie *Gaslight,* in which a man tries to trick his wife into thinking she is losing her mind so that he can take her money. He plays tricks that make her question whether her perceptual apparatus is reliable. For example, he dims the gas lamps in the house, but when she questions him about it, he says, "It's not getting any darker. It's all in your mind, my dear."

REFERENCES

Beck, A. T. (1974). Depressive neurosis. In S. Arieti & E. B. Brody (Eds.), *American handbook of psychiatry. Volume three: Adult clinical psychiatry* (pp. 61–980). New York: Basic Books.

Carter, E. A., & McGoldrick, M. (1980). *The family life cycle: A framework for family therapy.* New York: Gardner Press.

Haley, J. (1973). *Uncommon therapy.* New York: W. W. Norton.

Hampden-Turner, C. (1982). *Maps of the mind.* New York: Macmillan.

Henderson, L. D. (1983). *The fourth dimension and non-Euclidean geometry in modern art.* Princeton, NJ: Princeton University Press.

Keeney, B. P. (1983). *Aesthetics of change.* New York: Guilford Press.

Levinson, D. J., Darrow, C. N., Klein, E. B., Levinson, M. H., & McKee, B. (1978). *The seasons of a man's life.* New York: Ballantine Books.

MacKay, A. (1977). *Harvest of a quiet eye.* England: Bristol Institute of Physics.

Maturana, H. (1984, August). *Cybernetics.* Lecture given at Eastern Virginia Family Therapy Institute, Virginia Beach, VA.

Minuchin, S. (1974). *Families and family therapy.* Cambridge, MA: Harvard University Press.

Minuchin, S., & Fishman, H. C. (1981). *Family therapy techniques.* Cambridge, MA: Harvard University Press.

Minuchin, S., Rosman, B., & Baker, L. (1978). *Psychosomatic families.* Cambridge, MA: Harvard University Press.

Spencer-Brown, G. (1969). *Laws of form.* New York: E. P. Dutton.

Varela, F. (1976). On observing natural systems. *Co-evolution Quarterly, 10,* 26–31.

Watzlawick, P., Weakland, J., & Fisch, R. (1974). *Change: Principles of problem formulation and problem resolution.* New York: W. W. Norton.

17

Systemic Family Therapy and Family Development

LORRAINE M. WRIGHT
WENDY L. WATSON

University of Calgary

Systemic family therapy owes its origins to the brilliantly creative and innovative clinical team of M. Selvini-Palazzoli, L. Boscolo, G. Cecchin, and G. Prata (1978, 1980). These four Italian psychiatrists have had an enormous impact on the conceptualization and practice of family therapy in the 1980s in North America and throughout the world. Drs. Boscolo and Cecchin have functioned as meritorious mentors to us through several workshops presented in Calgary, Canada, as well as through many personal discussions with them both in Calgary and in Milan, Italy. During the past 3 years, Dr. Selvini-Palazzoli has had a significant impact on one of us (L. W.) through various presentations and discussions in both Milan and the United States.

This chapter presents our interpretation and practice of systemic family therapy, particularly its application to families experiencing difficulties with health problems (e.g., angina, multiple sclerosis). It addresses the issue of family development and how it is viewed by systemic family therapists. A detailed case example illustrates the conceptualization of human problems from a systemic perspective and how that conceptualization influences treatment and the developmental implications.

CASE EXAMPLE: THE HEARTBREAK OF PERCEIVED DISLOYALTY AND DISAPPROVAL

Context of Treatment

The Family Nursing Unit (FNU), University of Calgary, an educational and research unit, was established in 1982 under the direction of Dr. Lorraine

The Chronic Illness Project cited in this chapter, which is conducted within the Family Nursing Unit at the University of Calgary, is funded by a grant from the Alberta Foundation for Nursing Research, Edmonton, Alberta, Canada.

Wright for the interactional study and treatment of families with health problems (Wright, Watson, & Duhamel, 1985). Two other nursing faculty members, Dr. Wendy Watson, Education Coordinator, and Dr. Janice Bell, Research Coordinator, complete the clinical, research, and education team of the FNU. The FNU offers assistance to families when one or more family members are experiencing difficulties with a health problem. Families seen at the FNU are either self-referred or referred by health care professionals such as family physicians or community health nurses. On average, five to six sessions are provided to each family.

Master-of-nursing students who wish to specialize in family systems nursing spend two practicums within the FNU. The FNU is an excellent training facility, utilizing a suite of five interviewing rooms and one large observation room. Each interviewing room has a one-way mirror, so that interviews can be observed and supervised. Because of the excellent facilities, and because of our commitment to provide intensive and frequent live supervision, families normally receive the benefit of a team approach. Graduate nursing students conduct the interviews, and a supervisor (one of us) and other graduate students observe. All team members have input into the assessment and intervention with the families. Videotape supervision is provided bimonthly.

In addition to the training and supervision of master-of-nursing students, several research projects are conducted within the FNU. One of these is the Chronic Illness Project, which examines the relationship between family functioning and illness and the effect of systemic family interventions on family functioning and the illness. We work as a clinical team with the families seen in the project: For each session, one of us interviews, and the other observes from behind the one-way mirror.

PROFILE OF THE H FAMILY

The H family was referred to the FNU by a mental health professional, who had noted the intergenerational conflict between the adult daughter, Janet, aged 39, and her mother, Mary, aged 66, and the concomitant stress to each. Because the mother was presenting with angina, the family was enlisted in the Chronic Illness Project. The family received a team approach (Dr. Watson, interviewer; Dr. Wright, observer) for six sessions over a period of 5 months.

Mary was a retired legal secretary presenting with angina treated with nitroglycerine. She lived with her second husband of 30 years, John, aged 73. Janet had been married 20 years to Gus, aged 46. They lived 15 blocks away from Mary and John with their three children, Mila, 16, Tara, 14, and Sam, 12. Janet's father, Mary's first husband, Imre, lived in Hungary, from which Janet and Mary had immigrated 30 years ago.

On recommendation from the mental health professional, Janet contacted the FNU and gave the intake secretary a brief sketch of the presenting problem. She indicated that her mother was disapproving of how she (the adult daughter) was handling her life. Her mother thought that Janet should seek help from a psychiatrist. Janet also stated that Mary was having heart problems. Janet was concerned that the stress of their mother–daughter relationship might make her mother more ill.

Janet requested that the FNU not call her at home to arrange the appointment time. She stated that "the family" must not know about the conflict between her and her mother.

Based on this information, our team began to develop hypotheses about this adult daughter–elderly mother system. One hypothesis was that the reciprocity of concern between the daughter and the mother was a sign of overconcern, indicating an overly close parent–child dyad. The team was intrigued with the directive for the FNU not to call the daughter at home. The "secret conflict" information supported a hypothesis that the relationship between mother and daughter might be the most important "marriage" in the family.

One way in which systemic therapy (a nonnormative model) uses family development (a normative model) notions is in the generation of beginning/ working hypotheses about the connection between the symptom and the system. Thus a second hypothesis was developed in the presession: that Janet and Mary were having difficulty negotiating the normal developmental tasks of an aging mother and a middle-aged daughter. The elderly mother and her adult daughter constitute a system that, according to family life cycle stages, consists of the interfacing of the mother's "aging-family" tasks with the daughter's tasks of "families with teenagers." A developmental perspective on the elderly mother as a member of an aging family indicates that she would be concerned about the following:

1. Shifting from a work role to leisure and semiretirement or full retirement.
2. Maintenance of couple and individual functioning while adapting to the aging process.
3. Preparation for her own death and for dealing with the loss of spouse, siblings, and other peers (Wright & Leahey, 1984).

Concurrently, the adult daughter, Janet, would be focused on the following:

1. Development of increasing autonomy for her adolescents.
2. Refocusing on midlife marital and career issues. Certainly Janet and her husband were in the midst of this, as evidenced by the marital conflict present.
3. Beginning a shift toward concern for the older generation. It has been stated that the last developmental task of middle age is adjusting to aged parents (Havighurst, 1948). Neugarten (1979) has wisely observed that "concern over an aging parent or parent-in-law has come to be part of the psychological baggage that most adults carry around in their heads" (p. 259).

Silverstone (1979) recognizes the multiple demands, transitions, and tasks these women may be facing. She notes that the tasks of middle age include the following: giving up one's youth; adjusting to the "empty nest," which she terms a euphemism for the multitude of feelings this life cycle stage may provoke; facing one's mortality and aging; and taking on a filial role in relation to one's parents. It is the interdependence of these tasks that can complicate even further the potential conflicts among the filial, marital, and parental responsibilities of the middle-aged woman. The special burdens of members of this age group, who function as the "fulcrum of familial stresses" (Bloom & Monroe, 1972), have been unappreciated and unresearched.

Session 1

In the first session, the elderly mother–adult daughter conflict was described as being related to the daughter's having planned and taken a trip to see her father, Imre, in Hungary 2 years ago. Janet had planned the trip without consulting her mother: "I didn't want her to control this." When Janet anxiously told her mother that she was taking the trip, Mary was "stunned and then seemed to be out of her mind and became ill with her heart problems."

In systemic therapy, it is important to learn the family's hypothesis about the problem.

Therapist: When you saw that, how did you explain it to yourself? What did you think was happening?

Janet: I thought whenever she didn't want me to do something, she would have heart trouble.

Mary took an individual developmental perspective and attributed the conflict between her and her daughter to her daughter's "midlife crisis." Mary interpreted her daughter's planning and taking the trip as a "search for her real father" and as being untrue and "disloyal" to her mother and stepfather. Mary perceived her daughter as "firmly standing behind her father for the past 2 years and firmly *not* standing behind me for the past 2 years!"

Mary and Janet's relationship had reportedly deteriorated since the daughter's trip to visit her natural father in Hungary. Mary and Janet had in fact only spoken to each other in the context of family gatherings, to ensure that the "secret" conflict would be kept. During the first session, neither would acknowledge the other's presence or perspective. Mary presented her perspective of attempting to help her daughter and having that help "rejected." As Mary described the problematic cycle with her daughter, the process in the session was actually enacted in the reverse, with Janet offering to help her mother pronounce the word "wreck," and her mother disregarding the daughter's attempted assistance.

Systemic therapy considers the larger context in which a midlife crisis occurs. Mary and Janet presented a picture of a historically overly close mother–daughter relationship, which resulted from having come to a new country together and from there being no other children and no husband to divert their attention from and need for each other. In the context of this past, overly close relationship, "initiation" on the part of Janet was perceived as "rejection" by Mary.

The life-threatening potential of the mother–daughter conflict was further dramatized by their both believing that Mary would die. From Mary's point of view, her daughter's continued disloyalty would lead to her (the mother's) death! Her relationship with her daughter had "died" and so would she!

Therapist: I am trying to understand how a woman who could leave Hungary with a 10-year-old daughter and conquer the new world would find this present situation so terrible that it has affected you to the point that you might die.

Mary: Because to me my daughter was the most important in the world always. When I realized that I lost her, I felt I lost everything.

Feedback from the family to circular questioning in the first session led to the following hypotheses: (1) Mary's heart problem was life-threatening for her and was autonomy-threatening for Jane; (2) intergenerational conflict was an issue of loyalty and control; and (3) intergenerational conflict between Mary and Janet was related to the lack of differentiation between them and to the daughter's reconnection with her natural father.

Session 2

In the second session, support was given for the mother–daughter relationship being the "best marriage" in the family: The daughter had never felt "bonded" to her husband. She had hoped that when her mother-in-law died, she would be closer to her husband, but this did not happen.

A systemic view considers the nondevelopment of the daughter's relationship with her husband in the context of the very close relationship between her husband and his mother, and between the daughter and her mother. The converse is also important to consider, that is, the very close relationship between each spouse and their respective mother in the context of the lack of "bonding" between the younger couple.

Developmental issues are clearly systems issues. A change in autonomy in one part of the system is associated with a change in control in another part of the system. Increasing autonomy by Janet involves a relinquishing of control by her mother. The systemic therapist asks herself/himself the question, "In what context is the increasing autonomy being sought?" Thus the systemic therapist is cognizant of the interfacing of individual and family life cycle developmental issues. The adult daughter's midlife autonomy issues and her family-with-teenagers tasks interface with her elderly mother's aging issues (health concerns) and her aging-family tasks in such a way as to make launching, at this time, precarious at best and impossible at worst.

Steinman (1979) uses the family life cycle to point out transitions that require modification in both family structure and family relationships. This can place strain on family members and lead to conflict "because the urge is frequently to maintain the status quo. When a family is not flexible enough to withstand important developmental changes, conflict is likely to be a concomitant of transitional periods. If this conflict is not resolved, symptoms will frequently occur" (p. 128). During the second session, the polarization of the perspectives of Mary and Janet continued. However, with the use of triadic questioning by the therapist, they did agree on one issue—that they had been "too close" over the years and that they had not had a "normal" mother–daughter relationship.

Therapist: If your husbands were here today, how would they describe the relationship between the two of you as mother and daughter?

Janet: My husband would say we were too close. He was very threatened by it. Ours was much closer than "normal." My marriage was very traumatic for her.

Mary: Very.

Janet: It was a difficult separation. Later it eased with the children. But even now, for some things to make this much trouble for 2 years, you must realize that this is not the normal laissez-faire relationship.

The intersession hypothesis was that the intergenerational conflict served to maintain and/or create distance in a historically overly close mother–daughter relationship. The end-of-session intervention consisted of the following:

1. Pointing out similarities between the mother's and daughter's individual developmental issues at age 38 (i.e., that Mary did not seek advice from her mother regarding her decision at 38 to come to the "new world," and that when Janet was 38 and thought of another kind of "new world," she did not seek advice from *her* mother).
2. Discussing the significant developmental issues of the mother–daughter relationship (i.e., that their close relationship had developed in the context of coming to a new country; that the mother had no husband for support and the daughter, no siblings; and that they needed to turn to each other for support).
3. Systemically reframing the conflict as a distance regulator (i.e., "Had it not been all these unexpected things, the two of you would have found something else unexpected and dramatic to help the two of you be a little less close").

We then contracted with the mother and daughter for three sessions, to assist them as they determined how close they should be to each other at this time in their lives.

Since interventions are delivered at the end of the session to further perturb the system, the reaction of family members to the team's opinion constitutes a salient point. To the systemic reframing, the mother responded very positively, even clarifying the therapist's words, whereas the daughter was more hesitant and struggled to understand the team's opinion.

Therapist: To solve the situation of being so tight, you each did a good part to help you loosen. But now we think you've gone overboard. You've flown apart.

Mary: From one extreme to the other.

Therapist: Now you're looking to find the right distance between you as mother and daughter at this time.

Mary: In a medium way.

Mary (*to Janet*): Do you not realize it?

Therapist: We need you both to think about this. Some of these ideas you may agree with, some not. We see that you are continuing to keep this extreme distance between you by each of you believing that you see things the *right* way and by not being willing to see the other person's point of view.

Session 3

Considering Mary's very helpful reaction to the team's opinion, the team was surprised by the continuing symmetry between Mary and Janet in the third session. Just as Mary had "understood" the opinion at the end of Session 2 while Janet had not, now, in Session 3 Janet made "sense" of the intervention while Mary could not. In fact, Mary was more entrenched in her "correct" view that her daughter's trip to Hungary was an act of disloyalty toward her and that Janet was accepting her father and rejecting her.

Using the language of her past profession of legal secretary, Mary brought to the session three typewritten pages presenting her "testimony." Mary patronized her daughter throughout the session. Janet responded by becoming withdrawn and overwhelmed with the content and process of her mother's presentation. The more nonresponsive Janet became, the more in control and persistent Mary became, and vice versa.

During the intersession break, it was difficult for the team to shift from a linear hypothesis that the intergenerational conflict was maintained by the mother's very fixed beliefs. Slowly, however, the hypothesis became more systemic by considering how Janet's impotent response could assist in the cementing of her mother's fixed beliefs. Further discussion led the team to see that *both* parties had firmly held beliefs and that *both* showed impotence (Janet by becoming withdrawn, and her mother by attempting to take more control). Thus the systemic hypothesis was that the intergenerational conflict was maintained by the very fixed beliefs and the impotence experienced by both mother and daughter.

The team determined the necessity to (1) challenge the fixed beliefs of the mother and daughter, (2) empower each of them, and (3) maintain engagement with each of them. Fortunately, Dr. Bell, the FNU Research Coordinator, had joined Dr. Wright behind the mirror that particular day. This enabled Dr. Bell and Dr. Wright to reflect the conflict between the mother and daughter in the form of a split-opinion intervention. We wanted to use the "language" of the mother (i.e., the written word) and heighten the curiosity of the family members by preparing a letter available for pickup 3 days after the session. Therefore Dr. Watson told the family, "Something unusual has happened today. My two team members behind the mirror cannot agree. It's going to take time to come to a decision. Therefore we will write our opinion in a letter for each of you."

The verbatim letter is as follows:

Dear Mary and Janet:

After much further discussion, our team unfortunately could not reach agreement about the way they see the problems between the two of you. Therefore, the solutions to these problems also differ. Realizing that we may never agree on how we see the problem, we have agreed to present our differing views to each of you:

1. One team member found herself taking Janet's side:

Problem: This team member sees that the problem is one of a misunderstood daughter who cannot convince her mother that she, as a daughter, loves, cares and is loyal to her mother.

The reason that Janet cannot convince her mother is due to the fact that Mary, her mother, has very rigid, fixed beliefs which she is unfortunately not willing to give up at this time. Janet has tried to convince her mother that even if contact with her father, Imre, continues, this does not lessen her loyalty or concern for her mother, Mary.

Unfortunately, Janet's visit to her father in Hungary uncovered some deep, long-standing mistrust and misunderstandings between her father and her mother.

This team member congratulates Janet on her attempt to reconnect with her father, as understanding your heritage and family background is a very important part of becoming a mature woman. This team member sees that it was not necessary for Janet to ask for approval from Mary to visit her father, as this team member sees that a relationship between you, Janet, and your father is a separate relationship from your relationship with your mother . . . especially in the case where your mother and father have been divorced for many years.

Solution: This team member thinks that mother's inability to see her daughter's point of view and her continuing resentment toward her daughter has more power to break up the family than anything that Janet could do, or Imre could do, or that their husbands could do.

Therefore, the team member that takes Janet's side thinks that Janet should keep contact with her father, even though it may be infrequent. However, since knowledge of further contact with Imre generates too many bad feelings in Mary and also too many worries about the future, Janet should keep her contact with her father a secret from her mother. That is to say, as a loving daughter, Janet should not tell her mother, Mary, of her contact with her father, Imre.

2. One team member found herself taking Mary's side:

Problem: This team member sees that the problem is one of a misunderstood mother who cannot convince her daughter of the seriousness of her daughter's action in visiting her father, without first seeking approval from her mother and stepfather.

This team member sees that Janet is a loyal daughter but was not courteous and sensitive enough to ask her mother for permission to see her father and to seek her opinion and advice on the matter before making plans to go. It would also have been respectful for Janet to explain her reasons for wanting to see her father.

This team member congratulates Mary for caring so very much about the stability of her Canadian/Hungarian family. This intense caring makes Mary very sensitive to the possibility that knowledge of the details of her daughter's trip and knowledge of the conflict between mother and daughter may break the family up.

This team member thinks mother is very desirous to not have the breakup happen, for if it did, both mother and daughter would be left without family members and without each other as well. This would be tremendously difficult for a mother and daughter who have been so very close and connected to each other. This team member thinks that mother is doing everything she can do to prevent her daughter, Janet from having to experience the pain of having a family break up. This team member congratulates mother on her efforts to save the family.

Solution: This team member sees that mother and daughter are close but that Janet's inability to understand the seriousness of continuing contact with Imre may break up the family.

This team member thinks that Mary has made a valiant effort over the past two years to try to convince her daughter of the seriousness but sees that mother's efforts have not had much effect on Janet.

In fact, this team member thinks that the more Mary repeats the same facts, over and over again, the less that Janet listens. This team member is concerned that all of mother's efforts are being wasted on the deaf ears of her daughter. Therefore, this team member advises that Mary seek some new ways to encourage her daughter to discontinue contact with her father. Mary should not repeat anything that she has already said to Janet. Instead Mary should find some new reasons for no further contact with Imre. This team member also thinks that mother should continue to watch over the safety of her Canadian/Hungarian family and keep the conflict with her daughter a secret.

3. I (Dr. Watson) strongly disagree with both Dr. Bell and Dr. Wright. I think that the other two members of the team are not looking at the real issue. They are being sidetracked by their own emotions and are not willing to consider another point of view. By each of them sticking so firmly to their own view, I think that they are missing what is really going on between the two of you as mother and daughter.

Here is my opinion:

After hearing the disagreements of Dr. Wright and Dr. Bell, I am even more convinced that the real issue between you as mother and daughter is the following:

Problem: I see that the problem is one of a mother and daughter who have been too close in the past due to the circumstances of coming to a new country, having no other family members initially to interfere with your focusing on each other . . . that is, there were no husband and no other children in the family to talk with or do things with. Even with the addition of family members, your new husbands, the two of you as mother and daughter were very close . . . and perhaps the best "marriage" was between you as mother and daughter.

I believe that each of you was sensitive to this very deep closeness and was aware that it had the potential of interfering with your relationships with your husbands and other family members that you love and care about.

I believe that at an unconscious level each of you knew that something had to be done to loosen the very close bond between the two of you. Because of the intensity of the bond, you knew it had to be something very dramatic, something very unexpected . . . to be successful to give you a more natural mother–daughter relationship.

Janet's trip to see her father has served the purpose to loosen the bonds between you. Janet's taking the trip was very unexpected to Mary, as was Janet's not seeking permission first; Mary's response (becoming ill and continuing to be resentful) was very unexpected to Janet. Thus, the trip has helped the two of you to be less close. But the two of you have taken it too far . . . you have gone overboard in loosening the bonds. You have each distanced too much from the other. The more you distance, the more difficult it is to see the other person's point of view.

Something that had the potential for good . . . that is, loosening the bonds between the two of you, so that you each could be closer to other family members . . . you were each willing to sacrifice a bit of closeness in your mother–daughter relationship for the overall good of the family . . . this potential good, has been taken too far and now is turning to the detriment of all.

Let me emphasize that since you were both sensitive to the overcloseness in your mother–daughter relationship, if the trip to Hungary to visit Imre had not been the thing to distance you from each other, *you each would have found something else to help you not be so close to each other.*

Solution: You as mother and daughter have taken your task of trying to be close too far. You are now too distant. It is becoming more and more difficult to see each other's point of view or to hear what the other is saying. You both need to find a happy medium . . . a place that is not too close to each other so that other relationships are blocked out, nor too far apart so that you can no longer find each other. I am very willing to assist you in your efforts to find the right balance in your mother–daughter relationship. Finding the right balance will be a difficult but very worthwhile pursuit for two people who have such a great amount of caring for each other.
Conclusion:

With the very strong disagreement present in the team and the disagreements between the two of you, I think it is best that you carefully and thoughtfully consider the ideas presented in this letter. This will take time and concentrated effort.

I would therefore like to offer you your next appointment in three weeks. I will be looking forward to hearing your points of view at that time.

Sincerely,

Wendy L. Watson, R.N., Ph.D.
Education Coordinator, Family Nursing Unit
Associate Professor, Faculty of Nursing   cc Dr. L. M. Wright
University of Calgary   Dr. J. Bell

Three days after picking up the letter, Janet called Dr. Watson requesting an earlier appointment and stating that her mother and she had gone for lunch together the previous day. We decided as a team not to see the family before the scheduled time in 3 weeks, in order for the split-opinion intervention to have further time to percolate in the system.

Session 4

Mary came beautifully dressed to the fourth session. She brought her copy of the letter, announcing as she entered the therapy room, "This is the most wonderful letter I have ever received!" Janet had read, memorized, and destroyed her copy of the letter, to prevent her husband from accidently finding it and discovering the "secret" conflict. Mary spontaneously reported that she was going to go to the doctor for her heart condition. This was a *major* change from her previous stance of saying that she was just going to die and that she would not seek medical attention.

When the women were asked what stood out for them in the letter, it was clear that the letter had had further dramatic and system-perturbing effects.

Mary: I realized how very wrong I was in many places. It was like getting shock treatment on my head. Before I was discredited and alone. I was like a shivering "wo," "wor," "worm?" [Mother sought help from her daughter to say the word "worm." Another change.] But now I am myself again, I am like a bear and I want to help this overaged cub. She is a wonderful woman and I love her.

The daughter was surprised that the letter had "so much insight, so much more than she expected!" The daughter was a bit hesitant about having a team member take her side so strongly. She was weepy throughout the session and explained that it was such a relief to have a change in the relationship with her mother, a change that had eluded both of them for 2 torturous years.

The letter had prompted the mother and daughter to talk more, and they had been out to lunch together. They reported that "they could now solve their own problems; they could now get on with talking about the 'real' problem." *The context for change had been created.* Both mother and daughter brought "new" information to the session that day to share with the other. In each case, the "new" information clarified the fears of the bearer and illuminated instrumental and affective issues around the problematic trip to the "old" world!

A ritual was prescribed at the end of Session 4. To help their two hearts start healing, two "heart meetings" were prescribed. One meeting was to be initiated by Mary, the other by Janet. We structured the meetings, giving details regarding length (1 hour) and process (during the first 15 minutes, one would talk and the other only listen, and vice versa for the next 15 minutes).

Details on content were general. The rationale for the intervention was to enhance and facilitate the new balance of closeness and distance that this mother–daughter system had discovered. The mother's response to the suggestion of the ritual was, "This is the first time in 40 years my daughter and I have talked like this. Now my daughter will have time for me!"

Session 5

Session 5 was held 2 weeks later. Janet reported that the relationship with her mother was now filled with hope. She no longer felt guilty or that she had done something "bad or wrong" in taking the trip to visit her natural father. Mary reported that her daughter was "no longer on trial" and that she was now "willing to believe" her daughter. The two "heart talks" had resulted in Mary's being able to talk to her daughter for the first time in 2 years. "Too much pride" had prevented her from doing so before.

Mary's comments on their readiness to work on a new relationship were particularly systemic in nature: "I will give her freedom. She will give me freedom. I am not hanging onto her. She's not hanging onto me."

The session focused on having Mary and Janet convince the team members behind the mirror that there was another point of view to take, one that differed from that which the team members had so rigidly ascribed to in the letter. That is, the mother was able to present her daughter's point of view, and vice versa.

The women eagerly awaited the "verdict" of the team during the intersession break. Had they swayed Dr. Wright and Dr. Bell to take another point of view? The team again mirrored the perceptions of the mother and the daughter with the perceptions of Dr. Wright and Dr. Bell. To further perturb the system, each reflected position was taken a bit beyond what the mother and daughter had presented during the interview.

Therapist: The team member who originally could only see your mother's point of view could now see yours, Janet. That person was impressed that you could say so clearly and directly to your mother that Imre is an SOB but he is your father and that you want contact with him.

Mary: That's right.

Janet: I've come a long way!

Mary: Yes, I appreciate that.

Therapist: The team member who could originally only see Janet's point of view was able today to see Mary's view. This person is impressed with your ability and willingness to be less . . .

Mary: Stubborn! I'm going to push myself behind her! This is the first time in my life!

Therapist: This team member thinks that you will actually have a greater influence on your daughter by holding back. You'll be even a better mother by being able to hold back, being able to give her the freedom to make decisions, even at those times when you may not agree with the decisions. You may even need to say in the future when she comes to you for a decision (*Mother laughs*), "I have confidence that you can handle it!"

To continue to maintain the positive changes in the relationship and to deal with unresolved hurts, a "burial ritual" was prescribed. The mother and daughter were encouraged to (1) write on pieces of paper any "old hurts" that they were ready to bury, (2) place their pieces of paper in a box, and (3) bury the box. They were told that this would help their two hearts continue to heal toward each other. In the future, if they wanted to "dig up the old hurts," they would know where to find them. A follow-up session was scheduled for 3 months later.

Follow-up Session

Janet attended the follow-up session by herself. (Had the mother launched her daughter?) She had tried to encourage her mother to attend the session, but her mother perceived coming to therapy as indicative of problems being present. Since the problems were resolved, she saw no need to attend but had sent her feedback with her daughter. It was hypothesized that she was showing confidence in her daughter's ability to present her (the mother's) point of view. What a dramatic change!

Janet reported many improvements in the relationship and was most eager to tell about the changes in her mother, stating that the team would not recognize Mary.

Janet: She looks 10, no, 15 years younger. Her skin is smooth. She has a new hairdo with gentle curls around her face. She had really let herself go, but now she is dressing beautifully. She used to dress OK but it was always polyester! [The clinical research team decided this could possibly be a new outcome criterion: raw silk versus polyester!] She feels good about us. She takes *much* less medication and is willing to go to the doctor when she needs to.

Therapist: So her heart is healing. And the two hearts?

Janet: We're easy with each other. We didn't do the burial you suggested. There *are* no bad feelings. My mother says she can't imagine any bad feelings. It was so good to hear, the last time we were here, that she will trust what I'm doing and that I know what I'm doing and that it won't cause problems for us. That was a great thing for me to hear. It took a long time for me to hear it, I know. I never thought I would hear it!

Therapist: If your mother was here, what would she say she enjoys the most about your relationship these days?

Janet: The stress is not there.

Therapist: How would you define your relationship?

Janet: Easy.

FAMILY DEVELOPMENT AND SYSTEMIC FAMILY THERAPY

Systemic Family Therapy

Systemic family assessments focus on family relationships, family development, alliances/coalitions, and the process of communication between family members. The three fundamental principles necessary to conducting a systemic interview are hypothesizing, circularity, and neutrality (Selvini-Palazzoli *et al.*, 1980). All three of these principles are interrelated.

The assessment process is based on the formulation of hypotheses by the therapist about the family organizational patterns connected to the problem. The therapist first gleans information about a family from intake data, from previous experience with other clinical families, and from various theories and research regarding the presenting problem or the "type" of family and then generates one or two initial working hypotheses (Fleuridas, Nelson, & Rosenthal, 1986). Family development theories can be useful in pointing the therapist to "tasks" and attachments that may be taxing the presenting family. Throughout an interview, questions are asked in order to validate or invalidate alternative hypotheses. Based on the information gathered from the family, the therapist modifies or alters his or her hypotheses about the problem and about the family and continually moves to a more "useful" understanding of the family.

In our view, the hardest work that occurs in systemic therapy is in developing systemic hypotheses. Linear hypotheses are so much easier to generate, particularly judgmental linear hypotheses (e.g., a mother is too controlling of a father). Systemic hypotheses connect the behaviors of all family members in a meaningful manner (Tomm, 1984b). (For example, a father shows little initiative or concern regarding his future. The less concern he shows, the more concern his wife shows; eventually, she directs him in what to do. The more she directs him, the less he directs himself, and vice versa).

"Circularity" refers to the therapist's ability to develop systemic hypotheses about the family based on the feedback obtained during questioning about relationships (Selvini-Palazzoli *et al.*, 1980). Circularity is based on Bateson's (1979) idea that "information consists of differences that make a difference" (p. 99).

> Differences between perceptions/objects/events ideas/etc. are regarded as the basic source of all information and consequent knowledge. On closer examination, one can see that such relationships are always reciprocal or circular. If she is shorter than he, then he is taller than she. If she is dominant, then he is submissive. If one member of the family is defined as being bad, then the others are being defined as being good. Even at a very simple level, a circular orientation allows implicit information to become more explicit and offers alternative points

of view. A linear orientation on the other hand is narrow and restrictive and tends to mask important data. (Tomm, 1981, p. 93)

Circular questioning involves the ability of the therapist to conduct the assessment on the basis of obtaining information about *relationships* (Selvini-Palazzoli *et al.,* 1980). Linear questions tend to explore individual characteristics or events (e.g., How long have you had angina?), whereas circular questions tend to explore relationships or differences (e.g., Who in your family is the most confident that you can manage your heart problem?; Selvini-Palazzoli, *et al.,* 1980; Tomm, 1981, 1985).

If the therapist wants to validate or invalidate the hypothesis that a family is having trouble launching the eldest daughter, a useful circular question, directed to other children in the family, could be, "What will be different in the family when Susan leaves home?" Interventive (reflexive) questions induce a family to reflect and therefore think and act in a new way (Tomm, 1987). Although many kinds of questions have the potential for inducing new cognition, affect, and behavior, all questions are not created equal! Using the preceding family situation, consider the following interventive developmental question, directed to the parents of Susan: "If you decided to convince Susan that she was ready to leave home, how would you go about it?"

"Neutrality," the third principle of systemic assessments, refers to the ability of the therapist to respond without judgment or blame to problems, change, persons, and various descriptions of relationships. For example, if a family makes a connection between a developmental problem, such as a young adult's reluctance to leave home, and their belief that it is due to the young adult's having a chronic illness, the therapist would be as neutral as possible in his or her reactions to this description, but it does not mean that the therapist has to *accept* this connection. The assessment information obtained through circular questioning about the meaning and belief of developmental problems will greatly assist the therapist in intervening. However, it must be emphasized that it is necessary to intervene only if particular beliefs interfere with or block the problem-solving efforts.

Family Development through a Systemic Lens

In the systemic approach, families are viewed as self-regulating systems controlled by rules established over time through a process of trial and error (Selvini-Palazzoli *et al.,* 1978). If the rules do not allow for a natural progression through various family life cycle stages or for an accidental shift (e.g., chronic illness, divorce), a family member may develop a symptom as a "solution" to helping the family progress along its evolutionary path (Hoffman, 1981; Tomm, 1984a). The symptom, or presenting problem, represents an interactional dilemma that is derived from particular family beliefs. In this model, one of the therapist's goals is to offer the family an alternate "belief" or "reality" about the problem, which may then allow the family to discover its own solutions. More specifically, the therapist aims first at understanding the family's reality surrounding the problem and then at challenging this reality by introducing "new connections" between relationships, beliefs, and behaviors.

The family finds its own solutions once its ability to change has increased. This is accomplished following a change in the "reality" of, or in the beliefs about, the problem: new views of old problems. Ugazio (1985) emphasizes that the first phase of any systemic interview should focus on the family's interpersonal belief system and should explore family members' explanations, interpretations, and attributions of meaning and intentionality for their own and other members' behaviors. We concur with this focus and make it a routine pattern of our clinical practice to explore consciously and deliberately family members' beliefs about and meanings for the presenting problem (i.e., cause, course, cure, consequences).

Systemic therapists do not adhere to the belief that the past determines the present or the future. Rather, they find it more helpful, from a systems view, to believe that the past can illuminate the present and vice versa. The systemic lens enhances the therapist's ability to view the past in a variety of ways. In the case example we presented earlier, the intergenerational conflict between the elderly mother and her adult daughter was illuminated by the information about the intensity of their closeness in the past. This allowed for a more positive understanding of why they had "chosen" and applied their present solution (extreme emotional distance) to their past problem of extreme emotional closeness.

An understanding of developmental stages and transitions could generate an alternate useful hypothesis to illuminate the past emotional closeness and give another view of the problem. Most family life cycle stages are highlighted by the addition and/or departure of family members. The stage of families launching children is perhaps the most dramatic and traumatic in this respect. It is punctuated with numerous entries and exits of family members: the departure of young adult children, the addition of sons- or daughters-in-law, and the attrition by death of the grandparent generation. Families frequently find themselves involved in a series of adjustments and readjustments at this stage of development. How families cope with this particular stage is best understood if a three-generational view is taken (McCullough, 1980). For example, the amount of success parents encountered in dealing with autonomy and separation issues with their families of origin will, in turn, have a definite impact on their ability to deal successfully with these issues with their own grown children (McCullough, 1980). In the case example, the elderly mother had had great difficulty separating from *her* mother and had exhibited her autonomy by disagreeing with her mother's counsel that "suffering is part of being a wife" and thus divorced her husband and immigrated to Canada.

When a family encounters difficulty in accomplishing the task of parent–child separation, it is usually manifested in one of two ways (Wright, Hall, O'Connor, Perry, & Murphy, 1982). Wright *et al.* (1982) indicate that one common response is for parents and children to be so loyal to the nuclear family that they disregard their own individual development. In families characterized by a high degree of loyalty, it is often difficult for the young adult to individuate because individuation may be seen by the family as a form of rejection. Some young adults respond to this dilemma by remaining highly dependent on their parents for emotional and, sometimes, economic support, and they often provide companionship and nurturing for one or both parents. One could hypothesize that the adult daughter and the elderly mother in the case example responded to the threat of transition posed by the launching stage by being overly close for many years.

The second extreme response of families negotiating the launching stage is for parents and children to distance themselves emotionally from each other to such an extent that they *appear* to be totally disinterested in each other and totally consumed by self-interest. For example, young adults may declare their independence and cut ties completely with their family in an effort to individuate. When the women in the case example presented clinically at the FNU, they appeared to be exhibiting this type of extreme response. For example, they had not spoken to each other in 2 years. Their inability to accomplish the task of parent–child separation consequently thwarted reinvestment in each of their marriages. However, determining *what* direction their relationship would take was not the primary goal of the clinicians. Rather, the aim of the systemic therapy team was to create a context for change and to offer an alternate epistemology of the problem so that the family could discover their own solutions. Therapists must trust the solutions that families find and must recognize that the pace the family takes toward problem solving is often different from that which the therapist might establish (e.g., sometimes much slower, sometimes much faster). To induce the elderly mother–adult daughter system to find the direction and pace of its solutions, the therapists accepted each family member's perception of the problem (as highlighted in the split-opinion intervention) and also offered an alternate view, or "reality," of the problem. The aim of this systemic perturbation is to enhance the autonomy of the system.

The challenge for the therapist is not to become "married" to the alternate reality that is presented to the family or to think it more correct than the view a family holds. It is, at best, a more useful view, in the sense that the new reality frees up the problem-solving ability of the system. There are more realities than there are families, and these realities only need to be modified when they inhibit individual or family development.

An important difference between this model and other family therapy models is that the systemic approach utilizes a nonnormative model of family functioning while recognizing that there clearly exist various developmental transitions and stages. (It is intriguing to us that an understanding of a normative model enhances the learning of a nonnormative model). However, systemic therapists work against the impulse to direct families as to *how* they should function or develop. The use of the split-opinion intervention in the case example is an excellent illustration of how to intervene not only with the family but also with the therapeutic team, to prevent the latter from pushing the family to change in a particular direction and/or at a particular pace. If families are influenced in a particular direction, that will, in turn, direct family development and/or family functioning.

THE PROCESS OF CHANGE

To facilitate change in a family system is the most challenging and exciting aspect of family therapy. The process of change is a fascinating phenomenon, and various ideas exist about how and what constitutes change in family systems. Liddle (1982) has suggested that one of the basic issues of all of us who engage in family therapy is the interviewer's theory of change, "that is what mechanisms permit or force change to occur? Even more basic, what is the nature of change itself according to one's own model." (p. 248).

We concur with Bateson's (1979) notion that systems of relationships appear to possess a tendency toward progressive change. However, there is a French proverb that states, "The more something changes, the more it remains the same." This highlights the quandary frequently faced in working with families. Systemic therapists must learn to accept the challenge posed by the relationship between persistence (stability) and change. Watzlawick, Weakland, and Fisch (1974) suggest that persistence and change need to be considered *together* despite their opposing natures. They have offered a notion of change that is accepted by most systemic therapists, which is that there are two different types, or levels of change. One type they refer to is first-order change, or change that occurs *within* a given system, that is, in the elements or parts of the system, without changing the system itself. It is a change in quantity, not quality. First-order change involves using the same problem-solving strategies over and over again. If a solution to a problem is difficult to find, more old strategies are used, and they are usually applied more zealously.

Second-order change is change that alters the system itself. This type of change is thus a "change of change." (It appears that the French proverb is applicable only to first-order change.) In second-order change, there are actual changes in the rules governing the system, and therefore the system is transformed structurally and/or communicationally. Second-order change always involves a discontinuity and tends to be sudden and radical; it represents a quantum leap in the system to a different level of functioning. Systemic therapy focuses on facilitating second-order change. Our case example beautifully exemplified changes that were dramatic and rapid. A change occurred in the system itself, in addition to a change in the presenting problem.

In summary, we concur with Bateson (1979) that change is constantly evolving in families and that frequently we are unaware of change. This is the type of continuous or spontaneous change that occurs with everyday living and with progression through individual and family stages of development. These changes may or may not occur with professional input. We also believe that major transformations of an entire family system can be precipitated by major life events and/or interventions by family therapists. We view change as a systems/cybernetic phenomenon; that is, change within a family may occur within the cognitive, affective, or behavioral domains, but change in any one domain will have an impact on the other domains. However, we believe that the most profound and sustaining change will be that which occurs within the family's belief system (cognition).

Concepts of Change

There are certain concepts regarding change we have found particularly useful in our systemic clinical work with families. We will discuss the two most salient concepts here.

First, the ability to alter one's perception of a problem enhances the ability for change (Wright & Leahey, 1984). It is essential that both family members *and* family therapists alter their perceptions of a problem. If a therapist agrees with the way a family views a problem, then nothing new will be offered. How we, as therapists, perceive and conceptualize a particular problem determines how we will intervene.

When a therapist conceptualizes developmental problems from a systems/cybernetic perspective, his or her perceptions will be based on a completely different conception of "reality" as a result of these theoretical assumptions. Our clinical practice with families who present at the FNU with developmental problems is based on a systemic–cybernetic–communicational theoretical foundation. Interventions are based primarily on the systemic model (Selvini-Palazzoli *et al.,* 1980; Tomm, 1984a, 1984b;). These are some of our efforts to think systemically. But what of families?

Individual family members construct their own realities of a situation based on personal beliefs and assumptions. Families and family members need assistance in moving from a linear perspective of the problem to a circular one. This is possible only if the therapist doesn't become caught in linear thinking when attempting to understand family dynamics.

We have found that one way to avoid becoming linear in conceptualizing developmental problems is to avoid thinking that the views of a particular family member or of all family members are "right" or correct." The challenging position of the therapist is to offer an alternate perception, reality, or epistemology that will free the family to develop its own solutions to problems. This alternate reality is usually redefined as an interpersonal or relationship problem.

The second salient concept is that change does not occur as a result of therapeutic elaboration of a family's understanding of developmental problems. In our clinical experience, we have rarely found that changes or improvements regarding developmental issues occur by embellishing a family's view of the problem. Rather, we have observed that the solutions to problems change as the family's beliefs and interactional patterns change, whether or not this is accompanied by further insight. Systemic therapy avoids the search for lineal causes and seeks, instead, to provide systemic explanations of problems and impasses.

ROADBLOCKS TO FAMILY DEVELOPMENTAL CHANGE

Family therapists, regardless of theoretical orientation, have noticed that many families have not progressed smoothly or automatically from one life cycle stage to another. Their clinical interventions focus on the stressful transition points between stages. Certainly, in our own clinical work, we have sometimes succumbed to the temptation to focus on particular transition points that have become problematic. The potential trap is for systemic therapists to become too purposive, that is, to become too invested in a particular outcome and to then direct the family to function or be restructured in a particular way. Systemic therapists try not to "get in the way" of family development by not being *directly* directive. Thus the notion that families must progress smoothly through the family life cycle stages must be confronted. Smooth progression, in our estimation, is not characteristic of a developing family.

However, there are occasions when families have "derailments from the family life cycle" (Carter & McGoldrick, 1980, p. 9). This notion of derailments is useful, because it conjures up a much more optimistic view of family life cycle difficulties. One of the most common derailments that we encounter in our practice is the derailment by illness. The impact on the family of a chronic or life-threatening illness does not automatically result in a derailment, but it almost always interferes with roles, rules, and rituals. From a systemic perspective, a derailment also frequently occurs when family members are attempting to obtain meaning and clarification in a relationship. The greater the ambiguity regarding relationships, particularly at various developmental junctures throughout the family life cycle, the greater the chance for family and individual symptoms. In the earlier case example, both illness and an attempt to obtain clarification and meaning in the elderly mother–adult daughter relationship had manifested in a family life cycle derailment. A former family life cycle derailment, or nonnegotiation, and an attempt to obtain clarification and new meaning in the elderly mother–adult daughter relationship was associated with the presentation of angina in the mother.

With any derailment, it should not necessarily be the therapist's goal to have the family return to the original "track." Rather, it behooves the therapist to create a context for change for the family, to allow them to decide which track will provide the greatest opportunity for reduced stress and increased growth.

INTERVENTIONS THAT CREATE A CONTEXT FOR DEVELOPMENTAL CHANGE

There are numerous interventions that can be utilized to facilitate or create a context for change. However, we will discuss only *systemic* interventions that create a context for *developmental* change.

Offering Alternate Realities

Systemic family therapists frequently offer beliefs, opinions, or conceptions about problems without regarding them as interventions. However, when strategically thought out and planned, these various types of opinions serve as potent and useful interventions, offering an alternate reality to those experiencing particular problems.

1. *Information and advice.* Families find advice and information about developmental problems valuable and beneficial. Frequently, information about developmental issues (e.g., elderly parents' needs for "spatial but not social isolation" and for "autonomy with contact"; Banziger, 1979) can liberate a family so that the members are then able to resolve their own problems.

2. *Systemic opinion (reframing).* Presenting symptoms may serve a positive function for a family. A systemic opinion is offered by conceptualizing the presenting symptom as a solution to some other hypothetical or implied problem that would or could occur should the symptom not be present (Tomm, 1984b). In the case example, the intense intergenerational conflict was positively connoted as a distance regulator in an overly close parent–child relationship. The symptomatic behavior is systemically reframed by connecting it to other behaviors in the system. The connections are based on the information derived in the assessment through the process of circular questioning. It is essential, when offering a systemic opinion to a family, that the recursiveness of the symptom be delineated: The symptom serves a positive function for the system while at the same time the system serves a function by contributing and maintaining the symptom (Wright & Leahey, 1987).

3. *Redefinition of the context of therapy.* A powerful opinion can be given by redefining the context in which family therapy is provided. If a family objects to attending sessions for what they have defined as family therapy, then, based on the assessment, the family could be told that family therapy sessions will be discontinued and that developmental sessions will begin (Wright & Watson, 1982). It is not that the nature of the work between the

therapist and family changes but rather that the context, or "name," of the work is made more palatable. With the family described in the case example, the nature of our work was named research rather than therapy.

4. *Commendation for family and individual strengths.* Following a recent analysis, by three observers, of 28 sessions we conducted with four families in a hypertension project, one of the common themes identified was our routine practice of commending families on particular strengths at the end of interviews. Feedback from both research observers and families has made us cognizant that this practice involves more than just being courteous—it represents a significant intervention that can alter family members' realities of themselves.

5. *Split opinion.* We have found the split-opinion to be a most powerful systemic intervention. Normally, a split opinion offers the family two or more different and opposing views. Each point of view is equally valued and the family is left to struggle with the various views of reality. The split-opinion intervention in the case example was the single most powerful intervention delivered to the family. It enabled each woman to have her view of reality strongly supported while at the same time providing each with the opportunity to entertain a totally new epistemology with regard to the presenting problem. This intervention created a context for change that had previously been impossible because of the extreme rigidity of each family member's beliefs.

Prescribing Rituals

In designing and prescribing a ritual, a therapist requires that a family engage in behaviors that have not been part of their usual patterns of interaction. The existence of confusion is normally an indicator for the use of the ritual intervention. The confusion is due to the simultaneous presentation of incompatible injunctions within the family. Rituals introduce more clarity into the family system. In systemic work, the actual execution of the ritual is not as important as the feedback about what new connections the family has made and, consequently, what new beliefs or realities the family now entertains. In the case example, two rituals were prescribed. The "meeting of the hearts" involved ritualizing a talking–listening session for the mother and daughter, who, for 2 years, had not spoken to each other. The "burial of the hurts so the hearts could heal" provided a forum for further purging. The mother and daughter did not execute this second ritual. The mother had stated to her daughter that there were no more bad feelings for her. In fact, she could not imagine any more bad feelings! Selvini-Palazzoli (1986) indicated that some families respond just to the idea of doing something unusual. Thus the enactment of the prescribed ritual may not be essential to induce a change in the family system. Useful information to the family and the therapist may be provided through just the description/prescription of a ritual.

CONCLUSION

Traditional life cycle theorists and therapists imply with their clearly demarcated stages, tasks, and attachments, "WE know how your family should function." Systemic therapists use life cycle information to generate (1) working hypotheses about the connection between the symptom and the system and (2) questions to perturb the family system, so that the family can answer its own question, "What is the most useful way for our family to function at this time?"

REFERENCES

Banziger, G. (1979). Intergenerational communication in prominent Western drama. *The Gerontologist, 19,* 471–480.

Bateson, G. (1979). *Mind and nature: A necessary unit.* New York: E. P. Dutton.

Bloom, M., & Monroe, A. (1972). Social work and the aging family. *The Family Coordinator, 21,* 103–115.

Carter, E., & McGoldrick, M. (1980). The family life cycle and family therapy: An overview. In E. Carter & M. McGoldrick (Eds.), *The family life cycle: A framework for family therapy* (pp. 3–28). New York: Gardner Press.

Fleuridas, C., Nelson, T., & Rosenthal, D. (1986). The evolution of circular questions: Training family therapists. *Journal of Marital and Family Therapy, 12,* 113–127.

Havighurst, R. J. (1948). *Developmental tasks and education.* New York: David McKay.

Hoffman, L. (1981). *Foundations of family therapy.* New York: Basic Books.

Liddle, H. A. (1982). On the problems of eclecticism: A call for epistemologic clarification and human-scale theories. *Family Process, 21,* 243–250.

McCullough, P. (1980). Launching children and moving on. In E. Carter & M. McGoldrick (Eds.), *The family life cycle: A framework for family therapy* (pp. 93–119). New York: Gardner Press.

Neugarten, B. L. (1979). The middle generations. In P. K. Ragan (Ed.), *Aging parents* (pp. 258–265). Los Angeles: The University of Southern California Press.

Selvini-Palazzoli, M. (1986, September). *New work on psychosis and eating disorders.* Conference conducted at the Ackerman Institute for Family Therapy, New York.

Selvini-Palazzoli, M., Boscolo, L., Cecchin, G., & Prata, G. (1978). *Paradox and counterparadox.* New York: Jason Aronson.

Selvini-Palazzoli, M., Boscolo, L., Cecchin, G., & Prata, G. (1980). Hypothesizing, circularity, neutrality: Three guidelines for the conductor of the session. *Family Process, 19,* 3–12.

Silverstone, B. (1979). Issues for the middle generation: Responsibility, adjustment and growth. In P. K. Ragan (Ed.), *Aging parents* (pp. 107–115). Los Angeles: The University of Southern California Press.

Steinman, L. A. (1979). Reactivated conflicts with aging parents. In P. K. Ragan (Ed.), *Aging parents* (pp. 126–143). Los Angeles: The University of Southern California Press.

Tomm, K. (1981). Circularity: A preferred orientation for family assessment. In A. S. Gurman (Ed.), *Questions and answers in the practice of family therapy* (pp. 84–87). New York: Brunner/Mazel.

Tomm, K. (1984a). One perspective on the Milan systemic approach: Part I. Overview of development, theory, and practice. *Journal of Marital and Family Therapy, 10,* 113–125.

Tomm, K. (1984b). One perspective on the Milan systemic approach: Part II. Description of session format, interviewing style and interventions. *Journal of Marital and Family Therapy, 10,* 253–271.

Tomm, K. (1985). Circular interviewing: A multifaceted clinical tool. In D. Campbell & R. Draper (Eds.), *Applications of systemic family therapy: The Milan approach.* London: Grune & Stratton.

Tomm, K. (1987). Interventive interviewing: Part I. Strategizing as a fourth guideline for the therapist. *Family Process, 26,* 3-13.

Ugazio, V. (1985). Hypothesis making: The Milan approach revisited. In D. Campbell & R. Draper (Eds.), *Applications of systemic family therapy: The Milan approach.* London: Grune & Stratton.

Watzlawick, P., Weakland, J., & Fisch, R. (1974). *Change: Principles of problem formulation and problem resolution.* New York: W. W. Norton.

Wright, L. M., Hall, J., O'Connor, M., Perry, R., & Murphy, R. (1982). The power of loyalties: One family's developmental struggle during the launching years. *The Journal of Strategic and Systemic Therapies, 1,* 57-70.

Wright, L. M., & Leahey, M. (1984). *Nurses and families: A guide to family assessment and intervention.* Philadelphia: F. A. Davis.

Wright, L. M., & Leahey, M. (1987). Families and psychosocial problems: Assumptions, assessment and intervention. In M. Leahey & L. M. Wright (Eds.), *Families and psychosocial problems,* (pp. 17-34). Springhouse, PA: Springhouse Book Corporation.

Wright, L. M., & Watson, W. L. (1982). What's in a name: Redefining family therapy. In A. Gurman (Ed.), *Questions and answers in the practice of family therapy* (Vol. 2, pp. 27-30). New York: Brunner/Mazel.

Wright, L. M., Watson, W. L., & Duhamel, F. (1985). The family nursing unit: Clinical preparation at the Masters' level. *The Canadian Nurse, 81,* 26-29.

18

The Presence of the Past: Continuity and Change in the Symbolic Structure of Families

DAVID V. KEITH
Family Therapy Institute, St. Paul

CARL A. WHITAKER
University of Wisconsin

Indeed, it is not so much identical conclusions that prove minds to be related as the contradictions that are common to them.—Albert Camus (1942)

Families are endlessly enchanting. Each of us is part of one, and none of us understands his or her own. They are a rich nexus of human experience. They have a wonderland quality that attracts thinkers and clinicians from many disciplines. Families are filled with contradiction, as they stay the same through generations while constantly changing.

The effort to clarify the contradiction divides the mind, straining the corpus callosum as the left brain battles the right. The left brain loves family life cycle and developmental theories. The right brain cannot see them. The left brain likes the apparent order that life cycle and family development theories bring. The right brain feels eclipsed and cornered by the conceptual structure that does not fit experience because it desymbolizes experience. There really is no such thing as the family life cycle or a system of family development. Families are infinite in time and infinitely complex in process patterns. The life cycle–family development ideas are metaphors attempting to expand into concrete descriptions or explanations of dynamic family patterns. Both are in danger of becoming overextended and overcalcified. We prefer our metaphors unfinished and inconclusive. In work with families, inference is better than definition.

The following is an example of a family that was conceptually broken out of a life cycle pattern:

Although this chapter is written in the first person, referring usually to David V. Keith, it represents a collaborative effort that incorporates many of Carl A. Whitaker's ideas.

A 60-year-old transvestite plumber was brought by his wife to the medical clinic in an acute anxiety state. He had been caught shoplifting a pair of lacy panties and had to go to court. This was the first time his sexual pattern had been exposed to anyone outside his marriage. He was a rigid, overresponsible Lutheran, who led a quiet, sober life. He and his wife had three sons, aged 29, 26, and 17. The 17-year-old lived at home. Where would this couple fit into the life cycle? They were grandparents still having the fights of newlyweds about who was in charge and having the sexual maturity of preteenagers, yet worrying about the proximity of retirement and death.

I saw the couple eight times in therapy. I had an unusual number of sleepy episodes with them, which, to me, signals deepening unconscious contact. The husband had a series of powerful dreams, which he described with wonderment. He never knew that people talked about their dreams. During the week following the fifth interview, he was in a remote area with his youngest son, cutting firewood, when his truck broke down. A rage started to come over him, which he focused on his son. While his rage was gaining momentum, he remembered a time when his father blew up at him for a reason he never understood. We had talked about his father's anger in a therapy session, and it occurred to him that he was being as ridiculous as his father had been. He started laughing at himself, and his son joined in. He said the experience had him thinking differently about himself. He received a suspended sentence for his shoplifting escapade. He was not certain as to where he was with his life as a transvestite; he was still too frightened. Yet, something had changed in him. His crazy world of personal isolation had been invaded. He had a symbolic experience of the past in the present.

THE FAMILY GROUP PSYCHOSIS

This therapy experience foreshadows what I want to say about continuity and change in families in relation to symbolic experiences. The central concept has to do with the seeds of creativity and craziness in the bone marrow of the family. Although to some it may sound shocking, I want to refer to these experiential nodes of continuity and change as "psychoses." The psychosis of the psychiatric world is a socially identified experience that involves being overwhelmed by subjective experience, isolated, ambivalently extruded from an intimate relationship (the family), and objectified by the community. This existential psychosis refers to the experience of being in a territory outside of intellect, where social propriety is in abeyance and unconscious (preverbal) factors dominate. The subjective experience is powerful, but it is usually multi-personal, in the context of a group experience. It is usually culturally invisible —that is, the community does not notice it. Even though anxiety about the situation can be quite high, this affectively charged experience is regarded as "just normal." To go further, most psychoses begin in the same way, but if the group anxiety or anger is too high, a scapegoat is elected and extruded.

From our perspective, *individuals* have some capacity for being left-brained, but families have virtually none (Kramer, 1985a). Unconscious factors dominate family living patterns. Families need a clause in their rule systems that constantly acknowledges the unconscious components of their living. The phenomenon of group psychosis is brought into focus most sharply in families, and it is crucial in understanding the simultaneous process of change and continuity.

It would be easier to understand continuity and change if we had genes and chromosomes in our symbolic world. We could explain that the symbolic chromosomal structure is transmitted from generation to generation. It is modified through mating and the birth of babies. The genetic structure is also changed by mutations, or accidental and idiosyncratic events.

This chapter focuses on two themes that make up the warp and woof of the emerging fabric of the family. First, the family of the present is an imperfect distorting lens that takes the past and projects it onto the future. The family looks back at the past in an effort to see where it is going. Second, family rituals are the hot spots for the process of changing and staying the same. The paradigms are the processes that surround birth and death and their symbolic equivalents.

OUTGROWING THE FAMILY LIFE CYCLE

When I first became interested in families and family therapy, I was captivated by the concept of a family life cycle. It looked like a way to answer theoretical questions about families. But what is crucial in understanding families is their idiosyncracy rather than their uniformity. Fourteen years later, I find that the main use of the family life cycle is to feed intuitive thinking about hidden distresses in a family. This use is illustrated in the following example:

A family with four children, aged 7–17, came in for therapy because of chronic marital troubles and ongoing agitation between the father and the oldest child, a son. This son was a competent student and an athlete, and he worked responsibly at his part-time job. Nevertheless, he was viewed by his father as an impossible "screw-up." Life cycle thinking tells us that part of the trouble is the family's panic in anticipation of the beginning of the end of being a well-nested family. However, there was nothing in their discussions that would suggest this to be the case. It was out of their awareness, but once brought to light, it diminished their incapacitating, diffused anxiety.

To repeat, I do not think there is such a thing as a family life cycle. Individuals have life cycles, but families do not. Families are infinite. Our pattern of family therapy has little to do with the family in a sociological sense. Rather, we focus on the symbolic family—the personal family that I live in, the one you grew up in. The theory of family development and life cycles has more to do with those theoretical, anonymous families over there in the distant background.

The family we speak of is not a still photograph. It is a complicated movie with a distorted time frame. The past appears in the present, but with no warning or no punctuation. It is there, then gone, leaving an impalpable, quickly fading image.

SYMBOLIC REALITY: BLENDING FANTASY AND FACT

When working with a family in any clinical situation, it is important to keep in mind that what we are told in the history is not just fact. Family myth is always built in. As a bachelor medical student, I learned to take a careful developmental history on pediatric patients. I asked when the child walked, rolled over, and so forth. But after my own children came along, I became aware of how those landmarks were loose approximations, based on fantasy about the child as much as anything. In any piece of clinical history, the family's fantasy is mixed with that of the clinician.

I first discovered this obvious admixture of fact and fantasy when I was a medical intern. I had the now familiar experience of interviewing an individual about a relationship and forming a fantasy about the absent person based on the patient's fantasy, only to have it shattered upon meeting the other person.

A woman was referred to the attending psychiatrist because she was concerned that she had cancer of the breast, but the physical assessment showed no disease process. She was not relieved by the negative diagnostic evaluation. We asked about her depression, and she took off on a long story about her railroad engineer husband who had a woman at every whistle-stop. We asked that he come for an interview the next day. We expected Casey Jones, macho hero of the railroad, to arrive for the interview. Instead, in walked a version of Beaky Buzzard, a bewildered, skinny, tall man. At 58, he was old for his years and soon to retire from the railroad. He described feeling discouraged about himself and his recent sexual impotence. She had caught her depression from him. It infected her already injured self-esteem and appeared as a fantasied cancer.

THE LENS OF THE PRESENT: FOCUSING THE PAST ON THE FUTURE

The Greeks "saw the future as something that came upon them from their backs, with the past receding away before their eyes" (Pirsig, 1984, p. 7). Our modern unconscious sees the future in the same way. The dim light of the past is focused and augmented through us, the lens of the present. Our family living patterns, as they emanate from the past, combine powerfully with individual life cycle events and emotionally significant accidents to determine the present. The purpose of the symbolic experience of the three-generation family interview is to collapse the past and future into the present.

The following case illustrates the way the dim out-of-focus past comes clear in the dynamics of the present:

Bill, a skinny, bright-eyed, 42-year-old auto mechanic, was referred because of chest and upper gastric pain; no organic disease was found. Bill was very successful, having developed his automobile repair business into a large garage with ten mechanics. The business was going well. He had built it up by working 15-hour days for 20 years; now he needed to work only 4 hours per day. His father had been very successful as a salvage dealer. When his father was 44, the bottom fell out of his business, he went broke, and he lost his spirit, which was never recovered. Bill's unconscious felt himself being cornered by his father's past, the only future he knew. Our assumption was that Bill viewed his success as a precursor to failure in the fifth decade. Of course, he did not accept the inference that his present symptoms were in any way attached to his family past, nor would he bring his father to an interview. So, the idea remained only a part of the psychiatric fortune-teller's fantasy.

The "vulnerable child syndrome" (Green & Solnit, 1964) gives another slant on the recurrence of the past in the present. If there are problems in the family at the time of a baby's conception, gestation, and birth, the child is more susceptible to psychological troubles later. If the grandfather has a stroke around the prenatal period, the family may become oversensitized to physical symptoms in the baby. Or the parents' overprotectiveness may arise as a result of the baby's having been seriously ill in his or her early weeks. At any rate, this syndrome gives voice to the way the family unconscious maintains continuity of meaning.

We ignore these subintellectual, symbolic issues because we do not understand them, we do not know how the processes work, and worse, we do not know what to do about what we know. It is better to know things we can do something about. The whole idea sounds mystical, but we are not mystics. The fact–fantasy story needs to be folded into the family's unconscious picture of itself. The idea may provide healing. Or, if the family is overreasonable or too afraid, they will disregard it.

The vulnerable child syndrome expresses itself in the following example:

Joe was referred by the dean of students because he was so eccentric. He was brilliant in mathematics and an excellent student, but his paranoid mannerisms troubled both faculty and students. At the time of referral, the dean was trying to decide if Joe should be committed to the state hospital or awarded a cum laude degree. At our request, his family came from out of town for an interview, so that we could expand the context of his behavior.

Joe was conceived during World War II. When his mother was 4 months pregnant, her beloved brother, the family hero, was killed in combat in the South Pacific. She was thoroughly devastated. Suddenly, life had no meaning. She prayed the pregnancy would miscarry, because this world was too cruel to bring babies into. When Joe was born, she named him after her brother. She loved him deeply, the more so because his father was away much of the time on his construction job. Joe was anointed and took over the job of family hero. His high intelligence added to his qualifications. He went off to college to seek his degree in physics as a first step toward winning the Nobel prize. Then the big, bad world coldly intervened. He was drafted at the end of his second year, assigned to the infantry, and sent to Vietnam. He survived the year of combat duty, but 2 months after returning to the States, became psychotic. He was supposed to have died, you see (my association). It was written in the family symbolic genes.

This is an example of the power of the symbolic understructure of family living patterns. But understanding or acknowledging these symbolic components does not automatically change anything. The exegesis of the poem is not the poem. But, when the clinician ignores them, it does not help either. The therapeutic implication is that if the story can be told with enough anxiety in an expanded family group, the symbolic domination can be diminished. I fully admit that this point of view is only a vestige of my Presbyterian predestination training, but Walsh (1978) describes the increased incidence of schizophrenia in children born within 3 months of a grandparent's death.

The process that I am describing has a mystical quality. It is nonrational and turns us away. The vulnerable child concept makes psychological as well as intuitive and aesthetic sense. It expresses simultaneously the conscious and the unconscious. Robert Pirsig, author of *Zen and the Art of Motorcycle Maintenance* (1974), provides a helpful example here. Pirsig (1984) describes how his son, Chris, was killed in a street mugging in San Francisco 2 weeks before his 23rd birthday. The father and stepmother had to come back for Chris's funeral and to take care of his belongings. After things had settled a bit, Pirsig was back home contemplating where his son went after death. As we saw in *Zen and the Art of Motorcycle Maintenance,* he gets an idea and works and reworks it in bottomless, vertiginous depth, round and round in minutest detail. Where had his son gone? What happens to somebody after dying?

Mourning his son, he wondered,

> What was it I was so attached to? Is it just something in the imagination? When you have done time in a mental hospital, that is never a trivial question. . . . There is an old cultural habit of thinking of people as primarily something material, as flesh and blood. As long as this idea held, there was no solution. . . . What had to be seen was that the Chris . . . I missed so badly was *not an object but a pattern* and that, *although the pattern included the flesh and blood of Chris, that was not all there was to it. The pattern was larger than Chris and . . . myself and related . . . in ways that neither of us understood completely and neither of us was in complete control of.* . . . The pattern was looking for something to attach to and couldn't find anything. . . . The pattern is trying to hang on to its own existence by finding some new material thing to center itself upon. (Pirsig, 1984, p. 8; italics added)

In the midst of this pondering, Pirsig's wife became pregnant. The couple decided they would abort the pregnancy. Pirsig was in his late 50s. Both had raised children and did not want to have another baby with all the long-term implications. Thus they made an appointment to terminate the pregnancy. The night before they were to have the abortion, they began revisiting their decision. He described a powerful sense of uneasiness about it. They decided not to go ahead with the abortion. They were joyful about the birth of their little girl. "The hole in the pattern (was) being mended. . . . What is seen so much more clearly is that, although the names keep changing, the larger pattern that holds us all together goes on and on" (Pirsig, 1984, p. 8).

He describes by his experience and deep imagination a primitive, crazy idea. We belong to a larger pattern that we cannot quite bring into focus. Pirsig's article fills a hole in what I am trying to describe. As a therapist, I can see the other family's pattern, but I cannot quite see the patterns in my own family. We do not have to look too deeply into ourselves to realize that our own experience resonates constantly in that primitive stratum. This is the way that continuity and change are united—by patterns that are multipersonal and cross-generational. They affect us deeply but lie out beyond understanding. Life lives us, we don't live life.

To reiterate, what goes on is not the person but the living patterns around that person. A Russian gypsy friend in Toronto, disguised as a psychiatrist, says it another way. One of the traditional ideas about people is that when somebody dies, we think that the body stays while the soul leaves. But actually, it is the other way around. The body goes away and the spirit (ghost) remains, in the family. The family is peopled with the ghosts of the past (personal communication, F. A. Yaroshevsky, 1982).

BIRTH AS SYMBOLIC PARADIGM

An important model for the maintenance of family patterns is the birth experience. Births are "hot spots" along the family evolutionary trail because they are likely to bring families together with affect and whole-body stimulation. With the birth of a new baby, the family patterns are simultaneously maintained and changed. But the change experience is like the participation in a birth, with the rich interweaving of the biologic, psychological, and social implications.

Births are new beginnings and at the same time extrapolations of the past. They force a heightened level of intimacy on families. The grandparents remember when their babies were born. The new grandmothers describe their breast-feeding experiences to the new mothers, along with other richly embossed family stories. New rules are made, rules about who gets to hold the baby when and who is in charge of what. Father may learn at that point that he is too dumb to change a diaper. The men may be pushed out in the postnatal period, and they often stay out. Emotional skin is thinner, personal vulnerability increased. But with the possibility of more intimacy comes the danger of deeper disappointment and hurt feelings. This possibility may be reflected in the fact that divorces can begin around births. The legal divorce may not take place until later, but the marriage develops a hairline fracture then.

New rules for how to live are made at this time, and old rules are reactivated. Parents who are intellectual agnostics may get into a fight about whether the baby should be baptized in the church she does not believe in any more or in the church that he does not believe in any more. The baby's identity begins to emerge when the family says, "Oh, he looks just like his Aunt Mary!"

Birth is a prototype for the developmental psychosis, the experience of being out of our heads. The experience is a nonpathological, culturally invisible, multiperson, family psychosis, a model for an existential or thera-peutic psychosis. We believe we are all crazy anyway, covered over with a thin, water-soluble frosting of social adaptation. In this birth experience, we change or are changed because we lose our conscious grip on ourselves. The experience takes the family over. The quantum-jump quality that a birth stimulates is a paradigm for other quantum-jump experiences symbolically related to birth experiences. Thus profound personal experiences are seen as "rebirths." The collective unconscious must know something of the demand for these psychoses.

Death in the family is the other paradigmatic wheel of change. Death may be easier to ignore as a vessel of growth because something is taken away and that absence can be ignored. Something happens around death when the family wraps itself in the solitude of its mourning. The strange intimacy of loss is deep. The family soul is resurrected. The remark is often heard, "It's too bad he had to die to get us together like this."

RITUAL EXPRESSION OF THE FAMILY PSYCHOSIS

The simultaneous experience of continuity and change is maintained by rituals—weddings, bar mitzvahs, baptisms, and all the holidays. Christmas is a cultural celebration of birth and recapitulates the new baby's arrival in an enchanting, unconscious way. The psychological pregnancy starts in October (only 90 shopping days left). Gifts are purchased, and the family starts to murmur, "What should we do for Christmas this year?" The nest is symbolically refeathered and special food prepared for the arrival of the new symbolic baby. The symbolic baby is the hoped-for rebirth of the family spirit. The family begins to anticipate the fun, or they may have to recall the pain that occurs when Uncle Bill and Aunt Sarah have their annual dispute with Grandfather. I worked with a family where the father had rages on Christmas day for as long as anyone could remember. The family so feared them that they planned the day around an effort to be away from the father. He had no awareness of what they were talking about. This example gives a hint of the out-of-conscious quality of the family psychosis.

Christmas day is magical. Adults time-travel to feel like children again. Stories are told of family Christmases from past years. The time is joyful, yet tinged with the desperate feeling that there may not be enough new hope. Then comes the afterglow, as we savor the renewal over the next few days, reminiscent of those first days when the baby comes home from the hospital. After that, we return to business as usual; the joy still warms, while an edge of sadness emerges. The letdown, a feeling of something lost or something missed, seeps in. The warmth of renewed closeness is replaced by the pain of distance or indifference. January finds the postpartum blues creeping over us, and we feel alone.

The rituals of Christmas take us over, like the experience of birth. At the height of the celebration, there was the possibility of a new experience. It has components that are enriching and painful, renewing and stifling. And always at the end, there is the loneliness. The family has rejoined, refreshed its spirit, and recalibrated itself to the present.

Other family rituals carry this nonrational, out-of-the-head quality. A weddings is a good example of a situation that creates emotional nakedness. The following example illustrates a situational psychosis emerging in a normal family:

A radiologist told this story of a family wedding that took place while she was our patient. Her family of origin was socially prominent. Her 30-year-old brother was to be married for the first time. The bride-to-be had no family, being the only child of parents who had died 10 years previously. The couple decided to have a small wedding for the family only. But the groom's mother said she would "die" if there was not an elegant wedding. In an effort to save this mother's life, the couple agreed to let her take over. The old family patterns heated up, and the oils of the unconscious began to make things slippery, as seen in the following highlights: The mother attempted to dominate the planning with her usual pattern of vengeful hysteria. It now appeared that orchestrating the wedding could have a fatal outcome for her. She hosted a bridal shower and forgot to invite the bride. The couple had planned a Caribbean honeymoon. The groom's father, an obstetrician who should have known something about sex, took his son aside and insisted that the couple stay at the family home for 3 days, so that sonny-boy could spend some time with his grandmother, who "might not be around for long." The son agreed without consulting his wife-to-be. My patient, a grown-up 32-year-old physician, went to the prewedding picture-taking session. Her mother objected to the color of her dress. They got into a heated dispute, and my patient refused to be in the pictures. She told the story later with a sense of disbelief. "I can't believe it was really me." The magic spell of family patterns took over, disrupting time and social structure.

Even death offers this strange birth-like quality. Death and birth are the front and rear wheels for the family journey. They are united by this group psychosis experience I am seeking to illuminate here. The family therapeutic psychosis is constructed from elements of both. We die in being born and are born in our dying. In the family, there is a deepened intimacy that goes with death, which, in a feeling way, is not unlike the intimacy that goes with having a new baby. The family's past and future experience collapses into the present.

This is the culturally invisible psychosis of intimacy, the heart of the patterns of change and continuity. The collapse into the present induces the feeling of intimacy, of openness, of vulnerability, of confusion and stupidity. There are similar powerful moments in therapy with families, when it feels as if souls touch. For a moment, social convention means less and loses its power. I am deep inside myself, yet available for unusual contact with someone else. Those who are phobic of feeling crazy or intimate may turn oddly cold at moments such as these. It seems that from deep inside ourselves we can only touch someone who is inside himself or herself. A person who is professional or overfunctional can seem blank and aggravating at these moments. One aim in therapy is to go deep inside myself in the presence of others and to meet in the murky underwater world.

FAMILY PSYCHOSIS AND ILLNESS

Experiences with illness create a similar kind of vulnerability. Relationships are malleable and available for the kind of change that results either in new closeness or in distance, both with others and with ourselves. I wish that medical practitioners could break out of the trees and see the forest of symbolic implication that goes with illness. But this is a cultural, not just a medical, problem. The spontaneity that goes with the symbolic level is distrusted. Is it better that the symbolic meaning of illness stay covered? I think not. Illness diminishes the importance of social conventions, taking us into ourselves. It is in one of these psychosis-like experiences that we make contact with our primitive inside self. Through illness, we may deepen our relationship with ourselves and establish a reconnection to our bodies.

We worked with a family for 2 years in relation to the oldest daughter's profound withdrawal into herself. She benefited from the family therapy and rejoined the human race. Later, her father, a mathematician with virtually no psychological mindedness, who had seemed untouched by his daughter's distress, developed a benign, slowly growing cancer. We followed them intermittently for several years. We began to hear from another side of him. When he talked of his experience with cancer, there was a feeling of better connectedness with himself and a previously unnoticed warmth. It was as if the cancer, by causing him to pay more attention to his body, gave him more psychological contact with himself.

Patterns of illness usually have a ritualized quality in the family. Illness is linked to an effort to change and to an effort to stay the same. "Where there is caring, all pathology is sharing" (personal communication, J. Warkentin, 1968). Illness may develop out of the effort to postpone death or craziness.

Sue P, at age 23, had anorexia nervosa, complicated by Crohn disease (regional ileitis). She had diagnostic assessments, followed by prolonged nonpsychiatric hospitalizations, in three major medical centers. A married sister, age 27, lived in close physical and emotional proximity to her parents. When Sue was born, her mother had a severe depression, which resulted in a 3-month separation between mother and child. Sue's father's mother took over the mothering. Sue and her mother never did get securely connected; they had a difficult relationship, each feeling antagonized by the other. The family was rigidly religious, with constant emphasis on a "positive" view of life and its troubles. The parents were role models of the macho hunter-fisherman-businessman and the self-effacing wife-mother.

There was no capacity for grief or acknowledging loss. At age 16, when the older daughter was being "rebellious," Sue developed Crohn disease. Four years later, her father had two heart attacks, but the family did not worry about him because Sue's anorexia nervosa emerged at that time. It was like having a new baby to care for. Four more years passed, and the sister married and had a baby. Old jealousy erupted between the sisters as Sue lost her parents again, and again regressed to noneating. She was referred to a psychiatrist. When there was no progress, he invited us in for a family consultation. The family anxiety about the father's health had been raised. The mother's loneliness surfaced. They were upset by the interview and chose to avoid further family sessions.

This is a sad story of a family who overtly depended on positive thinking and positive action to solve the many problems that came their way. But covertly, they depended upon Sue's remaining an infant in order to drain off their anxiety about themselves. They avoided confronting their despair as a group and thus could not find enough desperation to unite their resources.

Because symbolic time arrest is possible, and because these experiential change inducers are not age related, a family developmental schema is hard to derive. Families are usually off the track.

A vignette from therapy with a couple gives another example of change through brief joint psychosis.

The marriage was boring. Jack, a Vietnam combat veteran, concealed his anger with dependency and tearfulness. Much of his personality style was the result of an effort to entomb the self of his years in Vietnam. Nancy complained too much. After a year, the relationship converted her into a wicked banshee, and him into a hapless wimp. One evening, as they prepared supper together, she began her usual badgering. He exploded and pulverized a cauliflower, and then he took her by the shoulders, shook her, and told her to "quit picking on" him. He reported this episode 3 days later in therapy. Then he recalled a dream in which he appeared as a young boy. In the dream, he became furious with his irritable, alcoholic mother, took her by the shoulders, and shook her. There are several impressive facts. The first is that the dream had occurred the night before the fight with his wife, but he did not remember the dream until the therapy hour, 3 days later. The second is that his wife had no recollection of him destroying the cauliflower or of shaking her. This was a mutual psychosis. Both were out of their heads at the time. As time passed, it was clear that that encounter had marked a turning point toward a newly enlivened marriage between peers. Six months later, when the therapist commented on the significance of that episode, neither remembered the experience.

THE PRAGMATICS OF SYMBOLIC EXPERIENCE

The family group psychosis is a naturally occurring process in families. It is not a therapeutic method, but rather an experience that may be induced by therapy. If we can move the family into an experience of this sort, they are available for change in ways their process will determine.

The following dream illustrates such an experience. My wife and I were in a large home with many, many rooms. All who lived there were children who had something wrong with them, but what was wrong was not obvious from what we could see. Our job was to get them into the hallway in small groups, take photographs of them, and then show the children the photographs. In the middle of our work, one of my long-time cotherapists showed up to help. Later in my dream, we were told that what my wife and I were doing was immensely helpful to the children, but we could not tell how. My association to the dream was that if we therapists can help the family get a picture of itself, the family can begin to self-heal.

The pattern of family therapy used by my colleagues and me seeks to give the family expanded access to itself so that it has the administrative power to deal with the community in regard to problems that the group or individual members may face. Family therapy patterns that eclipse the family's initiative or the family's creativity should be avoided. Seeking a life cycle framework or a developmental system is a way to gain control of the pattern that Pirsig (1984) admitted he could neither understand nor fully control. What happens to the therapist's personhood, his or her own symbolic substructure, in these encounters with the therapist's own family? We do not know enough about it. But if we have too much discomfort with the symbolic mystery of our own families, we therapists may seek control of our own mysteries, and we do it best by attempting to organize the mysteries of families that we work with.

Gathering Historical Facts

The family story needs to be collected from as many perspectives as possible, so as to add depth and richness as well as confusion and ambiguity. We think this is best done when the story is told with affect in the context of a three-generational interview. You do not learn about a family by talking to the father or to the mother. The most can be learned about the family when the stories are told in a multigenerational group. Often, few secrets are revealed; the power comes out of having the family's dynamic, expanded past and present picture on the table, so that the relationship between the stories and the stress network of the present becomes part of the family self-image.

The Framework of the Interview

The method I prefer in my practice is to have the vertically extended three-generation group present with as much horizontal extension as possible. Depending upon the size of the group, we meet for 2–6 hours, optimally with a 2- to 3-hour follow-up the next day. Instead of "family therapy," we call the meeting "family consultation." Two therapists are best. The purpose is for the participants to talk about how the family works now and how it has worked in the past. After the first half hour, no matter what is happening, one of the *therapists* ought to question whether the interview is going anywhere and to suggest that the family members are being too careful with one another.

The Symbolic Meaning of Experience

When told in this format, the family history weaves between fact and fantasy. The personalized distortions or interpretations of events are as important as, if not more important than, the facts. The description provided by one family member does not need to agree with that given by another. The distortions reveal the simultaneous experience of multiple meaning levels. The symbolic level challenges our logical, rational side. Something dangerous lurks there; most obvious is the danger of death or craziness, or maybe the threat of intimacy and isolation. One can define as "symbolic" anything that triggers our imagination.

Professional academic training diminishes the importance of the symbolic. Young practitioners learn patterns of rational–emotive encouragement or reassurance. Any orthodox pattern, even a humanistic one, gradually clears out the unexpected symbolic weeds and leads to reified craziness (deviance) elsewhere in the emotional system. A mother-to-be's panic about her approaching labor and delivery is not made up and must be listened to. Her distress may be a reflection of obstetric stories that go back two generations. She is frightened because of her mother's story of pain and because no one is listening.

We degrade another person when we challenge the symbolic meaning of his or her experience. It is a sin that is commonly committed with children: "You should not be afraid." Illness is overlaid with symbolic features. When is it appropriate not to intervene? Intrusive treatment that desymbolizes experience may disrupt a process in a family and thus prolong it. A permanent schism in a family with an ongoing battle about who defines reality is a pattern that underlies chronicity. The following case example illustrates such a pattern:

Mrs. Nichols, age 72, a Roman Catholic with five grown children, had been burdened by chronic headaches and insomnia for 4 years. She ran the family with her illnesses. Father attempted to control with his long-suffering demeanor and narrow-minded moralism. The Nicholses were wealthy, so cost was of no concern in the diagnosis and treatment of her symptoms. She had been evaluated extensively by a number of specialists and at two major medical centers. There was a reality component: A brain tumor of uncertain cell type had been removed 6 years earlier. It was considered benign, but there was a question. She had no relief. By accident, she was referred to us, and we convened the family. The parents were estranged from three of the five grown-up children. Another son had a chronic illness. Twelve years ago, their only daughter had given up for adoption an out-of-wedlock, mixed-race baby. The family had put her on extended probation for immoral behavior since then.

Mrs. Nichols was frustrated with us at the first three interviews. We offered no new medications or diagnostic techniques, suggesting only that she learn to suffer (Keith, 1980) and return with her family. I called the internist to tell him that I had given her and her family a massive dose of ambiguity and that there might be disturbing side effects. I explained that the ambiguity was what was needed and said that I hoped he would keep them coming back. He understood and added that he felt that as an internist he could never leave anything ambiguous. In that sense, her chronic illness was idiopathic. Her medical doctors could not face their impotence and thus kept inducing an attitude of hopefulness in Mrs. Nichols by offering new solutions which perpetuated her fruitless search. The unacknowledged schisms and the battles for validation in the family were a large part of her chronic health concerns.

At the fourth interview, she complained that we had not explained what was wrong. We told this Catholic family our impression that she had been a childless saint in an earlier life. She had returned to earthly life to have the experience of raising children and was unable to tolerate the sinfulness implicit in conceiving and raising five children.

The therapy process was complex and change gradual. The clearest change occurred in the 39-year-old daughter. At the beginning of the therapy, she appeared in an unadorned, aggressively plain manner. Her conflict with her parents became more explicit. It became clear that her mother and father had different feelings about her pregnancy. Her mother was far more forgiving than her father, who was still bitter. The mother and daughter had some impassioned discussions about their relationship; some ended bitterly and some with great tenderness. Then, over a period of several months, they both began to dress more stylishly and became more attractive. There was evidence of self-esteem. The observation may sound sexist, but it was a clinical fact. Some of the schisms in the family were still present, but they no longer dominated the family as they had.

At an interview near the end, after about 7 months of therapy, Mrs. Nichols recalled the time that I accused her of being a saint. "I am just one tough old broad now!" she said. Her headaches and insomnia did not disappear. But the symptoms became episodic and far less anxiety provoking.

This case illustrates the way in which diagnosis and treatment at the highest standard of medical practice may inadvertently become a sustaining cause of a symptom pattern if it does not allow full expression of a family's symbolic world. It is crucial that we allow ourselves to be surprised by the families we see and by ourselves. When we push into areas of behavior or history where we feel uncertain, it leads to spontaneity in the family's behavior.

As we have indicated, the family evolves through symbolic experiences. Birth is one of the most significant of these. Each family has its own solitary appreciation of itself, which is hard to get at in the clinic. Each family has a profound solitude of its own. Many of our modern psychiatric methods disrupt it, but inadvertently, out of a perpetual innocence. The best access is via a three-generation interview. Our effort is to help family members integrate their own evolving family image, not to adjust them to fit a predeveloped model. Integrating their experience demands that they integrate the experience of the past as well as of the present.

We (D. K. and Thomas Lutz, a cotherapist) had worked with a family as their 22-year-old son was emerging from a 2-year psychosis. He had coalesced into a lively, creative young man. Six months after the family had ended therapy, the parents came back, concerned about the fact that their 19-year-old, always-good daughter, Kim, had entered an explosive, angry phase with her parents. Most of her anger was focused on her mother. The daughter had moved out. They came in to grieve. The interview was one of those touching, late-stage interviews. The mother was concerned that she had made an error that could be rectified only by getting her daughter to move back home and work through the conflict. We thought that the separation process sounded healthy, though painful. We thought her rebellion was so over-determined because it had been delayed. We also thought it to be evidence of the parents' new marital security. The mother became very thoughtful. With glistening eyes, she said that she and Kim had fights that she was never able to have with her own mother. The she told a story of spending 3 hours at her mother's grave one afternoon, carrying on a one-sided battle. "I guess our family just goes on and on. I just didn't know it would be like this." She laughed a small laugh. "I bet my dad said the same thing, 'Let me out! I didn't know it would be like this!' Oh, I guess it must happen in every family. But no, it can only happen like this in our family. I didn't want to be like my mother, but sometimes I corner Kim just like my mother cornered me. I guess I am proud of Kim for standing up to me, for what she believes in." She was talking about the special quality that Kramer (1985a) referred to when he said that each family is its own masterpiece. Thomas Lutz, my cotherapist, was reminded of the Russian dolls within dolls, like grandmothers inside of grandmothers, going back through the generations.

The Therapy Process

A major goal of work with families is to make the symbolic experience of the family therapeutic psychosis available. My belief is that it is at the center of most effective psychotherapy, even though unacknowledged. Some of the steps involved in guiding the family toward a nonrational confrontation with themselves include:

- Discuss the present in the context of the families of origin. How do the patterns of living in the present correspond with the patterns from the families of origin and how are they different?
- Identify pivotal moments in the family history. These include significant deaths, moves, births, divorces, and other events that have effected the symbolic structure of the family.
- Challenge the role domination that diminishes personhood. The usual implication is that community obligation supercedes personal awareness and responsibility. A father is leaving for work. His six-year-old daughter is crying. His role responsibility leaves no alternative but to go to work. Personhood leaves open the possibility that he take the day off to play with his daughter.
- Challenge the family's desire to bury primary process thinking and experiences. Primary process is a specific psychoanalytic concept which we have distorted to describe a primitive, nonrational component of unconscious family living. When the overly passive father describes his fear of getting angry, he is describing his primary process fantasy that his anger would lead to murder. Or, there is the case of a mother and 15-year-old-son who have an embattled, ambivalent relationship. The mother comments that she wishes she had "a normal mother-daughter, er . . . I mean mother-son, relationship with him." In her error, there is glimpse into a primary process component of their relationship. It is our assumption that illuminating these fragments in the context of family therapy makes them less detrimental to family health. The process of play therapy is a helpful guide to working with primary process in family therapy (Keith & Whitaker, 1981).
- Disrupt the myth that things are changed by the passing of time.
- Disrupt the myth that things are *not* changed by the passing of time.
- Use cotherapy teaming, so that the team's mythology can form a solvent that enhances family change.
- Laugh at the family for its effort to stay the same.
- Congratulate the family for its capacity to stay the same.
- Fall in love with the family. This is an ever-deepening experience, where play becomes a given and not a technique. A therapy hour has social, educational, and therapeutic components.

The family is constantly exposed to contradiction; they are not allowed to find a resting place or a new orthodoxy. The hope is that they will reach a new world of creativity. "We have found the answer and it is us!"

CONCLUSION

What I have tried to say in this chapter is that developmental or life cycle theory does not help us in our work with families. Our life cycle thinking is quite loose, focusing mainly on births and deaths, real and symbolic. The difference is not always distinguishable. Families are too complicated to simplify with a theory of life cycle development. Simplification can disrupt the family's integration efforts. The strongest determinants for continuity and change are the patterns that emanate from past families, the patterns that look for something to attach to, shadowy fabricated patterns. The multigenerational birth experience is a paradigm for changing and maintaining the patterns.

REFERENCES

Camus, A. (1955). *The myth of Sisyphus and other essays* (J. O'Brien, Trans.). New York: Alfred A. Knopf. (Original work published 1942).

Green, M., & Solnit, A. J. (1964). Reactions to the threatened loss of a child: A vulnerable child syndrome, pediatric management of the dying child, Part III. *Pediatrics, 34,* 58-66.

Keith, D. V. (1980). The case of Helen D.: A woman who learned to suffer. *Family Process, 19,* 269-275.

Keith, D. V. and Whitaker, C. A. (1981). Play therapy: A paradigm for work with families. *Journal of marital and family therapy, 7,* 243-254.

Kramer, D. A. (1985a, October). *Breaking the family crucible: Symbolic-experiential family therapy.* Workshop presented at the meeting of the American Association of Marital and Family Therapists, New York.

Kramer, D. A. (1985b, October). *Three generations of experiential psychotherapy.* Workshop presented at the meeting of the American Association of Marital and Family Therapists, New York.

Pirsig, R. M. (1974). *Zen and the art of motorcycle maintenance.* New York: William Morrow.

Pirsig, R. M. (1984, March 4). An author and father looks ahead at the past. *The New York Times Book Review,* pp. 7-8.

Walsh, F. W. (1978). Concurrent grandparent death and birth of schizophrenic offspring: An intriguing finding. *Family Process, 17,* 457-463.

19

Developmental Thinking and the Family Life Cycle: Implications for Training Family Therapists

HOWARD A. LIDDLE
University of California, San Francisco

The generation of schools or models of treatment has dominated the field of family therapy in recent years. These approaches have specified a variety of ways of working with families and have given conceptual flesh to the bones of the personalistic family systems frameworks of the early days of family therapy. In terms of the field's development, however, one difficulty with the high profile given to the specification of family therapy schools has been the way in which other important content areas have lagged behind or have not garnered equal attention from clinicians, those in daily need of pragmatic models to guide their conceptualizations about and actions with families.

There is evidence that the field is becoming more mature regarding the specification of schools of thought. One change has been an increased call for integrative theories—models that can be comprehensive in scope and able to combine the best of two or more approaches into a consistent, unified whole (Gurman, 1981; Lebow, 1987; Liddle, 1982; Moultrup, 1981). Another example of increased maturity has been the particularizing, or we might say the *contextualizing,* of family therapy approaches in terms of specific populations, problems, or use in a certain life cycle stage. These models are beginning to be thought of in more clinically grounded, less overly generalized, more context- and problem-specific ways. This trend seems to be in accord with the psychotherapeutic field's essential question: Which model with which population with what kind of therapist will provide the most help under a certain set of conditions?

Work on this chapter was supported in part by a research grant from the National Institute on Drug Abuse (Grant No. R01 DA03714), "Structural–Strategic Family Therapy with Drug Abusing Adolescents."

DEVELOPMENTAL THINKING

Although developmental thinking in systems terms has been successfully adapted in other fields such as family sociology (Duvall, 1977; Hill, 1971; Rodgers, 1973), and increasingly in developmental psychology (Bronfrenbrenner, 1979; Lerner, 1983; Liddle, 1987a; Magnusson & Allen, 1983; Minuchin, 1985; Riegel, 1976; Rutter, 1983; Urban, 1978) it has been slow to develop in family therapy. The landmark works of Solomon (1973) and, of course, Haley's *Uncommon Therapy* (1973), which gave a developmental organization to the strategic work of Erickson and in the process posed a strong message to family clinicians (i.e., conceive of your work and the lives of your clients within a developmental context) were instrumental in instigating developmental and life cycle thinking in family clinicians.

Gradually, developmental thinking, generally conceived and portrayed in terms of the family life cycle paradigm, began to appear as a major content area of note in family therapy (Barnhill & Longo, 1980; Carter & McGoldrick, 1980; Liddle, 1983; Walsh, 1982). Increasingly, despite some conceptual and practical limitations in the clinical realm (Liddle & Saba, 1983a), the family life cycle framework has found its way into the clinical mainstream of family therapy as work has been produced that uses the family life cycle framework as a foundation for clinical intervention (Breunlin, Chapter 5, this book; Carter & McGoldrick, 1980; Combrinck-Graham, 1983, 1988; Ferguson, 1979; Kantor, 1983; McGoldrick & Carter, 1982; Stierlin, 1974; Walsh, 1983; Williamson, 1981).

The overall objective of this chapter is to examine the implications of the family life cycle and more broadly, the concept of developmental thinking for the training of family systems therapists. These are clinicians who do not see themselves as always working with entire family units; their unit of intervention is often at the family subsystem or even the extrafamilial level. It is their way of thinking and, to a lesser extent, their interventions that define them as unique in the world of psychotherapy.

The family developmental model has achieved a natural fit with family therapy. Thinking developmentally is something that has a natural resonance for most family clinicians. Major models of family therapy have acknowledged, at least in terms of the broad conceptual strokes of their approaches, the importance of the family life cycle (e.g., that symptoms tend to appear at developmental transition points, at which families become "stuck" negotiating the terrain of their developmental voyage; Haley, 1976; Minuchin, 1974; Watzlawick, Weakland, & Fisch, 1974).

However, in the training domains of the major family therapy approaches, the specific ways in which the family life cycle and developmental thinking are used to teach a particular approach are underdeveloped (Liddle, in press; Liddle, Breunlin, & Schwartz, 1988). This is understandable, since the training area shows some of the same developmental trends of the clinical fields, generally after they occur in the clinical arena, however. Currently, although the clinical field is moving away from schools of thought, the training field is still struggling for unified schools, or at least approaches or models of training. So, returning to the previous point, if these content areas are becoming more prominent in the clinical domain of the field, then, by implication at least, this trend is something that trainers need to pay attention to. This rationale is related to an overarching goal of the family therapy trainer (or any trainer of psychotherapists for that matter): to ensure that the trainees be kept up to date with changing developments in their field. That is, there is probably nothing more unforgivable than being trained in something that is obsolete.

If we are to consider life cycle and developmental thinking as an integral part of both the clinical and the training contexts, then what form does or should it take, especially in the training domain? How would we know that the concept of developmental thinking was given high priority in one training program and not in another? One guide to how content and process from the clinical domain appear to be or are replicated (sometimes intentionally) in training has been the isomorphic principle of training and therapy (Berger & Dammann, 1982; Doehrman, 1976; Haley, 1976, 1988; Liddle & Saba, 1983b, 1985; McGoldrick, 1982; Minuchin & Fishman, 1981). This notion asserts that the systemic principles that guide us in therapy also guide us in training. "Isomorphism" refers to at least two classes of phenomena. First, patterns or interpersonal processes can be found to replicate themselves at different levels of the training and therapeutic systems. Second, the organizing principles of our theory of therapy can be used as a pragmatic and conceptual guide in supervision (Liddle, 1988; Liddle & Saba, in press).

A further guide about the use of developmental thinking, or more specifically, the family life cycle model, in training has to do with a concept that has helped us to understand individuals in families. Here we refer to Koestler's (1978) notion of a "holon"—an entity that has the properties of a whole *and* a part. The family life cycle paradigm is a *whole* in the sense that it can be thought of as an internally consistent body of knowledge, with its own logic, language, and reality. However, it is also a *part,* a piece of the conceptual puzzle that the clinician and trainer need to take into account so that they may comprehensively and nonreductionistically understand complex clinical and training events. Just as we have understood and developed other aspects of the training process (e.g., live supervision and video supervision) from this perspective (i.e., any given entity being both a whole and a part), we now need to frame the life cycle and developmental paradigms in a similar manner. These paradigms have informed the ways in which we conduct therapy, and furthermore, the very existence and development of these content domains is illustrative of our field's evolution.[1]

This chapter explores a series of specific questions relative to one's overall training objective, including the following: (1) What are the general and specific ways in which the developmental paradigm can more precisely and pragmatically inform the conceptualizations and actions of the family therapy trainer? (2) How does the introduction of developmental thinking at a basic level of conceptualization affect the training context in the clinical, training, and supervisory domains? (3) What are the consequences for trainers, trainees, and families of bringing developmental thinking to the forefront as a central, perhaps indispensable, conceptual overlay (Liddle, 1985)? (4) How does the *developmental lens,* and its attendant content, fit in relation to other aspects of the training curriculum?

USES OF THE FAMILY LIFE CYCLE AND
DEVELOPMENTAL THINKING IN TRAINING

The family life cycle and developmental paradigms are relevant to both the content and the process of family therapy training. First, the family life cycle and developmental thinking can be viewed as *content overlays.* Here these domains are defined and illustrated as specific content aspects of training. This perspective deals with one of the trainer's essential questions: What do I teach? This body of knowledge informs the perceptions available to the clinician in a number of useful ways. In this first category of understanding, the content of the literature on the life cycle (research findings about particular stresses of life cycle stages and events) and on family and human development is primary. This category refers to the concept as a body of knowledge or block of content, an overlay that will shape the work of the therapist. A therapist must have a practically informed model of human development and life cycle development available, ready to be accessed.

Second, family life cycle and developmental thinking can be viewed as metaphors serving the function of *process overlays.* These paradigms are defined as metaphors that are useful to understanding key components of the training process. This second way of seeing these paradigms brings us into the familiar territory of the isomorphic nature of training and therapy. Here we examine that aspect of this principle having to do with the notion of development, developmental stages, and the crises of transitions as they are applied to the therapist (i.e., trainee/clinician development) and to the development of the trainer and the training setting.

THE FAMILY LIFE CYCLE AND DEVELOPMENTAL
THINKING AS CONTENT OVERLAYS: THEIR USE AND
TRANSMISSION IN TRAINING

The family life cycle and developmental thinking are *lenses of assessment* —through knowledge of this content and the perspective that it yields, the actions of a clinician can be organized in a highly practical manner. These templates suggest direction to the therapist, based, in part, on assessment of the life cycle stage and corresponding tasks of the family and of its individual members. Assessing the family's presenting complaint through a developmental and family life cycle lens allows goals to emerge naturally (e.g., from the lack of concordance between where the family is developmentally and where they might be).

This framework provides an *explanatory function* in the context of training. Trainers must define the how (methods) and what (content) of training (Liddle, 1984). This latter area, in most family systems contexts, will yield answers along the lines of developmental frameworks. The family life cycle and developmental paradigms provide a base of understanding that ground the family in functional and temporal ways. A therapist's standard assessment schema naturally includes questions about the life cycle stage and corresponding tasks of each family member.

Clinicians can choose to focus on one level of a family's functioning over another, with these selections reflecting theoretical and personal biases. Intergenerational therapists naturally focus on the transgenerational processes of families, whereas brief family therapists tend to ignore such dimensions and instead focus on the repeating acts of attempted solutions in the present. The discussion, along developmental lines, of a family's presenting problem and of its life in general helps to anchor the therapist in something other than sequences around pathology. The life cycle orientation and vision of the therapist embodies a *future orientation* toward family life, constantly pushing the family and its members to question where they want to be going, individually and as a family. Thus, this way of thinking not only orients the therapist away from a dysfunction-seeking set but also urges family members to think in terms of their own future, collectively and as subsystems. In sum, these paradigms are offered at this point as, at the least, assessment tools—schemata that help therapists ask relevant questions about the family's progression along its life course.

These assessment schemata help in *defining goals of therapy.* The present view assumes that the goals of therapy are co-created by therapist and family. Further, it is postulated that the family life cycle and developmental thinking allow for the assessments using these constructs to lead directly into goals of therapy. Defining problems in ways that are workable and solvable is a central goal of any clinician. This process involves having a framework of understanding that operates beyond the nonshared, personal conceptualizations of the therapist. Clinicians' models (ways of understanding families, problems, and change) become public as a result of the actions they take or decide not to take. The polemic at the outset of therapy about what the presenting problem *really* is (i.e., how it is to be defined and by whom) is intrinsically tied to, and able to be shaped by, adherence to the family life cycle and developmental paradigms.

Developmental and Life Cycle Constructions

The foundation of a therapist's pronouncement "Your son is having a hard time acting his age—what can the two of you do to help him through this crisis of refusing to grow up?" is not necessarily true or false but may be a way to establish a developmental frame around the presenting problem. Trainees must be helped with the technical aspects of how to construct such developmentally based conceptions of problems that organize therapy along non-pathology- and non-trait-oriented lines. But they also need to be assisted at the higher level of abstraction and consider the context and nature of such interventions. That is, for trainees to deliver certain themes or interventions, they generally must, in their own words, "be comfortable" with such interventions or at least understand their logic.

Although the need for such an understanding is especially important with regard to the so-called paradoxical interventions,[2] it is also important when using developmentally based reframes or constructions. Isomorphically speaking, just as the therapist takes great care in understanding the constructivistic nature of the clinical domain, especially at that stage of therapy where the problem is being co-defined, so, too, does the trainer. That is, trainers construct workable realities along family life cycle and developmental lines with their trainees (sometimes in relation to their own behavior and sometimes in relation to the family) just as therapists construct workable realities along these lines with the families they see.

Teaching Trainees To Think in Terms of Resources and Strengths

Teaching therapists how to perceive and mobilize the hidden strengths and resources of their cases is a major challenge for trainers. As we know, an induction process often occurs in therapy that renders clinicians (even the most skilled and experienced) distant, pessimistic, and even cynical about the possibilities for change in a particular family. In such cases, therapists accept the family's presentation of a belief in the impossibility of change. Viewing and framing a family's pattern of relating along family life cycle and developmental lines can help prevent therapist burnout and provide a forward-looking definition of the problem for the family.

Training Trainees To Think with Complexity

Introducing the developmental paradigm into the training context assists therapists in their quest to think more complexly about clinical phenomena, and perhaps about life in general. The introduction of this overlay, as well as others dealing with cultural, ethnic, economic, gender, spiritual, political, or moral issues, can help provide the developing clinician with continued exercises in systemic thinking—the art of simultaneously taking into account a multitude of factors and explanations (along with their inter-actions) about human behavior. Thinking along life cycle and developmental lines serves to contextualize human problems in easily understandable and common (in a nonpejorative sense) terms. Temporality (i.e., past, present, and future) is introduced into the family's and therapist's realities. The temporal dimension thus becomes a relevant, indeed central, aspect of the content of therapy.

Redefining Pathology

The developmental and family life cycle frameworks define therapeutic change as constituting a transformation from developmental "stuckness" to "unstuckness" rather than a move from a pathological state to a nonpathological one. The use of these frameworks makes therapeutic contexts less "unnatural"— the therapeutic situation becomes informed by concrete, commonsense prescriptions for human behavior in a familial context. This is not to say that the family life cycle and developmental paradigms prescribe the particulars of everyday behavior between intimates. In essence, families define for themselves what (from outside their boundaries) might be judged to be dysfunctional.

The Trainer's Challenge

Trainers are in a difficult position—they must know the specifics of developmental theory and must be aware of how this knowledge of human behavior informs a therapist's work. Some therapists have raised questions about the degree of training clinicians receive in these areas (Combrinck-Graham, 1983). Realistically though, we must ask how clinicians can remain current in or go beyond a field. That is, how can they be expected to do more in the realm of application than the content (i.e., the data of the theory builders and researchers) allows? Can we expect the trainer or therapist to go beyond the rudimentary level of development attained in the theoretical domain of life cycle theory? In one's teaching, can one transcend, in his or her specialty area, what the theorists are having a hard time going beyond?

Levinson's (1986) newest theoretical ideas (e.g., his conception of eras and, particularly, of life structure) are good examples of how the developmental paradigm can inform a clinician's thinking and actions. He frames a definition of life structure by asking particular questions of the individual (which can, of course, be adapted to families) that elicits responses about areas in which the individual needs help. Levinson maintains a contextual focus with this work; he considers the most important aspect of life structure to be the person's relationships with the external world. These questions are useful not only to the clinician (as in a classic assessment situation) but also to the client or family, as challenges or clarifiers.

Formulating Each Family's "Big Questions"

This section addresses how the developmental paradigm fits into therapy, specifically, how therapists use this way of understanding families to formulate interventions.

The "big questions" asked by a therapist to any given family are universally derived but idiosyncratically crafted. In part, they relate to the generic questions that are posed by family life, such as the following: What kind of marital relationship do I want? How should our children be raised? How should our family be run on a day-to-day basis? Levinson's life structure concept has relevance here—parents want to have more influence on the development of certain life structures than on that of others. Essentially, the therapist uses therapy to pose the big questions about life not only in a general or existential sense but also in a developmental sense, and further, in a way that relates to a family's own particular set of life circumstances. Thus the clinician asks probing, developmentally oriented (e.g., life task) questions that require family members to clarify (through thinking, experiencing, and acting) how they want to live their lives.[3]

This approach is a variation on the question that a therapist often asks himself or herself during an interview: What should happen in this session that is not happening at this time? The same kind of question is posed to the family in a more general sense, this time with a developmental or life cycle twist: "Given what you know about your child and about children in general, how do you think your 13-year-old ought to be behaving?" The therapist poses such questions through a certain formula: "Given _____, what do you expect _____, and what would you like to do about it?" These kinds of queries tap specific behavioral, cognitive/intellectual, and affective dimensions; the areas of a family's existence that deal with values and beliefs, and the family's hopes and dreams for the future as it has been shaped, sometimes cruelly, by the past (Liddle, 1985).

THE FAMILY LIFE CYCLE AND DEVELOPMENTAL THINKING AS METAPHORS: PROCESS OVERLAYS IN ACTION

The family life cycle and developmental thinking in general have tremendous utility as metaphors for conceptualization and teaching in the context of training. Just as therapists are interested in instilling in their clients an appreciation of human development in terms of how they view their families, so, too, is it advantageous for trainers to adopt the developmental lens when considering the training situation. Therapists are interested in the life course and life cycle eras of their families; trainers must similarly conceive of their trainees as being on the professional life course of becoming clinicians. The process of professional socialization of the family systems therapist has not received prolonged or substantive attention despite the field's sensitivity to the political and personal consequences of adopting a systems view.

Along these same lines, little has been written and even less researched about the developmental stages of the therapist. Two papers by Whitaker (Napier & Whitaker, 1973; Whitaker, 1976) are nonempirical but nonetheless useful characterizations of therapist behavior at different stages of the trainee or clinician life cycle. More recently, the work of Kantor and his associates (Kantor, 1983) in delineating macrolevel stages and attendant subphases of the teaching and learning process is a clear step in the right direction. Research on the outcomes of live supervision has begun to differentiate learning styles and preferences and has defined some predictable trainee responses from therapists who have undergone a live supervision experience (Liddle, Davidson, & Barrett, 1988).

Just as therapists think in terms of the stages of their training, so, too, trainers realize that learning proceeds in stages. There are transitions to be managed at every step of the way. Further, sometimes the stages or steps are not clearly marked, so as to make the journey for the traveler, as well as for those trying to track the journey for purposes of guidance and evaluation, very difficult. (For a discussion of the development of the training group in stages, see Dell, Sheely, Pullian, & Goolishian, 1977; Tucker, Hart & Liddle, 1976; Tucker and Liddle, 1978.)

Why is it useful for trainers to think along these lines? Does it truly inform their work, and if so, in what ways? A developmental approach provides a benevolent framework for trainers in understanding the actions of their trainees. This framework does not ask questions of ultimate truth or validity. As with any framework or lens for a therapist or trainer, issues of practicality and usefulness must prevail over ontological or epistemological speculation.

Trainee Development

Developmental crises in families can stimulate developmental crises in trainees. Are there predictable crises in trainee development? Crises produce a pull to go back, to return to previous forms and levels of functioning. By defining problems developmentally, the therapist keeps from pathologizing the family. Employing the same *modus operandi,* the trainer keeps from deskilling and pathologizing the trainee by maintaining a useful developmental attitude.

Successful therapy largely involves developing a useful mind set. Therapists have their own version of a "bad attitude"—a framing of reality, personality, relationships, and so forth, that does not lead to alternatives or hope about change. In training, our basic assumption about this less-than-helpful attitude on the part of the therapist is that it can, and indeed must, be altered. One approach that does alter such an attitude is the trainer's introduction and use of the family life cycle and developmental theory as guiding principles of a therapist's work. In training, supervisors can adopt problematic attitudes toward their trainees. These paradigms help supervisors frame therapist difficulties as crises and not as signs of an intractable, deep-seated dysfunction. This view allows trainers to actually *see* differently; it allows certain processes and alternatives to emerge (or to be constructed) in their expanded comprehension of the training situation. Observations that ordinarily might not be available are suddenly possible.

The leaving-home model (Haley, 1980) is an example of an approach that uses family life cycle and developmental thinking intimately in its construction of a therapeutic model and specific plan for each case. What would be the equivalent of this model in the training world? Trainees "leave home" in the sense that they finish training programs, graduate, and follow the path of private practice, agency, or institutional work. However, the leaving-home metaphor in training is incomplete and potentially problematic. It implies that there is an end point in one's development as a clinician, a place that one will come to, inexorably, after the successful completion of a training experience. Just as we do not think of people as being cured at the end of therapy (i.e., the family practice model of health maintenance visits), we cannot think of therapists as being "cured," or fully trained, at the end of their training.

What might be another disadvantage of thinking in this way? That is, what are the problems associated with thinking in terms of stages of trainee development? Just as therapists can think in an overly literal way about developmental theory, trainers can adopt a perspective based on *developmental determinism*—interpreting developmental and life cycle theory in an overly concrete and literal manner (i.e., this stage is followed by that, etc.; therefore one "knows" what will be coming next). From this erroneous perspective, the variety that is inherent in the human drama becomes flattened out in the wash of reductionistic, too tightly predicted, pseudodevelopmental theory. Here, our overly literal interpretation of developmental theory leads to a view of behavior, in a strict sense, as being "on time" or "off time." As we do when we apply this paradigm in therapy, we need, in training, to think in terms of a *range* of behavioral possibilities or probabilities.

The Trainee's Developmental Message

What are some examples of typical markers that can be seen at one stage as developmentally appropriate trainee thinking and behavior but at other stages as signs that a supervisor needs to target that thinking and behavior for special attention? The following are areas in which a therapist's developmental difficulties typically evidence themselves:

- Thinking systemically.
- Becoming accustomed to video and observation procedures or a model of therapy that express different values from one's original approach.
- Dealing with the complex issues of model integration. For therapists, it is often

difficult enough to do one model of therapy well; trying to blend many approaches into a coherent framework is a difficult task (Lebow, 1987; Liddle, 1982; Liddle, 1987b)

- Evaluating one's work.
- Engaging in time-limited therapy, as it exists in the context of a training program.
- Shifting to a nonpathology, resource-mobilization focus.
- Structuring interviews, doing a directive therapy, and using a paradoxical approach.

Thinking developmentally and using this metaphor allow the trainer to pay attention to what we might term the trainee's "developmental message." Thus the verbalizations and behavior of the trainee are accepted with a certain developmentally oriented hearing on the trainer's part. This yields assessments and interventions that focus on helping the trainee past developmental transitions.

This framework allows trainers to do their part in completing the other half of the cybernetic loop of the teaching–learning situation. As with therapy, the essence of training or teaching is in interaction. Teaching and learning are inextricably linked; they are interdependent processes. Teaching or training is not merely the pouring of knowledge (content) into the head of a trainee or learner. The framework that a trainer adopts can facilitate the translation of the trainee's feedback (about the training process, about the case, about the trainer) into some meaningful and useful language. Further, it provides a way of casting the teaching–learning situation into a cybernetic form, a way that uses the very concepts that we try to teach to our trainees and, in a different sense, to our clinical families.

This is a model of looking and listening to trainees, a model in which interaction is the key element. We are not speaking here merely of an unsystematic, always progressing kind of interaction. Interaction gets recalibrated—one responds to the trial-and-error aspects of situations and (re)acts accordingly. In therapy, therapists look for ways to read and interpret feedback from their families. The nature of this feedback and the different issues involved in its interpretation have been described elsewhere (Liddle, 1985). In training, trainers are alert for ways to provoke, read, understand, and, ultimately, adjust their own actions on the basis of this feedback. Thinking, listening, and looking in terms of the lenses of the family life cycle and therapist development are useful ways of informing the trainer along these lines. Although there are other useful, flexible, and necessary lenses a therapist can or should use with given therapeutic situation (e.g., the broader macrosystemic focus, ethnicity, and cross-cultural factors), the developmental optic remains a central and an indispensable perspective for beginners and experienced clinicians alike.

The framework of the trainee life cycle will allow that developmental perspective to emerge. This paradigm opens up a way of seeing, and therefore of responding. For the supervisor, this is crucial. Trainees will be seen as being on paths and within cycles of evolution that detour, forge straight ahead, or sometimes leap ahead discontinuously (Liddle & Saba, 1983a).

This framework permits trainers to gaze benevolently upon struggling trainees, who report that the contexts involving live supervision represent one of their most difficult professional challenges. More hope regarding change is often inherent in this framework than in other frameworks designed to make sense of therapist behavior. Trainers often talk of trainees in the same disrespectful, nonhopeful way that therapists talk about families. Who among us would like to be on the receiving end of those descriptions?

One alternative for trainers in this regard is to await the research findings on how therapists develop and on the stages of trainee development. Another strategy for trainers is to engage in a personal construction (reconstruction) of the model (just as one does with a model of therapy), which is a way of clarifying one's essential guiding premises (Argyris & Schon, 1974). This strategy has been referred to elsewhere (Liddle, 1982) as the establishment of a therapist's epistemological declaration—an articulation, not at a level of technique, but at a more basic, presuppositional level, of the values and content that often implicitly guide one's work. Trainers also engage in this kind of activity (Liddle & Saba, in press). One of the key aspects of this activity is the way in which trainers develop their beliefs about the people they train and supervise. In this sense, trainers must specify their theory of change, their best ideas about how therapists become skilled. To develop formulations about the phenomenon of therapist change, trainers need to have a conception of trainee or clinician development, including the notion of stages.

Theory of Trainee Change

What are the variables—the components and mechanisms—that are involved in trainee change? The following questions are among the important ones for a trainer to consider in constructing his or her model of trainee change and development:

1. How do different contexts affect trainee development?
2. How do current and previous orientations or allegiances to various therapy models affect the learning of a new approach?
3. How do different kinds of cases activate the various partial selves of the therapist?
4. How does a supervisor's style interact with the manner in which a trainee conducts his or her work?
5. What is the role of a trainee's personal life, and further, what is the trainer's position on inquiring about and intervening in this area in training?

Trainers need to look at trainees' actions and to listen to their verbalizations from the developmental perspective. What emanates from this observation are indications of where attention is needed as well as a frame of mind about the trainee's behavior that allows the supervisor to be in a position to help. It is on the basis of these constructions (the hearing and seeing of what's "out there") that the feedback loop is completed between teacher and learner. At such moments, the learner becomes the informer, giving the teacher vital information that needs to be coded in useful ways. Often, the information is presented in a language that seems indecipherable to the teacher; we have to use all of our senses and acuity to make sense of these sometimes obscure signals. It is through this interpretation and encoding of information (that we sometimes misinterpret or interpret in ways that are not helpful) that the trainers' decision-making processes regarding intervention are stimulated.

The Trainer's Life Stage and Phase of Professional Development

The trainee's life cycle is not the only developmental path that must be taken into account in a useful and comprehensive assessment of the training context. A trainer's professional development and its interaction with the variety of other factors in the training setting can also be examined in terms of developmental thinking and the life cycle. We know very little about trainer development. However, in a study with trainers and supervisors of the American Association for Marriage and Family Therapy and American Family Therapy Association, Saba and Liddle (1986) found that trainers desired an increase in opportunities for continuing professional development as well as theories or frameworks that could practically inform their work. These trainers were addressing professional needs at particular stages of development. By understanding what these supervisors seek, we can begin to know how they function. Clearly, such extrapolations are incomplete and inadequate. More work is needed in the area of trainer/supervisor development as well as in the application of life cycle thinking to these experienced professionals.

CONCLUSIONS

Family therapists' use of the family life cycle in the clinical and training realms is at a primitive stage. We only need to look at the sophisticated model-building efforts of such modern-day theorists as Bronfenbrenner, Riegel, Gould, and Levinson to see the challenge that lies ahead for family therapy.

However, even though this framework needs further thought and refinement regarding its full implications for intervention with families, therapists, and supervisors (and the field in general), this way of thinking has allowed us to move away from a pathology-oriented perspective. This achievement can be considered a major contribution within the field. Further, the concept of human development can be a conceptual overlay, a transparency that can guide and shape a therapist's actions and provide a frame of reference from which interventions can be made.

To what degree is all of this known to experienced trainers? Does this framework constitute common knowledge about trainee development? Is it already embedded in the "folk wisdom" of savvy trainers and merely has to be written down or empirically demonstrated? Certainly, the multiple uses of developmental thinking as content and process overlays in training seem straightforward and commonsensical. But a reminder might be in order here: Our fundamental notion in family therapy, that of contextual or systemic thinking, also began along similar simple, straightforward lines. In this regard, few would disagree that the "simple" and "commonsense" concept of context has yielded rich and valuable complexity and diversity in its formulation and application. In the same way, the continued formulation, refinement, and application of the similarly "uncomplicated" ideas of development and life cycle theory remain a worthy and worthwhile challenge for theoreticians and therapists alike.

NOTES

1. Other indicators of family therapy's evolution have been the struggle to define the place of epistemology, specification of the use of cultural and ethnic variables in therapy, an increasing honesty and concern about the achievement of decidedly mixed results in changing institutional structures and policies, greater appreciation of research and its role in the field, less rhetoric and more realistic thinking about expectations in family therapy, and a focus on gender issues as they relate to the conduct of marital and family therapy and to systemic theory in general.

2. Here, therapists need to understand the perspectivistic nature of reality and that paradox is merely another way of understanding events that we have been thinking about in a certain patterned, usually logical way.

3. This metaphor, helping families to pose and struggle with the universally derived, but idiosyncratically defined, "big questions," is one key aspect of the structural-strategic therapy model being refined and tested in the clinical research arena of the NIDA-funded Adolescents and Families Project. This research is concerned with, among other things, helping therapists to adopt developmental thinking and the life cycle paradigm as antidotes to a major nemesis of every clinician—pathology- or dysfunction-oriented thinking.

REFERENCES

Argyris, C., & Schon, D. A. (1974). *Theory in practice: Increasing professional effectiveness.* San Francisco: Jossey-Bass.

Barnhill, L., & Longo, D. (1980). Fixation and regression in the family life cycle. *Family Process, 17,* 469–478.

Berger, M., & Dammann, C. (1982). Live supervision as context, treatment, and training. *Family Process, 21,* 337–344.

Bronfenbrenner, U. (1979). *The ecology of human development.* Cambridge, MA: Harvard University Press.

Carter, E., & McGoldrick, M. (Eds.). (1980). *The family life cycle: A framework for family therapy.* New York: Gardner Press.

Combrinck-Graham, L. (1983). The family life cycle and families with young children. In H. A. Liddle (Ed.), *Clinical implications of the family life cycle.* Rockville, MD: Aspen Systems Corporation.

Combrinck-Graham, L. (1988). Psychiatry and family therapy training. In H. A. Liddle, D. C. Breunlin, & R. C. Schwartz (Eds.), *Handbook of family therapy training and supervision.* New York: Guilford.

Dell, P., Sheely, M., Pullian, G., & Goolishian, H. (1977). Family therapy in a family therapy seminar. *Journal of Marriage and Family Counseling, 3,* 43–48.

Doehrman, M. J. G. (1976). Parallel processes in supervision and psychotherapy. *Bulletin of the Menninger Clinic, 40*(1), 3–10.

Duvall, E. M. (1977). *Marriage and family development* (5th ed.). Philadelphia: Lippincott.

Ferguson, L. R. (1979). The family life cycle: Orientation for interdisciplinary training. *Professional Psychology, 10,* 863–867.

Gurman, A. S. (1981). Integrative marital therapy: Toward the development of an interpersonal approach. In S. Budman (Ed.), *Forms of brief psychotherapy.* New York: Guilford.

Haley, J. (1973). *Uncommon therapy.* New York: Norton.

Haley, J. (1976). *Problem-solving therapy.* San Francisco: Jossey Bass.

Haley, J. (1980). *Leaving home: The therapy of disturbed young people.* New York: McGraw-Hill.

Haley, J. (1988). Reflections on therapy supervision. In H. A. Liddle, D. C. Breunlin, & R. C. Schwartz (Eds.), *Handbook of family therapy training and supervision.* New York: Guilford Press.

Hill, R. (1971). Modern systems theory in the family: A confrontation. *Social Science Information, 10,* 7–26.

Kantor, D. (1983). The structural-analytic approach to the treatment of family developmental crisis. In H. A. Liddle (Ed.), *Clinical implications of the family life cycle.* Rockville, MD: Aspen Systems Corporation.

Koestler, A. (1978). *Janus: A summing up.* New York: Random House.

Lebow, J. (1987). Developing a personal integration in family therapy. *Journal of Marital and Family Therapy, 13,* 1–14.

Lerner, R. M. (1983). A "Goodness of Fit" model of person-context interaction. In D. Magnusson & V. L. Allen (Eds.), *Human development: An interactional perspective.* New York: Academic Press.

Levinson, D. (1986). Conceptions of adult development. *American Psychologist, 41,* 3–13.

Liddle, H. A. (1982). On the problems of eclecticism: A call for epistemologic clarification and human-scale theories. *Family Process, 21,* 243–250.

Liddle, H. A. (1983) (Ed.), *Clinical implications of the family life cycle.* Rockville, MD: Aspen. Systems Corporation.

Liddle, H. A. (1984). Family therapy training: Current issues, future trends. *International Journal of Family Therapy, 4,* 81–97.

Liddle, H. A. (1985). Five factors of failure in Structural-Strategic family therapy: A contextual construction. In S. Coleman (Ed.), *Failures in family therapy.* New York: Guilford.

Liddle, H. A. (1987a). Editor's Introduction I: Family psychology: The journal, the field. *Journal of Family Psychology, 1,* (1) (September).

Liddle, H. A. (1987b). Editor's Introduction II: Family psychology: Tasks of an emerging (and emerged) discipline. *Journal of Family Psychology, 1,* (2) (December).

Liddle, H. A. (1988). Systemic supervision: Conceptual overlays and pragmatic guidelines. In H. A. Liddle, D. C. Breunlin, & R. C. Schwartz (Eds.), *Handbook of family therapy training and supervision.* New York: Guilford.

Liddle, H. A. (in press). Family therapy training and supervision: A critical review and analysis. In A. Gurman and D. Kniskern, (Eds.), *Handbook of Family Therapy* (2nd edition), New York: Brunner/Mazel.

Liddle, H. A., Breunlin, D. C., & Schwartz, R. C. (Eds.). (1988). *Handbook of family therapy training and supervision.* New York: Guilford.

Liddle, H. A., Davidson, G., & Barrett, M. J. (1988). Pragmatic implications of live supervision: Outcome research. In H. A. Liddle, D. C. Breunlin & R. C. Schwartz (Eds.), *Handbook of family therapy training and supervision.* New York: Guilford.

Liddle, H. A., & Saba, G. (1983a). Clinical use of the family life cycle: Some cautionary guidelines. In H. A. Liddle (Ed.), *Clinical implications of the family life cycle.* Rockville, MD: Aspen Systems Corporation.

Liddle, H. A., & Saba, G. (1983b). On context replication: The isomorphic nature of training and therapy. *Journal of Strategic Systemic Therapies, 2*(3), 3-11.

Liddle, H. A., & Saba, G. (1985). The isomorphic nature of training and therapy: Epistemologic foundations for a structural-strategic family therapy. In J. Schwartzman (Ed.), *Families and other systems.* New York: Guilford.

Liddle, H., & Saba, G. (in press). *Supervising family therapists: Creating contexts of competence.* New York: Grune & Stratton.

Magnusson, D., & Allen, V. L. (Eds.) (1983). *Human development: An interactional perspective.* New York: Academic Press.

McGoldrick, M. (1982). Through the looking glass. In R. Whitte & J. Byng-Hall (Eds.), *Family therapy supervision: Recent developments in practice.* New York: Grune & Stratton.

McGoldrick, M., & Carter, B. (1982). The family life cycle. In F. Walsh (Ed.), *Normal family processes.* New York: Guilford.

Minuchin, P. (1985). Families and individual development: Provocations from the field of family therapy. *Child Development, 56,* 289-302.

Minuchin, S. (1974). *Families and family therapy.* Cambridge, MA: Harvard.

Minuchin, S., & Fishman, H. C. (1981). *Family therapy techniques.* Cambridge, MA: Harvard.

Moultrup, D. (1981). Towards an integrated model of family therapy. *Clinical Social Work Journal, 9,* 111-125.

Napier, A. Y., & Whitaker, C. (1973). Problems of the beginning family therapist. In D. Bloch (Ed.), *Techniques of family psychotherapy: A primer* (pp. 109-122). New York: Grune & Stratton.

Riegel, K. (1976). The dialectics of human development. *American Psychologist, 31,* 689-700.

Rodgers, R. (1973). *Family interaction and transaction: The developmental approach.* New York: Prentice Hall.

Rutter, M. (1983). Statistical and personal interactions: Facts and perspectives. In D. Magnusson & V. Allen (Eds.), *Human development: An interactional perspective.* New York: Academic Press.

Saba, G. W., & Liddle, H.A. (1986). Perceptions of professional needs, practice patterns and critical issues facing family therapy trainers and supervisors. *American Journal of Family Therapy, 14,* 109-122.

Solomon, M. (1973). A developmental conceptual premise for family therapy. *Family Process, 12,* 179-188.

Stierlin, H. (1974). *Separating parents and adolescents.* New York: Quadrangle Press.

Tucker, B., Hart, G., & Liddle, H. (1976). Supervision in family therapy: A development perspective. *Journal of Marriage and Family Counseling, 2,* 269-276.

Tucker, B., & Liddle, H. A. (1978). Intra- and interpersonal process in the group supervision of beginning family therapists. *Family Therapy, 5*(1), 13-28.

Urban, H. (1978). The concept of development from a systems perspective. In P. Baltes (Ed.), *Life-span development and behavior* (Vol. 1). New York: Academic Press.

Walsh, F. (Ed.) (1982). *Normal family processes.* New York: Guilford.

Walsh, F. (1983). The timing of symptoms and critical events in the family life cycle. In H. A. Liddle (Ed.), *Clinical implications of the family life cycle.* Rockville, MD: Aspen Systems Corporation.

Watzlawick, P., Weakland, J., & Fisch, R. (1974). *Change: Principles of problem formation and resolution.* New York: Norton.

Whitaker, C. (1976). The hindrance of theory in clinical practice. In P. Guerin (Ed.), *Family therapy, theory and practice.* New York: Gardner Press.

Williamson, D. S. (1981). Personal authority via termination of the intergenerational hierarchical boundary: A "new" stage in the family life cycle. *Journal of Marital and Family Therapy, 7,* 441–452.

Index

Numbers in italics indicate tables and figures.